DARK STAR

Henry Stevens

Adventures Unlimited Press

Other Books by Henry Stevens:

HITLER'S FLYING SAUCERS

HITLER'S SUPPRESSED & STILL SECRET WEAPONS, SCIENCE & TECHNOLOGY

DARK STAR

Unresolved Post-War Nazi Mysteries

Henry Stevens

DARK STAR
by Henry Stevens

ISBN: 978-1-935487-40-1

Published by:
Adventures Unlimited Press
One Adventure Place
Kempton, Illinois 60946 USA
auphq@frontiernet.net

www.adventuresunlimitedpress.com

DARK STAR

Unresolved Post-War Nazi Mysteries

Adventures Unlimited Press

Thanks to everyone who helped on this book.
Your research was invaluable.

DARK STAR

PREFACE

A few things should be noted before beginning this book regarding its style and content:

All German to English translations are my own. I am not a professional translator nor will resources allow employment of one. Computer translations are still not acceptable and in fact take as much time or more time to correct as to start from scratch. In the words of the late Patrick McMahon: "It isn't going to happen unless you make it happen." Pat was not talking about translations but about life in general, yet it certainly applies in this instance. I have had to translate things pertinent to this book myself otherwise the book would never have been written.

In the text of this book, foreign words are not italicized. There are so many foreign words in this book that italicized text would appear to the extent of distraction. Most of these words are German but other languages do appear. Many times a translation of those words will appear immediately thereafter in parentheses. Overall, I do not think this is a great problem. Text quoted from other sources, directly, is extensive and is italicized.

Quotes from other authors do appear in italics except for especially long quotes that have a line-bar before and after the quote. This same method is used to display documents that need to be clarified or enlarged. This also applies to translated documents.

This book was written with the assumption that the reader will possess some interest and knowledge of the subject matter.

This book begins and ends in the time frame of roughly 1933 to 1989 but references a few years either side of this stretch have been made. It is assumed that the reader already knows the general course of events of World War Two in Europe and knows the aftermath and political outcome, the Cold War.

It is also assumed that the reader is already somewhat familiar with the genre dealing with German technology and weaponry developed during the war and kept secret afterward. This genre, lacking a satisfactory name but called "Nazi High-Tech" on occasion, deals with related issues involving history, places, and the people involved in this technology. It is really just history missed by professional historians who have at least failed to connect the dots.

Contents

DARK STAR

Unresolved Post-War Nazi Mysteries

INTRODUCTION

Having established the reality of German flying discs in my first book, *Hitler's Flying Saucers* and the scientific-technical sea from which flying discs and other wonders sprung in my second book, *Hitler's Secret and Still Suppressed Science, Weapons and Technology*, with this third book we will look past the war and into a complete and total culture that survived the war but has been subsequently lost to established history. In researching this, we are going to explore some old rumors. Not all of these tales can be affirmed as well as one would wish. I would ask the reader to suspend judgment on particular cases in isolation and instead judge the overall interconnections, as it will be made by the end of the book.

This book, as were my other two, is predicated on the idea that new information and a new understanding of some historical events previously thought to have been understood has now surfaced. Most of these new facts and new understanding have emerged since the fall of the Berlin Wall and the collapse of the Soviet Union. This was matched by a relaxing of conditions in the West such as the Freedom of Information Act and similar legislation in other countries. Now, one of the constraints seems to be how much the Germans want to let be known as opposed to how much they want to keep to themselves for a time after the Americans are gone. This may be part of the "sleeping dog" concept that we will discuss later in the book.

As I and many other contemporary writers have shown, this science and technology extended far beyond the flash and bang of atomic weapons, flying discs, rail guns and other exciting technology. It extended into the everyday life of the post-war world. Hundreds of thousands of patents were taken by the Allies from German vaults at the close of the war. This was done without payment or even credit for these discoveries. Just as World War One had the hated Versailles with its onerous reparations, what came out of World War Two were reparations in the form of stolen science and technology. This science and technology form the basis of our modern world and surround you even as you read this. And when I say "hundreds of thousands of patents", this is not an exaggeration. In fact, the last patent taken from the Berlin Patent Office by the United States was numbered at 750,986. (1). This means the actual number of patents taken from all facilities at least approached one million and this certainly does not include the SS secret archives.

Sources for this type of work simply cannot be airtight. Speaking about these subjects can still get on in some kinds of trouble under certain conditions. One of my important sources for this hidden post-war world, Wilhelm Landig, has also been investigated and cited as a source by Dr. Joseph Farrell (2). The book by Dr. Farrell, just cited, also explains the post-war Nazi organization in some detail. For purposes of this book this detail need not be repeated since most individuals who have this book in hand will also probably be familiar with Dr. Farrell's work. We are going to look at the post-war Nazi world and its organization only with special emphasis on its formative years along with some other details and rely on Dr. Farrell's book for the overall perspective.

It may be impossible to deal only with the most credible sources, however, since we are pushing into the unproven. This is probably my last book dealing with these subjects so I want to relate as many of these stories as I can remember for future researchers. The principle of "where there is smoke, there is fire" has almost always born fruit in this research. If the "smoke" had been labeled "not-credible" at the beginning and discarded, we would have no knowledge on the reality of German flying discs, the German atomic projects, and so on.

The reader may notice that I am using the word "Nazi" far more in this book. We really have no way of knowing the political affiliations of all the scientists and individuals working on the flying disc projects or other aspects of German wartime secret science and technology while in Germany during the war. The situation is much clearer outside of the former 3rd Reich and after the war. It can safely be assumed that individuals taking part in the SS post-war organizations and their followers and employees were, in fact, Nazis.

So, we are going to take a look at rumors regarding the post-war Nazi world, especially those rumors coming from German sources, and then we are going where those rumors take us. Sometimes a seemingly well-known, well understood topic will be used to discuss other more exotic topics. Sometimes technology and events will be discussed with a fine point while a more general discussion is taking place about other topics that should coalesce in the end.

In other words, this book deals with technology but in describing this technology a more human tale will be told. On the surface this book deals with secret bases and fantastic U-boats. Here and there other interesting topics will be interjected. Some of these other topics as well as things discussed while discussing secret bases and fantastic

U-boats may come together forming larger themes. This technology has human and historic outcomes and we will try to trace some of these.

Literature Cited

1. **Georg, Friedrich, 2008**, "*Unternehmen Patentenraub*" 1945 Die Geheimgeschicher des Groessten Technologieraubs aller Zeiten, page 69, Grabert-Verlag, Tuebingen, Germany
2. **Farrell, Joseph, Ph.D., 2008**, *Nazi International: The Nazis' Postwar Plan to Control Finance, Conflict, Physics and Space*, Adventures Unlimited Press, Kempton, Illinois, Pages 12-23

Part One: German Secret Bases

THE FIRST CLUES

In looking for clues to what really happened regarding German secret bases in World War Two we should first look at the actual statements of those individual most directly involved. In this case top Nazis actually hinted at their intentions. We are going to look at some of their statements, translated into English, to see where we should go in researching this topic.

From the mouth of Adolf Hitler came these words as cited by W. Mattern:

> *"In this war there does not exist victors or vanquished, only the dead and the living, but the last battalion - that will be a German battalion"* (1).

Hitler was said to have uttered these words on February 24, 1945. Mattern calls this statement Hitler's end-of-the-war-prophecy. These words "last battalion" have given rise to a whole sub-story concerning the last days of World War Two, as we will see later.

Willibald Mattern was a German who lived in Chile after the war and he definitely was a Nazi. In fact, his work cited here is very strongly pro-Nazi, even though it was written many years after the war. Another Nazi, Ernst Zuendel, published Mattern's work with no date on the publication. It was approximately 1978, however. Zuendel compiled his own work on German flying discs after Mattern but in English. Zuendel's publishing company, Samisdat, announced an upcoming publication called "The Last Battalion" at about this time. This title was never published even though it generated considerable interest. I wrote to Zuendel in the 1980s about this title once or twice without success. Finally, other avenues of research opened up to me after the fall of the Berlin Wall and I realized who the source for both Zuendel and Mattern was concerning "The Last Battalion". The primary source was Wilhelm Landig, making Zuendel and Mattern superfluous. We will review what Landig has to say on the topic as well as more current revelations by other researchers, amplifying his case. But a question that should be kept in mind is: What was this Last Battalion idea really about and did it have to do with any of the statements made below?

Next we move to an earlier statement by Gross-Admiral Karl Doenitz in 1943:

> *"The German submarine fleet is proud of having built for the Fuehrer, in another part of the world, a Shangri-La on land, an impregnable fortress"* (2).

And another statement by Doenitz in 1944 at a cadet inauguration address in Kiel:

> *"The German Navy will have to accomplish a great task in the future. The German Navy knows all hiding places in the oceans and therefore it will be very easy to bring the Fuehrer to a safe place should the necessity arise and in which he will have the opportunity to work out his final plans"* (2).

The source cited here, Buechner and Bernhart are very credible informants. Besides being a Colonel in the US Army, Buechner was also a medical doctor. In fact, Col. Buechner was the first medical doctor on site as the Allies took over Buchenwald concentration camp. He was also a college professor. "Bernhart" is an alias, but the alias of a German submariner. In fact, Bernhart was a junior officer, the Chief Torpedo Officer; aboard the famous U-530 from August 1944 until July, 17, 1945 when it surrendered at Mar del Plata, Argentina, over two months after the war in Europe had ended. As we will see, U-530 was almost a magical vessel for a number of reasons.

Returning to the statements of Karl Doenitz, it must be remembered that he was the highest-ranking officer in he German Navy and became Fuehrer after Hitler's death. It was Doenitz who surrendered the three fighting divisions of the German military (Army, Navy, and Air Force) to the Allies, ending the war in Europe. Obviously, we cannot short-change anything this man has to say concerning secret bases outside of Germany or the Greater Reich.

At the Nuremberg Trials, Doenitz again spoke on this topic:

> *"...an invulnerable fortress, a paradise-like oasis in the middle of eternal ice"* (3).

This statement is actually more powerful in the original German:

> *"...uneinnehmbaren Festung, von einer paradiesischen Oase inmitten ewigen Eises"*

These words "uneinnehmbaren Festung" mean or convey the idea of an "untakable fortress", not just an invulnerable one. The words "ewigen Eises" are full of Hans Horbiger (Fire and Ice) connotations.

So we are getting the idea that this fortress is rather pleasant even though it is located in a cold place. Is this place in the mountains or near the poles? We are really not told since it has been said to be "on land" but also surrounded by ice. But the German Navy built it, indicating a connection with the ocean.

Finally, we have these words from Hitler himself, spelling out his purpose for the foreign base(s):

> *"And if the enemy overruns all of Germany, then the war will be carried on from foreign soil, surrender will not happen"* (4).

Researcher/writer O. Bergmann that is being cited here reports that these words of Hitler's were uttered at the beginning of the Polish campaign, in other words at the very beginning of the Second World War. Even at that time, Hitler seems to have formulated some sort of contingency planning.

O. Bergmann has done some very fine research, especially as it pertains to U-boats and secret bases. Personally, I think that Bergmann gets the details concerning the power plant of field propulsion saucers wrong. But Bergmann does contribute a wealth of details to the subject at hand and so cannot be discounted over my one, personal prejudice. In defense of Bergmann, nobody has ever been right about everything.

Jumping ahead, Bergmann introduces one idea that we should consider. He says the same type of power plant that propelled German flying discs was used in their very most exotic U-boats. In fact, he says that there is virtually no difference between German flying discs and German U-boats once we reach a certain level. If this is true, it would account for the USOs, unidentified submerged objects, seen worldwide and would account for their ability to rise from the sea directly into the air.

Returning to the topic of secret bases, we ought to ask ourselves exactly what were the reasons for the Germans to be considering building secret bases abroad? From the quotes cited above, it might seem the building of these bases was solely a contingency plan against a Nazi defeat. The reasoning given involves carrying on a war with the Allies from beyond the borders of Germany as well as a place of refuge for Hitler and presumably other important Nazis.

Another huge concern in building foreign bases, especially Arctic bases, was their function as weather stations. We have all heard of the importance of weather forecasting in the timing of D-day, the invasion of Normandy by the Anglo-Americans. But the Germans were fighting from the shores of the eastern USA in their U-boats all the way to the new industrial heartland of the Soviet Union, east of the Urals. They needed good weather predictions over a vast area of the Northern Hemisphere. To do this they needed to know the direction of storms spinning out of the Arctic as well as their strength and speed. The Germans built bases whose primary function was to gather this information and transmit it back to Germany. These weather stations stretched from eastern Canada to the Soviet Arctic including Norway, Greenland, Franz Josef Land, and Spitsbergen.

These same positions would be invaluable as listening posts, intercepting shipping as well as military information. We all remember the importance of the Norwegian, Icelandic, and Greenland listening posts and their associated military installations in monitoring Soviet submarine activity during the Cold War. Similar concerns would have been present for the Germans who were very interested in intercepting convoys of ships supplying Great Britain and even the Soviet Union from America.

All of these secret German bases supplied and assisted German U-boats whenever called upon to do this. So, all of these bases might be considered U-boat bases although the extent and scope and frequency of the assistance they were in a position to offer might vary greatly.

A well-positioned base in the Antarctic might have served as a way station for communication and trade between Germany and Japan should more direct bases, such as the Japanese base in Singapore, fall into enemy hands. Also, for military reasons, the Germans conducted warfare in the South Atlantic. This took the form of two successful raider vessels, the Penguin and the Atlantis that prowled the waters South of the Cape of Good Hope. These ships, camouflaged as merchant vessels, would spot another, enemy merchant vessel, approach it, and then drop their merchant guise as they opened up with cannon fire.

But even before the war in Europe started, the Germans had already secured a huge tract of Antarctic land in the region described in the last paragraph, just south of Africa. This region was known as Neuschwabenland. It was mapped and explored by the Germans. This was done under the auspices of Hermann Goering of the German Air Force. The question of German settlement or German bases in this region is a topic of concern that we will cover.

In 1944, Nazi realists saw the Reich slipping from their grasp. The war was not going well and that was an understatement. All hope of salvation rested in bringing the wonder weapons to an operational stage. Hitler argued for time to do just this and directed his military strategy toward the delay of the advancing Allies on all sides of Germany.

Also, as the war soured for Germany, there were certainly top Nazis who wanted Hitler out of the way, plotting a Fourth Reich. This Reich would be Nazi but without Hitler. The plot even had a name, Operation Avalon (5). How far this plot extended is unclear but it is clear that it was not actualized even though stationary for this Fourth Reich was actually prepared (6). Operation Avalon had the alleged backing of Dr. Hans Kammler, Dr. Manfred von Ardenne, Albert Speer, and Dr. Kurt Diebner. (7). Other names cited as present were: Fritsch, Ohnesorge, West, Grothmann, von Puttkamer, Teichmann, Weidehammer, Seufert and Schaub (8).

There is even a tale surrounding Operation Avalon and the real end of the Third Reich. It involves a meeting of the Nazi leadership on March 27th, 1945. Hitler was going on as usual with optimistic expectations of turning the war around once certain wonder weapons came on line. At one point Speer had heard enough of this. He rose and in a loud voice uttered the unthinkable to Hitler: *"Nein, Mein Fuehrer!"* Speer allegedly went on to say that there had already been enough death of enough son's treasured by their mothers and that the wonderweapons, especially the A-bomb would not be employed by the Germans as it was a murderous weapon aimed at the people (9). Of course, many top Nazis were trying to do a deal with the Allies, especially the Americans, to save their own skin and perhaps doing so while plotting Operation Avalon or using one or the other as a secondary plan.

If this Operation Avalon story is true, then it spelled to doom of the Third Reich even in the eyes of its most staunch true believer, Adolf Hitler. Hitler must have seen that without his wonder weapons, all was lost. It may not have come in a sudden realization, but over the days that followed the truth was plain to see. All Hitler's actions after this date can certainly be explained as resignation of a man who knows his is a lost cause. Even though plans had been made for Hitler's escape, he declined those plans. Instead, Hitler tied up the lose ends of his personal life, marrying Eva Braun, and contemplated the means of his own end.

This plan, Operation Avalon, would have involved the very top technology of the Reich, the Kammler Group and all its laboratories. If all this high technology was actually spirited out of Germany or to what extent this was done involving the plans of others remains an open question.

Others, including Hitler's Secretary, Martin Bormann, were more practical. They thought in terms of a post-war world in which they would exist as intact Nazis but not necessarily within the borders of what was called the Greater Reich. But they also included an element that seems to have been overlooked by the Avalon people. That one element was money. That money concerned Martin Bormann is no surprise since he handled financial affairs for Hitler.

A secret meeting took place in which a post-war world was discussed. In this eventuality, the Germans had lost the war. Everyone knew what had happened the last time Germany had lost a war. It was not only an economic catastrophe but a social and political one as well. The whole existing order in Germany was forever changed with that defeat. So, those attending this meeting wanted to insure some sort of continuity between the Third Reich and whatever world came next. They also wanted to assure the survival of their political ideas and goals as well as their own safety. Further, they wanted to take with them the financing necessary to do this.

They met in late 1944 at the Hotel Rotes Haus in Strasbourg, France. Hitler was not aware of this meeting. In that meeting, representatives of the military, government, industry and finance were present. A far-reaching agreement was made. Under Bormann's auspices, German industrialists began transferring abroad huge sums of money, counterfeit money, precious stones, gold, machine tools (tools used to build other tools), specialty steel, and secret blueprints to be utilized after the war was over (10). Scientists themselves were transported as well. Business considerations where not neglected so that corporations and shadow corporations were set up, clandestinely, to facilitate the money and technology transfers.

The purpose for the secret blueprints and the scientists was to reconstruct some of the wonder weapons being developed within Germany. It was also to carry out further work of high technology along the unique scientific avenues begun by those SS alchemists working for Kammler. If an organization has its own land, weapons, and money, it can rightfully call itself a "power" and this was exactly the aim of those participating. They saw themselves as a secret power or at least secret from common public knowledge.

What is unclear is it they wanted themselves and their organization kept secret from other countries or power blocks.

Bormann may have instituted the idea for this particular transfer but Martin Bormann would soon become lost to history. As with Adolf Hitler and Dr. Hans Kammler, tales of Bormann's demise are multiple. After Hitler's death on April 30, 1945, all parties inhabiting the bunker scattered, each man for himself. Among these late starters was Bormann. One report of him place his death outside the Solex carburetor factory in Berlin where he was allegedly hit by Soviet artillery, or if you prefer, ducking down some underground rat hole out of Berlin from which he never emerged. But whatever story you prefer, he completely vanishes and there is really no credible information that he survived he war or resurfaces elsewhere. As we will see, it did not matter: Nazi political types had lost all credibility in the eyes of the surviving SS and figured no role in their organization.

Dr. Hjalmar Schacht, the financial genius who almost single handedly had put the German economy back together after the Depression made the financial arrangements. Col. Otto Skorzeny, whom the Allied called "the most dangerous man in Europe", made the operational arrangements. In fact, Skorzeny, a legitimate war hero in the eyes of average German soldiers, took over the leadership role in the absence of Bormann (11). We will deal with the personalities involved as well as the Nazi organization as best cases of each present themselves.

One problem was the physical transportation of items of value to the safe areas. Germany really lacked a fleet of long distance heavy lifting aircraft. There were no Lancaster bombers or B-17s in the German Air Force on the squadron level. There were individual prototypes, as we shall see, but the bulk of the heavy lifting became the responsibility of the German Navy and the German Navy was, at this point in the war, the U-boat service. The details of each secret base are somewhat different as is their history so we will explore each, base by base, starting with their major point of departure and some of the secrets it still holds.

So, we will begin with the jumping off point, Norway, and its mysteries. Then, following Landig's lead, we will move to Point 103 somewhere in the Arctic. From there we will back track a bit to Greenland, its bases, including the probability of a new discovery called Beaver Dam. The Last Battalion legend as well as discussion of German flying discs will be interjected as they become relevant. We will then move to the possibility of sequestered German high technology in Switzerland and Tibet before coming to the controversial topic of Neuschwabenland, Landig's Point 211. From there we will move to Nazi post-war holdings and interaction in South America. Finally, we will move to the base that makes concrete the German secret-base concept and ties the far-flung bases together.

Literature Cited

1. **Mattern, W.**, *UFO's Unbekanntes Flugobjekt? Letzte Geheimwaffe Des Dritten Reiches?*, date unknown, page 23, Samisdat Publishing LTD, Ontario, Canada
2. **Buechner, Col. Howard A. and Capt. Wilhelm Bernhart**, *Hitler's Ashes Seeds of a new Reich!*, 1989, pages 172-173, Thunderbird Press Inc., Metarie, Louisiana.
3. **Mattern, W.** *UFO's Unbekanntes Flugobjekt*, page 38, see (1).
4. **Bergmann, O.**, *I Deutsche flugscheiben und U-Boote Ueberwachen Die Weltmeere*, 1988, page 4, Hugin Society, Wetter/Ruhr, Germany
5. **Mayer, Edgar and Thomas Mehner**, *Die Atombombe und das Dritte Reich*, 2002, page 19, Jochen Kopp Verlag, Rottenburg, Germany
6. ***ibid.***, page 237
7. ***ibid.***, page 236
8. ***ibid.***, page 244
9. ***ibid.***, page 243
10. **Infield, Glen B.**, *Skorzeny: Hitler's Commando,* 1981, page 179, St. Martin's Press, New York
11. ***ibid.***

NORWAY

Wilhelm Landig began his classic novel, *Goetzen Gegen Thule Ein Roman voller Wirklichkeiten, (Idols against Thule: A Novel Full of Realities)*, in Norway. Norway was the point of departure for this tale. Landig was interested in explaining things as had never before appeared in print. By this it is meant that he presents the Nazi viewpoint. Since Landig is not afraid to do this, perhaps we ought to consider things he says which have no legal or political consequences seriously. We do not have the luxury of reviewing the whole of Landig's work even if this were possible. All we can do is draw upon the examples and explanation he provides in the appropriate instances which are of immediate concern to us.

What Landig does is to immerse us into a completely alien post-war world. Here, the Nazis still retain their organization, ideals, and ability to operate in a limited, tactical manner. They have the machines of war at their disposal and no inclination to suddenly surrender to the Allies. An occupied Germany was not an attractive option for these men. Since these were young men, perhaps an analogy is appropriate. In this analogy, a young man is being asked to choose between two ugly sisters in terms of marriage. The two sisters are Communism and Capitalism. A life under Communism was out of the question for the Nazis but what most people do not understand is that the Nazis saw Capitalism as almost as bad as Communism. These new options were not too attractive to men who were happy with a simple and unambiguous chain of command, the Fuehrer Principle. Is it no wonder that so many Germans, especially German soldiers with Nazi leanings, who had lost everything in the war were unhappy or thought they would be unhappy in the "New Germany"? They looked around for options and looked toward the very men with whom they had served for the last six years. These men and this organization were their new family now. Considering this mind-set, let us now proceed to our first topic, Norway.

As far as I can tell there were three areas of German bases in Norway during the war that are of interest to us. Most of us have already heard of the Norsk-Hydro plant operated by the Germans for the purpose of production of heavy water. The Norwegians eventually destroyed this plant with the support of the British. This story has been told so often that it is really not of concern here. We are interested in facilities that have not already been thoroughly explored. The three areas of concern for us are the U-boat facilities at or near Kristiansand, the facilities on the central plateau of Norway, and the facilities at the far North of Norway. The Kristiansand facilities concern U-boats and are fairly well known. We will first touch upon the facilities in the far North.

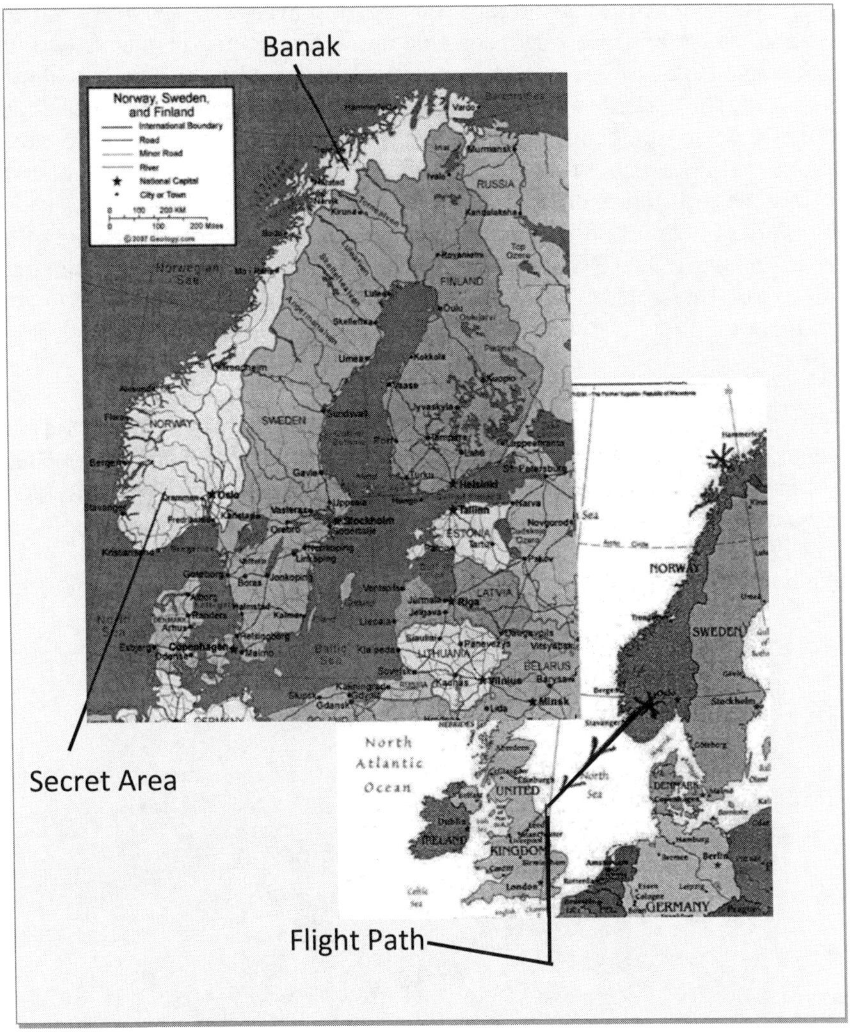

Map of Norway The area of Banak, at about 79 degrees N, discussed in the text as well as the highland plateau area of Norway should be noted. Also, the direction and approximate origin of the missile attack on Manchester, England is indicated.

"Goetzen" opens in such a base in the far North of Norway, probably near Banak at Latitude 70 N. Three men, soldiers, are flying West as the Reich is collapsing behind them in a prototype aircraft. In all probability or most such prototype aircraft were fleeing the Reich at this very moment and Landig describes two such prototype aircraft for us.

The first was a Junkers-Dornier prototype but perhaps built at the Heinkel works in Berlin. Interestingly enough, this machine already carried the Black Sun as its identifying symbol (1). This aircraft was an improved and reconstructed Junkers featuring a trilateral or three-sided construction. Apparently, it had a two-fuselage construction and a crew of three. Two crewmembers sat on one side and the third in the other fuselage. This aircraft was unarmed. It was equipped with very special engines, the Daimler-Benz 603A. The Daimler-Benz 600 series are well known; they are water-cooled in-line engines (2). The interesting point here is that Landig says two such engines were merged to turn one propeller (3). This construction was formalized in the DB 606 that were two DB 601 engines in unison (4). This improved version of the DB 601 was called the DB 603 with running changes and improvements receiving letter designation (5). Therefore, this prototype aircraft was one of the first four motor, dual propeller aircraft to fly.

Its speed was 725 kilometers per hour, about 442 miles per hour (6), with a range of 8,000 kilometers, about 4880 miles (7). This was a high speed for a propeller drive aircraft of its day but its range was simply outstanding! Presumably, this aircraft would have been used for high-speed reconnaissance.

Landig equates this aircraft with the Dornier Do 635 (8). Information does exist on

Dornier Do 635, Messerschmitt Me 264, and Junkers Ju 390

Dornier Do 635 - projected high-speed reconnaissance twin

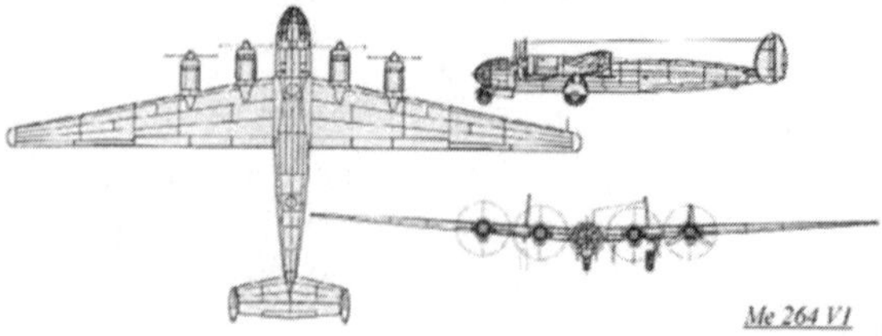

Me 264 V1

the Dornier Do 635. It is a peculiar aircraft, designed to tow huge gliders into the air or to assist large, heavily burdened aircraft airborne. This aircraft looked odd since it consisted of two Dornier Do 335s were joined together at the wing that both halves shared (9). A pilot sat on he left side of the "twin" with the radioman and another crewmember occupying the right twin. Fuel was stored in the central wing giving it extremely long range if used as an observation aircraft that is given by Kens and Nawarra as 7,500 kilometers (10). As in other aircraft, one could construct another firm's design if the government saw fit to do so. In this case the Dornier Do 635 became the Heinkel 111Z (the "Z" was for Zwillige or Twin in English) using the DB 603 engine in tandem with one propeller as described by Landig (11).

In Landig's Nordic Odyssey, this aircraft was brought to a secret base, Point 103, somewhere in the Canadian arctic. It was equipped with a strange instrument, the Himmelskompass or heavenly compass. This device has been described in my earlier books but it was basically a compass that did not orient itself to north using magnetic means. Remember, the true magnetic North Pole lays on the Boothia Peninsula that is well South of the geographic North Pole. This inconsistency would certainly cause confusion for aircraft of shipping approaching the magnetic north pole from the North.

Landig also mentioned a second mystery aircraft. He called it the "Dosthra". The Dosthra was a mid-wing monoplane with a five-cornered fuselage, when viewed in cross section. It resembled a giant insect; it was thicker in front than in the rear with a glass front end. Two black circles painted near the front of the craft only increased the insect-like look. These black circles were called the "Schwarze Runde" and were yet another version of the Black Sun symbol, the symbol used by SS survival groups. The wingspan was about 135 feet so it was about the size of a B-29. The insect look was further enhanced by the two gun turrets on either side near the front of the aircraft (12).

There were two things very different about this aircraft: the first was its construction. According to Landig, this aircraft was not made of ordinary metal. Landig calls this metal "Quetschmetall". The method of this metal's production concerned it being placed under pressure of four hundred thousand atmospheres that resulted in a high compression, high strength, but low weight metal. This super-skin of the aircraft gave it the highest possible tensile strength and functioned as a protective armor (13).

I have mentioned the Dosthra aircraft in my second book concerning super metals (14). This process is an outgrowth of the work of the Austrian inventor, Karl Nowak, who was very interested in cold, heat and changes in states of matter. Nowak will be more completely considered later but for now it should be noted that Nowak thought the applications of such changes of state could be used to power engines and create new industrial processes such as the one under discussion (15). There is much talk linking Nowak to the propulsion of German flying discs using the expansive qualities of helium as it is brought from the liquid to the gaseous state. There is even talk of a "molecular bomb" using such methods.

This is no small idea in our story. The SS alchemists took Nowak's lessons to heart. In fact, changes of state and outright transmutation of elements (in a nuclear reactor and perhaps other devices) were at the core of their research. Anyone familiar with Nazism will remember the Fire and Ice theories of Hans Hoerbiger that fits into this discussion nicely on a philosophic level, as does the concept of the Uebermensch, the Superman, who could be thought of as a transmuted human being. With so many converging ideas, concepts and philosophies coming together and seemingly reinforcing each other, it is no wonder that each success only served to reinforce the larger concept as a whole. We will see another application of these ideas when we discuss mystery U-boats.

Returning to the Dorsthra, it could carry as many as seven people but could function with a crew of five. It was designed to operate on rough runways, as the two landing wheels were four meters in diameter. It was powered by four radial Argus engines, turning four, four-bladed propellers. Other engines were present on the tips of the wings and in the tail section. These were jet engines for use at high altitude as in the later American B-36 bomber. The jets could also be used for steering when they were employed. The wings were of slotted construction and they were small in surface area and small to the overall size of the aircraft. The tail section slanted backwards.

The most astonishing aspect of the Dorsthra was its performance as claimed by Landig. Its top speed was cited as 830 kilometers per hour (over 500 miles per hour) with a range of 22,000 kilometers (13,420 miles) or 32,000 kilometers at high altitude (19,520 miles). Landig says this legend was able to fly to the United States from Europe and back again (16).

We are not told of the mission or purpose of the Dorsthra. Fuel storage must have taken up quite a portion of its available storage area. So we are left with somewhat of a mystery wondering if it was really to be a long distance bomber or simply a reconnaissance aircraft.

Wilhelm Landig is not the only writer to talk about exciting prototype aircraft fleeing the Reich in its dying days and this lends credence to Landig. Siegfried Heppner is a writer/researcher who delves into German flying discs and other mysteries surrounding the Third Reich. He gives us an eyewitness account of a "supermachine" which he actually saw fleeing the Reich with his own eyes as a boy of about fourteen years old.

Heppner discusses a novel written by famed writer/researcher Tom Agoston that concerns a mystery aircraft fleeing the Reich and then tells us that it actually happened, as he saw it. The following is my translation of his account:

> *"This aircraft really existed! I see it excitedly still today as it flew low to me in an uproar and over the house southward into Switzerland and disappeared. That was between 8:00 and 9:00 in the morning on the 9th of May 1945, as I stood in the window in he direction of the Reich's Bank at Constance. There appeared with a great uproar a double fuselage machine with the Balkan Cross of the German Air Force so low near the cathedral tower that I became afraid that it could strike the 101-meter high spire.*
>
> *It seemed to have been a one-off double fuselage research type of Dornier, D 635 with four motors, (two propellers in front, two on the tip of the tail), with an*

aggressive tear shaped glass cockpit in the center. This type was 900 kilometers per hour fast! Its chief superiority lay in the maneuverability through use of its front plus rear thrust!

I could observe the overflight from the northern side of he house for only a few seconds. The range of this supermachine was in any case up for a flight from Prague to Spain and from there (refueled) to South America." (17)

So, we have a second Dornier Do 635 being described as escaping Germany as it collapsed. But there are still other prototype aircraft which are still somewhat of a mystery. One of these is the Messerschmitt Me 264. This aircraft was a large, four engine bomber with a very long range. Its range was said to be anywhere from 6,000 kilometers to 12,000 to 15,000 kilometers. These higher figures would have allowed the Me 264 to cross the Atlantic from Europe and fly back carrying a 1000 kg bomb load (over one ton).

All German long distance bomber projects suffered from a series of changes of direction and starts and stops as the course of the war itself changed. At first two prototypes of the Messerschmitt Me 264 were built (18). The first prototype first flew on April 27, 1942. The second prototype was destroyed during a bomber attack even before it could be test-flown. But even before the first test flight occurred, the program was beset with problems. Messerschmitt simply had too many aircraft in production at the same time. But Willy Messerschmitt had meanwhile promised Hitler the Me 264 was the solution for bombing the east coast of the USA. Field Marshal Milch ordered five more examples to be built the day after Messerschmitt's promise to Hitler. The solution was to farm it out to another firm that was a common procedure. Unfortunately, none of the firms in the running was really capable of pulling off such a large, complex construction project.

One of the Me 264's early passengers at the Rechlin testing facility (if not an outright test pilot), a Captain Nebel, had been given command of his own Sonderkommando unit Sonderkommando Nebel. Sonderkommando Nebel had all the technical understanding and machinery necessary to built or at least assemble a Me 264, which they did. It is unclear to me if a subsequent air attack spoiled these plans or only set them back to February 1945. If the aircraft was completed it was to be an extremely long-distance reconnaissance aircraft (19).

What this all means is there may have been two Messerschmitt Me 264s available at the very end of the war for long distance hauling of materials and transport of human cargo.

Next we will consider the big daddy of all the German prototype heavy lift aircraft, the Junkers Ju 390. This was a six-engine long distance bomber. It was envisioned as an aircraft that could cross the Atlantic and return with no problems. The Ju 390 never made it out of the prototype stage in the same off and on, start and stop, scenario that plagued many German aircraft designs. There are mysteries concerning almost every step or phase in the Ju 390's history with advocates and deniers pushing forth their own versions of this aircraft's history.

As far as I can tell, two examples of the Junkers Ju 390 were built with certainty and possibly one additional example. These are given the designation V-1, V-2, and V-3, the "V" meaning variant. V-1 was certainly built and flown. V-2 was also built and tested along with V-1 at the German test facility at Rechlin. But shortly after a few test flights and a short trip to Laerz, Oberleutnant Joachim Eisermann who flew V-2 himself reports that it completely disappeared (20). But even earlier, Captain Hans Bauer, Hitler's personal pilot, had been presented an example of a Ju-390 for official government use. To further confuse things, the third example, the V-3, was to be completed before the V-2 disappeared if we judge by comparing dates (21). Meantime, sightings of a Ju-390 and even pictures of it in flight show that either extensive modification had been made to one of the existing aircraft or that other mystery examples of the Ju-390 had been built. In the end the advancing Allies found only one Junkers Ju-390, the V-1, in Dessau on November 15, 1944 (22).

So a mystery arises as to where the missing Ju-390s ended up. And this mystery is further confused by another mystery, what purpose were the Ju-390s being used? Solving the mystery of their purpose might shed light on where they ended up. Now of course, they were intended as long-range bombers but they were never used for this purpose except for possibly a dry run. Additionally, some of the modifications, such as the removal of defensive armament, lead one to the possibility that they were actually used for heavy lifting, long-haul operations.

The "dry-run" mentioned was the alleged trip from Mont-de-Marsan, France to New York City, or a point 20 kilometers (12 miles) from it in the Atlantic. The Ju-390, apparently having made a point to those in the Luftwaffe who were interested, turned around and few back to France. This tale is widely repeated and there apparently exists some documentation in the form of a British Intelligence report, somewhere, supporting this flight (23). In any event, this flight should have been no surprise to anyone since it was within the design capability of the aircraft involved and in fact the whole reason for its existence.

Returning to the tasks the Ju-390 was being asked to do on an operational basis, research/writer Friedrich Georg comes up with three:

1. *Secret intelligence operations.*
2. *As an escape vehicle for the Nazi leadership.*
3. *As a long-distance delivery vehicle connecting to Japan.*

All of these are really connected. Even the idea of giving the design to the Japanese is included in number three above. They would have found this aircraft useful, as it would have traversed the Pacific just as it would the Atlantic.

With the topic of Nazi escape always comes the question of Dr. Hans Kammler. In fact, Kammler had to be very familiar with the Ju-390 since it was built in Prague, his area of dominion (24). The problem with postulating the Ju-390 as yet another Kammler survival story (or Kammler death story) is that Kammler actually had a fear of flying and so probably sought other means of escape (25). Besides, I have a better Kammler survival story for you, to follow, and it is the first time this story has appeared in English.

There is a story that probably concerns this aircraft that bears repeating. On April 17, 1945 a secret message was sent from Kammler to Himmler. In this four-line message Kammler tells Himmler that he is unable to send Himmler the "L.K.W." that he is requesting. The only meaning I have ever heard given "L.K.W." is "Lastkraftwagen" or "truck" in American English. This discussion is not over a fleet of trucks, only one "truck". Tom Agoston repeats this story on page 55 of his book "Blunder How the US Gave Away Nazi Supersecrets to Russia". Evidently, Agoston takes this word "truck" at face value. This seems a strange request at best. But writer/researcher Friedrich Georg who sent me a copy of this document years ago had another take. He thought the word "truck" was code or slang for a very large, heavy lift aircraft. The Junkers Ju-390 is obviously what was being discussed.

What really ties the Ju-390 into our story of Norway is the fact that the Ju-390 flew to Japan, over the polar route, from Norway. My source for this is again Friedrich Georg who cites the material of Tom Agoston that was published in German (25). The Ju-390 left Norway from a base in the far north at Bardufoss, flew over the north pole, over the Bering Strait, then down the east side of the Kamchatka Peninsula to the island of Pamushiro which was within the Japanese Empire. From there it flew over Japanese-controlled Manchoutikuo to Tokyo. Confirmation of this flight comes from a radio report by the Japanese Attaches for Marine Aircraft in Germany, dated March 21, 1945 (26). Agoston gives a slightly less detailed account of this flight in his English language book (27). The purpose was to transport German high-tech weaponry secrets and some personnel involved with this work. This was exactly the same purpose as the famous U-234 voyage and the two methods of communication can be considered complimentary, each part of a larger whole. There may have been and probably were more flights involving the Ju -390 to Japan just as there were probably other U-boats delivering technology to Japan besides U-234.

An operational aircraft that we must consider for long-range operations was the Focke-Wulf Fw 200 Condor. This was originally a four engine passenger aircraft but the Luftwaffe adapted it for long-range reconnaissance and even as an anti-shipping bomber. This aircraft had flown in peacetime from Berlin to New York City, nonstop. Besides extensive work in the North Sea and Polar Regions surrounding Norway, this aircraft also transported supplies all the way to Stalingrad in 1942.

The reader will remember the 1944 conference at Strasbourg in which it was agreed that blueprints, machine tools, secret weapons, specialty steel, gold, money and scientists were to be transported outside the Reich for future use. The means of this transfer, according to one source, was the employment of Geschwader 200 (Squadron 200), an elite flying group of young men, many who had lost their families.

Geschwader 200 was the first choice of the Luftwaffe for truly dangerous missions. Geschwader 200 was, for instance, scheduled to fly the manned version of the V-1 to high value targets. This would have certainly meant the loss of almost all of the pilots, as the men themselves knew. Later, that project was abandoned but Geschwader 200 was involved in a suicide attack on a bridge spanning the Oder in the final stages of the war that was an attempt to slow the advancing Soviets.

In the transfer specified in the Strasbourg agreement, the goods and people necessary were loaded aboard Condor aircraft by Geschwader 200 and flown form points within the Reich to Madrid, then on to Cadiz. Cadiz is on the Mediterranean Sea. From there transport to South America was accomplished using both Fw 200 Condors of Geschwader 200 and U-boats (28) Additionally, the Azores or the Canary Islands were used as a stopover base (29). I would ask the reader to keep this last sentence in mind for further reference.

Two Heinkel He 177s were heavily modified in Prague. The bomb bay area was enlarged, the engines changed along with other modification encompassing the whole aircraft. The only reason for doing this type of work was to allow for a much larger bomb, presumably an atomic bomb, to be delivered by this aircraft. One was extensively damaged before the end of the war but the other was intact enough to allow an assessment of its ultimate purpose. Friedrich Georg supplies us with six pictures of this aircraft for documentation (30). The importance to our story is the willingness of the Germans to take existing machines and modify them for new purposes almost "in the field".

Modification of existing aircraft characterizes the last aircraft we will consider, the Dornier Do 217-K-2. This aircraft was another prototype or perhaps just a test-bed. It was based on the well-known Dornier Do 217. This was a two engine, late 1930s design that could carry a somewhat larger payload than the Heinkel He 117.

Meanwhile, Dr. Eugen Saenger and his mathematician wife Dr. Irene Brendt were engaged in designing a huge ramjet powered bomber. This bomber would circle the earth by vaulting its way up to the far upper atmosphere and then re-enter the denser lower atmosphere in a series of skipping states, before firing up the ramjets once more and repeating the process. Saenger's ramjets were monsters, approaching twenty tons of thrust. This put the Saenger ramjet in the same league with Dr. Wernher von Braun's A-4 (V-2) engines. Saenger's engines were built and ready but the orbital bomber project was canceled. Saenger then went off to work on ramjet interceptors at the Skoda Works, leaving the monster engines in his past. So, for whatever reason, as a test-bed or for possible delivery of an atomic bomb, the huge Saenger ramjet engines were mounted on top of the Dornier Do 217, which was re-designated the Dornier Do 217-K-2 and fell under the purview of KG 100 (31).

Two of these Dornier Do 217-K-2s were found in the post-war years abandoned and partially wrecked in Istres in Southern France. This would make the date of their abandonment somewhere in the second half of 1944, as this is the time the Germans lost this ground.

Were there other examples? Why not and why leave such a wonderful example of a high-tech engine as a free gift for the Anglo-Americans? Other examples may have been evacuated to Germany.

The question arises of how fast could the Dornier Do 217-K-2 have flown? The short answer is "as fast as the pilot wanted to go" since the strength of the airframe was probably the limiting factor. If anyone were going to flee the 3rd Reich during its moment of collapse, it is hard to imagine an aircraft better suited for this purpose. This one-time light bomber could certainly accommodate a high-value individual and his secret library of wonder inventions on a fast, one-way ride to Norway or even possibly beyond.

Friedrich Georg with the help of Antonio Chover has uncovered a real mystery regarding Norway. This is great research and draws upon seemingly unrelated facts and events which are pieced together to make a coherent whole which sheds a new light on the history of World War Two, German involvement in Norway, and German secret weapons.

The mystery starts with a night attack on Northwest England by air. In the early morning hours of December 24, 1944 a large attack of 50 Heinkel He-111, belonging to Squadron 53 (KG 53), crossed the English coast and headed for the northeast industrial region, launching 31 V-1s from the air at their target. All the V-1s impacted between 5:28 and 6:45 AM. But serious reports list this attack, not on December 24th but on December 23rd. And the attack was precisely pinpointed on Manchester. On December 23rd, the Heinkel He-111s were not even in the air and the range for either the V-1 and V-2 would not have allowed them to be fired directly from Holland. The conclusion drawn is that these were not one attack in which dates were confused but two separate attacks (32).

The Italian newspaper "La Stampa", Turin, reported that the Christmas Eve attack was actually not an attack by He-111s firing V-1s. The report credited five German scientists with receiving an award from Hitler for the invention and development of a new long-distance weapon (33).

Sources are clear that neither attack was the work of the V-2 rocket. So if this was not an attack in which V-1s were carried within range of their target, what was it then? The answer comes from a surprising source, a Polish vacationer and it comes years later.

Flash forward to 1948. A former Polish soldier, Kasimir Browski, is on his summer vacation at Misdroy, on the Baltic coast in the vicinity of Swinemunde on the Wollin peninsula. This area was a testing ground during the war, most notably for testing the high-pressure cannon (HDP) of August Coanders. Browski must have been an inquisitive and hardy soul. He noticed a large launching ramp of the type used for the V-1 in the ocean. Browski decided to dive down in the Baltic waters to see what he could see. Browski, without diving equipment, was able to dive down four to five meters (16 feet or so) into the Baltic waters.

What Browski saw was amazing! Near the end of the ramp he found a series of totally unknown flying objects. Apparently, they were there as the result of some sort of misfiring. Perhaps each had its own individual problem that resulted in its crash landing, we will never know. This flying device had a long fuselage with an engine mounted on its rear top as in the V-1. Where wings would be found on a normal aircraft, Friedrich Georg pictures in his book, small wings as in a canard design. At the rear, below the engine, are located larger wings with adjustable control surfaces on them. From the presence of these control surfaces with the lack of a pilot, the conclusion must be reached that the missile was remote controlled. A small rocket is described by Browski as being underneath the craft that was undoubtedly for rocket-assisted take-off. The color of the missiles was gray-gold with the engine being a dark color. The diameter of the missiles was estimated by Browski to be 80-80 cm. Only one of these missiles was completely intact, the others were missing one or more parts. Browski christened the missiles the "V-4" (34).

Friedrich Georg compares them to a small version of the later American Martin Matador. The firm who made these missiles remains a complete mystery. Georg suggests Junkers and the mystery missiles Vu, D-6000 which was also probably launched from a catapult and was developed by the SS in Pilsen (35). He also suggests this missile may have been called the "V-3", but of course the HDP, the super-long distance cannon, the "centipede", developed by August Coanders, also was given that title.

The engine is a real mystery. Was this a pulsejet like the V-1? Or was this a turbojet, or perhaps a ramjet? All might be considered a possibility. There was talk of an improved V-1, could this be it? Turbojets were expensive and difficult to build but were more flexible in operation than either the pulsejet or the pure ramjet engines. The ramjet has no moving parts and is the simplest of all jet engines. It simply uses air rammed into its leading orifice for compression rather than a complicated compressor but it needs to reach about 250 miles per hour before the ram effect comes into presence. The rocket-assisted take off as well as the catapult ramp might indicate a ramjet. Also, all available turbojet engines were spoken for in the hard-pressed military situation the Germans found themselves.

As an aside, I must make mention of one other rumor about the V-4 or a missile very much like it. That rumor, I call it so for lack of more evidence, is that the V-4 was teamed up with the V-2 in a horse and rider configuration. Or, alternatively, that the V-2 formed the lower stage and the V-4 delivered the warhead. Georg's informant, "Dr. X", a Peenemuende insider, claims a range of 3500 km. (2135 miles) with a warhead weighing well over two tons (36) Using totally different sources the Czech researcher Dr. Milos Jesensky and the Polish engineer Robert Lesniakiewicz describe a similar craft, a combination V-1, V-2 that they say was to be somehow employed at sea, being towed by a U-boat. They call the missile the "Urzel" (37). Georg mentions the fact that Swedish reports, starting in October 1944, mentions "ghost rockets", so this phenomena was not one of the post-war period but originated during the war (38).

The American Martin Matador

Was this 1950's missile a natural post-war outgrowth of the V-1 or was it inspired by a German second generation cruise missile? Wrecks of the "V-3-V-4" were found submerged beyond a launching facility in the Baltic.

Engine	4,600 lbf (20,000 N) thrust Allison J33-A-37 Turbojet sustainer engine; 55,000 lb (25,000 kg) thust Aerojet General solid fuel rocket, 2 s burn
Wingspan	28 ft 7 in
Operational range	700 miles
Flight altitude	35,000 ft
Speed	Approximately 650 mph (Mach 0.9)
Guidance system	"A" Radar directed radio command guidance system; "C" same plus Shanicle
Launch platform	Mobile Launcher

Mr. Georg found the next clue in the newspapers of those times. Mention has already been made of the "La Stampa" article in which Hitler honored five German scientists for their work in developing a new weapon. In this article the report of the 12/24/44 attack on Manchester by Heinkel He-111 firing V-1 missiles was debunked which led to the story about the five scientists. But there is more. Both Reuters and the Swedish newspaper " Suedsvenska Dagbladdet" acknowledged the possibility that the Manchester attack in question was launched from the district of Hardangervidda, in Norway, on the Hardanger plateau (39). Even the English newspaper, the "Daily Express" from January 15, 1945 reported that German flying bombs had originated from Hardangervidda in the plateau region of Hardanger (40).

Now comes the Spanish researcher, Antonio Chover, who writes to the authorities in Norway and asks them about secret German installations in this vicinity. He got many answers, all saying essentially the same thing: there were no Norwegian launching facilities for German V-weapons in Norway and nothing of note happened in Hardangervidda in the region of Hardanger. Even one of the participants in the destruction of the German heavy water generating facility, the Norsk-Hydro plant, by the name of Klaus Helberg reported to Mr. Chover the Germans had an aerial observation base in that area but he assures Chover that the Germans had no plans for missile launching in this vicinity or at least he had never heard of any (41).

Could this be the end of the story? After all, why would he Norwegians decline information if they had it? Well, let me suggest something. Anglo-Americans did not enter Norway in order to oust the German forces. Germany was entered through France and so in this direct route, Norway was a diversion. In other words, there was no military reason to enter Norway. Yes, the Western Allies, especially the British, did assist resistance in Norway but in the end, Norway was left on its own. The Germans occupied Norway until the bitter end. And in the end the Germans just surrendered and faded away—-or vice versa. But either way, the Norwegians may have felt they owed nothing to any other country.

Because of this strategy of bypassing Norway, there were no super-secret teams of Americans and British combing Norway for German high technology. The Norwegians perhaps felt very entitled to keep whatever was left behind and share it with nobody. After all, the Norwegians have always been rather independent people, even today. Their relationship with the EU and to the Euro is evidence of this independence. Have they been wrong with this self-confidence? Well, no, Norway does have the highest standard of living in the world. So perhaps there was a wall of silence, on some level, directed toward outsiders.

But like every good researcher, a little rejection did not deter Antonio Chover. Finally, a letter was received from Frode Saeland, museum director of the Norwegian Industrial Workers Museum in Vermonk that is in the region of the German heavy water production plant near Rjukan. Mr. Saeland had a completely different answer to the question of German facilities in the plateau region. He reported that in the vicinity of the Gaustad Mountain peak the Germans began a secret base in autumn 1944. The rumor at the time was this facility was connected to secret German V-weapons. Mentioned is the word "Radioinstallation" (radio installation). Mention is also made of a radar installation. These would be the tools necessary to guide remote controlled missiles. Only German workers were allowed on these sites and the whole area of these facilities was guarded, day and night, land and air. Opposite to these installations in the nearby valley heavy anti-aircraft provisions were made to guard against an air attack. A railroad wound its way to the mountain peak and the whole railroad line was guarded with cannons, munitions facilities and barracks (41), (42). Not only could have these facilities have been used to guide the new long range V-1s or V-4s to their target, but they could have also eventually been used to guide the A-9/A-10 missiles to America.

The central Norwegian coast is fjord country. These fjords harbored the German Navy during the war. At first it was the refuge of capital ships such as the Bismarck and Scharnhorst but later these facilities took on an even greater importance as U-boat bunkers in France were bombed and eventually overrun. The U-boat facilities in Norway became the home for the U-boat fleet and the U-boat fleet became the real German Navy.

It was from this area that U-boats were sent out in the final days of the 3rd Reich on all manner of desperate missions. Until the very end, U-boats apparently awaited Nazi bigwigs who never showed up for their journeys of escape. Later, we will recount the mission of U-234 as well as the U-boats of the legendary "Last Battalion" whose point of departure was exactly these waters.

But for now we must return to the springboard for the Nazi post-war world, the airbases of Northern Norway from which the Germans explored and watched over their holding in the Arctic. From here special long distance aircraft, including prototype aircraft salvaged from jaws of Germany's collapse, were operational. Also, something new was in the air, a new identity was forming. Not only Wilhelm Landig tells us this in 1971, German engineer Claude Schweikhart (sometimes aka Erich Halk) tells this to us for the first time much earlier. In the August, 1952 issue of the magazine Mensch und Schicksal, he states that often in the last days of the war, in areas of highest priority for the Germans, the symbol of the "Schwarzen Sonne" (black sun) was in use in portions of the German armed air defense forces. These "heretics" within the SS, as Schweikhart calls them, above all used the air base at Banak in Northern Norway as their base for long distance flights over the inner Arctic using the most modern long distance aircraft which they had obtained after these aircraft were designated as "failed constructions" by the official Luftwaffe. Speaking specifically of this base at Banak, Schweikhart says: " If they likewise used a special symbol, it is uncertain, but possible" (43). This "failed construction" methodology for procuring long-distance aircraft is repeated by Landig and said by him to include flying discs. These aircraft were the property of a sect within the SS and were re-branded with the Black Sun symbol according to Landig (44).

Meanwhile, back in the highland plateau region, the Germans there evidently had ideas of carrying forth the war from Norway or at last prolonging the war from there. In fact, the last known German unit to surrender on the European mainland did so at Haudegen, Norway, on September 4, 1945 (45). This date lacks four days from being four months after Admiral Doenitz officially surrendered the three German fighting divisions of the German military, the Army, the Navy and the Air Force. Please note that the SS apparently never officially surrendered.

With a positive attitude Landig's three SS men leave Northern Norway in one of these special long-distance aircraft in the novel "Goetzen Gegen Thule", bound for a secret German post-war base somewhere in the Arctic, "Stuetzpunkt 103", which is Base 103 or as it is called here, Point 103.

Literature Cited

1. **Landig, Wilhelm, 1980**, *Wolfzeit um Thule*, page 30, Volkstum-Verlag Wilhelm Landig, Vienna, Austria.
2. **Lusar, Rudolf, 1964**, *Die deutschen Waffen und Geheimwaffen des 2. Weltkrieges und ihre Weiterentwicklung*, page 153, J.F. Lehmanns Verlag, Munich
3. **Landig, Wilhelm, 1971**, *Goetzen Gegen Thule*, page 37, Hans Pfeiffer Verlag GmbH, Hannover, Germany
4. **Lusar, Rudolf,** *ibid*
5. ***ibid.***
6. **Landig, Wilhelm, 1971**, *Goetzen Gegen Thule*, page 25
7. **Landig, Wilhelm, 1971**, *Goetzen Gegen Thule*, page 37
8. ***ibid.***, page 25
9. **Kens, Karlheinz & Heinz Nowarra, 1968**, *Die Deutschen Fluezeuge 1933-1945*, page 172, J.F. Lehmanns Verlag, Munich, Germany
10. ***ibid.***
11. ***ibid.***
12. **Landig, Wilhelm, 1971**, page 185
13. ***ibid.***
14. **Stevens, Henry, 2007**, *Hitler's Suppressed and Still-Secret Weapons, Science and Technology*, pages 123-124
15. **Nowak, Karl, 1954**, *German Patent number 905847*, Klasse 12g, Gruppe 101, page 1
16. **Landig, Wilhelm, 1971**, page 180
17. **Heppner, Siegfried, 1997**, "Geheimnisse...dem Deutschen Volke", page 11, ISBN 3-929086-12-3
18. **Georg, Friedrich, 2000**, *Hitler's Siegeswaffen Band 1: Luftwaffe Un Marine Geheim Nuklearwaffen des Dritten Reiches und ihre Traegersystem*, pages 31, 32, Amun-Verlag & Heinrich-Jung-Verlagsgesellschaft mbH, ISBN 3-935095-02-3 and ISBN 3-930558-57-9
19. **Georg, Friedrich, 2000**, pages 35, 36
20. **Georg, Friedrich, 2000**, page 40
21. **Georg, Friedrich, 2000**, page 41
22. **Georg, Friedrich, 2000**, page 43
23. ***ibid.***
24. **Georg, Friedrich, 2000**, page 44
25. **Georg, Friedrich, 2000**, page 44, citing Tom Agoston's 1993 book, *Teufel oder Technokrat-Hitlers graue Eminenz*, pages 43-44
26. **Georg, Friedrich, 2000**, page 45

27. **Agoston, Tom, 1985**, *Blunder: How the U.S. Gave Away Nazi Supersecrets to Russia*, page 35, Dodd, Mead & Company, Inc., N.Y., NY.

28. **Haarmann, D.H., 1985**, *III Geheim Wunderwaffen Ueber den Krieg hinaus!*, page 96, Hugin, Geschellschaft fuer pol. phil. Studien e.V., Eigendruck, Germany

29. **Buechner, Col. Howard and Capt Wilhelm Bernhart, 1989**, *Hitler's Ashes*, pages 130-133, Thunderbird Press Inc., Metairie, Louisiana, USA

30. **Georg, Friedrich, 2000**, pages 54-56

31. **Georg, Friedrich, 2004**, *Hitlers Siegeswaffen Band 2: Star Wars 1947 Teilband B: Von der Amerikarakete zur Orbitalstation-Deutschlands Streben nach Interkontinentalwaffen und das erste Weltraumprogram*, pages 57-60, Amun-Verlag Schleusingen, Germany, in conjunction with Heinrich Jung Verlag, Zella-Mehlis, Germany

32. Georg, Friedrich, 2003, *Hitlers Siegeswaffen Band 2: Star Wars 1947 Teil A: Vn der V-1 zur A-9: unkonventionelle Kurz-und Mittelstreckenwaffen*, pages 220-221, Amun-Verlag, Schleusingen, Germany and Heinrich-Jung Verlag, Zella-Mehlis, Germany

33. ***ibid.***

34. **Georg, Friedrich, 2003**, pages 204-205

35. ***ibid***.

36. ***ibid.***

37. **Jesensky, Dr. Milos and Ing. Robert Lesniakiewicz, 1998**, *"Wunderland" Mimozemske Technologie Treti Rise*, pages 11, 15, Aos Publishing, ISBN: 80-86063-15-1

38. **Georg, Friedrich, 2003**, pages 205-206

39. **Georg, Friedrich, 2003**, page 221

40. **Georg, Friedrich, 2003**, page 219

41. **Georg, Friedrich, 2003**, page 221

42. **Georg, Friedrich, 2003**, page 220

43. **Schweikhart, Claude, August, 1952**, Mensch und Schicksal, 10/6, page 5

44. **Landig, Wilhelm, 1980**, *Wolfzeit Um Thule*, page 30, Volkstum-Verlag/Wilhelm Landig, A-1040, Vienna, Austria, ISBN 3-85342-033-8

45. **Georg, Friedrich, 2000**, page 45

POINT 103

Wihelm Landig is just about our only source for the secret base he calls Point 103. Landig uses every setting, every situation, to unveil something that happened during the war or some aspect of thinking or technology. When his three characters, the three German soldiers, land at Point 103 they are told of the "V-7", a German flying disc that has been brought there. They are told its developmental history and means of operation. They are likewise informed of other prototype aircraft that have been brought to this base and housed there as well as the extent and purpose of Point 103 itself.

Point 103 is set by Landig to be in the Canadian Arctic. We know that the Germans had a base as far West as Cape Chidley which is east of Hudson's Bay but Landig's locating this particular base in the Canadian Arctic rather than farther east may be literary license, we simply do not know. It is set on an island in a semi-circular basin surrounding Point 103. Tunnels were made in the rock and served as living areas and storage as was done by the Germans at many other of their secret facilities, Nordhausen, Jonastal, Der Riese, Zement, and so on. Since aircraft were flown into this base, it must have had runway facilities. Hangers were blasted out of the solid rock mountains surrounding the base and it was in these cave-hangers that experimental aircraft of all sorts were stored. This base contained workshops, research facilities, housing, cooking facilities, offices, corridors, and assembly halls. Hundreds of German soldiers inhabited this base on an ongoing basis. It functioned as a listening station, air base, weather station and most probably a U-boat facility (1).

Point 103 was connected to the outside world in this immediate post-war time frame by flying disc as well as by radio. Writer O. Bergmann states that Germans of the Arctic groups were in communication with other post-war German groups via in intermediate position in the Northern Andes. Each group had its own code-name. The group in the Northern Andes used the designation "Atlantis", for instance. He states that other post-war groups survived in bases in inner Asia, as well as Africa and that these along with the Arctic base formed a unit while another three group unit was formed by a group in Greenland, somewhere near Australia and somewhere in the Pacific (2).

he Canadian Arctic
larked are Cape Schidley, the Boothia Peninsula and Magnetic North Pole.

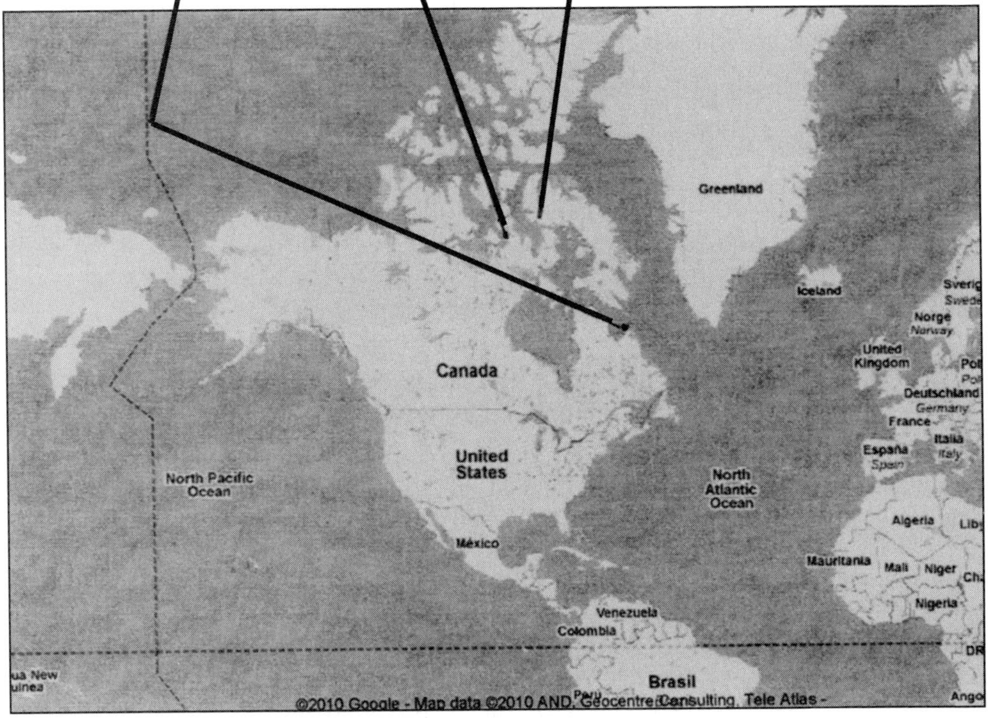

It seems that all branches of the German military were represented at Point 103, including the SS. The particular sub-group or inner circle of the SS present at Point 103 lent their esoteric symbol, the Black Sun, to the base as a whole. On their aircraft the standard German insignias were removed and in their place the Black Sun sign was displayed. This took the form of a deep, dark-red circle (3). It is quite obvious that the thinking behind this symbol came from the Thule Society and their belief in a kind of Nordic Atlantis in the far north from which sprung the Aryan peoples, particularly the ancient Germanics. The Black Sun symbol reached its zenith at Point 103. It was adopted by some mystery U-boats of German origin sighted after the war but it was apparently not used in Neuschwabenland, Landig's Point 211. The flying discs and possibly aircraft flying form Point 211 used the old German military insignias (4).

During the war, Wilhelm Landig had been in charge of security for the airport at Prague where three flying disc projects were housed. Since this area was the industrial heartland for the SS, Landig would have also been familiar with any aircraft projects under development by the SS. He would have also personally seen any prototypes flying to "his" airport from other facilities. Therefore, taking Landig at is word regarding things that fly is not stretching the imagination very much. But Landig does not stop with things that fly. He goes on to describe some other amazing aspects of alleged Nazi technology under development or operating at Point 103.

According to Landig, aircraft were guided to Point 103 by a special compass, called a Himmelskompass (heavenly compass). This compass did not work on magnetic lines of force generated by earth's magnetic field as most compasses do. This is because the magnetic north pole is not located at the geographic North Pole, but instead on the Boothia Peninsula, the third peninsula west of Hudson's Bay, hundreds and hundreds of miles south of the geographic North Pole. Instead of measuring magnetic lines of force with a needle, the Himmelskompass measured polarized light (5). So, using this device as a guide, an aircraft could be navigated to the proper coordinates without the use of a traditional compass and without interference from a defensive device employed at Point 103, the Magnetofunk.

The Magnetofunk was a compass in reverse. It generated a magnetic field and so would confuse any aircraft using a magnetic compass. It would influence the compass just enough to throw off anyone following it as a guide. Therefore, enemy aircraft would be passively diverted around Point 103 without the searching aircraft even being aware of its influence. A more detailed discussion of both the Himmelskompass and the Magnetofunk can be found in my previous book (6).

But Landig describes other amazing devices and research going on deep within the bowels of Point 103. He states that a kind of alchemy is at work here. This is not the old alchemy of gold making, conspiracy or black cats, but a new alchemy for modern times. Vril energy was being analyzed. Landig goes on to state that this Vril energy was suitable for powering aircraft. It was the same sort of energy sought by the ancient Indians for their flying craft, the Vimanas. Mercury was being used as a partial means of propulsion. Landig then goes on to make an amazing statement, saying that "our Indian friends" are busy reconstructing ancient secrets under security observation from these ancient sources (7).

In another paragraph Landig states that experimentation was ongoing involving the generation of electricity from a totally new perspective, in its "entire aggregate condition". In this work electricity is called a formless body. In fact it is gas-like, liquid and solid (8). This sounds like some of the strangest explanations I have heard cited by those close to Karl Schappeller regarding aether energy in its most fundamental (coldest) state.

More convention energy extraction was also said to be going on at Point 103. In this, latent heat from the atmosphere was being extracted and presumably used to generate electricity. This was a benzene-steam procedure, developed in 1944 by a deceased engineer named Doczeka (9). Latent heat is the heat given off or absorbed in the process of vaporization from the atmosphere, in other words at ambient temperatures. The extraction of latent heat can happen at very cold ambient temperature, even in Arctic conditions.

At some point we must consider the question of the actual reality of Point 103. Landig tells us that his story is a story “full of realities”. But there is the possibility that Point 103 was not where Landig says it was. In fact, there is a possibility that it was simply just a literary prop to explain other things. Since Landig is really our only source for Point 103, the question certainly arises as to any supporting documentation for this base. The supporting evidence is small but the following is what there is of it.

In an article that translates to: “A Strange Message from the Reich of the Polar People” (10), mention is made of a mysterious “Blue Island” in the polar sea. It seems that routine Canadian air patrols originating out of the Parry Islands began encountering something they could not explain. Several independent reports from around 1950 state more or less the same thing. It seems that these patrol flights (their purpose was not stated) would sometimes encounter what they described as an island, surround by an icy ring of high mountains. On this island building structures could just be made out. Further, aircraft of some sort and which could not be properly identified were seen. These “notable powered aircraft” could be seen landing.

But there was a big problem. All attempts to approach this island for a better look were met with a strange kind of resistance. Upon drawing closer to the island, the aircraft was surrounded by a “thick blue aether” which was impenetrable to the aircraft’s radar. The article goes on to suggest relationships within esoteric ideas of the immediate post-war Nazi world.

Now, this is not Reuters or some other reputable new agency. It would be very easy to dismiss this whole tale based upon its obscure source and the more or less factual treatment of some of the esoteric language included in the text. What is being said is that using this article as proof for Point 103 is not only non-sufficing, but it needs backup on its own.

But what if strong supporting documentation were found? Would this not serve as verification for the “Blue Island” story and additionally make this whole obscure story for Point 103 far more probably?

The Blue Island story rests on reports of routine Canadian overflights of the Arctic. For what purpose were the flights? At this very same time the Americans were doing exactly the same thing from their own Arctic bases in Alaska. And they were searching for UFOs. We know this thanks to Retired Col. Wendell Stevens (no relation to this writer) who was stationed in Alaska after the war, flying B-29s, whose mission it was to photograph UFOs, either flying or on the ice. Col. Stevens, a famous UFO investigator, has told this story many times over the years in print, at UFO conferences and in correspondence to me. The B-29s were stripped of guns and instead several types of cameras were mounted in the gun locations. Col. Stevens reports that sightings were made of UFOs, in the air and on the ice, photographed, with the film being sent via courier to higher-ups in Washington, DC in an undeveloped state. No feedback of any sort was ever made to those flyers taking the pictures. In retrospect, Col. Stevens has written to me that the makers and operators of those early flying saucers may have been Nazis.

Since the Canadians were doing exactly the same thing from their positions in the Arctic, it is safe to assume that the mission was substantially the same. The Canadians were looking for something that should not have been there, UFOs. What they may have found in the Blue Island was a base. What they encountered in approaching the island may have been some defensive device of which we know nothing.

But we have circumstantial evidence that is even stronger than this and it comes from the governments of Canada, the USA and Germany. This evidence is the movement of the famous German U-boat, U-234. This was the cargo U-boat, headed for Japan at the very close of the war, which somehow ended up surrendering to Allied forces between Halifax, Nova Scotia and Portsmouth, New Hampshire, a whole hemisphere away from Japan.

U-234 was a Type Xb minelaying submarine. The Type Xs were the largest submarine built by the 3rd Reich, displacing 2,000 tons. A bomb hit U-234 during construction in 1942 and again in May 1943. It was not commissioned until March 3, 1944 and spent a couple months in the Baltic on a shake down cruise. On or about August 30, 1944, U-234 returned to Kiel and from there to the Germania Werft U-boat yards where it was overhauled and refitted from a minelayer to a transport ship (11).

To structurally transform U-234, her 24 vertical mineshafts were removed. This left two large storage chambers running down the sides of the ship on either side of the conning tower and six vertical shafts in the center-forward area of the submarine. In addition, four horizontal deck storage containers, originally containing torpedoes were converted for cargo storage (12). U-234 was fitted with a snorkel, the latest and best radar as well as other electronic defense devices.

The point should be emphasized that this U-boat was reconstructed into something that it was not in its original design. My position is that older U-boats were rebuilt or reconstructed towards the end of the war and used for testing of designs that might once have called for a prototype submarine to be constructed from scratch. We know that U-boats were damaged by bombing or even sunk and resurrected. Were the original U-boat numbers kept or where new numbers assigned to reconstructed boats? Imagine the confusion this question alone would generate amongst the Allies who were desperately trying to sink U-boats and needed to identify each for purpose of evaluating tactics. We will come back to this idea later in the book.

Returning to U-234, in December 1944, it was re-launched and they proceeded with new trials. Ten weeks later the ship was ready for her first mission and began loading fuel and provisions. Everyone knew the destination, Japan (13).

The cargo aboard U-234 was to be a gift to the Japanese to benefit the Japanese war effort against the United States. At first the two major Axis powers had been cool toward each other as war partners. Hitler entered into the alliance thinking Japan could help him against the Soviets while the Japanese thought the Germans could help them against the United States. After Pearl Harbor, Hitler honored the treaty and declared war on Japan's enemy, the USA. But it was only toward the end of the war, as each partner saw how the other acted in adversity, that mutual respect led to increased mutual assistance. U-234 was not the first U-boat to transmit cargo to Japan and the German sent the Japanese gifts by other means such as long distance aircraft as we have already seen.

The cargo of U-234 consisted of microfilm of designs for secret weapons, drugs, radar, radio equipment and other electrical components, technical drawings, lenses, anti-aircraft rockets and other munitions, mercury, lead, zinc, a disassembled Messerschmitt Me 262 jet fighter (14), secret documents in sealed containers, a Panzerfaust and other anti-tank weapons, cameras, optical glass, and small rockets. Now we know beyond a doubt that U-234 carried uranium oxide in special containers for the Japanese Army (15). Dr. Ing. Heinz Schlicke, the electronic specialist who was onboard to advise the Japanese is said by Warrant Officer Wolfgang Hirschfield in his memoirs to have thrown overboard the microfilm for the America Rocket (presumably the A-9/A-10) just before being taken into custody by the Americans (16).

But there is more. Dr. Schlicke was said to be carrying designs for an infa-red fuse detonation system for an atomic bomb. This design was said to have been used a couple months after the capture of U-234 on the Trinity atomic bomb test in the New Mexico desert. Dr. Joseph P. Farrell cites researcher Carter Hydrick in his book Critical Mass as saying U-234 carried atomic bomb components and "presumably plans to build those weapons as well" (17). Dr. Farrell seems to endorse this view as he does Hydrick's work without reservation. Accompanying the chapter is a copy of the US Navy's microfilm records concerning the cargo of U-234. There are plenty of fuses aboard U-234 but these pertain to the ship's operation or perhaps other cargo. But there is a designation of "Dr. Schlicke's fuses" which are of particular concern here as Dr. Schlicke was an atomic expert aboard U-234 and not a member of the crew or a radar or missile specialist. There can be little doubt that these fuses are the fuses under discussion in regards to an atomic bomb.

Now I am going to tell you what people say "off the record". I have heard people familiar with U-234 say that not only were plans and components for an atomic bomb carried by U-234; an entire atomic bomb was part of the cargo! We know the uranium oxide was present. We know that fuses, a serious secret component that was perhaps lacking in the American scheme, were present. We know other very secret technology was present. Why not an actual atomic bomb? If this were true, it would go along way to answering the reasons for the obfuscation on the part of the US National Archives over this cargo (18). Does one make the explosive and the fuses before he has made the bomb?

We can say that U-234 was a very important U-boat for the Germans, for the Americans and for the Japanese who were eagerly awaiting its arrival in Japan. So what in the world was it doing off the coast of Nova Scotia? That destination is certainly not on the way to Japan. Someone has some explaining to do. Let's look at the U-234 timeline. This is mostly based on the Wolfgang Hirshfeld diary, published by Geoffrey Brooks.

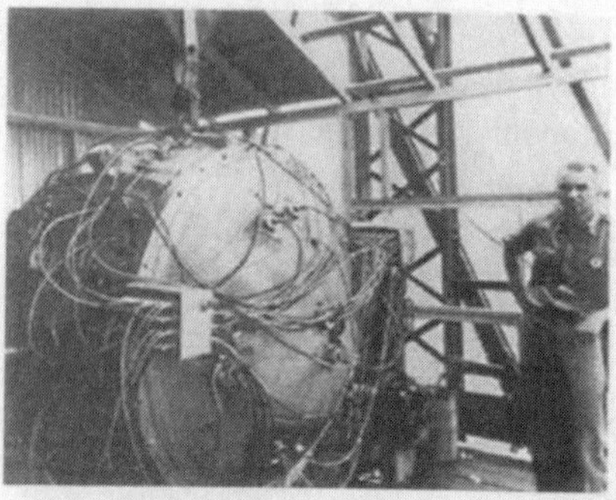

Trinity nuclear test bomb
(Detonated July 16, 1945)

Infrared Fuses Please note the cable-like devices covering the Trinity test atomic bomb. These are the infrared fuses.

March 25, 1945, U-234 leaves Kiel, Germany for Kristiansand, Norway. The next morning it picks up some escort vessels including three of the latest Type XXIII U-boats.

March 29, 1945, U-234 reaches the Oslo Fjord. A training run is announced for all U-boats equipped with a snorkel. During the training run, U-234 collides with U-1301. There is no dry dock available for U-234. Captain Fehler obtains a suitable steel plate and while anchoring near Kristiansand, submerges the bow 20 degrees by flooding the forward tanks, raising the stern out of the water.

April 1945. For the first week repairs continue using the ship's diesel engines as a power source to weld the steel plate in place. General Ulrich Kessler, Luftwaffe attaché to Tokyo boards U-234. Kessler is an anti-Nazi and anti-Goering that upsets Captain Fehler.

April 14, 1945, Hirshfeld, as communications officer, receives a message: "U-234 Sail only on my order. Sail at once on your own initiative. Doenitz",

April 16, 1945, U-234 leaves Kristiansand on route to Japan. But U-234 heads north, not south, up the Norwegian coast to at least the latitude of Bergen, Norway (19). Dr. Farrell, relying on Hydrick verifies this and points out that this is inconsistent with the ship's log and suggests a second "official log" may have replaced the log (20). This is the beginning of the inconsistencies regarding the movements of U-234.

Meanwhile, Wolfgang Hirshfeld gives us the details on U-234's course to Japan. He says U-234 proceeded at periscope depth and began "the long voyage to the Equator by snorkel". The course was south, along the coast of Africa, around the Cape of Good Hope, to the Indian Ocean, across "the wide ocean to the heart of Japan". This "wide ocean" can only mean the Pacific, so from a point south of Ceylon, U-234 was to proceed to the Pacific Ocean. This is Hirshfeld's commentary after giving the last confirmed date of April 16, 1945.

But then somehow Hirshfeld begins talking about the Iceland-Faroes Narrows and navigation problems. Fehler begins to run on the surface rather than at periscope depth. U-234 "breaks out into the Atlantic" in an environment of "sub-arctic swell".

May 1, 1945 or so, U-234 learns of Hitler's death.

May 4, 1945, a cease-fire for attack submarines is received. All attack submarines were ordered to return to Norway. Captain Fehler ignored this order since his was not an attack submarine.

May 6, 1945 U-234 receives notice that Japan considered all treaty agreements with Germany over and Germans in Japan would be considered enemy aliens and arrested.

May 8, 1945 U-234 learns of Germany's surrender. But according to Hirshfeld, Regional Commander of U-boats Bergen, Norway, Captain Roesing sent Fehler a message "in Japan cipher": "U-234 continue your voyage or return to Bergen, FdU". Hirshfeld says U-234 was moving at 16 knots to the southwest on a "Great Circle course in the mid-Atlantic".

Date Unstated, the Allies signal instructions for surrender for all U-boats. This was carried out by "particular sea area". U-234's port of surrender was Halifax, Nova Scotia, Canada. Captain Fehler and First Officer Richard Bulla monitor English language radio for the next five days.

May 13, 1945 U-234 makes contact with Halifax but Captain Fehler continues sailing south (21).

Date Unstated, Captain Fehler makes contact with the American destroyer, Sutton, and arranges surrender.

May 19, 1945 U-234 arrives in Portsmouth, New Hampshire, USA.

What is really going on here? We have a period of time, April 16, 1945 to about May 13, 1945 where U-234 is way out of position. First, it sails north, not south to near Bergen, Norway. Then it turns west, still not south, and ends up in the mid-Atlantic. Then it makes contact with Halifax while in that vicinity, the Canadian arctic, headed south. What ever happened to sailing south past West Africa to the Cape of Good Hope, let along the final destination of Japan?

I have to believe the original intention was to sail to Japan. Two Japanese officers were aboard U-234 who subsequently committed suicide after Hitler's death and then there was General Kessler, attaché to Japan. But something happened on the way that caused U-234 to reconsider this trip. This "something" was so extreme that the logbook had to be discarded and a new one substituted according to some. In all, we have to account for twenty-eight days, from April 16 to May 13, 1945 in which the exact whereabouts of U-234 are a mystery. What could have happened?

It is the opinion of Ferrell, citing Hydrick that a side trip to Hamburg to pick up Martin Bormann and Heinrich "Gestapo" Mueller was made on April 30, 1945 or May 1, 1945 (22). But this would involve going south, not north, after leaving Kristiansand. I think something else happened, something much simpler.

I think U-234 made a side trip to a base in Eastern Greenland. After doing whatever it was that brought them to Greenland, U-234 headed south and then west, probably in an attempt to visit the other large secret German base, Point 103. Perhaps they did visit Point 103 or perhaps not, but whatever happened, U-234 was headed south in Canadian arctic waters when it made contact with Halifax. Wolfgang Hirshfeld, the communications officer aboard U-234, says the U-boat surrender was by area and the area inhabited by U-234 at that time meant she was to surrender in Halifax.

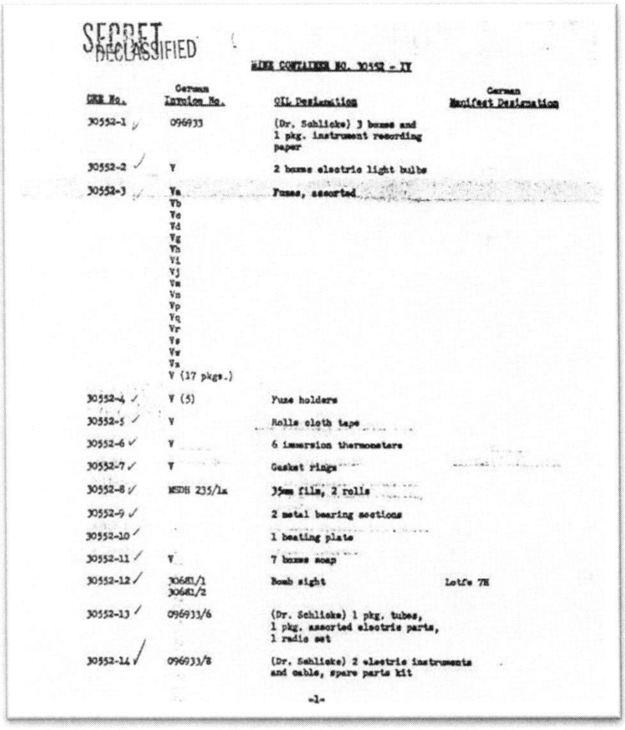

SECRET
DECLASSIFIED

MINE CONTAINER NO. 30552 - YY

CNR No.	German Invoice No.	OIL Designation	German Manifest Designation
30552-1	096933	(Dr. Schlicke) 3 boxes and 1 pkg. instrument recording paper	
30552-2	Y	2 boxes electric light bulbs	
30552-3	Ya Yb Yc Yd Yg Yh Yi Yj Ym Yn Yp Yq Yr Ys Yw Yx Y (17 pkgs.)	Fuses, assorted	
30552-4	Y (5)	Fuse holders	
30552-5	Y	Rolls cloth tape	
30552-6	Y	6 immersion thermometers	
30552-7	Y	Gasket rings	
30552-8	MSDH 235/1a	35mm film, 2 rolls	
30552-9		2 metal bearing sections	
30552-10		1 beating plate	
30552-11	Y	7 boxes soap	
30552-12	30681/1 30681/2	Bomb sight	Lotfe 7H
30552-13	096933/6	(Dr. Schlicke) 1 pkg. tubes, 1 pkg. assorted electric parts, 1 radio set	
30552-14	096933/8	(Dr. Schlicke) 2 electric instruments and cable, spare parts kit	

-1-

Dr. Heinz Schlicke's Fuses from U-234 It is the writer's opinion that the mystery fuses shown in the enlarged photograph are the infrared fuses used to detonate the Trinity atomic bomb. *Source: Department of Navy, Naval Historical Center, Washington, D.C. Microfisch obtained via F.O.I.A. Request.*

So, what caused this change of plan aboard U-234? Maybe stopping in Eastern Greenland was the plan all along. Or perhaps events in the open Atlantic further South from Kristainsand scared off U-234 and it sought refuge for a time before even considering taking up its mission to Japan. We are going to return to this possibility later in discussing the Last Battalion legend. Once conditions in Japan deteriorated for the Germans, surrender seemed like the best option. But it was surrender to the Americans, not the Canadians that was the goal of Captain Fehler. U-234 had to get farther south and somehow the logbooks had to show this last sprint for Portsmouth for the logbooks to have any credibility at all.

In considering the possibility of Landig's Point 103, we have the vague and somewhat legendary-sounding evidence of the "Blue Island". But, we know both the Canadians and the Americans were making routine flights over the Arctic looking for something secret as Retired Col. Wendell Stevens testifies. Finally, we have evidence that U-234 was heading south in Canadian Arctic waters after the war ended with the reasons for its presence never adequately resolved. Combine this with a know German Canadian Arctic weather station at Cape Chidley which went undetected and undiscovered for 37 years (23). Considering this combined evidence, the likelihood of Point 103 being a reality are at least 50-50 in my mind. Landig states that Point 103 functioned after Germany's surrender but not much longer. It was abandoned in favor of more hospitable refuges.

Literature Cited

1. **Landig, Wilhelm, 1971**, *Goetzen Gegen Thule Ein Roman voller Wirklichkeiten*, pages 123-132, Hans Pfeiffer Verlag, GmbH, Hannover, Germany
2. **Bergmann, O., 1989**, *II Deutsche Flugscheiben und U-boote Ueberwachen Die Welmeere*, page 134, Hugin Gesellschaft Fuer Politisch-Philosophische Studien E. V., Wetter/Ruhr, Germany
3. **Landig, Wilhelm, 1971**, page 137
4. **Landig, Wilhelm, 1991**, *Rebellen fuer Thule Das Erbe Von Atlantis*, page 570, Volkstum-Verlag, Vienna, Austria
5. **Landig, Wilhelm, 1971**, pages 27-28
6. **Stevens, Henry, 2007**, *Hitler's Suppressed and Still-Secret Weapons, Science and Technology*, pages 52-57. Adventures Unlimited Publishing, Kempton, Illinois, USA
7. **Landig, Wilhelm, 1971**, pages 276-277
8. **Landig, Wilhelm, 1971**, page 277
9. **Landig, Wilhelm, 1971**, pages 276-277
10. **Neues Europa, 1951**, "Eine seltsame Botschaft aus dem Reich der "Polarier" "Blue Island"-die geheimnisvolle Insel in der Arktis.-unbekannte Flugzeuge, die dort landen.-Blue Island", ein zweites Shangi-La? Was wissen die "Polarier" von der letzten Pruefung, die wir noch zu bestehen haben?, newspaper/magazine article from January 1, 1951, Stuttgart, Zuerich.
11. **Brooks, Geoffrey, 1992**, *Hitler's Nuclear Weapons*, pages 141-148, Leo Cooper (publishing), London, England
12. **Henshall, Philip, 1992**, *Vengence Hitler's nuclear Weapon: Fact Or Fiction?,* pages 122-123, Alan Sutton Publishing Ltd, Gloucestershire, England
13. ***ibid.***
14. ***ibid.***
15. **Stevens, Henry, 2007**, pages 8-10
16. **Brooks, Geoffrey, 1992**, page 166
17. **Farrell, Joseph, 2008**, *The Nazi International The Nazis'Postwar Plan to Control Finance, Conflict, Physics and Space*, page 125, Adventures Unlimited Press, Kempton, Illinois, USA
18. **Stevens, Henry, 2007**, pages 6-17
19. **Henshall, Philip, 1995**, page 125*ibid.*
20. **Farrell, Joseph, 2008**, page 124
21. **Henshall, Philip, 1992**, page 126
22. **Farrell, Joseph, 2008**, page 122
23. **Bergmann, O., 1988**, page 57

GERMAN FLYING DISCS, UPDATE

At this point we are going to take a little break from the topic of secret bases and explore some ideas about German flying discs.

In my first book, Hitler's Flying Saucers, the point was made that in this study there are worlds within worlds to consider regarding German flying discs. Some new information has come to light but first we must jump down one of these rabbit holes, so hold on.

There were probably two forms of German field propulsion flying discs, a large one and a smaller one. They each may have had different technical origins. In my first book the work of Karl Schappeller and further development of his ideas by the pre-war Reichsarbeitsgemeinschaft (Reich Works Association) was documented (1). This concerned the larger of the German saucers. I feel confident that this type of technology accounts for the larger discs although not exactly as I originally thought. New evidence has come in the form of two German engineers who have researched Schappeller. I do not want to give away identities or more details as one or two of these European researchers intend a book on this and other new aspects of the Karl Schappeller mystery but the new for me is that the two really first rate scientists who have investigated the world of Schappeller, on site, conclude that the Schappeller device is related to the work of Nikola Tesla. This makes Bill Lyne and his work look pretty good in my eyes right now.

The reader might remember that Schappeller described the central core of his device as "glowing magnetism" in which there was apparently some sort of glowing energy that had a magnetic field. Recently, I came across Tesla's own words that made think of Schappeller's statement. Tesla is discussing broadcast transmission of electrical energy that is quoted in a book edited by David Hatcher Childress and titled: The Tesla Papers Nikola Tesla n Free Energy & Wireless Transmission of Power, page 66:

> *"I gained this conviction through the discovery of a singular electrical phenomenon, which I described early in 1892, in lectures delivered before some scientific societies abroad, and which I have called a "rotating brush". This is a bundle of light which is formed, under certain conditions, in a vacuum-bulb, and which is of a sensitiveness to magnetic and electric influences bordering, so to speak, on the supernatural. This light bundle is rapidly rotated by the earth's magnetism as many as twenty thousand times per second, the rotation in these parts being opposite to what it would be in the southern hemisphere, while in the*

region of the magnetic equator it should not rotate at all. In its most sensitive state, which is difficult to attain, it is responsive to electric or magnetic influences to an incredible degree."

For me, a simple layman, a bundle of electric energy is certainly charged and a charged field that rotates generates a magnetic field. This must be Schappeller's glowing magnetism. More on this is coming later.

But there was another type of German field propulsion disc, the smaller one. The smaller saucers I call the "Magnetscheiben" or magnetic discs after a description related to me by Horst Schuppmann (2). Now, there may be a new and better explanation of the workings of smaller discs thanks to physicist Dr. Paul Potter.

Before starting on this explanation, I would like to make it clear that I have no evidence for operational German field propulsion flying discs in World War Two. My position is that they only experimented on these devices during the war. Later post-war observations of these devices, such as were called "Adamski craft", were further developed by Germans in South America, possibly Greenland, and possibly in the USA.

The smaller discs, called the "Vril discs" by most people, are given an origin as inventions of the Vril Society, a subset of the Thule Society. According to this line of thought, the arrangement of construction was channeled to Vril psychic mediums. Three counter-rotating magnetic fields, one on top of another, somehow supplied the lift (3).

Writer O. Bergmann, while not contradicting Juergen-Ratthofer the spiritual father of the Vril and Haunebu concept, gives us a better explanation of the workings in my mind. Please bear with my translation:

"The later flying discs (UFOs) have still only one revolving, rotating ring as is always reported by eye witnesses. This revolving ring causes the same effect, serviceably copying, heavenly bodies and planets as they circle about themselves whereby each its own gravity field will be generated, planets as in flying discs. Nature, the godly cosmos, is constructed upon wise, conformed, laws. Today mankind does not possess the ability to recognize these wise, conformed laws let alone to mimic the abolition of gravity by means of rotation in technical devices. We have already said that the German flying discs have made themselves independent of earth's gravity, just as from the gravity of other planets. They have no longer relinquished the powers of pressure and suction whereby the often observed zigzag flight at high speed is at once possible to them without harm for the (disc's) inhabitants or suddenly stand still in the air."(4)

Another version of the same idea comes from writer D. H. Harmann, writing even earlier, before the onset of Norbert Juergen-Rathoffer or Ralf Ettl. Again, my translation:

"All material bodies set in motion generate a magnetic field in this way because all material electrons contained are set free by rotation. This holds in the greater sense also for planets that through rotation generate their

electromagnetic or gravitation field as I have already said. This works if advanced in rotation or else held fixed in rotation as through the sun." (5)

I want to focus on the words of these two German writers but just so the reader will not think that this "planetary motion" idea is completely aberrant, or some peculiarity of the German mind, below are a couple paragraphs from William Lyne:

"According to Hannes Alfven, a giant electric current travels through space along lines of "frozen magnetic force" from the sun to the earth, passes through the earth and back to the sun's equator, imparting "angular momentum" to the earth in its solar orbit. This was based on earlier research by Kristian Birkeland, who in 1895 explained the aurora borealis as the effect of the currents later proven by Alfven, as they enter the earth's magnetic field is almost vertical, causing a glow similar to that of cathode rays in a laboratory.

J.J. Thompson, in 1893, restated Tesla's earlier finding (without attribution), "..if moving tubes of force entering a conductor are dissolved in it, mechanical momentum is given to it at right angles to the tubes and to the magnetic induction", adding that this momentum is " ...proportional to the vector product of electric and magnetic forces". This repeated what Tesla had said, since the momentum was proportional to the vector product of the electric and magnetic fields." (6)

So the point these writers seem to be making is that a force, gravity or electromagnetism or both can be generated through rotating bodies and that German flying discs or at least one type of German flying disc, used a rotating part, the saucer part, to achieve this energy production. In this way they mimic and are based upon planetary motion. This is not the same as the aerodynamic forces being generated by the Miethe, Schriever and Habermohl discs that also rotated about their axes. What is being discussed is totally different. It is a method of field propulsion. But outside of describing its motion, we are still at a loss to explain its workings other than the Juergen-Ratthofer reference to three moving magnetic fields.

In and around this discussion, all three writers cite and mention Renato Vesco. Renato Vesco was an Italian engineer who worked with the Germans during the war in the secret facility at Lake Garda. Vesco was fortunate enough to gain access to the British Intelligence Objectives Sub-Committee files in London. From this he gleaned most of his knowledge on flying discs. This access to British as well as American (Combined) Intelligence Objectives Sub-Committee reports as well as other reports on German wartime science and technology began in 1946 even as they were coming off the printing press. It was in 1946, one year after the war ended, that a period of good feeling and relaxation developed. Actually, it was more like a security meltdown since for some reason things never acknowledged before or since were allowed to leak out. This all changed from 1947 onward as relations between the East and the West cooled and then froze into the Cold War. Even since the Cold War has ended, the intelligence agencies of both the East and West have behaved as if this secrecy situation developed during the Cold War is going to be a permanent, ongoing, state policy.

Vesco, giving us a glimpse through the modern security-state secret window and into the world of that defeated technical wonder, Nazi Germany, speaks of one organization doing work on rotating bodies, Kreiselgeraete, GmbH. The word "Kreiselgeraete" means something like "gyroscopic devices". The relationship to flying saucers is obvious. Vesco explains the obvious fact that the cabin needs to be held steady in relationship to any rapidly rotating ring extending outward which the flying saucer might have (7). Vesco actually only devotes one paragraph to Kreiselgeraete but everyone since seems to have agreed that this company must have played some role in at least some German flying discs. Here are Vesco's words on Kreiselgeraete:

> *"In 1945 the National Physical Laboratory's division of applied physics had reexamined a system of direct gyroscopic stabilization. It was modeled on the same system that at the beginning of the century had made the "miracle" of the Monorail train possible (a curious vehicle that has never come into widespread use; it was kept balanced on a single rail thanks to the gyrostatic inertia developed by the small by heavy and rapidly spinning flywheel). In addition, the laboratory put to profitable use in its own studies the experience accumulated by the scientists of the Kreislegeraete G.m.b.H. of Berlin Britz, a dissolved company that had specialized in the study and construction of mechanisms employing gyroscopic phenomena. In 1943 Kreiselgeraete had succeeded in reducing the oscillations of a violently disturbed moving body to not more than one tenth of a degree." (8)*

The obvious next step is to get a copy of whatever information the government has on Kreiselgeraete. But what is it we are looking for exactly in consideration of Kreiselgeraete? This "information" is going to take the form of a government report that is going to have to be obtained using the coercive power of the Freedom of Information Act. We cannot expect the government to simply spill the beans and discuss flying discs in a report on a company which at best built sub-assemblies for such craft. The reader might remember the matter of Dr. Mario Zippermayr, his fuel-air bomb and the series of cover stories about "vortex cannons", all disinformation (9). In the initial FOIA request, five responses were received, each representing the next rung up the security ladder. Nobody without proper security clearance is going to get a higher-level report. Instead, a lower level report is generated which explains things only in general terms, giving away no sensitive issues.

So, again, what are we looking for? The answer is that we are looking for inconstancies or things left unsaid or unexplained. With this kind of understanding, let us review the government's report on Kreiselgeraete (10).

First and most importantly, we should note the date on which this information was obtained, February 9, 1945. This report was obtained during the war. In my experience reports written during the war are far more informative than the drab, monotone, minimizations written after the war. The report is based on one prisoner who was captured. His name is given as Herbert Franke. Franke was a skilled mechanic. He had worked at Askania (which is important as we will see) before coming to Kreiselgerate. Actually, at Kreiselgeraete, he was one of 15 skilled "research mechanics". He was with Kreiselgeraete until being drafted on July 25, 1944—those were desperate times for Germany. He is sometimes referred to in the report as "P/W" (prisoner of war).

Kreiselgeraete produced electrical gyroscopes of all types and sizes, gyroscope components, gyroscope frames, control boxes for submarines, tank turret components, and until 1943 they produced the Kommandogeraet for Marine flak.

Franke informs the Americans that Kreiselgeraete GmbH consisted of two plants, one in a suburb of Berlin at Zehlendorf and the other at Nieder Einsiedel. The Nieder Einsiedel facility was an experimental station and it was at this where Franke worked. Then Franke gives additional information that there was actually a third facility. From the report:

> *"**4.** There was another section or plant under this firm's title in Lodz, Poland. P/W claims that the firm was a subsidiary of Askania, since the director ROUX from Askania visited often and issued directives, etc."*

Franke would know this since he had worked at Askania. Somewhat later we are told:

> *"**25.** According to P/W this entire plant, plus the one at Nieder Einseidel, was used primarily for research. Any quality production was accomplished at Lodz, Poland. He had no definite production figures and would not hazard a guess at any."*

Franke provides a very detailed description of the individual buildings and a description and brief resume of the seven most important people working there. About 700 people in all were employed. Franke describes his activity at the experimental station at Nieder Einsiedel as:

> *"**44.** P/W was not certain as to the used of the experimental boards he was making but thought they were for some remote control apparatus with which the engineers in the laboratories were experimenting. As far as he could judge the boards were used to test the power of different types of electric motors."*

We learn more about this facility as Franke describes the actual building in which he worked:

> *"**48.** The first floor of he rear section was used as a work shop in which about 30 women were employed winding coils for electric motors. The second floor was the workshop in which the experimental boards were constructed, where P/W was employed with nine others. The third floor was the drafting room employing 7 or 8 men and 3 women."*

SECRET - 1 - 6824 DIC/MIS/NOI-515

Name: FRANKE, Herbert
Rank: Gefr.
Unit: 15 PD PJ Abt 33.
Capt: 17 Jan 45, HÜLFLINGEN.
Interrogated: 6824 DIC (MIS), 9 Feb 45.

Reliability: C-2.

I. PREAMBLE

1. P/W, 31 years old, BERLIN-TELTOW, Ruhrsdorfer Str. 67, was a skilled mechanic in civilian life. After finishing a four year apprenticeship he was employed at ASKANIA, BERLIN until 1932. He was without work for two years until he was given employment at KREISEL GERÄTE, GmbH, BERLIN/ZEHLENDORF in Feb 34. He worked for this firm until he was drafted on 25 Jul 44. In Dec 43 a group of 15 research mechanics including P/W, were moved from BERLIN to NIEDER EINSIEDEL, where he was employed until July

INDUSTRIAL
KREISEL GERÄTE, G.m.b.H. BERLIN-ZEHLENDORF
Feb 34 to 25 July 44

II. A. LOCATION

2. KREISEL GERÄTE GmbH
BERLIN/ZEHLENDORF
GÖRZ ALLEE 311

3. KREISEL GERÄTE GmbH
ZWEIGSTELLE
NIEDER EINSIEDEL
(Experimental station; see III)

4. (There was another section or plant under this firm's title in LODZ, Poland). P/W claims that the firm was a subsidiary of ASKANIA, since Director ROUX from ASKANIA visited often and issued directives, etc.

5. The factory (see sketch) in BERLIN/ZEHLENDORF may easily be considered as part of the old GÖRZ plant, which is now ZEISS IKON. The RR spur which runs through the KREISEL plant was originally intended for the exclusive use of the GÖRZ firm.

Kreiselgeraete GmbH This was the prime german company manufacturing gyroscopic devices. The testimony of a prisoner of war who worked for both Kreiselgeraete and Askania is that Kreiselgeraete and a third facility in Lodz, Poland which worked closely with Askania's plant there. Askania was said to have produced "aircraft motors" at Lodz. The prisoner also worked at Kreiselgeraete's experimental facility at Neider Einsiedel.

So, what have we learned about Kreiselgeraete GmbH? We now know it was really an experimental facility with levels of sophistication. First there was the more mundane work on gyros, tank parts, and submarine control boxes. Second was the secret, experimental work done on control boards, perhaps measuring output, and electric motors that may have been the subject of the control board monitoring. Production work was not done on secret work at either the Zehlendorf or the Neider Einsiedel facility but instead was done at Lodz, Poland in conjunction with another company, Askania. In fact,

Askania may have been directing this research work according to the testimony of Franke.

We have gone from a gyro plant to a plant that is really making experimental electric motors and associated test apparatus and then sending their work to a third facility or a related company in Lodz, Poland. This is strange. Lodz is at the very center of Poland, southwest of Warsaw.

This has to have been the most eastern part of Poland which German speakers and German culture felt comfortable for operation purposes. After the war Germans were resettled out of what was then an eastern portion of Germany and what is now Poland. German culture was gone with the wind. Place names were changed. Now, research into mysterious wartime happenings must be done and is done through a Slavic perspective. No Anglo-American post-war recovery teams ever make it to this region, so US/British government files are going to be of no value. We need to get lucky here.

SECRET

SECRET - 4 - 6824 DIC/MIS/NOI-515

D. OUTPUT

19. Electrical gyroscopes of all types and sizes.

20. Gyroscope components.

21. Gyroscope frames.

22. Control boxes for submarines.

23. Tank turret components.

24. Until 1943 they made the Kommandogerät for Marine Flak.

25. According to P/W this entire plant, plus the one at NIEDER EINSIEDEE, was used primarily for research. Any quantity production was accomplished at LODZ, Poland. He had no definite production figures and would not hazard a guess at any.

E. PACKING AND DISPATCH

26. P/W was very indefinite about this phase of the production. He knew that most of the shipment went out by truck, but the destination was not known. The control boxes were packed in crates and shipped by rail to KIEL and WILHELMSHAVEN, but he had no idea to which firm they were sent.

F. RAW MATERIALS

27. This plant used all types of metals which were delivered by truck - source unknown. There were many types of metals available, but the workers were always cautioned to be sparing. Electric motors were received from "OTTO BECKER", location unknown to P/W.

Kreiselgeraete GmbH More Combined Intelligence Objectives Subcommittee file content on Kreisegerate

SECRET

SECRET - 7 - 6824 DIC/MIS/NOI-515

47. The first floor (cellar) of street section is still being used for artificial flower making. The second floor of this section is used for storage of raw materials for the flowers. The third floor is used as living quarters for the plant owner.

48. The first floor of the rear section was used as a work shop in which about 30 women were employed winding coils for electric motors. The second floor was the workshop in which the experiment boards were constructed, where P/W was employed with nine others. The third floor was the drafting room employing 7 or 8 men and 3 women.

49. Bldg #3: Central heating plant 8 m long and 6 m wide with a smoke stack 25 m high which is the outstanding landmark in that vicinity. This plant was necessary for heating hot water which was used in the manufacturing process of artificial flowers. This building was also of stone construction.

MSH/gob.

For THOMAS C. VAN CLEVE, Lt. Col.
COMMANDING, 6824 DIC (MIS)

S. J. McCune

S.J. McCUNE,
Capt. A.U.S.
NOI SECTION.

23 Feb 45.

Kreiselgeraete GmbH More Combined Intelligence Objectives Subcommittee file on Kreisegerate

So what in the world is Askania and how do they figure into this puzzle?

It turns out that Askania is really no mystery. It is an old German company and information on it can be found on-line at a German language Wikepedia site (http://de.wikepedia.org/wiki/Askania). Askania is a maker of precision instruments. The Wikepedia site includes compasses for U-boats, distance measuring devices, pressure measuring devices, geophysical devices, time-keeping devices, gravimentic devices and in general devices servicing geodesic, aircraft, astronomy and navigation needs. Askania is centered in Berlin. The company's history, starting in 1871, is summarized except for their involvement in the Second World War for which they along with many other German companies understandably have developed amnesia.

But Askania did have a facility at Lodz, Poland which is evidenced at another German language website (http://www.ostwallinfo.de/Askania/mitte/askaniamitte.htm). Not only is there text here but many pictures since this site was unusual and needs some explanation.

Pictures of Askania Mitte

These are pictures of the underground facility at Lodz, Poland (Liztmannstadt), where Askania had its workshops. Askania worked in conjunction here with the Kreiselgeraete company on "aircraft motors". These were companies producing precision measuring devices, electrical devices and gyroscopic devices—not the pistons, engine blocks and cylinders of traditional aircraft engines. What type of "aircraft motors" could these have been?

Askania Mitte This is an entrance to the facility.

Askania Mitte This is an entrance for workers running parallel to the tunnel with special doors opening to it so that the workers could access the assembly line at any point.

Askania Mitte Another view of the tunnel, possibly showing tracks used for assembly work.

Askania Mitte This is a picture from the outside showing the roof.

The facility was called Askania Mitte and was about 40 km east of Lodz in a forest. In parenthesis behind the word Lodz is the German name "Litzmannstadt" which is evidently the name given it by the Germans. This site was the forward, temporary command post for the Fuehrer Headquarters at Wolfschanze. In October, 1940, construction people arrived and from December, 1940 to September, 1941 a massive project was undertaken in which two adjoining tunnels were carved out of the mountain and lined with two and a half meters of steel and concrete making them impervious to aerial attack. These two tunnels, one 380 meters long (about 1,235 feet) and the other 355 meters long (about 1,154 feet), were dug to house the special trains Hitler used for his purposes traveling around Germany. For instance, after dropping Hitler off at the Wolf's Lair, the train could be safely stored out of sight in one of these tunnels. A similar arrangement was found at other of Hitler's Headquarters facilities. Included inside this facility were 2.3 kilometers of railway, pumping (facilities), a communication and news center, an electricity generating facility, an additional bombproof, security bunker as well as housing for living and working. Because of security considerations, only German construction firms took part in this construction with as many as 4500 individuals working on this project at its peak.

As it turned out Hitler never stayed there, however, the facility took on a new role. In December 1944, the code designations of Goldamsel (Golden blackbird) and Huhn (fowl) were ascribed to this facility. Evidently, we are entering the period of time that shipments from Kreiselgeraete to Askania became increasingly important. This is also evident in its name "Askania Mitte" which means Askania Center. Finally, we are told of the purpose of this redesigned facility; it was used for the production of aircraft engines.

What? How is this possible? Askania did not build anything close to aircraft engines. Such engines require considerable heavy industrial facilities and effort in order to forge pistons and crankshafts alone. Nowhere can any record of aircraft engines being built by Askania be found as far as I know. This was simply not their area of expertise. Watchmakers do not make aircraft engines, no matter jet or piston.

This could not be possible unless these engines were being made out of the experimental electric motors produced for Askania by a Kreiselgeraete; a company that certainly would have been called upon should those engines revolved about a high-speed axis. Could Askania be using these experimental electric motors as well as other sub-assemblies and putting together engines to power another type of flying craft, one that spun on its axis and ascended vertically? Why else would "Flugzeugmotoren", aircraft engines be made by a precision instruments company, in a high security setting, deep underground, in hinterlands of the Third Reich? Can we say this place was the origin of the Magnetscheiben?

Let us be clear, there is no hard evidence yet that flying saucers were being made at Lodz. Secondly, if flying saucers were being produced at Lodz, they would have remained on the experimental level. The Askania facility at Lodz would have been a Forschungsstelle, a research facility only. Further development would have occurred at an Entwicklungsstelle, a developmental facility. Meanwhile, first generation (conventionally powered) flying discs were just going into assembly line production at Litomerice, in what is now the Czech Republic, at a facility called "Richard" (11). Richard was actually three facilities, Richard I-III or possibly code-named Elsaba, Kalkspat and Osram, respectively, according to the same source.

Sometimes the conventionally powered German flying discs are referred to with the work "Kreisel" (Gyroscope). Of course, this is because they spun on their axes. The Schriever and Habermohl discs are sometimes named with this word. But then there are references to something else, a "gyroscopic principle" which seems to mean a principle of flight. There is no gyroscopic principle in aerodynamics so this term must mean some form of non-aerodynamic flight. The following is a good example of the use of this term. The source was a newspaper article, here re-typed just as it was re-typed in a booklet self-published by UFO researcher William L. Moore of MJ-12 fame (12):

WASHINGTON (D.C.) DAILY NEWS, 14 MAY 1949; P.2, COL.1.

IN THIS OFFERING: A WEEKLY SIZED-UP BY MEMBERS OF THE WASHINGTON STAFF OF THE SCRIPPS-HOWARD NEWSPAPERS.

FLYING DISCS FROM SPAIN?

SOME AIR FORCE MEN THINK THEY KNOW WHAT THOSE FLYING DISCS ARE AND WHERE THEY COME FROM.

THEY BELIEVE THE DISCS ARE A NEW TYPE FLYING MACHINE UTILIZING GYROSCOPIC PRINCIPLE; THAT THEY COME FROM SPAIN.

THEY SAY NAZI SCIENTISTS KNOWN TO HAVE BEEN WORKING ON GYROSCOPIC FLIGHT DURING WAR DROPPED FROM SIGHT AFTER ROW WITH HITLER. INTELLIGENCE REPORTS HINT THEY ESCAPED TO SPAIN. CAPTURED DOMESTIC DOCUMENTS INDICATE GERMANS HAD GONE FURTHER THAN ANY WITH USE OF GYROSCOPIC PRINCIPLE FOR FLIGHT.

AIR FORCE PEOPLE ARE CONVINCED FLING DISC IS REAL. THEY SAY IT IS NOT PRODUCED IN THIS COUNTRY. THEY FEEL IT IS NOT PRODUCED IN RUSSIA.

CLINCHER CAME WHEN AIR FORCE GOT PICTURES RECENTLY OF THREE DISCS FLYING IN FORMATION OVER STEPHENSVILLE, NEWFOUNDLAND. NOT CLOSE-UPS BECAUSE THEY OUTDISTANCED OUR FASTEST SHIPS, BUT CLOSE ENOUGH TO BE CONVINCING.

Now all the above is really just a long introduction to the new information mentioned earlier, and the reader's patience has been appreciated. The new information is a working understanding of how such magnetically-powered flying craft would actually fly. For this explanation, we are indebted to physicist Dr. Paul Potter for writing his book *Gravitational Manipulation of Domed Craft*. Dr. Potter starts with an observation of heavenly bodies, particularly black holes, looking at the energy types and energy relationships involved that are studied and known to astrophysicists. It is upon this information that Dr. Potter bases his book. Given these observations, he asks the question, *how would they be employed to build what we would call UFOs?* To me, this is an important breakthrough in concept, since Dr. Potter is starting with empirical observation, not theory-first mathematics and chalkboard squiggles.

The reader will remember the German writers at the start of this chapter who also explained saucer flight in terms of the forces inherent in heavenly bodies. The rotation of the planets and the rotation of the planets around the sun were given as the reason for gravitation and electromagnetism. Likewise, and following this principle, it was stated by these German writers that the rotating parts of a type of flying disc generated a force which would make them independent of gravity.

What has happened is that the more poetic explanation of the two German writers has been amplified with scientific basis added. Dr. Potter makes this all understandable for us in his book and even uses a simple example, the Searl disc. The Searl disc was a flying saucer model. We know the Searl disc actually flew from the many pictures and eyewitness testimonies intertwined with its story. For descriptive purposes the Searl disc is wonderfully simple since it used only permanent magnets. A series of small magnets were arranged on the spinning wheel of the saucer and revolved around a larger, central permanent magnet at the center just like the planets rotate around the sun or the stars of a galaxy rotate around a central black hole.

Dr. Potter introduces us to magnetic reconnection. He says this concept is a known commodity in the astrophysics world and it is a bit surprising that it has not formed the basis of some patent, somewhere, but it has not. We all know a magnet is surrounded by what are commonly called lines of force. These lines start and end at the poles of the magnet with lines further away from the surface being more widely spaced, indicting that they are weaker. We could imagine magnetic reconnection as magnets in close proximity sharing lines of force. Permanent magnets are arranged in a circle around the larger, central magnet. As the disc is rotated, the existing lines of force shared by the central magnet and the outer magnets are pulled apart and then new, shared lines of force are immediately formed. This breaking and reforming of the lines of force is called magnetic reconnection (13).

By magnetic reconnection, electron-positron pairs are produced out of the zero-point vacuum (14). Positrons are positive electrons (15). In the process of magnetic reconnection the positrons and electrons separate, with the electrons being pushed outward and downward to the bottom edge of the disc and the positrons pushed inward and upward, forming a cone over and at the center to the disc. Potter describes this process as it relates to the Searl disc and the Searl SEG generator:

> *"Notably, this reconnection mechanism was mostly what led to the stressing of the air surrounding the discs of J.R.R. Searl (back in the 1970's), and which provided the copious supplies of charged particles which then became imbued with other kinetic forces, and which subsequently allowed Searl's generating rotors to defy gravity and to rise upward, not only by ionizing the surrounding air but by creating a projected field in the form of a rotating tube-field ahead of and above that disc, which the disc would simply fall upward into. The same reconnection electron-positron producing process is found in Searl's SEG power generator turbine which would also create copious supplies of electrons, which in Searl's turbine would be harvested by inductor coils and fed into an electrical storage circuit (and in an intelligent world such a mechanism would have then powered into a national grid, without the need for fossil fuels or nuclear-power rods)"(16)*

Once the mechanism is started auto-rotation results. Dr. Potter explains:

> *"Interestingly, with regard to those generators of Searl, he would have extracted those ferroelectric electron emissions by a form of magneto-electric-induction because his SEG rigs were not given any electrical input to start them running - and yet once they started to rotate they would continue forever. This would occur by the slightly miss-aligned magnetic field lines of the rotors and the stator bucking each other, thereby generating a kinetic rotational force that was self-sustaining and which resulted in a self-increasing rotational velocity. Once they started to increase in velocity these rotors would almost instantly have developed electric fields of 10 to the 6th volts/cm through the break-reconnection process." (17)*

Is there any hint at all that such a motor was under development during the Third Reich? If a hint of such a motor could be found, this along with the circumstantial evidence of Kreiselgeraete, Askania, and the strange site of Askania Mitte might lead us to the inescapable conclusion that the Magnetscheibe was an experimental reality. Yes, we do have a hint of such an engine.

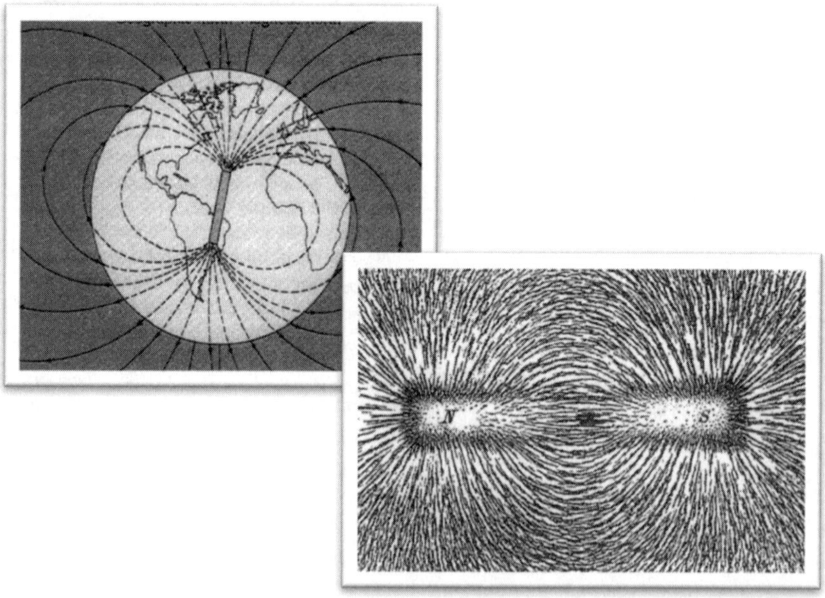

Magnetic Lines of Force. *The Earth's magnetic field is shown above with a bar magnet below. Imagine two earths or any heavenly bodies in close proximity, each spinning so that their magnetic fields interact. This would produce magnetic reconnection and the resulting generation of positrons and electrons according to Dr. Paul Potter.*

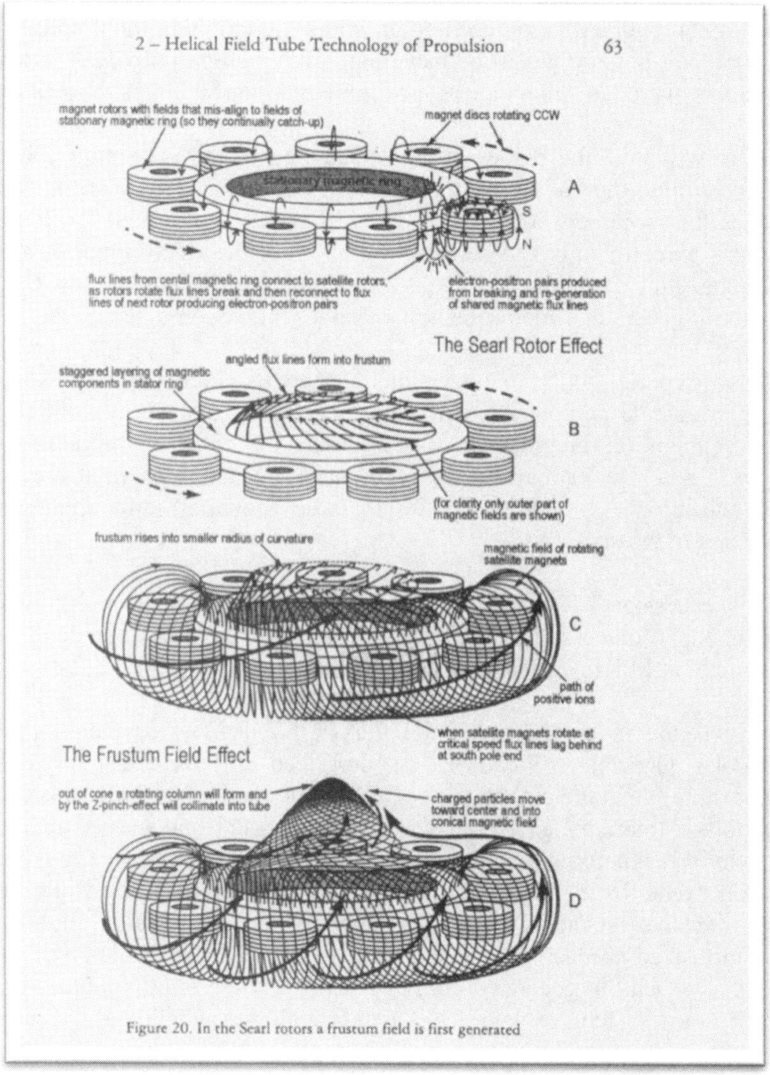

Dr. Paul Potter's diagram showing Magnetic Reconnection. Magnetic lines of force join and separate as they rotate, generating positrons and electrons.

Before citing evidence for this engine perhaps some problems need to be discussed. This problem has been called "retromoment". My understanding of retromoment is the opposing drag that would be caused when a magnetic motor self-inducts. By this I mean that the iron material forming the magnet or the core of an electromagnet when moving through a magnetic field would suffer the results of induction and be filled with eddy currents that would increase the strength of those magnets. If a ring of magnets were revolving around a central magnet, having been spun by an external force, the magnetic fields of the magnets moving past each other would interact; producing induction and the momentum of the wheel of magnets would suffer a breaking action. As any two magnets passed each other, their effect on each other would increase with their speed so that the momentum of their passing would be halted and even a slight retro-motion would occur as momentum is overcome unless a motor of some type can supply additional force.

Dr. Nieper will give the reader his understanding in the upcoming citation so the reader can determine the validity of each idea or determine if they are the same. The importance is this necessary idea of the "miss-alignment" of which Dr. Potter speaks. Somehow, this gyro-wheel has to be kept in motion for the electron-positron pairs to be generated. The "hint" mentioned above is a seeming breakthrough in how to achieve an electric motor or generator which somehow bypasses this retromoment.

Dr. Hans Nieper's book, "Conversion of Gravity Field Energy Revolution in Technology, Medicine and Society" mainly concerns a free energy conference in the 1980's and contains the citation. He is discussing the work of the late experimental physicist Dr. Bruce De Palma and his work on N-machines or what are now called homopolar generators. But, what applies to these generators also applies to electric motors as stated in the text:

> "The session of October 24 started with a presentation by Bruce DePalma, Montecito, California. DePalma is a former student and instructor at M.I.T. in Boston.
>
> He is the inventor of the high output N-machine, or the so-called Unipolar Generator. Faraday first described this principle in 1831, however. Nevertheless, it is to DePalma's merit that he studied the Unipolar Motor, called N-machine, in more detail and proved that the system of magnets rotating at high speed can deliver more electric energy than it needs for its operation. This, however, requires some expensive, cost-intensive technology. A subsequent video presentation showed a medium-sized N-machine in operation. It should be particularly pointed out that, when the generated current is tapped, there is no opposing drag effect in the system, as would be the case with a conventional dynamo or electric generator. The N-machine can operate only as a current generator, not as a motor, again in contrast to the conventional dynamo. DePalma made some comments regarding the overall phenomenon that were met with great interest. He especially mentioned some physical anomalies that were observed during the study of gyroscopic systems and heir interactions with the gravitational field. Thus, for example, the gravity acceleration of a gyroscopic system—-say, a rotating ball—-is different from that for a non-rotating ball. No explanation is available at this time.

DePalma also stated that most large planets should be viewed as Unipolar Generators or N-machines. This could explain, for example, the generation of high electric energies in the ring system of the planet Saturn.

"It is remarkable that DePalma referred to a 1941-42 paper by P. Boehning of the Faculty of Physics, University of Breslau. At the beginning of the war, Boehning had build a motor which, in contrast to conventional motors, operated without retromoment, i.e., its operation was similar to the N-machine. It is thus apparently possible to convert the principle of the N-machine to a positive motor drive. The Breslau papers were taken to the United States after the war, and were filed away there (FIAT reports)."(18)

Now, there is a lot to talk about here such as gyros, electrical generation, planetary motion, planets as N-machines, Saturn and its rings, and so on. But the most important issue for our discussion is the fact that Professor P. Boehning had found a way, apparently, to make a motor-generator that would simply spin freely. This must have been done using permanent magnets at least as test designs because of their simplicity. Also, this must have involved some sort of imbalance, keeping the motion going.

Since we are so deep into the rabbit hole let me digress to answer the question that you have just mentally formed: Where is the P. Boehning report? Let me say that of all the documents I have ever sought, this report is/was and probably will remain the hardest to obtain. I don't have it. Dr. Bruce DePalma is dead as is Dr. Hans Neiper. The University of Breslau no longer exists, neither does any city named "Breslau" - it is now a part of modern Poland. I have written to leading people in the free energy world in an effort to recover the report, all in vain. I have written the Library of Congress and the US Department of Commerce. These agencies did search in good faith but found nothing on Professor P. Boehning in the FIAT reports. I visited the U.C.L.A. Research Library and asked to go through their copies of the FIAT reports. They informed me that the FIAT reports were not available in the stacks, that they were in storage in a warehouse and that I would have to specify the report(s) I wanted and make an appointment at the warehouse. They made a list available to me of the reports on a computer. Naturally, nothing referencing P. Boehning, but I specified anything, any subject, which might be remotely connected and asked to see it. Trays of reports were produced on the appointed day but nothing appeared referencing P. Boehning or his mysterious motor. I am completely at a loss and any assistance would be greatly appreciated.

Now, we need to consider the craft allegedly made by the Vril Society. This device involved three magnetic discs stacked on top on one another.

What is next is basically a story frequently heard at UFO conferences. Many such stories are worthless but every now and then useful pieces of some partial truth can be gleaned. Some time ago UFO researcher Wendelle Stevens corresponded with me concerning German flying discs. In one of his letters to me he enclosed a copy of a letter he had received from a friend. Wendelle introduced this friend as a retired US Air Force Colonel and an air combat Viet Nam veteran. His letter to Wendelle was in response to a lecture on German flying discs Wendelle had given in Las Vegas, circa 2000, and which had been recorded electronically. Wendelle's friend sent a copy of the lecture to a retired CIA friend of his. This friend wrote back to the retired Colonel the comments below. Even though I have both names, that of the Colonel and the CIA figure, it would be bad form and perhaps even criminal to publish them. For those needing verification, I may be able to facilitate such verification or impose upon Wendelle Stevens to assist me in doing so. Following is one paragraph from the letter in which the retired Colonel relates the comments of the CIA person [Please note words in parentheses are mine for purposes of clarity]:

> *"You are correct about German saucer projects; however, one did get into production for combat. It had two rotating magnetic fields and a turbine engine and could get to 43,000 ' (feet) in 4-5 min. (minutes). One sprayed benzene in the air just ahead of a flight of B-17's, which caused them to blow up when ingesting it. Some Luftwaffe pilots were scheduled for transition training 15 May 45 to fly transport & combat missions. Some variations of these were taken to Murdoc and put in a hangar with a hinged roof. She said a friend verified this in 1965."*

The technical advisor I call Dr. Gordon Freeman once told me concerning the alleged "three rotating magnetic fields" that a clever engineer could do this with only two rotating magnetic fields. Think about this. The center magnet can be held stationary with the other two at the top and bottom moving in opposite directions. The fact that this saucer is described as having a turbine engine in addition to the magnetic fields indicates that the magnetic fields provided only levitation and that horizontal motion was provided by the jet engine and/or that "reverse moment" was being generated and had to be overcome with mechanical power.

This story raises the question if stacking the interacting magnetic fields involves the mechanism of magnetic reconnection as a means of levitation, if this method is an improvement over the arrangement favored by Searl, and if more powerful electromagnets were used or could be used in the stacked system. The story also brings us into the post-war world and introduces, yet again, the probability that the US Government obtained examples of German flying discs. Now I could go on with speculation concerning the Schappeller device with its monstrous magnetic field at this point but I will stop here.

The only real question remaining in my mind at this point is the origin of the Searl disc. There are really two mysteries. One is magnetic reconnection that generates electron-positron pairs and accounts for levitation. The second is method Searl employs to keep the disc spinning in spite of force(s) working to halt it. For the first, magnetic reconnection, Dr. Potter must be relied upon since this is totally beyond me. For anything other than a superficial mention of the subject, the reader must go to Dr. Paul Potter's excellent original work. Regarding the second mystery, how the Searl disc kept on spinning, the words of Dr. Potter are illuminating:

> *"The reader should note I am not here giving away the secret of Searl's magnetic rotors, of how their fields were configured so that they persistently rotated (mainly because I don't know how he did it...). That information is best obtained direct from John Searl himself, particularly via his current (circa. 20008*

websites at: http://swallowcommand.com and http://www.searlsolution.com)" (19)

By Occam' s Razor, making the least assumptions, it must be concluded that he used the very same method referenced by that other free energy pioneer, Dr. Bruce DePalma: that being the method explained in that elusive paper by Professor P. Boehning, University of Breslau. But Searl does not credit Boehning. Nor does Searl offer any logical progression toward his invention. As we all know, the history of science and technology is built upon the steps taken by predecessors. When the work of predecessors is denied, red flags should go up.

Searl claims that between 1946 and 1956 he designed and built the Searl Effect Generator, a device having "anti-gravity" powers as well as being a perpetual motion device (20). Searl claims to have arrived at this knowledge, (remember, this is anti-gravity and perpetual motion), solely as a result of a dream or a series of dreams between the years stated above (21).

Now, I can't beg, borrow or steal a copy of the P. Boehning paper. If it resulted or contributed to Dr. DePalma's work generating electricity in a better way, if it was one of the pillars of the SEG generator and the Searl disc, if it contributed to the stacked "Vril" disc which the Americans did get their hands on, well, no wonder! Someone working for the Security State certainly took Boehning's FIAT report out of circulation. But in the magic year of 1946, this FIAT report and others seemed to have been available for the mere asking.

Perhaps Searl, who began work in England as a young electrical engineer in 1946, did dream of a gyroscopic method of flight and energy production. But for my money, I'll bet at some point before the Searl disc actually flew, John Searl read the still-secret FIAT report in question and it was this technology, not a dream, which put him on the road to discovery.

But I do not know what is in John Searl's heart. Yes, I could be wrong. Maybe Searl did come by his breakthroughs, as he states, via a dream.

Or maybe it was a German dream.

Literature Cited

1. **Stevens, Henry, 2001**, *Hitler's Flying Saucers*, pages 144-194, Adventures Unlimited Publishing, Kemption, Illinios, USA
2. **Stevens, Henry, 2001**, pages 140-142
3. **Juergen-Ratthofer, Norbert and Ralf Ettl, 1992**, *Das Vril Projekt*, pages 27-28, STM-Tempelhof, Vienna, Austria
4. **Bergmann, O. 1989**, *II Deutsch Flugscheiben und U-Boote Ueberwachen Die Weltmeere*, pages 195-196, Hugin Gesellschaft, Wetter/Ruhr, Germany
5. **Haarmann, D. H., 1985**, *III Geheime Wunderwaffen Ueber den Krieg hinaus!*, page59, Hugin Gesellschaft, Wetter, Germany
6. **Lyne, William, 2001**, *Occult Science Dictatorship The official State Sceince Religion And How To Get Excommunicated*, pages 63, 63, Creatopia Productions, Lamy, New Mexico, USA
7. **Vesco, Renato, 1968**, *Intercept UFO*, page 247, Pinnacle Books, Inc., New York, USA
8. **Vesco, Renato, 1968**, page 248
9. **Stevens, Henry, 2007**, *Hitler's Suppressed and Still-Secret Weapons, Science and Technology*, pages 103-111, Adventures Unlimited Publishing, Kempton, Illinois, USA
10. Combined Intelligence Objectives Sub-Committee report, titled *Kreisel Geraete GmbH Berlin/Zehlendorf, 6824 DIC/MIS/NOT- 515*
11. **Jesensky, Milos Ph.D., and Robert Lesniakiewicz, 1998**, "Wunderland" Mimozemske Technologie Treti Rise, page 111-112, Aos Publishing, Czech Republic.
12. *Project V-7: Hitler's Flying Discs: An Illustrated Compilation of research and Source Materials, 1984*, page 6, William L. Moore Publications & Research, Burbank, California, USA
13. **Potter, Paul Ph.D., 2008**, *Gravitational Manipulation of Domed Craft*, pages 57-64, Adventures Unlimited Publishing, Kempton, Illinios, USA.
14. **Potter, Paul Ph.D., 2008**, pages 60, 62
15. **Van Nostrand's Scientific Encyclopedia, Third Edition, 1958**, page 1202, D. Van Nostrad Company, Inc., Princeton, NJ., USA
16. **Potter, Paul, Ph.Dl, 2008**, page 62
17. **Potter, Paul, Ph.D., 2008**, page 133
18. **Nieper, Hans A., M.D., 1985**, *Conversion f Gravity Field Energy Revlution in Technology, Medicine and Society*, pages 156, 157, MIT Verlag, Oldenburg, Germany
19. **Potter, Paul, Ph.D., 2008**, page 446
20. http://en.wikipedia.org/wiki/John_Searl
21. http://x-journals.com/2009/electromagnetic-flying-discs-the-story-behind-the-john-searl-story/

GREENLAND, PART ONE

Perhaps the reader will recall the second quotation ascribed to Gross Admiral Doenitz in year 1944:

> *"The German Navy will have to accomplish a great deal in the future. The German Navy knows all the hiding places in the oceans and therefore it will be very easy to bring the Fuehrer to a safe place should the necessity arise and in which he will have the opportunity to work out his final plans."*

This quote comes from 1944 and things were not exactly going the way the German leadership had planned. This statement sounds very much like a wartime contingency plan in which Hitler is evacuated from Germany and takes up residence somewhere hidden abroad. Further, it sounds a little Redemptionish in that it mentions working out final plans.

The Redemptionish School maintains that Hitler did not die in the bunker but escaped and is waiting in some undisclosed location, waiting for a precise moment in which to reemerge and win the Second World War. There are variations of this theme. For instance, Hitler is awaiting a fleet of spaceships from the star-system of Aldebaren. Or, he is waiting in the underground city of New Berlin at the South Pole. Or, he has joined like-minded individuals, Germans and aliens, living in the center of the earth.

Let me be clear. I believe Hitler died in the bunker by his own hand. The dental forensic evidence seems overwhelming unless a massive conspiracy, involving tens of individuals, all maintaining the same story while under intense pressure is postulated.

The simple fact is that Hitler could have survived if he had chosen to do so. He did not. There was a reason for this decision. While the man, Adolf Hitler, could have emerged from the bowels of the bunker and fled Berlin, he would have lost forever his status as a Germanic hero in the eyes of his supporters. A Germanic hero can ultimately lose the battle but he must always remain in control. This is the old "dying with a sword in the hand" thing. Running is losing control. If Hitler had run, what would have emerged from the bunker would not have been the Fuehrer of Germany nor probably even Adolf Hitler, but merely a broken man, running away, under an assumed name. In the end it really does not matter whether Hitler survived or not. The Fuehrer of Germany died in that bunker under the best conditions that he could manage in that situation.

This statement is not to begrudge those interested in Hitler's survival after the bunker. That research has its place since whenever evidence is reappraised, new facts may emerge which may have little to do with the original subject of the investigation.

But in 1944 Admiral Doenitz was doing the best that he could manage, the result being the planning if not the actual construction of a hide-away for Hitler and presumably his top military staff in a place from which to carry on the war. Neuschwabenland was half a world away. This would have been fine if hiding was all that mattered but in 1944 Norway was still firmly in German hands as was Greenland. From Greenland a war against those occupying Germany as well as the British and Americans was certainly possible if the second generation of wonder weapons had been a reality. Therefore, we just have to look at Greenland as a possible site for German secret bases.

Actually, as we shall see, we have to look at it twice as the Germans did. What this means is first we must consider it as just a place for weather stations and perhaps U-boat refueling but with the new reality of 1944, in which Germany was collapsing, we have to look at Greenland again as perhaps having a more expanded role.

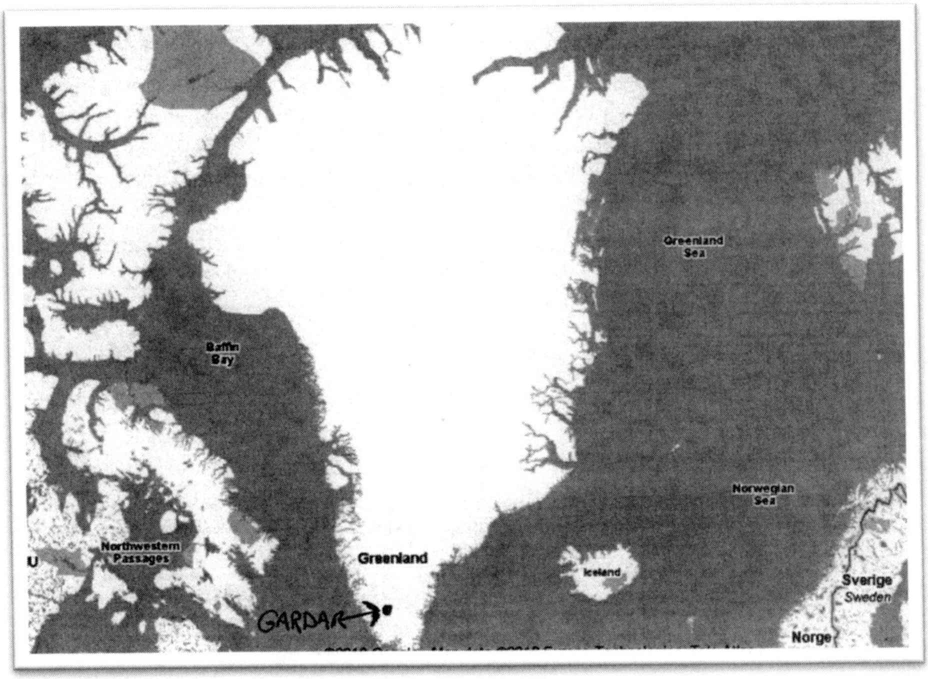

Map of Greenland Please note the eastern coastline, its proximity to Norway, and its numerous fjords, which are perfect for hiding a secret base. Greenland is also a stepping stone to the Canadian Arctic from Norway. Please note also the location of Gardar, which is discussed in a later chapter.

There is absolutely no doubt that the Germans had bases in Greenland. In fact, Rudolf Lusar, an engineer who worked for the German Patent Office writes in his book concerning German secret weapons that there were many German weather stations built in Greenland (1). A German language video documentary titled "Geheime Wetterstationen" states that there were indeed secret German bases of the east side of Greenland. It goes on to say that they remained hidden even though the Greenlanders and the Americans knew they were there but simply could not find them even after extensive searches (2) So the Americans and probably Canadians were certainly flying over Greenland and possibly exploring Greenland by ship but finding little or nothing. In other words, the German bases were well hidden. Another source suggests this failure might be attributed to the huge area that needed to be searched (3). This makes perfect sense since Greenland is the largest island on the planet.

But there is another reason that at least some of these bases could not be found. This is because they were actually tunneled into the bedrock of the island. This means the tunnels went though any snow and ice that might be present and also probably had an outlet into the sea so that U-boats might enter and exit without being seen. The tunnels would have been on the same order of magnitude as the huge underground facilities at Nordhausen, Richard, Der Riese, and Jonastal, for instance, at or near 2000 meters (about 6500 feet) (4).

For a better description of these bases and their history we will turn to a series of rather esoteric and historical sources. The first of these is Claude Schweikhart (aka Erich Halik), writing in 1952 in a publication called "Mensch und Schicksal". This publication billed itself as dealing in "Geisteswissenschaft" or spiritual science. This may be but in many instances this spirituality was a necessary post-war cover, necessary in order to discuss topics the wartime censors might frown upon. It was here that we are first introduced to the words "Dritte Kraft" or Third Power, which is called by Anglo-American writers the "Nazi International".

Schweikhart begins by introducing Louis Emrich, a real person, who was somehow charged with conducting an investigation, in fact, the first, as to the esoteric activities of the SS. In their work Emrich and his team either partnered with or relies on elements of the Yugoslavian intelligence service. Schweikhart tells a couple of interesting tales but one fits in well here. He says that in the last phase of the war at the time of the rumored construction of the Alpenfestung, (the German alpine fortress from which a last stand was to be made by the Nazis) a second fortress was actually built in Greenland. It was to serve as a base in which to carry on the war just as in Gross Admiral Doenitz's famous quote (5)

Perhaps even more astounding, Schweikhart tells us that fighting has continued in Greenland over this base to 1950. Commandos, presumably British or American, landed there and sporadic fighting, sometimes strong fighting, was carried on until the date given (6). Schweikhart goes off into some esoteric reasoning for this continued struggle which only Wilhelm Landig himself could interpret. In fact, judging from their choice of subject material and interpretations, it would not be surprising if Claude Schweikhart, Erich Halik and Wilhelm Landig had a very close connection indeed!

Next, we will look at a newspaper article in the Weiner Montag, dated December 29, 1947, titled: "Deutsche Kampfgruppe noch auf Groenland?" (German Combat Group Still in Greenland?). Following is my translation of the article:

German Fighting Group Still in Greenland?

Put in Place by U-Boats Almost Six Years in the Snowy Wastes

Vienna, December 28th. In several foreign papers there occur reports in the last few days which seem so fantastic that one must take them with caution. In any case, supplementary reports must be awaited in order to clarify the reports as to their validity. Eskimos reported, so it is said, to the commanders of an American military station that a 150 man strong German combat group was found.

The White Death Band

In the early part of 1942, therefore nearly six years ago, U-boats placed German soldiers in Greenland. Leader of the group was a captain named Hammerlein, who, prior to the war, had taken part in polar expeditions. The German soldiers who had named themselves the "White Death Band" were equipped with the best and most modern in contrivances. About 30 kilometers from the harbor of Angmagslik a station was erected from which Hammerleins troops radioed meteorological reports to Germany. Later came U-boats with provisions, medicines and two geologists so that one supposes that they were looking for uranium.

According to the reports of the Eskimos, later a German ship brought a collapsible aircraft. In the autumn of 1943 there appeared in the Eskimo settlement 50 German soldiers among whom a severe brawl broke out. Two of the soldiers committed suicide, obviously exhausted through the years-long sojourn in the snow and ice wastes of Greenland.

In the following years still more provisions, medicine and other materials were brought by U-boats and unloaded. In autumn 1944 the last transport came and brought an additional thirty men.

They bore the emblem of the Eskimos in uniform other than the soldiers who had been there since 1942 and so one surmised that this denoted SS individuals.

Firefight With Eskimos

The thirty newcomers occupied the same camp as the previous one hundred and twenty men but kept themselves completely separate from the others. In May of 1945, shortly after the capitulation of Germany, the 150 Germans completely disappeared in the area of Angmagsalik. The Eskimos believed the 150 men had given themselves up into American internment until shortly after they returned from a catch and reported that Germans were still presently to be found in Greenland. Two of the Greenlanders were shot as the Germans recognized them; the

Seite 3 "Wiener Montag", Montag, den 29. Dez. 1947 (!)

Deutsche Kampfgruppe noch auf Grönland?

Von U-Booten an Land gesetzt — Seit fast sechs Jahren in der Schneewüste

Wien, 28. Dezember. In mehreren ausländischen Blättern erschienen in den letzten Tagen Berichte, die so phantastisch anmuten, daß man sie mit Vorsicht aufnehmen muß. Jedenfalls wird man ergänzende Meldungen abwarten müssen, um Klarheit darüber zu gewinnen, ob die Meldungen in allem und jedem stichhältig sind. Eskimos haben, so heißt es, dem Kommandanten einer amerikanischen militärischen Station gemeldet, daß sich auf Grönland noch eine etwa 150 Mann starke. deutsche Kampfgruppe befindet.

Die „weiße Todesrotte"

Im Frühjahr 1942, also vor nahezu sechs Jahren, hatten Unterseeboote deutsche Soldaten in Grönland an Land gesetzt. Anführer der Gruppe war ein Hauptmann namens Hammerlein, der vor dem Krieg mehrmals an Polarexpeditionen teilgenommen hatte. Die deutschen Soldaten, die sich die „weiße Todesrotte" nannten, waren aufs beste ausgerüstet und mit den modernsten Behelfen versehen. Etwa 80 Kilometer von dem Hafen Angmagsalik entfernt, wurde eine Station errichtet, von der aus die Truppe Hammerleins meteorologische Meldungen nach Deutschland funkte. Mit Unterseebooten kamen später Lebensmittel, Arzneien und auch zwei Geologen, so daß man mutmaßte, die Deutschen wollen nach Uran suchen.

Den Berichten der Eskimos zufolge brachte ein deutsches Schiff später auch ein zerlegbares Flugzeug. Im Herbst 1943 erschienen in einer Eskimosiedlung 50 deutsche Soldaten, unter denen eine schwere Schlägerei entstand. Zwei der Soldaten, die durch den jahrelangen Aufenthalt in der Schnee- und Eiswüste Grönlands offenbar schon völlig zermürbt waren, verübten Selbstmord.

In den folgenden Jahren wurden noch mehrmals Lebensmittel, Arzneien und anderes Material von U-Booten aus an Land gebracht. Im Herbst 1944 kam der letzte Transport, mit dem auch 30 Mann an Land gingen.

Sie trugen den Aussagen der Eskimos nach andere Uniformen als jene Soldaten, die sich schon seit 1942 auf Grönland befanden und so vermutet man, daß es sich um SS-Leute handelte.

Feuergefecht mit Eskimos

Diese 30 Neuankömmlinge bezogen das gleiche Lager wie die 120 alten, hielten sich jedoch von diesen völlig abgesondert. Im Mai 1945, kurz nach der Kapitulation Deutschlands, verschwanden die 150 Deutschen aus der Umgebung von Angmagsalik. Die Eskimos glaubten, die 150 Mann hätten sich in amerikanische Gefangenschaft begeben, bis nun vor kurzem Eskimos nach der Rückkehr von einem Fang meldeten, daß die Deutschen sich noch immer auf Grönland befänden. Zwei der Grönländer waren, als die Deutschen ihrer ansichtig wurden, erschossen worden, die übrigen drei konnten flüchten und die Nachricht bringen, daß sie 170 Kilometer nördlich von Angmagsalik auf die Deutschen gestoßen seien.

German Battle Group Still in Greenland? According to the newspaper "Vienna Monday", Monday, December 29, 1947, an organized element of German military continued to function in Greenland long after the war ended.

O. Bergmann has another interesting report regarding Greenland. It seems that a question and answer session occurred in 1957 between a professor, a department head of a Southern German university, and an Austrian engineer. The engineer had contacts within the SD as well as the SS and so had a good overall picture of the lesser-known events leading up to the final moments of the 3rd Reich. This interview took place on September 24, 1957 and was recorded on audiotape. Either Bergmann or his publisher, Hugin, obtained a transcript of at least part of this interview, totaling 38 typewritten pages.

In the question and answer session, the Austrian engineer discusses the resistance movement. He states that there were two aspects to this resistance, positive and negative. The negative component concerned itself with sabotage and so on. We all know this negative resistance really went nowhere. The positive aspect of this resistance movement's aim was to establish a National Socialist, German, post-war country if not just government but not in occupied Germany. It is this thinking which concerns us here since central to this idea was the establishment of a position in the arctic from which a militant, esoteric group could carry out such a plan.

According to the engineer, this plan was put into operation even before the war ended. Elements of the Luftwaffe took the opportunity to spirit away arms and even facilities from the stores and reservoirs the Luftwaffe had at its disposal. This estranged faction of the Luftwaffe brought this supply of goods to the Artic. The engineer is explicit in saying that this was done without the knowledge of the Luftwaffe's high command being aware of it. Later, elements of the Kriegsmarine, the German Navy, also took part in this operation (7).

From this point on it gets somewhat confusing since there were always more than one group. In fact, there were three such groups, each with three sub-groups. Each group and sub-group had their own base and each group and sub-group had their own cover-name. This does not mean, however, that all these groups were sharing the Arctic, quite the contrary, these groups and their bases stretched far and wide all over the globe according to this report. But, there were two such groups in the Arctic. The group in the Arctic that had their primary or chief base in Greenland had three sub-groups below it. (8)

Since each group and sub-group had its own cover-name, in this system the group occupying Greenland received the name "Thuleka. Bergmann interjects that this name "Thuleka" was perhaps an abbreviation for Thule Kampfgruppe or Thule Combat Group in English. One sub-group of the larger Thuleka group is mentioned by name. This is the "Polaris" sub-group. This sub-group's home was so inner Arctic that Polaris's name is mentioned in the same breath as the legendary Ultimate Thule.

The Austrian engineer was asked about attempts to locate these bases by the Americans and Canadians. He repeats the story of the "Blue Island" which was mentioned earlier. He also goes on to compare the Arctic facilities with those erected by the Germans in Antarctica. In this comparison he includes electronic disruption of the airborne sensing devices seeking these bases.

One other group is worth mentioning in our story. This group is code-named "Atlantiker" (Atlantiens). Their sphere of influence was the Northern Andes. What is interesting about the "Atlantiker" is they had contact with both the Arctic and Antarctic groups and so connected all three groups since they were roughly half way between both. The exact means of this contact, by radio or other means is not stated (9).

The next bit of evidence came to Bergmann or Hugin from an employee of a German-language South American newspaper in the year 1988. Bergmann had published book one of his two book series on German flying discs and U-boats in that year so that this letter probably came as a response to that book. The one page letter is reproduced in Bergmann's second book in its entirety. Since both the sender and intended reader were well versed in the course of the war in Europe and post-war SS groups, there is little explanation of the course of events. For our purposes a bit of set-up is necessary so rather than translate it word for word perhaps the best treatment of this letter is just a discussion.

The writer of the letter did sign his name but this name has been partially obscured. The writer starts off by saying that he is not going to divulge real names or places that would identify the subject or informant the writer was using. Our writer, a newspaperman, met a former Captain in the SS in La Paz, Bolivia circa 1982 and got to know him. He told our newspaperman a very interesting wartime story.

It seems that this SS Captain was in charge of the defense of the dikes of Holland. We might instantly think of someone putting his finger in a dike but that image of a "dike" does not do justice to our story. Actually, the dike-system of Holland is massive and protects the entire country from flooding of the North Sea with levees, sea walls and gates. So, anyone in charge of this system would have a huge responsibility and a massive undertaking on his hands. What is most interesting is that this SS Captain's position, according to the letter, was completely bypassed by the invading Allies. We know this because the events of the letter take place in May 1945, and the British and Americans were already far into German soil having already pushed the German forces out of Holland. In fact, so the story goes, our SS Captain was called upon to surrender his little island of resistance, the dike, by the British twenty days after the capitulation of German or about May 28th 1945.

Of course, the British just assumed they held all the cards. After all Germany had unconditionally surrendered, this German unit was trapped between the British and the North Sea. Fighting their way out was senseless, there was no place to go since the war was over. But our SS Captain did hold some cards.

The SS unit had enough food and munitions stored up for at least a year. Secondly, they actually were in a strategic position. The SS Captain replied to the British that unless they were given a free pass back to Germany, with their weapons and colors, they would simply blow up the dike and submerge Holland in the North Sea. Well, we can all imagine the shock of the British. In fact there was a negotiation that lasted at least the twenty days mentioned. The British conceded terms as they were stated to the Germans. But since things took so long the Germans had lost trust in the British to live up to them. In the end, to consummate the deal, the Germans required the word of the Queen of England, which was given. The Germans returned home, through the British lines without restriction. There was imposed a press blackout of the whole incident for a whole series of understandable reasons.

But this is not our story; this was only the set-up to the story. Two days before the capitulation of Germany, so somewhere between May 5th and May 7th, 1945, a dozen German U-boats surfaced off the coast of Holland, in an area under the control of our SS Captain. Four landings were made by details from the U-boats taking on freight. Chests were taken aboard these U-boats from the shore. In the opinion of the Captain, the chests contained weapons and machine parts. Six officers of the Captain's SS unit were also taken aboard. The Captain knew one of these SS men since they were from the same town, Halle.
He told the Captain to tell his mother that he went missing but perhaps was still alive. Two years later the mother of this SS man did receive a letters from him, postmarked from Chile, Argentina and Columbia. The SS Captain and his men were sworn to silence about the whole affair.

The most significant thing about this story is the designations printed on the chests themselves. The SS Captain was able to make out the words "Thule 1 K" to "Thule 1 P", designations running in sequence. As this information came in the summer of 1988, the codenames "Thuleka" and "Polaris" had not been revealed by Bergmann and would not make it to print until a year later! The implication is clear. These chests as well as these

U-boats belonged to some sort of resistance group(s), perhaps the groups in Greenland. (10)

There seem to have been a distinct base in Greenland and by this I mean distinct in purpose and meaning from other Greenland bases. Landig puts this base on the east coast of Greenland and says it was military in nature as opposed to functioning as a weather station. It had no connection to the other bases and was staffed with from eighty to one hundred soldiers (11).
William R. Lyne says:

> *"Today, German flying saucer bases, such as the huge underground base built in Greenland, are probably maintained under joint Trilateral/ex-Nazi control."(12)*

At this point a digression must be made for a short story. I was requesting FOIA material and appealing negative outcomes from a large military facility. The reader would instantly recognize its name. This facility had hired a professional historian with a Ph.D. to respond to FOIA requests. This is nothing new. Now, all the large German firms do this as do the American firms. But, for some reason which escaped me at the time, this particular historian at this facility sent me a letter saying that perhaps it would be better for me to ask him "informally" for the information I wished and to describe it. This worked for a little while.

During this period of time I got a strange note or letter, forwarded by this historian, regarding German instrumentation. The writer was a former U-boat Captain or officer. He said at no time would a swastika be painted upon an instrument of the German military, the swastika was a political symbol and would have no place on such an object. Of course, he was not talking about U-boats. He and the historian had revealed themselves as knowing the topic of Nazi high-tech very well indeed because they were talking about William Lyne's compass. This was the compass Bill bought at auction as military surpluss. The compass is now famous as Bill interpeted it as coming from an electromagnetic German flying saucer. It features a round, Thule-type swastika and the letters "KT p2" painted at its center. Bill interpets this to mean "Kreisel Teller" (something like "gyro disc") with the p2 referring to the polarity of the craft.

At the time, I had no response. I had not the standing to debate or argue with a U-boat Captain. But later I saw footage of the Battle of Kursk in which a tank carried the same Thule-type swastika. I reasoned it must have been an SS tank and perhaps only the SS used such symbols in places where other organizations would not. Then I thought of the compass. Any field propulsion craft of this type would have been a very secret SS project. They would have made the parts in their own Pilsen/Prague facilities. This would have included the compass. They could paint whatever they wished on their gear, meant for their soldiers. Mystery solved? Maybe there is more of a mystery here.

What I mean is, given the account above from Holland, might the "KT p2" have another meaning? Might the SS have prepared this specific flying saucer for a specific Arctic Group if not base? In other words, might the "KT p2" have stood for

"Kampfgruppe Thule, Polaris Zwei" (Fighting Group Thule, Polaris Two)? It is just a thought but one not inconsistant with what has been presented here.

Returning to the general validity of German bases in Greenland, in his last book before his death, Heiner Gehring and researcher/writer Karl-Heinz Zunneck got a peak into the private files of Wilhelm Landig, just before his death in 1997. It is interesting to note that they cite Claude Schweikhart's 1951 work and give it credence, and using it as an example of a Nazi base that did not capitulate after May 9, 1945. (13) There seems little doubt that something of the 3rd Reich survived somewhere in Greenland after the official capitulation of Germany

Finally, I would like to move to a story sometimes mentioned in literature but never explained. It is a story that sometimes surfaces of UFO conferences or in discussion of secret Nazi facilities. This is the legend of the Laboratory of Death. I first heard this tale at a UFO conference and was told it was located in Norway. But, most commonly it is placed in Greenland so I will describe this legend and leave its location an open question.

I was told (on the UFO conference level of things mentioned above) that the Laboratory of Death concerns experiments in which humans are crossed with animals. This fusing of human and animal organs or characteristics was first told to me as a grafting process in which arms, legs and so on where transferred from one organism to the other. An alternate version involves "genetic experimentation" which somehow blends characteristics of humans and non-humans involving genes.

William R. Lyne's compass from a German flying disc
In this enlargement, please note the inscription KT-p2 below the Thule-style swastika.

The individual who first told me this story was an engineer. I completely disregarded it, thinking he had forgotten Biology 101. Rejection would certainly occur regarding body parts from two different species and in those days rejection drugs were unknown. Likewise, "genetic manipulation" in the late 1940's lacked the knowledge of the structure of DNA that remained undisclosed until Watson and Crick in the 1950's or 1960's, depending upon whose story you accept. Without knowing DNA's real structure, genetic manipulation as we know it is impossible.

Regardless of this story, the fundamental reference concerning the Laboratory of Death is Claude Schweikhart in his 1952 article in "Mensch und Schicksal "(14). It does not mention genetic manipulation or cloning or chimeras. Schweikhart reminds us of the investigation of the SS undertaken by the Louis Emrich team in conjunction with that Yugoslavian intelligence agency. Remember, they coined the word "Dritte Kraft" (Third Power) for the SS survival groups. Emerich and the Yugoslavians concluded that a base did exist somewhere in Greenland which they called "Laboratoriums des Todes" (Laboratory of Death) but this base remains a complete mystery.

They connect it with satanic activity. It is hard to connect experimentation of any sort with a religious concept, but this does occur again at a different place and time. Nazi hunter Ladislas Farago describes a special sect and its activities at Colonia Dignidad, the Nazi base in South America, as a combination of Nazism and voodooism (15). When I first read this I thought Farago was just using some sort of ploy to demonize the Nazis and disregarded it completely. Now I know better and so this activity will be discussed when we take up South America.

But that is not the big news coming from Schweikhart. The big news is that at the Laboratory of Death in Greenland a special type of flying saucer had been developed. This flying saucer had the ability to submerge in the ocean and from the ocean, fly into the air. In other words, it was a flying U-boat. Remember, Schweikhart was writing in 1952 so when he says this development took place in an unrepentant Nazi secret base on Greenland in 1951, we can only assume Schweikhart was well connected to say the least. (16) I do not expect any reader to take this statement, a statement from many years ago, from a mysterious source, describing an incredible event, at face value. But I would ask the reader to suspend judgment of the combination flying saucer - submarine until we can deal with that subject in some detail.

So picture, if you will, a base capable of such things. This base would have to be large indeed to accommodate both U-boats and flying discs. Bergmann describes what a Greenland base must have looked like as being essentially the same type of base needed at the South Pole at Neuschwabenland. It would consist of tunnels bored through ice and solid rock to a length of 2,000 meters. The entrance would have been camouflaged as to make it unfindable.

According to Bergmann, this type of base would have been protected by two kinds of weapons, both called "Strahlenwaffen" or ray weapons. First, there was the weapon he calls "Zuendunterbrechung" or ignition interruption in English. This word is simply a variant of "Motorstoppmittel", called magnetic wave by the Americans. This was a

1. AUGUST 1952 **Mensch und Schicksal** 6. JAHRG. / NR. 10

HALBMONATSSCHRIFT FÜR DAS GESAMTGEBIET DER GEISTESWISSENSCHAFT

Um Krone und Gipfel der Welt

Von Claude Schweikhart / Basel

„Wie bist du vom Himmel gefallen, du schöner Morgenstern! Wie bist du zur Erde gefällt, der du die Heiden schwächtest! Gedachtest du doch in deinem Herzen: Ich will in den Himmel steigen und meinen Stuhl über die Sterne Gottes erhöhen; ich will mich setzen auf den Berg der Versammlung in der fernsten Mitternacht; ich will über die hohen Wolken fahren und gleich sein dem Allerhöchsten."

Jesaja 14, 12—14.

Okkulte Kreise der Schweiz verfolgen mit großem, wachsendem Interesse die Bemühungen eines kleinen Ringes österreichischer Geisteswissenschaftler, die esoterische Bedeutung aktueller Vorgänge nachzuweisen, welche man zunächst für rein politisch-militärischer Natur halten möchte. Da wir in der Schweiz auch in okkulter Hinsicht doch etwas freiere Luft atmen dürfen, als unsere österreichischen Freunde und deshalb leichteren Einblick in Geschehnisse nehmen können, die sich der Sicht jener vermutlich überhaupt entziehen, sei mit Nachstehendem ein kleiner Beitrag zu ihrer intensiven Arbeit geleistet.

Okkulte Indiskretionen wurden im Altertum hart geahndet, weil sie oftmals in Vorhaben und Ereignisse Einblick gaben, deren Ziel und Zweck dem Wissen eines kleinen, priesterlichen Zirkels vorbehalten bleiben sollten, konnten und wohl auch mußten. Heute, nach mindestens 1952 Jahren Ringens um Menschenwürde und Gedankenfreiheit, halten wir es in gewissen esoterischen Dingen nicht mehr für angebracht, auf das Recht der Erforschung und nachfolgenden Publikation zu verzichten. Zudem ist die okkult interessierte Öffentlichkeit immer noch schmal und deshalb urteilskräftig genug, um der Gefahr einer Überschätzung der Meinung eines einzelnen nicht zu erliegen und sie weiß in ihren ernsthaften Teilen wohl Möglichkeiten von Tatsachen zu unterscheiden.

Hier wird der Versuch unternommen, esoterische Bewegungen und Bewegungsrichtungen in Umrissen zu charakterisieren, welche in aller Welt dem Ruf folgten, der im Jahre 1929 auf arithmetisch-kabbalistische Weise von Tibet aus, dem stellvertretenden geistigen Hochzentrum der Welt, erscholl und der in letzter Auswirkung, von Unwürdigen und Würdigen, von Berufenen und Erwählten vernommen, zu einem Wettstreit um die Protektion des „Großen Pol", der geistigen Potenz des arktischen Weltzentrums, führte.

Die Existenz dieses so heiß umworbenen Weltzentrums in der inneren Arktis läßt sich an Hand Hunderter Fakten beweisen und es sind diesbezüglich, wie jüngst, in dieser Zeitschrift schon mehrfach höchst bemerkenswerte Vorarbeiten und Hinweise publiziert worden. Viel schwieriger ist es naturgemäß, die gegenwärtige Situation zu erhellen. Manches kann deshalb über den Wert einer mehr oder weniger geglückten Mutmaßung nicht hinausgelangen.

Was bedeutet aber nun diese Existenz einer bisher verborgenen magischen Hochkultur, das Vorhandensein einer bis vor kurzem unentdeckten, oder besser gesagt nahezu vergessenen, weil dem profanen Blick entzogenen Insel auf dem physischen Gipfel des Erdballs, deren genaue Lage auf dem Astralplan fast nie eindeutig festgestellt werden konnte, für die Welt der Gegenwart?

Der Ruf zum Nordpol ließ alle Beteiligten nie darüber im Zweifel, daß dort oben, dem himmlischen Jerusalem der biblischen Verheißung, dem Ur-Shambhalla der Theosophen, die Krone der Welt für das unmittelbar bevorstehende Weltzeitalter des Wassermannes zu erwerben war und vielleicht auch heute noch zu erwerben wäre. Schon der während des 30jährigen Krieges verstorbene deutsche Mystiker Jakob Böhme weiß in seinem Werk „Aurora oder Morgenröte im Aufgang" zu sagen:

„Sieh, ich sage dir ein Geheimnis; es ist schon die Zeit da, daß der Bräutigam seine Braut kröne; rate, wo liegt die Krone? Gen Mitternacht, denn in der Finsternis wird das Licht hell. Von wannen aber kommt der Bräutigam? Aus dem Mittag, wo die Hitze das Licht gebärt, und fährt gegen Mitternacht, da wird das Licht hell. Was tun dann die gegen Mittag? Sie sind in der Hitze entschlafen, aber ein Sturmwetter wird sie aufwecken, und unter diesen werden viele zu Tode erschrecken."

Die beiden religiösen Gemeinschaften „Jehovas Zeugen" und die „Advent-Gemeinde" erwarten seit langem mit Sehnsucht die „Herabkunft" der „Himmlischen Stadt" auf Zion, aber sie haben leider übersehen, daß das palästinensische Zion so wie alle anderen sakralen Berge nur die Analogie und der Abglanz des einen Weltberges sind, ja sein müssen, dessen Gipfel als „Berg der Versammlung" in der fernsten Mitternacht, im höchsten Norden liegt. Sie haben nur eine Hoffnung, aber kein Wissen.

Wissen aber ist die Voraussetzung zu sinnvoller Tat.

Das gut zusammenwirkende Team des Psychoprognostikers Louis Emrich hatte es sich seinerzeit zur Aufgabe gestellt, die Bemühungen der deutschen Schutzstaffeln zur Erlangung der Gunst des geistigen Weltzentrums aufzuklären. Diese beschritten demnach zweifellos den zur Tat weisenden Weg des Wissens, obgleich sich dieses Wissen selbstverständlich auf esoterische Kreise innerhalb der nur äußerlich einheitlichen Schutzstaffeln beschränkte. Es dürfte jetzt genug Zeit verflossen sein, um die nachstehenden Tatsachen der objektiven Forschung zugänglich machen zu dürfen. Die erforderlichen esoterisch-historischen Recherchen wurden von einer kleinen, aber einflußreichen Gruppe forciert, die sich die

3

Cover of an article from *Mensch und Schicksal* magazine entitled "Um Krone und Gipfel der Welt". In the lower right hand corner the Louis Ermrich team—the first team to investigate esoteric aspects of the SS—is mentioned.

device that ionized the air within its range of operation and so short-circuited the ignition systems of enemy aircraft (17). The second weapon "Strahlenwaffe" goes undescribed by Bergmann but we may conclude it was a more directed beam weapon since Bergmann goes to pains to describe the result of the magnetic wave-type weapon (18). We will encounter both types of weapons again.

To flesh out our conception of such a base, we must assume parallel tunnels that are interconnected as they were in the underground facilities in Germany, Poland and the Czech Republic. Storerooms, living quarters, power generating facilities, heating facilities, and workshops would also be necessary. In addition, some sort of turntable for incoming U-boats would have been necessary in order to service them and then spin them around for launching again seaward. Access to a rough airfield would also probably be necessary for supplies and reinforcements from Norway.

What is the evidence such bases existed? Beyond these statements, however valid they may be, is there any brick and mortar evidence for such a base? Well, there may be a bit of evidence, but the reader is asked to bear with the story and allow the evidence presents itself.

Literature Cited

1. **Lusar, Rudolf, 1964**, *Die deutschen Waffen und Geheimwaffen des 2. Weltkrieges und ihre Weiterentwicklung*, page 356, J. F. Lehmanns Verlag, Munich, Germany
2. **Geheime Wetterstationen, a video film, Heitz and Hoeffkes**, Grabert Versandbuchhandlung, Tuebingen, Germany
3. **Bergmann, O., 1989**, *II Deutsche Flugscheiben und U-Boote Ueberwachen Die Weltmeere*, page 137, Hugin Publishing, Wetter/Ruhr, Germany
4. ***ibid.***
5. **Schweikhart, Claude, 1952**, *Um Krone und Gipfel der Welt, Mensch und Schicksal* (magazine), page 4, 6. JAHRG/NR. 10, August 1952
6. ***ibid.***
7. **Bergmann, O., 1989**, page 133
8. **Bergmann, O., 1989**, page 134
9. ***ibid.***
10. **Bergmann, O., 1989**, page 135
11. **Landig, Wilhelm, 1971**, *Goetzen Gegen Thule*, page 267, Hans Pfeiffer Verlag GmbH, Hannover, Germany
12. **Lyne, William R., 1999**, *Pentagon Aliens*, page 97, Creatopia Productions, Lamy, New Mexico, USA

13. **Gehring, Heiner and Karl-Heinz Zunneck, 2005**, *Flugscheiben ueber Neuschwabenland Die Wahrheit ueber "Vril", "Haunebu" und die Templer-Erbengemeinschaft*, page 172, Jochen Kopp Verlag, Rottenburg, Germany
14. **Schweikhart, Claude, 1952**, *Um Krone und Gipfel der Welt*, page 4, 6 JAHRG./Nr. 10, August 1952
15. **Farago, Ladislas, 1974**, *Aftermath*, page 388, Simon and Schuster, N.Y., NY. USA
16. **Schweikhart, Claude, 1952**, page 4
17. **Stevens, Henry, 2007**, *Hitler's Suppressed and Still-Secret Weapons, Science and Technology*, page 170-189, Adventures Unlimited Publishing, Kempton, Illinois, USA
18. **Stevens, Henry, 2007**, pages 198-208

GREENLAND, PART TWO: BEAVER DAM

Sometimes when the police cannot solve a crime within a few years using standard techniques and the case is closed, instead of filing it away somewhere, they turn it over to a special unit. This special unit specializes in closed, cold cases. They begin from square one and take a fresh look at everything. Sometimes this technique bears fruit and the case is solved.

Likewise, the Slavic researchers investigating mysteries of the Third Reich had no cultural connections to their neighbor to the West but plenty of underground ruins left from those people of those times. Sometimes the ruins were not even underground. Using their own methods, this group of Slavic researchers pieced together events from their own perspective. In this chapter we will take a look at some of their work.

Specifically, we will review "Wunderland" Mimozemske Technologie Treti Rise by Dr. Milos Jesensky, a museum curator and Robert Lesniakiewicz, a Polish engineer. My special thanks go out to Milos Vnenk who translated this book for me on audio tape and added his comments, supplying context which I would have been otherwise lacking.

Nothing in this chapter should be taken as being in conflict with the last or vice versa. Instead, the reader should probably integrate both sets of information into a larger overall picture of what happened during the 3rd Reich, particularly as it relates to the super-secret facilities in Greenland.

The strange trail leading us to the German secret base called Beaver Dam (Biber Damm) starts with the Soviet assault on Koenigsberg on the Baltic coast in modern-day Poland (Kaliningrad) in the dying days of the 3rd Reich. Even though Koenigsberg was defended by 35,000 German troops, it all came to naught for them as the Soviet Army overwhelmed the city, supported by 2500 attack aircraft and artillery. Koenigsberg went up in a tower of flame as the city was crushed. All the German defenders were either killed or captured. The Soviets looted the city in a drunken orgy, throwing valuables out as they searched for liquor and food. A city-full of German refugees seeking escape were mowed down by Soviet artillery fire. Koenigsberg died that night, utterly driven into the ground. In the larger scope of events German Silesia was gone with the wind, with the cities being renamed and resettled by Poles. Any German survivors were subsequently resettled West of the Oder River.

A short distance from Koenigsberg stood Wildenhof Castle. Wildenhof had served as the headquarters for the German General Schwerin who was connected to the defense of the city. This night the Castle was surrounded by Soviet infantry and attacked. The Soviet soldiers attacking Castle Wildenhof had been fighting the Germans for three years, coming all the way from Moscow in January 1942. They lived off the land, as the Soviets had no supply lines. They had been hardened through years of privation and combat with the Wehrmacht. On this night those hard, hard men burst into Wildenhof and, as their honed survival skills dictated, they went through every nook and cranny of the Castle looking for food, alcohol, and valuables.

Somewhere, buried in the bowels of Castle Wildenhof, those Soviet soldiers turned up a strong box. Naturally, they opened it immediately. Out fell a couple curious pieces of glass-like stone with some curious writing on it, two parchment scrolls, some photocopies of those scrolls and a recent military order marked "Geheimreichssache" which literally means "secret state matter". The soldiers turned the contents of the strong box over to the NKVD, which is Soviet Intelligence.

If it had not been for the official document marked "Geheimreichssache", probably little importance would have been attached to the matter. The glass-like stones turned out to be an amulet that was broken and glued back together. It dated from the Middle Ages as did the parchment scrolls, one in Latin and the other in Middle English. These objects have an occult and alchemical significance. They were taken to a central clearing facility, as were thousands of examples of war-related, displaced artwork. The "Geheimreichssache" document was altogether different, however, since it had a military context. In fact, it turned out to be an order, dated May 1, 1945, and signed by none other than the former Grand-Admiral Karl Doenitz and recently, as of that day, the second Fuehrer of Nazi Germany.

For some unexplained reason, Karl Doenitz took time out of his busy schedule to sign an order disposing of the amulet and parchment scrolls. Then, he went back to managing a collapsing military situation and negotiations with Allies concerning the surrender of Germany. Obviously, these documents were very important to Doenitz. The bottom line is that Doenitz ordered these items be taken to "Biber Damm" for safekeeping. "Biber Damm" (Beaver Dam in English) was obviously a place and the Soviet NKVD thought it might be a secret German base located on the East Coast of Greenland.

So with the Third Reich collapsing all around him, with Hitler dead and the Soviets in Berlin, Karl Doenitz is thinking about sending the contents of this little strong box to some place safe. Let us take another look at the words of Karl Doenitz in the quotation cited earlier:

> *"The German submarine fleet is proud of having built for the Fuehrer, in another part of the world, a Shangri-La on land, an impregnable fortress."*

And,

> *"The German Navy will have to accomplish a great task in the future. The German Navy knows all the hiding places in the oceans and therefore it will be*

very easy to bring the Fuehrer to a safe place should the necessity arise and in which he will have the opportunity to work out his final plans."

By themselves the amulet and the parchments have no significance in our story. Their meaning is only occult and alchemical. The amulet was apparently made in Eastern Europe or perhaps even further East in Asia during the Middle Ages. After falling into the hands of an Icelander or Greenlander who was probably employed as a mercenary in those lands, the amulet found its way to Greenland. From there it drifted to England and became the subject of some occult studies by John de Vincy and John Dees. How they got to Koenigsberg, to Castle Wildenhof, is a mystery. Perhaps this was just a step on a journey that was already underway when it was intercepted by the Soviets.

For whatever reasons, the NKVD failed to attach any value to the occult items, only to the order signed by Doenitz. But even this order and reference to a base called Beaver Damm seems to have faded in importance to Soviet Intelligence because it would be years before any importance was attached to any of this and then by a researcher already steeped in mysteries of the Third Reich, Dr. Ludwig Solchec.

Dr. Ludwig Solchec (1926-1978) was a prolithic Czech scholar who published thirty-five books in his career. Late in life, Dr. Solchec began to look into the mystery we are describing and it was largely his work which brought Dr. Milos Jesensky and Mr. Robert Lesniakiewicz to take yet another look at Beaver Dam and this whole mystery. Dr. Solchec published his work on this topic as part of his book whose title would be translated into English as "The Secret of the Amber Room".

At this point we must digress somewhat because this reference to an amber room is a huge World War Two mystery in Europe, especially for Germans and Russians. The threads of this mystery cross ours so that anyone involving himself in researching the amber room and looking at our situation involving the amulet, the parchments, Admiral Doenitz and a secret state order would be of great interest and help to us. The amber room or "Bernsteinzimmer" in German is a lost treasure and work of art that is almost unknown in the English-speaking world, but as a mystery, could be compared to the disappearance of Amelia Erhart for Americans.

The Bernsteinzimmer is just that, a room made of amber. Amber is a semi-precious stone formed from fossilized tree sap in an earlier geologic time frame. It washes up naturally on the shores of the Baltic Sea and so has been gathered by local people since the Neolithic and used as money and for trade. Fredrich Wilhelm I of Prussia presented the Russian Tzar Peter the Great with a room made of amber in 1716. Prussia needed an ally and Russia was a rising star at that moment. The amber room was shipped to Russia and set up in the winter home of the Tsar. It must have been a hit because Friedrich Wilhelm II sent a wall mirror frame consisting of splendid carvings in amber to the Russian. In 1735, the amber room, now a recognized art treasure, was moved to the Tsar's summer home. The hall in which the amber room was installed was approximately ten meters square and four and three-quarter meters high so this was a large, ornate, imposing mass of cut amber decking the walls. Russian amber carvers added to the room completely covering the ceiling with amber.

The Bernsteinzimmer remained as a Russian treasure through the Revolution being displayed near Leningrad at Empress Catherine's former palace in Pushkin. With the German invasion of World War Two, the amber room was packed up and moved East for safety sake. But only part of this treasure was actually packed up by the Russians and taken way. Some was not, including some of the upper frieze and the mirrors. We know this because Pushkin fell into German hands and the Germans packed up what remained of the amber room and moved it back to Germany. Some of it may have been moved to Thuringia but there is no doubt that a great portion of it went to Koenigsberg. Not only to Koenigsberg but to a castle near Koenigsberg and put on display. It was actually opened to the public in the summer of 1943 (1).

Was this "castle", Castle Wildenhof? I don't know but the chances are pretty good that it was. Of course this brings us to the Soviet advance on Koenigsberg which was discussed above. Now things start getting fuzzy. Hitler seems to have ordered the treasure onto a ship, the cruiser "Emden" along with the coffins of the Hindenburgs. The Emden arrived in Stettin two days later and then sailed for Kiel. At Kiel, the Emden was sunk in an air raid. In the words of researcher Ulrich Brunzel:

> *"Whether the Bernsteinzimmer was among the cargo is more than doubtful". (2)*

So, sometime between its presence at the castle in Koenigsberg and the sinking of the Emden at Kiel, the Bernsteinzimmer disappeared. In comparing the Bernsteinzimmer to Doenitz's amulet, the least we can say is that it seems Koenigsberg was a stop for treasure or valuables being spirited away from the hands of the Soviets. We know the amulet was supposed to be taken to a save repository, Beaver Dam. It is not unreasonable to assume that the Bernsteinzimmer in the same or a nearby location was also scheduled to be taken to that same safe repository. This probably intent links the two treasures and makes the work of Dr. Solchec who was primarily involved in researching the Bernsteinzimmer, so valuable.

But what was it that made Dr. Solchec believe that Beaver Dam was an Arctic base in Greenland? The answer is Dr. Solchec found, explored and researched the German Arctic training facility in the mountains of Bohemia, on the border between modern day Poland and The Czech Republic and found evidence there and elsewhere which led him to the location of Beaver Dam.

Dr. Solchec began his investigations in about the year 1969. He started by talking to old-time residents about things that transpired during the war years. There were fewer than might be expected due to the mass German immigration to the West but nevertheless Dr. Solchec found the information for which he was looking. In the border country between what is now Poland and the Czech Republic, Dr. Solchec was directed to a particular mountain where wartime mysteries still lingered. This mountain was named Kirkonoshe that is often called what would translate to " the Golden Peak" in English. On the Golden Peak was a camp or base that was used by the Germans each winter from

1938 to 1945. This base was cordoned off and guarded by security troops. Few if any local people were allowed on the base that was formed around the peak of the mountain.

According to the old-timers, Dr. Herdenerten ran the base. As Dr. Solchec would later discover, Dr. Herdenerten was an Arctic explorer. In fact, he did most of his work in Greenland. Dr. Herdenerten worked under the auspices of Hermann Goering who we all know commanded not the Navy but the German Air Force. In 1938 Goering launched the Umanku expedition to Greenland. Its purpose was to gather plants and animals and to acclimate people, plants and animals to that environment. To facilitate these goals he set up the Bohemian station on the Golden Peak, Kirkonoshe.

The reports given to Dr. Solchec were that Dr. Herdenerten set up the "Hawk Bungalows" in the high peak area of the mountain. Large, white sled dogs made an appearance at Kirkonoshe, which were engaged in training pulling heavy loads across the snow and ice in some sort of a training exercise. Greenland had an indigenous type of dog, a close relative of the Canadian Eskimo dog, called a Groenlandhund or Greenland dog that fits this description.

But besides the bungalows, most of the troops lived in tents. They did this at altitude and in the winter so it was obvious that living in these rough conditions was part of their training. Each winter the scene was repeated, right up until the Nazi collapse. But Dr. Herdenerten did not last that long as he was replaced by a biologist named Dr. Hans Knoespel.

Dr. Knospel added to the menagerie, bringing in large, white falcons. It seems that Dr. Knospel was interested in falconry. Dr. Knospel was another old Arctic hand that had done his share of exploration. While on expedition to the Spitsbergen, Dr. Knospel was involved in an accident that took his life in June of 1944. Nevertheless, combining the tenures of Dr. Herdenerten and Dr. Knospel accounts for the bulk of the war years as far as the base at Kirkonoshe is concerned. A local resident, Anton Pohoschaly turned the base over to Czech soldiers at the conclusion of the war and the base and its purposes were largely forgotten until the time of Dr. Solchecs interest in the place.

About 1969 Dr. Solchec began poking around at the base, talking to people and sifting through what was left of the facility. Gradually, he came to understand the purpose and scope of the base. The clincher came when Dr. Solchec found an old hat left behind by the Germans years before. It was an old fur hat, part of a Wehrmacht polar uniform. On the inside of the band of the hat and inscription could still be faintly read. It read: Po-Ra-Re Polar Versuchs Stab". The words "Polar Versuchs Stab" mean in English "Polar Research Staff" or alternatively "Polar Research Headquarters". This sealed the deal for Dr. Solchec. As far as he was concerned, this base had a direct relationship with the Arctic bases to the West, especially with that base of Greenland which Dr. Solchec found at the crossroads of his research into both the amulet and the Bernsteinzimmer, Beaver Dam. (3)

Greenland is a big place. We all know that it is the largest island on earth. So, exactly where was Beaver Dam in this land of unending glacial ice? How did Dr. Solchec set about solving this mystery?

From the start Dr. Solchec noticed the high number of place names of German origin on the East Coast of Greenland. He then began looking at the Arctic expeditions sent to Greenland and found a high number were originated by German explorers. Dr. Solchec reasoned that the Nazi government along with Doenitz and his Kriegsmarine had dusted off these reports and used them as an overview in looking for a likely spot for a base. Of course, the Germans were active in the area both with meteorological bases on land and ships stationed at sea in the particular Arctic region so they knew the terrain well.

Dr. Solchec reasoned that the base had to be in a relatively uninhabited place on Greenland. Most of the human activity centered on the southern tip of that island since Viking times, probably because the climate was more favorable in the South. Dr. Solchec therefore looked to the North. In fact, he began to zero-in on Peary's Land, named after a polar explorer. Peary's Land is the far Northeastern tip of Greenland that forms a peninsula jutting into the Barents Sea at about Latitude 80 degrees North.

But the clincher for Dr. Solchec was the presence of lignite in Peary's Land. Lignite is an energy source, being halfway between peat and coal. In fact another word for lignite is "brown coal". It is mined in the USA, Europe, Russia and Australia and is almost exclusively used as fuel to power steam-electric generation. This meant that a base built there which invested some effort in mining the lignite would be energy self-sufficient. We all know how desirable this would have been to the Germans. This natural supply of lignite had to be a huge consideration in choosing as site for a base.

At this point we should return to Bergmann's description of how an Arctic base would look and build upon this for a better understanding of how Beaver Dam might have appeared. Bergmann thought of other German underground bases in Europe and proposed tunnels of up to 2000 meters in length. He also thought such as base would be guarded by the new laser weapons and the magnetic wave weapons designed to render ignition-based aircraft inoperative. Jesensky and Lesniakiewicz are convinced that Beaver Dam had a connection with the sea. This means some sort of hardened bunkers accessible by U-boat such as the Germans built in the west coast of France and Norway. These were large, reinforced concrete, bombproof bunkers with overhanging ledges allowing a U-boat to sail right into and under the protection of the bunker. Considering the name "Beaver Dam", I think we can make some assumptions about the special nature of this particular base.

Beavers build a dam of branches on a stream, backing it up and forming a pond. In the center of the pond the beaver builds a lodge, a mound of interwoven branches containing a hollowed out central room where the beaver lives. To access this central room, the beaver builds or hollows out underwater tunnels from the pond to the lodge that cannot be seen from the surface of the water or the shore of the pond.

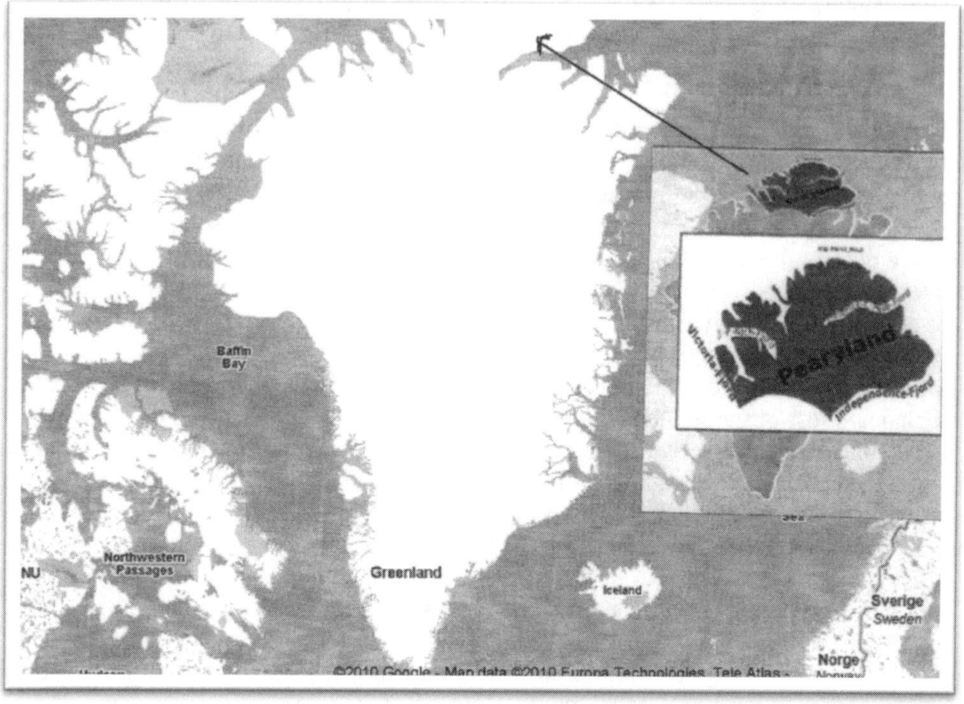

Greenland, Beaver Dam Please note the location of Peary Land in the extreme northern end of the island. Was this Admiral Doenitz' impregnable base? Allegedly, the presence of lignite for fuel made this secret base possible.

Obviously, this code-name "Beaver Dam" must mean something. In the absolute maximum of possibilities for Beaver Dam, I would picture it as breakwater or near breakwater, allowing only the tops of the waves into a central harbor. The central harbor would remain relatively calm for a U-boat, especially if it were submerged. To access the base itself the U-boat would dip a few feet underwater under an artificial ledge built into solid rock. Behind the ledge the U-boat would surface into a large hollow cavity completely cut off from the surrounding environment. The cavity would contain lights, dry-docks, machinery for on and off loading. Parallel tunnels would go into the solid rock for thousands of feet. These tunnels would be interconnected and contain living quarters, machine and workshops, storage facilities, advanced weapons and command facilities. It would contain some sort of camouflaged radar, electronic devices to throw off magnetic compasses, as well as the defensive weaponry mentioned above. The artificial breakwater and the reinforced cement ledge would be camouflaged to look like real rock or real rock might even be affixed on to it for this natural look. To aerial reconnaissance or even ships sailing past it, the base would blend into the natural surroundings. A small airfield was probably nearby since contact with Norway via air was necessary at least in the beginning.

If we are to believe the most extreme reports, this is the place the Nazis developed a flying U-boat in 1952. This blurs the distinction between a UFO and a USO. Besides flying discs and U-boats. Bergmann bases his two books on this concept. Bill Lyne as well as Dr. Jesensky and Mr. Lesniakiewicz believe UFOs used to spy on the USA were launched from Greenland, probably from this very base. The latter two researchers say the Nazis, using their flying discs, combed the atomic bases and facilities of the USA and the USSR in an attempt to appropriate atomic weapons. The latter two researchers even postulate the origin of the UFO that crashed at Roswell as coming from this base. This is in agreement with the central thesis just put forth by Dr. Joseph P. Farrell in his book "Roswell And The Reich".

But other weapons were kept at Beaver Dam according to Dr. Jesensky and Mr. Lesniakiewicz. Among these was the "Urzel". The Urzel was a combined V-1, V-2, mounted in a horse and rider configuration. This weapon was to be launched at the east coast of the USA and was to have contained an atomic warhead. Unfortunately for the Nazis, the atomic production facilities at Der Riese either could not produce the desired weapon in time or were overrun by the Soviets before they could do so.(3) The Urzel bears a close resemblance to the mysterious "V-3"/V-2 combination (based on that strange missile the Polish skin diver found while on vacation at the Baltic). Since this was also arranged as a horse and rider, one wonders if the two reports are the same weapon system.

Returning now strictly to the interpretation of Dr. Jesensky and Mr. Lesniakiewicz given in "Wunderland", we are informed that the mission and scope of Beaver Dam changed somewhat corresponding to the rapidly changing war situation. They list three stages for Beaver Dam.

In stage one, Beaver Dam would have been the impregnable fortress Doenitz promised for Hitler. Hitler was to be able to carry out war outside of Germany in this vision so U-boats and even tug boats would be necessary since containers carrying large rockets capable of hitting the United States would have been brought in. This base also functioned as a meteorological base until the bitter end for the war in Europe. Training for the men as well as testing and working out of details involving Arctic living would have been carried out at the polar research station at the Golden Peak, Kirkonoshe, in the Bohemian mountains.

In stage two the atomic warheads and very long range rockets could no longer be counted upon since the research, development and industrial facilities lying underground in the Owl Mountains of Poland were unable to provide them in a timely manner. Therefore, Beaver Dam took on a secondary function. It became a repository. Art, artifacts, gold and money from the Reich's Bank, blueprints for superweapons as well as prototype aircraft were brought to Beaver Dam for storage. Among these prototypes/superweapon blueprints was a flying disc.

In stage three the war is over. The base now served as a hide-away for prominent Nazis on the run but the most important function of Beaver Dam centered around the flying discs. This was their base and point of origin for spying missions directed at stealing atomic weapons and technology from the USA and USSR. Urzel weapons were also in storage. The Nazis at Beaver Dam still prepared for some sort of final battle, a Goetterdammerung, in which they would fight with advanced weapons and machines of all kinds.(5)

This last paragraph is definitely Redemptionist. In fact, Dr. Jesensky and Mr. Lesniakiewicz call a chapter related to this concept "Es kommt der Tag" ("The day will come"). According to these researchers the Germans there wanted to cause provocation between the East and West. Reinhard Gehlen, who ran a German intelligence network inside the Soviet Union during the war and was recruited by the CIA after the war to reconstitute the Soviet spy network and work for the West, is often accused of playing one side against the other, even manufacturing the Cold War, for the benefit of those he served and their ideals in the Nazi period. If the reality of a Third Power is accepted, could there have been some truth behind this?

Now, the Slavic researchers do not think Beaver Dam exists today. At some point during the last 60 plus years they believe the base ceased to function. They really do not say what might have happened but they do speculate about walking through the underground tunnels and finding abandoned, rusty flying discs and derelict U-boats. These researchers believe the evidence is there, only awaiting discovery. Imagine if it were true, if someone did find a secret German base, accessible only by tunnel to the sea, filled with U-boats and supporting machinery that had been in operation after 1945? That would settle the question of post-war German bases once and for all, right?

This may not be in the cards for Beaver Dam because this base just might never have gone defunct. Bergmann re-enters the picture with some thoughts which do not spell out the demise of Beaver Dam outright but inject a new player into this very area of Greenland's Peary Land: the Americans.

Bergmann informs us that just as Admiral Byrd led an expedition against the German base in the Antarctic, at Neuschwabenland, so too were expeditions mounted in Greenland, which Bergmann hints were for the same purpose (6). During the years 1947 to 1950 a Danish expedition commanded by Eigil Knuths was sent to Greenland. In the years 1947 to 1951 the French sent an expedition headed by and individual named Viktors. In 1951, the English got into the act with their own expedition to Greenland, which was led by Simpson.

But what is most amazing is that on March 27, 1951 the Danish, who own Greenland, found it necessary to enter into an agreement with the United States for the common defense of Greenland. Who were they defending Greenland against? Greenland is a sparsely populated land with no large cities, mostly inhabited by Eskimos still practicing variations of a hunter-gatherer lifestyle. The only military power in 1951 set up in opposition to the United States was the Soviet Union and it hardly had its sights set on invading Greenland.

Immediately, the US government began feverishly building some air bases in Greenland. Bergmann presents a map of Greenland showing three bases, Narsarssuak, Thule and Station North. The base at Station North is located exactly where Dr. Solchec, Dr. Jesensky and Mr. Robert Lesniakiewicz think Beaver Dam was located, on the northeast peninsula called Peary's Land.

So what happened here? The German were said to have just perfected their flying submarine at this time. How could the Americans and presumably NATO have a base in this exact spot or within a few miles of it? Again, William Lyne's comments about a German Greenland base are:

> *"Today, German flying saucer bases, such as the huge underground base built in Greenland, are probably maintained under joint Trilateral/ex-Nazi control."(7)*

But every now and then something even more sinister can be heard. Sometimes people whisper (at places like UFO conferences) that what we are calling Beaver Dam, a German base in Greenland, actually still exists and is under the joint control of Nazis and NATO. OK, this is usually at UFO conferences but these words have been uttered if not published.

A more likely scenario is that the Germans were displaced sometime in the years 1951 or 1952. They could have abandoned this base or these bases or they could have been forced out by the American military. They might even have entered into an agreement to cede the bases. If this is true, the March 27, 1951 agreement may have involved a secret party, one representing the interests of the Nazis. The hidden base itself with its hidden access to the sea may have been appropriated as a listening post and for use in clandestine activities directed at the Soviet Union.

Literature Cited

1. **Bunzel, Ulrich, 1997**, *Hitler's Treasures and Wonder Weapons*, pages 97-101, Heinrich Jung Verlagsgesellschaft mbH, Zella-Mehlis/Meiningen, Germany
2. **Bunzel, Ulrich, 1997**, page 101
3. **Jesensky, Milos, Ph.D., and Mr. Robert Lesniakiewicz, 1998**, "Wunderland" Mimozemske Technologie Treti Rise, pages 131-137, Aos Publishing, The Czech Republic
4. **Jesensky, Milos, Ph.D., and Mr. Robert Lesniakiewicz, 1998**, page 143
5. **Jesensky, Milos, Ph.D. and Mr. Robert Lesniakiewicz**, 1998, page 142
6. **Bergmann, O., 1989**, *II Deutsche Flugscheiben und U-boote Ueberwachen die Weltmeere*, page 132, Hugin Gesellschaft, Wetter/Ruhr, Germany
7. **Lyne, Willaim R., 1999**, *Pentagon Aliens*, page 97, Creatopia Productions, Lamy, New Mexico, USA

THE LAST BATTALION:

LEGEND AND RELATED EVENTS

Before leaving the North Atlantic the legend of the Last Battalion must be considered. I say "legend" because there is no real proof this event ever occurred as it is often described. There can be little doubt that the statement attributed to Hitler by W. Mattern had something to do with this legend. Again, the statement is:

> *"In this war there does not exist victors or vanquished, only the dead and living, but the last battalion that will be a German battalion." (1)*

Mattern calls this Hitler's end-of-the-war prophecy. This idea is closely bound with the idea that Hitler left the bunker and made his way to Norway. There, he boarded a U-boat so that the Fuehrer and a whole U-boat convoy sailed out of Kristiansand, Norway, on or about May 2, 1945. The part of the story that most concerns us now is that the convoy was intercepted by the British Navy, resulting in a large sea battle which has gone unrecorded in naval history. The Germans were said to have won the battle and continued on their way to Antarctica where the last battalion and accompanying legend take up residence.

As stated earlier, I believe Hitler did die in the bunker. But Hitler is only a prop in this story. The area we ought to concern ourselves with is the sea battle. Considerations of Neuschwabenland, the German Antarctic base, can be deferred to a later chapter.

Mattern's book containing this quote states no date and was published by Ernst Zundel's Samisdat Publishing, in Toronto. I know the time frame was the mid-1980s. Zuendel advertised a book devoted to this topic alone but never published it. By all accounts, the response to the advertised book was overwhelming. Something in the title "The Last Battalion" captivated the imagination. Later, I came across Wilhelm Landig's Wolfzeit um Thule and realized he was the source for Mattern and Zuendel as well as other writers.

In this chapter we will take a look at the sea battle in question and then consider ideas that may or may not be related to the Last Battalion but also involve sea battles roughly in this time frame, which have not been graced with a stamp of approval by conventional historians.

Wilhelm Landig published Wolfzeit um Thule in 1980. This was his second novel "full of realities". Landig actually opens the book with a description of this battle, the title of the chapter being "Die Verheimlichte Schlacht" (the secretive battle). Landig tells us the story mostly through the interactive conversation of two co-captains, Captain Krall and Captain Hellfeld, aboard a supply U-boat in the U-boat flotilla. Each U-boat had two co-captains for some reason. Our U-boat is not given a proper "U" designation, only being called "Boot 5XX".

Omitting the drama, I will try to recount and discuss the events as Landig describes them in his chapter titled "Die Verheimlichte Schlacht" which describes the naval battle.(2) This rendition of events can then be compared with later variations of the story.

Landig gives us the date May 2, 1945 for the fleet of U-boats putting to sea from Kristiansand, Norway. He calls it a "Geisterflottille", a ghost fleet. Among the U-boats assembled, Landig states that there is a Type XXI present. He also describes a totally different and totally new U-boat, not a Type XXI, Type XXIII or Type XXVI. This is obviously exciting but we will have to reserve discussion of this boat for a later time. Landig did not give any figures for the size of the ghost fleet.

The crews of these U-boats may not have been composed of standard operating crews. It is said that most are younger than 25 years old. Also, technicians and scientists are aboard. Some of these people, according to Landig, are already listed as missing so would not be sought or expected to return.

The men of this fleet left with the common understanding that the war in Europe was lost. They were not trying to change the course of the war and realized what we know today, that any hope of doing so had long since passed. They did understand that they were on a special mission. They also knew they were the bearers of an order (Nazism) that was hated by the rest of the world by this time.

These U-boats had all been upgraded to some extent and some possessed the very latest in technology. For instance, all had the schnorkel device that would allow fresh air to enter the U-boat while submerged at a shallow depth. This made it possible to run on diesel power or used the diesel engines to recharge the submarine's batteries, necessary to operate the electric engines for underwater running, while remaining relatively undetected.

Other devices mentioned by Landig are a round, dipole antenna used for warning the ship of an approaching enemy. Another device mentioned by Landig is called an "Ortungsgeraet" which pinpointed enemy ships with a range of eight nautical miles. I don't know if the "Ortungsgeraet" is a description of the device (Ortungsgeraet meaning positioning device) but I cannot find it as a codename for any device matching the description given. Additionally, Landig lists the Balkon-Horchgeraet as being used. This device is said by Landig to have a range of 40 nautical miles. It picked up the sounds of propeller screws. The name "Balkon" (balcony) referred to the balcony-like housing built on the U-boat to house the sensing head (3).

The fleet put out to sea with no difficulty and made its way North. Landig gives no real dates or time references beyond the May 2, 1945 date. He marks time by distance as when he says the fleet neared Iceland and continued north. He also marks time by discussing events known in a certain time frame.

The ship from which the story is told is called 5XX. It is a provision supplying U-boat but that is all we know. As was previously mentioned, two captains are on-board whose conversation serves to describe what is happening.

North of Iceland, Allied radio chatter is encountered so the Germans know they are in the area in some strength. But they also know that the Allies are not expecting such as sizable German force in the North Atlantic at this late stage in the war. The Germans are confident of their superior action-radius, based on the technology described and the speed of their U-boats.

A “flying object” from a German base outside of the Reich observes a group of hostile ships and the information is relayed by long-wave to the U-boats. This is significant. The Germans perfected long-wave communication during the war. This is Tesla technology in which long radio waves were sent by dipole transmitters through the earth. In this case “earth” also means the ocean so the Germans could pick up communications while submerged almost anywhere on the earth. Various regions had layers of water which best facilitated reception of these messages and the depths for best reception where mapped out by the German Navy, worldwide. The transmitter required was, naturally, very large and specialized. Transmissions could be received but not sent by the U-boats. The transmitter itself was in Magdeberg, near Berlin. The facility was code-named “Goliath” (4). We will discuss this technology in more detail in a later chapter.

This long-wave transmission is a problem, though. The “last” long-wave transmitter, Goliath, was destroyed by the advancing Soviets at about time. (5) This would make good sense since they had been at the gates of Berlin for some time. Remember, by May 2, 1945 Hitler is already dead and the Soviets have overrun the bunker. Could there have been a long-wave transmitter outside Germany? Landig says the transmission came from Point 103 that we know is outside of Europe. The transmission was picked up at a depth of 20 meters.

Another interesting statement by Landig is the “flying object” which made the original observation of the enemy ships was in fact a German flying disc, Landig calls it a “V-7” and it was based at Point 103. Of further interest was the means of communication used by the V-7. This was the “Kurier” (courier) device.

Just so it is clear, the Kurier device relayed messages from the V-7 to Point 103 and then as the story goes the messages were transmitted to the ghost U-boat fleet by long-wave transmission. The Kurier device relayed messages in a very unique way. Today, we call this method “burst transmission”. A great amount of date was dialed into the Kurier device and transmitted in a burst so that the enemy could not get a fix on the sender. This was extremely successful for the Germans. (6) After the war the first question asked of U-boat crews by the British was for the Kurier device. (7) Burst technology resurfaced forty years later, coupled with computers, in espionage settings.

With the enemy located and still operating undetected, the German U-boats attacked. Landig tells us that the weapon of choice for this attack was a particular kind of torpedo. Landig called it the "Typ TXI". He states that it operated at a depth of 50 meters, that it was steered by a sensor which honed in on the sound of propellers of the target ship, and that up to six such torpedoes could be fired at a time.

This torpedo is a variation of the "Zaunkoenig" torpedo. Lusar says of this weapon:

> *"The king among German torpedoes was the "Zaunkoenig" or "T-5". This torpedo was equipped with a magneto-striation transceiver that received, evaluated and then conveyed the direction from which the sound waves, issuing from the ship's screw, had been received to the rudder through a gyro-device. The torpedo first ran in an arc and then turned in the direction of the sensed target. A safety device had to be built in to ensure that the torpedo kept sufficient distance from the U-boat and did not hit it. This device initially provided for a fixed length of run, but when this turned out to be too short selective pre-setting was adopted. About sixty amplifying valves were fitted in the head of the torpedo.*
>
> *The "Zaunkoenig" was turned in to the screw-noise amplitude of the destroyers escorting the convoys and operated on a wavelength of 13,000 Hertz. When, however, the British, to whom the invention had been betrayed some six months before its introduction, had their destroyers tow noise-making devices (squawked buoys) which interfered with the "Zaunkoenig" sound locators an improved "Zaunkoenig" was designed - the "T-11", also called "Geier . The sound-locator of this torpedo was tuned so that it did not respond to the weaker noise of the destroyer's auxiliary engines. Consequently the torpedo would hit the destroyer itself. A further torpedo, the "T-14", with Walter turbine propulsion, was on the test bench at the end of the war and was not used operationally."(8)*

Lusar's Roman numeral TXI would correspond to Lusar's T-11.

As Landig tells the tale, the provision and supply U-boat 5XX had no weapons aboard and could only sit tight and wait out the battle. Eventually the captains raised the periscope and had a look around. All the British ships were either sunk or sinking. No British ships survived. After the battle, contact with the V-7s continued as was contact with Point 103.

Then the two captains discuss something that we will have to think about. In their conversation it is pointed out that now the Americans will know there is a German presence in the Arctic and they will certainly and actively seek the German base(s). This brings up the post-war episode of Americans searching the Arctic for flying saucers. As already mentioned, retired Col. Wendelle Stevens was among those involved in this search in those days. He has stated that B-29s were fitted with photographic gear and patrolled large tracts of the Arctic. In some cases, according to his testimony, contact was made with flying saucers, both in the air and on the ice and they were successfully photographed. The film was taken off the B-29s and sent to Washington, D.C. undeveloped. Col. Stevens never was given any sort of explanation as to the photo-interpretive results.

Returning to Landig and the captain's talk of Arctic bases, it was stated that all Arctic bases would be moved and relocated to the Antarctic where the Germans would have more room and security. Besides this, the probability of Hitler's death was discussed, as was the probability of the Arctic Blue Island legend. No firm conclusions were reached on either. This concludes Landig's discussion of the last sea battle of the war.

We should note that at no time does Landig use the words "Last Battalion". There is no mention of Adolf Hitler aboard the ghost fleet. Landig does mention a German flying disc but the only weapon mentioned by Landig was the sound-seeking torpedo.

Next we will move in chronological order to W. Mattern, who writes sometime in the mid-1980s, or a few years after Landig's *Wolfzeit um Thule*. In his book *UFO's Unbekanntes Flugobjekt? Letzte Geheimwaffe Des Dritten Reiches? ("UFO's: Unidentified Flying Object? Last Secret Weapon of the Third Reich?")* Mattern uses Landig's sea battle and greatly expands on it. This expansion is not in terms of proof or details but rather in terms of meaning. To Mattern, the sea battle between the ghost U-boat fleet somewhere near Iceland represents only a first adventure for what he calls "the last German battalion". It is his understanding that the German last battalion escorted Hitler—who did not die in the bunker—all the way to Antarctica to set him up in his new seat of power, Newschwabenland (9). As supporting documentation, Mattern only cites the magazine *Der Weg* and *El MercurioNews,* but gives no date or other identifying data so that it can be verified (10). Landig's ghost fleet has now become the "Fuehrer Convoy" (11).

There is another important difference. While Landig uses German flying discs for reconnaissance, Mattern makes them the very instrument of Nazi power. They become the vehicle by which the Nazis will perhaps achieve redemption and reassert themselves in the world's mainstream at some future time. In fact, this is the point of the book. There is still no mention of other exotic weaponry being used by the U-boat fleet itself.

One brief statement sets us up for what is coming from William R. Lyne in his sequence of events at or near this time frame. My translation of Mattern's words are as follows:

> *"It was perhaps Doenitz and not Goering who guaranteed the U-boat flotilla to the Antarctic and who also took over the security of the withdrawal of the Fuehrer from the bunker of the Reich's Chancellery, whereof Goering had no knowledge." (12)*

Please keep this idea in mind a few moments, while we consider other versions of the Last Battalion story.

D. H. Harmann relies on Norbert Juergen-Ratthofer, pulling a citation from a magazine article Juergen-Ratthofer wrote (13). In the last sentence of the otherwise standard rendition of the Landig story, Juergen-Ratthofer describes a new type of torpedo but also a totally different weapon that he calls the "Electrokanone" (electric cannon).

This "electrokanone" is most likely the rail gun that had been developed by the Germans during the war but never officially deployed (14), (15). The device would have worked well coupled with the huge batteries carried aboard a submarine. Unfortunately, neither Haarmann nor Juergen-Ratthofer offers any details or discussion on the subject.

Dr. Joseph Farrell provides us with some additional evidence for the special arms carried aboard German U-boats at this terminal phase of the war. Farrell, drawing upon sources Carter Hydrick and Geoffrey Brooks, comes up with the concept of "black U-boats" or U-boats that were off the official records and not under the control of the German Navy (16). Dr. Farrell sees these U-boats more in a secret supply role involving South America, which we will explore, but something he says about the technology on-board cannot go unnoticed. Farrell maintains that the Germans possessed some new sort of radar that spooked the Allies into not attacking, even when the U-boats in question were spotted. Further, citing Brooks, Farrell sees this new technology as an "energy field" that is disruptive to the engines of attacking aircraft:

> *"(iv) The last contacts appear to suggest that the submarines were now being seen on radar - perhaps the energy field was weakening - but as they entered the field the aircraft functions were jeopardized in some manner - 'if your aircraft starts to run rough for no apparent reason, pull away' ". (17)*

The answer fitting this description is "Motorstoppmittel" (or "Zuendunterbrechung" or magnetic wave) (18). This technology would find a perfect application on-board a U-boat. All attacking aircraft of the times were piston-based, ignition engines which were the targets of "Motorstoppmittel". Powering such a weapon would have been no problem for a diesel-electric U-boat whose diesel engines were often used to charge-up marine batteries from which the electric engines drew their power. Diverting the generators for employment of the Motorstoppmittel device would have been as easy as flipping a switch. The aircraft in question would have suddenly experienced ragged engine firing and finally their total failure as the aircraft continued on a straight-line trajectory and plunged into the sea.

Flights were directed over Germany specifically to investigate this new weapon. The rough-running engine was the telltale sign. American flyers were told to pull away from any target if this reaction was experienced. I reproduced a page of such a flying field investigation in an "F-38" (P-38 Lightning) from secret CIC Headquarters documents, dated January 24, 1945 in my previous book, a paragraph of which reads:

> *"3. In the beginning of his third pass his instruments began acting up and his left engine became very rough. He tried for approximately a minute and a quarter to correct the engine condition, that is, changing mixture control to auto-rich and back and changing FFM and manifold pressure. During this time the fuel pressure and FFM were fluctuating very extensively. Puffs of black smoke were*

observed from the turbo. After trying to correct the condition he observed flames coming from the turbo and fearing a fire he immediately feathered the engine."(19)

Just as with prototype aircraft, there was no tomorrow for further development. There was no reason not to try to use any advance the Germans could make work at this point. It is safe to say that in addition to advanced sound locating torpedoes, some German U-boats may have been fitted with rail guns, and some probably were fitted with "Motorstoppmittel" weaponry.

Colonel Howard A. Buechner and Kapitan Wilhem Bernhart describe this flotilla as the "Fuehrer Convoy" and state that up to 35 U-boats took part. They list their probable U-boat choices by number (20). These writers also state that the fleet made a stop at Kiel on their way to Kristiansand in which many addition crew members were added but that most torpedoes, ammunition and other armaments were stripped off the U-boats to make more room for the cargo and personnel (21). "Kapitan Wilhelm Bernhart" has a little more "street-cred" than most writers on this subject since, even though this is a pen-name, he claims to have actually been present in this flotilla as a junior officer aboard U-530.

Now we come to some variants of the basic story or perhaps some alternate explanations or perhaps some sea-tales occurring at about the same time that may or may not be related to Landig's basic work. The reader can sort this out for him or her self as well as anyone. These accounts really revolve around Gross-Admiral Karl Doenitz, after Hitler's death, as he ascends to the Fuehrership of Germany.

Hitler killed himself on April 30, 1945. The second Fuehrer of Germany, Gross-Admiral Karl Doenitz, surrendered the three divisions of the German military on May 8, 1945. So the question is what happened during those nine days and why? Why did it take nine days to surrender? It was obvious to all that Germany had lost the war. Numerous researchers have reported on Nazi higher ups and many of these apparently had made secret overtures to the Western Allies, seeking peace or trying to cut a personal deal for their safety or employment in the post-war world.

During this time Doenitz was physically on the border between Denmark and Germany in territory not yet overrun by the British and Americans. Was he using the time he had to do a deal? If so, why would the Western Allies give him the time of day—why would they listen? What sort of cards could Doenitz possibly hold? After all, he was boxed in with the Soviets charging hard from the East. Most of all the Nazis feared falling into Soviet hands as the war between the Soviets and the Nazis was particularly unforgiving.

William R. Lyne has an interesting answer to all this. He says a secret deal was done between Doenitz and the Americans.

"The Deutsche Antarktische Expedition (1938-39) laid out Germany's claim to part of Antarctica, which claim has been undisputed since the war. In the last coded message from Martin Bormann, references to "Terra del Fuego" (A.K.A., "Feurerland") were made, as the reins of power were transferred to Reichschancelor Admiral Doenitz, and his twenty-four German U-boats surrounded the United States, armed with I.C.B.M.s (A-9s), carrying neutron bomb warheads, and with celestial guidance systems. From this position of strength, Doentiz negotiated with the Allies, during a stalemate. The Russians were overrunning Germany, but Germany had its nuclear missiles trained on the heart of America. If Germany fired the missiles, the Russians would take all of Germany, and all would be lost for the Germans, who could have bombed America, yet would have had no home to return to. Under the circumstances, only America could save half of Germany, and so a deal was cut. Certain conditions were stipulated, and Doenitz was required to "scuttle all U-boats with all hands on board", as part of the amnesty agreement. Certain people were guaranteed amnesty, including Eva and Adolf Hitler, who were secretly provided with a cozy and secure home in Kassel Germany, for the rest of their lives, under the protection of the N.A.T.O. allies."(22)

These are extreme claims. The reader is probably asking himself/herself: What is the basis for these claims? Bill Lyne did spend time in the US Air Force, and, as he explains in his book, he had contact there with many people who claimed to know inside information. Since the first version of Bill's book first appeared in the late 1980s or early 1990s, he has had his share of "hits" regarding some of these claims. Therefore, I have learned to pay attention to Bill Lyne. But, returning to the question, what is the basis for this claim? Or, more properly stated, what is the evidence for this claim? Well folks, there is some.

Before going directly to the evidence, we ought to know what we are actually looking for in terms of military hardware. In other words, what sort of large missiles or rockets would have been launched by the Germans from their U-boats against the United States and how, exactly, would have this been done? Researcher/writer Friedrich Georg has done a great deal of work on this problem and compiled quite a bit of information, so it would behoove us to take a look at what he has found.

Friedrich Georg has uncovered three types of missiles that where meant for striking from surface to surface and could be launched from submarines. These missiles are all large enough to have contained non-conventional weaponry. By non-conventional weaponry it is meant miniaturized atomic warheads or, perhaps, red mercury warheads. There were three such missiles.

The first ought not to be a surprise at all; it was a sea-launched version of the V-1. We know that the V-1 was most frequently launched from ski-jump-like ramps but could be and were launched from bomber aircraft. The idea of launching a V-1 from a ramp mounted on the deck of a U-boat was first conceived in May of 1943. A supply-type U-boat was envisioned, a Type XIV. The project was de-prioritized, however, when as it was frowned upon by General Erhard Milch.

We pick up the thread a year and a half later, in November of 1944, at a meeting involving Himmler at Hohenlychen. There it was decided that Colonel Otto Skorzeny should proceed with all means to realize the concept of the sea-launched V-1. (23) At this point, there was only six months left in the war and so Germany's position was dire without the insertion of the wonder weapons. Himmler must have though that coming up with a new delivery system for wonder weapons would require almost a super-human effort to realize and so the appointment of Skorzeny, an engineer as well as a war hero, who had worked miracles for the Reich in the past.

The plan seems to have been to build a hanger on-board the deck of this large U-boat in which four V-1s would be housed. The U-boat would travel to within range (300 km or about 183 miles) of a large city on America's eastern seaboard, probably either New York City or Washington, D.C., at which time a ramp would be constructed on the deck of the surfaced U-boat and the missiles quickly launched. The U-boat would then quickly slip under the waves, thus avoiding detection.

The first big problem was that all the Type XIV U-boats had already been sunk. Of course, the new Type XXIs came into consideration but as far as I am aware, few of such craft existed, perhaps only three such craft were finished or nearing completion at this time. The idea that these Type XXIs would be stripped from the Kreigsmarine and put under the command of Skorzeny and the SS would certainly have displeased Admiral Doenitz to say the least.

But perhaps an even bigger problem involved the guidance system as it was currently constituted in the V-1 which was not all that accurate. It was fine if launched at a large city and from a fixed platform but on a tossing sea, the wave action at launch might greatly alter the pre-set flight path. A big wave at time of launch might send a V-1 miles off target.

It was pointed out in that meeting that new guidance systems were under development. One system involved radio guidance after launch via a second U-boat that had surfaced closer to the target for this purpose. Another suggestion was a homing device that could be placed at or near the target by agents put ashore for this purpose.

Another interesting suggestion was put forth, a homing device that we think of in terms of 1990s warfare. This was the "Radieschen" (radish) device (24). According to Georg, the device, developed for the Fritz-X missile and now housed in the nosecone, weighed only 15 kg. It used enemy radar as a homing signal and rode the radar waves to its target. It was to be used against the English Loran transmitters that provided the radar "cross-hairs" to Allied bomber squadrons over Germany (25).

The meeting broke up, resolving to a better guidance device for the sea-launched V-1. But Friedrich Georg suggests a couple of things. First, he wonders aloud what would have happened to Skorzeny's mandate to develop this sea-launched V-1 if General Milch had not frowned upon the original idea in May of 1943. Second, the use of agents to plant homing devices was already under serious consideration for other weapons designed to hit the American shore—why were these plans not coordinated with others also wanting to use this method? Third, he reveals that sufficient guidance devices already existed. He lists "Ewald II" and "Sauerkirsche II" as well as the impulse repeaters "Wespe", "Biene" and "Gluehwuermchen" (26).

Mr. Georg makes the point that using V-1s against New York City or Washington, D.C. would, by itself, with only conventional warheads, not be a war-changing event. If these missiles were equipped with atomic warheads, however, and the financial or governmental capitol were flattened, this might have given the Americans pause. With this in mind Mr. Georg goes on to prove that this capacity might have been at the fingertips of the Third Reich. To do this he highlights American weaponry of the late 1940s that was based on German prototypes.

After the war the Americans brought to the USA Dr. Wilhelm Fiedler, the man most responsible for the creation of the V-1. He was instrumental in building a virtual copy for the Americans that was called the "Loon". On March 7, 1948 a Loon was successfully launched from the American submarine USS Cusk.in just the manner already described except that it was guided remotely to its target. Three months later another submarine, the USS Carbonero repeated the exercise.

The Loon was a research rather than operational missile. It was the Regulus 1, a second-generation cruise missile, which first rose to operational status. But meanwhile, during the developmental lag between the Loon and the Regulus 1, a reserve of Loons were accumulated and stored. Strangely enough, an atomic warhead was developed for this missile while in "reserve", as of May 1948. It was designated the "TX-10" and described as a miniature Hiroshima-like bomb (26). Friedrich Georg compares it to the 28-cm atomic artillery shell, first conceived by the Germans and called the "Duesenkanone". This mobile cannon was actually under construction as the war ended, at Skoda under the auspices of the Kammler Group. The Duesenkanone or DKM44 was to launch a 28 cm projectile. Of course the Americans quickly reconstituted this cannon as the Atomic Cannon T-13 (28). This cannon was operational in the early 1950s and I am sure those old enough will recall newsreel footage of it being fired by the US Army, while shortly after a large explosion and mushroom cloud appeared in the distant desert. The point is that the Germans had expected a miniaturized atomic weapon for their cannon, it would also be available for the V-1, and as proof of this concept's validity, we have the Americans miniaturizing atomic weapons for both their cannon and their version of the V-1 in the late 1940s.

The second sea-launched rocket or missile that might have been aboard the U-boat fleet on its way to the American east coast was called the "Ursel". The reader might recall the discussion of a weapons system by a similar name, the "Urzel", by Dr. Milos Jesensky and Mr. Robert Lesniakiewicz. They described a combination V-1-V-2 in which the V-1 rode on top of the V-2 in a horse and rider configuration and which could be launched from a U-boat. We have also discussed the possibility of a more advanced version of the V-1 or possibly a new missile, the "V-3", as being employed in this way. What is being described in the reconstruction by Friedrich Georg of the Ursel is not this weapon but a completely different one.

But rather than fall into a name-trap, or trying to chose which description is correct or more correct, please consider that we are dealing with secret, undisclosed weapons dating back many decades, originating in a culture which is really extinct now, that of the Nazis. Nobody has ever been one hundred percent correct about their reconstructions such as this. Everyone changes or alters their view as new information surfaces. Since both resonstructions call for launch via U-boat, there are naturally going to be some similarities. There is undoubtedly truth in both reconstructions of the Urzel/Ursel. I would suggest that in spite of the similar names, both could be possibly considered as separate projects but more importantly as actual projects.

Again, we turn to Friedrich Georg for a description of the weapon in question. The essence of the Ursel is that of a rocket launched from under water by a U-boat. This stated on July 4, 1942 as a defense for U-boats. It took on two forms.

The first form was a Borsig solid fuel rocket of somewhere between 15 to 21 caliber. The word "Nebelwerferraketen" is mentioned in this context so a rocket which projects fog or smoke must be considered since this is what that word means. It was to be launched 10-15 meters below the water and in salvos. Actually, two projects of this type were undertaken, one by the Army and one by the Air Force (29). This may seem a bit strange until one learns that this was at Peenemuende, where facilities only existed for those two branches of the military.

In the second form, this project would be a larger Rheinmetall-Borsig 1.8-m, 89-kg rocket, but again with no guidance system. This project, like the first, went nowhere in terms of hardware, but something did stick. It was the idea of the underwater launch of a rocket. This idea seems to have transcended the original idea so that instead of merely a defensive weapon for a U-boat, the concept of an offensive weapon, possibly of "Vergeltung" status, was born.

At some point this concept made its way to several agencies. Among these were the CPVA, the Institut fuer Stroemungsforschung (something like the Institute for Fluidics) at Goettingen, the Forschungsanstalt (research installation) "Graf Zeppeline" in Stuttgart Ruit, and the Amtsgruppe FEP of the OKM. All of these facilities were assigned to develop this idea. It ended up under the direction of Dr. Lindberg at the CPVA that was the Chemische-Physikalische Versuchsanstalt (Chemical-Physical Research Facility) at the Austrian lake, the Toplitzsee.

The Toplitzsee is a deep-water lake, high in the Alps, surrounded by mountain peaks. The name "Toplitzsee" arises again and again not only as a test and research facility during the war but as a repository of secrets immediately after the war. For instance, as Mr. Georg explains, it was here that the sunken V-rockets were sighted by a driver, in this case a biologist named Dr. Fricke in 1987. This lake is suspected of being the final resting place for all sorts of exotic technology that the Nazis wanted hidden from the invading Allies. But also there are rumors of blueprints, gold and other treasure, and even printed British and American banknotes that were forged during the war by concentration camp inmates for the Nazis in Operation Bernhard. Through the 1960s divers would sometimes attempt to recover these valuable objects from the depths and almost as often turn up dead for their trouble. The Toplitzsee was and is an ongoing mystery.

At the Toplitzsee and still thinking defense of U-boats rather than long distance weapons, experiments were conducted in which rockets were launched as deep as 100 meters underwater. The problem with this idea as a method to defend U-boats then became apparent. The transition between operating in water and in the air was so drastic that the aim of those rockets was altered to the point beyond which the idea was practical.

About this time thinking apparently changed to the idea of an offensive weapon whereby a new firm, Wasag of Whttenberg was brought in. They arranged rockets with there own stands for launching on the U-boat. These rockets were greatly extended in range. To test these weapons they were first launched from small U-boats in the Toplitzsee and then guided to a target at the peak of one of the surrounding mountains. According to French agents, these rockets were V-2-like. At this point there is some confusion whether this was the Ursel rocket or the rocket associated with the Lafferenz Project which we will look at next and that also used V-2-like rockets only possibly smaller. This smaller rocket may have been the A-5 that was actually used as a model for the A-4 in spite of the numerical designation. I.V. Hogg describes the A-5:

> *"A-5. Test vehicle for the A-4 control systems. About 16 feet long and 2 ft. in diameter, it was powered by a Walter hydrogen peroxide rocket motor. Several were used in trials, both ground launched and launched from aircraft. A certain amount of confusion exists over this rocket since there were a number of experimental sub-models with changes in fin design which were given the appellation V-1, V-2, V-3 etc., to V-16. In this case the 'V' stands for 'versuchs' i.e. 'experimentation'. (30) The A-5 under consideration here was apparently given the appellation "V-7". It looked like a normal A-5 but was given a stronger engine of 1800 kp (one kp is the pressure of boiling water) as opposed to 1500 kp for normal A-5. (31)*

At the beginning of 1945 tests were conducted in the vicinity of Bornholm, in the Baltic in which two such rockets without warheads were launched from a Type VIIC U-boat underwater (32). It is very probable that this culminated the Ursel program and that these rockets were designed to be fired in salvo in a "Vergeltungs-attack", most probably at New York City.

Colonel Otto Skorzeny seemed confirm this in 1947 when commenting on the panic generated by the Orsen Wells radio program of 1939 concerning the fictional landing of Martians on the eastern seaboard. He is alleged to have commented:

> *"What would happen if only a pair of such rockets rained down in the middle of Manhattan?"*

But with a payload no larger than 15 kg per rocket, what would have caused the Germans to think such an attack would be a war-changing event? To do this the warhead must either be a radiological dirty bomb, an almost impossibly miniaturized atomic bomb or a red mercury bomb, emitting deadly neutrons as would a neutron bomb. As with many German weapons awaiting deployment, we are left with the lingering notion that they were expecting atomic weapons or other truly exotic and powerful warheads to materialize, momentarily.

If the Ursel was the rocket accompanying any German U-boat fleet on its way to attack the USA or not this concept certainly survived the war and was the basis for all the systems developed which fire long distance rockets from submarines, in both the East and the West.

The last possible method of attacking the USA using U-boat based missiles was the Lafferenz Project. The essence of the Lafferanz Project was a V-2 or V-2-like rocket which was encapsulated in a long tube, towed horizontally by a U-boat to within range of the US coast, righted to the vertical position, and fueled and fired by technicians in the U-boat.

Friedrich Georg tells us this idea first surfaced as the inspiration of Otto Lafferenz, then Director of the German Workers Front, in the fall of 1943. At this time he proposed the idea to Dr. Walter Dornberger, Director of the Army Research facility at Peenemuende. Evidently, he liked the idea because sometime in 1944 the concept was already being tested at the Topitzsee with a small U-boat and a V-2 or very similar rocket. I say "or a very similar rocket' because this project, like the Ursel, may have relied on a smaller version of the A-4, the V-2. Possible code names for this project were Testsland XII, Apparat F, and Projekt Schwimmweste.

The Lafferenz capsule is described as being round in section with four fins at its stern. A cap on the front end of the system popped off after the capsule was righted by flooding the ballasts. A gyro-stabilized platform steadied the missile for firing. There was a ring-shaped platform surrounding the A-4 or similar rocket, designed for servicing it. A ring-like exhaust tube re-directed the exhaust gasses up and out of the open cap at firing. Under this exhaust tube was the control room and tanks containing the propellant and oxidizer, probably alcohol and liquid oxygen. Below this was a second ballast tank in the stern.

It was calculated that a Type XXI U-boat could tow three such Lafferenz capsules at 12 knots per hour, underwater, on a 30-day trip to the US eastern seaboard. A smaller U-boat was only able to tow one capsule.

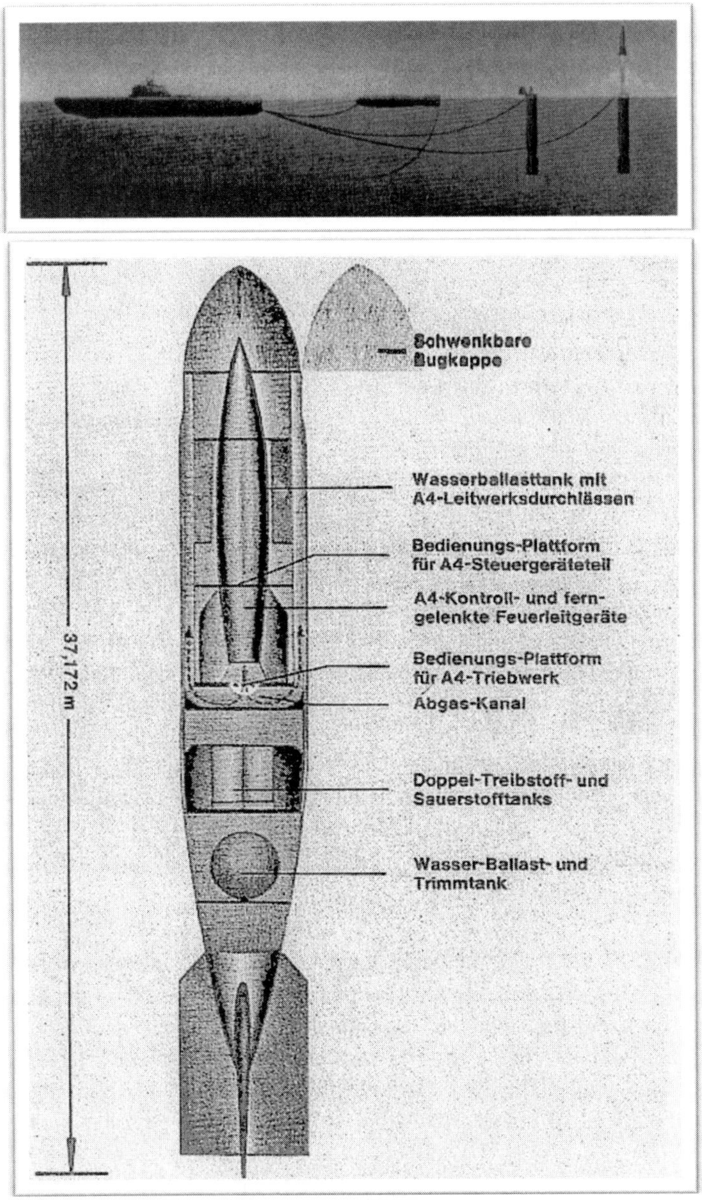

The Lafferanz Project

In this project German U-boats encapsulated V-2s to within range of the eastern seaboard of the U.S. Once in position, the rockets would have to be righted, fueled, and launched from control facilities in the U-boat.

Once the capsule had been positioned within range of its target, the proper ballast tanks would be emptied and flooded, the technicians would have entered the capsule from the U-boat, fueling and aiming the rocket. They would then return to the U-boat from which the actual ignition would have taken place (33).

The Lafferenz capsules themselves were made at the Vulkan Werft in Stettlin and the Schickau Werft in Elbing according to Mr. Georg. It is believed that 24 units were made in all. During the change of year between 1944 and 1945, U-1063 towed and evidently fired this rocket without any problems. Both Blohm & Voss in Hamburg as well as Weser AG in Bremen were involved in modifying U-boats; Type XXIs are mentioned, for the Lafferenz rockets (34). As with the previous projects, war-changing payloads come into question.

Mr. Georg tells us that In March 1945, a fleet of six Type VIIC U-boats refitted with snorkels departed under "Group Seawolf" (35).

At this point we will turn to the research of Mark Kneipp. Readers of my first book may recall that it was Mark who first identified some sensitive Paperclip reports. Even though Mr. Kneipp has not published, I considered the work of Mark Kneipp as being excellent to say the least. He wrote me many years ago with the saga that will follow. Incidentally, Mark's research regarding what will follow was originally prompted by a search for still unidentified Arctic German bases. In this search he was successful. Mark Kneipp found Arctic German bases in addition to those mentioned in this book. Perhaps the overall organization I presented encompassed them, but this is not a certainty. We all can only hope that Mr. Kneipp will someday publish the results of his research and the research he has done on other aspects of German technology, including German flying discs.

What follows is a summary of an article Mark Kneipp sent to me titled *Lafferenz and "Operation Teardrop"*. I am going to try to list points of contention or new points rather than go over material already mentioned. Mr. Kneipp used governmental sources, including those obtained under Freedom of Information Act, although he did not list references in his letter/article to me.

The idea of underwater rocket launch began in 1942 with a member of Peenemuende's engineering staff, Dr. Johannes Steinhoff, brother of Captain Freidrich Steinhoff of U-551. The idea was given approval and tests were begun on U-551, code named "Ursula". This method involved 21-cm solid fuel rockets mounted to the rear of the U-boat. Rockets were successfully launched with the objective of hitting an enemy ship. A test ship was hit and damaged 3 km away. Although successful, the project was dropped.

In 1944, with the course of the war in doubt, the project was resurrected. This time the goal was to discourage submarine hunters and another rocket was used, the Army's 30 cm "Wurfkoerper Spreng". Targeting was accomplished by sound location but the sounds made by the launching system itself would have alerted enemy ships to the presence and location of the U-boat. Again, the project was abandoned.

Meanwhile, Dr. Otto Laffrerenz suggested to Dr. Walter Dornberger the use of container tubes to tow V-2 rockets into range of American cities as explained earlier. According to Mr. Kneipp's research, the project was given to Volkswagen, AG at Wolfsburg for development. The finished Lafferenz tube was 30 meters long (98 ft.) and weighed 500 tons loaded with the rocket and fuel. The description of the Lafferenz device corresponds to that previously given, except that electricity for the launch was additionally provided by the U-boat.

A delay in the project resulted from a "hold" being placed upon it regarding the development of the V-2 to be launched. General Rossman and Dr. Walter Riedel directed a test model, a prototype, built at Peenemuende to be sent to the Toplizsee and launched by a Seehund, a two man submarine, there. The test launch, at least, involved the smaller A5 rocket. The tests were successful and picked up by French intelligence agents and passed along to the British.

Mr. Kneipp says that: "The contract was assigned to 5 separate dockyards near Peenemuende." These were:

- *The Stettiner Machinenbau AG, Vulkin Stettin (3 units built)*
- *The F. Schickau GmbH, Danzig (Elbing), (1 unit built)*
- *The Oderwerke, Stettin (12 units built)*
- *The Neptune Werft AG, Rostock (10 units built)*
- *The Flender Werke, Luebeck (4 units built)*

This totals 30 Lafferenz containers by my calculation. U-1063 carried out testing in the Baltic, one successful launch being conducted in late January 1945. By February, everything was fully tested an in place and a decision was made to put this weapons system into full operation.

The plan called for two waves of attacks. The first attack would use six Lafferenz containers while the second wave would follow up with a larger attack using twenty-four containers. On March 1, 1945 the 33rd U-flotilla was assigned the task. The six U-boats chosen were U-518, U-546, U-805, U-858, U-880 and U-1235 using the name Operation Seewolf. It was to begin on April 14, 1945.

The British informed US Intelligence of this operation, in part because of two German agents landed by U-1230 on November 29, 1944. An anti-submarine task force, code named "Teardrop" was assembled. It was composed of 4 aircraft escort carriers and 29 destroyer escorts.

From the outset the U-boats of Seewolf were on the defensive. On April 15-16, the USS Stanton and USS Frost sunk U-880. These same two American ships then confronted U-1235 on the surface. Wisely, the U-boat dived whereupon the destroyers fired hedgehog-exploding devices. After 90 minutes an explosion so massive occurred that it shook the USS Croatan that was twelve nautical miles away. Somehow, the USS Frost was damaged and withdrew to New York.

On April 21, the USS Mosley, the USS Lowe and the USS JRY Blakely made contact with a surfaced U-805. All three destroyers fired hedgehogs at the by this time submerged U-805. Underwater explosions were heard but thought to be evasive tactics of the U-boat.

On April 22, the USS Carter and USS Neal A. Scott located U-518 that exploded with all hands on board after the Americans attacked.

The next day U-546 was sighted on the surface south-southeast of Cape Farewell by aircraft from the escort carrier USS Bogue. An aircraft attack came up short. On April 24, the USS Frederick C. Davis made contact with U-546 and was joined by USS Hayter. U-546 counterattacked and sunk the USS Frederick C. Davis. Some of its crew survived and the battle was soon joined by the USS Otter and the USS Flaherty. U-546 was detected under the wreckage of the USS Frederick C. Davis by the USS Flaherty. U-546 responded by firing a Pillenwerfer. Confused, the USS Flaherty lost contact with U-546.

Meanwhile the USS Janssen, USS Hubbard, USS Neunzer and USS Varian joined the battle. Contact with U-546 was reestablished and several ships launched depth charges. Contact was again lost with U-546.

More US ships arrived—the USS Chatelain, USS Cockrill, USS Pope and USS Pilsbury. The USS Varian relocated U-546 and attacks were resumed. By now U-546 had been damaged and was using pumps. This noise hampered U-546 in sound location of enemy ships. Finally, a hedgehog blew a 15-inch hole in the pressure hull of U-546, releasing chlorine gas from its batteries. It surfaced and tried to torpedo the USS Flaherty, but missed. The USS Flaherty launched torpedoes in return, but also missed. Five of the destroyer escorts opened deck guns on U-546 and finally succeeded in sinking it, but the Captain and 32 crewmembers survived.

Mark Kneipp reports that the Captain, Kapitaenleutnant Paul Just, 2 officers and 5 specialists were placed in solitary confinement and were subjected to beatings each day. On April 30, 1945, the day Hitler died, Kapitaenleutnant Paul Just collapsed under such interrogation. He and seven others were sent to Washington with the other 25 crewmembers going to POW detention. In Washington, the same "interrogation tactics" were used on Just. On May 9, 1945, the day after Germany surrendered, Kapitaenleutnant Paul Just agreed to write a history of U-546, the objective of the interrogations. Evidently, the Americans were very interested in possible missiles aboard those submarines.

Returning to the sea battle, on April 27, USS Willis and USS Cockrill fired upon a probably U-boat. They were joined later that day by USS Swenning and USS Jannsen and on the next day by USS Hayter, USS Hubbard and USS Otter. On April 30, USS

Willis and USS Swenning investigated a possible contact by USS Core but no further U-boats where sunk.

After the war in Europe ended, U-805 and U-858 surrendered at sea. The Captain and crew of U-805 suffered the same level of "interrogation" that the men of U-546 had endured, and this was after the war had ended! Evidently, no Lafferenz containers were recovered by the US Navy but Mark Kneipp reports that U-805 had strange cables connected to the deck of the U-boat, cables that had been cut.

As an aside, U-873 under Kapitaenleutnant Friedrich Steinhoff also surrendered to the Americans at this time. He underwent the very same "interrogation techniques" described above. Kapitaenleutnant Friedrich Steinhoff committed suicide on May 19, 1945. This was the same Kapitaenleutnant Friedrich Steinhoff who had originally conducted tests for his brother, Dr. Johannes Steinhoff, originator of the "Ursula" concept.

Well, what do you think of Mark Kneipp's letter to me containing this information? I think it is explosive and I think it makes Bill Lyne and his report years before look very good in hindsight.

A few mysteries remain. During this time frame, the USS Mission Bay reported its aircraft had located a ship matching the description of the Tago off the coast of Greenland. This was a radar guidance ship that was designed by the Luftwaffe. Was it intended to guide the V-2s or A-5s or similar rockets to their target? Secondly, no Lafferenz containers were ever recovered by the Allies, at least officially anyway. Further, this whole affair, the Lafferenz Project, Seewolf, and Operation Teardrop were kept secret by the Americans for over fifty years.

Let us think about this last point for a minute. Conventional (establishment) historians will tell you in an instant that the Battle of the Bulge was the last German offensive in the West in December 1944. Was this a lie? Operation Seewolf was the last offensive in the West and it was in April 1945. Why would the US government mislead historians? Again, let me be charitable. The US government did not want to acknowledge the tremendous war-making capacity of the Lafferenz Project; they did not want to acknowledge the measures they took to block this attack from happening. But the underlying reason for both of these avenues of deception was the very high probability that those attacking missiles from 1945 contained a type of super-destructive warhead, and one that was miniaturized, which was unknown elsewhere for quite a long time to come, if ever.

At this point the reader may be asking why this seemingly documented Seewolf-Lafferenz-Teardrop saga is in the same chapter with the Last Battalion, Landig's undisclosed sea battle that was turned into a legend by others? Well, a few years ago Bill Lyne's tale about a US-Nazi stalemate and Doenitz's red mercury U-boats sounded even more fantastic than anything Landig ever claimed. Now, with some deep digging by the researchers named, that "legend" turned out to be mostly factual. My point is obvious: never count Landig out (or Bill Lyne for that matter).

Literature Cited

1. **Mattern, W., date unknown**, *UFO's Unbekanntes Flugobjekt? Letzte Geheim- waffe Des Dritten Reiches?*, page 23, Samisdat Publishing, Ontario, Canada
2. **Landig, Wilhelm, 1980**, *Wolfzeit um Thule*, pages 13-42, Volkstum-Verlag Wilhelm Landig, Vienna, Austria
3. **Hogg, I.V., 1970**, *German Secret Weapons of World War II*, pages 60, 61, Arco Publishing Company, Inc., New York, USA
4. **Lusar, Rudolf, 1960**, *German Secret Weapons of the Second World War*, page 211, Neville Spearman Limited, London, United Kingdom
5. **Brooks, Geoffrey, 1992**, *Hitler's Nuclear Weapons*, page 161, Leo Cooper (Publishing), London, United Kingdom
6. **Hogg, I.V., 1970**, page 78
7. **Lusar, Rudolf, 1960**, page 210
8. **Lusar, Rudolf, 1960**, page 213-214
9. **Mattern, W., date unknown**, pages 23, 24, 82
10. **Mattern, W. date unknown**, page 23
11. **Mattern, W. date unknown**, page 86
12. **Mattern, W. date unknown**, page 132
13. **Haarmann, D.H., 1983**, *GeheimWunderwaffen Zerrbild zwischen Taeushung and Tatsachen*, page 53, Hugin, Wetter, Germany Contained within this citation is Norbert Juergen-Ratthofer's article in the magazine Das neue Zeitalter titled Geheimwaffe UFO, May 9, 1980, Number 20, page 15
14. **Lusar, Rudolf, 1960**, page 160
15. **Stevens, Henry, 2007**, *Hitler's Suppressed and Still-Secret Weapons, Science and Technology*, pages 152 to 162, Adventures Unlimited Publishing, Kempton, Illinios, USA
16. **Farrell, Joseph P., 2008**, *Nazi International The Nazis' Postwar Plan to Control Finance, Conflict, Physics and Space*, pages 65; 96; 131, Adventures Unlimited Publishing, Kempton, Illinois, USA
17. **Farrell, Joseph P., 2008**, page 99, in which he cites Geoffrey Brooks, "Reports on Three Incidents Suggestive of Invisibility of German Submarines to Visual and Electronic Detection between 27 March and 4 July 1945", in which Brooks cites Wolfgang Hirschfeld, in personal communication, pages 192-202, Feindfahrten, 1983, Neff Verlag, (Pen and Sword Books for English version, 1997)
18. **Stevens, Henry, 2007**, pages 170-189
19. **Stevens, Henry, 2007**, page 174
20. **Buechner, Howard A., Col. and Kapitan Wilhelm Bernhart, 1989**, *Hitler's Ashes*, page 173, Thunderbird Press, Inc., Metairie, Louisiana, USA
21. ***ibid.***

22. **Lyne, William R., 1999**, *Pentagon Aliens* (third edition), page 97, Creatopia Productions, Lamy, New Mexico, USA

23. **Georg, Friedrich, 2000**, *Hitlers Siegeswaffen Band 1: Luftwaffe und Marine Gehime Nuklearwaffen des Dritten Reiches und ihre Traegersysteme*, page 177, Amun-Verlag, Schleusingen, Germany

24. **Georg, Friedrich, 2000**, page 178

25. **Hogg, I.V., 1970**, page 44

26. **Georg, Friedrich, 2000**, page 179

27. **Georg, Friedrich, 2000**, page 180

28. **Georg, Friedrich, 2000**, pages 144; 172

29. **Georg, Friedrich, 2000**, page 173

30. **Hogg, I.V., 1970**, page 13

31. **Georg, Friedrich**, 2000, page 175

32. ***ibid.***

33. **Georg, Friedrich, 2000**, pages 181-182

34. **Georg, Friedrich, 2000**, page 183

35. **Georg, Friedrich, 2000**, page 184

REPOSITORIES

We are going to take another little break here and discuss repositories. By this term I mean places where the Germans stashed high-value things for safe keeping after the war. This may mean aircraft or flying discs or blueprints, artifacts of value in Nazi ideology, money, or printing presses for making money. Some see the Antarctic as a repository and see the German base there only as an ice cave, a warehouse for storage. The same is true for the Andes region. We will deal with Antarctica and the Andes separately in appropriate chapters. Here I would like to concentrate on two possible repositories for the Nazis, Tibet and Switzerland, as strange as either might seem at first glance.

There is really no denying something going on between the Tibetans and the Nazis during the war. Expeditions were made by the Germans to Tibet. In truth, I really don't know how many were made. These expeditions were explained by the Nazis and explained by Nazi detractors, for all sorts of silly reasons. If we could identify the real reasons for making this difficult journey, we might get some clue as to the purpose for such expeditions.

The standard explanation given by, say, The History Channel, is that these Nazi expeditions were made first and foremost to find the origins of the Aryan people. Now, the term "Aryan" has fallen into disfavor since World War Two but it represents a legitimate concept. The politically correct term now is "Indo-European". The Nazis added additional meanings to the term "Aryan", those of racial purity and unique origin. Nevertheless, it was the Indo-Europeans of prehistory who are the common cultural antecedents of all Europeans except the Basque, Saami, Finns, and Hungarians. This means that the Slavs, Germanics, Romans, Greeks, Celts and all the other now extinct cultures of Europe owe a debt of origin to the Indo-Europeans. In fact today the languages spoken by the above-named peoples, plus those of the Iranians and Northern Indians are grouped into a classification bearing this name.

The problem was that European pre-history during the 1930s and before was centered about the Near East, so, allegedly, it was those people who were solely responsible for bringing "culture" to Europe. I say "Near East" but it took on tones of being bible-centric. The Nazis rejected this foreign origin of their culture and wanted to explore their own origins, both Indo-European and later Germanic.

The problem was that there were two "schools" to choose from in exploring native European origins. First there was the standard academic version, which, as I say, was certainly de-emphasized by mainstream archaeology and things would remain this way until the late 1960s. The other alternatives were the occult ideas of Madame H. P. Blavatsky, as reinterpreted by Guido von List and Lanz von Lebenfels, whose ideas found a home not in German science but in the Ahnenerbe, a Nazi organization which specifically sought Germanic-Aryan origins.

The Ahnenerbe became part of the SS in about 1940 and sent out expeditions of archaeologists and explorers in an attempt to establish a cultural and racial origin. Among these were the expeditions made to Tibet. Perhaps the Ahnenerbe thought the origins of the Germanics or the Aryans might be in Tibet, and so the grounds for measuring the populace in terms of typological anthropology, but this was not the view of the top scientists in German anthropology at the time, like Hans F.K. Guenther or Egon Freiherr von Eickstedt. So please, let us not ever confuse the Ahnenerbe with German science other than the fact that the scientists employed by the Ahnenerbe were willing to be used for this purpose. This is certainly not unique to the Ahnenerbe—American anthropology and indeed all social science was and still is chock-full of such prostitutes who are directly or indirectly funded by the government through academia and dare not deviate from current political correctness or lose their jobs.

But even if the Ahnenerbe entertained this racial-origin hypothesis on their first trip to Tibet, after that trip the reasons for continued expeditions must have been quite different. For instance, we know that biologist Dr. Ernst Schaefer's two expeditions sought the collection of rare animals, a hunt for the Yeti, and the collection of a rare Tibetan text, the Kangschur. True, an anthropologist or ethnologist Dr. Bruno Berger did collect human measurements and made facial casts but this line of reasoning, the Tibetans as Aryan ancestors, went nowhere, even within the most occult-oriented of the Ahnenerbe.

Tibetan monks did make their way back to Germany. A letter was brought back to Germany from the Dalai Lama, and it seemed that Tibet had a pro-German stance at the outbreak of World War Two. Nevertheless, the collection of Tibetan monks from a religion obscure to all but the professional German orientalists and a letter of support from a non-technological, essentially pacifist country could hardly be considered the makings of a successful expedition or have warranted further expeditions.

So the question remains: what did the Nazis want in Tibet?

"Claude Schweikert" aka Erich Halik (and perhaps other names) mentions Tibet in an occult-oriented, post-war article entitled *Um Krone un Gipfel der Welt ("Concerning the Crown and Pinnacle of the World").* Schweikert discusses Tibet under the occult terminology of "Agharta" and says of the occultist Ferdinand Ossendwoski that he was told a story concerning the retrieval of hidden science to the surface by an invading Khan (1). Agharta as well as Shamballah were underground kingdoms of hidden occult power usually centered in and associated with Tibet.

Next we will jump to Dr. Joseph P. Farrell and a rather rational description of what we might consider to be a German base in Tibet (2). He tells us of several Tibetan monks found dead by Russian soldiers entering Berlin:

likely possibility was sometime around the period of the massive German offensive on the southern Russian Front in the summer of 1942. It is a little known fact that the Wehrmacht sent armed long-range reconnaissance units as far east as Astrakhan on the northern Caspian Sea, but beyond sewing confusion behind Russian lines, there was little military value in such an operation. (here Farrell cites the German military historian Paul Carrell in the book "Hitler Moves East: 1941-1943") *However, it is possible that commando-engineered units of the Waffen SS might have been included in these units, and, once the units had penetrated as far east as was operationally save, the commando units would have been released to continue onward through Kazakstan and on into Tibet, utilizing Nazi intelligence contacts in these Muslim areas to smooth their passage through hostile territory. Once in Tibet, a makeshift airfield could have been constructed able to handle long-range aircraft. The Tibetans would have then been flown back to Germany. While a hazardous enterprise to be sure, it would have been far safer than attempting to smuggle monks out through British India and back to Germany via U-boat, which, in any case, would have required more trips than would have been required by even one of the large Junkers 290s or the enormous Junkers 390s. As for the purpose of such an operation, this is relatively transparent, for such expertise would have been required if Himmler's SS was to translate its copy of the Kang Shuur completely and accurately."*

"This requires some commentary. Since the 1938-1939 Schaefer Expedition is known not to have brought out large numbers of Tibetan monks, but only a copy of the Kang Shuur, the question becomes, when were these monks smuggled out of Tibet into Nazi Germany, by what route, and for what purpose?

This is a great point concerning the translation of the Kang Shuur. But there is really no evidence for even makeshift airfields. If there were, they would have been used on the yeti expeditions of the 1950s, and certainly on the attempts to climb Mt. Everest. Perhaps some helicopters were used in the 1950s, but nothing approaching the Junkers Ju 290 or Ju 390. And if you recall, the Dalai Lama had to flee Tibet on foot to India in the early 1950s after the Chinese invasion. Nevertheless, as Dr. Farrell points out, something is going on here because those monks certainly did not exit Tibet through India, which was in British hands during the war. All entrances and egresses to Tibet would have been very well guarded, and yet, somehow, they got into Germany.

Dr. Axel Stoll makes the point that the origins of some of the German flying disc technology may have been ancient India (3). Nobody really denies this is a possibility. Dr. Stoll, it seems, has really taken an interest in this possibility, translating the Vymaanika Shastra (evidently from an American/English version) into a scientific understanding in German language (4). The point for us is that Dr. Stoll believes that it may be true that this knowledge survives and is guarded somewhere to this day, and suggests this place may be Tibet (5).

Fortführung einer prägnant anti-vatikanischen Katharertradition zur Aufgabe stellte. Die Nachforschungen dieser deutschen „Ketzer" wurden in zwei Blickrichtungen vorangetrieben: Innerarktis und Tibet. Noch vor dem Jahre 1933 versuchte der junge deutsche Schriftsteller Otto Rahn im Auftrage dieser Leute, die polare Überlieferung der Cathari in Südfrankreich an Ort und Stelle zu rekonstruieren, worüber er ausführlich in seinen beiden hochinteressanten Werken „Der Kreuzzug gegen den Gral" und „Luzifers Hofgesind" berichtete. Er muß dabei mit den Beauftragten der um die gleiche Zeit entstehenden Pariser „Bruderschaft der Polarier" zusammengetroffen sein, die exoterisch in den Ruinen der Gralsburg Montsegur nach dem „Ketzerschatz", esoterisch aber wohl nach der Mani fahndeten. Ob diese „Polarier" später über Rahn mit den deutschen „Ketzern" zusammenarbeiteten oder fernerhin eigene Wege gingen, entzieht sich noch unserer Kenntnis.

Otto Rahn sagt uns nun sehr genau, was er unter dem Hofgesinde Luzifers versteht: „Darunter möchte ich jetzt schon diejenigen verstanden wissen, welche, das Recht und das Rechte suchend, ungeachtet der mosaischen Zwölf Gebote aus eigener Kraft Recht und Pflicht und Sinn gefunden haben; diejenigen, welche eigenmächtig und stolz nicht vom Berg Sinai Hilfe erwarten, sondern zu einem „Berg der Versammlung in der fernsten Mitternacht", wenn auch unbewußt gegangen sind, um Hilfe zu holen und den Menschen ihres Blutes zu bringen ..."

Was besagt der Ausdruck „Berg der Versammlung" und welcher Art kann die Hilfe sein, welche die in den Schutzstaffeln verborgenen deutschen Katharer für ihr Volk von dort erhofften?

Wir halten es für möglich, daß heroische Menschen, Gewaltige des Geistes, nach ihrem physischen Tode, gleichsam als Matrizen auf der anderen Seite der Welt, einen archetypischen Weg nach jener arktischen Insel nehmen, einer Urvorstellung der geistbetonten Menschheit folgend, welche am Pol des Nordens ihren Ursprung weiß. Verhält es sich aber so, dann besteht die Bezeichnung „Berg der Versammlung" zu Recht, dann kann dort oben mittels geeigneter Medien vielleicht alles erfahren werden, was positiver, schöpferischer Menschengeist je erdachte und ersann. Dann könnte es am Pol oder vielleicht schon in dessen Nähe möglich sein, nicht allzulang tote Wissenschaftler, Erfinder und Strategen um Kenntnisse und Erfahrungen zu befragen, die sie über die Schwelle mitnahmen und drüben noch ergänzten. Denn es ist auch eine alte Meinung der Esoteriker, daß die Todesschwelle von dem davon Betroffenen nahezu unmerklich überschritten zu werden pflegt, wenn er sich den Aufgaben dieser Welt intensiv widmete und ihnen etwa durch einen allzu plötzlichen Tod entrissen wird. Er geht dann einfach „durch den Spiegel"!

Interessanterweise registrierte das Emrich-Team, in solchen Belangen offenbar mit dem die „Dritte Kraft" jagenden jugoslawischen wissenschaftlichen Nachrichtendienst zusammenarbeitend, die Existenz eines „Laboratoriums des Todes" irgendwo auf Grönland, das als eine Burg des technischen Satanismus bezeichnet wurde und 1951 fliegende Unterseeboote erprobt haben soll. Hier dürfte nun allerdings der alte, verwirrende Fehler begangen worden sein, der Luziferianer und Satanisten in einen Topf zu werfen sich beeilt. Luzifer wurde von den deutschen Ketzern etwa als der erstgeborene Sohn Gottes definiert, der durch den zweitgeborenen Sohn Christus „unrechtmäßig" verdrängt worden war. Deswegen lautete auch seit jeher der Ketzergruß: „Luzifer, dem Unrecht geschah, grüßt dich!" Diese Verdrängung Luzifers, der als Luciphor — Phor — Pol — Ap o llyon — Bel — Baal — Ab e llio — Lucibel zu erkennen ist, war aber natürlich keineswegs ein theonisches Unrecht, sondern ein gesetzmäßiges Geschehen an der Schwelle eines Weltzeitalters mit seinen Werteumkehrungen. Luzifer mußte zum Dämon werden, damit der „Fischerkönig" erhoben werden konnte. Nun, da wir wieder an einer solchen Schwelle stehen, muß sich neuerlich die Umkehrungstendenz erweisen und der gestürzte Luzifer soll nach der Hoffnung seines Hofgesindes durch die Gewalt seiner Heerscharen als „Wassermann" auf dem Gipfel der Welt die Krone der Welt empfangen.

Luzifer wäre also nicht der unbedingte Widerpart Christi, sondern nur dessen (zeitweilig) verstoßener Bruder in der Hierarchie des Lichtes. Das Zentrum des Antichrist ist nicht am Nordpol, sondern in der Antarktis zu suchen. Die Spur des dort wirkenden Sonnen-Dämonismus soll aber in einem folgenden Aufsatz verfolgt werden. Hier sei nur angeführt, daß im esoterischen Inneren der deutschen Schutzstaffeln offenkundig die dort gleichfalls aktiven Satanisten über Luzifers Hofgesind nach außen triumphierten und das mystische Konzept eines zirkumpolaren Imperiums der Katharer durch die später auf so verwerfliche Art versuchte „Aufnordung" durch Rassenhaß und Rassenkult verballhornt wurde.

Ketzer und Satanisten haben höchstwahrscheinlich den Untergang der Schutzstaffeln überdauert. Im hohen Norden wie im tiefen Süden stehen sie sich heute geographisch wie ethisch als „vertikale" Weltmacht gegenüber: oben in der nächsten Nähe der Hochburg des Geistes, unten, tief unten, in den Labyrinthen der höchsten materiellen Zivilisation und Schwarzen Magie. Wir wollen aber hier nur den „Weg des Bräutigams" verfolgen und geraten auf ihm in den merkwürdigen und so gut wie unbekannten Bereich der militanten Esoterik, wie sie aus dem Verlauf des zweiten Weltkrieges resultierte.

Es ist wahrscheinlich bekannt, wenn auch nicht geläufig, daß von der deutschen militärischen Führung in der letzten Phase des Krieges neben der Einrichtung der berüchtigted „Alpenfestung" auch der Ausbau Grönlands als Basis zur Rückeroberung der verlorenen Mitte ins Auge gefaßt und eingeleitet worden ist. Vorkommandos waren bereits in Grönland gelandet und haben sich sporadisch bis 1950 (!) gehalten. Nach und nach sollten starke Streitkräfte folgen. Hinter dieser Strategie verbarg sich aber ohne Zweifel auch der Operationsplan der deutschen Katharer gegen den „Mitternachtsberg". Just in diese Zeit fiel nun die Konstituierung der Organisation der „Vereinten Nationen", die nach den Plänen Roosevelts, welcher nach den Ermittlungen des Emrich-Teams die Existenz des esoterischen Weltzentrums kannte, eigentlich zu einer Weltregierung erweitert werden sollten. Schon zu diesem Zeitpunkt mußten die deutschen „Ketzer" erkannt haben, daß die Idee der „Vereinten Nationen", hinter der möglicherweise die gleichfalls um das Polkonzept wissenden Rosenkreuzer-Verbindungen Kaliforniens standen, alle Chancen hatte, die Protektion des Großen Pol zu erlangen. Dies drückt sich, vielleicht nur als Verheißung, irgendwie schon im blauen zirkumpolaren Emblem der UNO aus. Es war also für die Deutschen sehr naheliegend, den Einbruch in die Bezirke der arktischen Hochburg mit allen technischen und militärischen Mitteln zu beschleunigen und es ist sehr wahrscheinlich und an verschiedenen Anzeichen zu erkennen, daß ihnen dabei wenigstens ein äußerer Erfolg beschieden war.

Zunächst verfügten die Schutzstaffeln über sehr gut ausgebaute Beziehungen zum Orden der Schwarzmützen in Tibet. Ferner waren sie eifrig bemüht, eine völlige Rekonstruktion der Alchemie durchzuführen, wohl ermutigt durch die apokryphen Verheißungen des Paracelsus vom alchemischen Schatz zwischen Bayern und Schwaben, und schließlich hatten sie offenen Zugang zu beträchtlichen Teilen des deutschen Kriegspotentials. Dies, und der Umstand, daß man bei der Suche nach möglichst tiefgelegenen Höhlen

Mensch und Schicksal Magazine, *Um Krone und Gipfel der Welt*. This page again names the Emrich team, claiming German bases in Greenland and a repository in Switzerland.

At a later point Dr. Stoll returns to Tibet in the book referenced above and describes it as a possible place for a secret German base (6). Here, he says outright that the Tibetans fought for Germany during the Second World War, so a good connection and rationale for such a base, at least in his mind, is evident. He says this would be an underground base and it would have been secured using electromagnetic means. This is what I have called the "electromagnetic vampire" in my book, *Hitler's Suppressed and Still-Secret Weapons, Science and Technology*. In chapter five of that book is a description of Dr. Stoll's electromagnetic security system (7). Suffice it to say that Dr. Stoll has his own unified field theory and in his interpretation, life force can simply be sucked out of an intruder using a sort of reverse-Faraday cage and the right electronics. In this underground secured base, among all the other things sequestered there, Dr. Stoll envisions flying discs (8).

So, the Nazis were interested in Tibet, possibly as a storehouse of ancient knowledge awaiting re-discovery through the efforts of the Ahnenerbe. We have evidence in the monks that people in some numbers were brought out of Tibet. It would have been almost impossible to smuggle them through India as Dr. Farrell points out. Dr. Stoll believes German underground base(s) would have been built, and that they would have contained, among other things, flying discs.

German flying discs, even the conventional ones, are credited by all German sources as being able to handle the Himalayas. Engineer Rudolf Lusar, who worked at the German Patent Office, gives a German flying disc the ability to climb, in three minutes, to an altitude of 12,400 meters or over 40,000 feet (9). It could hop over Mt. Everest. Traversing India after that would be no problem, since in the immediate post-war years the British had no real air defenses set up in India. So, if there were evidence for relatively large, man-made flying discs in operation at that time in this part of the world, would that not be compelling evidence for a German base in Tibet, one of the most out of the way places on planet earth to hide things? Is there such evidence? There is.

The evidence for a very large, obviously man-made flying disc comes from the British UFO Magazine (10). The article is entitled *Incident at Karachi.* This incident took place on March 23, 1955, almost ten years after World War Two had ended. Pakistan had separated from India in August 1947 when the two countries gained self-rule from Great Britain. Karachi is located on the plains of Pakistan, just south of the mountainous region leading up ultimately to Tibet. During and even after the war, this whole region south of Tibet remained within the British sphere of military influence. The Japanese had been defeated, the Americans had no presence here, nor did the Soviets, and the Chinese, the Indians and/or the Pakistanis had no capacity to build original high-tech flying craft at this time.

The disc was observed by thousands of people, mostly Pakistanis but also some British in the area, including one crew of military personnel coming back from their station in Singapore via flights and stopovers in Bangkok to Calcutta. The disc was first observed by these men at 3,000 ft, while aboard a DC-9 attempting to land at Karachi airport.

The teller of this tale is Mr. Frank J. Parker, who in the late 1990s was living in Hyde, Chesire, England. Mr. Parker, twenty years old at the time, was on-board the DC-9 in question and so first observed the flying saucer after some excited talk in the passenger cabin. Because the passengers from one side of the aircraft were standing up and moving to the other side of the aircraft, the captain ordered all the passengers back to their seats to avoid imbalance of the aircraft. Well, I have flown on a DC-6. It was a large, four-engine passenger aircraft. If it was in danger of becoming imbalanced, there were certainly many individuals moving from one side to the other observing this flying craft, and so it must have caused great excitement.

Upon landing, the militarymen boarded a bus for the 16 or 17-mile drive to Karachi. They could still see the flying saucer, stationary and suspended over the city. At first, according to Parker, from the air it looked like an orange ball, but took on a disc shape as they drew nearer to it. As they continued on toward it, Parker estimated that it was 300-400 feet in the air. The bus turned a corner on to "the parade grounds" where Parker describes the sight that met his eyes as "incredible". Thousands of people, mostly Pakistanis, were amassed on the parade grounds, and above them, as if suspended, was the flying disc. Many of the Pakistanis knelt on the ground, hands clasped as though they were praying. Parker and some companions exited the bus and began moving through the crowd towards the spot over which the flying disc hung. Nobody was afraid or upset, according to Parker, and so the British party was able to move through the kneeling crowd without taking their eyes off the flying disc. They came to a halt directly below the still-suspended disc, now only about 60 yards above them.

Parker describes the scene:

> *"This had to have been at least 150 ft across and two-to-three stories high—by that I mean about 75 ft, it was incredible."*

He goes on:

> *"Because it was hovering about 125 ft off the ground, we could see every detail. This was a 'nuts and bolts' spacecraft that looked man-made, because we could see what I could only describe as rivets, only perfectly aligned."*

In this assessment, we can certainly rely on Parker's judgment, since his job in the military was working on aircraft. He worked in the equipment section, and in Singapore had supplied aircraft parts to squadrons of British high-tech aircraft of the day, including the Vampire Jet. Mr. Parker continues his appraisal of this man-made flying saucer:

> *"I suppose because of its shape you could say it was a traditional 'flying saucer', like two bronze cymbals, one on top of the other. It was magnificent, made up entirely of this metallic bronze-colored metal that applied to the catwalks, ladders, portholes and aerials. These were all fixed to the exterior of the craft. At the underside, we saw a big black hole, which interested me because whatever was holding this thing up had to come from there. Well, we saw what looked like fans and I counted eight rotors, but every few seconds there would be a 'whooshing' sound and that created sparks and an array of laser-like effects."*

With catwalks, ladders, portholes, aerials, and rotors generating a downdraft, this craft was definitely not interstellar. Please keep the "rotors" in mind and the following details when we return to discuss this craft's exact engine. Parker continues discussing the 'whooshing" sound:

> *"Whenever this occurred, the entire craft would swing to the left and right and then come back again. This happened so many times that I believed whoever was behind the controls was experiencing engine problems... Every now and again,*

the craft ejected smoke towards the ground, and this gave off a strong smell of oil, but here's another curious thing - this stuff actually never reached the ground - rather it just seemed to evaporate... The craft made a constant noise not dissimilar to jet-engine propulsion, but nothing like as loud. This and the noise of the rotors would sometimes sound rough, as though they were faltering occasionally. Anyway, every now and again, it would force hot air downwards and this had the effect of blowing dust and pieces of paper all over the place."

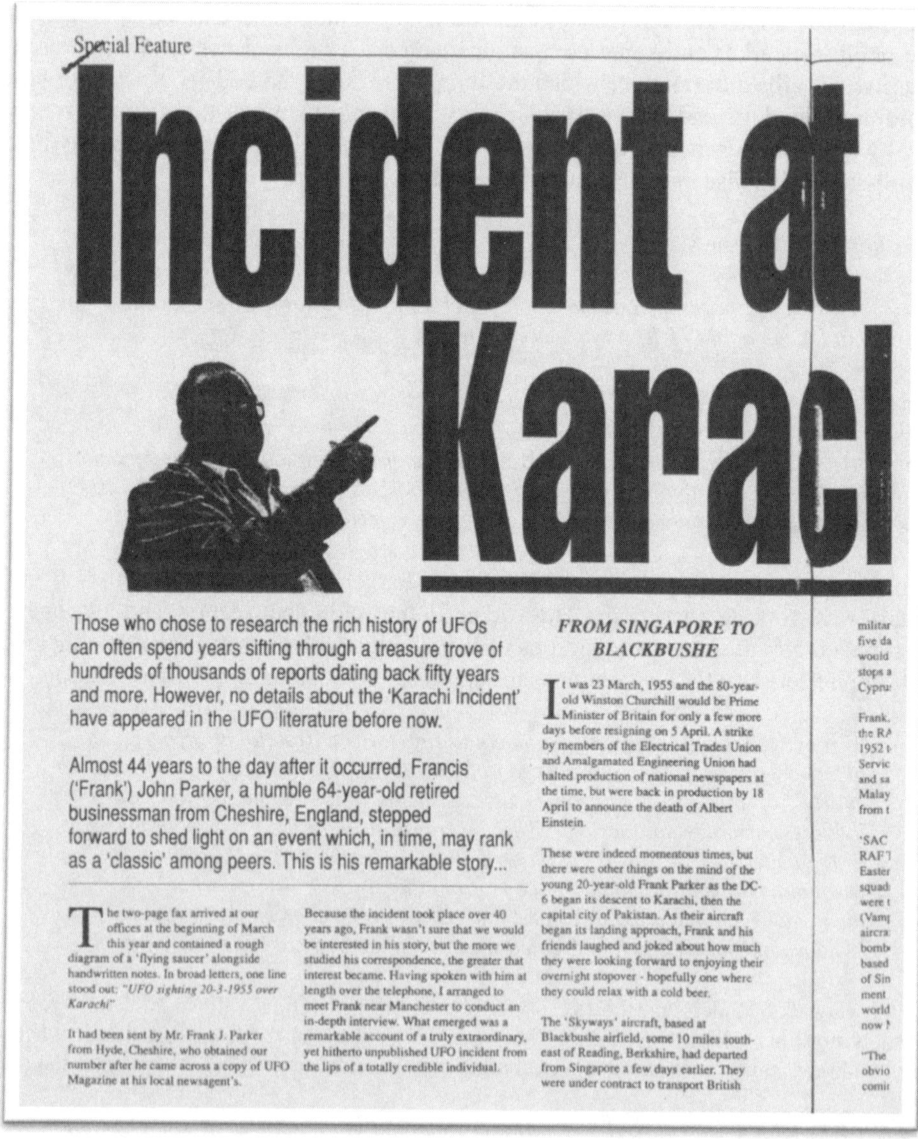

Special Feature

Incident at Karac

Those who chose to research the rich history of UFOs can often spend years sifting through a treasure trove of hundreds of thousands of reports dating back fifty years and more. However, no details about the 'Karachi Incident' have appeared in the UFO literature before now.

Almost 44 years to the day after it occurred, Francis ('Frank') John Parker, a humble 64-year-old retired businessman from Cheshire, England, stepped forward to shed light on an event which, in time, may rank as a 'classic' among peers. This is his remarkable story...

The two-page fax arrived at our offices at the beginning of March this year and contained a rough diagram of a 'flying saucer' alongside handwritten notes. In broad letters, one line stood out: *"UFO sighting 20-3-1955 over Karachi"*

It had been sent by Mr. Frank J. Parker from Hyde, Cheshire, who obtained our number after he came across a copy of UFO Magazine at his local newsagent's.

Because the incident took place over 40 years ago, Frank wasn't sure that we would be interested in his story, but the more we studied his correspondence, the greater that interest became. Having spoken with him at length over the telephone, I arranged to meet Frank near Manchester to conduct an in-depth interview. What emerged was a remarkable account of a truly extraordinary, yet hitherto unpublished UFO incident from the lips of a totally credible individual.

FROM SINGAPORE TO BLACKBUSHE

It was 23 March, 1955 and the 80-year-old Winston Churchill would be Prime Minister of Britain for only a few more days before resigning on 5 April. A strike by members of the Electrical Trades Union and Amalgamated Engineering Union had halted production of national newspapers at the time, but were back in production by 18 April to announce the death of Albert Einstein.

These were indeed momentous times, but there were other things on the mind of the young 20-year-old Frank Parker as the DC-6 began its descent to Karachi, then the capital city of Pakistan. As their aircraft began its landing approach, Frank and his friends laughed and joked about how much they were looking forward to enjoying their overnight stopover - hopefully one where they could relax with a cold beer.

The 'Skyways' aircraft, based at Blackbushe airfield, some 10 miles south-east of Reading, Berkshire, had departed from Singapore a few days earlier. They were under contract to transport British

Incident at Karachi A first-hand account published in *Flying Saucer* Magazine

No cameras were carried by the British servicemen, and they were not allowed to be in uniform due to this politics of these emerging states.

Let's review. The flying saucer had portholes, ladders, catwalks and aerials. The witness could see rotors and could feel a downdraft. An open hole or space on the underside was observed. He could smell oil and hear engine sounds that he really could not identify other than to say they brought to his mind jet engines but they were not as loud and so were not those of a jet engine.

Overall, this description is that of a German flying disc. Dr. Richard Miethe's legend includes multiple-rotor craft and Joseph Andreas Epp featured this design. The presence of portholes, catwalks, aerials, and a thrust exhaust opening on the underside with oily smelling air being forced downward argues *against* this craft being anything designed to fly in outer space and *for* a rather unsophisticated man-made saucer. It was obviously not British—otherwise Mr. Parker would have either known about it or been told not to report it. Other powers capable of building such craft were absent in the Indo-Pakistani area at this time. The only reasonable explanation is that it was a German flying disc, whose purpose had been to fly over the Himalayas or the other surrounding mountain ranges and land in Tibet, a country without facilities for landing conventional aircraft. Mr. Parker and his cohorts had seen this saucer either going or coming at a particular moment of engine trouble.

This brings us to the engine. What kind of engine would this be? It is not a jet engine. It is apparently a diesel engine or uses diesel oil for fuel, hence the smell. But diesel engines are not normally thought of as aircraft engines because of their increased weight. If an engine could be found which meets the description above *and* is capable of powering a flying disc, it would go a long way toward showing not only that this event could have occurred exactly as described, but also, by extension, that the saucer itself originated or was destined to service a base which is yet undisclosed.

There was such an engine. I did not set out to find it in order to fit the saucer sighting above; rather, it was discovered through an independent line of inquiry. Eventually, the pieces of this puzzle assemble themselves. The engine is called the Lutz free piston engine. It surfaced in a rather odd British communication on microfilm. What sometimes happens when something is requested using the Freedom of Information Act, especially with the US Air Force, is that you, as the requesting party, are directed to a particular microfilm roll that contains that information. Then you have to go through the roll of microfilm, document by document, until you locate the information for which you are searching. Of course, many times you stumble upon other interesting items, too. The Lutz free piston engine was one of these.

The British document was a June 23, 1945 memo from Air Ministry, A.I.2(g), Whitehall to the Director of Intelligence, Headquarters, U.S.S.T.A.F. (main) (For the attention of Colonel H.D. Sheldon) (USAF microfilm roll A-1007, 1652) This memo concerns an agreement apparently reached between the British and Americans regarding disposition of captured German technology. The memo reiterates the agreement and its

British writer introduces two British officers to facilitate this work. It also makes mention of a "Category 1 list" and discrepancies in this list between the British and Americans. It also describes the list that is in reality a wish list for the month of June, 1945, taking into account what was known of German technology to that date. The list names the following items:

1. *Me 163 parts (the Komet rocket interceptor)*
2. *Do 335 (the Dornier push-pull aircraft)*
3. *Jumo 222 (advance propeller driven aero-engine)*
4. *Jumo 004 (jet engine)*
5. *Lutz Free Piston Engine*
6. *BMW 003 (jet engine)*
7. *MK 214 (gun aboard Me 262 jet fighter)*

If the British valued the Lutz piston engine ahead of the BMW 003 jet engine, well, this is something that needed investigation! Then, in that same memo listing the items wanted, the British seem to have admitted they had two such engines that were appropriated at Volkenrode (a research facility near Nordhausen). There must have been some controversy stemming from this action, possibly resulting in this agreement to share technology between the two Western Allies, because the British were now explaining and agreeing to return one engine to the Americans.

This British memo may have been prompted by the results of a recent interrogation and a document reporting it. The document's stated origin was *Headquarters, United States Strategic Air Forces in Europe, Office of Asst. Chief of Staff A-2*, and it was entitled *Technical Intelligence Report No. I-22, Supplement* (on the same roll of microfilm). In this document, the C.I.O.S. (Combined Intelligence Objectives Subcommittee) Target Number 25/71, Dr. O. Lutz, was interrogated regarding his invention of the free piston engine. In that report, the disadvantages of such an engine are commented upon, one of which was:

(d.) "Decreasing scavenging efficiency with increasing load."

What caught my eye was the paragraph describing this problem:

> *"3. Objection (d,) is serious. Dr. Neugebauer of the Junkers factory, Munich, had shown that the charging efficiency, as measured by the ratio of air inspired to power output, dropped to 40% of its no-load value when the lead (delivery pressure) was 5 atmospheres. This fall was inherent in a gas generator where the motor and compressor pistons were fixed in tandem."*

Forget all the verbiage, what is important here are the words "Dr. Neugebauer". Readers may remember Dr. Franz Neugebauer from my first book (11). Dr. Neugebauer was a Paperclip scientist, brought to the USA to analyze new types of engines as related to their

Lutz Free Piston Engines

We had already received information that a R.A.F. officer, unknown to this Section, had removed two Lutz free piston engines from Volkenrode. We raised this matter with H.Q., 2nd T.A.F.(Main) and although we have not yet received an adequate explanation of the circumstances in which the engines were removed, we understand that one of them has been returned to Volkenrode. It is suggested that you should regard this engine as being available to American Research and arrange for its removal at your convenience. We presum that the second specimen is en route to this country, although we have no information on this point.

British Intelligence Document.

This document discusses the apparent misunderstanding or dust-up over the Lutz Free Piston engine.

weight and thrust values. This would be important for an atomic-powered flying saucer, and it is believed that this was Dr. Neugebauers forte. Prior to coming to the USA, Dr. Neugebauer was said to have worked on diesel aircraft engines. But the actual

wording of his Biographical Note in his official USAF Wright Field report (*The Effect of Power Plant Weight on the Economy of Flight*) gives away exactly which engine was involved:

> *"Dr. Franz J. Neugebauer is the foremost German authority on this subject. An expert on internal-combustion engines and a specialist for Diesel compound aircraft engines, he held leading positions at Junkers in Dessau and Munic from 1924 to 1943, and was director of the engineering department of the Institute for Aeronautical Research at Munich from 1943 to 1945."(12)*

Dr. Neugebauer worked on diesel compound engines. The Lutz free piston engine is a diesel compound engine. Dr. Neugebauer is strongly suspected of using his talents to analyze atomic powered saucers for the USAF and so it is possible if not probable that he did so for the Germans. Prior to atomic power, he is known to have worked on compound diesel engines so it is also probable that they were to be employed for this same type of flying craft. In fact, it is highly probable that Dr. Neugebauer worked on this very engine.

Now, we shall turn, not to the supplement (above) but to the interrogation of Professor O. Lutz himself in a document titled Headquarters United States Strategic Air Forces In Europe, Office of Asst. chief of staff A-2, May 23, 1945, Technical Intelligence Report Number I-22, Interrogation of Prof. O. Lutz with reference to his doughnut motor. This report describes the engine and its history. The idea was to use the engine to compress air was fed with the engine exhaust gas to a turbine. The turbine could then be used to drive a propeller or used strictly for thrust as in a jet engine. There are two types, the linear and the circular. The concept was invented in France by Pescara, tested and improved in Germany by Junkers.

The linear type involves two pistons in one cylinder that come together, compressing the fuel-air mixture and then moving in opposite directions as the compressed fuel-air is detonated. This design eliminates a cylinder head.

The circular or doughnut type of free piston engine was apparently invented by Lutz. Here is a description of this remarkable and strange engine from the report cited above:

> *"4. The Lutz engine has a single liquid-cooled cylinder with the axis a circle, forming a torus. Six pistons of 168mm diameter move in the cylinder at speeds up to 800 rpm., and are connected together in two groups. In the existing engine, three alternate cylinders and their connections were machined from the solid. The two groups of pistons have an intermittent advancing motion superimposed on the mean speed, thus varying the volume between pairs of pistons. During two thirds of a revolution, a piston advances from the intake port in the side of the cylinder, drawing air in. The following piston then advances, compressing the air. Fuel is injected and fired as in a Diesel engine, and the expansion occurs when the leading piston advances again to uncover the exhaust port. The following piston advances on the exhaust stroke and scavenges the cylinder. During the remaining one-third of the revolution, the leading piston advances past a second intake port, drawing in air for the compressor, which is compressed by the following piston to approximately 4 atmospheres. The compressed air is mixed with the exhaust gas, which is at the same pressure, and the resulting mixture is fed to a gas turbine at a temperature of about 450 degrees C. The cycles described is repeated in the six spaces between cylinders every revolution, but no shaft power is delivered by the engine. The piston motion is obtained from planetary gearing, with cranks on the planet gears operating like a scotch yoke in slots in a disc to which one set of pistons is connected. There are no valves."*

So, six pistons chase each other around in a circle. But in the last 1/3 of this circle their function is to compress air that is then mixed with the exhaust gas and ejected. This diesel engine is really a two-stroke power delivery system using another two strokes to compress air. Depending on the output required, such cylinder rings could be stacked on top of one another in a column-like arrangement.

Other facts mentioned in this report are that ahead of the air intake valve was a supercharger and a GM1 device. During this time period the word "supercharger" could also mean "turbocharger", with the difference being the first compresses air mechanically, using the engine itself as source of power, while the second compresses the air using the heat energy of the exhaust gases. For our purposes, it does not matter which was used. The nature of the GM1 device will be discussed later.

During this time period the word "supercharger" could also mean "turbocharger", with the difference being the first compresses air mechanically, using the engine itself as source of power, while the second compresses the air using the heat energy of the exhaust gases. For our purposes, it does not matter which was used. The nature of the GM1 device will be discussed later.

A request was made of the Engine Holdings of the National Air and Space Museum, 7th and Independence Ave, SW, Washington, D.C. 20560 that responded in part with their own summary of this engine as well as some diagrams and photographs of the engine itself. They provide some history, saying that it was invented in 1923 by Dr. Otto Lutz of the Goering Aeronautical Research Establishment in Braunschweig-Volkenrode (where we learned earlier that two examples were recovered by the British). They also go on to describe the intended application of this design:

> *Known as either a swing- or free-piston design, this unit was interned primarily as a combined high pressure compressor or gas generator for relatively high power gas turbine aircraft engines. These engines were intended for long-range transport aircraft, not requiring particularly high speed. The principal advantages of the swing-piston unit were greatly improved fuel economy, use of Diesel Fuel, and a compact design."*

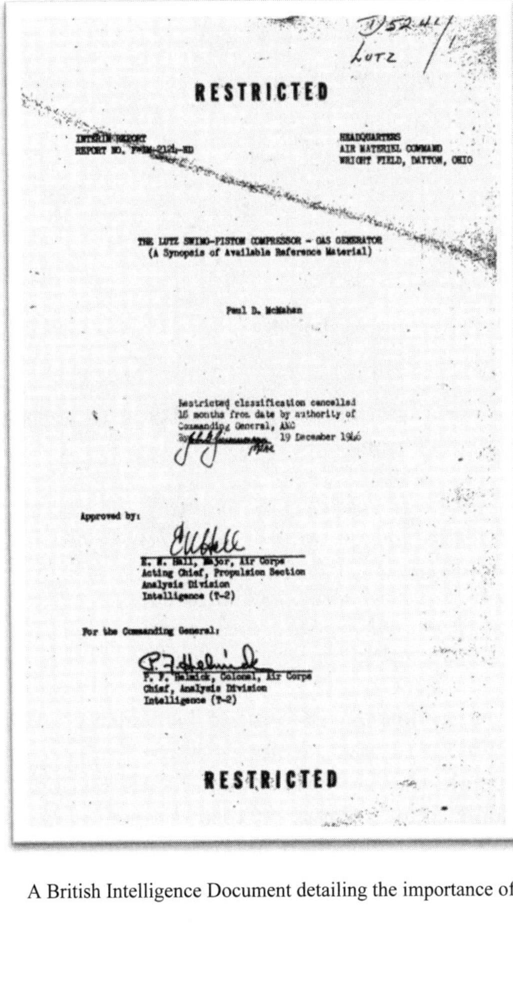

D/52.4L/1
Lutz

RESTRICTED

INTERIM REPORT
REPORT NO. F-SU-2124-ND

HEADQUARTERS
AIR MATERIEL COMMAND
WRIGHT FIELD, DAYTON, OHIO

THE LUTZ SWING-PISTON COMPRESSOR - GAS GENERATOR
(A Synopsis of Available Reference Material)

Paul D. McMahen

Restricted classification cancelled
18 months from date by authority of
Commanding General, AMC
By [signature] 19 December 1946

Approved by:

[signature]
E. W. Hall, Major, Air Corps
Acting Chief, Propulsion Section
Analysis Division
Intelligence (T-2)

For the Commanding General:

[signature]
F. F. Helmick, Colonel, Air Corps
Chief, Analysis Division
Intelligence (T-2)

RESTRICTED

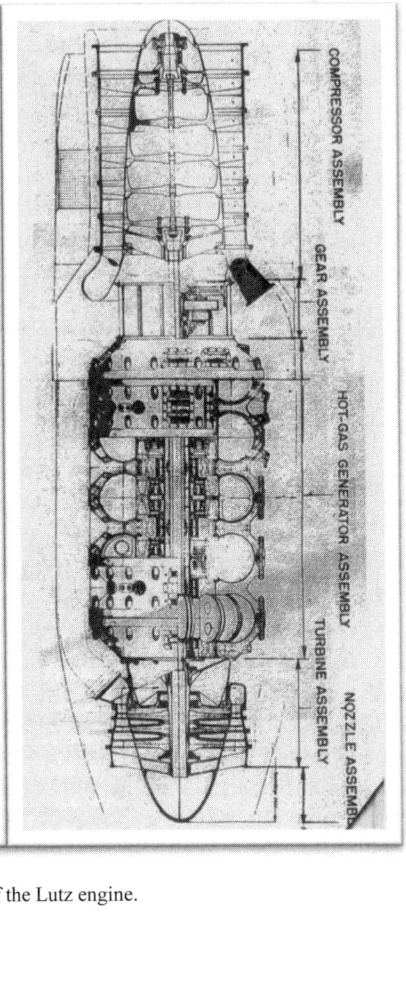

A British Intelligence Document detailing the importance of the Lutz engine.

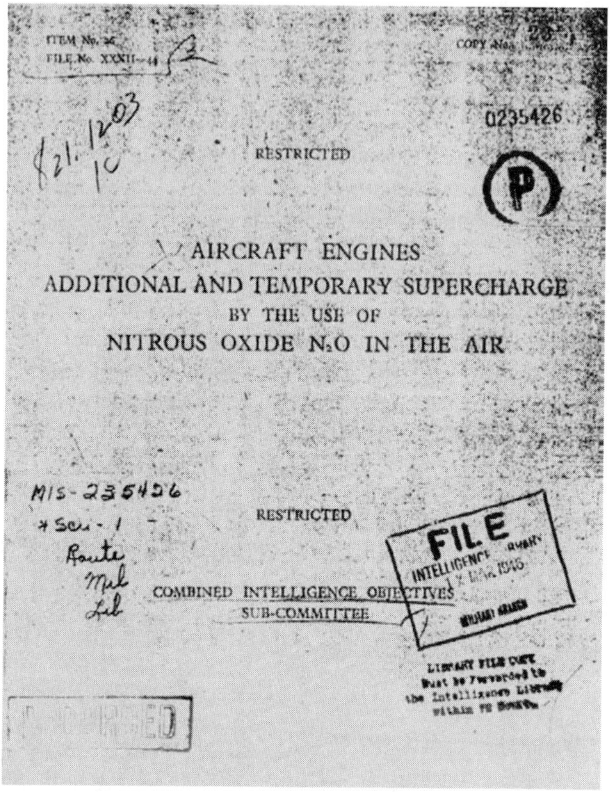

ITEM No. 26
FILE No. XXXII-44

0235426

RESTRICTED

AIRCRAFT ENGINES
ADDITIONAL AND TEMPORARY SUPERCHARGE
BY THE USE OF
NITROUS OXIDE N_2O IN THE AIR

MIS-235426

RESTRICTED

FILE

COMBINED INTELLIGENCE OBJECTIVES
SUB-COMMITTEE

Intelligence Article on Nitrous Oxide Injection

This engine, as stated with only one torus and six pistons, according to the above stated report, was rated at 400 horsepower at 800 rmps.

> *"Known as either a swing- or free-piston design, this unit was interned primarily as a combined high pressure compressor or gas generator for relatively high power gas turbine aircraft engines. These engines were intended for long-range transport aircraft, not requiring particularly high speed. The principal advantages of the swing-piston unit were greatly improved fuel economy, use of Diesel Fuel, and a compact design."*

Now we turn to an American report dated May 12, 1945, titled Headquarters United States Strategic Air Forces In Europe Office of Asst. Chief of staff A-2, Technical Intelligence Report I-5 by Frank L. Wattendorf, AAF Scientific Advisor, describing the two captured engines at Volkenrode in some detail. This is interesting since the war had ended only three days before and Americans already had both engines in hand. Evidently, the British then appropriated the engines somehow, causing a minor dust-up, and formalization of an agreement. The British then must needs explain the incident and return one engine. This report reinforces the low fuel consumption of this engine and states that the highest temperature of the exhausting gases is only 1100 degrees Fahrenheit "which means that uncooled turbine blades may be utilized." What this really means is that no special super-metals such as titanium needed to be used in the turbine blades, making this engine much cheaper and easier to build than contemporary jet engines.

So what do we have in the final analysis? We have an engine capable of turning the slow, carrying blades of the most unsophisticated of the German flying discs. In addition, exhaust gases could be vented to cause a jet effect, propelling the craft horizontally. Of course, we can imagine an afterburner being added. The engine itself was suitable for long distance flight because of its low fuel consumption. It was supercharged, giving it a capacity at high altitude. In addition and for short bursts of power at high altitude, a nitrous oxide injection system was provided. The engine was modular and could be ramped up to almost any size required. It ran on diesel fuel and so gave off a diesel exhaust. A flying disc that could land anywhere fits the evidence for Tibet, which had no landing strips yet was in communication with Nazi Germany. It fits all the parameters of the sighting by Frank Parker in 1955 and was in the correct part of the world to service Tibet as a repository site.

What is even more significant to the Nazi post-war world is the fact that many sightings of flying discs called “smoky saucers” occurred in South America in the immediate post war years that fit exactly this description. Their constraints would have been the same, mountains, jungle, long distances and no landing strips. It must be obvious that this type of Lutz free-piston engine was in operation almost worldwide in areas where this type of flying disc was in need.

From Tibet we will now turn to Germany’s neighbor, Switzerland as a place where the Nazis would store things of value. Actually, due to the proximity, secrecy, and neutrality of Switzerland, this would almost be a no-brainer for anyone seeking to hide valuables at that time and place providing a deal could be worked out with the Swiss. We have already reviewed the testimony of Siegfried Hepner in an earlier chapter who saw a Dornier Do 635 fleeing into Switzerland on the very last day of the war so what we shall do is to review other accounts that might lead to the same conclusion.

As an aside in discussing Switzerland, a bit of review is in order. In my first book, Hitler’s Flying Saucers, the Methernita Society’s Testatika generator was discussed on pages 169 to 171 with accompanying diagram. This electric generator has been featured in several video films. The device is started by spinning it by hand—the two Whimhurst electrostatic wheels are spun in opposite directions. The device self-corrects to an optimum speed of between 50-60 revolutions per second that is maintained by the machine itself, indefinitely. Paul Baumann is the “technician” almost solely responsible for this device’s creation and understanding. The device remains behind closed walls but has been shown to interested specialists. No fraud has ever been detected by those specialists. The Methernita Society, a brotherhood of Christians, has built several of these devices in varying sizes and outputs for their own use. It is my suspicion that this knowledge came to the Swiss Methernita Society as a result of The Second World War and the need to both preserve secret knowledge gained by the Nazis and the need for certain individuals to seek political shelter outside of Germany.

Lutz Free Piston Engine – Pictures and Diagrams

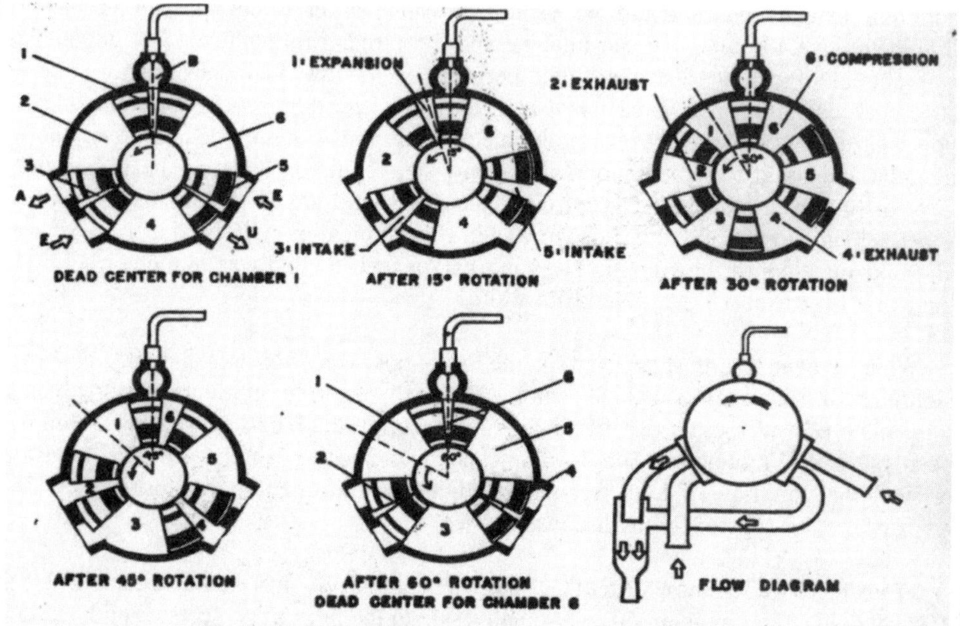

Fig. 1 - Schematic Diagram of the Rotating-Piston Principle

Fig. 2 – The two piston groups

Fig. 3 – Piston Groups and Synchronizing Mechanism

Discussion of Switzerland as a repository goes way back in time in August, 1952 and again with "Claude Schweikhart" in the magazine article which translates to: "Concerning the Crown and Pinnacle of the World". Incidentally, below the title the author, Mr. Schweikhart lists his locus as "Basel" (Switzerland), so he ought to know something of which he is talking.

This is the article that informs us that the SS has been investigated by Louis Emrich and his team. Specifically he means the relationship of the SS to Tibet as that is really the topic of the article but Schweikhart also mentions underground facilities the SS used for occult and alchemical work as well as for military purposes as being located between Schwaben and Bavaria. On the next page Schweikhart says that these underground military facilities have gone undetected to this time and that they extended from the Austrian alpine region and into Switzerland (16).

Dr. Axel Stoll reviews important UFO sightings and their meaning and so takes a look at the case of Eduard "Billy" Meier, a Swiss man. Meier produced probably the best, most clear and detailed UFO pictures ever in the late 1980s. Legend says that "Billy" first saw a UFO in 1942 along with his father but either believed or was told that this UFO was the product of the Germans of the 3rd Reich.

Much later Meier saw a UFO close-up as well as a UFO crewmember, a female named "Semjase". Semjase was described as a beautiful, petite, blond woman. Dr. Stoll is not buying this as he points out that this alleged extraterrestrial spoke perfect German to Meier. There followed a long series of sightings and clear pictures over a period of several years. Meier was given a rational for this interaction but it seems thin to many observes. Why would extraterrestials come all the way to earth only to single out an isolated, obscure, Swiss farmer for enlightenment? To Dr. Stoll the situation seems clear enough. The saucers Meier photographed were further developments of the "Haunebu" type of craft the Germans invented (17). The Haunebu is the name given to some larger field propulsion craft by some.

Billy Meirer Beamship
An alleged photograph and model showing the great number of spheres which could be likened to the Schappeller device or the Bell.

Taken as evidence neither of these situations is too convincing. First is an old semi-occult article by a guy who we know uses other names. The second concerns a UFO guy who has been involved in an ongoing UFO controversy, being alternatively debunked and defended for over twenty years now. But the news article that is coming is easily one of the strangest, most convoluted articles ever written by a real news agency.

For me it started with a reference by Michael Bar-Zohar. Bar-Zohar writes in the spirit of the "Nazi Hunter" genre although his book is titled "The Hunt for the German Scientists". He makes two references to "death rays" which is a catch-all term which was used before the words "laser" and "particle beam" became a part of our language. His first reference is unique and so elevates Bar-Zohar to the status of a "source" even though he gives few details nor cites a reference.

> *"There was also a vague report on the mysterious Zimmermann—the man believed to have invented the "death ray" and even to have used it effectively against the Russians in the Carpathians on 30 August 1944. The report said that he had been captured and taken to Russia just before the end of the war." (18)*

Having gotten my attention, Bar-Zohar concludes his book by saying that:

> *"At the present time scientists are living in comparative peace; except for a few underdeveloped countries which play at being sorcerer's apprentices with a few "brains" that they pay well but surround with barbed wire, men of science can consider themselves as enjoying a temporary freedom."(19)*

Evidently, Mr. Bar-Zohar lived on an alternative planet in 1967 or thinks that if German scientists didn't invent it, it was surely not an implement of war. But then he says something significant:

> *"But this does not prevent some of them from dabbling in preparations for war—like Dr. Hans Ehrhardt who was expelled from Switzerland for having experimented with a mysterious green death ray, and the unlucky English scientist who died from the microbes he was carefully cultivating for bacteriological warfare." (20)*

Forget the "English scientist" reference, I wanted to know who Dr. Hans Ehrhardt was and all about his green death ray. So, I did F.O.I.A. requests of the usual suspects and got absolutely nothing. Later when requested (F.O.I.A.) a list of Paperclip scientists, there was no Hans Ehrhardt on that list. This Bar-Zohar reference was a dead end—or so I thought.

Last year I was contacted by Mr. C. P., a Swiss researcher who specialized in Karl Schappeller. He had tremendous Internet search ability and came up with all kinds of elusive references. One reference that did mention Schappeller was titled "Schnee geschmoltzen" (melted snow). It was just a title on a page so I asked Mr. C. P. what in the world melted snow had to do with Schappeller? He sent me the entire article. It came from the German publication, *Der Spiegel*, and dated July 24, 1963. Der Spiegel is just about as solid a news magazine as exists. I read the article, thought about it, re-read it, with the result that the more I read and thought about its contents, the more impressed I was. The article is reproduced here in English. I am sorry but this particular article was difficult for me to translate for some reason so please forgive the rough treatment. It appears in the section of the magazine dealing with news outside Germany (Ausland).

AUSLAND

SCHWEIZ

TODESSTRAHLEN

Schnee geschmolzen

Ungewöhnliche Order lief Anfang vergangener Woche bei eidgenössischen Polizeidienststellen ein:

Die Gesetzeshüter wurden angehalten, nach einem Mann zu fahnden — freilich nicht, um ihn zu verhaften. Vielmehr sollte sichergestellt werden, daß der Gesuchte wirklich verschwunden ist und damit die eidgenössische Bürokratie von einer Blamage befreit hat.

Der Gesuchte nennt sich Dr. Hans Ehrhardt und hieß früher Hans Engelke. Als Amateur-Physiker war er — nach eigenen Angaben zusammen mit Wernher von Braun — in der Rüstungsindustrie des Dritten Reiches beschäftigt gewesen.

Dabei erfand er eine Wunderwaffe. Engelke wollte in den von feindlichen Bomberstaffeln durchflogenen Luftschichten dichte Wolken feinster Kohlenstoffpartikel „verteilen. Mittels einer Zündrakete sollte beim Herannahen von Feindflugzeugen ein Schlagwetter in der Atmosphäre erzeugt werden. Beim ersten und einzigen Versuch mit seiner Wunderwaffe, so fabulierte Engelke-Ehrhardt, seien im April 1945 gleich 36 Bomber auf einen Schlag vom Himmel geholt worden.

Nach Krieg und alliierter Internierung wandte sich Autodidakt Ehrhardt einem anderen physikalischen Phänomen zu. Er begann Versuche mit Strahlen, die laut eigener Aussage „im Frieden Kranke heilen und im Kriege Feinde töten" sollten.

Aus einer Gasplasma-Quelle gedachte der Erfinder mit großen Hohlspiegeln einen gebündelten ultravioletten Lichtstrahl herzustellen. Dieser Todesstrahl sollte einerseits 30 000 Kilometer weit wirken und eine „ungeheure Zerstörungskraft" (so Ehrhardt) entwickeln, andererseits aber Krebskranke von ihren Leiden befreien, „ohne daß Knoten oder Kapselungen zurückbleiben".

Erfinder Ehrhardt
„Ungeheure Zerstörungskraft"

In der Bundesrepublik gelang es dem modernen Cagliostro nicht, seine Ideen zu verkaufen, obgleich Deutschland stets ein dankbares Feld für Wundermänner war. Nach dem Ersten Weltkrieg gelang es dem geisteskranken österreichischen Landbriefträger Karl Schappeller, Ex-Kaiser Wilhelm II. große Summen für einen Plan zu entlocken, Deutschland „durch die Nutzung ungeheurer Energien aus dem kosmischen Raum zur ersten Weltmacht zu machen". Zur selben Zeit begeisterte ein Betrüger namens Franz Tausend den General Ludendorff mit seiner angeblichen Fähigkeit, aus Eisen und Blei Gold zu gewinnen.

Dem Strahlenmagier Ehrhardt glückte es hingegen Anfang 1961, die Kriegstechnische Abteilung (KTA) des Eidgenössischen Militärdepartements in Bern für seine phantastischen Projekte zu interessieren.

Die schweizerischen Landesverteidiger luden Ehrhardt am 24. Februar 1961 zu einer Besprechung ein und forderten ihn auf, schriftliche Unterlagen beizubringen. Eine Prüfung des Ehrhardt-Exposés durch Züricher TH-Professoren veranlaßte freilich die KTA am 31. Mai 1961 dazu, auf eine weitere Zusammenarbeit mit Ehrhardt zu verzichten.

Interessiert an den Künsten des deutschen Physikers blieb indes weiterhin ein Beamter der KTA: Adjunkt Eugen Burkhard, Chef der Rüstungszentrale der Kriegstechnischen Abteilung, erhoffte sich von Ehrhardts Ideen Entdecker-Ruhm und förderte den Deutschen in eigener Regie.

Als KTA-Beamten fiel es Burkhard leicht, dem Forscher Aufenthaltsbewilligung und Wohnung zu verschaffen. Im August 1961 siedelte sich der Waffenrevolutionär mit Gattin Ilse und vier Sprößlingen am Sarner See im Kanton Obwalden an.

Rückendeckung für die folgenden Versuche wurde Ehrhardt durch die „Bewilligung 2524" der KTA zuteil, in der dem Physiker gegen Entrichtung von 50 Franken Gebühr und 80 Rappen Porto routinegemäß erlaubt wird, „Prototypen zu Geschossen ohne Patronenhülsen bis zum Kaliber 30 mm herzustellen".

In Wahrheit experimentierte der Sarner Neubürger aber nicht mit 30-mm-Geschossen, sondern mit „Todesstrahlen". Mit diesen Produkten seines Erfindergeistes schmolz Ehrhardt im letzten Frühjahr — so erzählte er der „Deutschen National-Zeitung" — auf eine Entfernung von zwölf Kilometern binnen Sekunden anderthalb Meter hohen Gletscherschnee. Applaudierte die DNZ: „Erfinder Dr. Ehrhardt, Herr über Tod und Leben."

Ungemach näherte sich dem Herrn über Tod und Leben freilich, als Anfang Juni ein Photo erschien, das den Ehrhardtschen Todesstrahl als drohend himmelwärts gerichteten Finger über dem Sarner See zeigte.

Die eidgenössische Presse, von der schockierten Fremdenindustrie alarmiert, überhäufte die nichtsahnende Kriegstechnische Abteilung mit Vorwürfen wegen dieser „lebensgefährlichen Experimente", während die Sarner Gastwirte Schadenersatz für die Gäste forderten, die wegen der Todesstrahlen fernbleiben würden.

Das Militärdepartement ließ eilends verlauten, Ehrhardt habe „keinen Rappen" schweizerischer Steuergelder für seine Experimente erhalten. Zugleich interessierte sich die eidgenössische Sicherheits- und Fremdenpolizei eingehend für den Deutschen.

Dabei ergab sich laut Polizeibericht, daß Ehrhardt „über wesentliche Punkte seiner Person und seines Vorlebens unwahre Angaben gemacht hatte, so über seine Tätigkeit in der DDR".

Da witterten die Behörden die Chance, sich des peinlichen Gastes zu entledigen: Am 4. Juni eröffnete die Fremdenpolizei Obwalden dem Ehrhardt, daß sein Aufenthalt bis zum 15. Juli 1963 befristet sei.

Zwei Tage vor Ablauf der Frist, in der Nacht vom 13. auf den 14. Juli, verschwand Ehrhardt aus seinem Sarner Domizil, ohne sich abzumelden oder eine Adresse zu hinterlassen.

Mit seinem allzu stillen Abschied wurde Ehrhardt freilich gezwungen, vorerst auch auf die Verwirklichung eines Planes zu verzichten, den er in der Ende 1962 herausgegebenen Schrift „Der neue Weg" publik gemacht hatte: die Nutzbarmachung eines von ihm erdachten Perpetuum mobile.

„Über 30 000 Kilometer": Ehrhardt-Strahl am Sarner See

Melted Snow article (cover)

Switzerland

Death Rays

Melted Snow

An unusual order arrived at the start of last week at the Swiss federal police station.

The lawmen were stopped in their search to arrest a man, but not voluntarily. Furthermore it is guaranteed that the rumor does really disappear and thereby the shame is lifted of the Swiss federal bureaucracy.

The person for which they searched called himself Dr. Hans Ehrhardt and was called earlier Hans Englelke. According to his own account, he was an amateur physicist and together with Wernher von Braun he had been employed in the armament industry of the Third Reich.

At that time he invented a wonder weapon; Engelke wanted to distribute thick clouds of fine coal particles through the atmospheric stratums of the enemy's bomber squadrons. By means of a rocket ignition, and explosive mixed with air was to be created on the approaching enemy aircraft. With the one and only attempt with the wonder weapon, so Engelke-Ehrhardt went on to invent a story, it came to pass that in April 1945, as many as 36 bombers in one explosion were brought from the air.

After the war and Allied internment the self-taught Ehrhardt turned toward another physical phenomena: He began research with rays that according to one source would "in peace sickness heal and in war enemies kill."

From a gas plasma source the inventor thought to make a bundled ultraviolet light-ray with large concave mirrors. This death ray developed on one hand a useable range of 30,000 kilometers and a monstrous destructive power (according to Ehrhardt) and one the other hand could free you from the suffering of cancer, "without a node or capsule remaining."

In Germany the impostor and charlatan did not succeed in selling his ideas, although Germany was a constant grateful field for astonishing men; after World War One the insane Austrian postman Karl Schappeller succeed worming out of the Ex-Kaiser Wilhelm II great sums of money for his plan, to make Germany, through the use of enormous energies from cosmic space, into a world power. At the same time a swindler by the name of Franz Tausend inspired General Luldendorf with his alleged ability to produce gold from lead and iron.

The ray-magician succeeded, on the other hand, to interest the Technical War Division (KTA) of the Swiss Federal Military Department in Bern in his imaginary project.

The Swiss Defense Forces opened a discussion and a conference on

Interest in the skills of the German physicist remained, meanwhile, furthermore, an official of the War Technical Division Adjunct Eugen Burkhard, Chief of the Armaments Central of the War Technical Division hoped himself for Erhardt's ideas of discover-glory and advanced the German in a special state monopoly.

As a War Technical Division official Burkhard easily obtained the researcher a residence permit and habitation. In August 1961 the weapons revolutionary settled himself with wife Ilse and four offspring on the Sarner See in the Kanton of Obwalden.

Cover for the subsequent endeavor Ehrhardt would share though the permit 2524 of the War Technical Division in which to the physicist towards the payment of 50 Franks as fee and 80 centime postage were regularly granted, "Prototypes to projectiles without cartridge cases up to 30 mm to produce."

In truth the new citizen of Sarner did not experiment with 30 mm projectiles, but on the contrary, with "death rays". With this product of his inventive spirit Ehrhardt melted glacial snow, within seconds, at a distance of twelve kilometers, at a depth of one and a half meters thick early in the last year — so he told the Deutsche National-Zeitung. The Deutsche National Zeitung applauded: "Inventor Dr. Ehrhardt, master of life and death."

Discomfort drew itself nearer to the master of life and death to be sure as at the beginning of June a photo appeared that showed Ehrhrdt's death ray as a threatening finger pointed heavenwards over the Sarner See.

The Swiss press alarmed by the shocking exotic industry overwhelmed the silent War Technical Division with reproach because of this "life-perilous experiment." Whilst the Sarner landlord's compensation for the guests went ahead, which on account of the death rays would remain distant.

The Military Department made haste in hinting that Ehrhardt had "not a centime" of Swiss tax money received for his experiments. At the same time the Swiss Federal Security and Foreign Police took a detailed interest in the German.

With this a police report was issued and became known that "concerning material points of his person and his former life", Ehrhardt had made untrue statements as well as his activity in the Deutsche Demokratisch Republik (Translator's note: the former East Germany).

Here the authorities smelled the chance to rid themselves of their painful guest: On June 4 the Foreign Police in Obwalden disclosed to Ehrhardt that the time of his stay would be up until July, 1963.

Two days before the discharge of he appointed time in the night form the 13th to the 14th of July Ehrhardt disappeared from his Sarner domicile without announcing his withdrawal or forwarding address.

With his all too silent departure, Ehrhardt was certainly forced first of all also from the realization of a plan to renounce the published paper "The New Path" which he had made public at the end of 1962: making the use of his idea of perpetual motion.

So there we have the story. A German conman, at best an "amateur scientist", had unsuccessfully tried to fleece the Swiss military by pitching a death ray of his own design. Through the Swiss government's cooperation with *Der Spiegel* the story has been exposed to the public. The story ends and everyone lives happily ever after, right?

Wait a minute. Maybe in 1963 this story flew but the public is now much older and wiser in what a government advances through the press. In retrospect there are quite a few questions here that went unaddressed and unanswered. We are going to go through this story point by point and see if we can cut through the cover-up and get to the truth.

Ehrhardt as "amateur scientist" is the first red flag. This amateur scientist is alleged to have worked with Dr. Wernher von Braun and the Nazi government. The Nazis would not hire amateurs to head their programs anymore than the Swiss government would. In this story this "amateur scientist" is asked by the Swiss Defense Forces to bring proof for the basis of his work with is to be reviewed by professors of the Swiss Technical College. Then the War Technical Division offered this "amateur scientist" a contract developing secret weapons, complete with a built-in cover story. Let's be consistent. If consistent thought is employed, our amateur scientist would be met by an amateur committee of amateur professors who reviewed his work resulting in an amateur contract for amateur secret weapons.

What is unquestionably going on here is that "Dr. Hans Erhardt/Hans Engelke" had yet another name, his real name, and it was this real person who was a real scientist who worked for the 3rd Reich. Why he was using a false name is anyone's guess. He could have been doing so for a variety of reasons. Even after Dr. Ehrhardt left the employment of Switzerland, neither party wanted his real name disclosed.

Next we are told that he, Dr. Ehrhardt, invented the coal dust fuel air bomb. Wow! This was 1963. Until the late 1990s the US government who acquired the services of Dr. Mario Zippermayr, the real inventor of the fuel-air bomb, used a coverstory to hide this weapon from rival powers. They claimed Dr. Zippermayr invented a "vortex cannon", not a fuel-air bomb. Generations of historians read over each other's shoulders endlessly repeating this cover story to the delight of the American government. It was only late in the 1990's that the true facts were declassified and an accounting of Dr. Mario Zippermayr's true work was made public. I know this for an absolute fact since this writer is the person for whom the US Army declassified and provided the files under a F.O.I.A. request. (21) Nobody knew of the fuel-air bomb unless they had insider information within the 3rd Reich itself or had worked for Dr. Zippermayr.

But Dr. Ehrhardt disclosed something that was only recently known. The fact is that the fuel-air bomb had been tested in combat with success. I know this is fact because writer/researcher Friedrich Georg found an account of this test on microfilm that slipped through the hands of the censors. He published this account in two of his books. (22) (23) Actually, one book shows the first page of the report while the other book shows us the second page. What will be done here is that they will be re-typed and combined.

Then the report can be compared it to the disclosure of *Der Spiegel* based on the testimony of Dr. Ehrhardt.

SECRET

PW INTELLEGENCE
BULLETIN NO. 2/32

13. Fantasia, German Secret Weapons

Preamble. The following stories are from sources of doubtful reliability and may well be pure products of the imagination. However, in view of the striking similarity between them, they are printed for what they are worth.

First Story

Around 15 Sept 44, CP of 1127 Cron Rogt 559 Inf Div was in REINANGE at GSG3 4416/U1/912797. It was a warm, sunny day with a few scattered clouds and no wind. At about 1600 PW was standing near the church in REINANGE and observed a formation of Allied aircraft pass, flying from SW to NE, low enough to be recognized as four-motored planes. He counted up to 30 planes. They were flying in close formation.

While PW watched them pass by he saw what he believed to be a small fighter plane (grey color, no identification marks) climb and approach the Allied formation from an easterly direction. PW states that the "fighter plane" was flying at an abnormally high speed and that it penetrated into the midst of the formation apparently with being fired at. Suddenly there appeared where the "fighter plane" had been before, a red ball of fire, somewhat larger than the plane itself. A split second later, the ball of fire turned into a rapidly expanding red circle (parallel to the ground). This circle was bluish red at the edge, and as its diameter increased, the interior of the circle became an empty space. As the circle enveloped the planes, they seemed to just disappear. In a matter of seconds the entire formation of Allied planes had disappeared, and the sky was just as it had been before.

PW discussed the incident with several others who had witnessed it, including an Hptm of 1559 of Arty Rogt. This officer (who was subsequently killed) told him that the "fighter plane" in question was a wooden miniature plane with a speed of over 1000 km per hour and which was operated by remote control. The name of the plane is KOMET. The Hptm who told him that he had lived near an airfield where such planes were tested and that he had recognized it at once.

HITLER's Plans. About Oct 10 44, the CP of 1127 Gren Regt was visited by the 1st general staff officer (I-a?) of XIII SS Corps (an Oberstlt, name unknown). PW talked for about 10 to 15 minutes with this officer's driver, a Rottenfuehrer, who told him the following,

He, the Rottenfuehrer, had overhead a conversation between the general staff officer and HITLER and HIMMLER, who had visited the XIII SS Corps HQ a few days before. During the conversation he had heard HITLER say "the new secret weapon" would not be employed until a 24-hour mastery of the air and sea could be guaranteed. HIMMLER is supposed to have added that another prerequisite was a temperature of 10 degrees below zero.

SECRET

PW INTELLEGENCE
BULLETIN NO. 2/32

13. Fantasia, German Secret Weapons (Continued)

Second Story

One 6 Jan 44, between 1300 and 1400 hrs, PW saw a formation of four-motored American Liberators flying over STETTIN. He heard a noise like that of a V-2 taking off and saw a large red ball ascending toward the formation. It appeared to grow as it rose. There was a loud explosion and he saw broken parts of airplanes falling.

PW comments that there were three divisions (?) of flak in action at the time (3 x 72 pieces), but when he returned to PEENEMUENDE he was told by a friend who worked in the officer's club that this had been a first attempt with a new secret weapon and that 47 planes were brought down by the single shot. Another friend in Flak Rogt 11, STETTIN, told PW that the Flak had fired anti-personnel charges that day instead of usual Flak ammunition. When PW asked why, he was told that he ammunition as left over from AFRICA and had to be used up. PW's own comment (see also PW INTELLIGENCE BULLETIN 1/13 Item 17) is that it makes more noise and might be used to hide the noise of the secret weapon.

(Source: S/Gofr Franz KREIMER, 5 Para Mortar Bn 5 Para Div)

Here we clearly see two attempts at using a fuel-air bomb, one with an Enzian and the other with a Wasserfall rocket. Both types have been mentioned as being vehicles for fuel-air anti-aircraft weapons.

The question remains: *How could have Ehrhardt/Engelke have known about this weapon? Could he have worked with Dr. Mario Zippermayr at Tal Station?*

Now let us turn to Dr. Ehrhardt's description of he basis for the death ray. The article says that Dr. Ehrhardt used a gas plasma to generate his "death ray". Today, the words "death ray" have been replaced by the word "laser", so this archaic terminology can be dispensed with once and for all. Dr. Ehrhardt was talking about building a laser. Lasers can and are generated using gas plasma. Ultraviolet lasers are generated using argon gas plasma. (24) If we are to believe the *Der Spiegel* report that would have to be done with the assistance of the Swiss military, Dr. Ehrhardt was successful in this to the point of melting snow at a distance of 30 km or over 18 miles. Even half this is a phenomenal distance to have focused a laser in the early 1960's. If you are old enough you will recall that early laser research employed almost desktop distances. This lack of range was what separated the lasers seen on the TV program *Star Trek* from the reality. It was only with President Ronald Reagan and his Strategic Defense Initiative ("Star Wars") that serious talk of lasers as weapons was discussed.

Laser research in Nazi Germany has been discussed in a previous book (25). Researcher/writer Friedrich Georg discovered some remarkable laser experiments and diagrams on microfilm stemming from the I.G. Farben facility at Ludwigshafen. (26) So, if Dr. Ehrhardt knew this research so well, he must have worked at I.G. Farben, correct? But if so, how would he have known of the fuel-air bomb of Dr. Mario Zippermayr who worked at Tal Station in the Tyrol. Perhaps the solution is Tal Station or Hoch-Tal Station worked on lasers and we still do not know it. Or perhaps Dr. Erhardt worked at some sort of central clearinghouse for tip-top secret German technology such as the Kammler think-tank in Prague/Pilsen. We just do not know.

Finally, we come to the last paragraph in the *Der Spiegel* article, discussing Dr. Ehrhardt's plans to present a paper titled "The New Path" which discusses his ideas of perpetual motion. This title might indicate some new or revolutionary idea tht Dr. Ehrhardt is presenting. The fact that it would evoke the words and idea of perpetual motion, words and ideas synonymous with scientific heresy, is significant and could only have been supported if facts in the form of a working model had been presented. At this point I just cannot help but think of the coincidence of Ehrhardt's disappearance and the appearance of the Testatika device, in Switzerland, a few years later. The counter rotating wheels of this device simply spin indefinitely, by themselves, once set into motion. A seemingly free energy electric generator would certainly qualify as a new path forward. Could there be any relationship between Dr. Ehrhardt and the Testatika device of the Swiss Methernita Society? We just do not know. Or could there be another device?

One thing is clear, however. The Swiss government picked Dr. Ehrhardt's brain clean regarding the laser technology, probably had a working device, and sequestered this device and technology away in their secure underground facilities. Besides the laser technology, the Swiss undoubtedly debriefed Dr. Ehrhardt on other technologies, including the fuel-air bomb. We just do not know how much information Dr. Ehrhard had stored in this brain. But afterward, when Dr. Ehrhardt had given the Swiss all he knew, a whole variety of reasons were put forth which the Swiss used as grounds to rid themselves of Dr. Ehrhardt. And since Dr. Ehrhardt did not come to the Swiss with clean hands with regard to his true identity or real name, any complaint voiced by Dr. Ehrhardt would simply be minimized by the Swiss as the "sour grapes" of an impostor.

There can be little doubt that the Swiss know secrets of the 3rd Reich that we can only guess about.

Literature Cited

1. **Schweikhart, Claude, 1952**, *Um Krone und Gipfel der Welt, Mensch & Schicksal*, Edition 6, Number 10, page 4 and 5
2. **Farrell, Joseph P., Ph.D., 2008**, *Nazi International The Nazis' Powtwar Plan to Control Finance, Conflict, Physics and Space*, pages 383 and 384, Adventures Unlimited Publishing, Kempton, Illinois, USA
3. **Stoll, Axel, Ph.D., 2001**, *Hoch-Technolgie im Dritten Reich*, pages 15 and 16, Amun Verlag, Schleusingen, Germany
4. **Stoll, Axel, Ph.D., 1994**, *Vymaanika Shastra* (wissenschaftliche Uebersetzung as dem Amerikanischen, mit zahlreichen Anmerkungen und Hinweeisen des Uebersetzers, viele Abbildungen, 142 Seiten sowie mehrere Anhaenge), Berlin, Germany (privately published and referenced with Dr. Stoll's notes on the book reproduced here for competeness).
5. **Stoll, Axel, Ph.D., 2001**, page 16
6. **Stoll, Axel, Ph.D., 2001**, page 132
7. **Stevens, Henry, 2007**, *Hitler's Suppressed and Still-Secret Weapons, Science and Technology*, pages 27-29, Adventures Unlimited Publishing, Kempton, Illinois, USA
8. **Stoll, Axel, 2001**, page 132
9. **Lusar, Rudolf, 1964**, *Die deutschen Waffen und Geheimwaffen des 2 Weltkrieges und ihre Weiterentwicklung*, page 220, J.F. Lehmanns Verlag, Munich, Germany
10. **UFO Magazine (British)** date not shown but late 1990s, written by Graham W. Birdsall, pages 4,5,6,7,22,24, UFO Magazine web site: http://www.ufomag.co.uk
11. **Stevens, Henry, 2003**, *Hitler's Flying Saucers A Guide to German Flying Dsics of the Second World War*, pages 108-109, Adventures Unlimited Publishing, Kempton, Illinois, USA
12. **Neugebauer, Franz J., Ph.D., 1946**, *Effect Of Power-Plant Weight On Economy Of Flight* (Project No. NFE-64), page 11, Headquarters Air Material Command Wright Field, Dayton, Ohio, USA

13. **Combined Intelligence Objectives Sub-Committee Report No.26**, File No.XXXII-44, Aircraft Engines Additional And Temporary Supercharge By The Use of Niturous Oxide N2O In The Air, March, 1946, G-2 Division, SHAEF (Rear) APO 413
14. **Combined Intelligence Objectives Sub-Committee Report No 26**, File No. XXXII-44, page 14
15. **Georg, Friedrich, 2008**, "Unternehmen Patentenraub" 1945 Die Geheim- geschichte des Groessten Technologieraubs aller Zeiten, page 286, Grabert Verlag, Tuebingen, Germany
16. **Mensch und Schicksal, August, 1952**, by Claude Schweikhart, Um Kroen und Gipfel der Welt, pages 4 and 5, 6. Jahrig. / Nr. 10
17. **Stoll, Axel, Ph.D., 2001**, *Hochtechnolgie Im Dritten Reich Reichsdeutsche Entwicklungen und die vermutlich wahre Herkunft der "UFO",* pages 82, 83, Amun-Verlag, Schleusingen, Germany
18. **Bar-Zohar, Michael, 1967**, *The Hunt For German Scientists*, page 152, Avon Books, New York, USA
19. **Bar-Zohar, Michael, 1967**, page 222
20. ***ibid.***
21. **Stevens, Henry, 2007**, *Hitler's Suppressed and Still-Secret Weapons, Science and Technology*, pages 103-111
22. **Georg, Friedrich, 2003**, *Hitlers Siegeswaffen Band 2: Star Wars 1947 Teil A: Von der V-1 bis zur A-9: unkonventionelle Kurz-und Mittlelstreckenwaffen*, page 209, Amun-Verlag and Heinrich Jung Verlag, Schleusingen and Zlla-Mehlis (respectively), Germany
23. **Georg, Friedrich, 2004**, *Hitlers Siegeswaffen Band 2: Star Wars 1947 Teilband B: Von der Amerikarakete zur Obitalstation - Deutschlands Streben nach Interkontinentalwaffen und das erste Weltraumprogramm*, page 116, Amun-Verlag and Heinrich Jung -Verlag, Schleusingen and Zella-Mehlis, (respectively), Germany
24. http://www.rp-photonics.com/Ultraviolet_lasers.html This is a site tilted "Encyclopedia of Laser Physics an Technology.
25. **Stevens, Henry, 2007**, pages 198-208
26. **Detailed Interrogation Report, 3/13/45**, "Atom-Smashing Laboratory", report 6824-Dtc (MIS) M. 1075, US Government microfilm.

POINT 211

Because this subject has been so extensively covered by this time in print and on the internet (for better or worse), our time here would be spent most profitably, not be reviewing what most of you already know about Neuschwabenland, but by discussing new ideas about that base. A brief history of this base and subsequent developments can be found in my first book (1). The very best work on Neuschwabenland can be found in Rainer Daehnhardt's Dos Acores a Antarctida (2) Mr. Daehnhardt is the world's authority on the Ritcher Expedition as he has obtained two copies of the ship Schwabenland's log books and purchased the other two originals at auction. He is Portuguese, of Austrian ancestry, and attended grade school in Germany during the Second World War.

For those of you who have never heard of Wilhelm Landig's Point 211 or Neuschwabenland, a few words here must serve as an introduction. Just before the war in Europe started, Luftwaffe Chief Hermann Goering sponsored a voyage to Antarctica by the research vessel Schwabenland. Actually, this was a small fleet of vessels under the command of Kapitan Alfred Ritscher. The Schwabenland carried two catapult-launched sea planes and with these two aircraft the German dropped metal swastika flags on the ice, staking out their territorial claim to Antarctica which they named Neuschwabenland, New Swabia, in honor of the ship's name which carried them there. Besides staking out this claim, the Ritscher Expedition also explored this area of Antarctica, finding warm water lakes heated by geothermal vents. In fact, the same fault running from the center of Antarctica, bisecting Neuschwabenland, runs all the way through Africa (The Great Rift Valley) and into Western Asia, terminating at the Dead Sea. A mountain range runs along the coast of Antarctica roughly parallel to it but was broken by this fault line making the intersection of the sea the mountain range and the fault line the focus of Neuschwabenland.

During the Second World War the Germans claimed Neuschwabenland as a part of the Greater Reich just as they did Austria or any other territory they occupied at that time. Neuschwabenland appeared on German maps as part of their territory. Rainer Daehnhardt actually saw this on a map of the Greater Reich as a boy and a student in Germany at that time in textbooks (3).

If you look at the position of Neuschwabenland on a world map, it is noticed that it lies just South of Africa on the coast of Antarctica. This is certainly a strategic position given that ships must sail around the tip of Africa going to the Orient if the Suez Canal were ever blocked. Given commerce and communication between the Germans and the Japanese, one sees how important this sea way would be. So, during the Second World War there are rumors of building activity at Neuschwabenland in which the Germans turned this point on the map into a full-blown German military base. Willibald Mattern, living in Chile after the war and being greatly interested in this subject, reports that the Germans even grew vegetables at this base (4). This base would take the form of a naval base and since the German Navy was really a U-boat force, this base would logically take on the characteristics of a U-boat bunker. Additionally, German raiders—warships disguised as merchant vessels—operated in the South Atlantic. Among these were *The Penguin*, *The Thor* and *The Atlantis*, whose captain, before it was sunk, was none other than Captain Johann Fehler who we already met as the Captain of U-234 (5).

So what happened in Antarctica to Neuschwabenland in terms of development and a base there? There are many answers to this question with some of them seeming mutually exclusive. They cannot all be correct. We will take a look at a few of these ideas with some additional thoughts added.

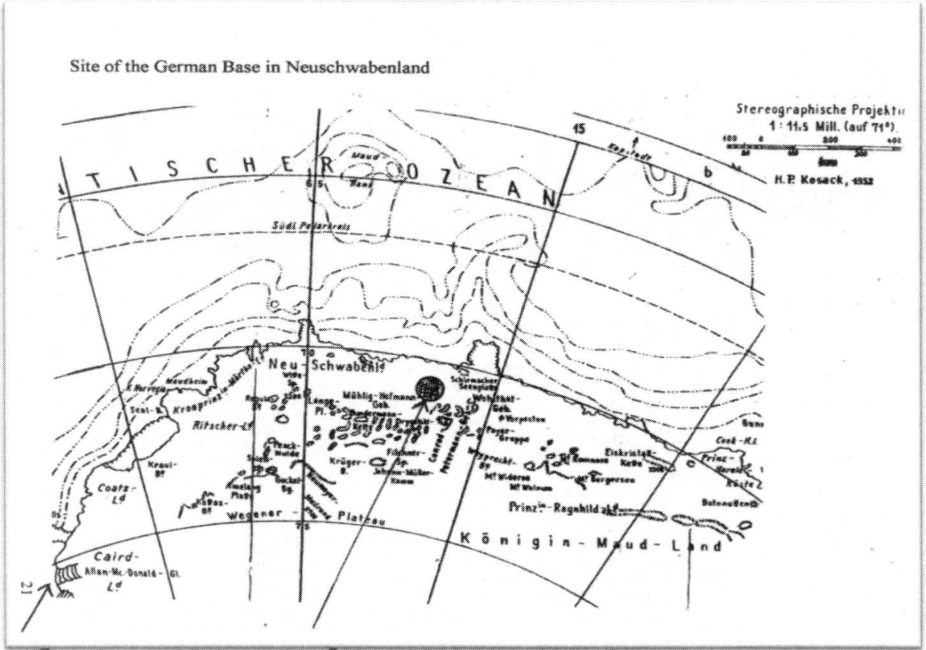

German Base of Neu-Schwabenland,
Point 222
From Haarmann, 1983

Coast of Antarctica

The ideas of Wilhelm Landig can serve as an overview. Wilhelm Landig saw the Ritcher Expedition as a military expedition cloaked as a scientific expedition. Its purpose, he says, was to find a suitable location for an Antarctic station. Starting in 1938, this station was built. After the evacuation of Point 103, aircraft as well as flying discs were relocated to the Antarctic station, which he names Point 211. Some of these flights were non-stop. All the personnel at Point 103 were relocated to Point 211. This must have included ships and U-boats although Landig does not specifically say so. This would also include survivors of the last sea battle with the British, called by Mattern "The Last Battalion". (6) To protect Point 211, Landig states that German flying discs, which he names "V-7" were employed. Also, Landig names a new weapon the Klystron-EG-Projector. Landig claims the air-burst atomic bombs detonated over Point 211 at the end of the 1950's were an attempt to knock out both these weapons using an electromagnet pulse. Landig tells us that the reason the Germans left Antarctica was not because they were forced out militarily, but because the germ-free environment of the Antarctic left the Germans there with weakened immunity systems that necessitated a return to an environment more heavily populated with humans. They relocated again to South America. Meanwhile, the United States and "weiteren interessierten Maechten", (further interested powers), signed a treaty on December 1, 1959 de-militarizing Antarctica. Landig is implying that one of these powers was the 3rd Power, or SS Nazis and their organization (7). Incidentally, yes, we will return to the subject of klystron tubes.

Deutsche Antarktische Expedition 1938/39

Fahrtteilnehmer:

Expeditionsleiter	Kapitän Alfred Ritscher
Kapitän des Schiffes	Alfred Kottas, DLH
Eislotse	Kapitän Otto Kraul
Schiffsarzt	Dr. Josef Bludau, NDL
Flugkapitän	Rudolf Mayr, Führer der Dornier-Wales „Passat", DLH
Flugzeugmechaniker	Franz Preuschoff, DLH
Flugfunker	Herbert Ruhnke, DLH
Luftbildner	Max Bundermann, Hansa Luftbild G. m. b. H.
Flugkapitän	Richardheinrich Schirmacher, Führer der Dornier-Wales „Boreas", DLH
Flugzeugmechaniker	Kurt Loesener, DLH
Flugfunker	Erich Gruber, DLH
Luftbildner	Siegfried Sauter, Hansa Luftbild G.m.b.H.
I. Meteorologe	Dr. Herbert Regula, Deutsche Seewarte, Hamburg
II. Meteorologe	Studienassessor Heinz Lange, R. f. W., Berlin
Techn. Assistent	Walter Krüger, R.f.W., Berlin
Techn. Assistent	Wilhelm Gockel, Marineobservatorium Wilhelmshaven
Biologe	Studienref. Erich Barkley, Reichsstelle für Fischerei (Institut für Walforschung)
Geophysiker	cand. geophys. Leo Gburek, Erdmagnetisches Institut, Leipzig
Geograph	Dr. Ernst Herrmann
Ozeanograph	cand. phil. Karl-Heinz Paulsen

I. Offizier	Herbert Amelang
II. Offizier	Karl-Heinz Röbke
III. Offizier	Hans Werner Viereck
IV. Offizier	Vincenz Grisar
Schiffsfunkleiter	Erich Harmsen
Schiffsfunkoffizier	Kurt Bojahr
Schiffsfunkoffizier	Ludwig Müllmerstadt
Leitender Ingenieur	Karl Uhlig
II. Ingenieur	Robert Schulz
III. Ingenieur	Henry Maas
IV. Ingenieur	Edgar Gäng
IV. Ingenieur	Hans Nielsen
Ing. Assistent	Johann Frey
Ing. Assistent	Georg Jelschen
Ing. Assistent	Heinz Siewert
Elektriker	Elektro-Ing. Herbert Bruns
Elektriker	Karl-Heinz Bode
Werkmeister	Herbert Bolle, DLH
Katapultführer	Wilhelm Hartmann, DLH
Lagerhalter	Alfred Rücker, DLH
Flugmechaniker	Franz Weiland, DLH
Flugmechaniker	Axel Mylius, DLH
Flugmechaniker	Wilhelm Lender, DLH
Bootsmann	Willy Stein
I. Zimmermann	Richard Wehrend
II. Zimmermann	Alfons Schäfer
Matrose	Heinz Hoek
Matrose	Jürgen Ulpts
Matrose	Albert Weber
Matrose	Adolf Kunze
Matrose	Karl Hedden
Matrose	Eugen Klenk
Matrose	Fritz Jedamczyk
Matrose	Emil Brandt
Matrose	Kurt Ohnemüller
Leichtmatrose	Alfred Peters
Decksjunge	Alex Burtscheid

A list of the German Personnel of the German Antarctic Expedition, 1938/39. Please note the names Heinz Sievert and Richard Wehrend, which are discussed in the text.

Writer/researcher O. Bergmann has done some very interesting research regarding the German base at Neuschwabenland. It seems that while giving lectures in Southern German lands, he met a merchant-navy captain who had occasionally served on both German speedboats and German submarines. In the course of his service towards the end of 1941 he met two German sailors by the name of Heinz Siewert and Richard Wehrend. Both had taken part in the 1938-1939 Ritcher Expedition to Antarctica. In fact, both their names appear of the list of personnel taking part in that expedition, Siewert being listed as an engineering assistant and Wehrend being listed as a carpenter.

These two sailors told the merchant-navy captain that after the return of the Ritcher Expedition to Germany, in the early part of the year of 1939, they again returned to Neuschwabenland on the ship Schwabenland and continued to do so four times a year in a regular to and fro rhythm from the home-port in Germany. The purpose of these voyages was to transport outfitting items and mining equipment to Antarctica. Among these were tracks for a railed line for trolleys and a huge milling machine used to bore tunnel systems in ice (8)

On the other hand, we have a story from Heiner Gehring and Karl-Heinz Zunneck (9). This was Heiner's last book and for it he read some of Wilhelm Landig's private archives. His partner for this book, Karl-Heinz Zunneck, has written an important book on secret German high technology and the finds at the Jonas Valley (10). This story involved a former officer in the "Gebirgsjaeger" the German mountain troops. The Gebirgsjaeger were sometimes Wehrmacht soldiers and sometimes SS soldiers. There was even a "Hoch-Gebirgsjaeger" or high mountain troops. In practice, they functioned as elite troops and turned up where ever the fighting was especially difficult, as did the Waffen SS. This account was included in their book along with the explanation that it came from an Internet discussion forum and that the entry was no longer available on the internet. Nevertheless, the authors felt the message deserves a hearing, so a translation is as follows:

> *"I was the police constable for the Gebirgsjaeger from 1942 to 1945 on a base with the official designation of Base 221 in the Antarctic area of Neuschwabenland. This base was established in the late summer of 1939 and served as the airfield for the control of the South Pacific from the air. During the whole three years which I was there three FW 200 Condors and several Me 109s were lying around, segmented, which were never mounted due to the lack of certain pieces of the engine which were necessary for the Antarctic climate.*
>
> *The Base 211, three kilometers inland, was provided twice a year with supplies and a change of personnel by U-boat. Half-tracked vehicles saw to the transportation from the coast to the base. All in all, by the end of the war there were 300 men stationed there, among these 70 belonged to the Luftwaffe and the remainder Gebirgsjaeger for the security of the facility.*
>
> *After the collapse of the German military radio-news-network, nobody knew what was happening. As a start, in the middle of July 1945, there appeared a British destroyer group that delivered the news of the end of the war. These*

ships brought the crew to Australia, everything else remained back there and may very well still lay there."

The careful reader may have noticed that the witness names "Base 221" as well as "Base 211". I do not know if this is a simple mistake; that is certainly possible. Or, it could also mean two bases, one that is an air base, and one further inland that is more of a naval base. If the later is the case then it is possible that the personnel of the more inland base were never evacuated by the British. It is also possible that all facilities there were evacuated, leaving the runways, underground base and machinery intact and waiting for reactivation that occurred in 1946 as Landig says.

In addition to the German raiders operating in the South Atlantic, Gehring and Zunneck tell us of at least one secret U-boat operation in Antarctic waters. This operation involved U-2603 under Korvettenkapitaen Horst Ristoff in the years 1943/44 (11). The purpose of this operation still remains cloaked in secrecy.

Now we turn to the nature of the base in Neuschwabenland as writers Colonel Howard A. Buechner and Kapitan Wilhelm Bernhart see it in their two books on the subject from the late 1980's.

Howard Buechner was a Colonel in the US Army, a medical doctor and a Professor of Medicine at both Tulane University and L.S.U. During the Second World War Colonel Buechner was with the 3rd Battalion, 157th Infantry Regiment, 45th Infantry Division which drove deep into Thuringia. Colonel Buechner was the first medical doctor to enter Dachau concentration camp.

Captain Wilhelm Bernhart is a pen name. In fact, this man was a junior officer aboard U-530. The full crew of U-530 is listed, including the junior officers; he is obviously one of these men. Since at the time of publication, Captain Bernhart lived in the USA, it would certainly be simple enough to locate him if one had the inclination, but what would be the purpose in doing so given that Colonel Buechner is obviously vouching for him?

Captain Bernhart says in the texts of these books that U-530, before surrendering at Mar del Plata, Argentina on July 17, 1945, two months after the war in Europe ended, voyaged to Antarctica beginning in March, 1945 where sixteen men put ashore and deposited relics of the 3rd Reich in a reinforced ice cave. One of these relics was the Spear of Longinus. This is the Christian holy relic said to have pierced the side of Jesus as he was dying on the cross. Captain Bernhard claims to have been one of those sixteen men who actually deposited these relics on shore in Antarctica (12). It then sailed to Argentina for its surrender. U-977, which surrendered at Mar del Plata on August 17, 1945, or one month later than U-530, sailed from Kristiansand, Norway, in the dying moments of the 3rd Reich, after receiving an air shipment containing the ashes of Adolf Hitler (13), bound for the same destination.

The site of this activity was a natural ice cave in the Muhling-Hofmann Mountains. These are the mountains described earlier as intersecting the fault line on the coast of Antarctica. We are told in the text that this cave was visited in the spring of 1943 by a

German U-boat whose mission was to build and install a large steel-reinforced door over the mouth of the cave (14). The location of the cave was further given as approximately 71 degrees, 30 minutes south by 14 degrees, 51 minutes west (15).

At this point things get somewhat confusing since this was evidently not the location of the base at Neuschwabenland. The writers describe it as follows:

> *"As previously indicated, plans for establishing a permanent base in Antarctica had been formulated as early as 1938. By the middle of 1940 submarines were bringing in vast stores of food, clothing, fuel and every other conceivable item necessary for setting up Hitler's refuge. Construction material, tractors, arms, distillation apparatus, machinery, radio equipment, personnel, engineers and scientists were included. During the next four years shelters were built and a mountain was scooped out. Here a facsimile of Hitler's "Eagle's Nest" home in Berchtesgarden was constructed.*
>
> *Inside this magic mountain Hitler and his staff would be able to grow fruits and vegetables and raise cattle and poultry in artificially heated beds and pastures of enriched soil. Everything was completely camouflaged. Here it would be possible for a large group of people to live for many years." (16)*

Besides the cargo of artifacts, it is claimed by these writers that Martin Bormann was a passenger aboard U-530 (17). Also, claims of an exotic propulsion system or an exotic component of the propulsion system have been made for U-530 (18). We will take this up in detail in our discussion of U-boats.

One question that has not been answered or even addressed is the exact relationship between Adolf Hitler and the Spear of Longinus. Trevor Ravencroft made much of this relationship in his book Spear of Destiny. The legend is that after piercing the body of Jesus, this spear point became an object of power. Any military leader—so the legend goes—who possessed this spear point was destined to rule and vanquish his rivals. This scenario seems to have applied to some famous German kings and even some Holy Roman emperors. Hitler, it is said, became fascinated with this relic as it stood on display in the Hofburg Palace and to have visited it many times in his days in Vienna before the First World War. On March 12, 1938, the day of "Anschluss", the day of Germany's unification with Austria, Hitler drove into Vienna, straight to the room which housed the Holy Lance, took it and made it his.

The question in all this is why would Adolf Hitler, who was not only a non-Christian but had anti-Christian leanings, venerate a Christian icon? If Hitler rejected Christianity, then this rejection would extend to Christian relics as objects of power, would it not? There is simply no power there for non-Christians.

This question always nagged at me after reading Trevor Ravencroft, and bothered me even more after reading Buechner and Bernhart. Not being a religious person, I began questioning anyone who might provide some clarity. Finally, I found Georg Breckmann who gave me an explanation (19). He laughed and said it was really not the Spear of

Longinus but instead the Spear of Odin. He went on to say, paraphrasing his words, that veneration of a spear would have been a pagan concept transposed into the Christian world. After all, Christians do not look upon weapons as objects of power. The symbolism using a spear represents Odin's pinpoint intellect but uses a martial object in keeping with his martial character. Famous weapons were given names in these times but even if this was not the true weapon Odin wielded the concept behind the symbol was a pagan one and one that was appropriated by the early Christians because it was familiar to the population they were trying to convert.

Unfortunately, I heard nothing of these words the first time around because his statement mentioning the "Spear of Odin" hit me like a lightening bolt. I had heard a lecture on Odin from an anthropologist while in college who presented the opinion that Odin was actually a real person, a war leader, who was then elevated to a divine status. The theory is drawn from a combination of archaeology, linguistics and cultural/social anthropology. I found a summary of this concept by and anthropology professor from 1939. This is Professor Carleton Coon in his book Races of Europe, page 322:

> *"Let us turn for a moment to consider the historical work of Snorre Sturlason. This erudite scholar deals with the gods as if they were men and treats their mythical actions as history. His rationalization seems to have been uncannily accurate. In the first place, Asgard, the home of the gods, was a town on the northern shore of the Black Sea. These gods fought a people called the vanir, with whom they eventually agreed to exchange hostages. Odin, the king of the gods, agreed to take Frey and Freya, two of the vanar, and these were soon deified along with their hosts. The gods then left Asgard; and moved northwestward; they sojourned in Denmark, and passed without much ado into Sweden. This country became their main home, and Uppsala their chief center. Odin worship, which arose among their descendants, the kings and jarls, was centered especially in this neighborhood and the worship of Frey and Freya as well.*
>
> *Thor, who was a rough-and-tumble bucolic god, is little mentioned in this Asgardian history; he was apparently an earlier god and the especial deity of the coastal people of Norway. Odin was a sophisticated personage, wearing a finely woven blue cape and carrying an iron spear; Thor, who clothed himself in skins, carried a hammer as his weapon, and drove about in a goat-drawn chariot. If we grant that Odin was the chief god brought in by the Iron Age invaders, and surrounded with their classically-inspired trappings of luxury, then Thor was apparently the god of the older people of the carl class and he represents in his person and attributes a blend between the robust Mesolithic hunters and fisherman, and the Megalithic and Corded people."*

Odin was a god of applied intelligence, on an off the battlefield. He is credited with bringing writing, in the form of the runes, to Northern Europe. But more importantly, Odin is the only Norse god of which I know who was associated with the spear and this is not an association that comes to mind with Jesus.

Returning to the Spear itself, the study of Bronze Age let alone Iron Age weapons is complex beyond description. But even if this spear turned out to be of Roman origin, traded and eventually reaching the shores of the Black Sea, that would only increase its value and potential war-power in this northern cultural fringe region. Odin's Spear can be imagined as a long lance with Odin's personal banner attached to it, riding in his chariot or carried by him on horseback, and serving as a rallying point for his troops.

There are precedents for the elevation of a war leader to a god in Indo-European culture. At the other end of the Indo-European world, in India, the invading Aryans deified at least one of their war leaders. This was Indra. Indra not only became a Hindu god but was somehow adopted by at least some Buddhists as I personally have seen a statue of Indra in a Buddhist temple in Thailand. Then, of course, there is Julius Ceasar who was deified by his Roman people. This idea of Odin as a flesh and blood person is not a new one and was certainly around in the 1930's.

When the Christians entered Northern Europe they met with considerable resistance in their conversion efforts. As they did elsewhere, the Christians adopted pagan items of culture and called them their own in an effort to induce conversion using cultural familiarity. In this way the Yule was re-branded as Christmas and Easter took on a Christian veneer. Pagan sites were destroyed and churches built on their ruins. It would not be surprising if a venerated pagan spear was simply appropriated by the Christians and given a new history. Later, the Spear was split in half and a nail, allegedly a nail from Christ's cross, was inserted in an effort to legitimize the artifact.

Remember, this scenario does not have to be correct, it only has to be plausible in the eyes of Adolf Hitler. If I could hear the tale of the Spear of Odin in California, halfway around the world from its display case in Vienna, you can bet that Adolf Hitler heard this story also in a world where the Spear was a major topic of conversation.

Returning to Buechner and Bernhart, my guess in reading their work is that these two were devout Christians and that this was at least partial motivation for their books. This seems to be so since they claim that an expedition was made in 1979 to Antarctica which recovered the Spear of Longinus, the urn containing part of Hitler's ashes, and other artifacts of those times. Some of these items are pictured in their books. Their position is that the spear that was returned to its case in Austria after the war is a fake. The problem is that there were more than two versions of the disposition of the Spear and so like other religious objects in dispute, we may never reach a final truth.

From here we move to yet another explanation of events in German Antarctica. Actually, there are a whole set of survival theories involving a continued Nazi presence at the South Pole. These range from that pole being a gateway to a hollow earth world to a the vast underground city of New Berlin. Dr. Michael E. Salla incorporates some of these things plus the idea that the Nazis were aided in post-war Antarctica by extraterrestrials which they originally contacted years before using telepathy after recovering a crashed alien saucer.

Dr. Salla has a political/foreign affairs orientation by education and profession. His presentation of these ideas follows along these lines. He presents these thoughts in a paper entitled *Foundations for Globally Managing Extraterrestrial Affairs—The Legacy of the Nazi Germany-Extraterrestrial Connection* (20). What will be done is a thumbnail summary of this paper and some comments on controversial and interesting aspects of it.

According to Dr. Salla, the Nazis began communication with at least one extraterrestrial species (ET) in the 1930s using a method we would call channeling. This is really nothing new as we have all heard of the alleged experiments in this field done by the Vril Society. In fact, Dr. Salla references the video film detailing all this, UFO Secrets of the 3rd Reich (which he references as "Secrets of the Third Reich"). To this he adds that the Germans recovered an alien saucer crash in 1936 or 1938 (depending on the story), either in what is now Silesia, Poland, or in the Black Forest of Southern Germany. As authority for this he references Robert Lesniakiewicz in a work titled: "The UFO Crashes in Poland" and an internet site referencing the words "Omega File: Nazi History" (21). The Nazis busy themselves back-engineering ET technology into their war effort. Naturally, the Allies are terrified and the Germans are emboldened. Well, in spite of all the help, things do not go that well for the Germans and they are forced to flee to Antarctica and South America with their newly developed flying discs, based on ET technology. The Allies counter with Admiral Byrd's failed Operation Highjump, by trying to scoop up all the German scientists they can find, by obtaining all the German technology they can get their hands on and by forming an alliance, a secret alliance, between themselves under UN auspices to contain the Nazis/ET enemy. The policy agreed upon included provisions of: 1. Non-Disclosure of Extraterrestrial Affairs, 2. Non-Disclosure of the ET-Nazi Connection and Countering Nazi Influence in South America, 3. Repatriation of Nazi Scientists/technologies and continuing Nazi Sponsored Human Projects, 4. Managing Extraterrestrial Artifacts Found Around the Planet, and 5. Cooperating to End the Nazi Threat. The whole matter is treated and presented as a policy paper and this itself is unique in my experience.

Some interesting ideas leap out at us from this discussion. The late Heiner Gehring wrote to me that he had been told that the efforts of the Vril Society at channeling continued after the war, until 1946. It is no secret that in the lore propounded by Ralf Ettl and Norbert Juergen-Ratthofer elements of the Nazi regime allegedly associated with the Vril Society launched an interdimensional flight to an extraterrestrial world seeking help in the Second World War. This flight communicated, allegedly, via medial transmission (or channeling). This medial contact, according to Heiner's source, continued until 1946 with the living crew of that ship when it was abruptly terminated. Of course, there is no way to verify any of this.

Another theme rampant in the UFO world is the idea that there are divisions within the US military and or US intelligence that work against each other. Usually, the reporting entity picks the side most aligned with his or her special interest group and then makes the other side the "bad guy". Here are Dr. Salla's words calling for an inquiry based on the work of one of these "whistle blowers":

"...Such official inquiries are needed to make the pubic more aware of how Nazi principles have infiltrated into the key national institutions responsible for managing ET affairs, and the threat his poses to democratic values and institutions. Evidence for infiltration of Nazi principles in the decision making bodies on ET affairs is given by whitlelowers such as dr. Michael Wolf who claims that "within the UFO Cover-Up here is a dark, covert renegade organization known as the 'Cabal'. He describes it as a 'well-orchestrated conspiratorial bevy of plotters... top heavy with the military, and headed by (a Navy Under-Secretary).' He claims that the 'paranoiac Cabal works against and deliberately undermines, the goals of peaceful negotiations with the extraterrestrial visitors."

There are probably many cabals. Alternatively, there are rumors of inter-agency fights. I strongly suspect that detractors or their sponsors of one particular cabal or another have issues to grind with the foreign policy orientation or alleged orientation of that agency which are totally unrelated to the UFO world and which Dr. Salla, speaking from a geopolitical perspective, ought to understand better than anyone. The Nazis may be the flash point eliciting this type of response but the underlying issues are of a more current nature and only tangential involve the Nazis.

Dr. Salla discusses mind control experimentation which certainly may have begun with the Nazis but undoubtedly flowered in the USA. He cites Andy Pero who mentioned some interesting things in experiments designed to optimize performance and so produce super-soldiers:

"I have also been used in the Montauk chair while at camp Hero, Montauk, and also in a chair in Atlanta, GA at Dobbins Air Force Base... The trainers would put me into a trance whereby I'd be told I could jump off a ladder of minimal height. In my mind, I believed that I was only jumping off a footstool or a short ledge. In actuality, I was progressively led to jump higher and higher heights to the point of successfully jumping off buildings and even out of planes without a parachute. When under mind control, I could do whatever I was instructed to do as long as I believed them. I would do 200 or more push ups in perfect form, sometimes as long as half hour straight, or until I was told to stop. I weight lifted 545 lb. on a barbell and squats while attending college and much more (500-1500 lb.) while I was under the mind control in training laboratory not far from Rochester, NY."

Training of super-soldiers to jump out of airplanes without the need of a parachute, even going low and slow is quite an achievement and certainly stunning news.

But the weak point in this presentation is in the premise that a crashed ET saucer resulted in some great leap forward for the Germans. I could find no such information in either web site cited. This may be due to the transitory nature of the Internet. There was mention of a crash in Poland and/or the Black Forest in the British UFO magazine but the wording was so vague and imprecise that I paid no attention to it whatsoever. It looked like a promotion of some article that would be written later, containing the facts. I have corresponded with Robert Lesniakiewicz and read his book on the subject of the 3rd

Reich's alleged interaction with extraterrestrials (21). At no time has he ever mentioned this crash to me but this information may exist or exist in another publication that I have not seen.

Now we turn to everyone's favorite Neuschwabenland tale: Britain's Secret War in Antarctica by James Robert. (23) This is actually a series of three articles appearing in Nexus magazine. This is probably the most exciting article ever written on the subject and one cannot help but believe this is by design. It reads like an adventure novel. It should be recommended if for nothing but its literary value alone. So, rather than review it and spoil the ending, what will be done here is to do the set up, as Mr. Robert did in the article, and then mention two or three aspects of it which are of importance to our discussion before moving on to a particular and controversial aspect which we will deal with just for fun.

James Robert's biography at the end of the article tells us he is a real guy. He is a civil servant for the UK Ministry of Defense as well as a World War Two historian and writer. His family has a military background. Mr. Robert has spent considerable time and gone to some expense in travel researching his history topics. The biography promises us a book and lists an email contact address that is no longer functioning. The central character and informant was an unnamed SAS soldier, active in the Second World War who Mr. Robert interviewed twice over a ten-year span of time.

The meat of the article starts out with the British Operation Taberlan. This was a wartime effort to monitor German activity in Antarctica. Yes, the British also had bases there and did detect the German base at Neuschwabenland. After the war, the British said nothing about what they suspected was on-going activity there by the Nazis. What is meant by "saying nothing" was they said nothing to the Americans, French or Russians. According to Mr. Robert, the British felt a little insecure concerning their share of German high technology recovered by the Allies. They also wanted a propaganda victory if, in fact, the Nazis were in Antarctica since they could then claim to have won the last battle of World War Two all by themselves.

The set up to the story is that our SAS soldier was not sent on the first mission. The first mission had apparently failed and his small force was the backup. The first mission radioed a garbled, confusing message for some time. There was a German military presence at Neuschwabenland, complete with an access tunnel leading to the Nazi stronghold. Only two survivors escaped back out of the Nazi base. In July 1945, all contact was lost after the final message said, in fear "the Polar Men have found us".

Well, the SAS man and his cohorts were trained in polar survival and then parachuted to within striking range of the German base. They gained access through a long, man-made tunnel and found a huge cavern, artificially illuminated with docks for U-boats and hangars for some sort of high tech aircraft. The facility was powered geothermally with a secondary power source of unknown origin. The mission was to blow this facility up.

Standing in their way, besides the German guards, were the Polar Men. These Polar Men were of unknown origin although it is said they were the products of Nazi science. They were completely covered in hair and possessed resistance to the intense cold. They also ate human flesh.

The remaining tale is about the mission and the attempt of escape thereafter. Some points should be made assuming, of course, the tale is true. First, it should be pointed out that the reason for the particular location of this base has everything to do with geology and energy. The cavern may have been a volcanic bubble but the geothermal activity is certainly associated with the fault line. Just as with the lignite at Beaver Dam, the Germans chose this side because they could take advantage of an existing energy source. Without this energy source already being in place, it is doubtful that any long-term presence could have been maintained.

What is unnecessary to this tale are the Polar Men. The Polar Men actually add nothing to the facts presented in this story. Since they add nothing to the fact-pattern and serve as a gateway to attack the story and the story certainly could be told without them, only two reasons present themselves. First, they are added to spice up the story, a sort of Guns of Navarone meets the Abominable Snowman. As such as ploy it certainly succeeds! But the second alternative is that this was exactly the way it was described to Mr. Robert. In other words, it is the truth regardless of how it sounds.

Nexus magazine does not print fictional stories so they must have done some checking on Mr. Robert. Assuming they did and found his biography or at least the more verifiable portions, like his employment at the UK Ministry of Defense, checked out, we are left with the problem that this portion of the tale may be true, that the Germans enlisted the assistance of an unknown race of hairy, cold-tolerant men who functioned as security guards for them in this environment. According to the tale, the British did manage to kill one Polar Man and he was a man, only covered in fur growing right out of his skin. But, because of the tale's internal weakness involving the Polar Men and without positive proof for their existence, this story is improbably and that is that.

There is the idea that hairy, cold-tolerant men could be produced using "Nazi science". The mechanisms for hair growth and cold-tolerance may exist somewhere in the human gnome. There is some evidence that Neanderthals and their ancestors were cold tolerant. For instance, within their caves fireplaces were not set up to maximize heat distribution within the living area and within that area it does not look like Neanderthals used the fire pits as their focus of attention as did modern humans. Also, we can all imagine Neanderthals and their earlier ancestors as having much more hair than do modern Europeans. Even if this is not a direct carry-over from a more primitive primate condition, Neanderthals would have needed this additional protection against the cold and so selection pressure would have existed to develop this independently and secondarily of the original hair loss.

The problem with "Nazi science" as an agent of activation for these characteristics is that the underlying genes for these traits would have had to have been activated and the structure of DNA was not known for certain until Watson and Crick in the early 1960's. Watson proposed the double helix in 1953 but it was one of several competing proposals. For instance Dr. Linius Pauling, who won two undivided Nobel Prizes, proposed a triple helix at the time. Without knowing the structure of DNA it would be impossible to manipulate and transfer individual genes.

So if these Polar Men were not created in a lab, then where did they come from? The next obvious avenue would be Tibet. Did the Germans capture a few abominable snowmen in their expeditions there? We know Ernst Schaefer looked for them and looked hard. According to Reinhardt Messner and speaking on a recent American television program, a 2009 show called Monster Quest, on the yeti, the famous Austrian mountain climber and old Himalayan-hand, says that Schaefer followed alleged tracks of a yeti to a cave in the Himalayas and shot two animals leaving that cave at its mouth. They turned out to be a kind of bear, a mother and child. Schaefer's widow gave Messner both skulls shortly after Schaefer's death. Schaefer, according to Messner, was afraid to tell the Ahnenerbe since they were hoping the yeti would turn out to be some kind or Aryan ancestor. But he did tell Messner, who wrote a book on the yeti, claiming they were a kind of bear, bigger than "our" brown bear with longer hair. Well, this description may lend itself to the thinking that these were not exactly what would be described as normal bears, these being the brown bear which exists throughout northern Eurasia and North America. What might fit this overall description of a cave-living, non-brown bear is the cave bear of Pleistocene Europe, Ursus selaeus, made famous in the novels of Jean Auel. This bear lived in caves at mid-elevations in the Alps. It might yet survive in remote Himalayan valleys since it was probably made extinct when Neanderthals ousted it from its home, caves, which they also sought to inhabit. Neanderthals did not extend eastward into Tibet. (http://en.wikipedia.org/wiki/Cave_bear)

Besides, how would the Germans ever get several yeti out of Tibet? We are back to the transportation problem involving British-controlled India and the Ju-390 verses the flying disc discussion. It must have been hard enough to get those monks out.

So we are left wondering where on earth the Germans would find a small populaton of primitive humans, ice age relics, and how would they be transported to Antarctica? Are there any possibilities here at all? Well, maybe, but it is a long stretch.

The theory goes that when modern humans entered Europe from the east, they slowly pushed the Neanderthals to the West and to the North. The last Neanderthals lived on the Atlantic fringes of Western Europe, up to 25,000 years ago. Prior to the Neanderthals, and ancestral to them, were a grade of human known as Homo heidelbergensis, "Heidelberg Man". Of course as Neanderthals took hold of glacial Europe, the older types were also pushed to the fringes just as they were pushed by modern man. During the ice age, all the polar land masses were connected by ice. It was possible to walk from Norway to Russia to Siberia, to Alaska, to Canada, to Greenland and then back to Norway without ever getting wet. So if early human species were pushed westward by incoming, more modern humans, then the place to look for early human relic populations would be in the land masses of the uninhabited North. Of course everywhere is inhabited but to make a long story short, the least inhabited area in the far North is Greenland and we already know the Germans had bases in Greenland. So the question becomes: is there any evidence for relic human people in Greenland. Well, again—*maybe.*

Cryptozoologist Mark A. Hall has collected Eskimo legends of the race that inhabited Greenland before them. In one report, Hall describes them as large, very strong and covered in hair. Old Viking legends, based on a man who had lived with the Eskimos in Greenland, say that these "trolls" still exist in the deep fjords of Greenland, living in caves.

Hall has also reopened an anthropological controversy from the 1920's, the Gardar skull. It seems that a portion of the skull and half a jaw of an extremely primitive looking human were found in a 12th Century Viking graveyard in Greenland at Gardar. Professor F.C.C. Hansen, University of Copenhagen, thought they belonged to a "throw-back", exhibiting the archaic phenotype of something close to "Rhodesian man". Indeed, if anything they look even more bestial. But Sir Arthur Keith, the leading voice in terms of human evolution of his day, looked at the pictures of the remains and Hansen's drawings and concluded they belonged to an acromegalic, a person suffering from a tumor of the pituitary gland, causing an overproduction of human growth hormone. Hansen died shortly thereafter, and so, Sir Arthur having spoken, the skull and whole affair were put in museum storage.

Perhaps an argument can be made against acromegaly; there are some inconsistencies. Keith's argument does not compare apples to oranges, as he uses a "giant", a person who developed a pituitary abnormality while very young and compares it to the Gardar remains, an individual of normal height and so affected after adulthood with the growth hormone overproduction. I say this is not comparing apples to oranges but it is comparing oranges to lemons. But any argument I could make would be less than 100 percent conclusive. The only such argument is a DNA test. An attempt will be made here to refute the acromegaly diagnosis of Keith, hoping that it might lead to further testing while combining two of my favorite subjects, cryptozoology/hominid relic survival and hidden Nazi history.

First, could a population of primitive humans have made contact with modern humans in the 12th Century? The Gardar skull was found in a Christian cemetery dating from that time. But, evidently, this individual was not entirely alone. In a sentence written by P.O. Pedersen who examined and photographed the remains in 1941, he says, as quoted in a website:

> *"The Gardar skull may be an extreme example of this "beserker" stock but similar less pronounced specimens have been recovered in the same cemetery."*

(http://www.cladonia.co.uk/acromegaly/though-the-ages.html)

If true this cuts the odds against the Gardar remains being pathological as the chances of finding two or more in the same burial are remote indeed.

If we take all these improbable eventualities and combine them, a group of such primitive, hairy, cold-tolerant humans could have been enlisted by the Vikings at Gardar as well as by the Nazis in World War Two as servants or slaves or just as body guards. We already know the Germans had an extensive presence on Greenland. They could have been moved to Antarctica by ship.

I have always had sympathy for Mark A. Hall's position in the cryptozoological sense. Mark Hall offers no anatomical argument countering Keith. Now, with the Gardar remains being the only possible link to the veracity of the Polar Men that I can find, some sort of countering, anatomical argument is in order.

So let us be clear about the positions of all involved:

> *Hansen*: Gardar is a "throw-back" to Rhodesian Man, now called Homo heidelbergensis.
>
> *Keith:* Gardar is a modern human with a growth hormone disorder, acromegaly.
>
> *Hall:* Gardar represents a relic population of H. heidelbergensis, rare but still living.
>
> *My Position (or at least the position I am arguing):* Gardar is a representative of H. heidelbergenis or H. neanderthalensis, probably the latter. (H. heidelbergensis was ancestral to H. neanderthalensis.) A small group of these men could have been captured by the Germans in Greenland, "domesticated", and their cold-adaptability used in their Antarctic base.

My burden: To show Keith's explanation inadequate, opening up the possibility of Hall's explanation and my position. To show Keith's explanation inadequate, I must show the abnormalities of the Gardar skull, in the ways they differ from skulls of modern humans, are not caused by an overproduction of growth hormone, but are unique to Neanderthals and so not caused by acromegaly.

Since the condition of acromegaly is central to this discussion, it ought to be defined and discussed. Acromegaly is a syndrome that results in the pituitary gland producing an excess amount of human growth hormone after the epiphyses plate closes at puberty. A number of disorders may increase the pituitary gland's human growth hormone output. Acromegaly most commonly affects adults in middle age and can result in disfigurement and even premature death. It is a disorder of slow progression. Acromegaly is associated with gigantism.

Gigantism is caused by an access amount of human growth hormone in children. Since it occurs in childhood, unlike acromegaly, it causes excessive height, from 2.1 to 2.8 m or from 6 feet 11 inches to 8 feet 11 inches. The difference between acromegaly and gigantism is one of development at the time excessive growth hormone occurs. If elevated growth hormone levels occur before the epiphyses close, gigantism occurs. If elevated growth hormone levels occur after the epiphyses close, acromegaly occurs. (http://en.wikipedia.org/wki/Acromegaly). The epiphyses are the spongy ends of the bones at which point those bones grow. A definition of adulthood might contain, for instance, mention of the epiphyses closing.

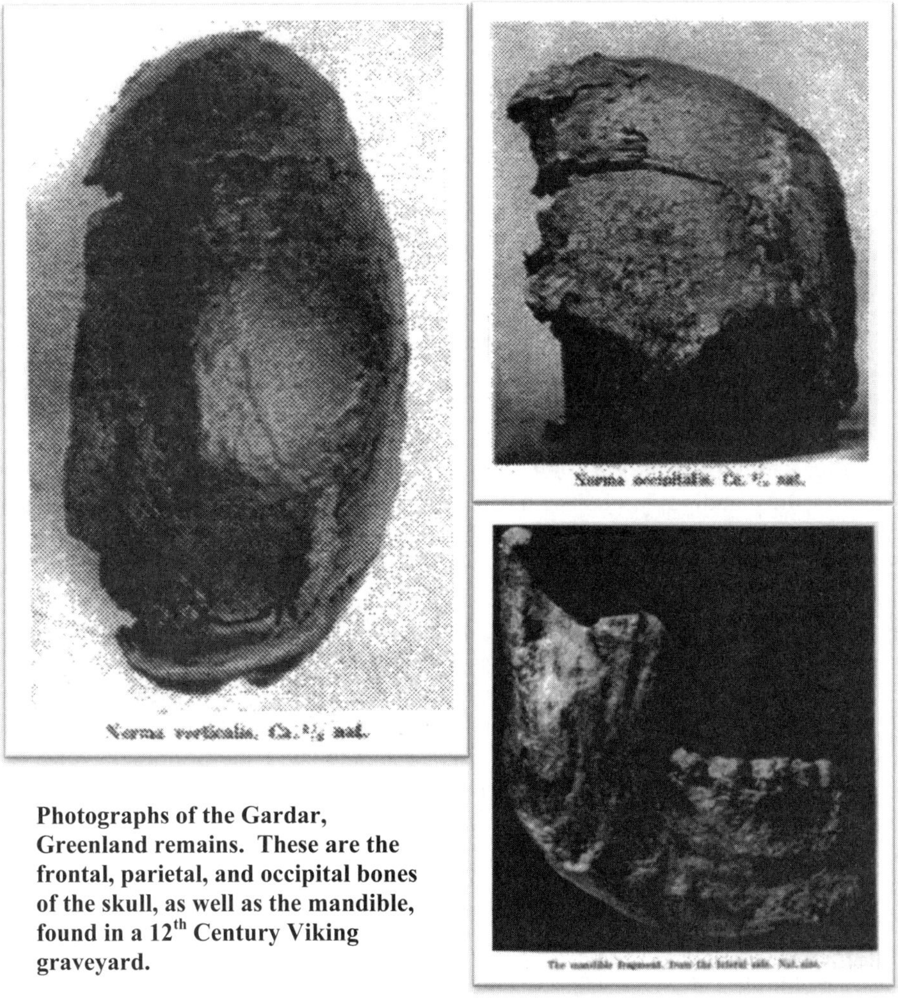

Photographs of the Gardar, Greenland remains. These are the frontal, parietal, and occipital bones of the skull, as well as the mandible, found in a 12th Century Viking graveyard.

So we have two related conditions, acromegaly proper and gigantism. The difference is the developmental stage of the individual when the syndrome started, adult or child. If it happened first during childhood, the individual would be very tall, over 6 feet 11 inches.

We should look at the symptoms of acromegaly. They are:

- *Swelling of soft tissue, hands, feet, ears, etc.. (We need not go on here since we have no soft tissue)*
- *Swelling of the soft tissue of the internal organs. (Again, we have none so it is irrelevant for us)*
- *Expansion of the skull at the fontanelle. (these are the soft spots on a newborn child's skull)*
- *Pronounced brow protrusion.*
- *Pronounced lower jaw protrusion, enlarged tongue, gapping between the teeth.*
- *Increased hair growth, darkening of the skin, increased sweating.*

Given we have half a jaw bone with premolars and molars only, no face, a partial skull with portions of the parietal, frontal, occipital and temporal bones and one femur which is undescribed except for its length, many of these criteria do not apply here. In general the bones of the face grow larger and longer and the nose increases in width. So increased growth hormone production would make an individual "look" more like a member of a pre-sapiens species in general. What we need are characteristics unaffected by increased growth hormone and specific to non-sapiens or pre-sapiens men.

Sir Arthur Keith, (February 5, 1866—January 7, 1955) was a medical doctor and one, if not the leading, authority of his time in terms of human anatomy and evolutionary theory. In his book The Antiquity of Man, Keith discusses the Gradar remains and makes an argument for acromegaly. But he does this largely by comparing the Gardar remains to a contemporary but deceased individual who was a giant in life. As mentioned above, this is not a wholly satisfactory comparison. Keith moves point-by-point making an argument of comparison to the skull of the dead giant and refuting Hanson. He lines up both skulls centering them of the three molars of the Gardar mandible. He compares the skull of his giant to that of Gardar, an individual of about six feet in height; a much smaller individual. But, because of space constraints, the fact that our primary concern in this book is recent history, not paleoanthropology, and simply because new methods of differentiating modern humans from archaic humans is now available, please forgive me if I save the complete rebuttal for another time and place and go directly to the new evidence not available to Keith.

Usually, an anthropologist can simply eyeball a skull and determine its place in terms of human evolution. This is sometimes called an evolutionary grade. We know examples of evolutionary grades by the names Homo erectus, H. heidelbergensis, H. neanderthalensis, H. sapiens, and so on. But, some anthropologists, in trying to infuse more scientific rigor to the discipline, have come up with objective methods to tell one species from another. We will look at two of these and discuss some species-specific traits applicable to the bones we have.

First, there is Carleton Coon's method of differentiating Homo erectus from Homo sapiens using arcs and cords. The effort dates to 1962 and was published in Coon's The

Origin of Races, page 342. Coon uses the markers recognized on the human skull by anatomists and connects them with lines. Nasion (upper margin of the nasal bones, located between the eyes) to Bregma (meeting of the frontal bone and parietal bones on the centerline of the skull), to the Lambda (meeting of the parietal bones and the occipital bone on the centerline of the skull) to the Opisthion (the rearward edge of the foramen magnum at the centerline of the skull). The foramen magnum is simply the hole through which the spinal cord enters the brain. Coon points to the difference between the straight lines of the cords with the skull contours that form the arcs and says that in the two human species there is a definite difference. He says:

> *"Homo sapiens is more curved in the frontal and parietal segments than Homo erectus; the opposite is true of the occipital segment."*

This is a description of head shape in which sapiens heads are rounded like a melon and erectus heads are made up of flatter angles, more like an American football, except the rear end of the skull is more rounded in erectus. Look at Hansen's reconstruction of the Gardar skull, which Keith uses. Clearly, the Gardar skull is more like the erectus skull and even more extreme in this than the example posted by Coon. Now, we do not have the exact Nasion since it is missing, nor do we have the Opisthion since the bottom of the skull is missing. We can estimate and if we did all the evidence would point to the skull being Homo erectus, even with the most generous estimates. But that is not proper evidence. We have one of the three arc-cords, the Bregma to Lambda cord-arc and it clearly is Homo erectus in character, being even more primitive than the Neanderthal condition.

Let us take a look at the Gardar jaw. We have most of the right half of the mandible, minus the chin and incisor teeth. We have the two premolars and three molars. Please note that the teeth are touching one another and not spaced apart as individual teeth as in the case of an acromegalic. Next, please note the space between the third molar, the wisdom tooth, and the ascending portion of the jaw. This space is called the retromolar space and is a Neanderthal diagnostic trait. It is not found before Neanderthals or after them. If a jaw were found today in Europe, for instance, and it possessed this gap, it would be instantly suspected of being from a Neanderthal. Even the famous Mauer mandible (from Heidelberg man) has no such gap and it is this species, Homo heidelbergensis that is believed to have been ancestral to the Neanderthals. Open your own mouth and look into the mirror at your lower jaw. If you have your third molar(s) intact, you will see the rearward margin of those teeth are behind the ascending ramus of your jaw, seen only by its flesh pink coating. If you were a Neanderthal, there would be a gap between the rearward border of this tooth and the beginning of the ascending ramus of the jawbone.

Now let us look at a set of criteria specifically formulated for sorting out Neanderthals from non-Neanderthals. This set of criteria was brought to me by the legendary Internet anthropologist, known only by the initials "C.A.". This occurred when I was fortunate enough to have had a small part in one of her projects. This set of criteria was originally formulated by Albert Santa Luca and Jean-Jacques Hublin in 1978. Please see diagram. (from Ian Tattersall's The Last Neanderthal The Rise, Success, and Mysterious

Extinction, page 118). As the reader can see, these are really overlooked little bumps and valleys on the skull. And most of these little bumps and valleys are at the rear of the skull, precisely the portion we have.

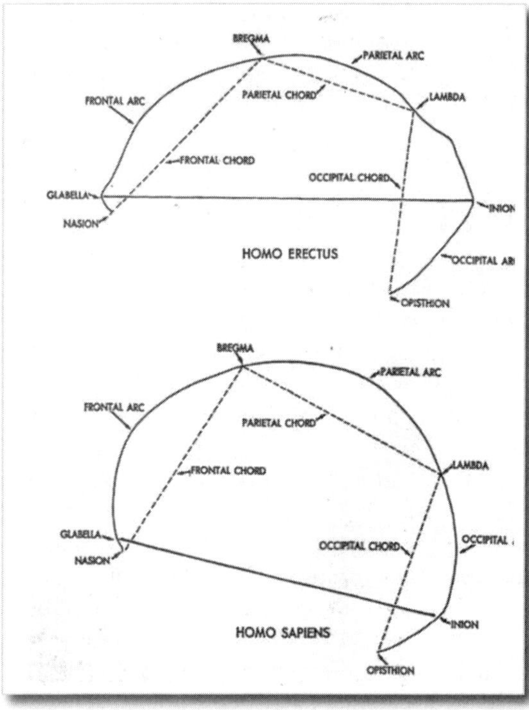

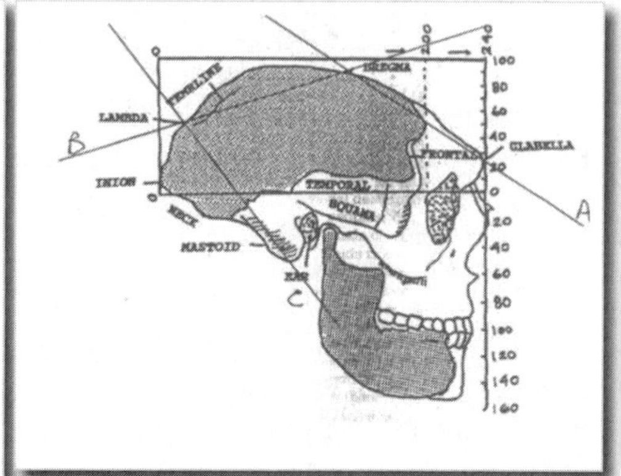

Carleton Coon's Arc-Chords. This is a method of distinguishing *Homo erectus* from *Homo sapiens*. The arcs are the skull bones themselves, while the chords are straight lines drawn between landmarks of the skull, extended in my drawing for clarity. In *H. erectus*, the arcs (of bone) are flatter than in *H. sapiens* in the front two measurements. This situation is reversed in the third, rearmost arc-cord. As you can see, Hansen's Gardar reconstruction, accepted and used by Sir Arthur Keith, is even more extreen and so more distant from *H. sapiens* than from *H. erectus*.

The occipital torus is a ridge of bone where the muscles of the upper back attach to the rear of the head. The Gardar skull had an occipital torus, a fact admitted by Keith in his book Antiquity of Man as he describes the Gardar skull. Modern men might have a slight ridge here if he had a huge and powerful neck but not a "torus" which indicates it is several magnitudes larger.

Just above the center of the occipital torus is a depressed spot on Neanderthals, the suprainiac depression. As the name indicates, it is just above the Inion, a landmark we used in reviewing the work of Carleton Coon. The suprainiac depression is just that, a hollow spot, which can be plainly seen in Hanson's drawing of the Gardar skull, a drawing used by Keith without alteration.

The next feature is the juxtamastoid crest, also called the occipitomastoid crest. Unfortunately, this area was broken off in the Gardar skull, so no conclusion about it can be drawn.

The last feature is the supramastoid tuberosity. This is an upward extension of the zygomatic arch, the lateral portion of what we call the "cheek bone". In modern humans, it just fades away, horizontally, into the temporal bone of the skull. But in the Gardar skull and in Neanderthals, this "fade away" area makes an upward turn, also running toward the back of the skull. If forms its own little ridge or tuberosity. It is hard to see, and the zygomatic arch is broken away, but it is there.

If you put your left hand on the corner of your left eye and then moved your hand back to your ear, you would feel the zygomatic arch as the slightly protruding bone paralleling your movement. Coming to the ear and following it upward with your hand you begin to feel a raised column of bone on your skull at the upper rear corner of your ear. It seems to just fade away moving upward. But in Neanderthals a larger column of bone would be present and it would continue to run up behind the ear with its forward margin merging with the zygomatic arch.

So, if we score a 1 for present or Neanderthal characteristic, 0 for non-determined, and -1 for absent or modern human characteristic, here is the way things break down.

Nasion to Bregma	(arch-cord)	0
Bregma to Lambda	(arch-cord)	1
Lambda to Opisthion	(arch-cord)	0
Jaw-presence or absence of retromolar space		1
Occipital torus		1
Suprainiac depression		1
Justamastoid crest		0
Supramastoid tuberosity		1
		5

Please note that there is not even one -1 characteristic, indicative of modern man, *H. sapiens*. The last series of values are the most important.

It is up to the reader if this attempt to rehabilitate the Gardar skull has been successful. But even in the most optimistic circumstance, this would not prove the Gardar skull was a Neanderthal or pre-Neanderthal living in 12th Century Greenland. What is realistic to claim is only that enough doubt is cast onto Keith's diagnosis of acromegaly to warrant a DNA test. Three intact molars exist, which should provide the necessary genetic material.

If Gardar turned out to be something other than a standard-model *Homo sapien*, then and only then could it be theorized that the Germans picked up a few of these relic, cold adapted men and enlisted them in a security force in Antarctic where cold adaptation was necessary. Until then, James Robert's Polar Men are just another post-war, Nazi mystery.

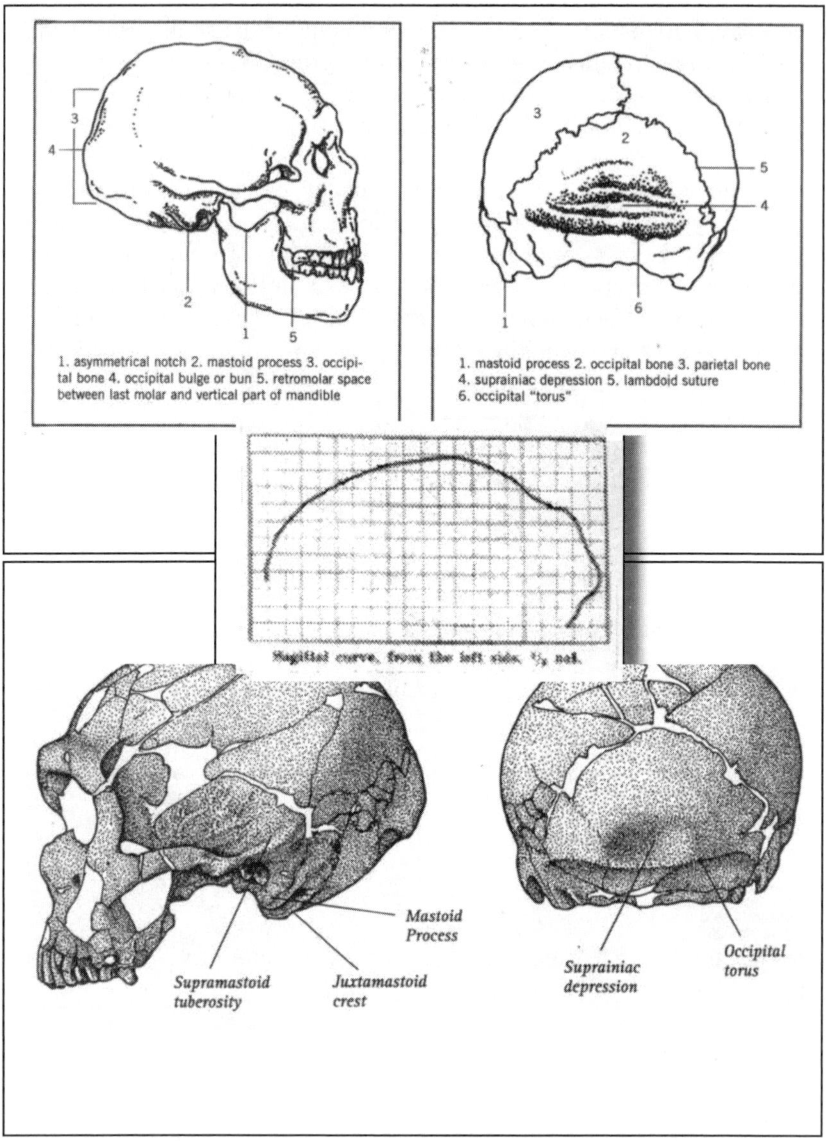

Neanderthal Diagnostic Traits
These are the characteristics discussed in the text. Acromegaly would have no bearing on the presence or absence of these traits, nor would it influence the basic shape of the skull. The Gardar skull's profile is shown for comparison with the Neanderthal condition.

Returning to Antarctica, we have to ask: where is Point 211 really? As would be expected, the base is located in a defensible position. It is situated near the Wohlfahrt Mountains, or Wohlthat Mountains, which form a 180-degree arch around the facility. After a short break, the Drygalske Mountains complete the circle. About 150 kilometers away are the Muehling-Hofman Mountains. Located pole-ward are the Schirrmacher warm water ponds, and to the east lie the Conrad Mountains, with their narrow valleys (up to 2000 meters deep) and unnamed projecting mountain peaks. The Conrad Mountains intersect the arch described the Wohlfahrt and Drygalske Mountains, and it is here at this intersection, seaward of the Schirrmacher ponds, where Point 211 can most likely be found. This is directly along the fault line containing the geothermal activity Buechner and Bernhart spoke of (25):

> *"It was found to be of volcanic origin and runs through the new German territory where it reveals itself in the form of warm water lakes, caves, crevasses and ice tunnels, most of which were found to be suitable for human habitation with the simple addition of electric lighting." (26).*

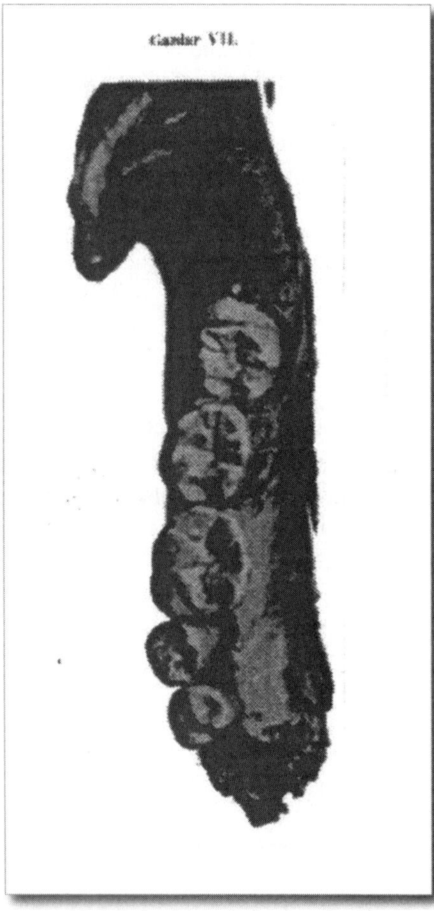

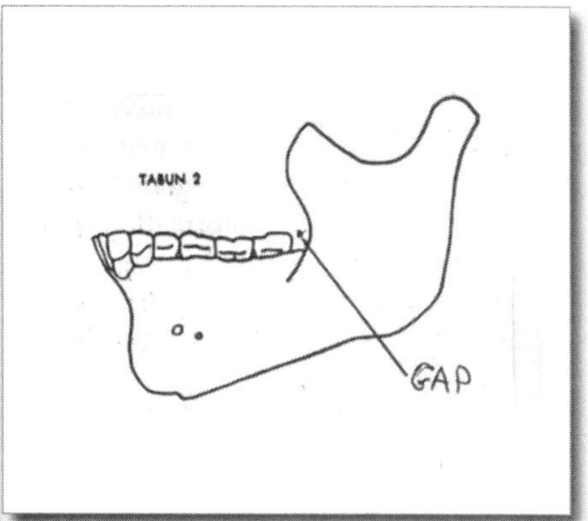

Garder Mandible

This picture shows the jaw fragment from the top down, exposing the gap between the third molar and the ascending ramus of the jaw. A Neanderthal mandible is also shown for comparison. This gap is only found in Neanderthals.

This compares very will with the description given by James Robert of the cavern illuminated by artificial lighting. In looking at a map, we can place the base at about 71 degrees, 30 minutes South by 14 degrees, 51 minutes West.

The existence of Operation Highjump has never been disputed by official history. The leader of this expedition, Admiral Byrd, was our most experienced Arctic and Antarctic explorer. Numerous books have been written about this expedition and the US Navy even saw fit to produce a film of this operation. This color film actually shows the ships and equipment involved and is narrated in the optimistic, "man overcoming nature and all obstacles" theme every school-age child of the 1950's remembers. The voices of the narration were done by three Hollywood stars of that period.

Operation Highjump was initially composed of three separate convoys that came from both the west coast and the east coast of the United States. Sailing south, they met in the Antarctic waters. Sub-dividing again, they reached the Antarctic Continent in January of 1947, the summer there. Besides the Americans, the British, Norwegian, Japanese, Russian, Argentine and Chilean Navies were invited to participate, giving the whole spectacle the air of a cooperative, international effort. The USA has since that time used the same ploy in ventures such as Korea, Vietnam, Iraq and Afghanistan, but throughout all of these it was clearly the Americans forcing the issues and calling all the shots.

Operation Highjump was outfitted for an eight-month stay in Antarctica (27). Admiral Byrd commanded a fleet from his flagship, Mount Olympus. There were the ice breakers Northwind and Burton Island. There was the aircraft carrier, *The Philippine Sea,* as well as the seaplane carriers *Pine Island* and *Currituch.* There were two destroyers, *The Brownsen* and *The Henderson,* as well as the escort ships *Yankey* and *Merrick* and the fueling ships *Canister* and *Capacan.* And finally, there was a submarine, *The Sennet* (28).

Accompanying this "scientific mission" were 4000 soldiers, and25 aircraft, including Dakotas and six helicopters (29), (30). Troop carriers included armored, tracked vehicles and a purpose-built Antarctic vehicle. The aircraft were equipped with special electronic sensing equipment. This equipment sent out an electromagnetic pulse that any target conductor—usually a metallic object—would convert into a small, temporary magnetic field that could in turn be picked up by sensors within the equipment. These specially-equipped aircraft were sort of flying metal detectors, working exactly as those used by millions of hobbyists around the world, but far more powerful. Their purpose was to locate metallic structures under the ice, although they had a very different official cover story (31).

This expedition, in spite of the propaganda effort, was what it was. It was a cold, naked, military operation. Byrd did not go directly to Neuschwabenland. Instead, his ground force remained on the other side of the Pole while his naval force a short way offshore from the German position. Byrd sent out feelers in the form of aerial surveillance in ever decreasing distance to the German base. Meanwhile, his ground forces were crossing Antarctica and would attempt to encircle Neuschwabenland. For some reason the first overflight of Neuschwabenland included the dropping of an American flag on the base (32). Some say a bomb was also dropped on the base at this time, allegedly done to let the Germans know they were no longer in isolation and security (33).

What happened next completely changed the character of Operation Highjump. A squadron of four aircraft that followed the scout airplane to the target, the one that dropped the flag and or the bomb, simply vanished as they over flew the German base (34), (35). Within 48 hours of this loss, Admiral Byrd gave the orders to cancel the expedition and made preparations to leave Antarctica (36). This means that Operation Highjump, scheduled to last eight months, lasted closer to eight weeks. In fact, Buechner and Bernhart put this date in February 1947 that may mean it did not even last in Antarctica one month (37)!

Anyone familiar with Admiral Byrd knows that he was, at times, outspoken. He was not afraid of his own ideas or conclusions, and at times spoke of them out loud. Fortunately for our story, one of those countries invited to participate for show was Chile. As we all know, Chile is close to Antarctica and so had a keen interest in the expedition, its purpose and its outcome. In fact, a Chilean newspaperman, Lee Van Atta, accompanied the mission, reporting for the newspaper El Mercurio in Santiago. By luck, Van Atta was aboard Mount Olympus, Admiral Byrd's flagship. Van Atta had access to the outgoing Admiral and penned articles on Operation Highjump that were published by El Mercurio.

For instance, when questioned over the necessity of the expedition, Byrd answered in the positive, saying: "Because the South Pole itself is located between us and our enemy". The question as to whom our enemy was, considering that the Axis Powers were officially eliminated, remained unanswered (38).

Catching Byrd in a particularly lucid state, Lee Van Atta inadvertently wrote a definitive piece on Operation Highjump that appeared in El Mercurio on March 5, 1947. The Spanish language article is pictured. I have no Spanish to English translation, but Wilhelm Landig provides a Spanish-to-German translation (39) that I have in turn translated into English:

ON BOARD MOUNT OLYMPUS ON THE HIGH SEA

ADMIRAL RICHARD E. BYRD INFORMED ME TODAY THAT IT IS NECESSARY FOR THE UNITED STATES TO TAKE DEFENSIVE MEASURES AGAINST ENEMY FLYERS THAT WILL COME FROM THE POLAR REGIONS. FURTHER, THE ADMIRAL EXPLAINED THAT HE DID NOT HAVE THE INTENTION TO SCARE ANYONE BUT THE BITTER REALITY IS THAT IN THE EVENT OF A NEW WAR THE UNITED STATES WOULD BE ATTACKED BY FLYERS WHO WOULD BE ABLE TO FLY FROM ONE POLE TO THE OTHER WITH FANTASTIC SPEED. THIS ASSERTION MADE ADMIRAL BYRD PERSONALLY BRING BACK TIMES AS EVENTS OF HIS POLAR RESEARCH AND TO BE SURE A CONFERENCE WITH THE INTERNATIONAL NEW SERVICE. CONCERNING HIS RECENTLY ENDED EXPEDITION ADMIRAL BYRD SAID: THE MOST IMPORTANT RESULT OF MY OBSERVATIONS IS THAT ONLY POWER GUARANTEES THE SECURITY OF THE UNITED STATES. THE FANTASTIC SPEED OF DEVELOPMENTS THROUGH WHICH THE WORLD IS ALWAYS SHRINKING IS AN OBJECTIVE LESSON THAT WE HAVE ACHIEVED FROM OUR OWN RECENTLY CONCLUDED INVESTIGATION OF THE ANTARCTIC. I CANNOT HELP, MY COUNTRYMEN, IN THE MOST FORCIBLE WAY TO WARN THAT THE TIME IS GONE WHERE OUR ISOLATED GEOGRAPHIC POSITION, THROUGH THE DISTANCING OF OCEANS AND POLES, FORMS A GUARANTEE OF SECURITY FOR US. FURTHER, SOUNDED THE ADMIRAL ANEW, IS THE NECESSITY TO STRICTLY WATCH OVER THE WHOLE ICE-GURTLE OF THE SIXTH CONTINENT BECAUSE THIS IS

There were other minor expeditions to Antarctica by the Americans and others but it does not seem that the German base was seriously challenged for eleven or twelve years. This period also constituted the golden age of flying saucers. Saucer sightings blossomed over North and South America during this time period.

President Truman was so shaken by the events that he called upon Albert Einstein for his opinion as to what had just happened. Einstein told Truman that he had no explanation for this occurrence (40).

To the German writers cited in this regard, the situation is clear. The Americans are being shown that they are not in complete control and that their most sensitive city and buildings can be attacked and they can do nothing about it. Mention should also be made that this was the exact time the Americans were taking charge and building military facilities in Greenland, possibly displacing the German base at Beaver Dam.

It was not until 1958 that the Americans returned to Antarctica to resume the attack. And again, they used "research" to hide their true aims. This was the International Geophysical Year, 1957-1958 and its attendant geological-geographical expeditions, tests, and so on. One of these expeditions involved a fleet that sailed to the South Atlantic. This fleet involved the destroyers *Warrington* and *Bearns*, the destroyer escorts *Courtney* and *Hammerberg*, the tankers *Neosho* and *Salamonie,* the seaplane carrier *Norton Sound,* and the full aircraft carrier and flag ship *Tarawa*. *The Norton Sound* had been especially prepared for the task at hand—Project Argus (41).

Following Landig's lead, in order to explain Project Argus we must delve into both the 1950's mind-set and history that was simply inconvenient and so untold. The Americans were intent upon destroying Point 211—a base that they did not even admit existed. How could this be done? In 1958 they are drawing near Neuschwabenland with a fleet of military ships. These ships are under cover as doing some sort of research about the earth. Strange as it may seem today, the both the USA and the Soviets, in those days, allege they were interested in "recovering" the Antarctic Continent. And according to this line of thought, recovering meant warming it up (42). What better to warm up a continent than with a few atomic bombs blowing off the continent's covering of ice? Either people familiar with the concept actually bought it *prima facie* or they bought it as a cover story to hide the real purposes for detonating atomic bombs over Antarctica.

In all fairness to the mind-set of those times, nobody had ever heard of global warming. Nobody had ever heard of the ozone layer. Nobody considered the fragile environment of the Antarctic because nobody considered the environment as "fragile". Those were "man against nature" days, with the goal of "conquering nature". During this time period above ground nuclear testing was going on in Southern Nevada, the only caveat being that it was done on days in which the wind was blowing away from Los Angeles.

According to Landig, a series of bombs were to be exploded over Antarctica, but they were not dropped from a bomber. That did not work out well for the Americans the last time around. This time a new, prototype rocket would be used. This was the RTV-3-Polaris rocket (43), a small, solid fuel rocket ultimately designed to be launched from beneath the surface of the sea by a submarine. In 1958, this system was not yet operational, so instead the RTV-3-Polaris rockets were launched from the deck of the seaplane carrier *Norton Sound.*

On August 27, 1958, a Polaris rocket arched up 480 kilometers high from the deck of the Norton Sound and then over the Antarctic Continent. It detonated as an air burst with the force of a 2-kiloton explosion. This was followed by another launch on August 30th, and yet another on September 6th (44). You already know the target coordinates.

Landig tells us that the real purpose of Project Argus was to knock out the defenses of Point 211 using the electromagnetic pulse of the nuclear detonations. Above all, they were fearful of the "die gefuerchteten neuen deutschen Klystron-EG-Projektoren", (the feared new German klystron EG projectors). But according to Landig, the Germans shielded sensitive electronics and so the electromagnetic pulse attack utterly failed. Actually, this is not so hard to do- a Faraday cage will suffice.

But, according to Landig, the Nazis did leave Point 211 and Antarctica. They moved to South America where they already had an extensive presence. The reason given for this move was not opposing military force but the power of a tiny organism. In a role reversal fom H.G. Well's War of the Worlds, the Germans left Antarctica because that Continent had almost no germs in its atmosphere. Without some virus or bacteria assaulting the human immune system, it becomes weak and ineffective. In time this loss of normal immunity would lead to a contagious outbreak whenever a visitor from the outside brought in even a sniffle (45). And since they were leaving, there would be no objection from "interested parties" to any new treaty de-militarizing Antarctica as already mentioned.

Now that the unofficial history of Antarctic is completed, we are free to return to something Landig mentioned, the klystron EG projectors, and the whole subject of German involvement with klystron tubes.

A klystron tube, invented in 1937, is a vacuum tube used to amplify microwave and radio frequency radiation. They can be very precisely controlled in amplitude, frequency and phase. Before modern semiconductors came into use, another type of klystron tube found wide use, the reflex klystron tube. An Internet site describes the workings this way:

> *"A klystron tube is used to produce microwave energy. In this application, it works in a similar manner to a pipe organ tube, except that the klystron tube uses electrons, while the pipe organ tube uses air. When the air in the organ tube vibrates, the pipe organ tube emits sound energy of a specific frequency that we hare as a single note. When the electrons in the klystron tube vibrate, the klystron tube emits high frequency microwave energy that can be detected by a radar receiver." (46)*

Polaris blastoff at missile range.

Photographs of a Polaris Missile launch, 1959
These photographs are from the book *Missiles and Satellites*,by James F. Scheer, 1959.

So electrons were put into sort of a chamber and energy applied to them until they reached the desired level. If released at this point, the output would be an electron beam. The electron beam can be "bunched" by electromagnets. This is precisely the language used by the first of three German studies on x-ray and gamma "death rays" (47). So something of this klystron technology is applicable to working those radiations into weapons. This energy could be transferred to radio frequency waves that include radar applications. The Germans used the klystron tube for their radar applications, probably because it was more precise than the magnetrons the Allies used (48). According to

Norbert Juergen-Ratthofer and Ralf Ettl as stated in their books and video films, the Germans used klystron tubes, mimicking the frequency of Allied radar units, to jam them, making the foo fighters which used klystrons invisible to radar. After expulsion of the desired energy/particles, a magnetic aiming device can be built around the klystron. This is a betatron, accelerating electrons within a circular glass torus. Klystrons can be built with a wave-guide to coupling microwave energy. This, if I understand correctly, allows them to produce high-power carrier waves that are the driving force for particle accelerators and synchrotrons (49). A synchrotron is a cyclic particle accelerator, circular in shape, in which the magnetic field and the electric field are carefully synchronized with the particle beam (50). It should also be noted that a klyston tube can be used to generate positrons and that this modernized, combined-compounded technology, as described, has been used in high energy experiments combining electron and positron beams in the 1980's (51). In other words, doing matter-anti-matter experiments.

The researcher asking the most pressing questions about klystons has been Thomas Mehner. In fact, he once emailed me and asked me what I thought was going on concerning the extensive use of klystrons by the Germans during World War Two. I had no answers. But pressing the issue, he found some answers using declassified F.O.I.A. material, which we will review. But he did not stop there. Sometimes, if you put out feelers regarding a certain topic, someone will come along and tell you what they know. Mr. Mehner and Edgar Mayer devote a whole chapter to "zyklotrons" in their book (52).

Mr. Mayer and Mr. Mehner present evidence that a huge, circular, particle accelerator was made by the firm Siemens-Halske and installed underground in the Jonas Valley. The activation of this device occasionally caused a light show that could be seen from a nearby castle. An anonymous source once sent me an unpublished report regarding these light shows. A geophysicist prepared it. It was his opinion that the device was so powerful that the light show was a reaction to the machine's interacting with earth's gravity. Misters Mayer and Mehner reviewed the witness evidence, which they cite, and conclude that the device was a klystron-betatron-synchrotron-type particle accelerator.

But that is really not the big news. The big news is the purpose for which this machine was used. An Internet article appeared in Polish that claimed to explain it all. (53) Please remember that the Slavic researchers have done excellent work in reconstructing events within the Third Reich, particularly in their geographic area of expertise, Western Poland, Bohemia and Monrovia, which were once part of Germany or areas heavily settled by Germans and under German influence during the war. A certain "Dr. D.L." came along and translated the Internet article for the German researchers and so it is available to us now. The German researchers are actively trying to track down the author of the article but even without an exact ascription, the article is so informative and powerful that it cannot be contained.

A bit of set-up is necessary. This is regarding uranium refining. We have all heard the story as it has played in current events. Uranium oxide, "yellow cake" is dissolved by a series of chemical reactions and forms into a gas, uranium hexafluoride. This gas is spun in a centrifuge. All the isotopes of uranium are separated according to their weight in the centrifuge since the heavier forms of uranium, even while in compound with fluoride gas, will move to the end of the centrifuge. The isotope of interest in a fission reaction, U235, can thus be separated from the other isotopes by its weight, that is its position in the centrifuge. This is called "enriched uranium". This is the way uranium has been enriched, at least in the USA, ever since. Plutonium originates in a nuclear reactor when another isotope of uranium, U-238, is placed in it and absorbs neutrons. It becomes U-239 and then decays to Pu-239, or plutonium.

Below are parts of the article that I have translated into English, along with comments and a summary, which appear outside the quotation marks (53):

The Other Method

> *"The other method sketched itself out for the Germans in the summer of 1942 and perhaps fulfilled itself under the influence of Albert Speer and the WHVA (Spandau), a radical change of point of view which befell the fate of the nuclear program. This change fulfilled itself during the secret conference of 4, June, 1942 in Berlin. It consisted of a new method of production of enriched uranium with the help of a specialized particle accelerator after the construction of Kerst." (footnote credits Kerst, an American, with the drawing of plans of a betratron)*

In the journal *Physical Review*, Donald W. Kerst and R. Serber published an article describing his first betatron. This was a small circular glass tube, an induced magnetic field, 7.5 cm. in diameter in which particles were accelerated with the energy of 2.3 million electron volts (MeV). The US government became interested. The first betatron was sold to the University of Illinois. Betatrons began to be thought of as smaller, cheaper substitutes for x-ray apparatus.

> *"The first accelerator produced a radiation corresponding to a gram of radium, which, at that time in Sweden, cost a million Krone."*

Soon, the subject caught the interest of Rolf Wiederoee who worked for the Norwegian firm of NEBB. He already worked in the field of high energy and soon wrote an article in September 1942, in the German publication Archiev fuer Elektrotecknik that was published in 1943. He wrote a second article, claiming the possibility of an accelerator in the order of 200MeV but this article never saw the light of day. Obviously, the German government was also interested in this research.

> *"In the early part of 1943 there appeared two German officials in Luftwaffe uniforms at Rolf Wiederoee's place of employment, the NEBB. Here it must be remembered that Norway was in German occupation from the early part of that year.*
>
> *Wiederoee found himself in a difficult position. On one side he would be suspected of collaboration and on the other he was invited to a luxurious hotel that he did not want to refuse. He said he would first have to solve the problem of his place of employment, but the German agents were perfectly prepared."*

What happened was that Wiederoee began work in Hamburg but was allowed trips to Oslo for "calculations". In fact, he was allowed a great deal of freedom, given all the circumstances. He was already working on his first assignment before his German employment, that of a 14 MeV betatron. Such devices were built and built up until the end of the war. But he also worked on further developments of the betatron and actually obtained patent rights.

"The next high performance betatron was to be set up in the vicinity of Heidelberg and reach a performance of 200 MeV. In July 1943 Wiederoee began work on this new accelerator. It must be mentioned here that Wiederoee as not responsible for the construction of this betatron. He functioned only as the author of the project (and diverse projects bound with it)."

In fact, Max Steinbeck (Siemens, Berlin) and Professor A. Sommerfeld interfaced between Wiederoee and the actual construction. Sometime in the second half of 1943, the new betatron reached the output of 287 MeV.

"With the beginning of the year 1944, the Ministry of Arms changed the decision for the place where the accelerator was to be set up. This was on account of the push of the Allies in Italy and the landing at Normandy (June 6, 1944). It was decided to place the accelerator in the area of Lower Silesia because, to the time, it seemed the most secure place. This decision also speaks to the conclusion of the problems which were connected now brought to completion in preparation of the underground production of rockets in the Kohnstein Massif (Dora) as well as the ongoings of Albert Speer in April, 1944 in the milieu of the similar programs, S III, originally begun with the central "Olga" in the area of Ohrdruf, a complex in the area of Lower Silesia. Hans Kammler was responsible for the execution and construction from the side of the SS."

References to Kohnstein and Dora are the Nordhausen complex where the V-1 and V-2 rockets were being produced. S III and Olga were part of the Jonas Valley complex system. From the last sentence in this paragraph, we know that as of 1944, Dr. Hans Kammler was running this program. In the next paragraph the Polish commentary touches again on Silesia, their area of expertise.

"Originally, there were three major projects: Fuerstenstein (Ksiaz), Riese (Bad Charlotenbrunn, today Walim), and Ruediger (Walderburg/Schlesia, today Walbrzych). Particularly Ruediger, in which many underground criss-cross burrows passed through, was selected as a nuclear laboratory. To this facility, which was completely self-sufficient, belonged electrical supply equipment, the oil heating unit, and a water supply. The facility had at its disposal a closed railroad track coming from Waldenburg. Every room contained its own steel door that opened only with the assistance of a special, coded identity card.

Ruidiger possessed a secret television connection to the important institutions of the Third Reich, realized over a central circuit that was located inside the facility Fuerstenstein. (The whole was a constituent of the 'Project Jonastal' that was under the supervision of the German Postal Service). Besides this there was a telephone network to the facility 'Reise' and other industrial institutions."

So in this area between the Jonas Valley and the Owl Mountains of Poland, there was a connected community of a dozen facilities of science that were united in the frame of nuclear programs. In July 1944, the huge accelerator became active in its underground home. Eventually, wartime conditions demanded that this accelerator and the nuclear leadership be evacuated. But we are told of its purpose and its efficiency:

> *"The chief main exercise of the accelerator was the production of enriched uranium, whereby the method was considerably more effective in reference to the American attempt."*

In the fall of 1944 something radically changed. After a idea from Paul Harteck, for the first time, the fuel in the form of fuel cassettes were discontinued (the fuel reactors were here also) from being shielded from the torus. As a moderator, beryllium was used and as cooling was assisted though the use of liquid nitrogen and liquid oxygen. At this point a fantastic idea took shape. It was to combine the fuel and production reactors!

> *" In November, 1944, steps were taken to realize a fantastic idea. With the goal of increasing the production of plutonium, both of the two facilities were united. Supported by the work of the French husband and wife team of Joliot-Curie from the year 1934 in the decomposition of beta+ radiation. The reactor built here was to use this beta+ decay. With this reactor success was realized in the transformation of protons in neutrons, accompanied by the emission of positrons (e+) and neutrinos. The process can be initiated during the time that the fissionable material is enclosed with gamma radiation.*
>
> *The source for the radiation was the accelerator. A stream of small particles, coming form the betatron, were directed though the so-called 'Schornstein' in the reactor. The Schornstein was already with the preceding reactors and served as introduction of the neutron source. In this a great quantify of plutonium was obtained. The Germans were without regard to the difficulties with the operation of the accelerator-very satisfied."*

The word Schornstein means "chimney" in English. The work continued until the end of March 1945. By the beginning of April, steps were already being taken to destroy the facility.

> *"How many kilograms of plutonium Germany possessed is hard to say. But probably it was a sufficient quantity in order to build an atomic bomb. Surely if it had been made, if they were capable, it would have been an intelligent value, intended for critical mass if the Germans knew this value with suitable accuracy."*

So by combining steps and reactors into one, the Germans were able to produce both uranium and plutonium more quickly than by the American system.

In addition to the "other method" there may be a third enrichment method. Edgar Mayer and Thomas Mehner report (54) that this method consisted of using a synchrotron, the outgrowth of the klystron and betatron. The synchrotron was also a development of

Wideroee as well as the experts Veksler and McMillian. According to the above named researchers, use of the synchrotron allowed the Germans the direct manufacture of enriched material necessary for an atomic bomb. In other words, this was a one-step transmutation of one element into another.

And evidently this synchrotron was much larger in diameter than any accelerator so far. Evidence for this object may still be seen in aerial pictures of the Jonas Valley. A faint outline can clearly be seen of a buried, circular object from the air. This, coupled with the reports of strange lights and energy emanations during the war years point to a large, unknown and undescribed particle accelerator being buried in one of the underground facilities there.

This brings us back to Wilhelm Landig and his klystron EG projectors. He claims that after the three nuclear missiles exploded over Point 211, nothing happened. The electromagnetic pulse attack failed due to German countermeasures. This included the klystron EG projectors. What were these klystron EG projectors?

Well, they obviously were weapons and mentioned along with the V-7 by Landig as defensive measures. Clearly, they were both air-defense weapons. We remember the x-ray/gamma ray weapons the Germans studied but did not build (55). The underlying German document mentioned "bundling" for the generation of these rays. This and the German history of x-ray production leads us to the almost certainty that these weapons, had they been built, would have used klystron tubes to generate the x-rays and gamma rays. So why were they not built?

The answer must be that there was an even better option almost within their grasp. This weapon would have also used a klystron tube as its basis but may have generated another type of radiation. Since the design study mentioned above includes discussion of a range of about three miles, we can conclude the Germans had added some sort of magnetic focusing, as in a betatron, to the klystron weapon. The result may have been a weapon that ionized the atmosphere as well as overloading each and every electrical circuit in the target aircraft. It would be like turning on a cell phone and throwing it into a microwave oven.

But, is there any evidence that this weapon was under development at the end of the war? Edgar Mayer and Thomas Mehner point to the F.F.O., (the Flugfunk Forschungsinstitut Oberpfaffenhofen). This was a research and development facility. In fact, they built klystrons as well as betatrons. Allied documents admit that the F.F.O. was working on an air defense weapons. Some of these included aircraft radar jamming equipment. This would have involved klystrons. In fact, klystons are mentioned everywhere in the report.

An interesting fact is that the most secret papers and equipment at the F.F.O. was taken or destroyed before the arrival of the Allied forces:

> *"All secret documents in the F.F.O. had been collected by the Librarian Dr. Kanzler who alleges he burned them before the Allies arrived. The above*

documents were obtained by asking individual members and from the head of the establishment Dr. Ahrens who collected them at investigators' request."(56)

So what the Allies knew of the FFO was what the German scientists were willing to disclose. One is reminded of Peenemuende where a code of silence kept the development and testing of a few examples of the A-10 rocket a secret (57). Then there is the testimony given regarding work on jamming devices which would be similar to the klystron devices of our discussion:

"Nearly all the following information was obtained from an interview with Dipl. Ing. Physiker Helmut Heine who was in charge of the station at Werteweil and who also worked at Oberpfaffenhofen. None of his equipment was seen and he reports that it was generally taken away or destroyed as where all classified documents. Further investigation of his laboratories at Warteweil and Oberpfaffenhofen should be made with him along."(58)

There is yet another clue concerning this klystron technology. This comes from an internet article whose title in German translates to "Research Site for Hitler's Death Rays" (Forschungsstaette fuer Hitlers "Todesstrahlen'' (*http;//www. mainnetz.de/nachrichten/region/aschaffenburg/aschaffenburgland/land/art3986,883119*).

The news here is that another research site specifically dedicated to "death rays" has been identified. In is near the town of Ringheim. This facility was said to be for the use of Leipzig Professor Ernst. Professor Schiebold's work on gamma/X-ray weapons was reviewed in my second book.. But from sources available at that time the types of weapons were designed only with the purpose of causing biologic harm to aircraft pilots. With the new information we learn that the purpose evolved into using the exact same ionizing radiation to disrupt aircraft engines rather than causing biologic harm to the pilots. This weapon would resemble the one described as "Motorstoppmittel" but instead of radiating out in all directions, this one would be specifically directed.

A large hall of all wooden construction was to house this research facility. It was to be about 35 feet high and about 57 feet wide and about 78 feet long. This single room housed the 15 million volt transformer with enough room so that flashovers would not occur. The device generating the radiation was a betatron, built in the same manner as were the devices built by the Norwegian physicist Dr. Rolf Widroee. Underground, side bunkers held the machinery and led off to an area where the personnel would be sheltered.

On September 20, 1944 Schiebold left project "Roentgenkanonen" for other work. This project's output must have been taken by the SS. To do anything else would have been irresponsible on their part and the acquisition of this technology would have fit well into their post-war plans.

The situation is even clearer with the FFO. It is clear that the Germans took the equipment and documents before the Allies got there. The German agency that would have desired this advanced technology and desired to deny it to the Allies was the SS. I believe the SS took a prototype klystron weapon from the F.F.O. as well as from the facility near Ringheim and it later surfaced in Antarctica in the year 1959 as Landig's klystron-EG-projectors.

Misters Mayer and Mehner state that the Allies took an extremely unusual interest in the klystron development at the F.F.O. Now we know why. Given the progressive development of klystron technology and how it was utilized by the Germans in so many ways, now we know one reason why it was of such interest to Mr. Mehner. We have him to thank for figuring this all out for us and we will mention another possible interest the Americans may have had for this technology in the final chapter.

But what was Landig's Klystron-EG-Projektoren really? My guess is they had to do with Tesla technology, specifically his quest for a broadcast energy system. A clue might come from Dr. Marc J. Seifer who, writing on Tesla's "death ray" says:

> *"...They suggest that Tesla's particle beam work is an outcropping of his experiments with X-ray machines from the same period, as well as from his independent idea of illuminating the skies with his magnifying transmitter by beaming up electrical energy to the stratosphere." (59)*

Another clue is the method Tesla proposed using a mountain top tower to actually broadcast the energy that was tied to a huge Tesla coil. But, the two, the tower and the coil, were physically separated. A discussion of their linkage is provided by electrical engineer Toby Grotz:

> *"A location at a high altitude is initially advantageous for reducing atmospheric losses which work against an efficient coupling to the Schumann Cavity. The high frequency, high voltage output of the coil will be half wave rectified using a uniquely designed single electrode X-ray tube. The X-ray tube will be used to charge a 130 ft. tall, vertical tower, which will function to provide a vertical current moment. The mast is topped by a metal sphere 30 inches in diameter. X-rays emitted from the tube will ionize the atmosphere between the Tesla coil and the tower. This will result in a low resistance path causing all discharges to flow from the coil to the tower."(60)*

Now the Landig's "Klystron EG Projektoren" may have just been the simpler directed beam of ionizing radiation that causes ignition-based aircraft engines to stop running. Or something may have been added to it to make it even more effective. In other words the X-ray tube, in our case the klystron or betatron tube generating X-rays, will ionize individual gas molecules, creating a path through the atmosphere, which more easily conducts electricity. It is like a virtual wire. A Tesla coil would then instantly generated a huge, high voltage current up (or perhaps down) the ionized pathway to the target aircraft, destroying it with something like a lightning bolt. It should be remembered that there is a potential difference between elevated objects and the ground, which is striking. With a pathway in place the lightning bolt could have easily traveled this pathway in its attempt to equalize the potential difference. Either way, the experimental study referenced in my second book concluded that x-rays could be generated which would cause biologic harm to the pilot of an aircraft over three miles away (61). This would give an indication of the minim range of what Landig describes as a klystron EG projector.

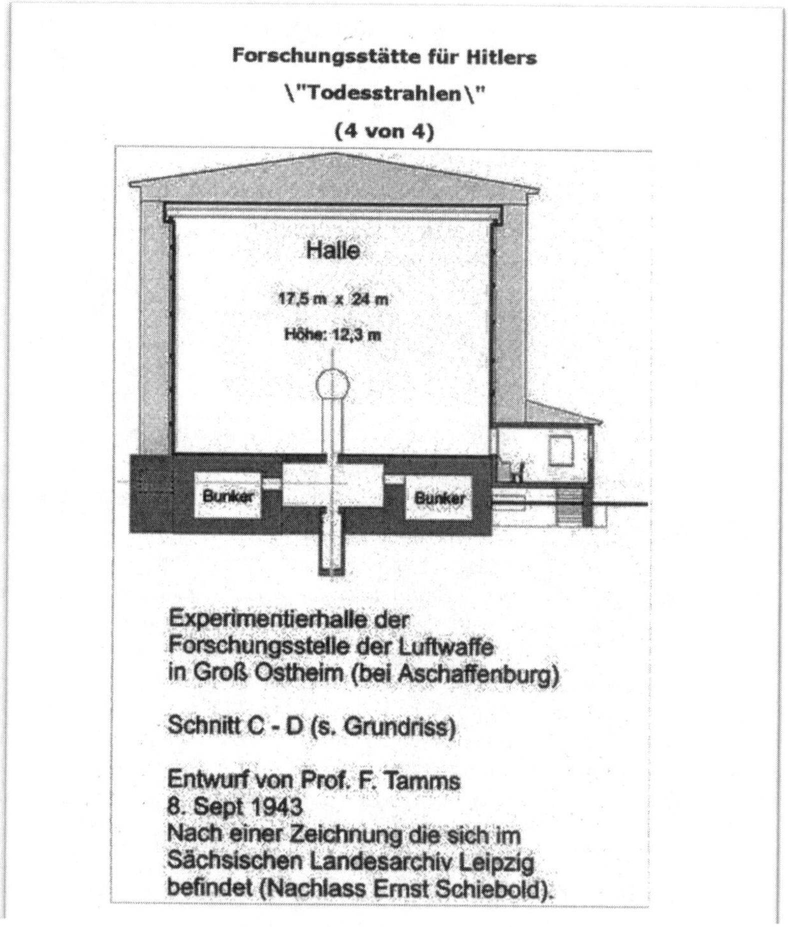

An actual "Death Ray" Research facility This diagram is of an experimental structure, designed for death ray testing, in Gross Ostheim, near Aschaffenburg. It is a drawing by Professor F. Tamms, September 8, 1943, after a diagram in the Saxon Archives, Leipzig by permission of Ernst Scheibold.

So, what can be said of Base 211? Was it a physical reality? Did this base possess tunnels, underground rooms, and high technology? Was it a U-boat base with hidden entrances and turntables for the submarines? Could people have remained hidden there for years? Well, a consideration of our next subject, Fuerteventura, may answer those questions.

Literature Cited

1. **Stevens, Henry, 2003**, *Hitler's Flying Saucers A Guide to German Flying Discs Of The Second World War*, pages 245-247, Adventures Unlimited Publishing, Kempton, Illinois, USA
2. **Daehnhardt, Rainer, 1998**, *Dos Acores a Antarctida*, Publicacoes Quipu, Lisbon, Portugal, ISBN 972-8408-08-0
3. *Personal communication via telephone in which Mr. Daehnhardt informed the author of this fact.*
4. **Mattern, W. , date unknown**,*UFO's Unbekanntes Flugobjekt? Letzte Geheimwaffe Des Dritten Reiches?*, page 89, Samisdat Publishing, Toronto, Canada
5. **Henshall, Philip, 1995**, *Vengence Hitler's Neuclear Weapon Fact or Fiction*, page 122, Alan Sutton Publishing Limited, Gloucestershire, England, ISBN 0-7509-0874-2
6. **Landig, Wilhelm, 1980**, *Wolfzeit Um Thule*, pages 29, 30, 87, Volkstum -Verlag/ Wilhelm Landig, Vienna, Austria
7. **Landig, Wihelm, 1991**, *Rebellen Fuer Thule Das Erbe Von Atlantis*, page 575, Volkstum-Verlag, Vienna, Austria
8. **Bergmann, O., 1988**, *I Deutsche Flugscheiben und U-Boote Ueberwachen Die Weltmeere*, pages 14 and 68, Hugin Publishing, Wetter/Ruhr, Germany
9. **Gehring, Heiner and Karl-Heinz Zunneck, 2005**, *Flugscheiben Ueber Neuschwabenland Die Wahrhiet ueber "Vril", "Haunebu" und die Templer-Erbengemeinschaft*, page 88, Jochen Kopp Verlag, Rottenburg, Germany
10. **Geheimtechnologien, Wunderwaffen Und Irdischen Facetten Des UFO-Phaenomens 50 Jare Desinformation und die Folgen, 1998**, CTT-Verlag, Suhl, Germany
11. **Gehring, Heiner and Karl-Heinz Zunneck, 2005**, page 91
12. **Buechner, Howard A., Colonel, and Captain Wilhelm Bernhart, 1988**, *Adolf Hitler And The Secrets Of The Holy Lance*, pages 148 and 149, Thunderbird Press, Inc., Metairie, Louisiana, USA
13. **Buechner, Howard A., Colonel, and Captain Wilhelm Bernhart, 1988**, page 158, 159
14. **Buechner, Howard A., Colonel and Captain Wilhelm Bernhart, 1988**, page 148
15. *ibid.*
16. **Buechner, Howard A., Colonel, and Captain Wilhelm Bernhart, 1989**, *Hitler's Ashes*, pages 156-157, Thunderbird Press, Inc., Metairie, Louisiana, USA
17. **Buechner, Howard A., Colonel, and Captain Wilhelm Bernhart, 1988**, page 167
18. **Buechner, Howard A., Colonel, and Captain Wilhelm Bernhart, 1989**, page 228
19. **Breckmann, Georg, 2008**, *Channeling the Visitors*, self-published
20. **Salla, Michael E., Ph.D., 2003**, *Foundations for Globally Managing Extraterrestrial Affairs -The Legacy of the Nazi Germany-Extraterrestrial Connection, Research study #6*, posted on the internet under the URLs www.exopolitics.org, http://www. exopolitics.org/Study-Paper-6.htm and http://www.fourwinds10.com/news/13-space/G-aliens-UFO/2003/13G-10-11-
21. *Dr. Michael Salla references the work of Robert Lesniakiewicz at http:// notizieufo.com/pol5.htm and The Omega File: Nazi History at http://www.think-abutit.com/Omega/files/omega3.htm* I could not find either reference. This may not be surprising given the transitory nature of the internet. I have not seen them all but most internet sites I have seen regarding this and related topics are junk. The only web-site that I have seen which I can recommend is Maurizio Verga's www.naziufos.com
22. **Jesensky, Milos, Ph.D., and Robert Lesniakiewicz, 1998**, *"Wunderland" Momozemske Technologe Treti Rise*, Aos Publishing
23. **Britain's Secret War In Antarctica, an article written by James Robert, Nexus magazine, October 2005**, page 41-46 and 81,
24. **Landig, Wilhelm, 1980**, pages 61, 62
25. **Buechner, Howard A., Col., and Wilhelm Bernhart, 1989**, page 151
26. *ibid.*
27. **Mattern, W., date unknown**, page 114
28. **Landig, Wilhelm, 1980**, page 192
29. **Buechner, Howard A., Col., and Wilhelm Bernhart, 1989**, page 230
30. **Mattern, W. date unknown**, page 114
31. *ibid.*

32. **Landig, Wilhelm, 1980**, page 193
33. **Mattern, W., date unknown**, page 114
34. *ibid.*
35. **Mattern, W. date unknown**, page 114
36. *ibid.*
37. **Buechner, Howard A., Col., and Wilhelm Bernhart, 1989**, page 230
38. **Mattern, W. date unknown**, page 111 Here Mattern cites *El Mercuro*, July 7, 1947
39. **Landig, Wilhelm, 1980**, page 195
40. **Haarmann, D.H., 1983**, II Geheime Wunderwaffen ...und sie fliegen doch!, page 23, Hugin Gesellschaft Fuer Politisch-Philosophische Studien E.V., Hoerschel, Germany
41. **Landig, Wilhelm, 1991**, *Rebellen fuer Thule*, page 571, 572, Volkstum-Verlag, Vienna, Austria.
42. **Landig, Wilhelm, 1991**, page 571
43. **Landig, Wilhelm, 1991**, page 572
44. *ibid.*
45. *ibid.*
46. What is a Klystron Tube? http://www.wisegeek.com/what-is-a-klystron-tube.htm
47. **Stevens, Henry, 2007**, pages 190 to 197
48. Klystron, Wikipedia, http://en.wikipedia.org/wiki/Klystron
49. *ibid.*
50. *Synchrotron, http://en.wikipedia.org/wiki/Synchrotron*
51. *Acceleration Characteristics of Positron Generator Linac*, http://www.slac. Stanford.edu/ pubs/slacreports05/linacB6-133.pdf
52. **Mayer, Edgar and Thomas Mehner, 2002**, *Die Atombombe und das Dritte Reich Das Geheimnis des Dreiecks Arnstadt-Wechmar-Ohrdruf*, pages 161-193, Jochen Kopp Verlag, Rottenburg, Germany
53. *The Other Method, internet article in Polish, http://www.republika.pl/skarbom and http://www.eksplorator.cud.pl/1.htm Also published in German translation: Edgar Mayer and Thomas Mehner, 2002, pages 182 to 187*
54. **Mayer, Edgar and Thomas Mehner, 2002**, page 188
55. **Stevens, Henry, 2007**, pages 190-197
56. **Combined Intelligence Objectives Sub-Committee (CIOS), Evlauation Report 156, 1st July 1945** of Flugfunk Forschungsinstitut Oberpfaffenhofen F.F.O. Establishments (Target Nos. 1/32, 6/50)
57. **Stevens, Henry, 2007**, pages 228-238
58. Combined Intelligence Objectives Sub-Committee CIOS) Evaluation Report 156, 1st July 1945 of F.F.O. (see above)
59. **Seifer, Marc J., Ph.D., date unknown**, *Nikola Tesla: The History Of Lasers And Particle Beam Weapons*, an article appearing in *The Tesla Papers Nikola Tesla n free Energy & Wiresless Transmission of Power*, 2000, edited by David Hatcher Childress, Adventures Unlimited Publishing, Kempton, Illinois, USA
60. **Grotz, Toby, B.S.E.E., date unknown**, *Wireless Transmission Of Power Resonating Planet Earth*, an article in *The Tesla Papers Nikola Tesla on Free Energy & Wireless Transmission of Power*, 2000, edited by David Hatcher Childress, page 81, Adventures Unlimited Publishing, Kempton, Illinios, USA
61. **Stevens, Henry, 2007**, pages 190-197

FUERTEVENTURA

Fuerteventura is a small island in the Canary Islands. It is one of the easternmost islands of that chain, nearest Africa. There is no longer any doubt that a secret German base existed on Fuerteventura during the Second World War. One is reminded of the statement by Admiral Karl Doenitz about how the German Navy knew all the ocean's hiding places. Well, this is certainly one of them—a secret base in plain sight.

This base has been mentioned by me in both my earlier books. Others have discussed this base, writing in German language. For some reason general knowledge of this base has not penetrated the conscience of the English-speaking world, probably because of the language barrier. I say this because the real description of the base is in German that has never been translated into English.

Fuerteventura is a resort spot but an out-of-the-way one. From discussions I have heard there is a small tourist town there that includes a bar. Rumors of the secret German base have always been discussed and questions asked about it, mostly by tourists. Evidently, everyone or most everyone on the island denies these rumors in public but affirm them in private. But everyone, even you dear reader, have heard of this base in a roundabout way. This was the secret U-boat bunker featured in the George Lucas/Steven Spielberg film "Raiders of the Lost Ark". In that film a U-boat sailed right inside the island, using a tunnel, into a huge cavern that was perhaps an ancient volcanic blister. There, the Nazi bad guys had erected submarine support equipment, turntables for U-boats, along with supporting manpower.

In 1971 Stern magazine published an article about the father of this base and the base itself in an article titled (and translated to English) "The Fantastic History of Don Gustavos, His Secret House and the U-Boat Base" (1). According to the rumors and the facts on the ground, the father of this secret base was a German General, Gustav Winter. General Winter built a large, white villa on the high point of this island. The rumor was that a staircase descended down into the bowels of the island, connecting to this secret base.

Researchers Heiner Gehring and Karl Heinz-Zunneck did some research on General Winter, which is illuminating. Winter was born in 1893 in the Black Forest and was trained as an engineer. He died in 1971, a few months before the Stern article. Gustav Winter performed some outstanding service for the Germans, which we will discuss later, and for that service he was granted land on the southern peninsula of Fuerteventura. During the Second World War, Winter was the driving force behind a project to build a secret U-boat bunder on the island. He was also an agent for the Abwehr, one of the German spy services (2). The major feature of this bunder was a huge natural cavity that was connected to the sea by tunnels bored into the solid rock. Ventilation shafts were also dug upward towards what was now the Villa Winter. This facility functioned as a military base during the war and was heavily armed and guarded. After the war a portions of the facility, with the exception of the airport, were destroyed with explosives. Today part of this site belongs to a nature park but part is still in private hands.

The best information to date comes, not from Stern, but from another German magazine, Nugget. Nugget is not a flying saucer magazine or new age magazine nor does it deal with strangeness or even World War Two as a rule. Nugget is a magazine of treasure hunters. Below the title "Nugget" is written the words (in English) Gold, Minerals, Treasure Seeking, Adventure. Most readers are familiar with this genre. The "adventure" involved is the mild adventure associated with finding or traveling to the treasure in question. Two articles were written titled: The U-Boat Bunker of Fuerteventure in the July, 1984 and August, 1984 editions. So what will be done is that we will take a look at these articles translated into English and see it they hold any clues to our story of German secret bases (3).

Exclusive: The U-Boat Bunker of Fuerteventura

Seven Tons of Gold in a Nazi Base

In a secret U-boat bunker off the Spanish island of Fuerteventura lie still today two U-boats, which were officially reported as sunk.

Thousands of vacationers who spend their vacations every year on the Canary Island of Fuerteventura have no idea what secrets this island, near the African coast conceals. The history of the U-boat bunker of Fuerteventura is mysterious and threatening at the same time. Murder and manslaughter holds on to this remnant from the Second World War and as the past shows, it is not always absolutely healthy to want to prove the secret.

The story began during the Second World War. Admiral Doenitz, commander of the U-boat fleet, wanted the established action radius of the "sharks" consolidated, above all in the Atlantic.

To be sure, the Spanish were neutral but the strategy of the National Socialist government found a way to circumvent this neutrality. The basis for a complete and independent presence of the German U-boats in these waters was a solid basis from which would have to offer even possible technical advances which were required for such undertakings. The difficulty was that not every place was suited for the construction of a U-boat base. The Spanish mainland was not considered because of the distance they had in mind. Also, the islands of Gran Canary and Teneriffa were dropped because these islands were too heavily populated. Hierro was too small and Lanzarote, on the account of volcanic characteristics, likewise was out of the question. The optimal offering was Fuerteventura. Lying only one hundred kilometers from the North African coast, a better island certainly could not be found. Also, the coastline was made for what was in mind.

The Spanish government soon made up its mind. Large parts of Fuerteventura were purchased. The owner was considered to be General Winter who, at the same time, was authorized with the fortification and construction of a base. The activity that immediately would develop was then also enormous. From Germany special troops were brought whose problem it was to search for water and to bore wells. The water supply was already at this time a large problem on this island of the Canaries.

A Villa Serves As Direction Finder

In order to make the possibilities of transportation easier, a narrow gauge railroad was especially built whose remains still can be seen today. With the construction of the base the construction commandos made use of the fact that at many places huge air bubbles had been molded through volcanic activity. These natural domes of which certainly most were only reachable from the sea, were outstandingly suited for a secret base.

In the South of the island a magnificent villa was built in terrain that enabled a very good view. It can be assumed that the villa with its tower served as an orientation and direction finder for U-boats making land. There today, no sort of construction plans can be hunted up any longer. They were either destroyed because of security reasons or, because of explosion, they were kept under lock and key. It was assumed that in one vicinity of the villa near Barranca a dry stairway was dug out. In this way it must have been possible to push through to an air bubble from the land.

In the phase of the construction work the greatest part of the population were evacuated. Possibly, this was for a reason, whereby with nobody on hand, nobody will know of the U-boat bunker. It is known that the construction work must have gone on in a very satisfying manner because soon there after a large freight ship made port on the island.

Two large multi-ton lathes were transported to Fuerteventura where they disappeared in the U-boat base. At the spot where the Barranca was found a cement roof was perhaps drawn over on top and so over that the original state of affairs were again set in place.

Also, at least two entrances to the subterranean installation must have existed since this was the only bunker that would have to be accessed underwater.

For U-boats of the 7-C Class it was thoroughly possible to take bearings at periscope depth and to near this point at a crawling speed.

The sense and purpose of this secret base must have been created on a completely independent basis, which was also administered and conducted completely autonomously.

It remains open if the real purpose, above all, was the smuggling of tungsten, which was known to have been wrapped up with this

7 Tons of Gold for the Base

One thing is certainly clear: every autonomous base must be financially independent from the Reich. At least it was ever so certain that there was the availability of an adequate, well-fortified cash box. That it must have dealt in gold is without a doubt.

Gold was, in such cases, a legal tender that was superior to all other monetary means. According to similar and corresponding statements, the amount dealt with was about 7 tons of gold. The base was prepared for action and, likewise, always for whatever secret action.

Fuerteventura - 1974

A large yacht moved itself about for a day in the waters around the island. The crew, two Spaniards and an Austrian, acted like tourists. Where ever they surfaced they were well received because of their gregarious, likable manner had made them many friends among which were not the government look-outs whom did not exactly have their blessings. But one thing attracted attention again and again. They always brought up conversation concerning the topic of the Second World War and also of the missing U-boat base and where exactly it could be found.

Again and again the yacht cruised the southern waters of Fuerteventura. One day the members of the crew dropped anchor. While one man remained on the yacht, two divers slipped into the water from the side of the ship away from the shore. They purposefully neared the coast, where, in about 6 meters in depth, gaped a large dark opening—-doubtless the entrance to the bunker. To be sure, the seabed here in the course of time is heavily choked with sand but the opening is still almost five meters high. A strong current prevailed with made it hard for both divers to move and also made the visibility at the bottom of the tunnel not more than two to three meters. Becoming wide in the interior of the tunnel, they deposited a flashlight that they had brought as a reserve for emergencies.

Gradually the water became shallower and after some meters they ran into a cement wall. The end of the tunnel has been reached. They climbed up over the wall on an iron ladder and for the first time immediately put away their diving gear. When they let their searchlights of their underwater lamps stretch over the interior of the huge cavern they were pale and it seemed to time that the blood froze in their veins...

What they saw as so monstrous that they both had to immediately sit down.

Part II

Two Spanish journalists succeeded in finding the underwater entrance to the U-boat bunker. They surfaced inside in order to investigate the secret of the bunker. What they saw inside was so monstrous that they immediately had to sit down.

In the defused light of their underwater flash lights they recognized machines in the background of the once natural cavern. But there were shadows which left the blood in their veins completely frozen. The cone of light of their flashlights swept over two U-boats of the 7-C class. As both divers caught hold of themselves they went towards the "sharks" to investigate closer. The U-boats were marked with the fastening of steel lines in the Atlantic surf, which were strongly noticeable. The attempt to open the U-boat on the left wall failed. They tried it on the U-boat to the right. Here they succeeded to open the turret hatch. They were now prepared for the worst. But as they carefully climbed down the tower nothing happened. In the light of their flashlights they recognized that everything had been lift in an orderly state. There was no sign of hasty flight or panic at all. It seemed as if the U-boats were ready to put out to sea.

Nautical Maps of South America

A pile of nautical maps stirred up their attention. One map especially caught their eye. The map of the coast of South America! Six points were marked with the letter "T" in a circle. Between the maps they found newspaper clippings.

They both laid everything back in their piles and climbed back out of the boat. After they closed the turret hatch they noted the number of the U-boat. Meanwhile, after the time came in they decided on a return dive to the ship and, on the next day, to come again to salvage the objects and particulars they had found.

The current had, in the meantime, become worse. They barely reached the diving gear that they had deposited which they had left behind in the case of emergency. They climbed back into the boat, again from the side that did not face the island, where the third man, the Austrian, awaited. After they had communicated their discovery, they verified, in a manual, the numbers of both U-boats and experienced, once again, a surprise. The numbers of the U-boats lying in the bunker were officially considered to have been sunk!

As they lay with their boat turned in a southerly direction, the villa Winter, with its small tower was like a fortress in the sparse landscape of Fuerteventura.

This night nothing special occurred on this small Canary Island other than that of a fire breaking out on a tourist ship with a

1977 Gran Canary

I got to know a man in a restaurant who was already here since the end of the war. "Charlie" as everyone here calls him, was a fighter pilot and after an accident he was sent to the command of a U-boat unit. Here in Gran Canary, Charlie is a general servant for everything. For the present he accompanied a German film team that shot a film here and on Lazarote. One day I brought up conversation of attack German U-boats. The veteran told me that they once surfaced inside a bunker. Immediately, I broke in with the story of the Fuerteventura bunker. With a doubting voice in opposition, I was told that such a thing was impossible. And now Charlie is not available. He himself has made the surface bearings about a mile from the island. The reference point is two rocky points which produce a "U". One point is round and large while the other point is small.

In conformity with Charlie's statement they moved themselves at a creeping speed back and forth in front of the island for four hours. There, according to the statement of his commander, the entrance was only possible at a certain time. Besides this the entrance should sometimes be visible on the upper margin in heavy surf. As I asked a couple of questions, Charlie described to me the inside of the bunker. Finally, as he spoke of two giant lathes, I knew that it must concern the secretive bunker.

Further, Charlie explained that the Commandant of the base blew up the land path in the early part of 1945. From here on the refuge was accessible only by means of water. And now came Charlie's story of adventure, like a blow from a hammer.

Vanishing Point for War Criminals

The base was said to have been active to 1950. With the knowledge of the American government, from here were allegedly brought wanted war criminals and Nazis to overseas destinations. Originally, there had been three U-boats but one was actually sunk in the vicinity of Florida. The idea occurred that both remaining U-boats likewise be noted as sunken. On my inquiry, because the crew remains present, the old ply for hire is the answer. The crew would have lived a civilized life on the island and would have only been active in response situations.

How did he know these things so exactly, I questioned him? But Charlie had a plausible explanation for this. Here on Gran Canary still lived a few of his former comrades, he explained. You know, when veterans meet we don't always talk about women. Then, often times the talk is of the past times. That was clear to me. But what was not clear to me was the whereabouts of the gold. "You can't forget the gold", laughed Charlie. "Look once around Fuerteventura yourself—-what do you see for buildings?" "Well, hotels", I answered. "You see, and these hotels have cost much money." "When you look to whom these crates belong you will find many German names."

Nothing has really changed here since the war. The fascists always still pay attention that nobody asks any unpleasant questions and if anyone becomes unpleasant, well, for them something is always found. What is really behind the secret one will never know because the Spanish authorities as well as the Germans have too great an interest to keep the background veiled. Who knows something doesn't talk about it because the conversation could be highly dangerous. This is also the reason why, in this story, nowhere does a name appear - except that of Charlie. And Charlie lives no more!

Therefore it is perhaps very well that a secret remains because there are people who are convinced that the truth could lead to a serious crisis and crisis we have indeed already enough of.

Appendix

On November 2, at 2:33 P.M. a caller reported to the editing department. He did not want to give his name but he had information about the article U-boat Bunker. The unidentified caller explained that he had been on Fuerteventura since February 1949.

In May, 1948, the personnel were informed that in ten days a "transport" would be due. In the middle of May, twelve Germans entered the villa Winter. Among these, according to the caller, he recognized Martin Bormann and Dr. Josef Mengele. The remaining ten people were not recognized by him.

On the next day, the fugitives were led to a staircase in the cellar of the villa, which led to a passage to the bunker. In the afternoon at 5:00 P.M. they put out to sea. Also, according to the caller, deposited in a room in the cellar of the villa is a large mass of documentary material and plans. What kind of data this is, he does not know. A comrade told him that this transport was carried out by the organization "ODESSA", which now, three years after the end of the war, still functioned. The transport to South America, according to the caller, arrived there safe and sound...

Here in the Canary Islands was an SS base that operated after World War Two. In fact, two U-boats were on-call and continued to be on-call for some time even after their last mission. We know this because the informant, "Charlie", includes the detail that the crew lived in the Canary Islands.

This base functioned at least up until 1950 and with the knowledge and consent. This would be the intelligence services of the USA, probably the CIA. We will get into this relationship later but we begin to see that this relationship between the surviving SS organizations, which became the "Nazi International" or The Third Power, was not always adversarial.

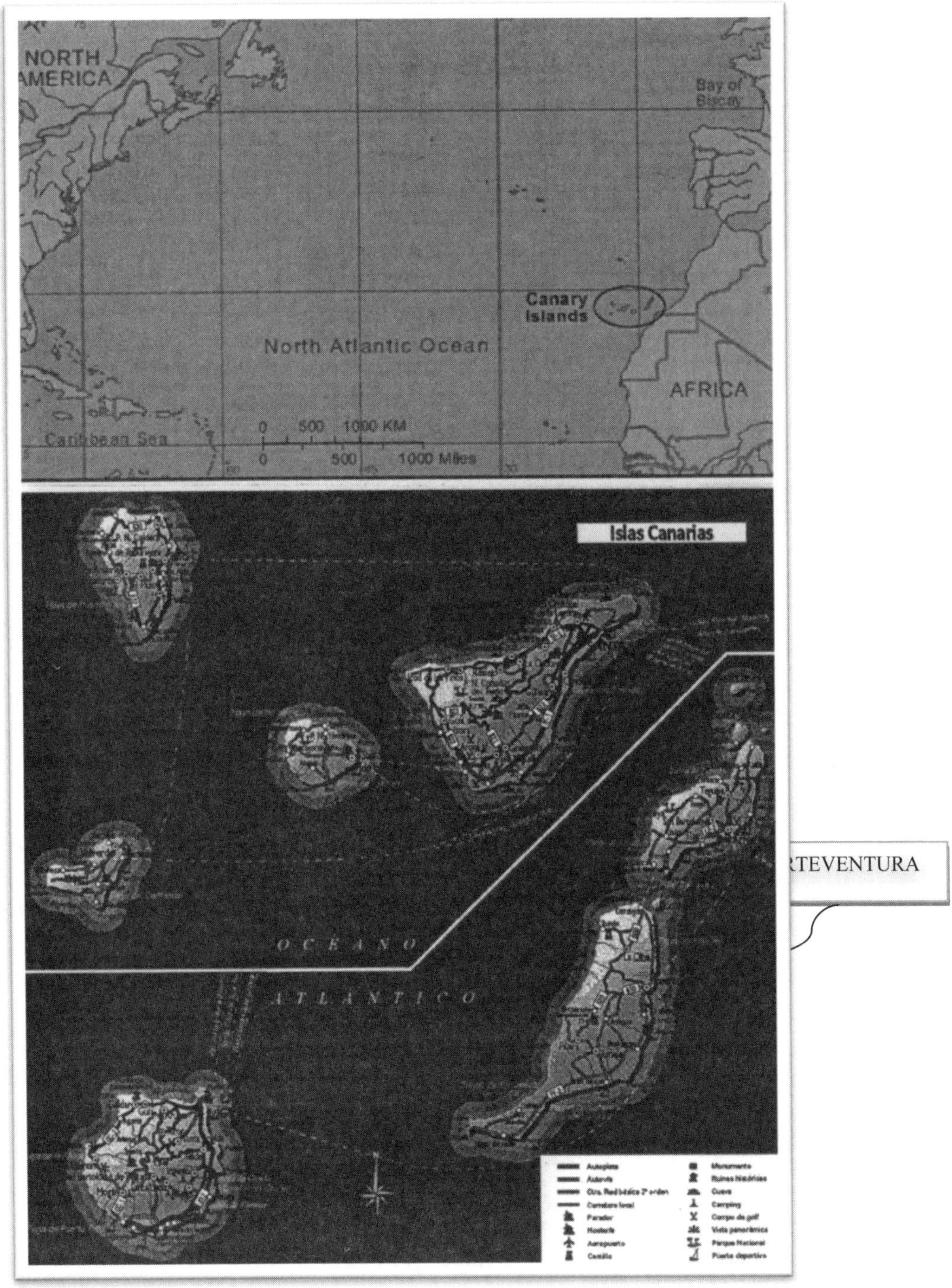

The Island of Fuerteventura
Fuerteventura is part of the Canary Islands just off the coast of Africa

Nugget Magazine Articles from 1984
Titled "Der U-Boot Bunker von Fuerteventura", this two-part article details the discovery of an underground German U-boat base.

Exclusiv:

Der U-Boot Bunker von Fuerteventura

Sieben Tonnen Gold im Nazi-Stützpunkt

In einem geheimen U-Boot Bunker auf der spanischen Insel Fuerteventura liegen heute noch zwei U-Boote, die offiziell als versenkt gemeldet sind.

Tausende von Urlaubern, die jedes Jahr ihre Ferien auf der Kanareninsel Fuerteventura verbringen, ahnen nicht, welches Geheimnis dieses Eiland vor der afrikanischen Küste birgt. Die Geschichte des U-Boot

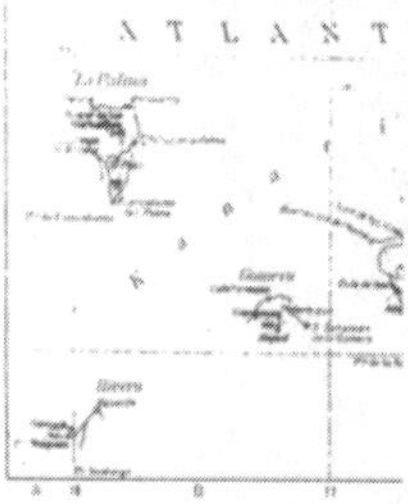

NUGGET 7/84

Exclusiv:

Der U-Boot Bunker von Fuerteventura

Teil II

Zwei spanischen Journalisten ist es gelungen, den unter Wasser liegenden Eingang zum U-Boot Bunker zu finden. Sie tauchen hinein, um das Geheimnis des Bunkers zu ergründen. Was sie darin sehen, ist so ungeheuerlich, daß sich beide erst einmal setzen müssen.

Im diffusen Schein ihrer Unterwasserscheinwerfer erkennen sie im Hintergrund der einstmals natürlichen Höhle Maschinen. Zwei riesige, bedrohliche Schatten aber waren es, die ihnen das Blut in den Adern schier gefrieren ließ: Die Lichtkegel ihrer Lampen streichen über zwei U-Boote der 7-C-Klasse. Als sich die beiden Taucher wieder gefangen haben, gehen sie daran die „Haie" näher zu untersuchen. Festgemacht mit Stahltrossen dümpeln die stählernen Röhren in der Atlantikdünung, die selbst hier in dieser Höhle noch stark bemerkbar ist. Der Versuch, das Boot an der linken Mauer zu öffnen mißlingt. Sie versuchen es am rechten Boot. Hier gelingt es ihnen, die Turmluk zu öffnen. Sie sind jetzt auf das schlimmste gefaßt. Aber als sie vorsichtig in den Turm steigen, geschieht nichts. Im Schein ihrer Lampen erkennen sie, daß alles in ordentlichen Zustand verlassen wurde. Kein Anzeichen von überstürzter Flucht oder gar Panik. Es sieht so aus, als wäre das Boot zum Auslaufen bereit. Sie suchen weiter.

Seekarten von Südamerika

Ein Stapel Seekarten erregt ihre Aufmerksamkeit. Besonders eine Karte fällt ihnen ins Auge: Die Karte von der Küste Südamerikas! Sechs Stellen sind mit dem Buchstaben „T" in einem Kreis markiert. Zwischen den Karten finden sie Zeitungsauschnitte.

Die beiden legen alles wieder an ihren Platz zurück und klettern wieder aus dem Boot. Nachdem sie das Turmluk wieder verschlossen haben, notieren sie die Nummern der U-Boote. Nachdem inzwischen Ebbe eingetreten ist, beschließen sie, zum Schiff zurückzutauchen und am nächsten Tag wiederzukommen und die gefundenen Gegenstände und Unterlagen zu bergen.

Die Strömung ist mittlerweile noch schlimmer geworden. Mit Müh und Not erreichen sie das deponierte Tauchgerät, das sie für den Notfall hier zurückgelassen haben. An der Land abgewandten Seite klettern sie wieder ins Boot zurück, wo sie der dritte Mann, der Österreicher, erwartet. Nachdem sie ihre Entdeckung mitgeteilt haben, prüfen sie im Handbuch die Nummern der beiden U-Boote nach und erleben abermals eine große Überraschung. Die Nummern der im Bunker liegenden Boote gelten offiziell als versenkt!

Als sie mit ihrem Boot abdrehen in Richtung Süden, liegt die Villa Winter mit ihrem Türmchen wie eine Festung in der kargen Landschaft Fuerteventuras.

In dieser Nacht ereignet sich auf der kleinen Kanareninsel nichts besonderes. Außer, daß auf einem Touristenschiff ein Feuer mit einer anschließenden Explosion ausbricht. Zwei Touristen kommen dabei ums Leben! Der dritte Mann ist später nicht bereit, auch nur das geringste zu dem Unglück und den vorangegangenen Unternehmungen zu sagen.

1977 - Gran Canaria

In einem Restaurant lerne ich einen Mann kennen, der bereits seit Kriegsende hier ist. „Charlie" – wie ihn alle hier rufen, war Jagdflieger und nach einem Unfall wurde er zu einer U-Booteinheit kommandiert. Hier in Gran Canaria ist Charlie das Mädchen für alles. Momentan begleitet er ein Deutsches Filmteam, das einen Film hier und auf Lanzarote dreht. Eines Tages bringe ich das Gespräch auf die Feindfahrten Deutscher U-Boote. Da erzählt mir der Veteran, daß sie einmal getaucht in einen Bunker eingefahren seien. Sofort fällt mir die Geschichte des Fuerteventura-Bunkers ein. Mit zweifeln-

12 NUGGET 8/84

Nugget Magazine Articles from 1984
Titled "Der U-Boot Bunker von Fuerteventura", this two-part article details the discovery of an underground German U-boat base.

Knowledge of this base and its continued existence after the war brings up claims of other facilities, laboratories, being operated by the SS after the war. Yes, there are those that say this is so and was done, not over the horizon in some never-never land, but right in Europe itself!

Misters Mayer and Mehner publish parts of a letter received presumable after publication of earlier investigative works. This letter was from a Mrs. Maria W. whose husband had worked as the chief of the construction-planning department of the German Post Office (Deutschen Reichspost). The Reichspost functioned as a research and development arm of the German government at that time. This was particularly true of atomic research being done in Germany of which the Deutschen Reichspost was a major player. Mrs. W. establishes herself as a credible witness by describing historical and biographical details that would only be known to governmental insiders of those times. In her letter she discusses secret facilities she knows will be of interest, particularly to Mr. Mehner, those concerning the Jonas Valley. She says in her letter, describing Marineheim near Sitzendorf in Schwarzatal that this area was not known to the Americans and Russians. This probably means the significance of these areas were not known to the Americans and Russians since they both obviously had maps. This area had "Anlage" in her words, which I translate as "facility". This facility had a close connection to Arnstadt (Jonas Valley), the U-boot supply and the Mitteldeutschen Werk (probably meaning the Nordhausen V-weapons plant). Mrs. W. says the SS operated this particular facility until 1952 (4). This, obviously, is inside Germany!

Not only that. She goes on to describe a small train track running to Bienstein (presumably also from the area of the Jonas Valley) that ran into a mountain. The Russians found the train track but did not ever follow the track fully into the mountain. This was the entrance to a German facility underground. For whatever reason, the Russians did not find the German facility there. Mrs. W. says this was a "Fusionsanlage" an atomic fusion facility. Not fission but fusion, as in hydrogen bomb! The big news is that this facility operated until 1952! At that time it was shut down but remains ready to fully resume operation (5).

Copies of the two U-boat Bunker of Fuerteventura articles were sent to researcher Mark D. Kneipp who had some interesting comments. He wrote to me in a letter that he believed the two U-boats may have been U1020 and U1021. According to his work, these were both type VII-C-41s that "were completely rebuilt with the latest sound detection and weaponry just before the end of the war." A premise under which I am working is that towards the end of the war the German Navy did not produce a totally new class of U-boats in which to test new engines and weaponry as the did with the Type 26, building a test type, the Type 17b. Instead, they refitted damaged or archaic U-boats as they presented themselves on an individual basis.

But the thing which should most concern us is the description of the base and its almost certainty of actual existence. If you accept the description of the base as a huge, hollow, natural volcanic bubble, connected to and accessible to the sea by tunnels, being full of machinery necessary to run a U-boat bunker, almost in plain sight, overflown and monitored on the surface by Allied aircraft and ships, then the proposition must be taken seriously that the Germans also had similar bases in areas where they would have been able to construct them unhindered. The fact is that the German base at Fuerteventura alone makes the case for the strong possibility if not the probability of similar bases in the Arctic and Antarctic.

But if that is not enough, there is one more tiny piece of evidence, which was promised and to which we return now. By this it is meant that "outstanding service" performed for the Germans by General and engineer Gustav Winter, for which he was given land on Fuerteventura and oversight of the base there. Before the war engineer Gustav Winter worked on research, using a strong magnetic field, to influence the compasses of ships and U-boats (6). This could only be the Magnetofunk device that was said to have been employed at Point 103 and perhaps elsewhere to divert enemy aircraft that were seeking these bases in order to destroy them (7). Even legends sounding crazy at first blush can have a basis in reality.

Literature Cited

1. **Gehring, Heiner and Karl-Heinz Zunneck, 2005**, *Flugscheiben ueber Neuschwabenland Die Wahrheit ueber "Vril", "Haunebu" und die Templer-Erbengemeinschaft*, page 165, Jochen Kopp Verlag, Rottenburg, Germany
2. *ibid.*
3. *Nugget* (magazine), July and August 1984 editions, *Der U-Boot Bunker von Fuerteventura*, Two part story in consecutive editions
4. **Mayer, Edgar and Thomas Mehner, 2002**, *Die Atombombe und das Dritte Reich*, page 203, Jochen Kopp Verlag, Rottenburg, Germany
5. **Mayer, Edgar and Thomas Mehner, 2002**, page 204
6. **Gehring, Heiner and Karl-Heinz Zunneck, 2005**, page 165
7. **Stevens, Henry, 2007**, *Hitler's suppressed and Still-Secret Weapons, Science and Technology*, pages 52 to 57, Adventures Unlimited Publishing, Kempton, Illinois, USA

ELECTRIC SCHAUBERGER

We are going to take a little break before beginning with a discussion of Nazi secret bases in South America. And here I would like to make an apology. In my first book I discussed the Schauberger saucer and mentioned that rather than use air or water, which were Schauberger's mediums, the German government would have been more interested in taking the principles, the basis by which the Schauberger saucer flew, and incorporating these principles into a saucer design but one which used modern electronic components rather than air. Comments are made about this statement, such as by Dr. Joseph Farrell (1). My apology is not about this statement itself which is true and should serve as an introduction as to why we are discussing Schauberger at this time. My apology is rather that I did not originate these words or the underlying concept of using modern electronics to replicate Schaubergian principles. Instead, a truly first-rate mind came up with it, that of "Dr. Gordon Freeman'. I only repeated it without proper ascription of its source. Sorry Dr. Freeman. Believe me, I have tried to enlist Dr. Freeman in writing a book which would explain this and other concepts to the rest of the world but he has declined. Dr. Freeman is busy frying bigger fish.

Let us return to Viktor Schauberger and the idea of building a saucer using Schaubergian principles but out of electric components. Schauberger's saucer and ideas are explained by Coats (2) who devotes a book to it, by me in my first book, (3) and again by Farrell (4). Actually, this "electronic component"-thing will become self-apparent if we just look at his saucer from another perspective. We have to do a little table-setting first. We are going to go over the publicized test of the Schauberger saucer and try to uncover some of the physics that would allow this to happen.

During the war Schauberger worked for the Nazi government and probably the SS at Castle Schoenbrunn. But prior to that, in 1940, Schauberger built two saucer models, one of which was tested at the place were it was fabricated, the Kertl company in Vienna. Schauberger had two objectives according to Coats:

"The purpose of these prototypes was two-fold:

1. *the further investigation of free energy production, and*
2. *the validation of Viktor's theories on levitational flight.*

Whereas the first case required the upper aerodynamic portion to be permanently fixed to the base, the 2nd case required its attachment to a quick-release coupling to permit its ascent once auto-rotation and the generation of levitational force had had been achieved. To initiate the energetic process, a small high-speed electric motor was used, capable of producing between 10,000 and 20,000 rpm.

Despite its compact size, this machine generated such a powerful levitational force that when it was first switched on (without Viktor Schauberger's permission and in his absence!), it sheared the six 1/4 diameter high-tensile steel anchor bolts and shot upwards to smash against the roof of the hangar. According to Viktor Schauberger's calculations, based on the data from previous tests, a 20 cm diameter device with a rotational velocity of 20,000 rpm world have generated levitational forces of such magnitude that it would have lifted a weight of 228 tonnes."(5)

The exact "levitational forces" have always been a mystery. Everyone has had a shot at explaining it.

The Schauberger saucer was made of copper, a conductor. As stated above, it was 20 cm in diameter. The pictures show it with a top and without but the completed saucer flew with the top. The top was perforated with several holes that allowed air to enter from the sides and perhaps the top. The rapidly spinning saucer then guided the air downward and then at right angles toward the periphery of the saucer, being forced between two undulating plates. As the air made its way to the periphery, it was rolled over by the centrifugal motion of the spinning saucer and formed into several mini-tornadoes. The air exited at the outer edge of the saucer where it was forced by vanes all pointing in the same direction into imparting the torque necessary for continued rotation. Dr. Freeman made the point that the air entering the saucer was also formed into vortices, one within another and extending a distance beyond the hat-like structure. The extension would also be horizontal and in the exact opposite direction of the vortices inside the saucer making their way toward the periphery. Coats goes on with another detail:

"In addition a glowing bluish white discharge akin to ionization is produced." (6)

The suspicion here is that it was an electrical effect. For instance, Coats points to triboluminscence in explaining the above (7). In addition, cooling is observed around the saucer. What could cause all of this? What, that is, in our known physical world and without resorting to physical processes or mechanisms which are not yet in evidence?

Air would enter the top, or hat, portion and be drawn downward simply because the saucer was being spun at 10,000 to 20,000 revolutions per minute. As a result, the centrifugal force of the air already within the saucer was being ejected, creating a low pressure area inside the saucer that would simply draw more air in. This is caused by the small electric motor spinning the saucer, ramping it up to auto-rational speed. There is nothing strange here. But there is an electrical phenomena, the bluish-white light and the levitational effects which still remain unexplained. For this we have to start where Schauberger starts, with Lord Kelvin's water thread demonstration.

Lord Kelvin's apparatus, shown below, demonstrates water's ability to accept and conduct an electrical charge. It has been given several different names over the years, including *Kelvin's water-thread device* and *Kelvin water dropper*.

Inside the device made by Kelvin, two small jets released a stream of water droplets from a common reservoir. Each drop from the jet, or dropper, fell through a ring of conducting metal—usually copper. After traversing the ring, the individual drops fell into their own individual retaining reservoirs, which were generally made also of a conductive material but remained electrically insulated from one another. Finally, conducting wires connected each ring to the opposite reservoir.

This is what happens. Some tiny imbalance occurs so that one retaining reservoir becomes slightly more positive or more negative than the other. There could be several reasons for this—an applied voltage or even tiny imperfections in the apparatus itself will give rise to slight differences in the fields acting on the two drops as they travel along the length of the stream.

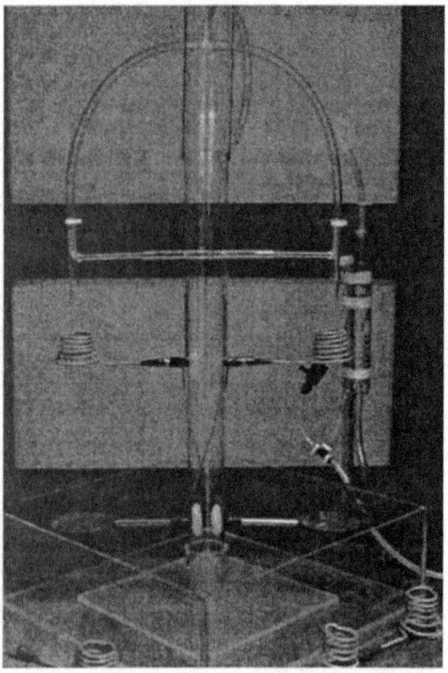

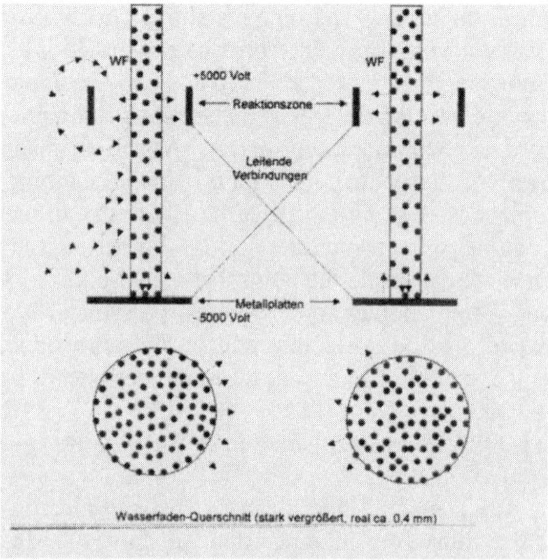

Lord Kelvin's Water Thread Demonstration
Kelvin's apparatus demonstrates the electrical conductivity of water through the electromagnetic induction of streams of tiny water droplets by separating and amplifying small potential differences in individual drops.

Since a conducting wire electrically connects each reservoir to the opposite ring, any small excess charge picked up by one drop at the end of its journey will be transferred to the ring that the next droplet on the opposite side will be traveling through. For a positive increment of charge transferred to the ring, a positively-charged droplet leaving the jet will want to take the "more negative" path, while a negatively charged droplet will move toward the "more positive" reservoir below. The result is a positive feedback loop, with each increment of charge introduced to the apparatus contributing to a greater attraction for more like charges. Thus, natural incremental charges are amplified again and again, quickly building up the opposite charges in the two reservoirs through electrostatic induction.

Eventually, both retaining reservoirs become highly and oppositely charged. A spark may leap from one ring to the other and/or drops may become electrostatically repelled and start to fly upward! Both these conditions are ways the systems seeks to discharge itself (7).

The point is that small drops of water can carry an electric charge and manifest electrical effect. Viktor Schauberger built and studied this machine himself. But the obvious question is how in the world would Kelvin's concept be related to the levitation of a flying disc inside a manufacturing plant? There would be no fog or clouds inside the Kertl factory to serve as a pathway for electrical effects, so how would tiny droplets of water manifest themselves in this setting?

We must look at Bernoulli's Principle. It states that as the velocity of a fluid (air should be considered a fluid in this case), the pressure exerted by that fluid decreases. This is counter-intuitive at first. It says, for instance, that air in motion has less pressure than air standing still but this is correct, nevertheless. (9) An airplane wing works using Bernoulli's Principle since the air passing on the upper (wavy) surface must travel faster that on the underside (straight) surface to reach the same point at the rear edge of the wing. This more rapid air flow on the upper surface causes a low pressure area to form at the spot on the wing where the wave occurs, causing the higher pressure underneath the wing to push it upward, keeping the aircraft in flight. Bernoulli's Principle is also involved with fluid or air in a tube. If the tube is constricted, causing the air to flow more rapidly, the resulting air pressure is decreased. This might seem familiar, as it is how a carburetor works. The constriction is called a "Venturi" (an application of Bernoulli's Principle) and it is at this point of lowest pressure that fuel and vacuum hoses are joined to the air-fuel intake system (10).

We all know that air holds water as water vapor. When the temperature drops or when the air pressure drops, the atmosphere cannot hold as much water as it can at higher pressure or higher temperature. Fog or clouds form if this happens. This sometimes even happens at odd moments. For instance, sometimes behind the leading surfaces of aircraft (where pressure would be lowest) a fog can briefly form. I have even seen this happen on large big-rig trucks in which the area behind their external rear-view mirrors develops a fog when they are going fast enough under certain atmospheric conditions.

So, what is happening inside the Schauberger saucer? Air is forming a vortex, extending outward and sideways long before it enters the saucer. Once it enters the saucer this vortex is strengthened. Air speeds are at least tornadic and probably much higher. Schauberger tells us the temperature of the air drops. With both a temperature drop and a drastic pressure drop, water droplets condense from even a dry atmosphere. These water droplets, rubbing against each other as they do in thunderstorms and/or colliding with the copper body of the saucer itself, pick up and carry an electric charge. In fact tornadoes are often observed to have lightning bolts descend straight down their walls toward the ground. Whether the individual vortices within the Schauberger saucer actually carry a DC current is really immaterial. They carry an electric charge and they are moving, violently. This moving charge means each one of the many Schauberger vortices within the saucer is generating a magnetic field, just as every wire carrying an electric current generates a magnetic field.

Each internal vortex is running in the same direction. If two conducting wires, for instance, are sending electricity in the same direction, their moving magnetic fields attract each other. Each vortex would be held equidistant from the next by these forces. More importantly for us, each vortex would be interacting with its neighbor and the central flowing center in the same way the seral disc did with its magnets, which is the basis of magnetic reconnection. It is this magnetic reconnection that generates electrons and positrons each time lines of magnetic lines of force are broken and reconnect. It is this migration of electrons to the bottom and positrons to the top of the craft that is responsible for levitation. This imbalance is what I'm calling a super Biefield-Brown Effect that causes movement toward the positive charge. In this case it means levitation.

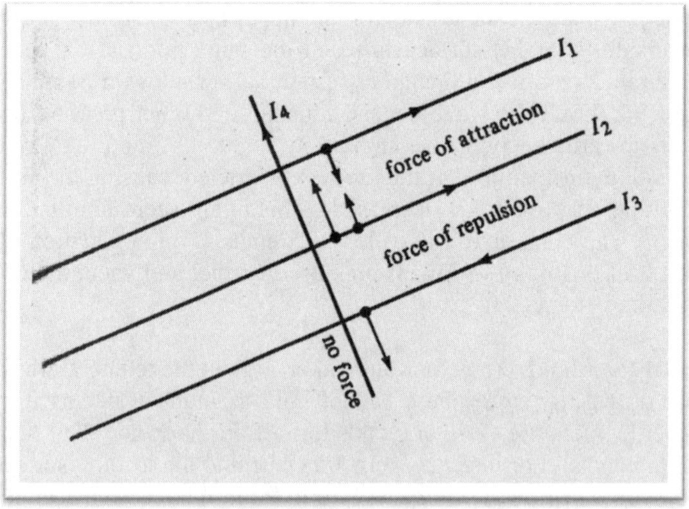

Parallel Electric Currents

Moving electrons constitute an electric current, and electric currents generate their own magnetic fields. If two conducting wires carry a current that is moving in the same direction, the wires will be attracted to one another. If their currents flow in opposite directions, an opposite, repulsive force will exist between them.

Meanwhile, the saucer body is spinning, being pushed as in a jet aircraft by the mass of the air being ejected at a slight angle by the directing vanes. This torque is important to remember. But as this is all happening and the saucer is being pushed to 20,000 rpms by the small electric motor, to auto-rotational speed, feeder vortices are forming at the inlets on the hat's sidewalls and perhaps top. The very same thing is happening here. The decrease in temperature and pressure is causing droplets to from which are rapidly spinning in the vortex, picking up electric charge.

Not only does this cause levitation but other electrical phenomena such as luminescence. "Reverse moment" resulting from any interaction between the magnetic fields involved would be overcome by the torque generated by the thrust of exiting air, deflected at an angle as it exited the saucer.

So now we can say the Schauberger saucer and the Searl disc both levitate in the same way. One uses air and one uses electric components, although primitive ones. Magnetic reconnection is responsible for the flight characteristics of both and when you think about what happened; both had the same fight characteristics.

Literature Cited

1. **Farrell, Joseph P., Ph.D., 2004**, *Reich of the Black Sun Nazi Secret Weapons & The Cold War Allied Legend*, page 216, Adventures Unlimited Publishing, Kempton, Illinois, USA
2. **Coats, Callum, 1996**, *Living Energies*, Gateway Books, Bath, UK
3. **Stevens, Henry, 2002**, *Hitler's Flying Saucers*, pages 121-129, Adventures Unlimited Publishing, Kempton, Illinois, USA
4. **Farrell, Joseph P., Ph.D., 2004**, pages 206-221
5. **Coats, Callum, 1996**, page 287
6. **Coats, Callum, 1996**, page 292
7. *ibid.*
8. *Kelvin Water Dropper, Wikepedia: http://en.wikipedia.org/wiki/Kelvin_water- dropper/*
9. *Bernoulli's Principle, Wikepedia: http://en.wikipedia.org/ wiki/ Bernoulli's _prin ciple*
10. *Venturi Effect, Wikepedia: http://en.wikepedia.org/wiki/Venturi_effect*

SOUTH AMERICA AND OTTO SKORZENY

By far, the largest numbers of post-war Nazi bases were located in South America. Nazi money would purchase tracts of land that became secure areas. Of course, hand in hand with the purchase of the land was the purchase of the politicians in power since both were needed for the land or the base to be truly secure. In Latin America, exchanging money for political favors is not simple corruption. On the contrary, this is doing business and this is the way all business is done on all levels. Sometimes this is hard for others to understand, as are the political aspirations of Latin American politicians. Politicians in Latin America do not want to ascend to power in order to change the system. They want to ascend to power in order to avail themselves of the system. Money makes this world go around. But South Americans would have equally damning things to say about other political systems, so let us just accept this political reality as it is and try to understand it as we proceed.

Secondly, we cannot understand the Nazi presence in South America, the SS self-help groups, the Nazi International, or the 3rd Power, without and understanding of the man instrumental in setting up this hidden world within a world, Otto Skorzeny. It is true that Martin Bormann set up the financial foundation as well as the general understanding of responsibility in what would be called the Nazi International. The problem was that Martin Bormann, Hitler's beancounter, was not in evidence after the war. As mentioned earlier, some think he did not make it out of Berlin after fleeing the bunker upon Hitler's death. In any event, he did not manifest himself to collect the huge sums of money and other valuables squirreled away in South America and other places by the Nazis toward the end of the war.

Let me say, just to set the record straight, as mentioned before I do not believe Hitler ever saw May 1, 1945 or that Bormann ever made it out of Berlin. But that does not mean I do not encourage those that do research these aspects of World War Two. On the contrary, there is a whole political philosophy which has morphed into a kind of political correctness which says everything about World War Two is known and understood and to question their understanding is politically incorrect and should be discouraged. This includes those researching Hitler possibly surviving the war. All aspects, everything, every assumption about World War Two should be questioned, researched, and everything which is propounded as fact should be backed up with as much proof as possible. Since the Berlin Wall fell, our understanding of German high technology has changed from night to day. Perhaps this is true in other aspects of the war's story. Has shinning light on a subject ever hurt honest brokers of the truth?

Back to Skorzeny: It was Colonel Otto Skorzeny who was present along with Bormann at the outset of the planning at the Rotes Haus in Strassburg on August 10,

1944 with those industrialists and bankers. In fact it was Skorzeny who was in charge of physically transferring the assets to neutral countries. (1) Dr. Hjamar Schacht was responsible for showing the industrial and financial concerns how to camouflage foreign assets on paper. (2) Dr. Schacht was Hitler's National Socialist financial genius who pulled Germany out of the Great Depression in 1933 and made it a financial world power while other countries were still wallowing around in doom and gloom. It was Skorzeny, assisted by Schacht, who showed up in South America, in the late 1940s, to collect the Nazi treasure that had been on-loan to political interests there. But Skorzeny had added some wrinkles to the original Rotes Haus plan. We need to take a look at Skorzeny and his achievements and those "wrinkles" in order to understand what finally happened in South America as well as what finally happened with the post-war SS organizations.

Otto Skorzeny wrote about himself and his exploits in his book, "Meine Komandounternehmen" (My Commando Operations). I have read bits and pieces of this book. The problem with it is that he was running the SS world while he was writing it. Even some of the information about happenings during World War Two seem out of character. The reason for this may have been that many people, some countries and some organizations, were always actively seeking to find a way to prosecute Skorzeny because he was an unashamed and vocal Nazi. He never disavowed Hitler and this just plain drove people crazy. Skorzeny was tried for alleged war crimes and acquitted but there was always the possibility that some other entity would try it again. So, "Meine Komandounternehmen" sometimes reads like Skorzeny's lawyer wrote it.

So, for a more objective view of Skorzeny, we have to turn to someone else. Glenn B. Infield, who was an American bomber pilot during the war and who was a professional writer, comes forth and fills this need. Infield is not without problems in his 1981 attempt, as he tries to paint Skorzeny, not as a war criminal, but as a terrorist. In fact Infield tries to paint Skorzeny as the origin of all terrorist organizations, in tactics if not politics. As is customary in the use of the pejorative term "terrorist", Inflield brands those he dislikes in the modern world terrorists and omits those on the other side using the same tactics, even if those omitted had actually originated the terrorist tactics. Nevertheless, Infield is the best available. He even went so far as to interview Skorzeny in Madrid shortly before Skorzeny's death in 1975. The following is a synopsis of his treatment of Skorzeny.

Otto Skorzeny was born in Vienna in 1908. His father owned an engineering business and so Otto was sent off to the Technical College of Vienna to study engineering. At college this large, strong, aggressive individual joined a dueling society. This club fought duels with swords in a ritualistic way. The combatants held the sword, so I am told, with both hands making downward strikes and upward blocks aiming at the opponent's head. Sometimes these were grudge matches but one of the objectives of a person's dueling career was to receive a cut to the head and have it stitched up rather badly, leaving a dueling scar as a mark of honor. At this time in Germany citizens preferred their professionals to have such marks as it implied a college education as well as personal courage. Skorzeny graduated with his dueling scar and began his own career as an engineer.

In 1938 Skorzeny stepped between two groups of Nazis preparing to beat each other up leading at the time of Austria's unification with Germany. Evidently, it was the force of Skorzeny's personality that prevented the bloodshed and this did not go unnoticed by Nazi higher-ups.

Skorzeny had learned to fly an airplane, so in 1939 with the outbreak of the war, he volunteered for the Luftwaffe. The Luftwaffe decided Skorzeny was too old at 31 and rejected him. Skorzeny was shunted to a communications depot in Vienna where he was unhappy. Meanwhile the Waffen SS was looking for people with a technical background and this was a perfect escape valve for Skorzeny. He was now an officer-cadet in the Waffen SS.

Otto Skorzeny

This picture was taken during Skorzeny's rescue of Benito Mussolini after a rival Italian government had secretly imprisoned him. This "prison" took the form of the Gran Sasso Hotel on a table-top mountain. Skorzeny led a glider attack, secured the light rail line leading from the mountain, and flew Mussolini off the mountain in a very light aircraft. After depositing Mussolini in Vienna, Hitler was so impressed and overjoyed that he instructed the Wehrmacht General in charge at Vienna to take off his own Iron Cross and personally pin it on Skorzeny's chest.

Skorzeny always wanted to succeed in his assignments and did so even if the rules had to be bent. After a few episodes of bent rules Skorzeny's chances of high rank seemed in serious doubt. A bar room brawl in Holland followed, caused when Skorzeny demanded a picture of Prince Bernhard of the Netherlands be taken down. Skorzeny was restricted to the base for 6 weeks. Evidently, the German military was not looking to promote "bad boys" which was hurting Skorzeny's career chances.

Then Skorzeny's unit was transferred to Yugoslavia to fight partisans. Skorzeny was the technical expert in charge of keeping the regiment's vehicles in repair. Three days into Yugoslavia Skorzeny happened to notice a large group of enemy soldiers walking towards one of his vehicles. Skorzeny quickly hid his men in the bushes. As the enemy soldiers were appraising the broken down truck, Skorzeny popped out from behind a tree with a rifle and along with his men took these soldiers as prisoners. Skorzeny marched fifty-four soldiers and three officers back to headquarters in custody. To quote Infield:

> *"Skorzeny's past transgressions in Holland were forgotten and he was made an officer on the spot." (3)*

Shortly thereafter Skorzeny experienced health problems in the form of a recurring gall bladder attacks. The severity of this problem eventually resulted in doctors declaring him unfit for front-line service. By this time, after the success in Yugoslavia, it must have been clear to everyone coming in contact with Skorzeny that "active service" was the only area where Skorzeny shinned. This was a big, aggressive, intelligent, technically trained man who was not afraid to take a risk. He possessed an ability of natural leadership. Finally, he had achieved some notoriety at what he really did best. Now, he was given an assignment at a repair depot near Berlin where he was expected to sit out the remainder of the war. Skorzeny must have been crushed.

Skorzeny's old friend and fellow Austrian Dr. Ernst Kaltenbrunner paved the way for an appointment to AMT VI-S, a division of the RSHA or Reich Central Security Department, a part of the SS. By this time he had made Captain. Part of his job involved interfacing with the Abwehr, the counterintelligence unit of the German high command run by General Wilhelm Canaris. This put him in contact with a wide variety of Reich insiders and under sometimes confusing chains of command. One benefit was that he sometimes took direct orders from Hitler and had personal access to him (4). Finally, he was promoted to leader of his own commando unit headquartered in Friedenthal near Oranienberg, northwest of Berlin. It should be noted that this area was a hotbed of all sorts of secret weapons development.

Skorzeny's commando unit has been called a James Bond type affair since it used new, strange and high tech weaponry which was of the small arms kind. He was given access to KG 200, the squadron first recruited to fly the manned version of the V-1. This was considered a suicide mission, although not publicly acknowledged as such. After Hitler canceled the manned V-1 program, Skorzeny still had access to this squadron of flyers ready to take on any challenge where danger and death were possible or probable outcomes.

On July 26, 1943 Skorzeny was flown to Rastenburg to be interviewed by Hitler at his Wolf's Lair headquarters. At Hitler's teahouse there Skorzeny found himself one of six apparent candidates for something as they were all going to be interviewed by Hitler. Each candidate reviewed his career for Hitler. Skorzeny quickly determined he was the only Austrian in the group. He was also the only one familiar with Italy that seemed to be important to Hitler. Hitler stood there, eyeing Skorzeny after his little talk. He then asked Skorzeny:

> *"What is your attitude toward Italy and the Italian people?"*

Skorzeny replied:

"I am an Austrian and our attitude toward Italy is prejudiced by the happenings in the previous World War and by South Tyrol."(5)

According to Infield, a slight smile appeared on Adolf Hitler's face. This must have been the knowing smile of a fellow Austrian and the smile of one who knows he is not being deceived. Skorzeny had just spoken "truth to power" as we say now. Italy had done a flip-flop during the First World War, (as they were destined to do in the Second). The peace settlement had given the region of the South Tyrol and its ethnic German lands to Italy, angering not only the South Tyrolians but all German speaking peoples. Hitler undoubtedly felt some of this and recognized Skorzeny's reaction as genuine. Hitler dismissed the other candidates.

Now Hitler confided in Skorzeny that his mission concerned Benito Mussolini, who had just been taken prisoner in a coupe – a forced resignation. His leadership role was assumed by King Victor Emmanuel, who Hitler knew would trade Mussolini to the Allies and join them in a flip-flop just as soon as the moment was opportune. "El Duce", Mussolini, had preceded Hitler to power and Hitler considered him a pioneer in terms of Fascist doctrine. The two men had grown close over time, Hitler being drawn to Mussolini perhaps as he was to no other man. The Fuehrer told Skorzeny:

"The Duce is, in my view, the last Roman. He is he last visible symbol of the proud old Rome that once ruled the world. His life, his rise, and his deeds are only comparable with those of an old Roman ruler. The Duce is more to me than a confederate, more than the representative and founder of Italian fascism. He has come close to me as a human being as few men before. He is my great friend. And I never leave my friends in the lurch.

"You, Skorzeny, will free my friend Mussolini and prevent the terrible fate which our enemies have conceived for him."

At this point Hitler reached out and took Skorzeny's arm, looked him directly in the eyes and said:

"Bring me my friend Mussolini. I know you will do your best and succeed."(6)

Obviously, failure was not an option here. Hitler placed resources at Skorzeny's disposal for this operation, but the big problem was that nobody really knew where the new Italian government was keeping Mussolini. Skorzeny brought 50 of his own commandos, camouflaged as part of a larger paratroop unit being sent to Rome to help stem the Allied advance in Italy. The mission had to be kept secret from the existing German forces in Italy and was known only to General Student, who was to assist Skorzeny in terms of resources.

In recounting this adventure, most concentrate of the actual physical mission itself. For this discussion the processes by which Skorzeny found Mussolini are perhaps even more important. Here, Skorzeny used every bit of his intelligence, education and training in addition to his native inborn assets to his advantage. This is in stark contrast to the situation which got him into so much trouble in Holland.

Once Skorzeny arrived in Italy he quietly questioned the people responsible for intelligence about the whereabouts of Mussolini. Nobody knew where the new government was keeping him prisoner. In fact, the Italian civilian population was puzzled by Mussolini's disposition as well. Frustrated, Skorzeny began circulating in restaurants and bars, engaging Italians in various ways to see it someone would open up. Skorzeny hit upon a plan. He would first raise the issue and then insult anyone claiming to know where Mussolini was being held, hoping to get a strong rebuttal and additional information.

Have you ever wanted to be a fly on the way in observation of history? My all-time trivia "fly" moment would be the time Skorzeny badgered an Italian sailor who fell for Skorzeny's insult strategy and became so incensed that he pulled a knife on Skorzeny in a bar. The six-foot four, wide spanned, 235 pound Skorzeny who had years of dueling experience behind him involving, essentially, just long knives, must have seen the irony in the reaction he had just perpetrated. To be a fly on the wall as Skorzeny's own men retold the episode must have been something also.

An Italian naval officer told Skorzeny in a bar that Mussolini was being held on the island of Ponza but he was transferred to La Spezia. Skorzeny, using his ploy, accused the Italian of trying to impress women in the establishment. The Italian naval officer became incensed and threw his glass at Skorzeny, a reaction Skorzeny considered appropriate if this was the truth. After checking this specific information it was determined that Mussolini was being held at both locations but had been recently moved.

After an intercepted letter indicating Mussolini was being held on Sardinia led to another island, Isola di Picco, both of which proved false, a young prostitute told Skorzeny Mussolini was being held at La Maddalena, a small island just north of Sardinia. A German spy, disguised as an Italian sailor, was sent and verified Mussolini's presence at a villa on Maddalena

Skorzeny wanted more information to formulate a rescue. He obtained use of a Heinkel He-111, a bomber with a glass nose. Skorzeny positioned himself at the nose with his Lecia camera, ready to snap pictures of the villa, presumably in a prone position just as enemy aircraft were sighted. Skorzeny ordered the pilot to stay on course, but one of the aircraft destroyed one of the two engines on the He-111, causing it to plunge downward. Skorzeny had just enough time to grab onto something as the aircraft nosed underwater and shattered the glass nose. But fortune was with that mission, because there was just enough air in the forward section of the aircraft for it to nose up as if it were gasping for breath. Skorzeny escaped with his life.

Hitler was advised of a plan for an aerial assault on La Maddalena by Skorzeny, who had been summoned back. Hitler approved, but meanwhile Mussolini had been moved again. Time was running out. The Italian government was finalizing negotiations with the Allies and there was no doubt that Mussolini would be given to them in that agreement. The German position in Italy was also deteriorating.

Finally, Skorzeny got word Mussolini was being held east of Rome in the Abruzzi Mountains at a place called Gran Sasso. Gran Sasso was a tabletop mountain with a hotel on top. A small railroad connected the hotel to the valley below. Of course, Skorzeny wanted another reconnaissance flight, so this time Skorzeny, camera in hand, knocked out the glass window of the light aircraft and leaned out, snapping pictures while his second in command secured him by holding his feet.

It was decided that the only way was a glider attack, landing directly on the tabletop in spite of the numerous boulders upon it. The gliders were constructed of tube metal and fabric, and were being provided by General Student. Skorzeny kidnapped an Italian general who was to order the Italian guards to put down their arms. Skorzeny was to land in the third glider. A Fieseler Storch—a light, two-man reconnaissance aircraft—would would land and fly Mussolini away.

The attack was underway when the first two gliders disappeared in a cloud. On the other side, both had somehow vanished and visibility was poor. Skorzeny cut a hole in the fabric of the glider in order to direct the pilot to the mountain. As they approached it became clear that a landing was impossible due to the rocks that lay directly on the area on which they planned to land. Skorzeny ordered the glider flown low and slow, and then suddenly ordered the pulling of the parachute's ripcord. The parachute was designed only to slow the glider once it was on the ground. The glider crashed down the last few feet to earth with a sudden stop. Skorzeny jumped out, Italian general in tow, ran to the hotel and obtained access to Mussolini without a shot being fired. Skorzeny's words of introduction were:

> *"Duce, the Fuehrer has sent me to set you free."*

To which Mussolini responded:

> *"I knew my friend Adolf Hitler would not abandon me"*

Meanwhile, the Italian solders were amassing below to retake Gran Sasso. Skorzney had only about 90 of paratroops on the mountain with him so time was of the essence. Conditions made it clear that the two other escape options they had considered were not going to work. Skorzeny called in the Fieseler Storch, flown by Captain Heinrich Gerlach, General Student's personal pilot and it managed to land on the tabletop and was waving for Skorzeny to load Mussolini aboard.

We all remember Mussolini and remember that he was not a small man. The Fieseler Storch had only a 240-horse power engine and was designed for two men and flyers in those days were usually not overly large men. The situation was that the aircraft could not take off against the wind, as is customary which means the lift generated at take off would be diminished. Further, the "runway" was not near long enough for a take off, the only option at this point was to run the aircraft off the side of the plateau and hope it would gain enough air speed before crashing into the valley below.

Skorzeny pushed Mussolini into the Fieseler Storch and then climbed in himself! Captain Gerlach flatly told Skorzeny "nein". Skorzeny politely told Gerlach this was his mission and essentially, his fate was intertwined with that of El Duce. If the aircraft crashed, well, Skorzeny would have been shot, so he might as well come along. Now, Captain Gerlach was obviously a pilot, Skorzeny was a pilot and Mussolini was a pilot so they all knew what was involved here.

The aircraft drove off the side of the cliff and began its 3,000-foot plunge to the valley below. Gerlach let it dive, attempting to gain airspeed. All were speechless except for Skorzeny who was at this point certain they would crash. Gerlach eased the stick back and the slow-flying Fieseler Storch had just enough lift to pull them out of this hole.

They flew to Pratica de Mare where a transport aircraft flew Mussolini to Vienna, still accompanied by Skorzeny where they landed and checked into a hotel. Himmler called Skorzeny to congratulate him. As Skorzeny was finally easing into relaxation, a full colonel burst into the hotel, and, on Hitler's orders, took off his own Knight's Cross to the Iron Cross and pinned it on Skorzeny chest. At that moment the Fuehrer called and said:

> *"Today, you have carried out a mission that will go down in history. You have given me back my old friend Mussolini. I have given you the Knight's Cross and promoted you to Sturmbannfuehrer" (major). (7)*

This was the start of the Skorzeny legend. There are about four missions in all that we need to understand. For the next mission, I am going to describe the legend and only partly rely on Infield. It was the legend surrounding Skorzeny in South America and firmly established by the time he got there. It is for us even more important than reality, if it differs from it, since legend had become reality by this time.

This mission is sometimes referred to as the "Horthy kidnapping". It is strikingly similar to the Mussolini mission in some ways. The similarities in September, 1944 were that German intelligence had ascertained that Hungary was about to do a flip-flop. Hungary had been occupied by the Wehrmacht and its regent, Mikki von Horthy, a World War One Naval hero and Admiral, was in league if not an ally of Germany's. About a million German soldiers were stationed in Hungary. Hungary had important oil reserves upon which the 3rd Reich relied. Hungary's seat of power was the Burgberg or Castle Hill where government offices were maintained in "the Citadel". This whole Burgberg/Castle Hill complex was near Budapest but separate from it in an ancient fortified town sitting on top of a hill. The whole matter was a problem inside a problem for the Nazis. Hitler, again, had a fire on his hands and so he called for his fireman:

> *"We have received confidential reports that the regent of Hungary, Admiral Horthy, is trying to establish contact with the enemy in order to negotiate a separate peace. If he is successful it would spell the loss of our army in*

Hungary. You, Skorzeny, are going to prepare for the occupation of the Burgberg in Budapest. When I give the order, you will start the operation. In order to permit you to obtain the necessary men and weapons, I shall give you written orders which will give you extensive power."(8)

In fact, Hitler placed a great deal of military muscle and men under Skorzeny's control for this mission, far more than was the case in Italy. The "order" Hitler was talking about was called a "Hitler Befehl" (Hitler Order) in which the bearer could order things done, anything done, in Hitler's name as if Hitler himself had given the order. This was a very, very powerful document and order.

Skorzeny wanted this coupe accomplished without destruction of the Burgberg. Remember, Skorzeny was an Austrian and Austria had been a part of the Austro-Hungarian Empire for three hundred years and had only been separated since the end of World War One. Skorzeny chose to travel to Budapest under an assumed name and survey the situation before finalizing a plan. He was to keep in contact with Berlin, periodically, reporting by radio. For some reason the codename for the operation was "Nikki Maus". At times Mikki von Horthy had gone by the nickname of "Nikki" as did his son, Mikki Horthy, Jr., a young man regarded as little more than a playboy.

The legend is that while on-route to Budapest and traveling alone, Skorzeny stopped in an inn for the night and a good meal. Skorzeny was a big Cro-Magnon-type and needed his meat. Wartime restrictions were such that it was rationed. Skorzeny, traveling incognito, wanted red meat or sausage for dinner at the inn. The proprietor argued with Skorzeny saying they had no meat or sausage as a result of the war. Skorzeny did not believe this and so the argument became more and more heated. Finally, Skorzeny pulled out the Hitler Befehl and ordered meat essentially in the name of Adolf Hitler. The proprietor complied; Skorzeny got his meat dinner. This was the only time the Hitler Befehl was used by Skorzeny.

Skorzeny arrived at the Burgberg and assessed it for an assault by various elements of the German Army. There was no place for paratroops to land and the densely packed old town was full of Hungarian soldiers. Skorzeny sought a more subtle method to subvert this government rather than outright attack.

To make matters worse, SS General Erich von dem Bach-Zelewski had arrived in Budapest with his huge 650 mm mortar and was pressuring Skorzeny to level the Burgberg at once. To add even more pressure Mikki von Horthy was not at the Burgberg in his office at the Citadel. Instead he was meeting with representatives of Marshal Tito who was acting as a go-between for the Soviets. Something had to be done immediately.

Skorzeny learned that Admiral von Horthy's eldest son, Istvan, had been killed when his aircraft crashed on the Russian front. Since the accident the regent had bestowed all his affection and hope upon his second son, Mikki Horthy, Jr. Young Horthy had been little more than a skirt-chaser and drinker but had tried to straighten up in the aftermath of the death of his brother and his father's new expectations. Skorzeny decided to kidnap the younger Horthy and then demand continued allegiance to Germany from his father as a price for his life.

The legend is that the kidnapping plan was radioed to Berlin but this was simply too much for the radio operator. He decided to change the code-name of the operation from "Nikki Maus" to "Mikki Maus", either in confusion over the name similarity or out of a sense of humor. The Walt Disney character Mickey Mouse had become a household word, worldwide. In any event, Berlin acknowledged the kidnap plan.

The actual kidnap plan was do be conducted by Skorzeny and some of his men in civilian clothes. Mikki Horthy Jr. was heavily guarded and to make matters worse, the time and place was set for the kidnapping when young Horthy was to be meeting with representatives of Tito in an office building. As Mikki, Jr. was exiting the meeting he was set upon by several elements of Skorzeny's men coming form different directions. Skorzeny himself was parked across the street, pretending to have an automobile breakdown. A gunfight ensued. Skorzeny threw a hand grenade at the entrance to the building to prevent more of Mikki Jr.'s bodyguards from joining the fight. The outcome was Mikki Horthy Jr. being captured, rolled up in a rug, taken to the airport and flown to Germany. Berlin was notified by radio that Operation Mikki Maus had succeeded.

The problem was that the elder Horthy, the regent, Admiral and leader of his country, told Skorzeny to just go ahead and shoot his son. He was not going to aid Germany at this point.

Berlin was again notified that in spite of the fact that Operation Mikki Maus was a success, the outcome of the operation was not really successful. The legend is that from this time on, in both German and English languages, anything that worked but not well was labeled in slang as a "Mickey Mouse Operation".

Skorzeny had no alternative but to initiate assault plans on the Burgberg. Again, I'll go with the legend. It was explained to me that Skorzeny drew Wehrmacht to the Burgberg in overwhelming force. Still, he wanted to minimize bloodshed. Skorzeny obtained a Kubelwagen, a military Volkswagen that looks something like a jeep, and with the top down, bullhorn in hand, he led a column of tanks toward the Burgberg. Skorzeny would rely on his loudspeaker to convey his voice, in German but with an Austrian accent. He reasoned that no Hungarian had fired upon an Austrian in three hundred years and if he could use this fact just to make the Hungarians hesitate, he might be able to bluff his way to the Citadel. He neared the first barricade and began talking. Now, nobody really wanted a battle. Skorzeny just found the right words, spoken in just the right way with, of course, the right accent. Without firing a shot he was in the Citadel, now ordering the Hungarian officer in charge to lay down their weapons. The Hungarians complied. Skorzeny had captured a vacillating Hungary without firing a shot. He had prevented the German Army there from being captured and saved the oil production facilities for Germany.

Berlin was notified. Skorzeny was told to assume military regency of Hungary for the time being. Mikki von Horthy was taken to Bavaria where he spent the rest of the war as a prisoner of the Reich in luxurious style.

A week later Skorzeny was again in Hitler's office at the Wolf's Lair. Hitler told him he was about to take part in an offensive, the offensive called by the Americans "The Battle of the Bulge". This was an attempted push on the western front to Antwerp by the Germans. It was the last German offensive of the war. Skorzeny's guile was to be used to advantage.

Hitler was telling Skorzeny that he must race ahead of the attacking tanks in American uniforms and American jeeps and secure certain bridges. He was to be given German soldiers fluent in English for this mission. In reality, Skorzeny had to round up most of the jeeps and uniforms himself. After the capture of the bridges Skorzeny's men were to function as spies, reporting on the strength of units they encountered. They were also to cause any mischief they could behind the American lines.

Now this misdirection mission was taylor-made for Skorzeny. To quote Infield:

> *"One of his groups passed through a breach in the American lines and advanced to Huy on the banks of the Meuse River. The leader, Firtz Bussinger, checked the bridge carefully, although it was guarded by American soldiers, and then decided to walk through the town itself to get an accurate understanding of the situation. Greeting American soldiers he met and saluting all officers, he spent several hours in Huy without incident. As he was getting ready to return to his companions waiting of the outskirts of the city, an armored vehicle leading a convoy of tanks approached. The lead vehicle stopped near him and the officer in the right seat asked Bussinger the way to Marchin. He promptly pointed north, the opposite direction of Marchin and explained that the Germans had captured several of the roads leading to the city of Marchin and they would have to make a wide detour. Unaware that he was being led astray, the American officer thanked him for the information and led his convoy away...in the wrong direction.*
>
> *Another of Skorzeny's commando units, led by Wilhelm Giel and wearing a military police insignia, took over the duty of directing traffic in a small village behind the American lines. When a regiment of the 84th Infantry Division arrived, Giel and his men directed them down the wrong road. Later they listened to American broadcasts that the regiment had been missing for three days. A later investigation of the incident by U.S. officers failed to turn up a trace of any military police who had been at this particular intersection, so Skorzeny's report of the incident was verified."(9).*

But the big news was a rumor, a false one, which Skorzeny did not want to quash. The rumor among the Americans, once they found out of Skorzeny's work behind their lines, was that Skorzeny's real mission was to assassinate General Eisenhower. By now they knew of Skorzeny's work saving Mussolini and his involvement that kept Hungary on the Axis side. The Americans freaked out! They put Eisenhower under guard and his movements became somewhat restricted. Check points were set up and everyone challenged everyone else. At one point the British Field Marshal Bernard Law Montgomery who had jumped on the opportunity to more freely circulate on the front lines in Eisenhower's absence, was stopped in all this confusion and asked for proper identification. Montgomery told his driver to keep moving. The Americans promptly shot out the tires of his command car and forced Montgomery and his driver into a guard shelter at gunpoint. Finally, a British colonel was called to positively identify Montgomery, which he did. It can only be imagined how angry the Field Marshal was at this indignity.

The German offensive finally played out and the Wehrmacht retreated. Now the British and Americans were advancing from the West to the East and the Russians were on the eastern borders of Germany advancing from the East to the West. The Third Reich was in its death throws.

This time it was Heinrich Himmler giving Skorzeny orders. Himmler, who by this time had gotten himself named commander-in-chief of the Army Group Vistula, was essentially ordering Skorzeny to save has bacon since he, Himmler, was obviously incapable of command himself. Himmler ordered Skorzeny to proceed to Schwerdt, a small city on the Oder River, form a bridgehead on the eastern side, and launch an offensive from this position. Two million extremely battle-hardened Soviet soldiers, tanks, support and aircraft were advancing to the Oder. Once across, a strike on Berlin was the only step remaining in the war. Also, the area from the Oder to Peenemuende was full of secret weapons test facilities, advanced aircraft production plants, rocket production facilities, and so on.

Skorzeny was given the order but nothing else. In American politics this is called an "unfunded mandate". Finally, Himmler came up with 1000 men. One thousand men against two million are not great odds. Skorzeny set out for Schwerdt nevertheless. But a strange thing happened on his way to Schwerdt. Soldiers who found themselves unattached to their units or whose units had ceased to exist because of losses began bonding to Skorzeny. The personal power of his presence was drawing volunteers. And this was not going to be an easy mission or even a mission from which one would expect to return. Skorzeny took up a position near Schwerdt.

Somehow, Hermann Goering heard of the situation and called Skorzeny. Goering sent Skorzeny 600 men from his own Hermann Goering Division who were supposed to guard Karinhall, Goering's country home. Skorzeny somehow appropriated fifteen 75 mm guns from an abandoned factory. They were not the famous 88s but they could still be used against Soviet T-34 tanks. Skorzeny also found a supply of MG42 machine guns and some anti-aircraft guns.

On February 17, 1945 the Soviets moved to overrun Skorzeny's position. The Hermann Goering Division coolly let the Soviets advance to within about 100 yards from their position before they unleashed an anti-tank rocket barrage. The tank advance was halted and now burning as the German snipers picked off the Soviet soldiers scrambling out of their burning tanks. The Soviet Army was now being held from advancing by a small force. This situation lasted six days when finally Skorzeny ordered his men across to the western side of the river.

Himmler was furious and ordered Skorzeny back to his headquarters. Himmler wanted the officer in charge on the ground to be shot and generally went off on a rant as he had probably seen Hitler do many times. Skorzeny just sat there and absorbed this tirade. When Himmler had spent himself, Skorzeny spoke:

> *"You sit back here where it is safe, where you have all you want to eat and drink, and you have the nerve to order a brave officer shot because he used good judgment and retreated to fight another day. All we ever received at Schwerdt from you were orders. No ammunition, no food, no reinforcements, nothing." (10)*

This was the second time Skorzeny had spoken truth to power. Himmler backed down. Skorzeny held out at Schwerdt until the end of February,1945. This delay in the Soviet advance allowed the evacuation of Peenemuende as well as the Nordhausen V-weapons works. It allowed the evacuation of all those secret aircraft and their test facilities in this area. More importantly, all the documentation concerning the actual building of this weaponry, the blueprints, were microfilmed by the SS and other entities and put in safe-keeping.

But there is even more to this conversation and our understanding of the post-war SS. A new dynamic had taken over the SS. After the death of Adolf Hitler in another month it became almost law. In the post-war world the ideologues of the Nazi movement lost their special standing. They had failed in the eyes of the rank and file soldier. These men no longer wanted to hear from the likes of Himmler, even if he had survived. Outside of political doctrine, he was at best a desk soldier. From now on the rank and file took their lead from real soldiers, the soldiers who had led them for six years of war. Only these men had the moral authority to command at this point.

This brings us to Martin Bormann because, at best, Bormann was Hitler's accountant. Whether Bormann survived the war or not is irrelevant. Bormann did not surface in South America to put in a claim for the Nazi fortune from those South Americans who had meanwhile usurped it. Nor did Bormann put in a claim for leadership of the post-war SS. He would have been disallowed even if he had done so. The Nazi leadership had been discredited in the eyes of the rank and file soldiers. By now the only people listened to by the expatriate German fighting men in South America or anywhere else in the Nazi post-war world were the men who had earned their respect by their fighting record in the war. Skorzeny was at the top of this list.

The war ended at which time Otto Skorzeny surrendered to the Americans. There was some confusion at first but they eventually figured out who he was and Skorzeny, for the most part, cooperated with the Americans, answering there questions so long as they did not touch on his post-war SS plans. The American recognized Skorzeny's value on several levels and recognized his deep and genuine anti-Communist feelings. The problem with Skorzeny was that he was a Nazi and, as such, was unashamed. This really pissed some people off, including some people in the US government.

In my first book on German flying discs the topic of extraterrestrials within the US government was discussed. It is a kind of tower of babel affair in which extraterrestrials are denied on one level but on the next level they are affirmed, suggesting the lower level intelligence was a cover story. At the next level they are denied again and so on up the tower. Nobody really ends up knowing anything. Well, it is the same way for political issues including the Nazis- only here it is a horizontal landscape.

One governmental agency wants to use the Nazis and contrives methods to "clean them up" for their purposes. The governmental need was manifested, for example, by Operation Paperclip. This was also true for the anti-Communist intelligence activities in which the Gehlen Org. was incorporated into the US intelligence effort and later spun-off and became the West German intelligence apparatus. But there were also facets of the US government who assumed a very anti-Nazi position, seemingly and at times actually at odds with other governmental agencies with other goals. The Paperclip people were always grooming and spotting up the records of Germans they wanted to work for them in the USA. Meanwhile, the "Nazi-hunter" types in the Department of Justice were actively trying to make a case against these very same people. Dr. Arthur Rudolf is an example of a person who was originally cleaned up by Paperclip until the goal of a moon landing was realized and then turned over to the Department of Justice for alleged use of slave labor at Nordhausen in spite of the fact that he had no control over slave labor there. In fact, the individual in control of the slave labor at Nordhausen and throughout Germany seemed to have been immune from prosecution or even efforts at the location of his whereabouts. This was, of course, General Hans Kammler. Kammler was just too big to prosecute.

Back to Skorzeny: Skorzeny simply was one of those individuals—Hans Ulrich Rudel was another—who simply would not say they were sorry for their Nazi past. Skorzeny, when located, was seemingly always giving news conferences. The favorite questions he would be asked concerned the Eisenhower assassination rumor, which he denied, and his possible involvement in flying Hitler to safety from the bunker in the last days of the war. Once, at a news conference, Skorzeny was asked if he flew Hitler from Berlin to Madrid in a two seater Messerschmitt Me 109. Skorzeny laughed and responded that if the Messerschmitt Me 109 could have flown from Berlin to Madrid, Germany would have won the war. It was statements like this rather than anything Skorzeny did during the war that led to him being put on trial for war crimes. He simply pissed off too many people.

The charges involved using poison bullets and the killing of individuals while in the uniforms of Allied soldiers. At first it looked bleak but Skorzeny had an American lawyer who believed in his innocence. In two courtroom stunners, Skorzeny refuted the rather weak evidence brought to bear by the prosecution. The first charge was a case of mistaken identity, as the poison bullets had been confused with another type of bullet. Brought to testify for the defense was a famous British commando, Wing Commander Forrest Yeo-Thomas, who testified that he had done exactly the alleged act for which

Skorzeny was being put on trial himself, acting under orders and on behalf of the British government. Skorzeny was acquitted.

Skorzeny was released for a time but taken into custody again by the new West German government as part of their de-nazification process. This was an appraisal and classification of individuals, ranging from criminal to those opposed to Nazism. Most Germans did not want the latter classification as it seemed to brand them as traitors, so the classification of "simple fellow traveler" was considered the optimum. Skorzeny could not get classified and so could not be released. Skorzeny informed his keepers that he had been found not guilty of war crimes and was under no obligation to stay, nor would he. Nobody listened to him. Finally, three American military police showed up and demanded Skorzeny be handed over for new charges. The West German governmental officials complied and Skorzeny was handed over.

Once they were out of earshot, Skorzeny was released by the three "Americans" who turned out to be former SS men with an American vehicle and uniforms. Who provided the props, the uniforms and vehicle? Skorzeny would later say that it was the Americans themselves (11).

Eventually, Skorzeny found his way to Madrid, where the Nazi-friendly Franco government posed no threat. There, he set up an engineering firm. In reality, Madrid was the locus of the post-war SS. It was both the intelligence center and the center for management of SS business. This was not something Skorzeny thought up while in American custody—it was something he had planned long before the war ended.

Remember, Skorzeny had been present at the August 10, 1944 meeting wherein Martin Bormann met with all the industrial and financial heads of Germany. Money, secret weapons and high tech blueprints, specialty steel, and machine tools were spirited out of the 3rd Reich for overseas destinations for use after the collapse of Germany. The industrialists were encouraged to set up firms in neutral countries. Dr. Hjalmar Schacht, the financial genius, was made available for assistance in accomplishing this transfer and camouflaging it on paper from prying eyes. Otto Skorzeny handled the physical transfer of assets to neutral countries. The understanding was as follows:

> *"Bormann promised them Nazi funds for this purpose with the understanding that the Nazi survivors would be able to draw from the profits of these firms later." (12)*

When Bormann failed to appear after the war, it was Skorzeny who enforced this understanding, and it was Skorzeny who took it upon himself to recover any and all moneys which had strayed from Nazi control in the time elapsed since the war had concluded.

At this point we have to consider Reinhard Gehlen and his Gehlen Org. This was sold to the Americans as an existing anti-Soviet spy network that could be activated by Gehlen. Although this plan would later be abandoned, there were always suspicions that Gehlen still worked for Germany first. In other words that he had never severed his Nazi ties or his Nazi allegiances. Furthermore, the Gehlen Org. has been accused of actually stirring the pot, so to speak, in the East-West conflict that was the cold war. By this it is meant that he may have over played his role and overstated or manipulated some threats to the West to keep the Cold War alive.

Dr. Hjalmar Schacht, who would become Skorzeny's father-in-law in the post-war years, knew where the money was buried and how it was buried and who was owed what. In other words, just as the Mafia in the USA had Meyer Lansky, who kept all the financial relationships and accounts between family leaders buried in his brain, the post-war Nazis had a similar store of information in Schacht, who effortlessly kept track of the money and moved it around the world.

Finally, there was Skorzeny, a man of tremendous ability in the eyes of the Allies, who could get things done behind the scenes with both the power of his personality and an ability to utilize the considerable human and mechanized assets of the Nazis in a kind of post-war shadow world.

The three continued to communicate with one another, and at times worked together for toward reaching goals each considered desirable. If these goals coincided with those of the Americans or British, they were willing to work with them as well. But this seems to have fostered specific issues for the post-war SS and Schacht while on a broader range for the Gehlen Org. Of course, they could also work at odds with the western powers at times, making the relationship a fluid and dynamic one. Indeed, it looks to me like there were periods of cooperation and periods of warfare between the postwar SS and the Americans in particular, followed by reproachmont and a period of cooperation.

Less clear is the relationship between the postwar SS and the Soviets. Yes, even though communism and the Soviets were their least-favored political entities and opposition to them helped define their existence, it appears that there was some sort of contact and some sort of relationship, at least at times. For instance, Infield reports that a disgruntled former SS man, using the name "Kluf" reported to the US Consulate in Marseille that the Soviets had formed an organization composed of former SS men within the Soviet Block to work with the Russians against the interests of the West. Implicit in Kluf's testimony is that Skorzeny knew of this organization and had some sort of contact with them.

> *"Kluf said he did not like the Russians and told Skorzeny he was not in favor of working with them. Skorzeny allegedly promised him he could return to Germany to work independently (not for Russia, nor for America, but for Germany) but that Viy gave him different instructions. These were that he, accompanied by a courier from the Russian zone, would return to Germany and report to the organization's headquarters in Hamburg. Kluf said he was not n accordance with this so he left the courier after crossing he French border and came to the consulate in Marsielle." (13)*

The post-war SS organizations had some sort of contact with the Soviets, which, like relations with the Americans, could be used for their own purposes.

Here is a thumbnail chronology of the postwar SS. Of course there were many more names than this, code-names within code-names, but here is a sketch. First was the "Skorzeny Movement". This organization was alleged to be interested in resisting Bolshevism and ending Allied occupation of Germany. Next came "Die Bruderschaft" (the brotherhood) came about while Skorzeny was still in West German detention. The movement was growing in numbers as former SS members recognized they were in trouble and needed organization. The West did not discourage it (14). This morphed into the O.D.E.S.S.A, an acronym for "Organization der Entlassene SS Angehorige" (organization of those former SS members who were released). This morphed into "Die Spinne" (the spider). Now the focus was on assisting former SS men escape from Germany to other countries. A legal arm of Die Spinne was the HIAG, an acronym for "Hilfsgemeinschaft auf Gegenseitigkeit" (mutual assistance association). After setting up shop in South America and having helped most members disentangle themselves from legal problems, by hook or crook, a more pro-active stance was possible. This was the Nazi International phase. In this phase real international projects could be taken on, calling into play major German industrial firms as well as leading scientists and engineers. This was coordinated from Skorzeny's engineering firm in Madrid. This usually worked when a country did not want the involvement of the US or the Soviets since either brought the CIA or KGB. So, instead, the Nazi International could be called upon without the intelligence entanglements. This usually worked with the consent of both the East and West since neither wanted the other to gain a foothold and the Nazi International was an alternative for all concerned. Dr. Joseph Farrell titled a book on this subject that should be seen as a reference (15) as should Ladislas Farago's work (16).

So, as a small example, in the 1980's, during the Iraq-Iran War, both sides wanted to increase the range of their Scud missiles. It was obvious that German scientists worked for both sides doing this job. Infield gave many more examples.

In light of possible new evidence, I am going to make a distinction between the Nazi International and what the German writers call "Die Dritte Macht" (The Third Power). The Third Power was a power on its one as opposed to the First Power, the West and the Second Power, the Communist Block. The German writers such as Haarmann and Bergmann make the point that the Third Power held many technical secrets that were unknown in both the West and East. The idea may be that The Third Power sold or exchanged information and/or technology for favors it wanted from either or both other powers as the situation warranted. We will return to this later. What I want to do now is to give an example of how this barter system originated and from that one can get the idea of how it would have worked on a higher level. What I am talking about are the Churchill letters.

In the years immediately following the war and culminating with the Korean War, there was a push in the United States to utilize Germans who where considered hardened Nazis in the effort against communism. Some Nazis were released from US custody as a result. Churchill was not a part of this and refused to do the same in Great Britain. Skorzeny, now free, sent word through contacts in the US requesting that Fritz

Knoechlein, an SS officer who had been convicted of war crimes in Britain, be released. Churchill flatly refused. In fact, Knoechlein was put to death. Skorzeny bided his time, knowing he had something with which to fight Churchill.

He struck a year later Churchill was again running for office. It was rumored that between 1927 to the end in 1944, Churchill had been secretly corresponding with Benito Mussolini, even when the two countries were at war with each other. What these two leaders discussed we will never know but it is absolutely certain that the average British voter would have taken a dim view of their pen-pal relationship during the war if they had known about it or if the letters ever surfaced. Politics would have been a memory for Sir Winston.

Skorzeny sent word to Churchill that he wanted a meeting with him in Venice in August 1951. Subsisting, for the moment, on a diet of crow, Churchill took time off the campaign trail and went to Venice to meet with Skorzeny, whom he had snubbed and disdained during the Knoechlein affair. But how could Skorzeny have possibly gotten his hands on something that explosive?

Skorzeny had noted that during their mutual escape from Gran Sasso, Mussolini was not able to bring a briefcase with him in the cramped Fiesler Storch. This briefcase seemed to have some special value for Mussolini if he wanted it on his person at such a desperate time. Skorzeny was not only a brave soldier who had some real and exceptional ability, he was also as smart as a whip and it seems that in this aspect of his makeup he was underestimated because even in the heat of the moment at Gran Sasso, Skorzeny made a mental note of the briefcase and its apparent importance. But since El Duce and the briefcase had to part company, it was taken by German troops to Skorzeny's base at Friedenthal by aircraft. Of course it was opened and the contents read. Skorzeny was notified and instantly understood the value of the letters. Mussolini could use the letters to purchase his own safety and eventual freedom should he ever be taken prisoner or surrender to the British. Mussolini even instructed his wife to ask to be handed over to the British should she be taken prisoner (17).

From the moment Skorzeny understood the meaning and value of the letters, an SS man was stationed at Mussolini's side to track the letters. At the end, on April 25, 1945, as Mussolini and his mistress Claretta Petacci were fleeing Milan, Oberstumfuehrer Franz Spoegler was stationed at their side. This relationship did not bother Mussolini, since it was the SS and Skorzeny who had saved him at Gran Sasso and he trusted Skorzeny. Spoegler was a young, handsome man, according to Infield's description, and had made friends with Mussolini's mistress, Claretta Petacci. So as they were fleeing, Claretta Petacci asked Franz Spoegler if he would return to Milan and pick up some additional clothes she had there. Spoegler agreed, and in addition to packing up the clothing she requested, managed somehow to get his hands on the very subject of his being stationed at Mussolini's side—the Churchill letters. Three days later, both Mussolini and his mistress were swinging from the end of partisan nooses, but Skorzeny had the Churchill letters.

Now, six years later, the investment was paying off with interest. The only witness to the Churchill-Skorzeny meeting was Paul Foerster who accompanied Skorzeny. He reported:

> *"Sir Winston received some wartime items he wanted very badly and in turn we received hope that some of our comrades in prison might obtain early releases." (18)*

Miraculously, Churchill's office as well as the Americans released Gottlob Berger, SS General sentenced to 25 years; Hans Lammers, Reich Chancellery, 25 years; Paul Koerner former head of Hermann Goering Works; Heinz Jost, SS; Frans Alfred Six, Adolf Eichmann's superior; Edmund Veesenmayer, SS comrad of Skorzeny's and Kurt Meyer, SS General sentenced to death.

What is significant is the pattern that would be repeated. The former Allies want something, the post-war SS supplies it for a price and that "price" might not necessarily be money.

So this was the man and the legend, Otto Skorzeny, who strode ashore in Argentina in 1949 with the purpose of regaining the Bormann SS treasure and other accompanying assets. The reason that the fortune had to be "reclaimed" is rooted in the actions of two custodians of the fortune who had made some bad decisions in the power vacuum left in the absence of Bormann. These two were named Rudolf Freude and Heinrich Doerge. Somehow, Juan Peron's new bride, Eva, had talked these two into depositing the fortune in bank accounts bearing her name for safe-keeping. This all allegedly had to do with the status of Nazi Germany and the fact that Argentina had, under pressure from the USA, declared war on Germany in the waning days of that conflict and so assets belonging to the 3rd Reich might be subject to seizure.

Skorzeny had already been apprised of Juan Peron and his wife Evita. The rule of the first Peron Administration was very much a partnership and Skorzney was briefed that Evita Peron was the real brains of the outfit. He realized that recovering this fortune was going to be a tricky operation, as tricky as anything he had done before.

Skorzeny was a huge hit in Argentina. Imagine all those "Generals" and politicians coming out of the military (which was the usual route to power) who bore a chest full of metals yet who had never actually fought in a real war ingratiating themselves to and with the presence of a true war hero in Skorzeny. Skorzeny, for his part, did not mention the SS fortune at first. Instead, he served Peron in small ways such as organizing intelligence and police forces. Infield reports that he made it a point to ignore Eva Peron.

In July 1949 Skorzeny was tipped off that two navy officers were planning to murder Evita. This grudge went back some time and involved Juan Peron but the two plotters thought they could even the score by harming Juan's wife. Skorzeny raided the apartment where the two were living but they were not home but there he found the details of the plot including the exact locating the two would use. Skorzeny stopped Eva on her way to inspect facilities at one of her charities. He informed Mrs. Peron of the plot to murder her. Eva simply did not believe anyone in Argentina would harm her but invited Skorzeny to accompany her. As they neared the Home for Working Women, the charity involved, Skorzeny suddenly leaped from the car and ran inside a building. He emerged with the two plotters at gunpoint. Evita Peron was surprised and overcome with gratitude and from this moment on saw Skorzeny as her hero.

Skorzeny later admitted that his men had located the two plotters after his raid on their apartment, arrested them, and then positioned them in the very places they had specified in their plot to assassinate Eva Peron. Skorzeny had simply picked up and taken charge of the two from his men who were holding them out of view of Eva Peron. Thereafter, according to the research of Infield, Eva Peron and Otto Skorzeny carried on a torrid affair behind Juan's back on trips together and at country estates (18).

This did pay off as Skorzeny assumed about one quarter of the SS fortune on a purely voluntary basis. Hjalmar Schacht learned through his banking contacts that Evita Peron "and her associates" had forty numbered bank accounts in Switzerland. Schacht and Skorzeny believed this money to be the Nazi fortune. But about this time Eva Peron suddenly contracted cancer and died on July 26, 1952. But Juan Peron had a couple little problems. Juan Peron asked for Skorzeny's help. Skorzeny managed to have the Swiss assets moved into funding for her charity, the Evita Peron Foundation. But some of Evita's associates moved to administer the funds as befits a charity. Then, Juan Peron took control of the Foundation using his power as chief executive of Argentina and gained access to the funds himself. But there was another problem. Under Argentinean law, Evita's brother, Juan Duarte had an equal claim to her assets as did her husband, Juan Peron. Durate wanted half the fortune himself. In fact it was brother Juan who acted as a courier for Evita in depositing the funds in Switzerland in a series of trips there.

The problem for Juan Durate is that he was just a man, one man. He got a visit from Otto Skorzeny after which Juan Durate decided to transfer his claim on the funds to Juan Peron. Now redundant, Juan Duarte was found dead on April 9, 1953, a victim of an apparent suicide. Now Juan Peron controlled almost 200 million dollars in Nazi assets.

Meanwhile, Skorzeny was having success in bending the arms of the industrialists who had promised repayment for Nazi investments during the war and dating to the August 10, 1944 meeting in Strasbourg, a meeting in which Otto Skorzeny was present and instrumental. Skorzeny managed to collect on agreements with Dr. Fritz Thyssen and with the Krupp family.

Juan Peron was having difficulties holding on to power. His partner and probably the brains of the partnership, Evita Peron was dead. Peron's political enemies were gathering strength. In September 1955 it finally collapsed and Juan Peron escaped Argentina in a Paraguayan gunboat. Of course Otto Skorzeny came to his assistance and with his contacts and history in Spain, he was able to negotiate asylum for Peron in Spain.

"At this time Skorzeny played his trump card. He arranged for Peron to live in exile in Spain through his intercession with influential friends in the Franco government. The price? The remainder of the Bormann funds!"(19)

Skorzeny had recovered all the SS fortune for the use of the post-war SS. Skorzeny had the control and absolute loyalty of the former SS men in South America. And Skorzeny had control of the scientists, blueprints, machine tools, specialty steel and any other assets the Germans had spirited out of the country before its collapse.

Literature Cited

1. **Infield, Glenn B., 1981**, *Skorzeny Hitler's Commando*, page 179, St. Martin's Press, New York, NY, USA
2. *ibid.*
3. **Infield, Glenn B., 1981,** page 18
4. **Infield, Glenn B., 1981**, page 24
5. **Infield, Glenn B., 1981**, page 30
6. **Infield, Glenn B., 1981**, page 30, 31
7. **Infield, Glenn B., 1981**, page 45
8. **Infield, Glenn B., 1981**. page 67
9. **Infield, Glenn B., 1981**, page 86
10. **Infield, Glenn B., 1981**, pages 104-105
11. **Infield, Glenn B., 1981**, page 151
12. **Infield, Glenn B., 1981**, page 179
13. **Infield, Glenn B., 1981**, pages 211-212
14. **Infield, Glenn B., 1981**, page 178
15. **Farrell, Joseph P., Ph.D., 2008**, *Nazi International The Nazis' Postwar Plan to Control Finance, Conflict, Physics and Space*, Adventures Unlimited Publishing, Kempton, Illinois, USA
16. **Farago, Ladislas, 1974**, *Aftermath Martin Bormann and the Fourth Reich*, Simon And Schuster, New York, NY, USA
17. **Infield, Glenn B., 1981**, page 187
18. **Infield, Glenn B., 1981**, page 188
19. **Infield, Glenn B., 1981**, page 199
20. **Infield, Glenn B., 1981**, page 204

SOUTH AMERICA

To start off this chapter it is necessary for us to review what was brought to South America in some of the preceding chapters and color in the sketch we already have.

In August, 1944 Martin Bormann called a meeting in the Rotes Haus Hotel in Strasbourg. That meeting was to plan for survival after the Third Reich had fallen. Dr. Hjalmar Schacht was put in charge of financial matters. He set up dummy corporations and using them he moved money to other countries outside Germany. Other benefits were also probably promised these firms as Bormann evacuated German high technology that included blueprints of secret weapons and probably other secret devices and technical methodology, machine tools, and specialty steel as well as the scientists themselves. Naturally, these firms must have believed they would benefit from this technology in the long run. In turn, they pledged to return the loaned money, coming from the Reich treasury as well as future consideration. Most of the focus went to South America.

SS Colonel Otto Skorzeny was put in charge of the actual physical transfer, called "Aktion Fuerland" by Farago (1), and referencing the Terra del Fuego region of Argentina. Skorzeny already had been in contact with Kampfgeshwader 200 (Battle Wing 200) or KG 200 for short. Headed by Werner Baumback, this was the unit that had already agreed to fly the manned version of the V-1 buzz bombs, a project which Skorzeny had headed but was canceled by Hitler. KG 200 has often been rumored to be the unit that was to provide pilots for the German saucer program. It was also rumored to have been chosen to fly the huge Horton Ho 18 to New York City when the atomic bomb payload was finished. In fact, KG 200 participated in suicide or near-suicide missions on a regular basis, using a variety of aircraft, including the suicide attack on bridges spanning the Vistula River that the Soviets needed for crossing. Skorzeny again, was given access to KG 200, however, each mission had to be approved by Himmler (2). Farago tells us:

> *"Up to June 1944, heavily guarded armored trucks carried the consignments across Germany and France to ports in southern Spain, where U-boats were standing by in hidden bases near Cadiz to take on Bormann's precious cargo. In Spain, General Wilhelm Faupel, a former ambassador and had of the Latin-American Institute, and now stationed in Madrid with a diplomatic cover, managed the operation." (3)*

The U-boats picked up their clandestine cargo and deposited it in Argentina according to all sources. But now we know about Fureteventura. It will be recalled that our treasure hunters found a map of the coastline of South America on one of the U-boats still there. If we check a map, Fuerteventura is not quite mid-way on this voyage. But considering it was mid-way between Beaver Dam and Point 221 as well, this small base must have served as quite a central switching station for a period of several years. It must be assumed that Fuerteventura had communication devices equal to this task and in contact with the two bases mentioned as well as Argentina.

Farago picks up the tale and reacquaints us with some old friends:

> *"On April 18, 1945 Agent Alarcon submitted a report, captioned "German Disembarkation at San Clemente del Tuyu", to the Ministry of the Navy (a copy of which was logged in under number CF-OP-2315 at the Coordinacion Federal). Brief as it was, the report gave an insight into the operation, pinpointing two of its principals. One was Ludwig Freude, described as "an agent of the Third Reich". Alacon had succeeded in planting on Freude on of his informers, called "Natalio" in the report. Natalio ascertained that Freude "had made extensive deposits in various banks" in the name of the other key figure in the plot, "the well-known radio and stage actress Maria Eva Duarte Iburguren". (4)*

Freude was mentioned earlier as a German agent who had allowed the SS fortune to fall into the hands of Evita Peron. In fact, this "other key figure" is better known as Evita Peron. Farago continues:

> *"Natalio learned from Freude himself that, on February 7, 1945 "a U-boat of Admiral Doenitz's submarine fleet" had arrived at a secluded spot in Samborombon Bay off Punta Norte near the village of San Clemente del Tuyu, 150 miles south of Buenos Aires. According to what Freude told Natalio, the U-boat had brought "shipment No. 1744" to Argentina, consisting of an unspecified number of crates and bags "containing", as Alarcon write in his report to the Navy Ministry, "a treasure designed to help the rebuilding of the Nazi empire." (5)*

Freude established two radio stations at Tandil and Bella Vista to guide in the U-boats. (6) Farago as well as Buechner and Bernhard in their two books describe the ranches, owned by Germans, where the cargo was off-loaded. This U-boat traffic was even said to have pre-dated the Rotes Haus meeting (7) and it certainly went on at a high rate toward the end of the war. This area of Southern Argentina, south of Buenos Aires, is a gulf into which empties the Plata River. In fact, the gulf is called Mar del Plata on maps. According to these experts, as many as 35 U-boats participated in this trafficking at one time or another. In illustrating the extent of this traffic, Buechner and Bernhard repeat an anonymous poem that seems to address the on-going, repeated voyages by the German submarines to this part of the world:

> *"Oh! Choosers of the Slain,*
> *Said he, Maidens of Valhalla,*
> *Bury me beyond the Sea,*
> *In a place called Mar del Plata." (8)*

Now we have the money, materials, blueprints, scientists and so on, shipped by U-boat, in Argentina. Otto Skorzeny arrives and frees-up the SS fortune. Dr. Hjalmar Schacht was back in circulation to assist with business knowledge and to move money. Also a new player was "coming on line" as we might say now. He was Reinhard Gehlen and his Gehlen Org. Gehlen had worked for the CIA reactivating his Nazi-era spy network for the Americans after which he was set up by them as essentially "West German Intelligence". It is now recognized that, at least at times, he functioned as a double agent, feeding the post-war SS information as well as, at times, exaggerating the Soviet threat to the Americans, keeping the Cold War going. With his SS contacts, he might even played a triple or quadruple game with Soviet contacts. This appears to have been accomplished sometime around 1952. The question is now: What is being done with this money and this technology by the Germans who have now come to settle in South America? How did it all work in terms of politics? Answers for these questions are readily supplied by Farago and more importantly by Wilhelm Landig. Once we address these questions and understand how this all works, we can go on, as we did with Antarctica, to some more interesting bits and pieces of information and some surprising ramifications regarding yet another principal player in the larger mystery of The Third Power.

The post-war Nazis used their money to buy political influence or in other words their own security. They also used their money and new influence to obtain huge tracts of land throughout South America. Remember, the political system in South America incorporates instability. Therefore, the post-war SS had to be able to pick up its leadership and go from country to country if conditions changed. Ideally, the tract of land would be rather remote and able to be secured in the military sense. The Germans called these "Sperrgebeite".

This whole Sperrgebeite system was described by Wilson (9). It was briefly discussed in my first book (10). One of these larger bases, called Colonia Dignidad, served as the home and site for the fusion experiments of the German scientist Dr. Ronald Richter that was discussed in my second book (11). Briefly, they did just this; they bought large tracts of land and controlled them like a country within a country. Within this safe zone they were able to live, build houses and farms, do manufacturing work and operate scientific laboratories. One report describes 230,000 square kilometers, 230 kilometers of streets, 70 bridges, 200 canals, two light aircraft and a radio homing beacon (12).

But the open-air ranches were not the most exciting of the SS facilities. The most exciting were the underground bases. Yes, according to Wilhelm Landig, the post-war SS obtained truly monumental underground facilities and used them to build the highest technology on the planet. This was based on the findings of the pre-war SS Ahnenerbe explorer Edmund Kiss and his expeditions to South America. It is claimed that Kiss found a tunnel system on the western side of the Andes. This tunnel system was huge and had an array of interconnecting tunnels and huge vaulted rooms at some intersections. The tunnel entrances were well hidden. The tunnel system ran from the Altcama Desert in Chile to Equador! The origin of these tunnels are a mystery. It might be they are a natural phenomenon or that they are the work of some pre-Inca civilization or a combination of both. It was in these hallways that work stations were erected, just has they had been done in underground installations in Germany during the war (13).

The construction of these underground laboratories and work stations was going on at the same time that activity was taking place in Point 211 in Antarctica. In fact, according to Landig, the two bases were in communication and supplies were being brought to Point 211 from South America using flying discs.

Again, we have to look at energy as a major reason for these underground facilities. The reader may recall that Beaver Dam relied on a supply of legnit, somewhere between peat and coal, as a source for fuel. Point 211 in Neuschwabenland relied on geothermal power and perhaps other artificial sources. These underground bases, which Landig calls "Mimes Schmiede" (14) relied, at first, on diesel generators mounted at the openings of the tunnels. Then, finally, they developed thermal power plants (thermischen Kraftwerken) that supplied the electricity necessary for operation (15).

This name "Mimes Schmiede" may be a bit obscure. As children, European royalty are not educated at home. They are sent away to school, a practice that still operates today. Mimes Schmiede refers to the legendary Siegfried, the focus of Wagner's opera, The Ring of the Niebelungs. Siegfried was sent away to an apprenticeship with Mime who was a master blacksmith. In Iron-Age Europe, the blacksmith was the rocket-scientist of his time. To be sure, blacksmiths made farm implements but the most skilled blacksmiths made weapons of war, especially swords. Famous swords bore names and were the subject of legend. The maker of a famous sword also became a legend. This was Mime. The word "Schmiede" is smithy in English. So Mimes Schmiede was a place where the highest tech weapons of war would have been forged. It is no accident that this name was ascribed to this particular place.

The purpose of Mimes Schmiede is absolutely clear. It came into existence so that the post-war SS could build or rebuild or salvage the German armaments and secret weapons technology (16). The exact aim of this enterprise might come into better focus if those involved were named. Two groups of SS weapons technologists or engineers worked here to recapture that high-tech pinnacle, first achieved in Germany (17). For this part of the story we must jump ahead to Landig death and the work of Heiner Gehring and Karl-Heinz Zunneck. Gehring read some of Landig's private material and it contained some additional information. It seems that one of these groups was called the Ruestungsesoteriker or Armament Esoterics (18). This group formed after 1945 and seemed to have been a loose association of individuals who were educated in both the rather occult ideas involved in these field propulsion flying disc and high technology. In this respect Dr. Gordon Freeman, whom I have mentioned many times, would have fit into nicely were he two generations older and inclined to participate. The Ruestungsesotiker operated, according to Landig's private notes, in hidden bases. They kept the saucers flying all those years exchanging ideas and joined in this enterprise and goal (19). This association of armament esoterics may have even extended world-wide as the need for replacement parts increased. Their work on flying discs is given as an example so their scope probably extended to other high technology projects beyond simply flying discs.

Gehring and Zunneck say that some of their esoteric knowledge may be based on what they call kabalistic computations (kabbalistischen Berechnungen) of a triangular aircraft that was "in play". This aircraft was built under the designation "Phi 300" or "FI 300". In Poland, say these researchers, this "magic" technology was coupled with long-distance flying frames (20). Maybe we will return to flying triangles at a later time.

Dr. Gordon Freeman explained this to me years ago. This "kabalistic computation" is a symbol, the merkaba. But the same concept is also conveyed using other symbols such as a simple "+" symbol or the figure "8". This is the principle behind the Bloch Wall (21). It simply involves energy input at the poles, output at the center and recycling of that energy through the poles once more. This concept has other names.

Gehring and Zunneck also reveal possible origins of the second group. In fact, he names the possibilities as the Thule and/or Vril Groups, the Herrn von Schwarzen Stein (DHvSS) and or the Herren vom Schwarzen Adel (the gentlemen of the black stone and the gentlemen of the black nobility, respectively. This last group probably refers to the SS leadership with a certain agenda). This information came from an informant named Hans Rittermann more of whom we will learn later. These groups along with the "Tempelhofgesellschaft" are esoteric organizations, first brought to us in the writings of Norbert Juergen-Rathoffer and Ralf Ettl. Rittermann, a no-nonsense informant, also says that these groups still exist today. Finally, Gehring and Zunneck name the Goldern Rose as another possibility. The Golden Rose is said to have been a resistance group within the German arms industry (22).

So, in post-war South America the SS have an underground tunnel network with huge connecting hallways in which they are allegedly constructing very high technology. But they are going to need more than just the brains of their scientists, even with blueprints. This could not be done without the high-tech infrastructure necessary to supply the raw materials as well and the manufactured materials necessary for any aerospace industry. This does not seem readily available in some remote jungle or mountain setting. So how was this done?

It was done as it is done today. A major aerospace firm designs a new aircraft. It really does not matter how large that firm is, it cannot possibly build all the components for that new aircraft itself. The major firm sub-contracts with mid-sized firms for sub-assemblies. For instance, this could be the engine or the electronics package or the radar. Those sub-assemblies would be sent off to the major contractor but even the mid-sized firm would contract out for many components. This would employ smaller firms all across the country. Of course, each step down, employees ask about the components and sub-assemblies they are producing. And, of course, they are given an answer but that answer may or may not be the truth and because the employees are not in a position to judge, any secrecy involved in the new aircraft can be maintained.

This is exactly what the SS did in South America. They drew up specifications and sent them out to aircraft firms or manufacturing firms all over the world to be built. The firm filling the order had no idea what they were building and probably didn't even care. The major supplier was the United States. Jan Holberg explains it this way to Michael X. Barton:

> *"In secret "Saucer" bases, hidden in the wilds of South America, South Africa and elsewhere, German scientists are busy assembling large-sized flying discs. All work is done in secret underground factories, just as during World War II. (as at Nordhausen, Traumstein, Bleicherode, etc.) However, actual parts for the discs are not made at the bases, but manufactured by independent companies in the United States. Each company makes a different part, but has no idea what that part will be used for. All parts are subsequently shipped by each company to some office in South America. From there, the parts are sent to the various secret bases. As Richard Ogden has suggested, the Germans may have perfected an Electro-Magnetic powered Saucer since 1947. Based on Viktor Schauberger's work, for example." (23)*

Flying saucers are the most visible sign of SS post-war high technology. They are probably the indicator that other high-tech projects are underway that are less easily observed. In the UFO Universe, flying saucer reports appeared very early in South America. They appeared as early as they did in the USA, that being the summer of 1947. Some of the first flying saucers to appear were the "smoky saucers" and they seem to have persisted in South America for a long time. This is exactly the type of flying disc which was sighted in Karachi, Pakistan at about the time in question and which was discussed in an earlier chapter. This type of craft would have provided great service in the isolated base locations of South America. Michael X. Barton devotes a whole chapter to smoky saucers in this book titled *The German Saucer Story*. But these Germans were also trying to produce saucers of a much higher technology. Let us take a look at what was being said about South America by Germans of those times and at what South Americans said about the origin of their own flying saucers.

The German community in South America is/was a rather closed one. Once an Argentinean researcher preempted my anticipated request and told me not to ask him to try to infiltrate Germans or German establishments in his city for information on this subject since that course of action did not lead to long-term health in his estimation. Actually, we are fortunate in this quest since an expatriate Austrian, to whom information was available but who had no love for the Nazis, was willing to spill the beans. This was Fred Andract, an engineer who had immigrated to Uruguay from Austria and wrote of flying saucers in South America and their origins sometime in the late 1970's. Apparently, the back-story is that Andract responded to an article in *El Diario*, or wrote an article for that publication which was picked up and/or summarized in other Spanish language publications. Below are two of these summaries. The first one was translated into German by O. Bergmann and then into English by me. The second came from *En Contacto*, a Mexican UFO magazine. This was translated for me into English from Spanish.

Flying Saucers with Swastika

Montevedeo, 8 (UPI) The so-called flying discs are not extraterrestrial space ships, on the contrary, works of Nazi scientists who were themselves not satisfied to have given up the Second World War and who themselves prepare for a coming conquest, said the engineer Fred Andract, an Austrian living in Uruguay.

He has been living in Uruguay for two years and owns a chemical laboratory. He was a college teacher in Switzerland and worked in Argentina.

In explanation to the opposing morning paper "El Dario", he pressed his interpretation to this question: "It is not only a theory, it is the truth. At the moment I am still not disposed concerning the persuasive proof with science demands, of which nobody from my point of view can draw doubts. But I have thrown up the problem on a higher plane because it is obvious that the situation of preventive measures is required and not carelessness.

Behind this there is more than only a mass of gold, but also an interest group that has very much power and is interested that it will not be known. Also, I must consider my security because those responsible will try to prevent, at any price, it from becoming known."

He remembered that Germany, before the Second World War, tested the newest weapons and Hitler wanted to convert the county into a testing field.

"Still, there are many Germans on the other side together with others who have decided to follow them and who believe that the last war is not over and that they could still be able to attain power."

He said he can not reveal where the base is located, out of where they operate and who they allow to peer through at them, the Argentine and North American military could know this truth or a portion thereof or at least have divined it.

In closing Andract said that he will shortly take part in a conference about the UFO question with interested Uruguayans and assured that his goal to attain was that Uruguay is the primary concern (as his voice raised in appropriate scope) against the aggression, as proof ordains (24).

Next is the En Contacto version:

The Ovnis (UFOs) Are Weapons of the Nazis

The Austrian engineer, Fred Andract, resident of Montevideo, Uruguay, affirmed that the unidentified flying objects are not the creation of extra-terrestrials but are the creation of Nazi scientists who desired to obtain revenge for a past world war.

The engineer Andract, who lived in Uruguay for the last 28 years, owns a chemical laboratory, has taught in Switzerland and has worked in Argentina.

In his previous declarations to the newspaper El Diario, he insisted that the concept of this problem was one, not of theory, but it was the truth. For the meantime the proof necessary for me to show exactly what I mean as science requires and in this sense nobody can contradict me. But I have already shown other people in high places that what is evidently required now are methods of prevention and not for us to trust anybody.

But given his abundant affirmations he declared:

"In between all this there is a lot of money involved, but also, people who have great power are interested that nobody find out about this. I even have to watch out for my own security because the people who are responsible for this are going to try to prevent me from making any accusations or declarations on for any of this to come out in the open. They will use any methods necessary to accomplish this."

The person who declares this is convinced that those who survived the Nazi regime are the ones who do the fabrication and that are controlling the engineers or the people who have been able to identify these extra-terrestrial objects. He said in the text there are a lost of German people who are still convinced that the Second World War is not finished and is still going on and that the power can still be regained. He used an example of actuality of these experiments that are being done with new arms or weapons, which is taking place in Spain during their civil war. He affirmed that he could not reveal where this base is located, where the Nazi UFOs still exist but he suggested the military or Latin Americans or North Americans could reveal this location if they concentrated. Soon he will participate in a study of UFOs in Uruguay. And he declared that his main goal is to let Uruguay give an announcement and alert of this problem when the necessary facts have been determined.

But does this sound like old history? The declarations of engineer Andract are not news because for the last 50 years this movement was started by the United States in their effort to calm the people who thought here was going to be an extra-terrestrial invasion. But in reality it was really the UFOs that were the secret weapons of the Nazis. This is not an easy subject, analyzing this in much detail, it is obvious that this information does not have any consistency because it the Nazis or the Russians had these weapons of the characteristics of UFOs they would have gone after their enemies without any delay.

This news that the Nazis created UFOs was exploited when it was still fresh in the memories of people. It is obvious that if this was done with the intention to distract attention from other things but, if this engineer Andract exposed the theory, but realistically, we think it is all in the past two decades." (25)

en contacto...

- REPITEN UNA EXPLICACION SIN CONSISTENCIA
- HACE 800 AÑOS UN CUERPO EXTRAÑO SE ESTRELLO EN LA LUNA
- FOTOGRAFIO SU AVISTAMIENTO UN PROFESOR BRASILEÑO
- LA TV TERRESTRE PUEDE SER CAPTADA EN EL ESPACIO
- AHORA TAMBIEN SE VEN OVNIS EN BOLIVIA
- UFOLOGOS Y ESCEPTICOS SE ENFRENTAN EN "PLAYBOY"

"LOS OVNIS SON ARMAS DE LOS NAZIS"

● El ingeniero austriaco Fred Andracht, residente en Montevideo, Uruguay, afirmó que los Objetos Voladores No Identificados no son vehículos extraterrestres, sino creaciones de científicos nazis que desean obtener la revancha desde la pasada Guerra Mundial.

El ingeniero Andracht vive en Uruguay desde hace 28 años y es propietario de un laboratorio químico; antes fue catedrático en Suiza y trabajó en Argentina.

Al hacer declaraciones al vespertino *El Diario*, insistió en que su concepto del problema "no es meramente una teoría, sino una verdad. Por el momento no dispongo de pruebas absolutas como las que exige la ciencia, para que nadie discuta mi punto de vista, pero he planteado el tema en las altas esferas porque evidentemente la situación exige adoptar medidas de previsión y no descuidarse".

Abundando en sus afirmaciones, aclaró: "Detrás de esto no sólo hay mucho dinero, sino sectores de enorme poder interesados en que no se conozca nada al respecto. Incluso yo debo velar por mi seguridad, porque los responsables tratarán de evitar ser descubiertos valiéndose de cualquier medio".

El declarante está convencido que son los sobrevivientes del nazismo quienes fabrican y controlan esos ingenios que la mayoría de la gente identifica como naves extraterrestres. Dijo textualmente: "Aún subsisten muchos de aquellos alemanes secundados por otros convencidos recientemente, que creen que la Segunda Guerra Mundial todavía no termina y que el poder aún puede conquistarse".

Como ejemplo de lo que están haciendo en la actualidad habló de los experimentos con nuevas armas llevados a cabo en España durante la guerra civil. Afirmó que no puede revelar dónde se encuentra la base desde la que operan los OVNIS nazis, pero sugirió que los militares, latinoamericanos y norteamericanos, podrían deducir su ubicación si se ponen a pensar en el problema. Por último comentó que próximamente participará en una mesa redonda con estudiosos uruguayos del fenómeno OVNI, y recalcó que su meta es lograr que "Uruguay sea el primero que lance la voz de alerta sobre este problema, cuando se cuente con las pruebas necesarias".

PERO... SUENA A HISTORIA VIEJA

Las declaraciones del Ingeniero Andracht no resultan nada novedosas, pues durante los años cincuentas existió un verdadero movimiento propugnado por los Estados Unidos, quizá con el fin de calmar a quienes esperaban una invasión extraterrestre, en el sentido de que los OVNIS eran armas secretas de los nazis. Desgraciadamente el asunto no es tan sencillo. Analizándolo detenidamente es obvio que esta explicación no tiene consistencia, pues de poseer los nazis, o los rusos, como se dijo en su oportunidad, armas secretas con las características de los OVNIS, ya las habrían lanzado contra sus enemigos sin perder tanto tiempo probándolas sobre territorios donde los contrarios podrían apoderarse de ellas.

La noticia de que los OVNIS eran una creación de los nazis fue explotada cuando todavía estaba fresco en la memoria de las multitudes el recuerdo de sus atrocidades, y es obvio que se hizo con la intención de desviar la atención pública hacia otros derroteros.

El ingeniero Andracht expuso su teoría con un lamentable retraso de más de dos décadas.

6

En Contacto Article This Mexican UFO magazine article details the German basis of UFOs in South America and was written by an Austrian engineer.

To this I would like to add another report, discussing flying saucer research in South America. This report was turned in to the FBI by a European couple acting as go-betweens in an attempt to sell flying saucer designs in Austria. The second part of the report is an alleged English translation of an original German language letter from the inventor. Actually, there is yet another second letter that is not reproduced here since it is of little value.

This report was originally sold by UFO researcher William L. Moore of Majestic 12 fame. Sometime later, Moore soiled himself by saying he had acted as "a government asset". But even prior to that I knew I needed an original copy from the FBI, not one handled by Moore. I requested it under FOIA. Naturally, it was rejected, claiming the FBI had no knowledge of the report in question. I sent the FBI their exact file number and a copy of Moore's report, asking for an original. Not in my wildest imagination could I have guessed what was to transpire.

A couple days after firing off my second request (I did not call it an appeal), I was awakened by telephone at some early hour by a female voice stating that she was an FBI librarian. She was rather upset with my request since I already had a copy of the file. I was groggy without my morning coffee but finally my head cleared and I lit into her, telling her that for verification, I needed an unspoiled, clean report.

She then told me I could order their complete UFO package for $110.00, including the file I wanted as well as their extraterrestrial stuff. I told her I did not want their other stuff, only the file in question so I should not have to pay the $110.00. She backed down but tried another tactic. She said that my file was the original file since William L. Moore had re-typed all the files in the $110.00 package and then the originals were thrown away! Moore even retyped a cover page using FBI stationary! His initials (WLM) appear on the retyped cover letter, dated 7/84, and followed by the words "A True Copy", a totally meaningless statement if not coupled with an affidavit, so swearing, under penalty of perjury. And in fact, the first document, retyped below, bears a stamp running 180 degrees in opposition to the text stating: "copies destroyed 270 Nov 19 1984. Naturally, in Mr. Moore's retyping effort there does not exist an FBI file number, without which all denials are possible. Fortunately, we have a second cover letter, a copy of an original, which contains the hand written FBI file number of 62-93494-338.

So, the file I wanted no longer existed because they had allowed a (then?) non-governmental, non-FBI (?) worker to waltz in and type them up after which the originals were thrown away and the retyped copies became the official FBI files. This was explained to me by a "librarian". Yet most FBI agents are law school graduates. With that general level of legal understanding walking the hallways, how is this sloppy evidence chain even possible? Is it any wonder that the FBI does not want to try terrorists in a Federal Court?

Nevertheless, here is the report as I received it originally from William Moore. In spite of my objections to the chain of evidence, I have no reason to believe it has been altered in substance. Consider the above discussion a disclaimer and statement of full disclosure. For the redacted words (blacked out) I am going to use a series of X, XXX, XXXX, about the letter-length of the redacted portion. I am going to forego retyping the cover letters and go right to the text. The first is the FBI's work. The second is an English translation of the inventor's proposal.

Confidential

On January 12, 1954, XXXXXXXXXXXXXXXXXXX East Orange, NY, appeared at the Newark Office and advised that he had received a letter from one XXXXXXXXXXXXXXXXXX West Austria on or about December 20, 1953.

XXXXX stated that the letter requested him to attempt to sell a number of inventions, which he, XXXXX had developed. XXXXXX stated that the request was to contact Aircraft Companies and sewing Machine Companies in the United States and attempt to interest them in these devices.

According to XXXXXXX requested that no governmental agencies be contacted. XXXXX stated that the intentions, which XXXXX had developed were new type of sewing machine and a flying saucer was of some importance in the national defense of this country. XXXX stated that he has never met XXXX but that XXXXX was given his name by XXXXX brother, XXXXX who resides in Graz, Austria, and who is employed at XXXXXXXXXXX, Graz, Austria. XXXXXX stated that his brother worked with XXXXX at one time, and he believes that XXXX is a chemist or some type of engineer. XXXX stated that the contents of the letter seemed fantastic to him and that if the letter were not written in such an intelligent manner, he would have doubted XXXXXX sanity. He stated that XXXXXX claims to have sold a new principle of aero-dynamics, which made it possible to construct a practical flying saucer and that XXXXX had developed a model that flies without the usual hazards. According to XXXX the letter continues by stating that XXXXX has been in contact with other men throughout the world, who have been attempting to develop the saucer and he has been the first to win real success.

By way of background, XXXXX stated that he was born in the vicinity of Leoben, Austria in 1925 and arrived in New York city on March 29, 1952 from Bremerhaven, Germany. He is employed at the XXXXXXXXXXXXX in Haplewood, NJ.

On January 30, 1954, XXXXXXXXXXX East Orange, NJ, appeared at the Newark Office and advised that she was the wife of XXXXXXX. She stated that another letter had been received from XXXXXXXXXX by her husband, XXXXXXXXX. She stated that her husband did not want to furnish the information in this letter to the FBI. She stated that he was not aware that she was furnishing this information and wished to keep the interview confidential.

XXXXX stated that the letter received recently by her husband, from XXXXX contained information that XXXXX had been contacted by Communists in Austria, who wished to take him to Switzerland in order that he might further, XXXXX to increase his efforts to sell XXXXXX new invention in the United States.

By way of background, XXXXXXX advised that she was born of German parents in South Russia and at the time of the German invasion of Russia, during World War II, she and her family were resettled in Germany. After the war, she married XXXXXXX and came to the United States with him.

XXXXXXXXXXXXX Item No. 1
New Jersey, U.S.A. 12/23/53

Dear Mr. XXXXXXXXX

Your brother will probably have communicated with you about me as we became acquainted with each other at a construction job. I had told him a few things about inventions or utilization. Dear Mr. XXXXX be not angry with me because I am now turning to you. I hesitated such a long time, as my wife does not wish to go abroad. Enclosed I am sending you 2 inventions, that is, ideas and I leave it to your own power of judgment whether one or both, or none of these inventions is suitable. If one seems to e profitable to you, you should apply for a patent in your own name as is the best possible way and enter for me and for yourself 45% each of the net profit and 10% for your brother. I am giving you entirely a free hand, as you will undoubtedly try to attain the greatest possible profit.

And now, dear Mr. XXXXX I am taking the liberty of telling you something about an invention that the entire world wants to have. (I am only writing the most important facts.) Before the war I intended to make a toy, something which flies, and purely accidentally I discovered a hitherto unknown aerodynamic law. I experimented further. I improved and informed several comrades. They were enthused and emmigrated to South America. There they tried it on their own responsibility. People were killed and they failed to perfect the incomplete invention. They approached me again. As they were only artisans, these flying machines were, of course, built primitively. The first experiments to fly with a motorcycle motor attained the result of 250-300 km. Not bad for the years 1938-1939: with a powerful motor they then flew 2600-2800 km (hour kilometers).

After the war they came to me again and told me about their misfortune, that about 60% of all flights had been fatal. To make it very clear, they wanted to find out how I construct my flying apparatuses, because with a device, which endangers lives, they could not, of course, appear before the public, and, therefore, all this is still, so to speak, a private secret. In America, this flying machine is called "flying saucer," and since among my former comrades a quarrel broke out and they distrust each other and none of them has the intelligence, which this invention demands, they have not progressed over there.

I imagine that they have stubbornly adhered to some construction, that is, become involved in it that they cannot advance. It has taken me years to reach the point where I can already say with respect to the construction plan that now the machine is safe for flying. Thereby I am losing, however, some speed, but, in return for it, safety is secured and this is the main thing. This machine is so simple in its construction that, if one gives me and engineer and experts, I can build this apparatus in 5 to 6 weeks at the most (but only experimentally for a crew of 1 to 3 men). Then this machine attains, with an automobile motor of 80 to 120 h.p. about 700 to 1,000 km. If a firm would exist, which does not shun the costs, I can, because of the simple construction of the machine, build the first machine immediately in such a manner that it exceeds the 2000 km. limit per hour.

Because of the new aerodynamic law it is possible without any difficulty (everything without propellers) to reach such speeds. Now the idea has come to me to build some kind of popular flying machine that is cheaper than an automobile. One does not need any starting or landing strip and one would have a traveling speed of about 500 to 700 km. per hour. I believe that America would be the most favorable place in the world for it. You will now understand that I am very anxious to establish contact with a firm that is greatly interested in this invention. But as I have no knowledge of English, it is for me, from the beginning, an affair that will come to nothing. If you, dear Mr. XXXXX can start the matter, you will not have done it in vain. I am not niggardly and besides I want to go to the U.S.A. to realize there a still larger project for which I need co-workers. The circular flying machines shall bring me the money for my future plans, for I believe popular flying machines, according to my model and besides 100% safe from crash, will be a gigantic business. I do not know the magnates over there; perhaps HENRY FORD or an airplane factory, possibly a helicopter plant would be interested in it.

But I shall announce the names of my comrades only after I have received a contract pertaining to license or gratuities and after my arrival in the U.S. However, it must be added that I shall not any out the money for the passage if some firm accepts me for the construction of the flying machines. But in addition to all that I need someone who lives over there and who knows the English language, and now I am asking you, my dear Mr. XXXXXX whether you can function as my manager as they say in the U.S.A. Well, you know that the manager receives payment, and I believe that you will enjoy working with me later on inventions when I am over there. Incidentally, I mentioned that I took a course as a chemist. (The "Do" apparatuses, later called fog - or rocket-missiles, originated with me and also many other things.) I hope that you can decipher my hieroglyphic script. Such small writing is not in my line. So that you may see that I am not exaggerating, I declare upon oath that the invention, known by the name of "flying saucer,." is my own, that I know the men who are building these machines in South America, and that I can construct the above-described machine myself and attain at least 2000 km.

/s/ XXXXXXXXXXXXX

I hope that you will be interested in it. I am awaiting your communication very hopefully,

with friendly greetings,
Respectfully,
/s/XXXXXXXXXXXXXXX

As documentation, all that can be offered is my telephonic conversation with the FBI and the source for the original retyped documents (26).

This last document is certainly a strange one. The "inventor", for lack of his name, claims he can use motorcycle or automobile engines to power a flying saucer. He also claims that no propeller is used (presumably also no rotor as in a helicopter). He claims a new aerodynamic principle. What could be going on here?

With no propeller or carrying screw, this could not be a Schriever or Habermohl type of saucer. Likewise, it could not be a Miethe type saucer since it involves no jet or rocket engines. That only leaves field propulsion, but with motorcycle and auto engines?

The inventor says such a saucer can be built with a motorcycle engine but a more powerful, faster one can be built with an automobile engine. Both only produce rotary movement of their crankshafts. The motorcycle engine would produce higher revolutions per minute but evidently this is of no benefit to the speed of the saucer. More speed can be obtained with a higher horsepower auto engine. The difference seems to be the auto engine produces more torque even though it turns less rapidly. So, what would fit the bill is a saucer that needed an excess of torque, the rotary force of the engine, obviously to turn something that would somehow be translated into speed, that is, saucer speed in proportion to simply torque of the engine. Perhaps we can just hold these thoughts for a while and return to our overall picture of the SS post-war world in South America.

Here is the overview so far. The post-war SS is working on high technology in their hidden underground bunkers. This post-war SS or Nazi International is making deals involving the utilization of German scientists and German firms associated with the Nazis, probably through Otto Skorzeny's engineering firm in Madrid acting as a clearing house. The Nazi International is being used on high-tech projects where the local government fears too much involvement with either the East or the West or when using the Nazi International is a compromise arrived at by both East and West. Meanwhile, farms, towns, all of human infrastructure is being carried on in their rather open secured areas run by these Germans, probably throughout South America but centering on southern South America. As friendly governments rise and fall, the relationship with the Nazi International adjusts and perhaps settlements move.

But there are a little more to the secured settlements themselves than meets the eye. And this fact and new understanding about it opens up a whole new chapter and new scope concerning the Nazis and their post-war Nazi world. Ladislas Farago provides the initial clue, although I must admit that I did not understand it at first blush. He says:

> *"The geographical centers of Nazism in Chile were in the area east of Valdivia, and in Parral, just south of Santiago. Located in the latter region is the weirdest Nazi encampment of the postwar world, housing a sect that combines Nazism and voodooism." (27)*

Something about Nazism and voodooism just to not mesh. Farago must be talking about some other aspect of the occult that he simply does not understand or wants to ascribe to the Nazis as a way of demonizing them. At first, I thought this must be the Thule or Vril people or Juergen-Rathoffer's "Uranus 13" or "Sonderbuero 13". But a conversation with Georg Breckmann set me straight. Farago was closer to the truth than he ever could have guessed while still being wrong.

It was explained to me that the Ahnenerbe set up a special research unit, Sonderkommando H, to research the Inquisition and the persecution of witches. Georg Breckmann was so kind as to send me some information on this subject.

From *Fortean Times*, 1981, comes an article written by Nigel Pennick titled: "Hexen! German Witches Burned Again". This article starts by recounting an exhibition at the

Landesmuseum in Karlsruhe concerning witches in Germany. One sub-section got the most attention:

"Although it was a minor part of the exhibition, the section on Sonderkommando H, a research office of the Nazi SS, attracted the greatest interest fro the press. In the 1930s, Heinrich Himmler, Reichsfuehrer SS, set up the department to research mediaeval German witch trials. His civil servants scoured the record offices for actual trial documents and created considerable dossiers on the holocaust undertaken by the church."

From the same publication, Patricia Clough supplies more details in her article: "Himmler's Witch Hunt":

"Hidden away in the mysterious Archive Department seven of the Reichssicherheitshaupamt — SS chief Heinrich Himmler's Headquarters in Berlin — SS men, academics and assistants known only by their initials pored over mountains of old documents, cataloguing, filing and indexing. By the time someone stopped them, they had produced some 3,621 files containing 30,000 pages."

She continues:

"...The project was halted in 1944 when the mounting allied air raids on Berlin forced the Nazis to move it to a castle at Slava in Silesia, where Himmler ran political indoctrination courses. After the war, the Poles stored the records in an archive known only to a handful of scholars."

The reason for this work was given by both authors as an attempt to find fuel to attack the Catholic Church. This seems unrealistic to me. If the Catholic Church was ever the enemy of the Nazis, certainly by the 1940's it was not even a slight threat compared to the Allied Powers. By 1944 the only projects undertaken by the SS, Ahnenerbe or not, was a quest for immediate weaponry. So, if the SS was working on something in this time frame, it was a weapon. But the answers are provided by the final document Georg Breckmann sent me, although I do not know its origin. It appears to be of Internet origin. This version might be compared to the many web-sites on German flying discs discussing worm holes and aliens from Aldebaran in that it states the most radical, sensational, and frankly fictional position possible. On the other hand, it does provide color and flavor regarding the Karoteckia legend and so illustrates why this topic is exciting. This article should be prefaced by saying that the word for "witches" is "Hexen" in German, the word "library" in German is "Bibliothek" and the word for "card" is "Karte".

History Of The Karotechia

The roots of the Karotechia are deep and varied. When the unit was officially created within the Ahnenerbe in 1939, it drew its members from within the Ahnenerbe, the disbanded Thulegesellschaft, and a little known section of Archive Department VII of the Reichssicherheitshauptamt (RSHA, Reich Security Central Office) called Sonderkommando-H. Created in 1935 under direct orders from Heinrich Himmler, Sonderkommando-H (for Hexen, German for witches) collected records of the Catholic Inquisition against witchcraft from libraries in Germany and Austria. These records were collated into the Hexenkartothek, a catalog of over 33,000 index cards, each providing the details of a victim of the witch trials. While most of the Hexenkartothek concentrated on witch trials in Germany, Sonderkommando-H researched cases from as far away as India and Mexico.

The research of Sonderkommando-H was meant to provide propaganda that would justify an SS crackdown on the Catholic Church, as well as discover the ancient Germanic religion that Himmler believed had been eradicated by the Inquisition. The SS officers that collected the Hexenkartothek came to informally refer to themselves as the "Kartothekia", and what they discovered were arcane formulae and necromantic rituals. Enough was learned by Sonderkommando-H to create some one hundred and fifty know witches, warlocks and alchemists termed "the resuscitating of the ye vital saylts." This formulae was first successfully put to effect by SS-Hauptscharfueher Dieter Scheel when his team resurrected 17th century sorcerer Jurgen Tess. It was this incident that created a new department within the Ahnenerbe to exploit the occult in service to the Reich; the Karotechia.

Occult research had been conducted by various arms of the SS for quite some time before the creation of the Karotechia. In the Ahnenerbe, the "Abteilung zur Ueberpruefung der Sogenannten Geheimwissenschafter" (literally, Department for the Examination of So-Called Secret Sciences) had analyzed the occult since 1933. Also since 1933, Karl Maria Willigut and his Department for Pre- and Early History had been Himmler's premier occultist, a position that was undermined soon after the creation of the Karotechia. Suitable members of these organizations were drawn to the Karotechia, as were former members of the Thulegesellschaft and scholars from Nazi-allied regimes and occupied countries. Kabbalists and Gypsy practitioners were even forcibly recruited out of concentration camps, as well as those occultists rounded up through Aktion Hess.

More so than any other group researching the paranormal for their government during the Second World War, the Karotechia sought to exploit the occult to its fullest. With the full backing of the SS and the Nazi state, they raided the libraries and museums of Europe in an insatiable search for arcane power. No avenue of study was left unexplored, no matter how ridiculous it might seem to the more established academics of the Ahnenerbe. The Karotechia was shielded form inquiry within and without by direct patronage of Himmler, who passed certain information on to Hitler (the Fuehrer remained basically unaware of the Karotechia). Members of the Karotechia were known by their initials in SS documents, and by their rune-names in internal correspondence, the names given upon induction into the unit. They were identified by the sonnenrad runes worn on the lapels of their black Allegmeine-SS uniforms. This insignia and the men that wore it were equally feared and respected throughout the SS.

The Karotechia never had a central headquarters, as each project maintained its own base of operations, reporting directly to Himmler. When the Karotechia was required to perform some ancient Germanic ritual for Himmler (virtually always ineffectual), they were called to the SS-order castle at Wewelsburg. However, the isolation and provincial boredom of the place meant that the Karotechia officers preferred to conduct their operations elsewhere. This also allowed them to operate with great independence.

Never as successful as their reputation belied, the Karotechia did score a number of impressive victories during the war. In particular was the discovery of a Gothic version of the Necronomicon in the spring of 1944, which opened up several new projects to exploit its potential. Most of these projects ended in failure, causing great destruction, such as the incident at Castle Naudabaum in early 1945, where seven Karotechia officers and seventy-three support personnel were killed and the castle destroyed during an abortive attempt to summon an extraterrestrial being called Azathoth.

This disaster led to the final Karotechia operation of the war: Aktion Gotterdammerung, the attempt b the Karotechia to reenact the Naudabaum disaster without aborting the sequence to summon Azathoth. Aktion Gotterdammerung was foiled by the American Delta Green organization. In the end, of the one hundred and sixty-four members of the Karotechia, fifty-four were assassinated by the Allies, six died of natural causes, three died during Allied bombing, four were executed for disloyalty, fifteen were killed while conducting experiments, nine committed suicide, eleven were institutionalized, twenty-four vanished while on operations, and thirty-seven escaped the destruction of Nazi Germany though the ODESSA network.

In the German popular mind, whole words are agglutinated as they are contracted whereby National Sozialist Partei became "Nazi", for instance. Likewise, the words Hexen Karte Bibliothek ultimately became "Kartotekia" or "Kartothekia". The above version contains fictional aspects. There is an on-line, video, role-playing game whereby the bad guys, Karotechia, are pitted against the good guys, called Delta Green. In fact if you google Karotechia, almost all the hits speak of Delta Green. There was no Delta Green. Its presence indicates the role-playing game. Good sources on Karotekia simply do not exist in English.

There is a more factual version found on-line at *http://de.wikipedia.org/wiki/Hexenkartothek* in the German language but it is the exact converse to the one above in that it is totally sterile and a book exists on the subject, also in German, titled: "Himmlers Hexenkartothek. Das Interesse des Nationalsozialismus" an der Hexenverfolgung by Soenke Lorenz, Dieter R. Bauer, and Wolfgang Behringer.

A certain computer expert and expert at Internet searches, "Mr. K." found records for this organization at the Bundesarchiv, Koblenz, Germany, and showed me a webpage on this. These were the actual records, sequestered in Poland and since returned to the German Archives. I have subsequently lost the website and all searches using Sonderkommando-H, Karoteckia (and variants), have failed me but I believe the records exist there.

My informant, Georg Breckmann, who had access to an SS man, told me the SS greatly feared this internal sub-group, Karotechia. This is the "voodoo" Farago discusses in the southern Chilean German secured bases. And according to Georg Breckmann, Karotechia lives to this day, a feared element within a feared organization. I have to believe the research done by Karoteckia was ultimately an occult weapon, otherwise it would have been discarded by the SS.

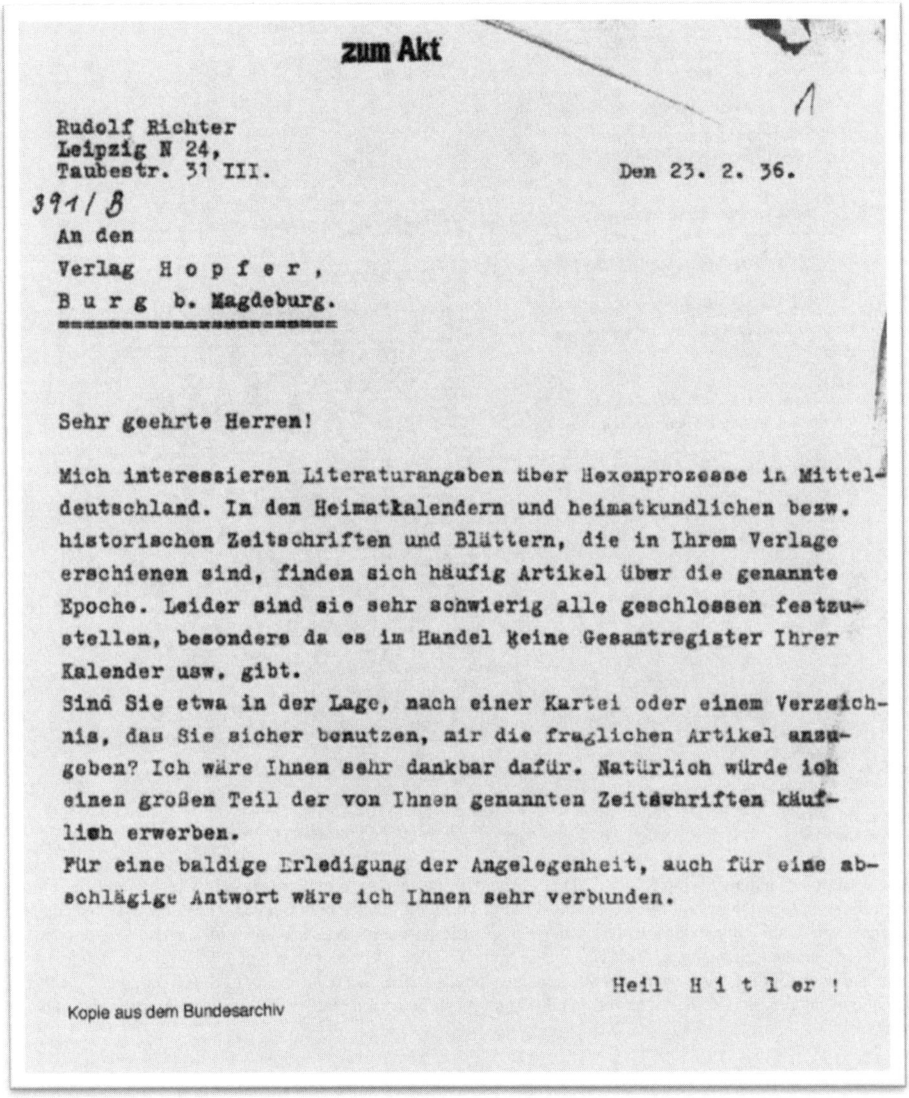

zum Akt

1

Rudolf Richter
Leipzig N 24,
Taubestr. 31 III.

Den 23. 2. 36.

391/B

An den
Verlag H o p f e r ,
B u r g b. Magdeburg.

Sehr geehrte Herren!

Mich interessieren Literaturangaben über Hexenprozesse in Mitteldeutschland. In den Heimatkalendern und heimatkundlichen bezw. historischen Zeitschriften und Blättern, die in Ihrem Verlage erschienen sind, finden sich häufig Artikel über die genannte Epoche. Leider sind sie sehr schwierig alle geschlossen festzustellen, besonders da es im Handel keine Gesamtregister Ihrer Kalender usw. gibt.
Sind Sie etwa in der Lage, nach einer Kartei oder einem Verzeichnis, das Sie sicher benutzen, mir die fraglichen Artikel anzugeben? Ich wäre Ihnen sehr dankbar dafür. Natürlich würde ich einen großen Teil der von Ihnen genannten Zeitschriften käuflich erwerben.
Für eine baldige Erledigung der Angelegenheit, auch für eine abschlägige Antwort wäre ich Ihnen sehr verbunden.

Heil H i t l e r !

A Document from Karoteckia Requesting Assistance? This is a February 32, 1936 request to a publisher specializing in esoteric issues to forward some relevant information and diagrams regarding the activity of witches in central Germany. Unfortunately, no official letterhead is present, only the name of the sender, Rudolf Richter. This letter was found on the Internet and sourced to the German Federal Archives—see bottom, *"Kopie aus dem Bundersarchiv"*

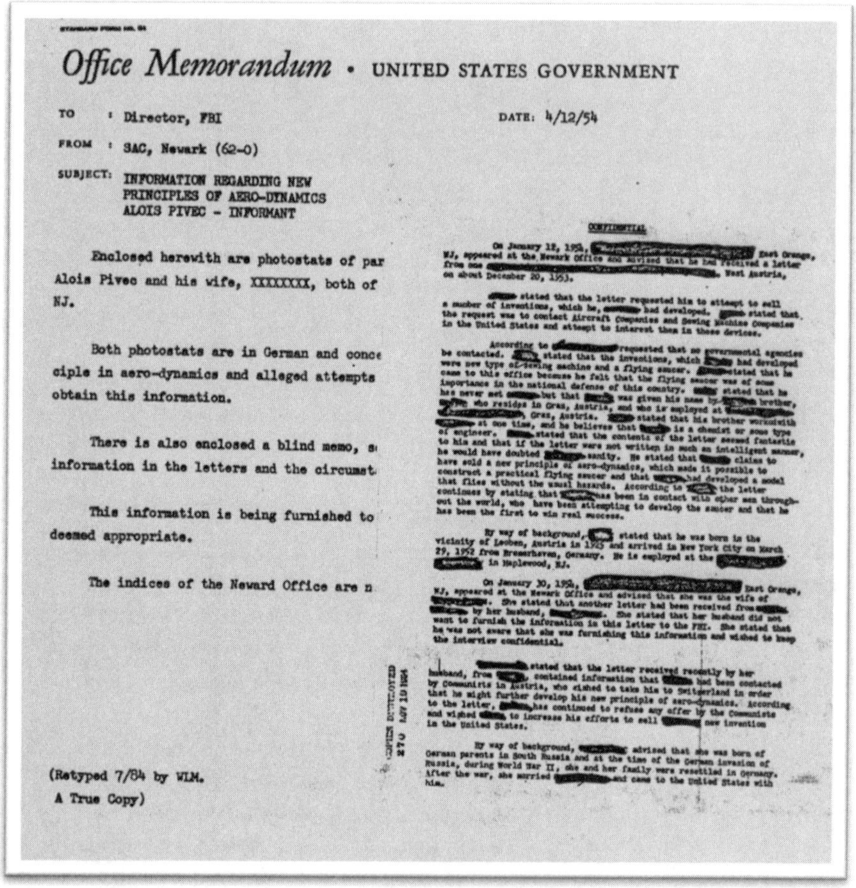

Office Memorandum • UNITED STATES GOVERNMENT

TO : Director, FBI

DATE: 4/12/54

FROM : SAC, Newark (62-0)

SUBJECT: INFORMATION REGARDING NEW PRINCIPLES OF AERO-DYNAMICS ALOIS PIVEC - INFORMANT

Enclosed herewith are photostats of par
Alois Pivec and his wife, XXXXXXXX, both of
NJ.

Both photostats are in German and conc
ciple in aero-dynamics and alleged attempts
obtain this information.

There is also enclosed a blind memo, s
information in the letters and the circumst

This information is being furnished to
deemed appropriate.

The indices of the Neward Office are n

(Retyped 7/84 by WLM.
A True Copy)

CONFIDENTIAL

On January 18, 1954, [redacted] East Orange, NJ, appeared at the Newark Office and advised that he had received a letter from one [redacted], West Austria, on about December 20, 1953.

[redacted] stated that the letter requested him to attempt to sell a number of inventions, which he, [redacted] had developed. [redacted] stated that the request was to contact Aircraft Companies and Sewing Machine Companies in the United States and attempt to interest them in these devices.

According to [redacted] requested that no governmental agencies be contacted. [redacted] stated that the inventions, which [redacted] had developed were new type of sewing machine and a flying saucer. [redacted] stated that he came to this office because he felt that the flying saucer was of some importance in the national defense of this country. [redacted] stated that he has never met [redacted] but that [redacted] was given his name by [redacted] brother, [redacted] who resides in Graz, Austria, and who is employed at [redacted], Graz, Austria. [redacted] stated that his brother worked with [redacted] at one time, and he believes that [redacted] is a chemist or some type of engineer. [redacted] stated that the contents of the letter seemed fantastic to him and that if the letter were not written in such an intelligent manner, he would have doubted [redacted] sanity. He stated that [redacted] claims to have sold a new principle of aero-dynamics, which made it possible to construct a practical flying saucer and that [redacted] had developed a model that flies without the usual hazards. According to [redacted] the letter continues by stating that [redacted] has been in contact with other men throughout the world, who have been attempting to develop the saucer and that he has been the first to win real success.

By way of background, [redacted] stated that he was born in the vicinity of Leoben, Austria in 1925 and arrived in New York City on March 29, 1952 from Bremerhaven, Germany. He is employed at the [redacted] in Maplewood, NJ.

On January 30, 1954, [redacted] East Orange, NJ, appeared at the Newark Office and advised that she was the wife of [redacted]. She stated that another letter had been received from [redacted] by her husband, [redacted]. She stated that her husband did not want to furnish the information in this letter to the FBI. She stated that he was not aware that she was furnishing this information and wished to keep the interview confidential.

[redacted] stated that the letter received recently by her husband, from [redacted], contained information that [redacted] had been contacted by Communists in Austria, who wished to take him to Switzerland in order that he might further develop his new principle of aero-dynamics. According to the letter, [redacted] has continued to refuse any offer by the Communists and wished [redacted] to increase his efforts to sell [redacted] new invention in the United States.

By way of background, [redacted] advised that she was born of German parents in South Russia and at the time of the German invasion of Russia, during World War II, she and her family were resettled in Germany. After the war, she married [redacted] and came to the United States with him.

An FBI Report on German Flying Discs This report describes a new propulsion system which could be powered by conventional motorcycle or automobile engines! This would only have been possible if all that was needed from those engines was a spinning motion to be used for a specific purpose. Was this specific purpose to overcome the back-torque of interacting magnetic fields? Please note that this report was retyped by William Moore (UFO researcher and later admitted "government asset"), whose initials appear in the lower left of the cover pate. The inset is the first page of the report. On the lower left-hand margin it can be seen that the FBI destroyed the originals. Our tax dollars at work!

The rise of Sonderkommando-H within the SS may have coincided with the demise of Karl Maria Willigut. For this reason alone it is of interest to those who study the Nazi Occult. Anyone who has ever read this genre knows there is, well, plenty of non-, dis-, and false information and gossip associated this topic. It can only be hoped that one or more of the reputable writer/researchers in this field, such as Nigel Graddon, Peter

Levenda, Dr. Stephen Flowers, or Nigel Pennick will obtain the Koblenz records and bring the real story to us in English.

So our picture of the post-war SS world is one in which there are outposts of Nazis at both poles and in South America who engage in an off-again, on-again, rather low level conflict with the United States and probably the other former Allied Powers. The conflict is one of forced withdrawals as in Greenland, EMP bomb attacks as at Point 211, and UFO overflights as in Washington, D.C., in 1952. The cooperation involves using German scientists and technical companies for projects that were for political reasons were unacceptable for either the Western or Eastern block countries to undertake. The mutually agreed upon solution by both East and West as well as the country involved was to use the Nazi Internatinal to fulfill these needs. In addition to monetary reward, the price for either the East or West probably involved something desired by the Nazi International following Otto Skorzeny's model with Churchill. And as with Churchill, neither the First nor Second World wanted to disclose or even admit the existence of the Nazi International.

But there is some new information in the next chapter which may add another dimension to this story and may serve to verify that the Nazi International was not the final incarnation of the post-war SS world; that an organization existed which has never really been properly described, the Third Power.

Literature Cited

1. **Farago, Ladislas, 1974**, *Aftermath Martin Bormann and the Fourth Reich*, page 204, Simon and Schuster, N.Y., NY., USA
2. **Infield, Glenn B., 1981**, *Skorzeny Hitler's Commando*, pages 25, 26, St. Martin's Press, N.Y., NY., USA
3. *ibid.*
4. **Farago, Ladislas, 1974**, page 265
5. **Farago, Ladislas, 1974**, page 265-266
6. **Farago, Ladislas, 1974**, page 209
7. *ibid.*
8. **Buechner, Howard A., Captain and Capt. Wilhelm Bernhard, 1988**, *Adolf Hitler and the Secrets of the Holy Lance*, page 157, Thunderbird Press, Inc., Metairie, Louisiana, USA
9. **Wilson, Harvey, 1964**, Article in Police Gazette
10. **Stevens, Henry, 2001**, *Hitler's Flying Saucers*, pages 249-253, Adventures Unlimited Publishing, Kempton, Illinois, USA
11. **Stevens, Henry, 2007**, *Hitler's Suppressed and Still-Secret weapons, Science and Technology*, pages 258-305, Adventures Unlimited Publishing, Kempton, Illinois, USA
12. **Haarmann, D.H., 1985**, *III Geheim Wunderwaffen Ueber den Krieg hinaus!,* page 77, Hugin Gesellschaft Fuer Politisch-Philosophische Studiern E.V., Wetter, Germany
13. **Landig, Wilhelm, 1980**, *Wolfzeit um Thule*, page 167, Volkstum-Verlag Wilhelm Landig, Vienna, Austria
14. **Landig, Wilhelm, 1980**, page 171
15. **Landig, Wilhelm, 1980**, page 173

16. **Landig, Wilhelm, 1980**, page 172
17. *ibid.*
18. **Gehring, Heiner, and Karl-Heinz Zunneck, 2005**, *Flugscheiben Ueber Neuschwabenland Die Wahrheit ueber "Vril", "Haunebu" und die Templer-Erbengemenischaft*, page 73,74, Jochen Kopp Verlag, Rottenburg, Germany
19. *ibid.*
20. *ibid.*
21. **Stevens, Henry, 2001**, pages 179-181
22. **Gehring, Heiner and Karl-Heinz Zunneck, 2005**, page 70
23. **Barton, Michael X., 1968**, *The German Saucer Story*, page 53, Futura Press, Los Angeles, CA., USA
24. **Article from La Razon, Buenos Aires, Argentina, circa 1977-1978**, as translated and cited by O. Bergmann, 1988, *I Deutsche Flugscheiben und U-boote Ueberwachen Die Weltmeere*, Hugin Gesellschaft, Wetter/Ruhr, Germany
25. *Article from En Contacto titled: "Los Ovnis Son Armas De Los Nazis"*, date unknown but probably the late 1970's, Mexico
26. **Moore, William L., date unknown but middle 1980s**, *Project V-7: Hitler's Flying Discs An Illustrated Compilation of research and source Materials*, item F-233, and "Nazi Flying Saucers: An Addendum to Publication No. F-233", William L. More Publications & Research, Burbank, CA., USA
27. **Farago, Ladislas, 1974**, page 388

THE THIRD POWER

The idea of a "Dritte Macht" or Third Power and the claims for it are not new. They have been around for over twenty years in the minds of some German writers who discuss lost and hidden technology. These claims stem from the dying days of the Third Reich and the frantic quest to drive prototypes into completion that have implications for the age which followed it, the Cold War. The writers O. Bergmann, D.H. Haarmann and others use this term. What they are talking about is a separate power from the West or the East, a power based on the advanced technology of the Third Reich. This included flying discs of the field propulsion type that were seen worldwide and attributed to extraterrestrials by the U.S. government using various ploys of their intelligence apparatus. This also included mysterious and fantastic U-boats that were powered in unusual ways and perhaps even in the same way as were the flying discs. In fact, writer O. Bergmann makes no distinction between the two, the UFOs and the USOs, saying they were both based on German technology. Of course, neither the USA or the Soviet Union nor other countries, especially the former Allied Powers, ever wanted to acknowledge the existence of the Third Power. To do so, a nasty appendix would have had to be written into the history of World War Two. The Third Power functioned with the Nazi International and the Gehlen Org. that by this time had made a comeback, and these were two components of the Third Power. The reason that a distinction is made between the Nazi International and the Third Power will become apparent as we proceed.

While we are on the subject, let us digress and review what is claimed to have happened at this time regarding field propulsion flying discs. Remember the SS post-war laboratories that remained in operation after the war. Well, according to Michael X. Barton's German informant, Carl Mayer:

> *"There are or were," Carl Mayer revealed, "post-war, some SECRET RESEARCH PLACES in the Black Forest, attempting to eliminate GRAVITY influence from the flight of objects, etc. It is supposedly some MACHINE, which I heard of some five years ago. What became of it, I do not know, but forecasts of 'surprises' were made in several newspapers." (1)*

Barton then turns to a UFO researcher of his time, Richard Ogden, who read Barton's 1960 book, "We Want You Is Hitler Still Alive?" Ogden says:

> *"Your book accurately describes the early post-war period of the Nazis in Argentina. This was up until 1952. Those saucers that were developed and flown in 1945 used JET POWER not electromagnetic power. The work on an electromagnetic powered saucer was done in German laboratories in Argentina and such a craft was perfected and flown in 1952." (2)*

Combining these two statements, this means the work underlying field propulsion was done in Germany. It was either done by Germans under supervision of the United States or it was done in still-operating SS laboratories. But if it was done under the auspices of the USA, then the secret was passed, via the Gehlen Org., to friends in South America. The Nazis probably had it before the Americans could build examples in New Mexico. Incidentally, I believe they are speaking of the larger German flying disc, the Haunebu type or Adamski type, powered by Tesla technology appropriated by Karl Schappeller and developed by a sequence of others and not the smaller Magnetscheibe or Vril. I believe the latter were already flying.

The important thing to remember is the Third Power relied on information, not military force. This information was the information both the West and East failed to get their hands on after the collapse of the Third Reich. In other words, it depended upon those sequestered caches of hidden documents and microfilm and those who knew where it was and exactly what it was. Not even the Americans instantly realized the total value of this German technology that could not be illustrated better than their complete non-understanding of digital computers and their applications (3). So, as the East and West came to appreciate what had been developed in Germany during the war, there was the Third Power to provide it to them or a shortcut to it, but of course for a price.

This whole idea rests upon information which was never taken as booty from Germany after the war. We have already discussed SS laboratories that remained functioning after the war and loyal to the SS. We have discussed the probability that laboratories operated by the Allies in Germany after the war had the product of their inquiry spirited off to the SS world by agents of the Gehlen Organization. But there were even whole caches of information, documents and microfilm, which never fell into the hands of the Allies, either because they were never informed of them and failed to find them on their own, or even more shocking, caches which they did find but where snatched from them in the waning days of World War Two in an SS damage-control effort. I documented one such case in my first book (4) but another instance or instances should be discussed.

For this glimpse deep into the inner, inner workings of the Third Reich and the SS, we are indebted to Friedrich Georg and Thomas Mehner (5) and the eyewitnesses to this history that have come forth and told their stories. I am going to summarize the testimony of the first two witnesses whose names were withheld. These individuals had problems in revealing their stories. These problems involved naming names of some still living that might be adversely affected. Also there were "health" problems since these secrets might upset still-powerful people. And finally, oaths were given not to reveal certain things. The witnesses worked around those problems and said what they could say. Besides this, certain testimony, especially the testimony of the third named witness was so explosive and destabilizing in the modern geopolitical sense that certain portions of it were withheld by the writer/researchers. Other caveats will be addressed as they are encountered.

The first eyewitness has already been cited once. This was the facility at Gossel that operated after cessation of hostilities at the close of the war. Both witnesses each describe in, separate detail, two large and yet unknown German rockets. In fact it seems that the facility at Gossel, between Arnstadt and Ohrdruf, was primarily a rocket production site after Kammler's original choice, at Ebensee, Austria, code-named "Zement", was moved and refitted to make synthetic fuel/oil. This facility was very near the other underground facilities of the Jonas Valley but unconnected to them. The intellectual leadership had connections to Kammler in Prague/Pilsen and the slave worker labor force did not come from Buchenwald as did the other nearby facilities but was separate from it.

I am not going to describe the large rockets. Just saying they exist and briefly describing them is unconvincing. What is needed to accept this as real is the detail provided by these writers in this and other books. In this it is like the German atomic programs or like the German flying disc programs that require an entire book to make the description concrete, allowing for their existence in the mind of a skeptical reader. The remainder of this testimony is shocking enough.

The first witness tells us by way of introduction that he belonged to the circle around Kammler, the "Adel" (Nobility). This group has also been called the Schwarze Adel, or black nobility in other places. This was a resistance group that wanted to remove Hitler and form a Fourth Reich. It is equated with the Avalon group of which Speer was part. The "nobility" in this case would be dissenting high SS officials. One begins to see why he was reluctant to give his name. At this point our witness also states that Wernher von Braun was not among his friends ("*nicht zu meinen Freunden gehoerte*") so we take from this that Dr. von Braun was not among the Adels.

The witness returns to "his facility", meaning Gossel, and says that it was so well camouflaged that it was impossible to identify, even though traffic went by it every day. In fact the researchers obtained detailed aerial photographs of this relatively small area and they still cannot find it. The Americans absolutely did not find it and as far as the Russians who took over the area are concerned, our witness cannot comment. He did say the facility was in operation after 1945, it was connected to a water supply, providing drinking water, and provisioned for some years. (6)

The second eyewitness is like the first witness but on steroids. He is now over 90 years old, started his work in Peenemuende, then went to the Reichspost and finally to Dr. Kammler. Then, immediately after saying he worked for Dr. Kammler he says "*auch nach 1945*", in English "also after 1945", meaning he worked for Kammler after 1945! He says he was a "Techniker" which means a technical person or even engineer in research and development. He was convinced of the doctrine (Nazi doctrine) but unconvinced of the war, the handling of the war, the "death" (caused by the war), and the military under the Wehrmacht and under Hitler. He says, he was on the side of the resistance, the Adels, in connection with Kammler and Speer and their goals. He says he was proud of German science and their creations.

The reader might recall that last official conversation between Kammler and von Braun from Tom Agoston's book *Blunder* (7) in which von Braun, awaiting an audience with Kammler, overheard his plans to hide from the Americans by "assuming the garb of the Benedictine order". Von Braun then rushed away from his doorway listening post just as Kammler's visitor, a Colonel Strack, exited and allowed von Braun entry to Kammler's office. Kammler and von Braun then both assumed a politically correct dialogue about relocating Peenemuende to the South and carrying on the war. According to von Braun, both realized this was impossible. This conversation was allegedly to have taken place in the first week of April 1945 at the Haus Jesu Christi Hotel, Kammler's headquarters at the time.

Well, there is more to the Kammler-von Braun relationship than that completely bogus conversation. According to the second informant, on February 4, 1945, a convoy left Peenemuende in the direction of Bleicherode and Gossel. At that time nobody knew about the "Nest" at Gossel, according to the second informant, as it was not even on the normal map. The convoy contained the whole Peenemuende technical archives, some 13.5 tons of material as well as Dr. von Braun and his co-workers, about 450 engineers. The convoy had three destinations that were Nordhausen, Bleicherode and Gossel. In Nordhausen von Braun met with Kammler where a discussion or perhaps an argument took place. Kammler laid it out openly and on the table. He, Kammler, along with his SS scientists, the Reich Research Council, the Reichspost with Dr. Manfred von Ardenne, and Dr. Kurt Diebner and his nuclear researchers had other goals: the erection of a Fourth German Reich with the gentlemen of the nobility (Herrn des Adels) in charge. This was followed by another conversation between Kammler and von Braun, this time with Albert Speer present, at Geraberg. But it came to nothing with von Braun and in the end Wernher von Braun and his team were not even allowed entrance into Gossel. In fact, they were probably never even made aware of Gossel's existence although our second informant does not say this. He only says they were not given entry to Gossel. It was at this point that von Braun set off for Oberammergau where he would eventually surrender to the Americans along with his team. At that time (presumably for the first time), von Braun learned that it was Dr. Kammler who headed the developmental work at Skoda. According to Agoston, the last meeting between the two took place at Oberammergau at the Hotel named but if our informant's tale is true, this meeting would have had its issues resolved earlier and so would have made no sense.

After his and his team's surrender, Dr. von Braun gave away the production sites in Nordhausen and those near Gossel to the Americans as well as knowledge of the research teams of Dr. Kammler and Dr. Diebner. Dr. von Braun also informed the Americans of the 13.5 ton archives from Peenemuende which Dr. von Braun had directed by sequester in Holzhausen (Thuringia) and Doerten (Northern Harz Mountains) by this men Huzel and Tessmann. Von Braun needed this library to show his work credible to the Americans. The Americans wanted to keep the information about the Doerten cache from the British (presumably it was in their sphere of influence). The SS and Dr. Kammler got wind of the attempt to claim the documentation at Holzhausen and cleaned out 2.5 tons of material before the Americans got there. They stashed the archive in a tunnel location, which shall remain unnamed and known to only a few SS members. This cache is there still to this day. (8) Our informant continues, saying that with this stash Dr. Kammler had a guarantee by which he could deal with the Americans as well as with the Russians.

The informant then states that Dr. von Braun was angry because: Dr. Kammler had his technical foundation; that Kammler had two rocket propellant components (for solid-fuel rockets) and he was angry because Helmut Groettup and Hans Rittermann had given the Russians the wind tunnel and laboratory at Nordhausen, the research area and production facilities at Lehesten, the firm Duema in Wechmar and the launch facilities (heavy rocket facilities) at Ichtershausen/Rudisleben to the Russians. The important thing is a third-party confirmation of the importance of Hans Rittermann whom we will met presently. Incidentally, our informant justifies the actions of Groettup and Rittermann, in essence saying that by giving up certain things, they saved other more important things from the Americans and the Russians including the saving of "objects of high technology of the German scientists" upon which the researchers Dr. Diebner and Dr. von Ardenne worked. He then states that not only did both the above named scientists work on the atomic bomb but also on the molecular bomb of which two examples were sequestered in Tresor, in the Stadtilmer school. (9) Of this weapon and the A-bomb the informant states that Speer and Kammler had the world-power in their hands along with the large rockets which they were also in possession. (10)

To have been a fly on the wall at this meeting....

For those readers who still do not believe the Germans were the first to detonate an atomic bomb or that the three atomic bombs in the possession of the U.S.A. could not possibly have been of German origin, I can only reiterate my position. Anything I could offer summarizing the work of those researchers living near Jonastal or the work of Friedrich Georg would be unsatisfying. This is also true for the delivery systems the Germans had built. But, English language readers are now able to get the first three of Friedrich Georg's books, his Siegeswaffen series, in English under the title of *Hitler's Miracle Weapons* (see www.amazon.com). If the reader is interested in these subjects or just plain doubts my opinion, please stop at nothing and obtain these works and see just how lazy establishment historians have been and just how far establishment media, in both the East and West, have led you astray.

Now for the testimony of Hans Rittermann: Hans Rittermann is an enigma. He certainly existed as his name appears throughout discussions of the secret underground facilities at the Jonas Valley. By way of introduction, Hans Rittermann was the Sonderbeauftragter (Special Commissioner) of the Reichspost (the German Post Office which did scientific/war-related research) and of the OKW (Over-Command of the Wehrmacht) in Thuringia for Sonderbauvorhaben (Special Construction Design) (11) and then came, by his own admission, under the command of Sonderfuehrer SS Gruppenfuehrer Kammler (12). In other words, Rittermann worked for the SS and Kammler doing some sort of specialized construction, underground. In doing such work he had not only access to the several massive underground installations in that vicinity, in fact, he was partially responsible for building them. He worked on the huge underground facilities at Jonastal. This is a deep insider, pardon the pun.

Immediately after the war, Rittermann was on-site and in fact disclosed the location of some facilities to the Soviets as was discussed above by a previous informant. Rittermann spoke English and since Patton's 3rd Army originally took over this area from the Wehrmacht and the SS, Rittermann was invaluable to the Americans before the relinquished the vicinity to the Soviets under treaty agreement. This did not diminish Rittermann's appeal as an employee since he also spoke Russian. In fact, Rittermann continued in some sort of advisory/contractual role with the Soviets, apparently until the early 1980s.

For instance, Rittermann writes that circa 1982-1983 he entered the facility code-named "Burg" (actually the last Fuehrer Headquarters and one of the underground facilities at Jonastal) with a Soviet officer. Rittermann was showing this Soviet officer around as this particular part of the facility had remained unknown and unexplored by both the Americans and the Russians. In the darkness, Rittermann walked up to an old light fixture and flipped the switch—and the light came on! (12)

Eventually, Rittermann left Germany forever and immigrated to the USA. At some point Rittermann believed he had concluded his fiduciary duty to both the Russians and the Germans and so became willing to talk.

At this point in time he was about 90 years old and in poor health. In fact, he dictated his communications, his letters, to several interested parties. His purpose was to shed some light on some of the most murky and mysterious happenings of the war, happenings of which he had special knowledge.

Thomas Mehner, who was one of the recipients of these letters, attempted to verify the letters as best he could. Of course, there really was a "Hans Rittermann" of that he is certain. But there is a possibility that the sender of these letters was someone using his name. But, it was concluded, even if that were true, the sender would have to have been someone with utterly exceptional knowledge and insider information.

Rittermann talks about many things, some of which have been redacted by Mr. Mehner since they might be sensitive to the world-political situation. He refers to "sleeping dogs" and we all know it is better to let sleeping dogs lie, sometimes. Perhaps, someday, Germany might see it in its own self-interest to raid the fine wine basement and uncork some of the secrets.

Mayer and Mehner devote over eighty pages to the Rittermann letters of which there are many. Rittermann throws light on many a murky issue. But here, we are going to focus on what Rittermann says about his old boss, Dr. Hans Kammler as contained in a segment of their book (13), which contains the information given below.

To preface, Rittermann's letter mentions Hitler and the mistaken assumption by the Americans that he was in the Castle Wachsenburg, since Hitler was sighted in this area and Wachsenburg is the only "Burg" in the area on the map. Actually, Hitler was not at the castle but in his headquarters, code-named "Burg". Also, Rittermann mentions some aircraft that were aircraft of such an exotic type that the Americans had never seen before and quickly snatched away. Also remember that Kammler planned a sort of coup with Operation Avalon or Schwarze Adel, so he might have been considered to have been part of the "resistance" if one were willing to stretch the term.

There is no good way for me to break the news about Kammler to the reader so I will translate Rittermann's own words from a letter:

"Kammler found himself in the facility 'Burg' till 4/1/45 in the region of the so-called special storehouses and arranged the security of facilities according to the Army Service Provisions 316, Prt I and II. He then flew at noon from the field airport Eichfelt/Bittstadt to Hradisko, the center of that place. With him was Ober-Engineer Wagner who had to come from Pilsen.

On May 6th, 1945, the laboratory part in Pilsen was taken by the 5th U.S. Army. On the same day there occurred a conversation between General Patton and Kammler. On May 9th, 1945, General Patton with Kammler decided upon Kammler's suicide and made it known.

Kammler was from May 28th, 1945 with high US military/scientific people in the vicinity of Ohrdruf and Arnstadt using the name Dr. Hausmann. He lived with an American in the Wachsenburg castle. At this time the mistake of the Americans was cleared up, Hitler was at the Burg (Wachsenburg). On the American maps the Wachsenburg Castle was designated as 'Burg' which the Fuehrer Headquarters referenced was the facility Burg.

With the hindrance of Kammler the facilities of the plant were relocated to Bergbad and the research aircraft to Ohrdruf. In the valley and the Fuehrer HQ at this time Kammler was not even present. On May 28th, 1945 at 14:30 hours they flew in three aircraft from the field airport in Eichfeld.

For reasons of security the US military could not bring Dr. Kammler to the USA so Kammler was brought again to the Castle Hradisko relative to the object there. In a decision between the Americans and Russians (also the Czechs) Kammler was sheltered with a Czech uncle of the chief German secretary of the Gestapo Augusta Sinkovwa (Sink), birth name Bruenn, in the village of Skalka (Prostejov). Kammler could speak Czech. He was given up to the Nazi pursuer of scientists and distinguished with Russian and Czechoslovakian resistance declarations. Kammler received a new name. I know his name, and he die in March, 1972. If he was buried in Skalka or elsewhere is not known to me. The Americans concluded an agreement with the Russians concerning Kammler, that he was at the disposal of both powers. I have myself spoken with Kammler in 1959 and 1964. The Americans as well as the Russians came by the following facilities: Pilsen, Skoda-Works, Dittmannsdorf, Ohrdruf, Lehesten, Stettin, Horst, Sussnin, Heidelberg, Stechowitz, Tharandt, Arnstadt, Stadtilm, Peenemuende, Koenigsberg, Schlowa, Ludwigshafen.

As a living being he was a questioned person for both sides. From 1967 he was attended too by Dipl.-Engineer Klein (formerly SS Oberfuehrer-General) who was in Arnstadt in the plant and also in the facility "Burg" many times. He was of the BRD. Klein was brought into the international camp at Dachau, he was completely conned by the Americans as chief of the Skoda Works, and as equivalent for Kammler delivered to the Czechoslovakians, there condemned and in 1967 exonerated. From this point on he lived in the BRD and was until death, Kammler's right hand.

Kammler had no contact with his family after 1945."

So, we are finally told what we suspected. Kammler's "death" and/or suicide was a fabrication but actual confirmation in terms of an eyewitness is a bombshell! Not only that, our eyewitness, Hans Rittermann, spoke with Kammler in his new position long after the war ended, not in hiding in South America but in Prague, sustained by both the East and West and, surprisingly, working for both sides, the Americans and the Soviets. Kammler's wartime crimes were ascribed to Klein and then Klein was pardoned.

From this situation we can glean some facts. Kammler was not a prisoner. Prisoners do not get another name. There is no reason to do so; they are in custody. Likewise, prisoners do not get assistants. Kammler cut a deal with both sides. Both sides evidently wanted to use Kammler's knowledge as to where thing, high technology, was buried on microfilm. Neither could expose the other without political fallout. In fact, neither side even wanted to mention the name "Kammler" as was discussed in my first book. (14)

Like von Braun, Kammler must have sent intermediaries ahead to cut a deal before his actual surrender. And he must have had a plan so that after he disclosed some facet of technology, the bargaining power would live up to its end of the bargain. This might have been, for instance, sending someone ahead to divide the file in question into two parts. Or it simply may have been the fact that the Americans and Soviets desperately needed his continual input.

What is meant is, again, illustrated with digital computer technology. The Americans simply did not recognize its importance in the post-war world, even though it was employed to guide V-2 missiles to their targets by the Germans. It was sometime before they woke up. (15) The comment of those finding microfilm detailing German technology in the hold of U-234 were correct when it was said the Germans were in advance (of us) of something like 100 years. But at very least the German scientists of the Nazi years built the technological second half of the 20th Century. But they were so far ahead that it was not always possible to see, understand and apply those advances. So, Kammler had to sit back and wait until he was called upon.

Can we imagine his circumstances? Kammler had worked in and made his career in what is now the Czech Republic. Kammler spoke Czech. Prague is a world of its own, neither fully Slavic nor German, but an island in between. This was a place where both German and Czech language could be heard on the street. Kammler was home! He must have been give comfortable surroundings, an allowance or salary. He must have been supplied with whatever else made him happy.

Also, Kammler must have had connections to the Skorzeny as well as the Gehlen Organization. Kammler would have been able to get word out or, perhaps, the others found him. Either way, the Nazi International and Kammler were really all in the same business, the high technology of Nazi Germany. Both would have used the Gehlen Org. and vice versa.

Kammler supplied high technology to both the East and West in exchange for something. The Nazi International was able to build this relic technology of the Third

Reich that would have amazed the Americans and Soviets. The flying saucers are a great example but we will touch upon some others. The Nazi International would have been able to move around the planet in their flying discs and mystery U-boats at will. The Gehlen Org. would have given them a "heads up" to any problems and supplied them with insider, secret information about both the East and West. Gehlen, by some accounts, stoked the fires of the Cold War, inflating some intelligence to keep the confrontation going. This all worked together so well. In a way, Kammler had his Fourth Reich and he was Fuehrer.

The axis of this "Fourth Reich" or Third Power as it should be known, was Madrid (Skorzeny), Munich (Gehlen), and probably the Prague/Pilsen area for Kammler that he knew so well. The workshops were in South America, being supplied with sub-assemblies and parts for "Mimes Schmiede" most from the USA. Money was no problem since Dr. Hjalmar Schacht was alive and well and the 3rd Power was probably making money on its own on an ongoing basis. This trade in Nazi science and technology and the relationship with both the East and West probably had its ups and downs but went on until the early-mid-1970s when Kammler died (1972) and Skorzeny died (1975). This was about thirty years after World War Two and the older generation must have been considering retirement. With the coming of the 1980's, the must have been some sort of change of leadership and perhaps new goals and outlooks.

Earlier I said we were going to use Rittermann's testimony to focus on Kammler. Well, I am going back on this for a couple instances. These are things already discussed in this book.

Rittermann is describing the work done in the vicinity of Arnstadt-Ohrdruf (Jonas Valley). He says that in 1943 tests on armor penetrating weapon by means of a "Lichtstrahltechnik" (light ray technology). Rittermann later comes back to this weapon and calls it "Energielicht" (energy-light). There is no doubt that he is talking about a laser. (16) Rittermann states that tests were conducted in the vicinity of Luisental and Rippersroda on the "Rundflugzeugen" (round aircraft) which is just another way of saying flying discs or flying saucers. (17) He then mentions tests conducted on "Todesstrahlen". This word is sometimes used when meaning what has been called here "Motorstoppmittel", (means to stop motors) or "Zuenderunterbrechung" (ignition disruption) or "magnetic wave" by the Americans. Finally, Rittermann mentions tests done on "Elektromagnetische Schockimpulse". This could only be Landig's "Klystron-EG-Projektoren", klystron-EG-projectors which he says were used against the Byrd air attack at Point 211.

The question will arise as to why some extreme Nazi, Hans Rittermann, should ever be believed, especially when discussing the history and accomplishments of the Nazi period. Did I mention Rittermann was an enigma? The fact is that even though Rittermann worked on the most sensitive German underground facilities in Germany, helped build them and certainly had full access to them as well as anything in the area, Hans Rittermann was a person to whom the Nazis did not even consider to be a real German. And this was no secret. Rittermann melded seamlessly into instant credibility with both the Americans and later the Russians since he seemed politically correct to both and spoke both languages. In fact, the Americans did not know if he was a prisoner or a free worker. This is all possible because Rittermann's Nazi identification papers clearly showed him to be a Jew. (18)

In fact, Rittermann's letters were posted from Jerusalem during the year 2000 where he was known by the name "David Hans Hoffmann" and where Rittermann died shortly thereafter. But before living in Israel, Rittermann had lived in the USA and reports that he wrote a report of approximately 800 pages on "Sonderbuero 3" (Rittermann's name for the combined underground complexes of "Burg", "Jasmin" and "Olga" in the Jonas Valley) which he gave to the "Geheimdiensten", the secret services, of both the USA and Israel. (19) Now, perhaps, we begin to appreciate the wisdom of letting sleeping dogs lie.

Literature Cited

1. **Barton, Michael X., 1968**, *The German Saucer Story*, page 23, Fortuna Press, Los Angeles, CA., USA
2. **Barton, Michael X., 1968**, pages 23, 24
3. **Stevens, Henry, 2007**, *Hitler's Suppressed and Still-Secret Weapons, Science and Technology*, pages 18 to 23, Adventures Unlimited Publishing, Kempton, Illinois, USA
4. **Stevens, Henry, 2003**, page 204. This damage-control was actually done by the Speer Ministry on May 1, 1945 but, by this time, after Hitler's death, most everything of a sensitive nature was actually ordered by the SS. This reference is based on I.V. Hogg's *German Secret Weapons of World War 2*, page 48, Arco Publishing Company, Inc., N.Y., NY. USA
5. **Georg, Friedrich and Thomas Mehner, 2004**, *Atomziel*, New York, pages 253-264, Jochen Kopp Verlag, Rottenburg, Germany
6. **Georg, Friedrich and Thomas Mehner, 2004**, page 264
7. **Agoston, Tom, 1985**, *Blunder How the U. S. Gave Away Nazi Supersecets to Russia*, pages 51-53, Dodd, Mead and Company, N.Y., NY., USA
8. **Georg, Friedrich and Thomas Mehner, 2004**, page 267
9. **Georg, Friedrich and Thomas Mehner, 2004**, page 258
10. *ibid.*
11. **Mayer, Edgar and Thomas Mehner, 2002**, *Die Atombomb und das Dritte Reich Das Geheimnis des Dreiecks Arnstadt-Weckmar-Ohrdruf*, page 17, Jochen Kopp Verlag, Rottenburg, Germany
12. **Mayer, Edgar and Thomas Mehner, 2002**, page 30
13. **Mayer, Edgar and Thomas Mehner, 2002**, pages 17-33
14. **Stevens, Henry, 2003**, pages 252-253
15. **Stevens, Henry, 2007**, pages 18-23
16. **Mayer, Edgar and Thomas Mehner, 2002**, pages 32 and 33
17. **Mayer, Edgar and Thomas Mehner, 2002**, page 33
18. **Mayer, Edgar and Thomas Mehner, 2002**, pages 37
19. **Mayer, Edgar and Thomas Mehner, 2002**, page 25

MOLECULAR BOMB

The question arises as to what in the world a "molecular bomb" would be. To give the reader some idea, something similar, in a way, to the molecular bomb is now in fashion among teenagers. It is called the dry ice bomb. These two are certainly not identical, the dry ice is not cold-compressed to the density as was the molecular bomb, but it does illustrate the power of expansive sudden reheating *(http://en.wikipedia.org/wiki/Dry_ice_bomb).* In a dry ice bomb, a one-liter plastic container, usually used for beverages, with a screw-on top is filled about 1/3 of the way with water. Then a small cube of dry ice is fitted through the top into the water and the lid screwed on tightly. Within 10-30 seconds the water sublimates the dry ice to a gas and this pressure of sublimation causes the plastic container to fail, producing a hand grenade like explosion. This is very dangerous and should not be attempted but anyone who has seen this demonstrated on U-tube will get an idea of a tiny part of what is under discussion with the molecular bomb.

Since testimony has been given that Kammler had possession of two examples of the molecular bomb, perhaps a description of it should be given. In my previous book this topic was mentioned and briefly discussed (1) as it has been elsewhere (2), (3). Dr. Joseph Farrell's summary (2) is the best overview:

1. The "Molecular" Bomb: The Hydrogen Bomb?

"The idea of a "Superbomb" was first patented prior to World War Two in Austria, and a modification of the idea was patented in Germany in 1943 (Farrell cites Patent Number 905.847, March 16, 1943 and other authorities from Mayer and Mahner's Hitler und die „Bombe", pages 158-159). Its inventor Karl Nowak, explained the reason for his invention as being to create a superbomb without the radioactive fallout effects that were evident from atomic and thermonuclear explosions! In other words, the Nazis were already looking past the thermonuclear age toward the creation of second and third generation weapons systems that would give the same offensive and strategic "punch" but without the side effects! In theory, the bomb is workable, but was way beyond the technological capacities of Germany, or any other power, in that time period. Basically, the idea was to create a state of matter in which, through ultra-low temperatures approaching absolute zero, matter would be super-compressed. The idea was then to detonate this material, subjecting it to sudden stress and heat, to create a sudden and massive expansion and explosion, and therewith, an

enormous, H-bomb sized blast. Thus, there may have been a basis in actual German secret research for the incredible claim of the Japanese military attaché in Stockholm's 1943 report to Tokyo that the Germans were investigating the properties of super-dense matter for weaponization."

The interesting thing is that every writer—except Friedrich Georg and Thomas Mehner's second informant (cited earlier)—states that this device was not built. The second, unnamed source says it was built twice and was in the possession of Kammler at Tesor in the Stadtilm School there (4). This witness is very definite about this. Therefore, it is possible that Dr. Hans Kammler had two such molecular bombs at his disposal, both hidden and potentially the subject of negotiation with both or either the USA or the USSR.

We also must bear in mind that, at least the USA, did not always understand the advanced weapons and technology developed by the Germans during the war. Nothing could make this case better than the American's blindness to the German-developed digital computer technologies. Both the computer programming and magnetic tape storage technologies were completely minimized by Americans and therefore passed over (6). The same could certainly be said of laser technology (7), since the Americans did not even have a word for the technology at the time and only acknowledged its existence after 1964, when Charles H. Townes was awarded the Nobel Prize in physics for his "development of laser principles". This was twenty years after the Germans had a working model. There are several more examples, as well as that famous but legendary comment about the microfilm hold of U-234, which, after review by the Americans, was said of it that the Germans were one hundred years in advance of the Allies. So, the point is that Kammler probably had to wait on the Americans and Soviets to rediscover German technology—or at least the need of this technology—before he was in a strong position to "deal".

According to everyone, the fundamental ideas allowing for the development of a molecular bomb were stated in Karl Nowak's patent of 1943. So first we must take a look at this patent for verification and a better understanding of this idea and other ideas related to it. Nowak's patent was mentioned in my first book along with a copy of the first page, but a fresh, more detailed look should be undertaken now so a drawing explaining the process involved is pictured below.

This patent is titled: "Method and arrangement to the Change of Material Characteristic or Manufacture of Strongly Expansive-Capable Materials". The German word I am translating as "materials", "Stoff", could also be translated as "matter" but in most instances "material" makes more sense. This is the very patent apparently applied for and granted to Karl Novak in 1943 as the small print under the title says:

"Patented in the domain of the Federal Republic of Germany from 16 March 1943 to patent announcement of 18 June 1953, patent - granted - made public - on 21 January 1954."

This is a mystery. Was this patent lost after the war or simply taken by the Americans? Was this the reason a new patent application had to be made and a new patent granted? Also, why when Germany was forbidden to invent and produce new weaponry, for about the first ten years after the war, was a patent granted dealing with high explosives with obvious military applications?

This is a short patent but patents are unusually boring. They seem to be a cross between two conflicting concepts: they attempt to describe a new idea in a way that incorporates as many potential applications as possible, while at the same time adhereing to the Bruce Lee Principle of *"Just enough is enough"*and carefully presenting both in the language of patent attorneys. This ensures that the most interesting descriptive concepts will be translated, while the rather boring processes behind remain only summarized (along with the patent claims at the end, which are already self-apparent in the description).

This patent does describe an exact process, which seems rock-solid—at least on a small scale in the laboratory—so I am wondering why at least two others writing on this topic say it was out of reach with the technology at hand. As we know, though, sometimes larger industrial-commercial-military processes are done differently, and this is what we would expect in this instance. But lacking industrial methods would not preclude the making of the material necessary for two examples of the molecular bomb in the laboratory, using the methods described.

As context, Nowak starts:

> *"The inventor references a method and arrangement of changing material characteristics or manufacture of strongly-expansive-capable materials (relating to explosives) and consists therein that the material to be changed with deep cooling appropriate, as much as possible, to the vicinity of absolute zero (in the condition of superconductivity) and will be or is put under pressure.*
>
> *It proves itself to be that through the reciprocal super cooling and compression treatment of a material atomic structure can be changed.*
>
> *The invention is based on the consideration that it must be possible, through the exercise of an outside pressure with deep temperature the characteristics of a material to change; and certainly in the following directions:*
>
> *With the heating of deeply cooled, compressed materials there forms a corresponding atomic distance but which must not correspond to the previous atomic order (lattice). Especially it is in this sense possible various materials to alloy with each other through linking of their crystal lattice in a special way.*
>
> *If the material remains with its compressive volume reduced, so it will, following heating, exercise an exceptional expansive pressure, showing the strongest explosion or expansive-effect."*

At this point Nowak refers the reader to the diagram of the container and describes the actual process of densification of matter which is summarized as follows:

The processes described take place in a special, triple walled container ***1***. The material to be influenced, densified, or otherwise manipulated is in the lower center ***2***, having been brought there via stopper ***3***, which, when sealed, is air tight so that the air can be pumped out. The outer portion of the container is encased in a heat isolationing mantle ***5***. Between the mantle ***5*** and the acted-upon material ***2***, another layer ***4*** exists, into which a means of cooling—liquid nitrogen, hydrogen or helium—is pumped. Over the subject material ***2*** a piston ***6*** and piston shaft *7* are arranged so that pressure can be put on the subject material. The shaft *7* operates through a special stopper ***8*** within stopper ***3***. Using an upward stroke of piston ***6***, air is exhausted via tube ***9***, creating a vacuum. The refrigerant, one of the liquid gasses mentioned above, enters through tube ***10***. A temperature gauge, ***12***, is set up for monitoring. Once cooling has been achieved, the cold liquid gasses are exhausted through tube ***11***. Nowak comments that a special three-stage mercury diffusion pump should be used for this purpose. Container ***1*** is provided with internal electrodes ***13*** and ***14*** used for testing the conductivity of subject material *2*. Nowak contends that in some instances superconductivity or near superconductivity can result from this densification process. Nowak also comments that, interestingly, no heat seems to be generated from the compression process.

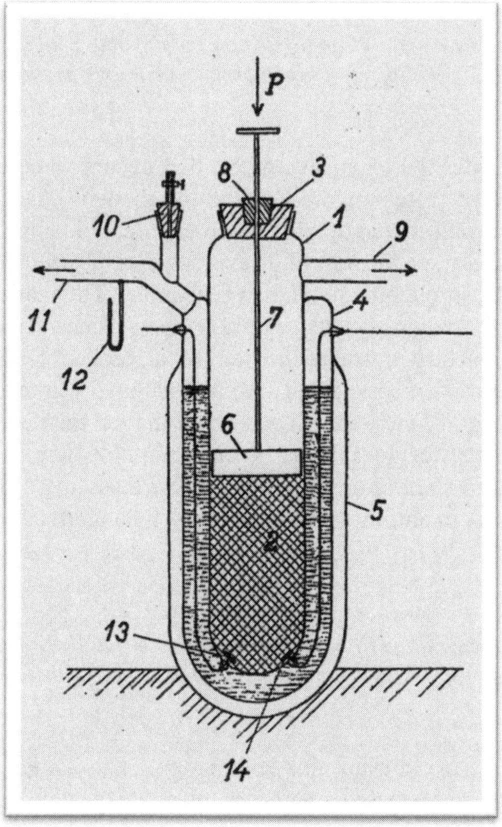

A diagram of the Karl Nowak Patent

Since there are several applications within the overall concept, specific and individual procedures would come into play for each individual result desired. Nowak mentions some of these. Parts of the claims within the patent involve alloying dissimilar materials. This happens because the atomic lattice has been altered by this process so that these dissimilar materials now share the same lattice. So, for example, molten material to be alloyed or even the pulverized powder of two dissimilar materials can be acted upon in the reaction area ***2***.

Then Nowak says something that I have never heard repeated and find exciting:

> *"It can, if the occasion arises, be profitable to influence the atomic formation of the reaction material through a vibration of the same means, sound or ultra-high frequency, (ultra sonic) (somewhere over the piston, 6.)"*

So high frequency vibration in the form of sound is sometimes employed to shake into place this densification through mechanically assisting in reshaping the atomic lattice? This sounds like work for Dr. Ronald Richter (8).

Nowak goes on to expand upon his explosives claims:

> *"For the manufacture of strongly expansive-capable explosives, it can be practical to multiply the effect of common chemical expansion material through super-compression."*

This means that besides the expansive affect that occurs when common materials are reheated, the expansive effect would be multiplied if the material undergoing densification from the outset was explosive in nature. So high explosives could be cooled, compressed, and their already high explosive value would be further multiplied because of the cold, densification and sudden reheating. The reader can imagine, just as the Germans must have imagined, what would happen if red mercury in its liquid state, already charged with neutrons and densified in a nuclear reactor, were then cold-compressed by the Nowak process, fitted into an insulated warhead and detonated. The result would greatly magnify the explosive value of the red mercury but the neutron burst would leave no permanent residue. What is really possible here is to greatly miniaturize the explosive warhead in such an insulated chamber, attaching a battery and electrodes, and using it, for instance, in anti-aircraft shells or even hand grenades.

Nowak goes on:

> *"The deeply cooled expansive material can also be used for rocket propulsion whereby the thrust-speed by means of the temperature of the cooling-mean can be regulated."*

So rocket fuel can be made using this technology. This statement even seems to say the thrust of the rocket can be varied, somehow, using this technology.

The patent then goes into a rule for operation, saying that the material to be manipulated, ***2***, should be of a higher atomic number than the cooling material ***4*** in the jacket.

Finally, patent claims are made as in every new patent. Nowak claims that his invention:

1. *Involves a procedure of changing the characteristics of a material or of matter by cooling to as near to absolute zero as possible and compacting.*
2. *Incorporating number 1 above, a procedure resulting in superconductivity.*
3. *Incorporating 1 and 2 above, a procedure for bonding two dissimilar materials.*
4. *Incorporating 1, 2, and 3, above, a procedure resulting in the vanishing of superconductivity.*
5. *Incorporating 1 to 4 above a new means of chemical expansion.*
6. *Incorporating 1 to 5 above, a means of regulating the output of rocket propulsion.*
7. *Incorporating 1 to 6 above, a means of manufacturing materials within container **1** above, material of a lower atomic number will be employed.*
8. *Incorporating 1 to 7 above, the material used to change the worked material, **4**., will be of a lower temperature than the acted upon material, **2**.*
9. *Incorporating 1 to 8 above, that the material in position **4** will have a lower melting point than that of position **2**.*

Norbert Juergen-Ratthofer is the one who first brought this whole concept to the fore. He is less abstract about this, getting much more specific and practical. Here is a translation of what he has to say on the topic (9).

> *"The principle of the "molecular bomb" can be described as follows: Under normal conditions with matter the dimension of molecular expanse is in the order of magnitude of 10-8 cm (1 hundred millionth of a cm) and the atomic (expanse) of 10-13 (1 ten-billionth of a cm). If mater is now cooled in the range of absolute zero, then there ensues an electron movement of almost stillness, whereby the electrons very strongly near their atomic nucleus at any given time. In the range of absolute zero matter now, without high expenditure of energy, matter can be strongly compressed. In conditions of this "super compression" the molecular distance resembles the atomic distance (10-8) to (10-13 at the atomic level) so that a contraction of nearly 15 volumes takes place. The deeply cooled conditions of easily compressed and densified matter develop, however, with re-warming, extra ordinarily strong molecular expansive power, which with a sudden, strong, heating of the supercompressed, deeply cooled matter produces an explosion over 10 to the 10th power (10 billion times). Volumetric increase is obtained through which this "molecular bomb" obtained the explosive force of a hydrogen bomb and, by the utilization of supercompressed chemical explosive, this even still more exceeds. In comparison: Chemical explosive that was not deeply cooled and super-dense yielded, at explosion, only that up to 10 to the 3rd power (thousand fold) its original volume. Molecular bombs undergo, though a normal heat generating chemical explosive start at its center, an enclosing*

"mantle" of deeply cold, super-compressed (liquid) gas, for example hydrogen, or with room-temperature liquid chemical explosive, for example nitro-glycerine, and an outer shell of likewise normal heat generating chemical explosive. Between the bomb's center - mantle and outer shell is found a thermo-isolation layer. The ignition of he molecular bomb results, as with nuclear bombs, through the normal chemical explosive start combine and parallel with direct electrical ignition. As with all other bombs, the molecular bomb was also planned to have a metal outer hull."

It must be left to scientists and engineers to comment regarding the molecular bomb vs. the hydrogen bomb in terms of explosive energy. But whatever the outcome, the molecular bomb is certainly an inexpensive, powerful device and certainly a something worth having in a country's military arsenal. If the second unnamed informant who described the actual existence of two such working bombs to Mr. Mayer and Mr. Mehner is true, and they were apparently at the disposal of the SS and so ultimately fell under the control of Dr. Hans Kammler in the post-war world, well, then without a doubt, they represent a strong bargaining chip on the table for Dr. Kammler to deal with the Americans and/or the Soviets.

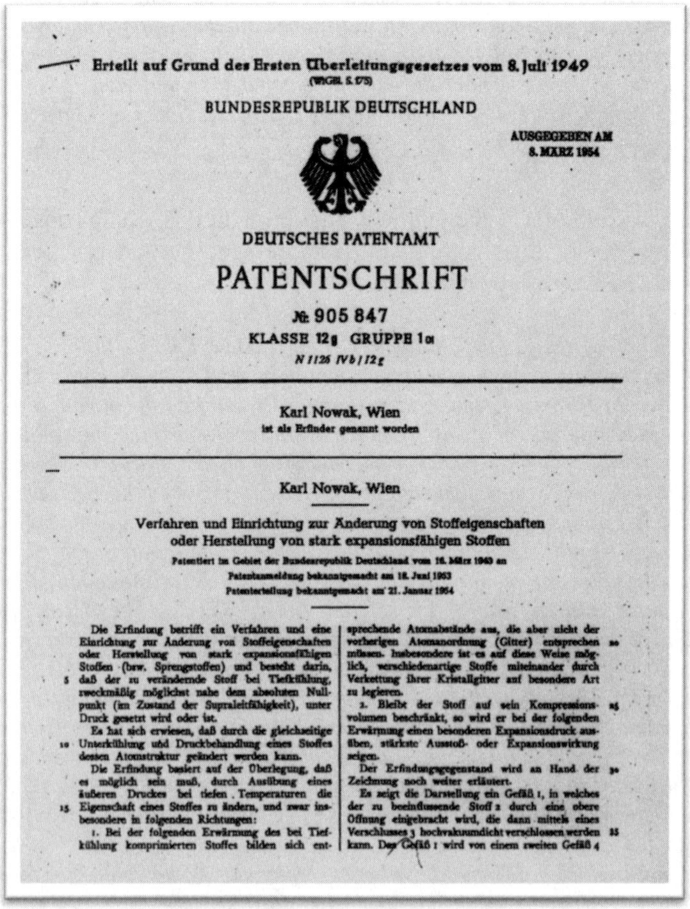

Erteilt auf Grund des Ersten Überleitungsgesetzes vom 8. Juli 1949
(WiGBl. S. 175)

BUNDESREPUBLIK DEUTSCHLAND

AUSGEGEBEN AM
8. MÄRZ 1954

DEUTSCHES PATENTAMT

PATENTSCHRIFT

№ 905 847

KLASSE 12g GRUPPE 1α

N 1126 IVb / 12g

Karl Nowak, Wien
ist als Erfinder genannt worden

Karl Nowak, Wien

Verfahren und Einrichtung zur Änderung von Stoffeigenschaften oder Herstellung von stark expansionsfähigen Stoffen

Patentiert im Gebiet der Bundesrepublik Deutschland vom 16. März 1943 an
Patentanmeldung bekanntgemacht am 18. Juni 1953
Patenterteilung bekanntgemacht am 21. Januar 1954

Die Erfindung betrifft ein Verfahren und eine Einrichtung zur Änderung von Stoffeigenschaften oder Herstellung von stark expansionsfähigen Stoffen (bzw. Sprengstoffen) und besteht darin, daß der zu verändernde Stoff bei Tiefkühlung, zweckmäßig möglichst nahe dem absoluten Nullpunkt (im Zustand der Supraleitfähigkeit), unter Druck gesetzt wird oder ist.

Es hat sich erwiesen, daß durch die gleichzeitige Unterkühlung und Druckbehandlung eines Stoffes dessen Atomstruktur geändert werden kann.

Die Erfindung basiert auf der Überlegung, daß es möglich sein muß, durch Ausübung eines äußeren Druckes bei tiefen Temperaturen die Eigenschaft eines Stoffes zu ändern, und zwar insbesondere in folgenden Richtungen:

1. Bei der folgenden Erwärmung des bei Tiefkühlung komprimierten Stoffes bilden sich entsprechende Atomabstände aus, die aber nicht der vorherigen Atomanordnung (Gitter) entsprechen müssen. Insbesondere ist es auf diese Weise möglich, verschiedenartige Stoffe miteinander durch Verkettung ihrer Kristallgitter auf besondere Art zu legieren.

2. Bleibt der Stoff auf sein Kompressionsvolumen beschränkt, so wird er bei der folgenden Erwärmung einen besonderen Expansionsdruck ausüben, stärkste Ausstoß- oder Expansionswirkung zeigen.

Der Erfindungsgegenstand wird an Hand der Zeichnung noch weiter erläutert.

Es zeigt die Darstellung ein Gefäß 1, in welches der zu beeinflussende Stoff 2 durch eine obere Öffnung eingebracht wird, die dann mittels eines Verschlusses 3 hochvakuumdicht verschlossen werden kann. Das Gefäß 1 wird von einem zweiten Gefäß 4

The Karl Nowak Patent cover page

Literature Cited

1. Stevens, Henry, 2007, *Hitler's Suppressed and Still-Secret Weapons, Science and Technology*, pages 92-101, Adventures Unlimited Publishing, Kempton, Illinois, USA
2. Farrell, Joseph P., Ph.D., 2004, *Reich of the Black Sun Nazi Secret Weapons & the Cold War Allied Legend*, page 190
3. Stoll, Axel, Ph.D., 2001, *Hochtechnologie im Dritten Reich*, pages 99, 161, Amun Verlag, Schleusingen, Germany
4. Georg, Friedrich and Thomas Mehner, 2004, *Atomziel*, New York, page 258, Jochen Kopp Verlag, Rttenburg, Germany
5. Juergen-Ratthofer, Norbert, undated but late 1980's, *Flugscheiben und andere deutsche und japanische Geheim- und Wunderwaffen im Zweiten Weltkrieg*, page 40 (page numbers are problematic), Privately Published, Sierdorf, Austria.
6. Stevens, Henry, 2007, pages 18-23
7. Stevens, Henry, 2007, pages 198-208
8. Stevens, Henry, 2007, pages 258-305
9. Juergen-Ratthofer, Norbert, undated, see footnote 5. above, page 40

THE GENTLEMEN AND THEIR LUGGAGE

Before moving on to the next section of this book we are going to take a break and discuss something directly which always forms a backdrop for any discussion on Nazi post-war survival, the survival of Hitler himself. Of course, there are many reports of Hitler surviving the war. These are always interesting as they have to be interesting or nobody would pay attention to the seventy years later. Some contain great detail and the reader has probably heard some of these tales. But none of them that I know allege to be official documents. This one does.

As stated above, I believe Hitler died in the bunker but I would encourage anyone wanting to do research on this topic as it might lead to other heretofore unknown avenues of knowledge. This document was circulated several years ago concerning Hitler and his survival after the war. If it is described as a "hot" document or a document one would not want to be linked with in polite company, perhaps this would convey its utter political incorrectness. Nevertheless, Heiner Gehring and Karl-Heinz Zunneck did publish it in their book "Flugscheiben ueber Neuschwabenland", ascribing it to American Gregory Douglas as published in the magazine "The Military Advisor". (1) The document as see in the book referenced above is reproduced here. I have another copy but it is in even worse condition. Before reviewing the document, I want to partially translate it as best I can. Some parts are just too faint to read. Please compare this to the original.

Secret Commando Matter
Heinrich Mueller   Principal - Matter Only Through Officer   (illegible) 26. April 1945

(illegible)
3 Dispatches

1 Dispatch
Regarding: Fuehrer Special Trip to Barcelona

1. The Fuehrer and his accompaniment left the airport Hoerching on 26, April, 1945 at 20.00 hours
2. Hereby are found in those in accompaniment of the Fuehrer:

The Fuehrer
XX (redacted)XXXXXXXX
XX (redacted)XXXXXXXX
Reich Leader Bormann
SS-Gruppenfuehrer (Major General) Mueller
SS-Gruppenfuehrer (Major General) Fegelein
(Major General)
General of the Infantry Burgdorf
Intelligence Person of Special Utilizaton Hewel
SS-Oberstumbahnfuehrer (General) Betz
SS-Sturmbahnfuehrer (Major) Dr. Stumpfegger
SS-Hauptsturmfuehrer (Captain) Gross (?)
Frauline Braun
Frauline Manzialy
4 Man Accompanying Kommando (RBD) + 3

The luggage of the proceeding named gentlemen has been delivered to the commander of the Airport Hoerching on 16.00 hours.

SS-Gruppenfuehrer (Major

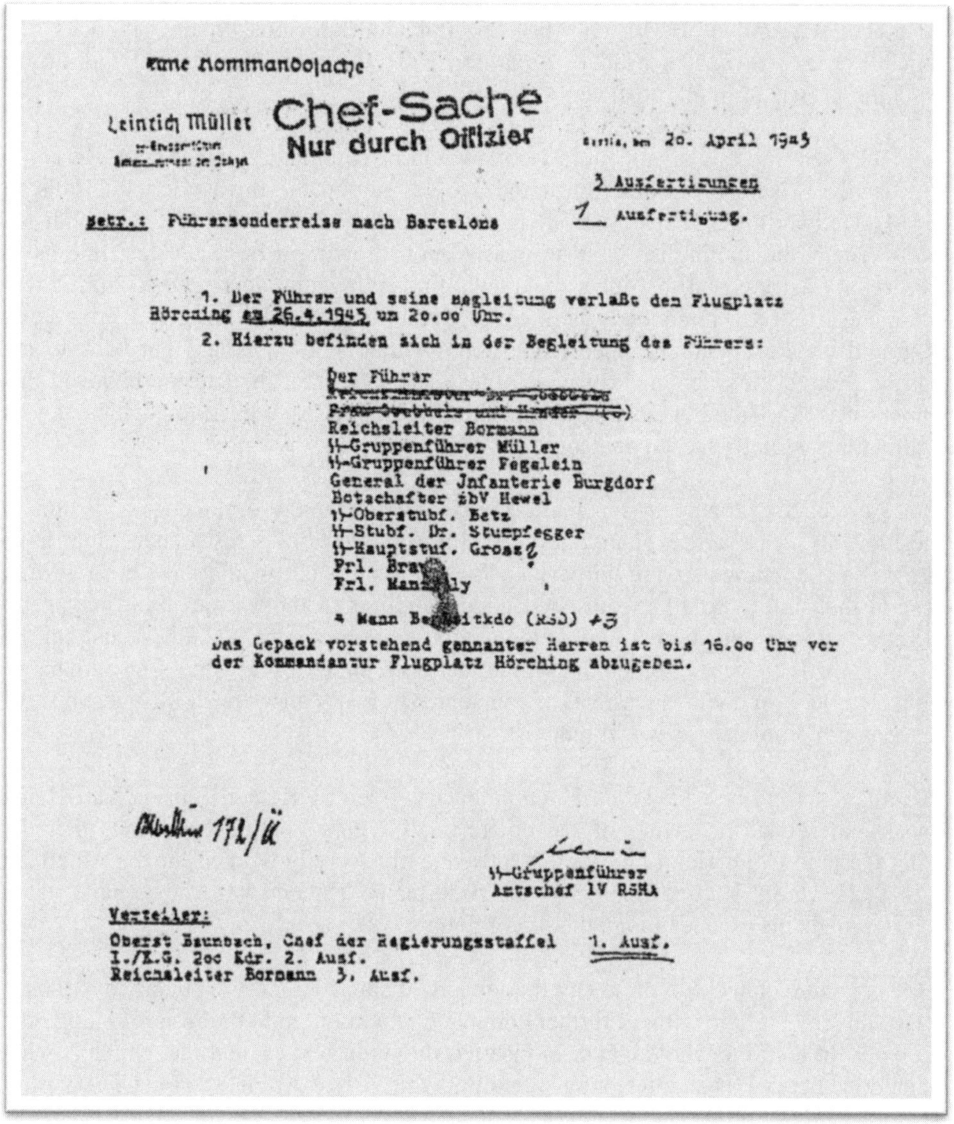

Geheime Kommandosache

Heinrich Müller

Chef-Sache

Nur durch Offizier

Berlin, den 20. April 1945

3 Ausfertigungen

1 Ausfertigung.

Betr.: Führersonderreise nach Barcelona

1. Der Führer und seine Begleitung verlaßt den Flugplatz Hörching ~~am 26.4.1945~~ um 20.00 Uhr.

2. Hierzu befinden sich in der Begleitung des Führers:

Der Führer
~~Reichsminister Dr. Goebbels~~
~~Frau Goebbels und Kinder (6)~~
Reichsleiter Bormann
SS-Gruppenführer Müller
SS-Gruppenführer Fegelein
General der Infanterie Burgdorf
Botschafter zbV Hewel
SS-Oberstubf. Betz
SS-Stubf. Dr. Stumpfegger
SS-Hauptstuf. Grosz
Frl. Bra...
Frl. Man...ly

4 Mann Be...itkdo (RSD) +3

Das Gepäck vorstehend genannter Herren ist bis 16.00 Uhr vor der Kommandantur Flugplatz Hörching abzugeben.

Müller 172/II

SS-Gruppenführer
Amtschef IV RSHA

Verteiler:

Oberst Baumbach, Chef der Regierungsstaffel 1. Ausf.
I./K.G. 200 Kdr. 2. Ausf.
Reichsleiter Bormann 3. Ausf.

The Gentlemen and Their Luggage

This is an alleged wartime document purporting to show Hitler and other important Nazis leaving the bunker on April 20, 1945. (RSHA was Reich Central Security Department).

One version of this document is marked "SECRET" at its top and with a date-stamp of 4 Sept. 1951 below. This would indicate it had become the property of the American government and held by them.

So what we have here is an alleged government document recording in a matter-of-fact way that Hitler, Eva Braun, Gestapo Chief Heinrich Mueller, Martin Bormann and some others flew out of Berlin on April 26, 1945 to Barcelona, Spain. It looks like Colonel Werner Baumbach, head of Squadron KG 200, was in charge of the airport Hoersching in Berlin. It all looks very official.

Someone sent me this document, no explanation or commentary other than it was too hot to handle. I sent it to some interested people, among these was Gerhard Hallstatt (formerly Kadmon). Gerhard is an artist, musician and writer who writes in both his native German and in English, and he insists upon drawing a hard and fast line as to factual reality as opposed to flights of fancy. In sending this document to him it was hoped his artist's right brain analysis might yield an insight. I did not give Gerhard any background on the document since I had none at that time. Gerhard got back to me saying he thought this document was a forgery. Beyond that, he said he believed this document was fabricated by an English-speaking source. His stylistic-linguistic analysis was something I totally lacked and could not even approach.

But I doubt this document for another reason. How many times does a document written seventy years ago explain and answer all the questions a researcher might have today? Those documents were not written for our benefit but would have been written for use at that time with all the unstated understandings of those times built into them. Government documents almost never completely solve problems. The best that can be asked of them is to verify something which has been stated by a witness or perhaps to contain testimony of a witness which, of course, never really answers all the questions we have today as completely as we would wish.

To this it should be added that the commentary given by Heiner Gehring/Karl-Heinz Zunneck states that the owner of the document, Gregory Douglas, contends that the missing Gestapo Chief Heinrich Mueller subsequently secretly worked for the American CIC in Switzerland! In questioning by the Americans, Mueller was said to have stated that Hitler made his escape though the use of doubles (2).

Gehring and Zunneck go on to say that experts dismiss Gregory Douglas' hypothesis as false and leave it here without further comment, leaving it up to the reader to judge the document. In fact, the whole matter in inserted into their text as an aside, which is what is being done here. It is an interesting sideline, as the M-J 12 Affair is to the UFO world.

Literature Cited

1. **Gehring, Heiner, and Karl-Heinz Zunneck, 2005**, *Flugscheiben ueber Neuschwabenland Die Wahrheit ueber Vril, "Haunebu" und die Templer-Erbengemeinschaft*, pages 128-129, Jochen Kopp Verlag, Rottenburg, Germany. These authors cited a articles by Gregory Douglas in the magazine *The Military Advisor*, 1992-1993, Third Edition, number 11 and 12 as well as Fourth Edition, number 11. In those writings Mr. Douglas claims he is in possession of the document.
2. *ibid.*

PART TWO: FANTASTIC U-BOATS

PREMISE AND INTRODUCTION

There is the idea that near the very end of the war in Europe, the German Navy refitted some damaged U-boats with non-conventional propulsion systems. This was unlike other developments by the German Navy, which involved extensive testing and prototypes and perhaps a whole line of test U-boats. These strange U-boats seemed to have been one-off and done on an individual and perhaps opportunistic basis. After the war, these U-boats may have continued to function as sort of a phantom navy for the post-war SS. As was done for the discussion of secret bases, some early reports of this practice will be cited.

The first example is Michael X. Barton in his first book, originally published in 1960 and written under the name "Michael X". Barton's 1960 work was really a pre-quill to his 1968 classic on German flying discs, *The German Saucer Story*. It was with this second publication that German informants came to Barton and described a truly inside picture of events. What is amazing is that as early as 1960 Barton had the inkling of a story, some informants, and some details concerning the Nazi presence and high technology in South America. What follows was written fifteen years after the war ended, while Dwight Eisenhower was President, the year Chubby Checker invented the twist, before the Berlin Wall was erected.

> *"FREE ENERGY, if released to this planet, could change things on earth as they have never been changed before. It could — undoubtedly — usher in a New Order of The Ages. Imagine it. A constant supply of free electrical energy taken right from the atmosphere by everyone. Yes, a universal power such as Free-Energy cold release man from many of the burdens now present in our world money systems. But who has such a secret?*
>
> *The Nazis! If they have the original Viktor Schauberger "Electro-Magnetic" engine — or improved versions of it — they have Free Energy. The UFO engine runs of power taken directly from the atmosphere. and that is quite inexhaustible.*
>
> *I have talked with a brilliant man from Europe. Holland, I believe, is his native land. It is, however, no effort for him to speak seven different languages fluently... including German. I asked him if he could give me any pertinent facts about the Nazis' use of Free-Energy, since I knew he had access to certain "inside information".*
>
> *'Yes', my friend replied, 'it is known that the Nazis have a Free-Energy motor, and used it in 1958 to propel a U-boat between Europe and Buenos Aires. It is*

also believed by many of us that there is an underwater station — built by the Nazis — somewhere in the Atlantic Ocean between Germany and Argentina. A stopover place, no doubt, for Nazi subs and UFO's.' "(1)

Well, the "underwater station" has certainly been identified as Fuerteventura.

We now turn to Buechner and Bernhart for a small portion of their description of the German submarine U-530 that surrendered in Buenos Aires on July 10, 1945, two months after the war in Europe had ended.

"It is to be remembered that the U-530 was exceptionally fast. What kind of miraculous power plant propelled her on her swift course and what kind of wonderful fuel did she burn, which was efficient, same, cheap and clean? Would the general use of this fuel have made the petroleum industry obsolete? And would it have unbalanced the economy of the world? Somewhere deep in the confidential archives of World War II, the answers to these questions await the coming of another era." (2)

It is to be kept under consideration that one author of the above, Kapitan Wilhelm Bernhart, is an alias. In life he was a junior officer aboard this very U-boat. (3) He ought to know what he is talking about.

And finally as introduction, we have O. Bergmann who sums up things to be investigated in this section of the current book. Translating from German:

"At sometime and someplace, at secret U-boat bases outside the German motherland, U-boats of the German Navy must have been weighted-out, and, during the great withdrawal in April/May 1945, missing U-boats must have been equipped with new revolutionary technology and also must have been converted with electromagnetic propulsion. With this these (U-boats) may, (have been) arranged with the same possibilities and technologies as the German flying discs (called UFOs)."(4)

Actually, this may not have been quite so simple as the above paragraph indicates. There were several different technologies involved that were perhaps competing in delivering new, long distance propulsion systems for German U-boats. What is going to be done in this section of the book is to take a look at each one of these possibilities and as much of the story behind each as we are able to find.

Literature Cited

1. **X., Michael, 1960**, *We Want You: Is Hitler Alive?,* page 35 and 36, Future Press, reprinted 1969 by Saucerian Books, Clarksburg, WV., USA
2. **Buechner, William, Col., and Kapitan Wilhelm Bernhart, 1989**, *Hitler's Ashes*, page 228, Thunderbird Press, Matarie, LA., USA
3. **Buechner, William, Col., and Kapitan Wilhelm Bernhart, 1989**, page 289
4. **Bergmann, O., 1988**, *I Deutsche Flugscheiben und U-Boote Ueberwachen Die Weltmeere*, page 18, Hugin Gesellschaft Fuer Politisch-Philosophische Studien E.V., Wetter/Ruhr, Germany

PRELIMINARY ISSUES

Before discussing the exciting issues of alternative new U-boat propulsion, some things need to be dispensed with. The Germans did recognize the value of a nuclear submarine. The German rocket scientist Dr. Kraft von Ehricke reported that the propulsion specialist, Dr.Thiel, had shown to him in 1942 a report and drawing for a steam-driven nuclear power plant which had been written and prepared by Professors Heisenberg and Pose in Leipzig. Speaking with Professor Heisenberg in 1944, Dr. von Ehriche was told that, in his opinion (Heisenberg's) there was an urgent need to utilize an atomic reactor for the purposes of propelling a U-boat (1).

So the Germans (as well as the Japanese) had already realized the value of a nuclear submarine during the war years. As far as I am aware, neither the Germans nor the Japanese ever built an atomic submarine, however. In fact, there is no evidence that such a submarine was ever built by the SS in any of their secret bases at all. Therefore, we can dispense with any discussion on this topic.

The electric generators of Hans Coler were financed at the end by the German Navy. The German Navy was a submarine force by this time so their aims were obvious. Coler built a 6-kV device which could be ramped up to higher outputs. The problem seems to have been reliability. The devices of Hans Coler were mentioned in my first book and a bit more extensively in my second (2). There is no point in doing this a third time.

The Karl Schappeller device had a wonderful application of turning the propelling screws of a ship. Schappeller had even spoken with a representative of the British government between the two World Wars about utilizing his invention to power ships of the Royal Navy (3). The British decided instead to convert from steam to the more known form of power, diesel. We now know the Schappeller device was a spin-off of Tesla technology. Two European researchers, aided by some first-rate scientists/engineers, are now researching this topic, so any extensive discussion of Schappeller, in isolation, at this time, would be pointless.

This brings us to a discussion of conventional German U-boats. These were powered by a combination of two types of engines. First, a diesel engine powered the U-boat while it was running on the surface. These diesel engines burned oxygen—usually, this meant atmospheric oxygen. While running on the surface, the diesel engine also ran a generator that charged the extensive battery array used to run the secondary electric motor. The electric motor does not need oxygen and so was used underwater or perhaps for escape when silent running was necessary. The downside to the electric motor was its range. Relying on batteries, it could only run as long as the batteries held electric charge. Once depleted, the U-boat had to surface or just lay there, dead on the bottom.

As the war progressed the U-boats were increasingly being attacked on the surface, even at night. The British and Americans were using radar to locate them on the surface and attack them from the air, seemingly out of the blue, in compete surprise. Surface running became dangerous for the Germans. But as things stood, it was necessary to run on the surface to charge the batteries in order to dive at all. In 1944 the Germans invented the Schnorkel, also called snorkel or "snort". This was a hollow tube that could be raised by the U-boat during shallow, underwater running, which connected atmospheric oxygen to the engine room for the diesel engines. Now, long distance voyages were possible and the batteries could be charged while the U-boat was technically under water. This snort could sometimes still be seen on radar but it was a big improvement. U-boat operation was again possible.

But throughout the war, two other alternative motors for U-boats were being pursued on an on-again, off-again basis. These were the Walter engine and the Draeger engine.

The Walter engine was a product of chemist Dr. Hellmut Walter. This is the same Dr. Hellmut Walter who produced the rocket-assisted boosters for heavy aircraft as well as the engine for the Messerschmitt Me 163 Komet, the rocket-propelled interceptor. The Walter engine relied on Dr. Walter's observation of the oxygen-carrying characteristics of hydrogen peroxide, H_2O_3. A high concentration of 80-85% hydrogen peroxide was used to react with a potassium permanganate catalyst, producing water vapor at 600-700°C and large quantities of oxygen. Since there was no visible combustion, this process was called a "cold jet process". If fuel is added, a "thermal jet process" takes place, in which the excess oxygen burns the fuel (here, diesel fuel). This can raise the temperature inside the combustion chamber up to 2,000°C, making it necessary to inject water into the combustion chamber for cooling. The water, which is instantly vaporized into steam, cools the combustion chamber to about 500-600°C. The high pressure of the steam produced (36 to 40 atmospheres), can then be used to turn a turbine connected to the ship's propeller. The Walter system was to be used as a secondary engine, in most cases, for underwater use and attack while leaving the diesel engine for standard operation. This engine would produce a great deal of power very quickly. In fact, it was an underwater rocket (4).

The Type XXI U-boats were slated to have this engine but due to technical difficulties involved in bringing this engine to a state of reliability necessary for military use, no Type XXI actually had the Walter engine. The one Type XXI that the Germans were able to make officially operational was powered by the standard diesel-electric engines.

The second type of alternative engine the Germans spent a great deal of time on was a system developed by Dr. Heinrich Draeger. This was an oxygen recycling system—almost. In this design a standard diesel U-boat motor was used along with a large pressurized oxygen tank. Rather than being vented away, exhaust gases were collected and cooled using a seawater heat exchanger, then passed through a carbon filter to remove the carbon dioxide. The gas was then enriched with a bleed from the oxygen tank so that, in effect, "artificial air" was created. This air was fed into the motor's air induction setup and burned again, cooled, scrubbed of CO_2, enriched and fed through again, and so on (5), (6). Presumably, this closed system could work under water, while on the surface atmospheric oxygen would have supplied the engine's needs.

Schematic Diagram of the Walter Propulsion System

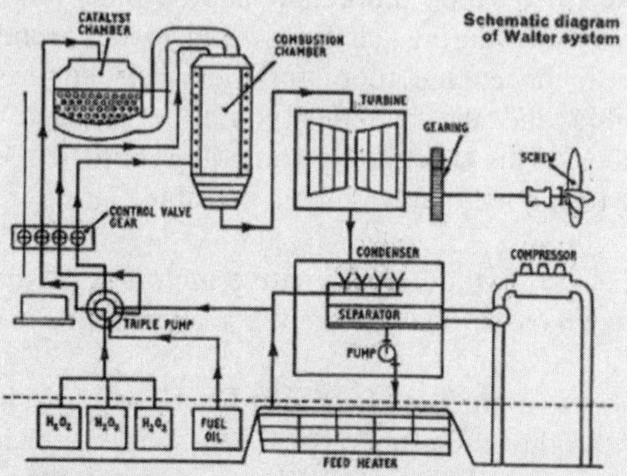

Unfortunately I haven't got the name of the kind person who kindly contributed with

Schematic Diagram of the Draeger Propulsion System

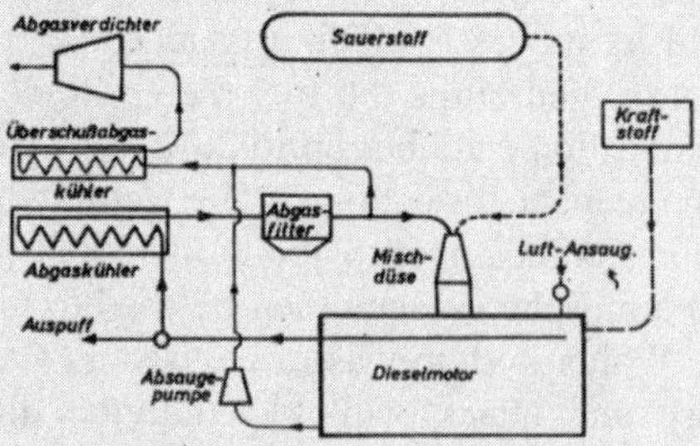

Schematische Darstellung einer Diesel-Kreislaufanlage
(für Uboottyp XVII K)

Sauerstoff=Oxygen
Abgas=Exhaust Gas
Abgasverdicter=Exhaust Gas Compressor
Abgasfilter=Exhaust Gas Filter

Luft- Ansaug=Air Intake
Dieselmotor=Diesel motor
Misch-Duese=Mixing Injectors
Kuehler=Cooler

For some reason, though, this idea never lived up to its promise. The power output of an engine fitted for his recycling or "Kreislauf" was never what was expected of it. Besides, the system required a U-boat to carry a large container or many small containers of liquid oxygen that would eat up space within the submarine. This idea, like the Walter system, was started and stopped and restarted and restopped many times during the course of the war.

Meanwhile, circa 1944, proponents of the "electro-boat" idea were making themselves heard within the Kriegsmarine. In the electro-boat, the electric motor becomes ascendant, with the diesel motor supplying the role of electric generator. This was made possible by an improvement in battery technology (7).

All three of these technologies seemed to compete for space aboard the new U-boat designs. The older Type VII and Type IX were slated for replacement with the Type XXI, Type XXII. A whole type, Type XVIIB, was created to test configurations for the Type XXVI. Hitler had pinned his hopes on turning the war in his direction, partly through use of these the new U-boat types. A great deal was riding on new U-boats but the realization of a totally new, revolutionary, superior U-boat type as a total package, seemed beyond the possibilities of the deteriorating war conditions, or, in other words, beyond the scope of the time frame involved.

All this experimentation documents the urgent need the Germans felt for an alternative to existing, conventional U-boat propulsion. But the official experimentation was bogged down in a bureaucracy and a convention of developmental prototypes. As with aircraft, what O. Bergmann was saying in the piece translated at the start of the U-boat discussion is that the Germans, at their individual U-boat pens, seemed to take it upon themselves to retro-fit older U-boat models which had been damaged or damaged and sunken boats which had been refloated with new equipment, on their own, without official permission or orders, at least from the very top. This can certainly be said after the war ended since "official permission or orders" did not exist. The older models in question would have had to by Type VII as well as some Type IX U-boats.

Before moving to those alternative options, we must take a quick glance at what have been called "mystery submarines". These are submarines of unknown nationality that were seen immediately following World War II, right up until this day where we call them USOs (Unidentified Submersible Objects). Of course, not all USOs are pirate German U-boats, the descriptions do not fit in every USO case. But for a few years after the end of the war this was certainly the case.

Submarines of unknown nationality were especially prominent in reports from Norwegian fjords. This was the area of operation for the German U-boat fleet and waters they knew very well. What was happening was that a submarine of unknown nationality would be picked up by sonar or sighted off the coast of Norway, eventually being penned into a fjord there. NATO and of course the USA would jump on this, trying to force the unknown submarine to the surface with depth charges and other weapons. Sometimes this cat-and-mouse game would go on weeks! It would always be reported in the European press and sometimes in the USA. Eventually and always, the submarine would slip away and the mystery would continue.

The problem was that this was the period of the Cold War. Obviously, NATO believed these were Soviet submarines and wanted to catch one for propaganda value. It was not absolutely clear that they were all Soviet in origin, especially in the beginning. So we will rely, instead, on instances where the nationality can be conclusively determined as German.

The first and most obvious instance is of the two U-boats that were in service of the SS and still resided in the U-boat bunker at Fuerteventura. Perhaps these U-boats were part of the Black Fleet, the black U-boats described by Dr. Joseph Farrell (8). Dr. Farrell says there may have been as many as six of these U-boats. Is there any wonder that there is so much confusion about the final resting places of so many U-boats, or the exact number of U-boats operational at the time of German surrender or the number of U-boat unaccounted for? Years ago, researcher Mark D. Kneipp wrote me about the Fuerteventura U-boats and said they might be U-1020 and U-1021. He said they were both Type VIIc-41s, completely rebuilt with the latest sound detection and weaponry at the end of the war but which went missing after the war.

Two other U-boats that operated in an immediate post-war environment were U-530 and U-977. Both surrendered months after the war ended in Buenos Aires, Argentina. U-530 surrendered on July 17, 1945 while U-977 surrendered a month later on August 17, 1945. Both were Type VII U-boats. Obviously, they both had been doing something since the war in Europe ended on May 8, 1945. Both were accused of transporting Hitler to South America. Kapitan Wilhelm Bernhart claims U-530 spent the time on a voyage to Antarctica and he claims to have made the voyage and the landfall in Neuschwabenland (9). His co-author, Howard Buechner, accepted this and he was a Colonel in the US Army, a college professor and a medical doctor. In fact, he was the first American medical doctor to enter the concentration camp at Buchenwald, so he had a reputation to lose.

There is a tale told concerning U-977 which Buechner and Bernhart repeat (10):

> *"Finally, there is one more mystery about the U-977. It is said that, she too, made a rendezvous at sea with another submarine. In this case it was a soviet vessel carrying nuclear scientists and a very high-ranking Russian official. In exchange for German plans of a highly sophisticated neutron weapon, the Soviets agreed to block the implementation of the Morgenthal Plan that would have crippled post war Germany and reduced her forever to an agricultural state. This incident has not been verified."*

This incident is certainly not verified but the German fear of the Morganthal Plan was certainly very real and would certainly motivate any German to the extreme. Of all the things mentioned in this book perhaps my retelling of the Morganthal Plan would be the least credible. Rather than do so in any detail one should see Wikipedia's version (*http://en.wikipedia.org/wiki/Morganthal_Plan*). This was a plan to remove industry from Germany, turning the whole country into pastureland. It was the brainchild of American Secretary of State and chief executive of the US State Department, Henry Morganthal who actually persuaded British Prime Minister Winston Churchill to agree to

the plan. It was never implemented, fully, but lived on in the American Zone as occupation directive JCS 1067.
Wikipedia says:

> *"In 1945 the German Red Cross was dissolved, and the International Red Cross and other international relief agencies were kept from helping ethnic Germans through strict controls on supplies and on travel. The few agencies permitted to operate within Germany, such as the indigenous Caritas Verband, were not allowed to use imported supplies. When the Vatican attempted to transmit food supplies from Chile to German infants the US State Department forbad it.*
>
> *In early October 1945 the UK government privately acknowledged in a cabinet meeting that, German civilian adult death rates had risen to four times the pre-war levels and death rates amongst the German children had risen by 10 times the pre-war levels. In early 1946 US President Harry S. Truman finally bowed to pressure from Senators, congress and public to allow foreign relief organization of enter Germany in order to review the food situation. In mid-1946 the average German adult received less than 1,500 calories a day. 2,000 calories was then considered the minimum and individual can endure on for a limited period of time with reasonable health."*

In September of 1946, the American government abandoned its version of the Morganthal Plan. If the U-977 story is true, evidently the Germans could imagine a situation in which all of Germany was subjected to such a plan and took drastic measures to prevent this from happening.

Unlike the other two instances of German U-boat activity after the war, the legend of the U-977 must remain in the realm of legend until evidence surfaces. But there is yet another bit of evidence for German U-boat activity after the war, the story of the Juliana. Buechner and Bernhart cite a French newspaper article from France Soir, dated September 25, 1946 that they translate and reproduce:

> *"One and one half years after the end of the fighting in Europe, an Icelandic whaleboat was stopped by a German U-boat. The whaleboat has been identified as the "Juliana" which was located in the waters near the island of Malvinas and the Antarctic zone, when it was stopped by a German U-Boat of magnificent size, bearing the German mourning flag (red with black borders).*
>
> *The commander of the U-Boat approached the whaleboat with a raft and gave orders to captain Hekla to surrender a part of the ship's provisions. The captain of the whaleboat had no other choice than to comply with the orders given by the German Navy officer. This officer spoke accurate English and paid for the provisions with U.S. dollars. In additions, he also paid a premium of $10.00 to each crewmember. The officer gave the captain of the whaler information pertaining to the location of whales. The ship later went to this described location and harpooned two whales. The rumors concering U-Boats of the German Navy in the waters of "Fireland" and the Antarctic zone are now a fact (Telegram from AFP, dated Paris, September 25, 1946)."(11)*

OK, just one more. This is involves the recent raising of U-534. This operation has its own website (*http://u534.coolfreepages.com/Basis_Frame.htm*). At the very end of the war U-534 refused to surrender as ordered to do. Instead, she headed north from Denmark to Norway with two other U-boats. From that website:

> *"May 5th, 1945 U-534 was sailing in the Kattegat, North-West of Helsingor. Although Admiral Doenitz had ordered all his U-boats to surrender as from 08:00 May 5th, U534 refused to surrender. U534 - with two other U-boats in company - was heading north towards Norway, without flying flag of surrender. Their departure was noted by Danish fisherman (?) and passed on to RAF Coastal Command that at her turn sent out an air-patrol.*
>
> *A Liberator from 547 squadron attacked U-534. With all three U-boats firing at her she was shot down and crashed in to the sea. One survivor was rescued by a boat from the nearby lightship. By that time the two other U-boats dived, leaving U534 alone on the surface."*

A British surface ship then attacked and sunk U-534 leaving three dead and forty-nine survivors. But the story is that the other two U-boats got away! These two U-boats did not go through an attack unecssarily. It was necessary in their minds. The only possible conclusion is these U-boats did not want to surrender. They did not want to become part of Occupied Germany. In fact, they wanted and they were at this very moment volunteering to become part of a kind of post-war, Nazi, black U-boat fleet.

Literature Cited

1. **Georg, Friedrich, 2000**, *Hitlers Siegeswaffen Band 1: Luftwaffe Und Marine Geheime Nuklearwaffen des Dritten Reiches und ihre Traegersysteme*, page 188, Schleusingen, Germany. Also available in English as Hitler's Miracle Weapons, (first book)
2. **Stevens, Henry, 2007**, *Hitler's Suppressed and Still-Secret Weapons, Science and Technology*, page 58-63, Adventures Unlimited Publishing, Kempton, Illinois, USA
3. **Bahn, Peter, Ph.D.**, and Heiner Gehring, 1997, *Der Vril-Mythos Eine geheimisvolle Energieform in Esoterik, Technik und Therapie*, pages 120-131, Omega Verlag, Duesseldorf, Germany
4. **Lusar, Rudolf, 1964**, *German Secret Weapons of the Second World War*, pages 129 and 202, J.F. Lehmens Verlag, Munich, Germany
5. **Lusar, Rudolf, 1964**, pages 207, 208
6. **Roessler, Eberhard, 1996**, *Geschichte des deutschen U-Bootes Band 2*, pages 300, 301, Bernard & Graefe Verlag, Augsburg, Germany
7. **Roessler, Eberhard, 1996**, page 441
8. **Farrell, Joseph, Ph.D., 2008**, *Nazi International The Nazis' Postwar Plan to Control Finance, Conflict, Physics and Space*, pages 65, 96, 131, Adventures Unlimited Publishing, Kempton, Illinios, USA
9. **Buechner, Howard A., Col., and Kapitan Wilhelm Bernhart, 1988**, *Adolf Hitler and the Secrts of the Holy Lance*, page 223, Thunderbird Press, Metairie., LA., USA
10. **Buechner, Howard A., Col., and Kapitan Wilhelm Bernhart, 1989**, *Hilter's Ashes*, page 228, Thunderbird Press, Metairie, LA., USA
11. **Buechner, Howard A., Col., and Kapitan Wilhelm Bernhart, 1989**, page 179

CONVERTED U-BOATS

This is O. Bergmann's concept that during the war and perhaps afterward, German U-boats were hauled up and refitted with new technology. It is his idea that sometimes this refitting took the form of exotic engine propulsion.

There was an idea a few years back that U-boats so refitted were then given a U-boat designation of another U-boat known to the Allies as having been sunken. This idea makes for confusion and that was the purpose for it as given. In this theory, the Allies would never know the exact strength of the U-boat fleet and would not even really know if a particular U-boat that they had thought sunk, was sunk. Add to this the problem of tracking down and accounting for all the U-boats themselves that were active towards the end of the war. There are organizations in Germany that do this, not for some concerns of conspiracy, but because those on board were valued people, they were the sons and husbands of Germany, defending it and so ought to be accorded the honor of knowing a final disposition. Problems seem to arise sometimes when a new sunken U-boat is positively in one place but the official accounting has put its location somewhere else. Then, a reshuffling takes place in the official accounting of where all these U-boats ended up. Almost seventy years later, this is still going on. An individual can now go on line with these organizations and be updated. There is no doubt that these agencies have great information about U-boats and U-boat-related things. But there is some mystery here no matter how absolute and final and authoritative all those experts and their websites seem to be.

While going through individual U-boat records and histories on some of those websites, one often sees descriptions of damaged or even sunken U-boats being raised, repaired and/or refitted and re-commissioned. To make this point two examples will be considered. One, U-234 is perhaps the best-known U-boat in terms of on-going mysteries. For a look at what happened to U-234 we will rely on the work of Geoffrey Brooks and Philip Henshall, two of the most rock-solid researchers around. The second U-boat whose refitting we will consider is U-530, a completely different story, told by a completely different source, "Wilhelm Bernhart", an alleged junior officer aboard her at the time.

U-234 was converted from a minelayer to a cargo ship. It was originally a Type XB but three other Type IXD/1 U-boats, U-180, U-195 and U-219 were also converted to cargo carriers in 1944, with the express purpose of bringing high tech items to Japan (1). U-234, it seems, could not wait for refitting as it was damaged by a bomb while still under construction in May 1943, so it was not launched until December 23, 1943. (2) In late August 1944, U-234 arrived in Kiel, German Werft for a refit. Twenty-four of the thirty-nine vertical shafts used to carry and lay mines were removed to make two large lateral holds. The other shafts were reworked to serve as cargo holds. A new radar unit with a small tower was installed, in addition to the latest snorkel model. (3) Upgrading old U-boats with a snorkel and modern electronics was an almost universal modification. Upon completing this refitting, U-234 left Kiel and formed up with three of the latest Type XXIII U-boats with the final destination of Norway using, at times, neutral Swedish waters. On a training voyage, U-234 collided with U-1301, puncturing the fuel tanks and causing a five-foot gash in her side. (4) The dry dock facilities at the closest base, Kristiansand, was full. Captain Fehler was directed to Bergen, three days sailing time away. Rather than take this option, the Captain decided on a radical course of action. He flooded the forward tanks, raising the U-boat 20 degrees out of the water and having members of his own crew weld a piece of steel plate onto the skin of U-234. (5) This took the better part of a week. (6)

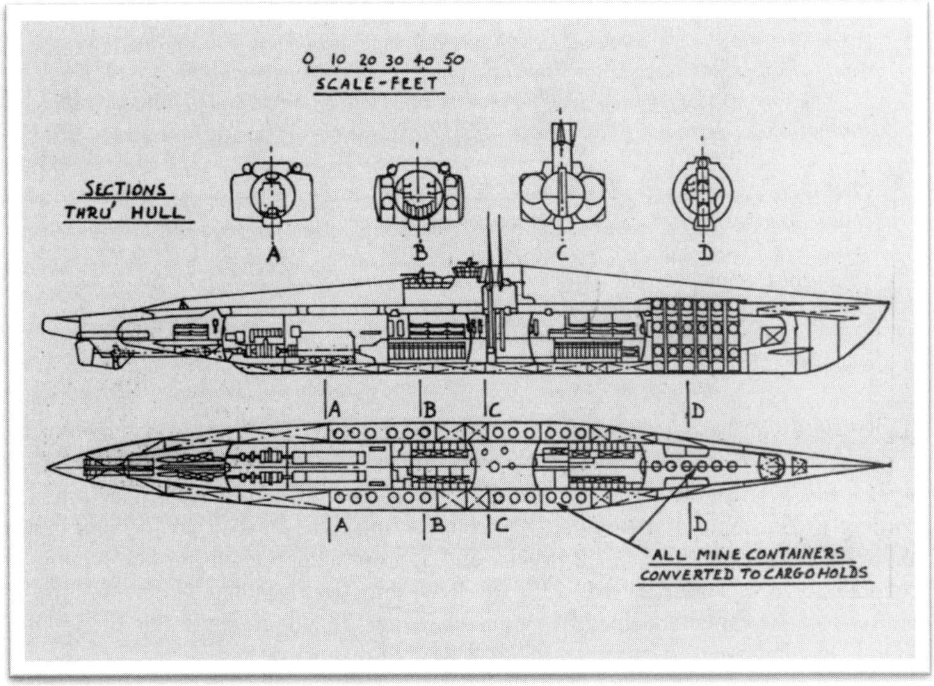

U-234, A Converted U-boat

This is a diagram of U-234 prepared by Philip Henshall (Vengeance: Hitler's Nuclear Weapon, Fact or Fiction) in which he points out modifications made to change its mission. This was done in the last days of the war.

In reality, this is like pipe welding. Pipe welding is done to a high standard as the pipe in question is subjected to pressure so that the weld itself must be done precisely and in a certain way. In the case of U-234, a long pipe, the precision of this weld or lack thereof carried with it the lives of all on board. The fact that Captain Fehler was willing to do this speaks of the competence of those crewmembers but also of the willingness and mental flexibility of the Captain and the ethos of the U-boat service. If he was willing to undergo a drastic field repair such as this and trust it going into action, then it is entirely feasible that other captains would be willing, also, to have their boats refitted in the field with untested, perhaps unauthorized machinery.

Regarding U-530, a Type VII c U-boat, we will rely on the eyewitness account of "Kapitan Wilhelm Bernhart". His name is in quotation marks because, as has been mentioned, this is a penname for one of the junior officers aboard this ship. The names of all aboard including the junior officers are known and listed in the book cited here so this "secret" is really an open one as anyone with littler research skills would be able to ascertain the real name. Bernhart begins setting up the story:

> *"At first glance the U-530 appeared to have been a highly unlikely choice for a long ocean voyage and the accomplishment of one of the most unusual missions of all times. She was old and leaky and had come to be known as an "unlucky" ship. In fact, she had recently been rammed by a freighter and at the time when her secret mission was to begin she was in dry-dock undergoing repairs (the author cites "National Police Gazette, 1977).*
>
> *The mystery of the selection of the U-530 for special duty is easily solved. A new boat had been produced and equipped with improved engines, extra battery power, schnorkel and other advanced features. For reasons known only to Admiral Doenitz she was assigned the duplicate number U-530 and hand picked by the Admiral for a highly secret mission. Above all else the new U-530 was fast. She is said to have been able to travel at 30 knots, even when submerged."(7)*

U-530 left Kiel harbor on April 13, 1945, first stopping in Denmark to take on some supplies and then on to Kristiansand, Norway, arriving on April 20, 1945, prepared for a long sea voyage. She departed on May 1, 1945 as part of a convoy of phantom ships, according to Buechner and Bernhart. And according to them the real U-530 would be found by the Allies in a dry dock in Kiel and appropriated entered into the records and accounted for. (8) This meant U-530, the new ship, was absolutely free to carry out whatever role the captain deemed fit. Somewhere near this point in the story U-530 hears Admiral Doenitz' order to surrender to the Allies but disregards it.

> *"Somewhere in the vicinity of the South Sandwich Island, the U-530 made contact with the U-465, another ghost ship which bore the number of a class VIIC vessel reported to have been sunk on May 5, 1943. She was now a type XIV known as an ocean going transporter or 'Milkcow.' " (9)*

From here U-530 is said to have traveled to Antarctica and deposited Nazi relics there. Bernhart claims to have been on the shore party as mentioned. Afterward, all evidence was eradicated and a new, substitute log was created. The ship sailed to Argentina and surrendered on July 10, 1945, but, according to the authors, it took the government of

Argentina three days to notify the government of the USA and seven more days before they actually arrived and took charge. In the meantime, anyone who did not want to be found or anything that needed to be hidden was taken off U-530:

> *"...and faded away like ghosts into the Nazi underground." (10)*

The Americans arrived and took the Captain and crew into custody, moving them to the USA and subjecting them to intense "interrogation". U-530 was placed undertow and began a long voyage to Boston, Massachusetts, or did it?

This is really the crux and proof of concept regarding exotic U-boat propulsion because if this existed as the two authors say it did, this U-boat would have been scrutinized intensively by the US government, in secret and in private. The results would not have been released to the public and the whole matter would have been kept top secret. A cover story would have been concocted. This is exactly what the two authors, Buechner and Bernhart contend.

> *"It would seem that the strange adventures of the U-530 were now at an end, but not quite. She was still to take part in one more interesting deception. At some point near the eastern limits of the Caribbean sea, the towing vessel veered off to the west, and a look-alike U-530 appeared und tow and took her place. For the second time the U-530 changed identity.*
>
> *The substitute submarine was taken to a port on the eastern seaboard. The original U-530 was towed through the Panama Canal and then northward past Central America, Mexico and California to the United States Naval base at Mare Island in San Francisco Bay. Here the once proud U-530 was demolished piece-by-piece and bolt-by-bolt. The purpose of this action and any secrets that might have been discovered, have never been make public.*
>
> *In November 28, 1947 the substitute U-530 was sent to the bottom of the Atlantic Ocean by torpedo fire off the coast of cape Cod, Massachusetts. Under an agreement with the Soviet Union allowing their observers to witness the death of captured German submarines, the Russians watched the fake U-530 go to her watery grave." (11)*

Remembering the earlier quote concerning the U-530's unconventional engines, very fast but which ran on some "miraculous power plant " with some kind of "wonderful fuel" which was "safe, cheap and clean" and which might make "the petroleum industry obsolete" (12) the authors say:

> *"...What seems to have been the final mystery of he astounding underseaboat 530, appears to be related to its ignominious fate of Mare Island in San Francisco Bay. Here the once proud vessel entered dry dock and was systematically reduced to a miscellaneous pile of parts. The U-530 became a nameless, a useless, and unidentifiable thing; worse than a ship at the bottom of*

the sea; a vessel which had ceased to exist. Why was this done? Was there a message hidden within her hull or was it the secret of her engine room which was of such great concern?" (13)

This is a fantastic story! We do not have the U-530 to examine now. Certainly, the American government would not release this information via a F.O.I.A. request. But, really now, would the US government stoop so low as to smuggle an entire U-boat into the country? If this behavior could be documented, it would go along way towards verification of this tale. But the US government would not be able to do this or do this in reality, right?

Wrong. Friedrich Georg caught them at this trick, red handed. He discusses the appropriation of German submarine hull design without proper ascription when he reveals (my translation):

"Actual proof has been uncovered that there could have been more here than only a design drawing. The US Naval Technical Mission had in November, 1945, on its own lifted a 195 ton German U-boat with a crane and freightered it to the USA. It is notable that no small German U-boat Type of this weight class is known. It is therefore very well possible that we are dealing with a research U-boat of the RPF with "(tear) drop form". A 195-ton water displacement fits very well with a length of 36 meters and a width of 5 m. In comparison, the Walter U-boat U-1406 displaced 415 tons and was more than double as heavy."(12)

This is quite a find. The US government did spirit away a research U-boat for points unknown and the records, the proof, had to be dug out of some totally obscure source rather than being fed to some malleable historian with an appropriate cover story as was the common practice at the time. This story did not surface until twenty years after Buechner and Bernhart published their book but it goes a long way in establishing a basis for their story.

Regarding the other U-boat, the U-1406, this was a research U-boat of a strange type. It was a rare Type XVIIb. The Type XVIIb, in total, consisted of three U-boats, U-1405, U-1406, and U-1407. These were built to test the feasibility of the upcoming Type XXVI U-boats. What they had in common was the Walter propulsion unit, the hydrogen peroxide power unit which had once again fallen into favor. The Type XVIIb was not an operational or attack U-boat but just a test-bed. (15)

But the first Walter units were not installed in a Type XXI, or a Type XXII, or a Type XVIIb, they were installed in the older Type VIIa units. Four of these were built, U-792, U-793, U-794, and U-795, all commissioned between November, 1943 and April, 1944. They were assigned to the 5th U-boat Flotilla but were retained for testing rather than seeing active, combat duty. All were scuttled on May 4 or May 5, 1945. Two, U-792 and U-793, were raised by the British for more testing. (www.uboat.net)

SECRET

Bremen
Bremerhaven
Naples
Genoa
Rotterdam
Antwerp
Le Havre
Cherbourg
Marseilles

Two German floating cranes, one of 350 tons and the other of 250 tons, were used in loading equipment on ships.

An estimated 750,000 board feet of lumber were used for crating.

In Paris, the incompleted roadway by-pass tunnel around St. Cloud, used formerly for German Torpedo Stores, was used as a crating and storage depot until an epidemic of thefts made it necessary to move this activity to the Navy garage which was under a relatively more effective guard. The St. Cloud tunnel continued to be used, however, for crating any item weighing more than one ton.

Some of the major jobs in which the Shipping Sub-Section participated were:

→ (a) disassembling and shipping a factory from Ludwigshaven;

ID (b) lifting a 195-ton submarine aboard a ship for transport;

(c) crating and shipping several V-1 and V-2 projectiles;

(d) placing 39 airplanes aboard an airplane carrier in Cherbourg;

(e) moving tank cars of concentrated H2O2 to Cherbourg and Antwerp and on to ships for transportation;

(f) disassembling, crating, and shipping a wind tunnel, from Southern Germany.

Disbursing Sub-Section

In the early days of the Mission, the Supply officer took care of disbursing duties.

DECLASSIFIED
Authority NND 873065
By JE NARA Date 8-9-07

Mysterious Booty U-boat

German researcher Friedrich Georg found a recently-declassified U.S. document discussing the shipping of a captured 195-ton U-boat back to America

The point is that there was exotic technology being tested by the Germans at the tail end of the war. New, exotic technology was tested first in older U-boat designs. U-boats were refitted throughout the war with new technology. Having established that there were exotic U-boats, U-boats at least exotic enough to attract the attention of the US government and for it to maintain secrecy thereof, we can now turn to some explanations of that exotic technology.

4. Interrogation of Type 17B U-boat officers at Wik Barracks, Kiel:

(a) Ober Lt. Werne Klug, CO of U-1406

(b) Ober Lt. R. E. Heitz, CO of U-1407

(c) Ober Lt. (Eng.) W. Schenck, Eng. Off. of U-1406

The U-1406 and U-1407 were experimental boats equipped with the Walter propulsion units. They were launched prematurely at Blom and Voss, Hamburg, taken to the Kiel area to avoid capture, sabotaged and scuttled by their crews near Cuxhaven on May 6 and have since been raised and are on the docks at Kiel. P/W (a) had made 9 operational cruises as first watch officer of U-552, had served on U-794 (prototype Walter boat) and took command of U-1406 on 8 February 1945. P/W (b) had made 5 cruises as torpedo officer of U-507 and U-664, was CO

-6-

[redacted]

Interrogation of Type 17B U-boat officers at Wik Barracks, Kiel (Cont'd.)

of U-792 (prototype Walter boat) and took command of U-1407 on 29 March 1945. P/W (c) had made 9 cruises on U-107 and had served on U-792 before becoming engineering officer of U-1406 on 8 February 1945. The U-1406 had been dived 3 or 4 times to shallow depths near Kiel and the U-1407 twice. The Walter propulsion unit was used only once, for about 5 minutes, on the U-1406, and not at all on the U-1407, due to missing components.

The P/W's were interrogated separately but agreed in all respects. They had been given only qualitative information about the Walter unit, and did not know what fuel was used except by its code name of "T-Stoff". The engineering officer P/W (c) had been given a brief course in the mechanical features of the turbines, but had never handled or operated the equipment. During the few times that the Walter units on the U-792, U-794 or U-1406 had been used, an engineer from the Walter Werke came along to operate them. The subject was treated as top-security and they were not allowed to know more. They were under the administrative command of the 5th U-boat Flotilla at Kiel, but had no superior officer who was informed about the Wlater propulsion units.

The two CO's had expected to experiment for themselves as to the tactical uses of the high speed. They had been given no instructions as to tactics. Both considered the Walter units as auxiliaries to be used only for attacks. The U-1406 (one turbine) was expected to operate at 20 knots for 4 - 5 hours; the U-1407 (two turbines) at 22 to 23 knots for 5 - 6 hours. Both CO's were slated for command of Type 26 boats when ready and expected to use Type 17B's to gain experience, but they had been told very little about the new type.

Prepared by:

Dr. M. S. LIVINGSTON
Technician

U.S. Naval Technical Mission in Europe, Technical Report No. 287-45. Officers aboard three working Walter U-boats are interrogated.

Literature Cited

1. **Brooks, Geoffrey, 1992**, *Hitler's Nuclear Weapons*, page 139, Leo Cooper/Pen & Sword Books Ltd, Barnsley, UK
2. **Brooks, Geoffrey, 1992**, page 144
3. **Brooks, Geoffrey, 1992**, page 149
4. **Henschall, Philip, 1995**, *Vengeance Hitler's Nuclear Weapon Fact or Fiction?,* page 124, Alan Sutton Publishing, Ltd., Gloucestershire, UK
5. **Brooks, Geoffrey, 1992**, page 157
6. **Henschall, Philip, 1995**, page 125
7. **Buechner, Howard A., Col., and Kapitan Wilhelm Bernhart, 1989**, *Hitler's Ashes*, page 189, Thunderbird Press, Inc., Metairie, LA., USA
8. **Buechner, Howard A., Col., and Kapitan Wilhelm Bernhart, 1989**, page 186
9. **Buechner, Howard A., Col., and Kapitan Wilhelm Bernhart, 1989**, page 187
10. **Buechner, Howard A., Col., and Kapitan Wilhelm Bernhart, 1989**, page 220
11. **Buechner, Howard A., Col., and Kapitan Wilhelm Bernhart, 1989**, page 222
12. **Buechner, Howard A., Col., and Kapitan Wilhelm Bernhart, 1989**, page 228
13. *ibid.*
14. **Georg, Friedrich, 2008**, "Unternehmen Patentraub" 1945, *Die Geheimgeschichte des groessten Technologieraubs aller Zeiten*, pages 230-231, Grabert-Verlag, Tuebingen, Germany. Here Mr. Georg cites: RG38, Operations CNO, Records of the Office of the Chief of Naval, Office of Naval Intelligence,Naval Technical Mission to Europe, 1945-47, Entry 72, Box 15, (Serials and Enclosures 312 to 198) Serial 338.
15. **US Naval Technical Mission In Europe, released to the public April 22, 1996**, Technical Report No. 287-45 titled: *Tactical Planning For High Speed U-boats*, September 1945, pages 23-22 (page numbers problematic), US Naval Mission In Europe, C/o Floot Post Office, New York, N.Y., USA.

TESLA

There are several aspects of what are called here converted U-boats that involve the ideas Dr. Nikola Tesla. In fact, they all do in one way or another, to a greater or lesser extent. As an example and to introduce the reader to this way of thinking, perhaps it would be best to recount the conversation that first brought me to these ideas.

This was in the early 1990s. I had gone to a UFO conference with a friend who was also very much interested in German flying discs. My friend was an old hand at UFO conferences but this was my first one. It was held in a large meeting room of a hotel with several alcoves surrounding the main room. While walking through one of these alcoves my friend and I met a man known to my friend. We began talking for a moment when my friend excused himself, having to attend to some pressing. He told us both he would be back in a few minutes and suggested we settle into some sofas the hotel provided in the alcove. We sat down and my new acquaintance began talking.

He was an engineer or some sort of technician for a large aerospace company in Southern California. But he began the conversation by attempting to enlist me in aiding him recover some books and research material he had loaned our mutual friend. This was a little uncomfortable so I tried to change the subject. I brought up the video film we had just seen, "UFO Secrets of the 3rd Reich", a production by Norbert Juergen-Ratthofer and Ralf Ettl.

Well, my new acquaintance liked the film and then began talking about one of the historical characters in the film, Dr. W.O. Schumann (incorrectly called "H.O. Schumann" in the film). He told me some interesting things that I had not heard before.

My new acquaintance told me that Dr. Schumann was primarily known for his work in radio frequency radiation. Seeing that I had no idea of who Dr. Schumann was outside the movie we had just seen, he went on. He told me that it was "this" Dr. Schumann who was responsible for "discovering" the Schumann Resonance. He explained that this resonance was like the ringing of a bell and the bell was planet earth. He said our planet "rings" within a narrow range of radio frequency energy like a bell. This was a natural phenomenon, caused by lightning strikes hitting our planet, worldwide and constantly. He said that the waves produced traveled right through the earth and rebounded at the surface, re-entering the earth again. The waves themselves, he said, were very, very long, called ELF waves or "extremely low frequency" waves.

My new acquaintance then went on to say that the Germans had built something similar to an ELF wave generator during the war but with waves that were only slightly shorter. I asked why they would do that? He told me that one transmitter could communicate with stations all over the world using these waves, or even under the sea. I repeated "even under the sea" and he said "yes" because the radio communications system built by the Germans using this long wave technology was purposefully designed to communicate with U-boats underwater anywhere in the world!

This was news to me and hard for me to accept. Seeing this, he went on saying that it was undoubtedly Dr. Schumann who had built this system for world wide U-boat communication and since it was intimately bound with the Schumann Resonance, he had probably known about that during the war, not when he published its presence in 1952. But then he said something that really got my attention.

My new aquaitance, the engineer or technician at an aerospace company, said that he thought the Germans used this same technology for charging the batteries of their U-boats. It is only a half step further, he explained. Instead of just receiving radio messages, why not set up transmission facilities and have the U-boat tow a wire antenna a mile or so long? The ELF waves themselves were so long that the waves were huge, stretching perhaps a mile from crest to valley, so that it would be necessary for a U-boat to tow an antenna at least half the length of the wave or possibly a multiple of the wave or half of it or a quarter of it, he did not know exactly. But the antenna would be long, trailing behind the U-boat. The Germans must have at least looked at this idea—this was originally a Tesla idea, he said.

The Americans are probably using this system right now, he said. I asked if the Americans got the information. "Oh, hell yes", he said, "they got it right from the horse's mouth—Dr. Schumann was brought over to the USA as a Paperclip scientist. We certainly got the long-wave communication system, he explained. "Our submarines have had it for years as do the Soviets."

About this same time I had heard on talk radio. Here I must digress for a moment. This "talk radio" was that of the early 1990s before the special interest groups using their corporations bought out all radio descent and homogenized it into the "ditto heads" and "great Americans" we have today. All that talk radio is gone today. Anyway, during this memorable program, the conversation I heard then was of a electromagnetic propulsion system which was said to be used on some American "nuclear" submarines. Whoever this was talking (I never got the details) said this device worked under cover inside the engine room door of the submarine and was marked as "Danger-Nuclear Radiation". It was quite a good cover.

Both these occurrences sparked my curiosity, and so being somewhat motivated, a check was made into the reality of the German long wave communication facilities. This existed. It was code named "Goliath" and was located near Berlin at Magdeburg. Rudolf Lusar describes it:

> *"Very Long Waves*
>
> *Experiments with various wave-ranges showed that very long waves, those of about 28,000 m., can penetrate the surface of the sea to a depth of about 12 to 14 m., depending on the composition of the sea water. This fact was used to convey wireless messages to U-boats submerged at that depth. At fixed times, the situation permitting, the boats dived to that depth to receive instructions without being detected by enemy reconnaissance. The depth to be maintained by the boats was called "programme depth". The transmitter of this very long wave, "Goliath", was near Calbe, not far from Magdeburg; the transmitter and its secret fell into British hands. When the Russians occupied the Calbe area the Goliath transmitter installations had already been dismantled." (1)*

Having established that half of the basic idea—that of the communications system—was real, the next step would be to investigate the energy transmission system. For that we have to turn to the other half of the same technology used for the Goliath system, the energy transmission system, which was also invented by Tesla. Actually, they are almost the same thing; the objective is different so some of the tuning would be different.

This is not so much Tesla's transmission of energy through air that is under discussion but a similar system in which one terminal is grounded, thus transferring the energy right through the earth. Tesla found that very long waves transmitted through the earth would reach the other side and be reflected back to their point of origin. In fact, there is a completely natural radio frequency, about 8 cycles or Hertz (Hz), which does this every moment of every day. It is caused by the multiple thousands of lightning strikes hitting the earth, worldwide, and makes the earth "ring like a bell". Tesla's idea was to generate similar long waves at a period just on the return strike back at the point of origin on the earth. This is like pushing a child on a swing. At first a shove must be given but once the child is actively swinging, only a slight nudge needs to be given to maintain the height of the swing. Or, additional energy can be applied and the child will go even higher but since momentum has already been built up, no tremendous output of energy approaching the initial, first swing is necessary.

Since the transmitting device is timing each new input to coincide with the return beat bouncing off the earth at the other side of the world, a standing wave is formed. This is a wave that does not move. Imagine two pebbles being thrown into a pond a few feet apart, hitting at exactly the same moment. Waves would form from each pebble and intersect at the point half way between each. Where they intersect the waves overlap but just seem to stand there, not moving until the disturbance subsides. These are standing waves.

ELF waves can range from 3-30 Hz. The Germans used 15 to 60 kHz, centering on 16.55 kHz, on their Goliath communications system that is called a VLF transmitter,

(VLF is for Very Low Wave). It had a maximum output of 1800kw and was the most powerful transmitter of its time (2). The US government and the Soviets used 50-85 Hz on their submarine communications (3). These are true ELF waves. They are also very long, sometimes spanning 28 km. (over 17 miles) in length or even more! This would mean an antenna used for their reception would normally have to be half that length or a resonant multiple of that length. This would mean an antenna of over two miles in length, at least.

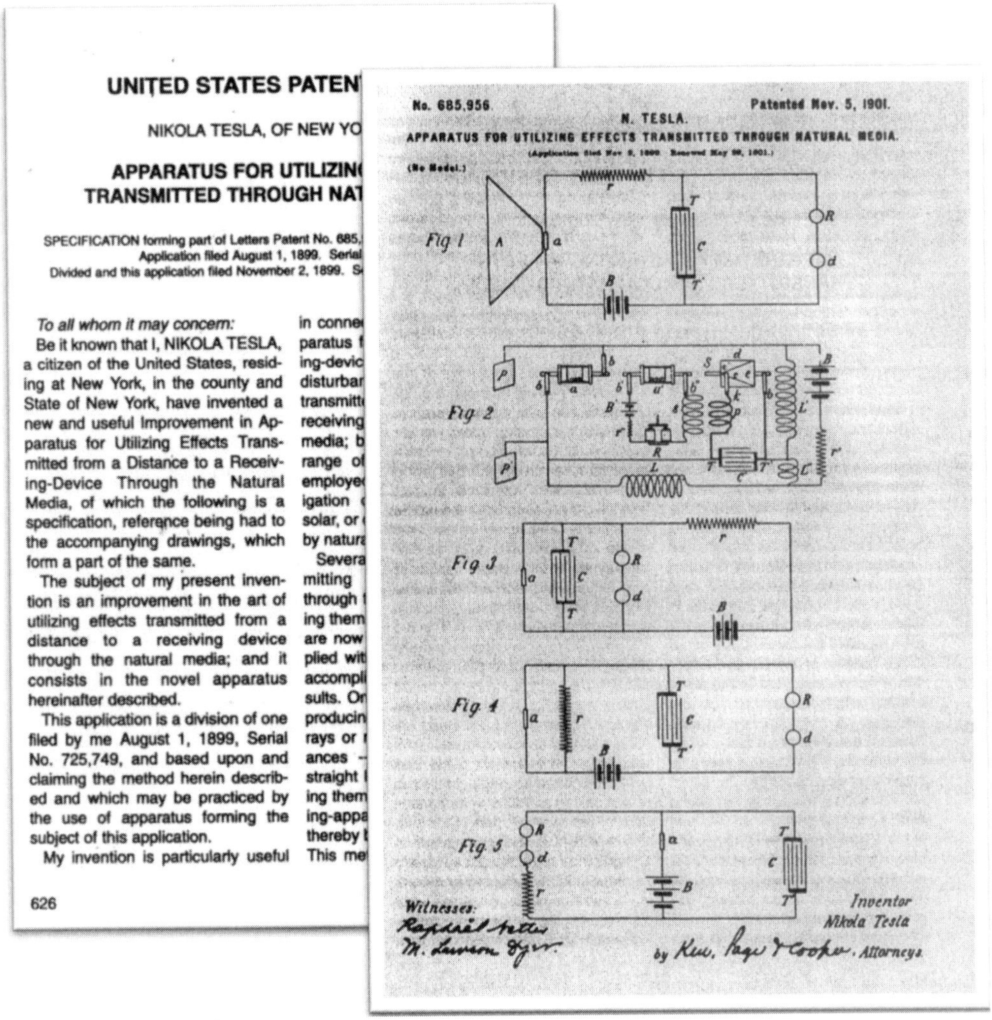
UNITED STATES PATEN

NIKOLA TESLA, OF NEW YO

APPARATUS FOR UTILIZIN
TRANSMITTED THROUGH NAT

SPECIFICATION forming part of Letters Patent No. 685,
Application filed August 1, 1899. Serial
Divided and this application filed November 2, 1899. S

To all whom it may concern:

Be it known that I, NIKOLA TESLA, a citizen of the United States, residing at New York, in the county and State of New York, have invented a new and useful Improvement in Apparatus for Utilizing Effects Transmitted from a Distance to a Receiving-Device Through the Natural Media, of which the following is a specification, reference being had to the accompanying drawings, which form a part of the same.

The subject of my present invention is an improvement in the art of utilizing effects transmitted from a distance to a receiving device through the natural media; and it consists in the novel apparatus hereinafter described.

This application is a division of one filed by me August 1, 1899, Serial No. 725,749, and based upon and claiming the method herein described and which may be practiced by the use of apparatus forming the subject of this application.

My invention is particularly useful

626

Tesla Patent Number 685,956: Apparatus for Utilizing Effects Transmitted through Natural Media. Tesla worked on ways to convert radio frequency waves, once received, into something which could be intelligently used. In other words, Tesla was looking to build a device which could convert radio waves originating from afar into signals or energy which could be used on the spot. He had several such patents.

Tesla designed the transmitter for these signals. The sender as well as a receiver (probably for communications) can be seen in his patent, patent number 787,412, of April 18, 1905 (4). Tesla's transmission work does not seem to have begun until his residence in the USA but a similar receiver to the American patent about was filed in Germany in 1901 as German Patent Nr.139-464 even though those records clearly state Tesla was living in New York at the time. The receiver is important because Tesla devised a way to compact the antenna, not requiring miles and miles of wire in a straight line.

Tesla envisioned a transmission system in which any particular point on the earth could be instantly filled with energy. He even patented a method for controlling a boat on the ocean, even if the sender were on the other side of the earth (US Patent number 613.809, German Patent number 142 842). This is made possible as explained in this US Patent number 787,412 (referenced above) describing the "Art of Transmitting Electrical Energy Thorough the Natural Medium, in which he says:

> *"By impressing upon the earth two or more oscillations of different wave length a resultant stationary wave may be made to travel slowly over the globe, and thus a great variety of useful effects may be produced".*

This means the standing wave could be moved anywhere on the surface of the earth, under control and at will.

But the most interesting Tesla patent for this discussion is his American Patent No. 685,012, issued October 22, 1901. This is a "Means for Increasing the Intensity of Electrical Oscillations (US Patent number 685,012, German Patent number 136 841). Tesla determined that to induce the greatest reaction in the receiver, the antenna, the inductance must be maximized and the resistance minimized. Tesla wanted to use a resonant receiver and depicts a coil wire that is identical to the coil wire used as a sender. The greatest reaction is achieved, according to Tesla, when there is a loose connection between resonant coils or in other words, if they are some distance apart. He called this a "freely-oscillating circuit". Resistance in a wire can usually be overcome by simply using a thicker wire but Tesla determined this increase led to diminishing returns in some situations. Instead, for this patent, Tesla chose to cool the sending and the receiving coils in a bath of liquid air. Tesla says:

> *"Briefly stated, then, my intention consists in producing a great increase in the intensity and duration of the oscillations excited in a freely-vibrating or resonating circuit by maintaining the same at a low temperature."*

Continuing this thought he says:

> *"My invention, it will be understood, does not primarily contemplate the saving of energy, but aims at the attainment of a distinctly novel and valuable result — that is, the increase to the greatest practical degree of the intensity and duration of free oscillations. This may be usefully applied in all cases when this special object is sought, but offers exceptional advantages in those instances in which the freely-oscillating discharges of a condenser are utilized."*

This invention is illustrated simply using a cut away drawing of an insulated (apparently wooden) tub in which a coil and antenna are mounted. The "tub" is probably a closed tank. In both tubs the coil is covered with liquid air. In this patent Tesla actually claims:

> *"In such as case the cooling of the conductor A, which may be effected in any suitable manner, results in an extraordinary magnification of the oscillation in the resonating-circuit B..." (5)*

Tesla writer George Trinkaus credits Tesla with the early work on superconductivity with this invention. He says:

> *"Prior to recent breakthroughs, superconductivity and supermagnetism were low-temperature (cryogenic) phenomena, occurring when circuits were cooled down to near absolute zero. The new superconductivity at least drastically reduced temperatures developed out of the cryogenic work of the last twenty years, and this may be in debt to Tesla, who patented a similar idea way back in 1901. Tesla's patent observes that the deep cooling of conductors with agents like liquid air 'results in an extraordinary magnification of the oscillation in the resonating circuit.' Imagine the performance of a supercooled Tesla coil." (6)*

Liquid air is something in which the Germans of this period were very interested. Liquid air will be taken up later but here we should realize that the Linde method for making liquid air was just coming into its own, the Germans were manufacturing quantities of it and looking around for additional applications of this technology. Foremost among these was the Reichsarbeitsgemeinschaft, the Reichs Works Agency, which looked for alternative sources of energy for Germany before the war. They discussed applications for liquid air technology (7).

According to electrical engineer Toby Grotz, Tesla's electrical distribution system could be up to 90-94% efficient as opposed to 70-74% for standard, hard-wired systems, the difference being in the resistance of the wires themselves in the hard-wired system (8).

The question I have is *was there enough energy in these long wave transmissions to be of practical value in charging up a U-boat's batteries?* If this is true, and there was enough energy, then why not take matters one step further and tap the best ELF wave generator, the earth itself? Tesla did extensive experiments with lightning in mind and so knew precisely that it was lightning striking and "ringing" the earth that caused these huge, low frequency, long waves to rebound again and again beneath the earth's outer shell. Tesla describes bouncing waves off the other side of the earth, the characteristics of those waves for energy transmission in his US patent number 787,412 which certainly should have given Dr. W.O. Schumann who was investigating this problem some important ideas:

> *"Second: It is necessary to employ oscillations in which the rate of radiation of energy into space in the form of Hertzian or electro-magnetic waves is very small. To give an idea, I would say that the frequency should be smaller than*

twenty thousand per second, though shorter waves might be practicable. The lowest frequency would appear to be six per second, in which case there will be but one node, at or near the ground-plate, and, paradoxically as it may seem, the effect will increase with the distance and will be greatest in a region diametrically opposite the transmitter. With oscillations still slower the earth, strictly speaking, will not resonate, but simply act as a capacity, and the variation of potential will be more or less uniform over its entire surface."

Electrical engineer Tobly Grotz connects Tesla to the basic understanding of the Schumann Resonance:

"Although it was not until 1954-1959 when experimental measurements were made of the frequency that is propagated in the resonant cavity surrounding the Earth, recent analysis shows that it was Nikola Tesla who, in 1899, first noticed the existence of stationary waves in the Schumann cavity. Tesla's experimental measurements of the wavelength and frequency involved closely match Schumann's theoretical calculations. Some of his observations were made in 1899 while Tesla was monitoring the electromagnetic radiations due to lightning discharges in a thunderstorm which passed over is Colorado Springs laboratory."(9)

Could not have a machine been constructed to receive these ELF waves, even if at another frequency after being bounced around inside the earth, and combine them into one stream of electrical energy suitable for charging the batteries of a U-boat? This might be done using a series of antenna able to receive waves coming in at different directions as they bounce around the earth's interior like pin-pong balls and perhaps at slightly differing wavelengths. The rectifying device would then combine these waves, now turned into electrical impulses, into one stream of energy in a diode-like device that merges two such streams together as two roads become a one-way street. But this is not such a simple question since there are several factors involved. Tesla says:

"The intensity of the effect of a transmitting-circuit with a free or elevated terminal is proportionate to the quantity of electricity displaced which is determined by the product of the capacity of the circuit, the pressure, and the frequency of the currents employed." (10)

Tesla built a small capacity unit, charged as much as possible with a rounded sending antenna in his final patent for this type of device (number 1,119,782). In the case of the lightning-driven Schumann Resonance, the capacity of the circuit is the earth itself that seems vast, at least to me. The "pressure" is the lightning itself, again seeming very strong. It is only the frequency of the wave itself that must remain low. The feasibility of actually using the Schumann Resonance is something for physicists and engineers to figure out but the Germans must have at least considered this on some level. And likewise, they must have considered using either the Goliath system or some other similar system to charge up those U-boat batteries using a Tesla or Tesla-like system.

Returning to artificially transmitting long waves, the Goliath facility used 15 to 25 kHz, longer waves than real ELF waves but sufficient to communicate with submerged

U-boats worldwide. Since this sufficed and the frequency was higher (see above comments of Tesla). Was this sufficient for the transmission of energy?

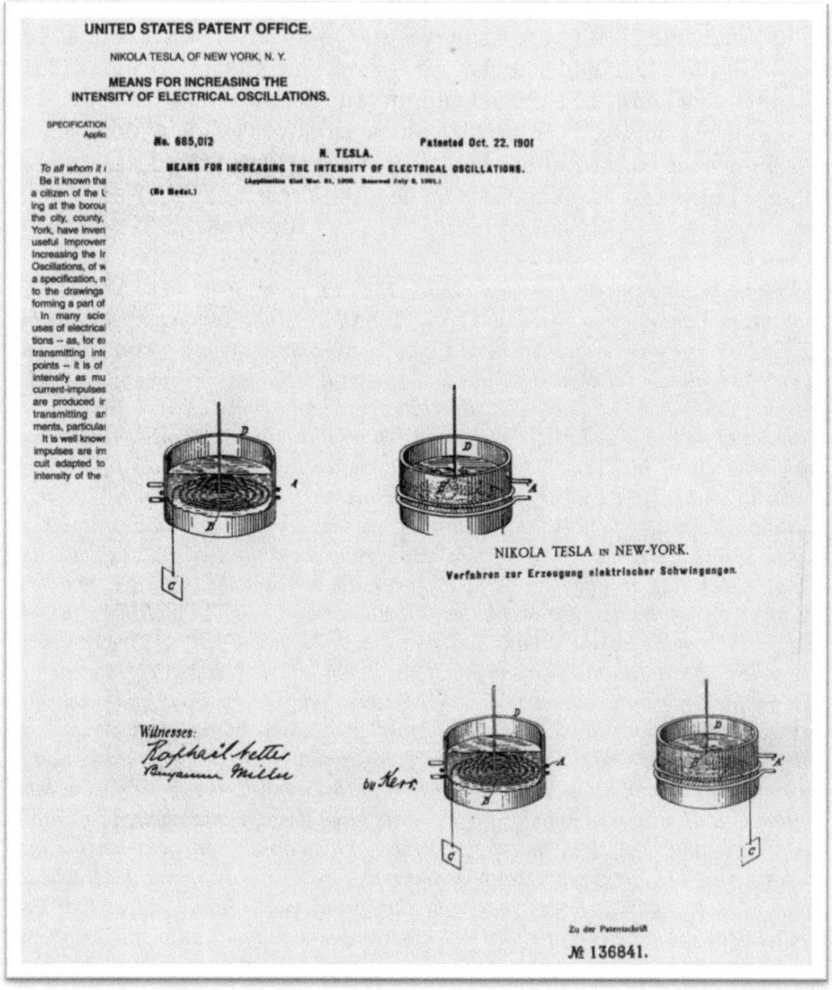

Tesla's American and German patents for increasing the signal of incident radio frequency radiation. The American and German patents are identical. They use a liquid gas to super-cool a coil antenna—in this case, liquid air.

We know there was another ELF wave generator in Germany but the dates given for it were apparently wrong. This was a facility that has been recently detected under Berlin's Tempelhof Airport. This was code-named "TeddyBaer" or "Teddybear" in English. The problem is the source seems to think this facility was built by the

Americans in the 1980's and used in Cold War espionage *(http://www.fosar-bludorf.com/Tempelhof/)*.

But there is another possibility for a huge ELF wave generator. ELF waves can be made using a loop antenna. In other words a huge coil wire can be laid down on the earth and made to generate ELF waves. There was such a huge coil wire, both at Teddybaer and at another facility, this time one that was of wartime vintage. This was the strange circular facility lying under the earth at Ohrdruf. The outline of this facility is still visible from the air in the same way as archaeology uses aerial surveying to locate ancient earth works. And since the purpose of this book is to investigate unsolved Nazi mysteries, Dr. Axel Stoll, a geophysicist, is going to be quoted, full-force, after which we can consider implications for U-boats. (My translation):

> *"In my view, and in this I am not alone, it is that point number 5 (exotic UFO propulsion manipulating space and time) (translator's note: from points made by Dr. Stoll on previous page) has been solved by German scientists during the time of the Third Reich. That also speaks to, among other things, H. Faeth discussing for the first time, respectively, the Germans carrying out the Thuringian "Manhattan Project" during the Second World War; the creation of a German atomic weapon. In Jonastal by Arnsadt, respectively, in the region of the troop exercise yard at Ohrdruf, is found deep in the shell limestone, openly, a huge particle accelerator facility. Auto engines, among other things, stop, still, when traveling in a determined area (Dr. Stoll references and early chapter: see Chapter 4 Physical Phenomena). Pictures taken from the air rove that the arrangement of this facility resembles a Celtic cross or the symbol of the Black Sun. The symbol of the Black Sun one can view beautifully in Wewelsburg (Himmler's castle) in the "Gruppenfuehrer-Room". There is a strong suspicion that the facility mentioned was not simply interested in German atomic research, on the contrary that it served for the purpose of time and space manipulation. In other words, one worked on the problem of time-trips and the accompanying possibility of surmounting the speed of light. Just as well, the development and production of electromagnetic waves may have been researched. (Dr. Stoll references: Bearden, 1996, and the appendix of his book). I am convinced of the actuality that the last sentence may sound unbelievable to the uninitiated. Those who, however, occupy themselves with this problematic firmly assert that the German scientists and technicians must have reached important major progress as is generally conceded. In order to, for example, manipulate space and time (one can create or obliterate space and time) an electromagnetic longitudinal wave must be generated (the normal situation as, for instance, light and others are electromagnetic transverse waves). These longitudinal waves move straight through the body of the earth and the oceans and would be able, at once, to obliterate numerous targets. Therefore, these are extraordinarily interesting for high-tech weapons utilization." (11)*

Well, OK! The reader has been given a good, big dose of very exotic German high technology by one of the few doctors licensed to prescribe it. Recovering from this high-tech infusion, it can be seen that our concern, ELF wave generation, is not really a huge problem and fits right in here. What is meant is that here at Ohrdruf we have a large particle accelerator, at the disposal of researchers. To accelerate a particle to near-light speeds the forces of magnetic attraction and repulsion are put into play. But just as in a rail gun, this may not have been done with magnets. Instead, large electric cables follow the track to be taken by the accelerated particle. One cable sends electricity of a suitable character in one direction while its neighbor on the other side of the particle's pathway sends electricity the opposite direction. A cross section of the cable would show an outward spiraling of the cable's magnetic field. Since each cable is going the opposite direction, the particle is being squeezed by opposing magnetic poles faster and faster as it travels down its pathway. But even if electromagnets were used in the instance of the particle accelerator, the electric wiring described would be in place to charge them up. This "electric wiring" would be in the form of a large loop.

Since the large looping cable, the antenna, is already in place, all that would need to be done is to turn off one cable. Now electricity is being pumped at tremendous pressure one way around the track, generating a powerful electromagnetic wave. With some tuning, a sufficing wave could be generated with which to test the feasibility of charging the batteries of a U-boat on the other side of the planet, if not actually do this on a regular basis.

We are going to see the hand of Tesla again, at almost every step of the discussion concerning fantastic U-boat propulsion but first we are going to discuss one Tesla-free U-boat option.

Literature Cited

1. **Lusar, Rudolf, 1964**, *German Secret Weapons of the Second World War*, page 211, J.F. Lehmans Verlag, Munich, Germany
2. Goliath Transmitter, Wikipedia, *http://en.wikipedia.org/wiki/Goliath_transmitter*
3. Communication with Submarines, Wikipedia, *http://en.wikipedia.org/wiki/Communication_with_submarines*
4. **Ferzak, Franz (production) and Ulrich Heerd (editor), 2000**, *Nikola Tesla Collected German and American Patents*, pages 645 - 653, MVV Peiting, Peiting, Germany ISBN 3-89539-246-4
5. These quotes can be found in the book referenced in (4), all under the individual patents referenced in the text.
6. **Trinkaus, George, 1988**, *Tesla The Lost Inventions*, page 10, High Voltage Press, Portland, Oregon, USA
7. **Taeufer, Johannes, 1930**, "Vrill, Die Cosmische Urkraft Widergeburt von Atlantis", page 18, Astrologischer Verlag Wilhelm Becker, Berlin-Stegilitz, Germany
8. **Grotz, Toby, E.E., date unknown**, *Wireless Transmission Of Power Resonating Planet Earth*, as appears in *The Tesla Papers Nikola Tesla on Free Energy & Wireless Transmission of Power*, 2000, as edited by David Hatcher Childress, Adventures Unlimited Publishing, Kempton, Illinois, USA
9. *ibid.*
10. **Tesla, Nikola, 1914**, *Apparatus For Transmitting Electrical Energy*, US Patent number 90,245, page one, US Patent Office, contained in Nikola Tesla Collected German And American Patents, see Ferazk, Franz, above.
11. **Stoll, Axell, Ph.D., 2001**, *Hochtechnologie im Dritten Reich Reichsdeutsche Entwicklungen und die vermutlich wahre Herkunft der, "UFOs"*, pages 106, 107, Amun Verlag, Schleusingen, Germany

LIKE WALTER-PROPULSION ONLY BETTER?

Like Walter-propulsion, only better! Well, this is the claim of a few Reich insiders regarding a new and totally unknown type of U-boat propulsion which resembles the Walter systems, but is better. These same Reich insiders also claim that at least one such U-boat was built and put to sea.

Like many other things in this book, the legend starts off as a description in a "novel" by Wilhelm Landig, in this case "Wolfzeit um Thule", as the ultimate Reich insider, the Deepthroat of Nazi Germany, begins telling us of the German Navy's most highly guarded secret. There is a great deal of translation for this and the subsequent sources, so please bear with me. Landig begins:

> *"Then there existed a further U-boat, a completely new, three thousand ton boat type, which was fitted with a two-turbine composition as power plant and had a 50-man crew. They were placed under the strictest security, since they did not make use of the hitherto means of operation. A completely new kind of fuel was filled into bottles and put under pressure. The method of propulsion was a substance that oxidized in the presence of oxygen. When mixed with seawater, this new substance effervesced and the oxyoid-sea water-compound was blasted under enormous pressure into the turbines at six hundred atmospheres. Out from there the mixture was led through a diversion, first through a regenerator and then to a separation process with which reclaimed oxygen was again conducted back to the U-boat. The remaining substance was then conducted through a hollow shaft to the ship's screws. Through the taking of the mist from the ship's screws through a suction effect the speed can be increased. With the freely working ship's screws the new boat-type made 75 knots underwater. And with the help of the reclaimed oxygen it was even possible to travel underwater for a year. Such a salt or carbide-like substance functions in chambers that are adjustable. A very small amount suffices to turn the turbines. The traveling speed is regulated through an adjustable valve. These boats with the completely new type of propulsion were the most highly guarded secrets of the German Navy and would have to be withdrawn at the attack of the enemy. U-558 of this new series had a mechanical breakdown upon a special sortie near Iceland and disappeared. The aforementioned number of the series (meaning U-558: translator's. note) occurs no more anywhere again, just as infrequently as other numbers..."(1)*

Next we turn to O. Bergmann. This genre of exotic, strange and mysterious U-boats is one of Bergmann's specialties. He tells us why all this confusion concerning the numbering of U-boats was necessary and then adds some additional information to this specific account:

"In order to out-perform enemy espionage and organized treason, it can be given out that at the time official German statements about depth of dive, horse power, knots, and so on, were simply underestimated. Therefore, also again and again differences are to be determined between statements from unseized data as they are to understand in the technical literature on one side, and records of reports of experienced witnesses of individual U-boat men of the other side. Here is an example..."

Before reviewing Bergmann's example we should be aware that after the war this practice, which I call "undervaluation", was continued and almost a policy set in stone among the former Allied Powers, especially the Americans. This had to have been at first a purely propagandistic practice, since the Allies did not want to admit that the Germans had technology and machines that could greatly outperform their own (2). It may have also been a part of Cold War strategy, in which one power, having gained a full measure of a new technology, sought to undervalue it in the eyes of its competitor. Returning again to Bergmann:

"In the general U-boat literature in the class VIIC U-558 belongs and is named, led by Captain Krech, which on July 20, 1943 off Northern Spain, northwest from Cape Ortegal was scuttled after and attacked from the air. In the minutes register submitted by a Marine, Franz We...(Translation note: here Bergmann references Geheim Wunderwaffen, Book I, page 47 which will also be reviewed later in this treatment). His U-558 does not belong to the VIIC class, was not commanded by Captain Krecht, on the contrary by Captain zur See Schermann. It was not scuttled near Ortegal but sank after mechanical failure near Iceland, and found itself in a U-boat assembly under Korv. Captain Moehle, who was most probably bound for Mar del Platta, Argentina with the aim of withdrawing it from circulation. On the basis of other reports we know today, for example that the numbers of scuttled boats were renewed and taken over by the revolutionary new boats, so it must have been in the case of U-558, but most probably only when these new boats with their re-renewed numbers would no longer engage in general war sorties, but were instead brought to a whole new destiny. The U-boat described by Franz We... had two turbine components with 12,000 horsepower each and attained a still not to be found speed of 75 knots and had a Walter-type but till better propulsion. The U-558 commanded by Krecht was already lost in the summer of 1943 while Franz We... explained:.' ...still in the year 1943' (which means the year's end) we took over the new boat with the number U-558." (3)

Now we can go to the reference cited by Bergmann, that of D. H. Haarmann in the first of his "Geheim Wunderwaffen" series. Here we finally get to meet Franz We... Haarmann explains to us:

"Definitive eye witness reports from the last years of the war concerning the propulsion method of the most secret U-boat types, with declarations which in the general U-boat literature are no doubt hard to find. In order not to receive any legal, patent difficulties, some technical declarations are altered.

Transcript of a conversation that took place on March 22, 1980 in Klausenleopoldsdorf, a part of which, also on tape recording, is taken.

Present: Rudolf J. Mund; Franz We...; Karl La...; . Mr. W. handed over four photos: two are photos of a U-boat. One photo of him in uniform with his father in civilian clothes and one picture of him in a circle of his comrades.

Mr. W...reported the following as a former Marine; ' I reported for duty to the recruit company in the year 1943 to Biels. Later I was transferred to Neustadt in Holstein—to ULD, that is the Lehr Division. There Korv. Captain Moehle was already our commandant. We were there trained on 20 boat, that is 2,500 ton boats. From there we were transferred to Kiel and took over a boat there that we generally did not know. That was still in the year 1943. By means of a dive-saver (Drager Tauchretter) (this is perhaps a rebreathing device, I do not know—translator) I gained admission to the boat. If I had been caught, I would have been hanged. (Two photos of the Krupp-dockyard).

In the Krupp works we took possession of this boat. It was a 3,000-ton boat, and that was a big boat, with a 50-man crew and two-turbine composition, each 12,000 horse power. It was driven by a substance that was oxidized in oxygen. It was three...which oxidized with a sea water mixture blown up like a spray. This oxidation - seawater compound was blown under enormous pressure, 600 atmospheres, in the turbines. From there the mixture was led over a diversion through a..., there separated and the reclaimed oxygen again led back into the boat.

The remaining substance was led through a hollow shaft to the ships screw. By suction effect we took away the mist from the ship's screws so we could travel faster. The ship's screws could work better because they had no suction-effect. Yes, and there we made 75 nautical miles under water. With the oxygen that was reclaimed we would have been able to travel for a year underwater (remain underwater). It was a waste of time to return back for fuel. The fuel was in cylinder bottles. They were equipped with a pressure seal. The substance looked so similar to... in its structure. This (substance) was carried back in chambers that were adjustable. The amount that was inducted amounted to, at the most, a half a thimble with was blown to the turbines.

I do not know if they had ever seen that before. It was a whole wall full of valves. Depending upon traveling speed we have to adjust. If one wanted to go 'full speed' one had to put everything down and open the suction valves. Thereby, one had gotten the most water and most fuel. The boat drew itself up and took off.

Question: How large was the effective range? Yes, it was 12-15,000 nautical miles but when we had more bottles on board... One would not know how many bottles there were on board. Only the Captain knew, that for us, was secret. Because, at any time, the more bottles on board so much more dangerous would be the situation. That was not a normal boat. Only just in captivity we learned that the boat would explode if water were to force its way in. For this reason, prior (than in captivity) because to Iceland the Captain had scuttled the boat as we were on the trip to Argentina.

The boat had mechanical failure prior to Iceland. A broken shaft had to be welded. For that purpose the boat had to half-surface and was, therefore, capable of maneuvering. The Captain of the boat was Scher ...Captain zur See. The whole flotilla was led by Krov. Captain Moehle.

We wanted to run to Argentina. We had crates on board which we were to deliver. We were to have run to Mar del Plata; there we were to deliver the crates and would have gone into captivity or internment. What happened to the boat, I do not know. We traveled as U-558, 26 Tb (type), 1000 registered gross tons displacement (3,000 tons), 50-man crew, we were the 5th Seal - Kiel. U-558 under Scher...

You will see that U-558 nowhere in a database. You will find 522, 527 then 600. Nowhere U-558. " (4)

If the three accounts are combined, well, this all adds up to quite a tale. U-boats that were scuttled by the Germans had their U-boat number re-issued to fool Allied intelligence. A new type of propulsion system, *like the standard Walter system but better*, had been developed and installed into one of these phantom (or perhaps "black") U-boats. The new propellant was stored in bottles held in chambers within the U-boat's hull. Most shockingly, this U-boat was of the Type XXVI, which had not officially ever gotten wet!

Is there any confirmation for this tale? There are some clues that support two of these claims. The first is regarding the existence of a new type of fuel which, though perhaps not identical to the "substance" described above, did possess some similarities. The second concerns a strange U-boat diagram. For the fuel we will turn to a standard source of information on German wartime technology, engineer Rudolf Lusar, who spent the war years in the German Patent Office and has published a book, with many subsequent editions and upgrades, about this technology and weaponry.

Lusar speaks to us in this context not of U-boat propulsion but of a new means of powering torpedoes. Professor Walter worked on both. The question is whether this type of propulsion could be used for other purposes besides torpedoes.

"Towards the end of the war a torpedo was being tested which, powered by back-thrust propulsion, was to have reached a speed of 60 knots. Professor Walter, when starting his tests in 1933, had the idea of developing a back-thrust propulsion torpedo but shelved the tests to investigate take-off aids for aircraft. During he war, however, the tests were resumed. Hydrogen peroxide (H2O2) and a fuel (e.g. diesel fuel) (water being added for cooling purposes) were burnt in a combustion chamber without steam generator and converted into a useful pressure. After intensive tests a new fuel, "Helman" - a hydrazine hydrate fuel mixture - was used, which could, however, be stored for a few weeks only and had to be injected shortly before the launching to the torpedo. These gas

compounds were at first use in a piston engine and their effect fell short of expectations; therefore turbine was chosen which supplied 500 PS (horsepower) at 30,000 r.p.m, generating a pressure of 40 atmospheres at a temperature of 500 to 550 C. These torpedoes had a speed of more than 50 nautical miles per hour and a range of 20,000 meters. Torpedoes with pure jet propulsion had only a short range. The course of these two torpedoes was not given away by bubble trails, as those particles of the combustion gas which were not absorbed by water made bubbles on the surface which were imperceptibly small." (5)

The new propellant, "Helman", does not exactly correspond with the "substance" described earlier, the strange new fuel described in the report of Franz We…, but it is similar. It is said to be a hydrazine hydrate, N_2H_4. We have already seen this formula once in reference to German flying discs (*cf* my book on that subject) as it was said to have been the fuel used in one F.B.I. account that was provided by a prisoner of war (6). It was also designated "B-Stoff" by the Germans, and when mixed with methanol (wood alcohol) designated "M-Stoff", and whith water designated "C-Stoff" *(http://en.wikipedia.org/wiki/Hyrazine)*. C-Stoff was mixed with "T-Stoff" (80% concentrated hydrogen peroxide, 20% oxyquinoline) in the combustion chamber of the famous Messerschmitt Me 162 B rocket interceptor *(http://en.wikipedia.org/wiki/List_of_Stoffs)*.

We are looking for something a little more, though—a fuel which can be stored and is in a more solid form. There are two derivatives of hydrazine that might interest us. The first is monomethyl hydrazine. This is another rocket fuel and is said to be "stable enough to be used in regeneratively cooled rocket engines" *(http://en.wikipedia.org/wiki/Monomethyl_hydrate)*. The second is 1,1-Dimethylhydrazine (UDMH). It is also a stable rocket fuel that can be kept loaded in fuel systems for long periods of time *(http://en.wikipedia.org/wiki/DMH)*. The increased stability of the second option sounds more like the "substance" we're looking for, but our substance is apparently a solid or at least has the consistency of paste.

Constituting as solid or semi-solid may not be a problem. Remember dynamite? It is composed of a very unsafe, unstable fluid called nitroglycerin. It is a great explosive, but like our hydrazine it is hard to work with. Alfred Nobel simply soaked clay or sawdust with nitroglycerin and made dynamite, incorporating the explosive properties of nitroglycerin in a form that could be more safely handled by people. What I am suggesting is that something similar happened with the German's hydrazine compound.

Now let us turn to the ship, the phantom U-558 itself. This was a big boat. What could it have been? Again, we can turn to Lusar for some general information.

"While these boats were under construction bigger boats, too, were begun, the "U-796 and "U-797" (type XVIII), which had a displacement of 1,485/1,650 tons, were 40.7 m long and 6.2 m in the beam. They were to have been powered by a 2,000 PS (this means horsepower but left in the original German abbreviation) diesel engine for surface travel and two 7,500 PS (horsepower) Walter turbines with reduction gears for underwater operations. Their speed would have been 17.5 knots on the surface and 24 to 25 knots submerged. The boats were intended for operations in the Atlantic and were expected to be commissioned in 1945. A further order was placed for 100 boats, the "U-4501"

to "U-4600", to be powered by 7,500 PS Walter engines (type XXVI), but this order was canceled shortly after construction had begun. " (7)

The type XVIII was certainly big enough. Franz We… says, however, that his U-558 was a type 26 (type XXVI). But as far as conventional history goes, it was not the type XVIII that was the prototype for the type XXVI, it was the type XVII B (8). The type XVII B consisted of three prototypes, U-1405, U-1406, and U-1407. All had "conventional" Walter-type hydrogen peroxide engines. The type 17 B was made possible by fitting older U-boats, U-794 and U-792, for instance, with the Walter engine.

So, Franz We… could be correct if there was another kind of type XXVI U-boat which was designed for another type of engine. I don't know if this would be the type XVIII or not but it would require a prototype if German consistency counts, and that prototype would be first a reconditioned boat or at least a boat which was unexpected as a prototype by Allied intelligence. Perhaps a boat reported and accepted as scuttled by the Allies?

There is something very odd which appears in Eberhard Roessler's Geschichte des deutschen U-Bootbaus (The History of German U-boat Construction). This book is a two-volume U-boat bible. It is one of those painstakingly researched, carefully written, fully illustrated with diagrams and pictures, lifetime work of the author (9). There is a section of this book that describes U-boat Projects with "Kreislauf-Antrieb". Kreislauf is another word for the Draeger System of oxygen recycling in which oxygen is added to the intake of a diesel engine, the exhaust from this is filtered removing the carbon dioxide, cooled and ducted to the intake where it is again enriched with oxygen. The air goes around and around, hence the name "Kreislauf" or circularity running. The reader might remember from the introductory words of this system that it was worked on, abandon, and constantly brought up again during the war but the performance of this method was disappointing in terms of power output. Regarding the future of this method, Eberhard Roessler states:

"A further improvement of the Kreislauf propulsion concerning U-boats could only still be expected with an oxygen generator on board." (10)

But in this discussion, it even seems to get more implausible. This new type 26 K, which had to be a world-beater at this point in the war, with the "Kreislauf" (Draeger oxygen rebreathing) propulsion system is to store its oxygen, not as liquid oxygen as usually depicted in this system, but as compressed gas stored bottles, stored in chambers, in the hull of the vessel.

We are all familiar with this method. Compressed bottles of air are what scuba divers use. How long do they stay down with two bottles? Perhaps two hours? Even using pure oxygen, given a diesel engine of over 1000-horse power and running at least 450°F, as opposed to slightly less than 100°F for a human, how many hours could such an oxygen supply last? Maybe this system was just to be used for underwater travel. But then where are the hundreds and hundreds of gallons of diesel fuel stored? The reader might think that this U-boat is getting bigger with each consideration. But this is not necessarily the case, since a diagram does exist which shows exactly how this Type XXVI U-boat with its oxygen bottles would have appeared.

Roessler's depiction of the Type XXVI K Kreislauf boat comes complete with rows of bottles stored in chambers. Of course Roessler himself said this could not have worked, since the available storage area would have been simply too small. Then why did he create the diagram? Surely the concept-level engineers involved would have, at first blush, disregarded this idea for the Type XXVI out of hand. Yes, there was a discussion of larger boat using this method of storage—in particular, a Type XXIX K was mentioned. But this does not get the Type XXVI K diagram off the hook, so to speak.

The only rational explanation is that this diagram of a Type XXVI U-boat would not have carried atmospheric oxygen in its bottles. On the contrary, the only explanation that suffices is that in these bottles something was carried that served as a fuel, but that "something" is never stated, not in the diagram and not by Roessler. The only thing which fits this scenario is the description given above by Franz We… of a very different type of fuel, mixed with sea water and possibly a derivative of hydrazine. The records of this fuel, along with those of the German U-boat that used it have simply vanished from conventional history.

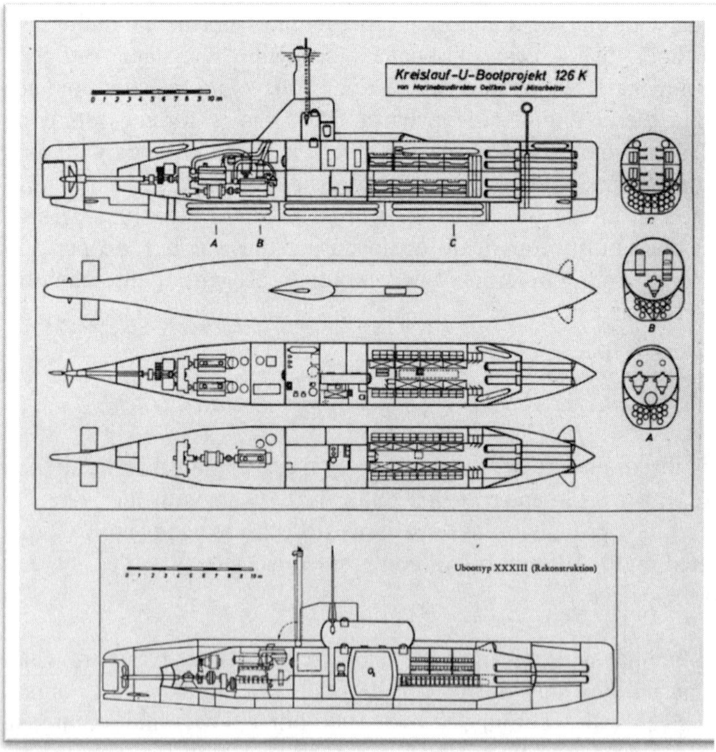

Walter-like Propulsion Only Better? This is a strange diagram of a proposed Type 126K U-boat. It is shown as a "Kreislauf" design, meaning it carried oxygen, but this was not in the conventional design using a single large flask. Instead, this design used many small bottles stored below the living compartments. Was this explanation the forerunner or a cover for another system using a complete fuel stored in the same way as described in the text? Below is another design featuring the standard single-flask design for oxygen.

Literature Cited

1. **Landig, Wilhelm, 1980**, *Wolfzeit um Thule*, pages 14 and 15, Volkstum-Verlag Wilhelm Landig, Vienna, Austria.
2. **Stevens, Henry, 2007**, *Hitler's Suppressed and Still-Secret Weapons, Science and Technology*, pages 6-17 "The Stonewall and Undervaluation", Adventures Unlimited Publishing, Kempton, Illinois, USA
3. **Bergmann, O., 1988**, *I Deutsche Flugscheiben und U-Boote Ueberwachen Die Weltmeere*, page 6, Hugin Gesellschaft Fuer Politisch-Philosophische Studien E.V., Wetter/Ruhr, Germany
4. **Haarmann, D. H., 1983**, *Geheim Wunderwaffen Zerrbild zwischen Taeuschung und Tatsachen*, pages 47, 48 and 49, Hugin Sesellschaft Fuer Politisch-Philosophische Studien E.V., Wetter, Germany
5. **Lusar, Rudolf, 1964**, *German Secret Weapons of the Second World War*, page 212, Neville Spearman, London, UK
6. **Stevens, Henry, 2003**, *Hitler's Flying Saucers*, page 216, Adventures Unlimited Publishing, Kempton, Illinois, USA
7. **Lusar, Rudolf, 1964**, page 205
8. **US Naval Technial Mission In Europe, Technical Report Nol 287-45, 1945**, c/o Floot Post Office, NY., N.Y., USA, obtained though USAF, Wright-Patteson AFB, USA
9. **Roessler, Eberhard, 1996**, *Geschichte des deutschen U-bootbaus Band 2 Entwicklung, Bau und Eigenschaften der deutschen U-Boote von 1943 bis heute*, pages 447-448, Bernard & Graefe Verlag, Augsburg, Germany
10. **Roessler, Eberhard, 1996**, page 449

Tesla's Self-Acting Engine, Part One

Nikola Tesla discusses this concept at some length that will be reviewed. The idea that this system might have been used by the Germans in World War Two for U-boat propulsion was brought to us by William R. Lyne. In fact, he seems to describe three different types of electrical propulsion that were (possibly) used in exotic U-boats without separating them from one another, distinctly. His sources for this information are a man from Virginia named Dort, a man with whom Bill is acquainted whose initials are P.M., and what he heard in military intelligence on the subject. Bill was kind enough to correspond with me, explaining these issues beyond what has been printed in his books. Since Mr. P.M. was named only in private correspondence, his initials will have to suffice for now as he is probably still living and may not want to see his name mentioned here. Bill believes another informant, Mr. Dort, then in his eighties circa 1980, is dead by now but I do not have his first name. Bill tells us that Mr. Dort's father developed the Tesla engine under discussion here and that it was used by the Germans in a U-boat. Bill Lyne discusses all three systems together, and, evidently, he thinks they could have been used in combination, one adding to and reinforcing another. The first system, Tesla's broadcast system, has already been discussed so we are moving to the Dort machine.

This machine was an electrical generator but a very unusual one as it relied on liquid air for fuel. In conception, the electrical generator (Dort machine) is coupled with a Linde ice machine. The Linde unit had been invented in Tesla's time and was in use worldwide. It had the ability to cool air down to the point where it liquefied. As we know, the Germans had great plans for liquid air and made a great quantity of it. The importance of liquid air in the scheme of things is made clear by the fact that liquid air and the Linde method are the only other energy yielding systems discussed by the "Reichsarbeitsgemeinschaft", (Reich Works Association) the pre-Nazi organization charged with making Germany energy independent (1).

German engineer Dr. Carl Paul Gottfried von Linde invented his refrigeration unit in the early 1870s. The Linde "ice machine" might be explained starting as follows: A bank of hollow, refrigeration coils is placed in the space to be cooled. These pipes are filled with a special fluid whose boiling point is lower than the temperature of the space to be cooled so that this special fluid is turned into a gas, absorbing it as the heat of vaporization, while passing through the coils inside this space. This subtracts heat from the space to be cooled. The gas is pumped into a compressor and then discharged into cooling tubes. In a U-boat both the compressor and the cooling tubes would be cooled by incoming seawater. At any depth this water would be no no warmer than 38-40°F or about 5°C and could be even colder than this. The heat of vaporization would be transferred to this seawater and the gas would become a liquid again. This water would be ejected and since the U-boat is moving, no pumping would be required. The cold liquid would be pumped back into the area to be cooled and the cycle repeated until the air within the space to be cooled was itself liquefied (2). Linde added one important feature which was essential to Tesla's thinking. The Linde machine used a counter-current heat exchange technique that used the cold air produced by expansion of the cooling fluid into a gas to chill the new ambient air entering the system. (*http://en.wikipedia.org/wiki/Carl_von_Linde*). At first the warm machine would have given up heat to this incoming air but after some operation, the machine itself would have gotten colder and colder as would have the Dort (Tesla) electric generator itself which was connected to it.

The First Linde "Ice Machine"

The liquid air would be stored in a large tank aboard the U-boat. This large tank of liquid air might have a coiled antenna within it for use as a receiver of broadcast radio frequency energy as was explained in the Tesla patent discussed in the last chapter but in any event it would have supplied the Dort machine with energy for its operation. A portion of the liquid air supply would have been allowed to sublimate, to turn back into gas. Liquid air is of the same constitution as is in our atmosphere, mostly nitrogen and oxygen. Oxygen turns to liquid at -118.8°C, but at -118° the pressure of oxygen returning to a gas is 49.7 atmospheres. For nitrogen, it turns to liquid at -147°C but at -147.1° its vapor pressure is 33.5 atmospheres (3). In other words, a supply of liquid air turning back to a gaseous state would have a pressure of over 40 times standard air pressure at sea level. This pressure is what powers the Dort (Tesla) electric generator.

> *"The German government had wasted no time in taking Tesla seriously, when Tesla's laboratory was burned down in 1895, Linde filed his patent on the liquefaction of air, identical to the system developed and tested by Telsa in conjunction with running his oscillator. The German Ministry of Marine purchased Tesla's turbine right after the US Navy rejected Tesla's attempts of interest them in it first. By 1905, German chemical interests had already begun liquefying and storing thousands of gallons of liquefied air in steel bottles, in anticipation of their need for it in the coming submarine warfare."(4)*

What Mr. Dort's father had to do with this engine, I really do not know beyond what Bill tells us. What is known is that Tesla had a patent for this very type of electric generator in the USA and in Germany. The American patent was issued in 1894, patent number 511, 916 and the German patent was dated 1896, patent number 87269. The application date in both countries is the same, 1893. Both patents are exactly the same.

These patent descriptions are bewildering for some reason, so it is hoped that Bill Lyne will not mind if his simplified and much clearer diagram is used here:

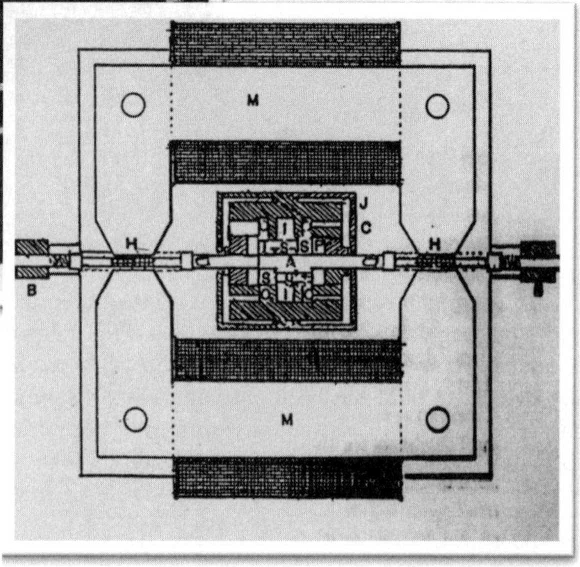

Picture and Schematic of the Tesla electric generator, from William Lyne's *Pentagon Aliens*.

Vorrichtung zur Erzeugung elektrischer Ströme von gleichbleibender Schwingungszahl.

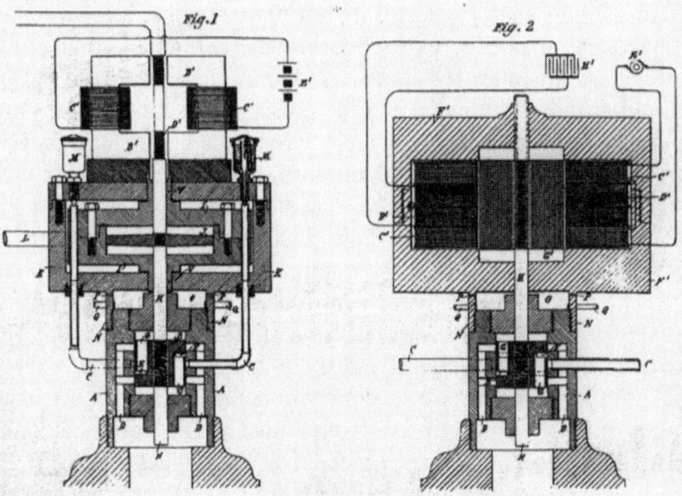

Zu der Patentschrift

№ 87269.

UNITED STATES PATENT OFFICE.

NIKOLA TESLA, OF NEW YORK, N. Y.

ELECTRIC GENERATOR.

SPECIFICATION forming part of Letters Patent No. 511,916, dated January 2, 1894.
Application filed August 19, 1893. Serial No. 483,562. (No model.)

To all whom it may concern:

Be it known that I, NIKOLA TESLA, a citizen of the United States, residing at New York, in the county and State of New York, have invented certain new and useful Improvements in Electrical Generators, of which the following is a specification, reference being had to the drawings accompanying and forming a part of the same.

In an application of even date herewith, Serial No. 483,563, I have shown and described a form of engine invented by me, which, under the influence of an applied force such as the elastic tension of steam or a gas under pressure, yields an oscillation of constant period.

In order that my present invention may be more readily understood I will explain the conditions which are to be observed in order to secure this result.

It is a well known mechanical principle that if a spring possessing a sensible inertia be brought under tension, as by being stretched, and then freed, it will perform vibrations which are isochronous, and as to period, in the main, dependent upon the rigidity of the spring, and its own inertia or that of the system of which it may form an immediate part. This is known to be true in all cases where the force which tends to bring the spring or movable system into a given position is proportionate to the displacement.

In the construction of my engine above referred to I have followed and applied this principle, that is to say, I employ a cylinder and a piston which in any suitable manner I maintain in reciprocation by steam or gas under pressure. To the moving piston or to the cylinder, in case the latter reciprocate and the piston remain stationary, a spring is connected so as to be maintained in vibration thereby, and whatever may be the inertia of the piston or the moving system and the rigidity of the spring relatively to each other, provided, the practical limits within which the law holds true that the forces which tend to bring

Tesla's American Patent Number 511,916 and German Patent Number 87269.
These identical patents are the basis for the "Dort Engine"

Two huge horseshoe-shaped iron magnets face each other with a small gap between the two. A coil for induction of the output electric current wraps around each iron magnet at its center. A small tube runs between the magnets facing each other. In that tube are two small conducting shafts whose internal diameter just allows them to slip inside the tube. A space, an air pocket, exists between the two small conducting shafts. On each side of the tube are air inlets for compressed air. These are from the liquid air storage tank. The liquid air has sublimated and the pressure of sublimation is applied as the two inlets are opened. The two conducting shafts are pushed together rapidly but stop when the air between them compresses to a degree stronger than the incoming pressure of sublimation. This is really a spring. Tesla calls it an airspring. At this moment the conducting shafts pass over an outlet, an air hole, just like the exhaust port in a two-stroke engine. This port lets the air out of the compressed air side, the side facing the inlets, away from the center of the mechanism. This release as well as the compressed air in the center, in the air spring, pushes the conducting shafts back outward. The shafts cover the exhaust port on their way outward and the process is repeated. This process results in a rapid back and forth motion of the conducting shafts that can be imagined by the buzzing sound they produce as this process continues. The conducting shafts are rapidly breaking the magnetic lines of force between the two magnets and so inducing an electric current in the collecting coils wound around them. The square area in the center of the machine is: "…the air-powered mechanical oscillator which drives the horizontal shaft" (4). This mechanical oscillator is yet another Tesla patent (US patent number 514,169, German patent number 84 335). This mechanical oscillator could function as an air pump but in our special instance it is replaced by the Linde unit generating air pressure by sublimation. The air exhausted from the electric generator is simply fed back into the Linde machine, re-cooled, re-liquefied and stored in the liquid air tank.

Tesla's original generator was to work on steam or compressed air. It had an oiling system for the conducting shafts. At the temperatures under discussion here, either special lubricants would have to have been used, graphite powder, or improved air bearings, since the fit between the conducting shafts and the tube which housed them allowed some passage of air for lubrication purposes. The water in the liquid air would probably have to have been removed. This is no problem, however, given water's high freezing point. In fact, Linde could separate out and distill oxygen from liquid air if this was necessary.

Another interesting point is the similarity between the total set up here, the combination of the Dort (Tesla) electric generator and the Linde machine, and the work of Karl Nowak. Further, as we hear Nikola Tesla's words that will soon follow, the reader is asked to bear in mind issues of raising negative entropy and Black Sun theory as presented in my first two books (6), (7).

Tesla thought this combined Linde machine - electric generator, perhaps, might even somehow cheat the Second Law of Thermodynamics, (or more specifically the Carnot Theorem), meaning getting something for nothing, or said another way, function as an over-unity machine. He had more than one thought on this subject, as we will see later.

For now it is very interesting to read Tesla's own words about how this combination might work (8):

A Departure From Known Methods—-Possibility Of A 'Self-Acting' engine Or Machine, Inanimate, Yet Capable, Like A Living Being, Of Deriving Energy From The Medium—- The Ideal Way Of Obtaining Motive Power.

When I began the investigation of the subject under consideration, and when the proceeding or similar ideas presented themselves to me for the first time, though I was then unacquainted with a number of the facts mentioned, a survey of the various ways of utilizing the energy of the medium convinced me, nevertheless, that to arrive at a satisfactory practical solution a radical departure from the methods then known had to be made. The windmill, the solar engine, the engine driven by terrestrial heat, had their limitations in the amount of power obtainable. Some new way had to be discovered which would enable us to get more energy. There was enough heat-energy in the medium, but only a small part of it was available for the operation of an engine in the ways then known. Beside, the energy was obtainable only at a very slow rate. Clearly, then, the problem was to discover some new method that would make it possible both utilize more of the heat-energy of the medium and to draw it away from the same at a more rapid rate. I was vainly endeavoring to form an idea of how this might be accomplished, when I read some statements from Carnot and Lord Kelvin (then Sir William Thompson) which meant virtually that it is impossible for an inanimate mechanism or self-acting machine to cool a portion of the medium below the temperature of the surrounding, and operate by heat abstracted. These statements interested me intensely. Evidently a living being could do this very thing, and since the experiences of my early life which I have related had convinced me that a living being is only an automaton, or, otherwise stated, a "self-acting engine," I came to the conclusion that it was possible to construct a machine which would do the same. As the first step toward this realization I conceived the following mechanism. Imagine a thermopile consisting of a number of bars of metal extending from the earth to the outer space beyond the atmosphere. The heat from below, conducted upward along these metal bars, would cool the earth or the sea or the air, according to the location of the lower parts of the bars, and the result, as is well known, would be an electric current circulating in these bars. The two terminals of the thermopile could now be joined through an electric motor, and, theoretically, this motor would run on and on, until the media below would be cooled down to the temperature of outer space. This would be an inanimate engine that to all evidence would be cooling a portion of the medium below the temperature of the surrounding, and operating by the heat abstracted.

But was it not possible to realize a similar condition without necessarily going to a height? Conceive, for the sake of illustration, an enclosure T, as illustrated in diagram b, such that energy could not be transferred across it except through a channel or path O, and that, by some means or other, in this enclosure a medium were maintained which would have little energy, and that on the outer side of the same there would be the ordinary ambient medium with much energy. Under these assumptions the energy would flow through the path O, as indicated by the arrow, and might then be converted on its passage into some other form of energy. The question was, Could such a condition be attained? Could we produce artificially such a "sink" for the energy of the ambient medium to flow in? Suppose that an extremely low temperature could be maintained by some process in a given space; the surrounding medium would then be compelled to give off heat, which cold be converted into mechanical or other form of energy, and utilized. By realizing such a plan, we should be enabled to get at any point of the globe a continuous supply of energy, day and night. More than this, reasoning in the abstract, it would seem possible to cause a quick circulation of the medium, and thus draw the energy at a very rapid rate.

Here then, was an idea that if realizable, afforded a happy solution of the problem of getting energy from the medium. But was it realizable? I convinced myself that it was so in a number of ways, of which one is the following. As regards heat, we are at a high level, which may be represented by the surface of a mountain lake considerably above the sea, the level of which may mark the absolute zero of temperature existing in the interstellar space. Heat, like water, flows from high to low level, and, consequently, just as we can let the water of the lake run down to the sea, so we are able to let heat from the earth's surface travel up into the cold region above. Heat, like water, can perform work in flowing down, and if we had any doubt as to whether we could derive energy from the medium by means of a thermopile, as before described, it would be dispelled by this analog. But can we produce cold in a given portion of the space and cause that the heat to flow in continually? To create such a "sink," or "cold hole," as we might say, in the medium, would be equivalent to producing in the lake a space either empty or filled with something much lighter than water. This we could do by placing in the lake a tank, and pumping all the water out of the latter. We know, then, that the water, if allowed to flow back into the tank, would, theoretically, be able to perform exactly the same amount of work which was used in pumping it out, but not a bit more. Consequently nothing could be gained in this double operation of first raising the water and then letting it fall down. This would mean that it is possible to create such a sink in the medium. But let us reflect a moment. Heat, though following certain general laws of mechanics, like a fluid, is not such; it is energy which may be converted into other form of energy as it passes from a high to a low level. To make our mechanical analog complete and true, we must, therefore, assume that the water, in its passage into the tank, is converted into something else, which may by taken out of it without using any, or by using very little, power.

For example, if heat be represented in this analog by the water of the lake, the oxygen and hydrogen composing the water may illustrate other forms of energy into which the heat is transformed in passing from hot to cold. If the process of heat transformation were absolutely perfect, no heat at all would arrive at the low level, since all of it would be converted into other forms of energy. Corresponding to this ideal case, all the water into the tank would be decomposed into oxygen and hydrogen before reaching the bottom, and the result would be that water would continually flow in, and yet the tank would remain entirely empty, the gases formed escaping. We would thus produce, by expending initially a certain amount of work to create a sink for the heat or, respectively, the water to flow in, a condition enabling us to get any amount of energy without further effort. This would be an ideal way of obtaining motive power. We do not know of any such absolutely perfect process of heat-conversion, and consequently some heat will generally reach the low level, which means to say, in our mechanical analog, that some water will arrive at the bottom of the tank, and a gradual and slow filling of the latter will take place, necessitating continuous pumping out. But evidently there will be less to pump out than flows in, or, in other words, less energy will be needed to maintain the initial condition that is developed by the fall, and this is to say that some energy will be gained from the medium. What is not convened in flowing down can just be raised up with its own energy, and what is converted is clear gain. Thus the virtue of the principle I have discovered resides wholly in the conversion of the energy on the downward flow.

First Efforts To Produce The Self-Acting Engine—-The Mechanical Oscillator Work of Dewar and Linde—Liquid Air

Having recognized this truth, I began to devise means for carrying out my idea, and , after long thought, I finally conceived a combination of apparatus which should make possible the obtaining of power from the medium by process of continuous cooling of atmospheric air. This apparatus, by continually transforming heat into mechanical work, tended to become colder and colder, and if it only were practicable to reach a very low temperature in this manner, then a sink for the heat could be produced, and energy could be derived from the medium. This seemed to be contrary to the statements of Carnot and Lord Kelvin before referred to, but I concluded from the theory of the process that such a result could be attained. This conclusion I reached, I think, in the latter part of 1883, when I was in Paris, and it was a time when my mind was being more and more dominated by an inventions which I had evolved during the preceding year, and which has since become known under the name of the "revolving magnetic field." During the few years which followed I elaborated further the plan I had imagined, and studied the working conditions, but make little headway. The commercial introduction in this country of the invention before referred to required most of my energies until 1889, when I again took up the idea of the self-acting machine. A closer investigation of the principles involved, and calculation, now showed that the result I aimed at could not be reached in a practical manner by ordinary machinery, as I had in the beginning expected. This led me, as a next step, to study of a type of engine generally designated as "turbine," which at first seemed to offer better chances for a realization of the idea. Soon I found, however, that the turbine, too, was unsuitable. But my conclusions showed that if an engine of a peculiar kind could be brought to a high degree of perfection, the plan I had conceived was realizable, and I resolved to proceed with greatest economy of transformation of heat into mechanical energy. A characteristic feature of the engine was that the work-performing piston was not connected with anything else, but was perfectly free to vibrate at an enormous rate. The mechanical difficulties encountered in the construction of this engine were greater than I had anticipated, and I made slow progress. This work was continued until early in 1892, when I went to London, where I saw Professor Dewar's admirable experiments with liquefied gases. Others had liquefied gases before, and notably Ozlewski and Picket had performed credible early experiments in this line, but there was such vigor about the work of Dewar that even the old appeared new. His experiments showed, through in a way different from that I had imagined, that is was possible to reach a very low temperature by transforming heat into mechanical work and I returned, deeply impressed with what I had seen, and more than ever convinced that my plan was practicable. The work temporarily interrupted was taken up anew, and soon I had in a fair state of perfection the engine that I have named "the mechanical oscillator." In this machine I succeeded in doing away with all packing, valves, and lubrication, and in producing so rapid a vibration of the piston that shafts of tough steel, fastened to the same and vibrated longitudinally, were torn asunder. By combining this engine with a dynamo of special design I produced a highly efficient electrical generator, invaluable in measurements and determinations of physical quantities on account of the unvarying rate of oscillation obtainable by its means. I exhibited several types of this machine, named "mechanical and electrical oscillator." before the Electrical Congress at the World's Fair in Chicago during the summer of 1893, in a lecture which, on account of other pressing work, I was unable to prepare for publication. On that occasion I exposed the principles of the mechanical oscillator, but the original purpose of this machine is explained here for the first time.

In the process, as I had primarily conceived it, for the utilization of the energy of the ambient medium, there were five essential elements in combination, and each of these had to be newly designed and perfected, as no such machines existed. The mechanical oscillator was the first element of this combination, and having perfected this, I turned to the next, which was an air-compressor of a design in certain respects resembling that of the mechanical oscillator. Similar difficulties in the construction were again encountered, but the work was pushed vigorously, and at the close of 1894 I had completed these two elements of the combination, and thus produced an apparatus for compressing air, virtually to any desired pressure, incomparably simpler, smaller, and more efficient than the ordinary. I was just beginning work on the third element, which together with the first two would give a refrigerating machine of exceptional efficiency and simplicity, when a misfortune befell me in the burning of my laboratory, which crippled my labors and delayed me. Shortly afterwards Dr. Carl Linde announced the liquefaction of air be a self-cooling process, demonstrating that it was practicable to proceed with the cooling until liquefaction of the air took place. This was the only experimental proof that I still wanted that energy was obtainable from the medium in the manner contemplated by me.

The liquefaction of air by a self-cooling process was not, as popularly believed, an accidental discovery, but a scientific result which could not have been delayed much longer, and which, in all probability, could not have escaped Dewar. This fascinating advance, I believe, is largely due to the powerful work of this great Scotsman. Nevertheless, Linde's is an immortal achievement. The manufacture of liquid air has been carried on for four years in Germany, on a scale much larger than in any other country, and this strange product has been applied for a variety of purposes. Much was expected of it in the beginning, but so far it has been an industrial ignis fatuus. But he use of such machinery as I am perfecting, its cost will probably be greatly lessened, but even then its commercial success will be questionable. When used as a refrigerant it is uneconomical, as its temperature is unnecessarily low. It is as expensive to maintain a body at a very low temperature, as it is to keep it very hot; it takes coal to keep air cold. In oxygen manufacture it cannot yet compete with the electrolytic method. For use as an explosive it is unsuitable, because its low temperature again condemns it to a small efficiency, and for motive-power purposes its cost is still by far too high. It is of interest to note, however, that in driving an engine by liquid air a certain amount of energy may be gained from the warm, each two hundred pounds of iron casting of the latter contributing energy at the rate of about one effective horsepower during one hour. But this gain of the consumer is offset by an equal loss of the producer.

Much of this task on which I have labored so long remains to be done. A number of mechanical details are still to be perfected and some difficulties of a different nature to be mastered, and I cannot hope to produce a self-acting machine deriving energy from the ambient medium for a long time yet, even if all my expectations should materialize. Many circumstances have occurred which have retarded my work of late, but for several reasons the delay was beneficial.

One of these reasons was that I had ample time to consider what the ultimate possibilities of this development might be. I worked for a long time fully convinced that the practical realization of this method of obtaining energy from the sun would be of incalculable industrial value, but the continued study of the subject revealed the fact that while it will be commercially profitable if my expectations are well founded, it will not be so to an extraordinary degree.

The way this would work in the submarine is that air would be continuously brought into the mouth of the Linde machine, cooled first by the expanding gas coming out of the compressor ducted around it, then cooled, compressed, cooled by seawater, allowed to expand resulting in more cooling, until the gas collapses into a liquid. The liquid air would be stored in a large tank. Using gravity, as small portion of the liquid air would be bled into a smaller tank. At least one pump, probably two, would be necessary. The heat from these two machines would be ducted towards vaporization of the liquid air in the smaller tank. This air would then be ducted into the oscillator, causing the conducting shaft to cut magnetic lines of force for production of electricity. The air, still very cold, would then be guided back into the mouth of the Linde machine for another round.

As the machines work together, they get colder and colder. In an ideal world the gas's liquefaction requirements would be tied to the amount of compression-expansion of the pump so that no energy is wasted. Likewise, if any additional heat were required for vaporization (sublimation) of the liquid air, it would come from the outside environment (ambient temperature of the environment). A gas might be chosen, as was oxygen in this example that required less energy to liquefy but would provide adequate pressure through its vaporization pressure. It does take some additional energy to collapse air into a liquid but there is also a release of energy in the expanding gas and so it is in the efficient use of these changes of state where this particular engine shines. These machines might be fined tuned to work with only one or two degrees of difference arising anywhere within the machines themselves.

U-boat Designs with Large Oxygen Tanks.
Here are two more German designs involving large oxygen tanks.

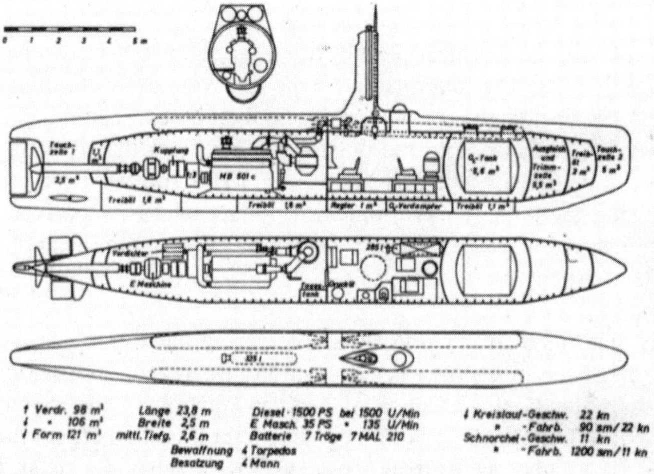

Ubootyp XXXIV Vergrößerte Ausführung mit festem Schnorchel von Grim und Kurzak

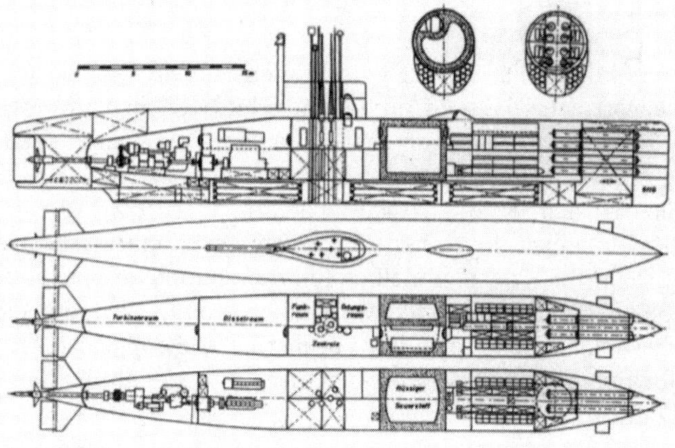

Ubootyp XXXV (Rekonstruktion von Beuter 21. 7. 1945)

Of course the purpose of the combined engine would be to produce electricity to charge the batteries of the U-boat. But, additionally as mentioned above, the storage tank of liquid gas might surround an antenna designed to receive and magnify incoming ELF waves that could then be converted to electricity. This additional electricity might either be used to charge the batteries or, if already charged, to manufacture additional liquid gas. And if the gas used was oxygen, this might be used to burn diesel fuel, either as enrichment or solely if traveling underwater, in the Kreislauf (Draeger) system.

This is not a free-energy machine. But it is certainly a very efficient one and it might allow additional types of energy to be utilized as explained in the last paragraph. Compare this to an automobile's engine in which 25-40% of the energy produced is wasted as excess heat and an additional (perhaps double digit figure) amount of energy is wasted friction when the piston rings scrape over the cylinder walls.

An automobile engine is a heat pump. It works because heat can cause expansion in an environment that is colder than itself. If the environment were the same temperature as the burning gas inside the combustion chamber of the engine, the gas would not expand nor would it exhaust into the outside environment that is acting as a heat sink. The Dort (Tesla) engine is doing the opposite. It is cooling itself down as much as possible and using the outside environment to induct heat to vaporized liquid air. This outside heat is just enough to sublimate the liquid. Our engine is acting as a heat sink, not the outside environment.

My view is that this engine works though lowering the entropy of the engine. As the heat is taken out of the machine it becomes more organized, less random. This and the fact that it uses cold, or the absence of heat, in relation to the ambient environment, would make it the darling of Karl Schappeller, Viktor Schauberger, fire and ice theory founder Hans Hoerbiger, as well as Tesla. This is what physicist Michael Watson describes as Reverse Thermodynamics (9). For me, this is another example of the densification, reverse thermodynamics, change of state, change of energy technology that I call the Black Sun concept.

OK, so it is cool, but what besides the testimony of Mr. Dort do we have to presume that this engine was actually used during the Third Reich or afterwards by the Nazi International/3rd Power for the purpose of powering U-boats? Well, how about the design drawings of what would have been the Type XXXIII, XXXIV, and XXXV U-boats (10), which all had large tanks designated as to be used to carry liquid oxygen? This was at a time in which the Kreislauf, oxygen recycling (Draeger), system had fallen out of favor. Perhaps the Kreislauf method fell back into favor once it was realized that it could be combined and compounded with other propulsion methods, hence the new designs. But these tanks could also have been what they appear to be on the surface—storage tanks for liquid air or liquid oxygen, used in a straightforward way to power an electric generator as in the Dort engine.

Literature Cited

1. **Taeufler, Johannes, 1930**, *"Vril" Die Kosmische Urkraft Wiedergeburt von Atlantis*, page 18, Astrologischer Verlag Wilhelm Becker, Berlin-Steglitz, Germany
2. **Van Norstrand's Scientific Encyclopedia, 1397**, page 1759, D. Van Norstrand Company, Inc., Princeton, NJ, USA
3. **Van Norstrand's Scientific Encyclopedia, 1958**, page 1759
4. **Lyne, William R., 1999**, *Pentagon Aliens*, page 286, Creatopia Productions, Lamy, N. M., USA
5. **Lyne, William R., 1999**, page 285
6. **Stevens, Henry, 2003**, *Hitler's Flying Saucers*, pages 181-187, Adventures Unlimited Publishing, Kempton, Illinois, USA
7. **Stevens, Henry, 2007**, *Hitler's Suppressed and Still-Secret Weapons, Science and Technology*, pages 312-322, Adventures Unlimited Publishing, Kempton, *Illinois, USA*
8. ***Tesla, Nikola edited by David Hatcher Childress, 2000***, *The Tesla Papers Nikola Tesla on Free Energy & Wireless Transmission of Power*, pages 52-58, Adventures Unlimited Publishing, Kempton, Illinois, USA
9. **Stevens, Henry, 2003**, *Hitler's Flying Saucers*, pages 181-183, Adventures Unlimited Publishing, Kempton, Illinois, USA
10. **Roessler, Eberhard, 1996**, *Geschichte des deutschen U-bootbaus Band 2*, pages 449, 451, and 452, Bernard & Graefer Verlag, Augsburg, Germany

U-530

Regarding U-530 we have something unique. A junior officer writing under the penname "Wilhelm Bernhard" has become an eyewitness for us, disclosing many things which contradict established history. U-530 has already been discussed as a converted U-boat. Bernhard accuses the US government of taking possession of U-530 and then transporting it, allegedly to the American east coast but switching boats near the Panama Canal and towing it westward, through the Canal and to San Francisco on the west coast. Here, it was dismantled bolt by bolt, obviously in a search for something important, yet it was done in a deceptive manner, as if whatever they were looking for was a major secret to be kept secret at all cost. We have seen that the American government did ship another U-boat back to the USA in secret, and that the records for this "abduction" apparently surfaced only by accident, contained within another discussion.

In order to try to determine the nature of this exotic propulsion, the statement by Buechner and Bernhard needs to be reviewed again:

> *"It is to be remembered that the U-530 was exceptionally fast. What kind of miraculous power plant propelled her on her swift course and what kind of wonderful fuel did she burn, which was efficient, safe, cheap and clean? Would the general use of this fuel have made the petroleum industry obsolete? And would it have unbalanced the economy of the world? Somewhere deep in the confidential archives of World War II, the answers to these questions await the coming of another era." (1)*

Earlier in the story these authors reviewed the capture and interrogation of Captain Wermoutt, commander of U-530. One of these questions was:

> *"How had she (U-530) been able to operate so long without refueling?" (2)*

This question came about because U-530 had last refueled in Norway on March 13, 1945, and surrendered in Mar del Plata, Argentina on July 10, 1945 (3). This was a voyage of over four months' duration, during which she crossed the entire Atlantic (U-530 was off the American east coast when Hitler died) and then sailed all the way down to Argentina without refueling.

Dr. Axel Stoll provides us with the obvious answer (my translation):

> *"A whole series of U-boats from the German Reich surfaced continually in the Antarctic waters, in order to, most probably, transport men and material thereto. Among these were found, towards the end of the war, real "under water fortresses", which, without surfacing, had a range of 45,000 kilometers and were equipped with an anti-radar system. Viewed technically, they were, compared*

with Allied developments, ahead by ten years. Hydrogen served as fuel, a clean form of energy that was obviously produced from seawater. This permitted these U-boats speeds of one hundred kilometers per hour under water! Unbelievable? Hardly!" (4)

One hundred kilometers per hour is slightly over sixty-one miles per hour. Setting this claim aside for a moment, what is of most interest here is the fact that seawater was being used, according to Dr. Stoll, to manufacture hydrogen gas. Water can be broken down through electrolysis into its constituent elements, oxygen and hydrogen. Two electrodes, in this case two metal plates (such as platinum or stainless steel), are placed in a container of water and each electrode is attached to the power source. The conduction of electrical current through the water causes individual water molecules to break down into their two constituent parts, with the positively-charged hydrogen components moving toward the negatively-charged electrode and the negatively-charged oxygen componentsmoving towards the positively-charged cathode. The reaction actually works much better for seawater, in which dissolved salts serve to increase the water's conductivity as in an electrolyte (*http://en.wikipedia.org/wiki/Electrolysis_of_water*).

Between the two World Wars there was an effort in Germany to investigate forms of energy other than petroleum, which Germany in particular lacked. One of these forms was hydrogen. It was proposed that hydrogen be produced by electrolysis at German power plants at times of the day considered "off peak". This hydrogen could then be stored and transported and used by engines specially fitted to do so (5). In other words, hydrogen could be used to exchange or transport energy over distances or over time—it could be used as an energy bank.

The Germans actually had practical, working hydrogen engines before World War Two. These specially-fitted engines were designed by German engineer Rudolf Errens. They did not differ much from a standard internal combustion engine. The main modification was a gas-injection system fitted on the cylinder head, which allowed hydrogen to be injected directly into the engine when all the valves were closed. This was necessary since allowing hydrogen to mix with the incoming atmospheric gases caused backfiring and potential explosions. The hydrogen injectors could be set to enhance existing fuel combustion or be used exclusively as a hydrogen fuel. Hydrogen injection has been compared with supercharging. With hydrogen injection, engines ran cleaner and achieved better efficiency ("better milage"). These were called the "Erren Engine", or "Erren Process", or "Erren System". The Nazi government even considered wholesale conversion to the Erren System, since there was apparently no downside (6).

Naturally, the question of using both hydrogen and oxygen in their pure forms as engine fuels comes to mind. In fact, this seems to have happened:

"Two other Erren inventions, the 'oxy-hydrogen' submarine and the trackless torpedo, attracted some attention in Britain in 1942. The trackless torpedo, fueled by oxygen and hydrogen, was beguilingly simple in concept. Erren started from the realization that torpedoes leave 'tracks' of exhaust-gas bubbles. Because hydrogen and oxygen recombine into water vapor, condensing back into

the seawater, no bubbles were formed, and thus there was no giveaway trail. And the oxygen-hydrogen-burning submarine eliminated almost entirely the need for big batteries and electric motors for underwater running. Instead, during diesel-powered surface runs the sub's engine also drove an electrolyzer, generating oxygen and hydrogen, which were then stored away under pressure. When diving and running submerged, the same diesel engine burned the oxygen and hydrogen without any exhaust bubbles. " (7)

Further,

"All major engines in use at that time were modified, including those manufactured by MAN, Daimler-Benz and Beardmore." (8)

Rudolf Erren

Rudolf Erren: Modifying Engines for Hydrogen Fuel

Engineers in Germany and England first began investigating the use of hydrogen as an automotive fuel in the early 1900s, but one of the first and most influential engineers to modify the internal combustion engine to run on hydrogen was Rudolf Erren, who in the 1920s began modifying both Otto cycle and Diesel cycle engines to operate on hydrogen fuel. Erren was a combustion engineer who developed a fuel injection system that allowed the hydrogen to be fed directly into the cylinder, thereby eliminating the carburetor, which was poorly suited to inject a gaseous fuel. The remaining engine components were unchanged, thus the conversion cost was relatively small, and the vehicles were able to operate on either hydrogen or other hydrocarbon fuels while in operation with the flip of a switch from inside the vehicle. All major engines in use at the time were modified, including those manufactured by MAN, Daimler-Benz and Beardmore.

In World War II, the Allies captured a German submarine that used hydrogen to power both their Errenized "trackless" diesel engines and torpedoes. Conventional fuels leave tracks, which are a trail of exhaust bubbles, but when only hydrogen and oxygen were combusted in the engine, the resulting water vapor condensed into the seawater, thus no bubbles were formed that would drift to the surface for a giveaway trail. During surface operation, the submarine's diesel engines also powered an electrolyzer, which separated water into hydrogen and oxygen. These gases were then stored under pressure until needed when the submarine was diving or running submerged. The hydrogen-fueled submarine eliminated the need for large heavy batteries and electric motors needed for underwater operation. The weight and space savings allowed the submarines range to be extended by 15,000 miles and because the hull was strengthened, the vessel was able to dive deeper and faster.

Rudolf Erren This is from a website by Harry Braun of the Phoenix Project Foundation in Phoenix, Arizona. It states that a German U-boat employing hydrogen propulsion was captured by the Allies.

MAN was the major supplier of diesel engines for German U-boats. And yes, this is correct—Erren not only contacted the German Navy but also the British Navy between wars in an attempt to further develop his inventions. In fact, he spent the war years in

Britain. Rudolf Erren is an example of why it can be a mistake to overuse the word "Nazi" in reference to wartime Germans.

It should be mentioned that the electric generators used to recharge the U-boat's batteries were not ideal for electrolysis. Marine batteries, large and slow in their charging and discharging rates, would have had a current profile somewhat different from the optimum for electrolysis (more on this later).

According to the Phoenix Project Foundation, cited above and here:

> *"In World War II, the Allies captured a German submarine that used hydrogen to power both their Errenized 'trackless' diesel engines and torpedoes." (9)*

Could this have been the famous U-530, or was it another, as of yet undisclosed, mystery U-boat?

At this point any engineers or scientists reading this book are rolling their eyes and thinking that there is no such thing as free energy, no violation of the Second Law of Thermodynamics is possible, something cannot be gotten for nothing, and if hydrogen and oxygen are being produced on board a U-boat, it is being done at the cost of burning diesel fuel, *one makes up of the other—so what is the point?* Here is what Tesla has to say:

> *"The hydrogen liberated in the electrolytic decomposition was to be burned or recombined with oxygen, not with that from which it was separated, but with that of the atmosphere. Thus very nearly the total electrical energy used up in the decomposition of the water would be recovered in the form of heat resulting from the recombination of the hydrogen." (10)*

So almost all the energy produced by electrolysis could be recaptured by using the resulting hydrogen in conjunction with atmospheric oxygen, while running on the surface or through the snorkel underwater. But it gets better. Meanwhile, the oxygen produced could be run through the Linde machine and turned to a cold liquid gas. This is stored in its tank, a facility well suited to house an antenna for the reception and amplification of ELF waves. These could perhaps be turned into electrical energy for charging the U-boat's batteries, electrolysis of seawater, or to make more liquid oxygen via the Linde machine. A balancing act would occur. If the liquid oxygen supply was low, resources could be directed there. If hydrogen supplies were full, it could be bled into the diesel engine using the Erren System. Hydrogen and oxygen could run the U-boat while submerged or diesel and oxygen could run it submerged or diesel fuel and hydrogen plus oxygen could run it, all depending on circumstances. So, by using resources not originally brought by the U-boat: seawater, atmospheric oxygen, and perhaps ELF radiation, and by converting this energy into other forms of energy, and using matter to transport and save this energy as well as the use of change of states of matter, the U-boat is able to so smartly manage its resources that a kind of free energy effect does come to mind.

It gets even better still when we consider the type of electric generator best suited for electrolysis, the homopolar generator (HPG). The HPG is well suited to utilization for electrolysis because it is a DC generator and its electric current profile is low in voltage but high in amperage. In current profile the HPG is exactly the opposite of the Coler device, for instance, which is another DC generator that was being developed by the Kriegsmarine during the war.

A homopolar generator consists of a conductive, circular disc that is rotated between two magnets on a shaft. Due to some fluke of physics, both the center of the disc and the periphery have different electrical potentials. This means that if a brush or electric pick-up is mounted at the very center of the disc and another brush, literally brushing the outside of the conductive wheel as it turns, and electric current will be generated. The "fluke" part comes from the fact that standard theories of induction by Maxwell do not account for the electrical generation caused here. New ideas had to be developed. The homopolar generator was invented in 1831 by Michael Faraday and due to this "fluke," the homopolar generator was termed the Faraday Paradox for many years (*http://en.wikipedia.org/wiki/Homopolar_generator*).

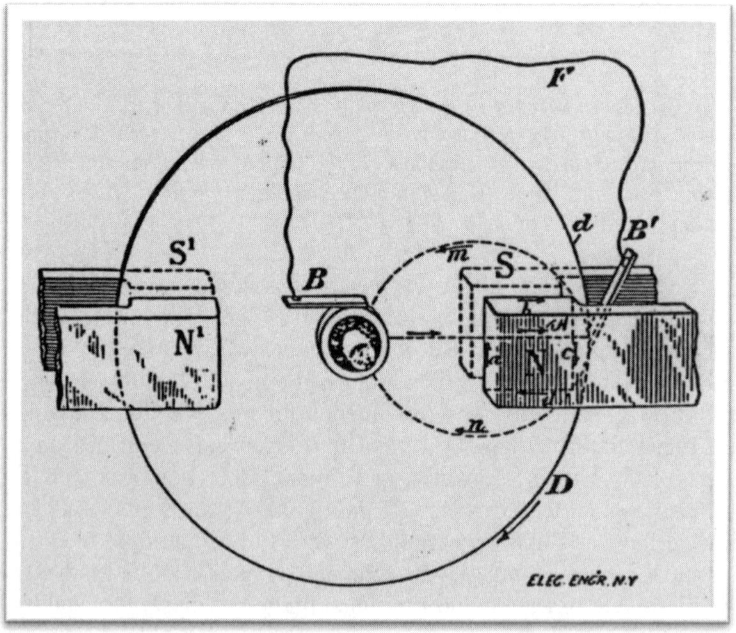

Homopolar Generator Basics. When a conducting disc is rotated within a magnetic field, there is a potential differenc between the points at the center of the disc and points along its periphery. Here, four magnets are situated as shown on bot sides of a conducting disc with brushes *B* at its center *B'* at the periphery. The direction of rotation is shown by *D*. If a loac such as a small lamp, is placed on the circuit represented by wire *F*, then an electric current will flow from *B* to *B'* along *F*, an the lamp will light up. There are three basic variables which influence the output of a homopolar generator in direct proportio the radius of the disc, the speed of its rotation, and the strength of the magnetic field (here supplied by the four stationar magnets). Increasing any one of these variables, then, results in a proportional increase in the generator's electrical output.

The output of the HPG is increased if the radius of the wheel is increased, and if the magnetic field of the HPG is increased, and if the speed of rotation is increased. Inversely, if the wheel is decreased, if the magnetic field is lessened and if the speed is decreased, the output will suffer. In addition, some conductive materials turn out to be better than others, especially for given parts of the machine. Also, back torque, the bane of all electrical generators, can be reduced in a HPG by using various materials for the brushes and smart types of off-loading the electric current generated.

But the HPG is a very efficient device in taking mechanical energy (the turning force which must be applied to the wheel) and turning it into electrical energy. Figures of 90% efficiency are common. For this reason, it is the darling of free energy researchers. Whole papers, books and conferences are devoted to making this device 100% efficient or better, making this an over-unity device in which it generates more electrical energy than it needs for its own rotation (11). This means that a homopolar motor can be spun using electrical current and it can be used to spin a HPG. All that is necessary is an output from the HPG of greater than 100%. Claims are periodically made and discredited so this is an ongoing, intense study among physicists and electrical engineers.

Back to U-boats, suppose a HPG could be mounted directly into the diesel drive train, like a flywheel on an automobile? Now suppose current being drawn off only at odd moments such as between gears when the diesel engines are wasting fuel, idling? This is the same concept as the hybrid automobile engine. Hydrogen and oxygen could be generated during these times with much smaller negative consequences for diesel fuel supply. Back torque would only be present during actual electrical generation so the remainder of the time the unit would just spin as does the flywheel of a car.

Now imagine a HPG with almost no back torque at all. It might be employed almost constantly at any engine operating condition other than full load without much in terms of consequences. In fact the current generated could be modified for use in the U-boat itself and to charge the batteries. If this were possible, then only one generator need be used on the U-boat, a very efficient one by all accounts. A HPG with no back torque was evidently claimed by Professor P. Boehning at the University of Breslau in 1942 as was discussed in an earlier chapter, with the result being the output drove the generator. (12) And without this or very similar technology, someone still must explain how the Searl disc auto-rotated.

The point is that through the use of the HPG, excluding any wild and crazy discussion of over-unity, another dimension is added to our already very efficient U-boat in addition to those already mentioned. But in the next chapter we will take on these very "wild and crazy" ideas and discover that they are not too crazy after all.

Literature Cited

1. **Buechner, Howard A., Col., and Wilhelm Bernhard, 1989**, *Hitler's Ashes*, page 228, Thunderbird Press, Inc., Metairie, LA., USA
2. **Buechner, Howard A., Col., and Wilhelm Bernhard, 1989**, page 221
3. *ibid.*
4. **Stoll, Axel, Ph.D., 2001**, *Hochtechnologie im Dritten Reich Reichdeutsche Entwicklungen und die vermutlich wahre Herkunft der "UFOs,"* page 122, Amun-Verlag, Schleusingen, Germany
5. **Hoffman, Peter, 2002**, *Tomorrow's Energy: Hydrogen, Fuel Cells, and Prospects for a Cleaner Planet*, page 34, 35, The MIT Press, Cambridge, MA, USA
6. ibid.
7. ibid.

8 **Braum, Harry, date unknown**, John Lorenzen & Rudolf Erren: *Energy Pioneers* (H2 Exhibiton Project), page 2, (www.phoenixprojectfoundation.us/.../John_Lorenzen__Rudolf_Erren.pdf) Phoenix Project Foundation Phoenix, AZ. USA

9. ibid.
10. **Tesla, Nikola, edited by David Hatcher Childress, 2000**, *The Tesla Papers Nikola Tesla on Free Energy wireless Transmission of Power*, page 43, Adventures Unlimited Publishing, Kempton, Illinois, USA
11. **Valone, Thomas, M.A., P.E. (now Ph.D.), 1994**, *The Homopolar Handbook A Definitive Guide to Faraday Disk and N-Machine Technologies*, Integrity Research Institute, Washington, D.C., USA
12. **Nieper, Hans a., Ph.D., 1985**, *Conversion of Gravity Field Energy/Revolution in Technology, Medicin and Society*, page 157, M.I.T., Management Interessengemeinschaft fuer Tachyonen-Feld-Energie GmbH, Oldenburg, Germany

TESLA'S SELF-ACTING ENGINE, TWO?

Again, the legend from Michael X. Barton writing as "Michael X." talking to his European informant:

> *" 'Yes,' my friend replied,' it is known that the Nazis have a Free-Energy motor, and used it in 1958 to propel a U-boat between Europe and Buenos Aires. It is also believed by many of us that there is an underwater station — built by the Nazis — somewhere in the Atlantic Ocean between Germany and Argentina. A stopover place, no doubt, for the Nazi subs and UFO's." (1)*

With Fuerteventura, the second half of this statement has proven itself true. All we have to do is find the first half.

In this chapter we are going to focus on the idea of the homopolar generator as a source of electricity for a U-boat, all on its own. William Lyne gave us this idea in his writings as a result of his own experimentation and conversations with the man called Mr. Dort. Dort has already been mentioned in the discussion of Tesla's oscillator in combination with the Linde machine. Dort seems to have known important details of this engine that were based on this father's invention, an invention he claimed was used in German U-boats.

Bill Lyne says that Tesla discovered a special generator which is still a complete secret and which is locked up "in the Los Alamos vault". It was made of three metals, copper, aluminum, and iron together with weak magnets. Mr. Dort chimes in saying aluminum was the best reflector, copper the most active (conductor) and iron the magnetic core material. Overall, the device most resembled a homopolar generator. Bill Lyne recognizes the resemblance of the homopolar generator to the common household electric meter, the old one with the moving metal wheel. With all these things in his mind, Bill got two such meters and did a little experimentation on an apartment house he owned:

> *"In 1979, I took two old 115-volt Tesla electric meters—-which ware at least 70 years old—-and connected them together in a 'peculiar way', attempting at first*

to measure two separate 115-volt currents coming into an apartment. There are four unlabelled posts on each (of) these old meters, so I didn't know how to connect them, so I just took a shot in the dark. Due to the manner in which I connected them—-which was apparently wrong—-the two meters behaved strangely. At a low current drain, the disks rotated faster than when the current was greater. At a sufficiently high current, the disks stopped, hummed loudly—-which I refer to as "snoring"——and even reversed, at a still greater energy consumption in the apartment. As the current usage went up and down, there was commensurate change in the "snoring" and disk directions in the two meters.

By actually using more electricity in the apartment, less usage was recorded by the meters, as well as the main meter, for my entire complex, and the electric bill for my whole complex dropped by about one-third. The meters were generating power, perhaps enough to power the entire apartment. Sometimes, when the disks were running in reverse, the meters were generating more power than that being used, and when they were running slowly in the opposite direction, the meters were generating less, but overall, the one-third drop in the bill indicated they were running that apartment, one-third of my complex.

Mr. Dort—-the Virginia man whose father invented the special generators stolen by the Nazis and used on their "Electro-U-boats"—-said that, when the 'snoring' was at its peak and the disk stationary, that the meter was at the "center of load", which meant that the amount of current being used was equal to that being generated by the meters! When the disks reversed, the 'meters' were generating more current than than that being used, and were putting electricity back into the grid! After I removed the old meters from the circuits, my bill increased by one-third." (2)

How could it be possible for two electric meters, even given they were homopolar motors, to stop while in operation and even reverse direction and generate electricity on their own? Well, first an electric motor can usually be made to generate electricity by overrunning it. By this I mean spinning it faster that it is designed to operate, using outside mechanical force. And what is all this "wrong" connection talk? When I hook up something electrical and it is "wrong", it either does not work at all or it blows up. I think Bill is being a little modest here because he certainly has seen the Tesla design for a homopolar generator and read the astonishing commentary Tesla provides on the matter.

In 1889 Tesla was granted a patent on a homopolar generator, Patent number 406,968. The invention is referred to as a "unipolar" generator, another name for the homopolar generator. Tesla's unique contributions appear to be two in number. First, he combines two homopolar generators into one unit in a unique way:

"I prefer to construct the machine in such as manner that the direction of magnetism or order of the poles in one field of forces is opposite to that in the other, so that rotation of the disks in the same direction develops a current in one from center to circumference and in the other from circumference to center." (3)

In this way, current produced by the first generator is fed into the second, amplifying the electrical output "for free", or without any additional input required. This, or something much like this, is what Bill Lyne did with his four terminals and wiring.

Second, Tesla used a metal belt, which ran along the outside of both disks and served as a brush in connecting them electrically to one another. In this way, current can be drawn uniformly from the rotating disk rather rather than from a single spot, reducing the brush's contribution to the system's back-torque.

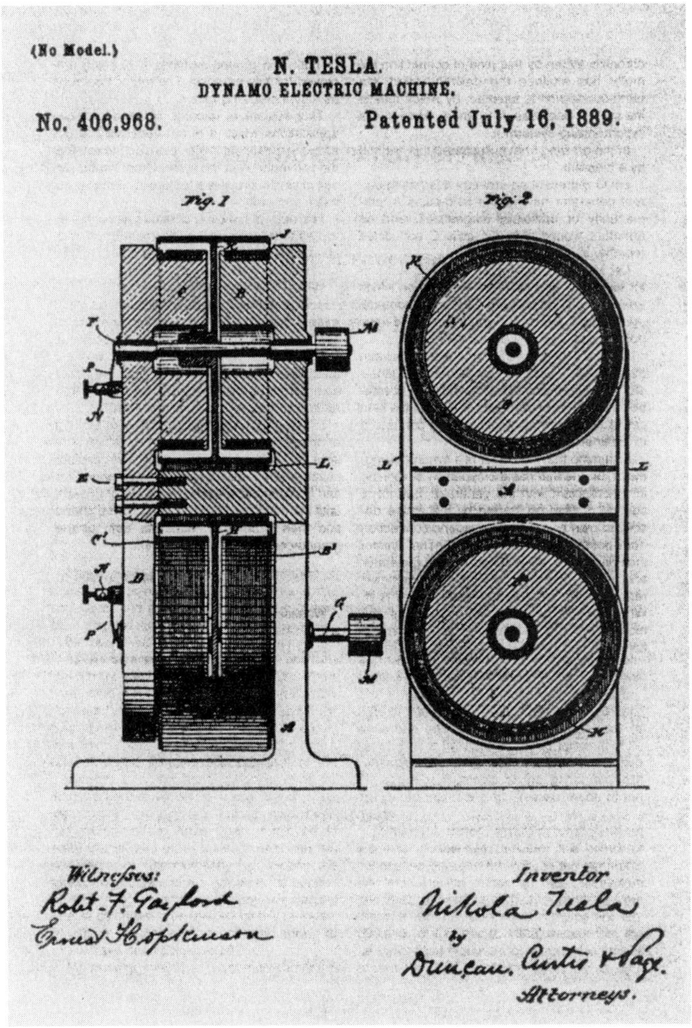

Tesla's Homopolar Generator. This is Tesla's U.S. Patent Number 406,968. In this design, two homopolar generators are combined so that a belt can run between them. The belt functions as the outer brush for picking up electricity. The brush provides a greater contact surface for the flow of current, minimizing the production of eddy currents and the back-torque they induce.

But it is really not his patent that is so exciting, rather his discussion of the homopolar generator in the September 2, 1891 edition of a journal, *The Electrical Engineer* (4). This is because Tesla discusses eddy currents and back torque in an entirely new way. Eddy currents can be used, according to Tesla, to increase or decrease the strength of the field magnets though that the disc is rotating. In his diagram of a homopolar (unipolar) generator, he makes the point that the area of the conductive disc inside or under the magnets, that is, through which the disc is being rotated, is the most active for electrical generation. Tesla says that the current will flow from the center (one pole) to the periphery (other pole) in this area as this is the shortest distance of this electrically active area. Two pathways are possible which Tesla marks "m" and "n". Given the direction of rotation of the disc, "D" (clockwise), eddy currents in pathway "m" would weaken the magnetic field strength of the energizing magnets, while if the pathway "n" is chosen, these eddy currents would reinforce the field strength of those magnets and actually adding to them. This was Tesla's breakthrough! Eddy currents, once thought of as only counterproductive, could be used to strengthen the magnetic field. Since the strength of the magnetic field is one of the variables influencing a homopolar generator, with increasing strength resulting in increasing electrical output, the energizing of the machine though positive application of eddy currents increases the electrical output.

> *"...the figure shows that one of the two branches of the eddy current, that is , A B'n B,will tend to demagnetize the field, while the other branch, that is A B' m B, will have the opposite effect. Therefore, the branch A B' m B, that is, the one which is approaching the field, will repel the lines of the same, while branch A B'n B, this is, the one leaving the field, will gather the lines of force upon itself."*

Tesla suggests a couple ways to use this idea. First, he suggests using two pairs of weak magnets positioned on the periphery of the disc, opposite poles alternately facing each other, upon which Tesla winds a coil of wire. Electrical current would be taken right off the surface of the rotating disc. As the disc started and increased output, the coils would energize and strengthen the weak magnets. It would seem this could continue as the speed of rotation increased up to a high level of magnetic field strength.

Since the now electromagnets are opposite in relation to each other, they serve to drive the disc between them and forward just as two strong electric wires whose currents are going in opposite directions, propel a conducting projectile down their length in a rail gun. More on this in a couple paragraphs.

Second, Tesla suggests segmenting the conductive disc in spiral segments. In his diagram he again shows how such a system could either retard or drive the disc in a given direction depending upon which way the current comes off, just as he does in the earlier explanation. If the disc is segmented to that the least path of resistance are the solid lines, in other words engineered as a segmented spiral, so that current flows along the solid lines, the field strength ought to be increased. If current is allowed to flow on the dotted lines, back torque and a weakening of the field would occur.

So Tesla talks about these eddy currents strengthening the field magnets and so increasing output as well as exciting the machine or eddy currents demagnetizing the field magnets if traveling in the wrong direction, and slowing it down. But there is more:

> *"To return to the principal subject: assume the conditions to be such that the eddy currents generated by the rotation of the disk strengthen the field, and suppose the latter gradually removed while the disk is kept rotating at an increased rate. The current, once started, may then be sufficient to maintain itself and even increase in strength, and then we have the case of Sir William Thomson's 'current accumulator."(4)*

This means if the eddy currents could be arranged most advantageously, they, the eddy currents alone, might serve as the field magnets if they were removed gradually. The field magnets are replaced with eddy currents that are generating their own magnetic field.

There is another thing. Remember that back torque caused by (negative) eddy currents physically retards the rotation of the disc. Well, Tesla discusses increasing the field strength of the magnets involved using his positive positioning of eddy currents but does it also have an effect on rotation itself? If so, would not this be especially true for Tesla's system of increasing the field strength of weak magnets using a coil of wire, an electromagnet? As mentioned before, flowing electrical energy has a magnetic field that endlessly spirals outward. If you grabbed an electric wire, for instance, with your right hand so that your fingers curled upward and your thumb ran along the wire, the spin of the magnetic field would be in the same direction as your fingers were pointing. Current flowing the other way has the opposite field spin. This spin is what pushes against the metal conducting material of the disc, either in the direction of the rotation or against it, depending on the direction of rotation and the direction the current is flowing as it is being taken off the disc. Since the now electromagnets are opposite in relation to each other, they serve to drive the disc between them and forward just as two strong electric wires whose currents are going in opposite directions, propel a conducting projectile down their length in a rail gun.

This use of eddy current to positively spin the conducting disc is my interpretation, for whatever it is worth, but at least Tesla had apparently solved the back-torque issues within the disc itself. This only leaves back-torque issues of the brushes and perhaps current exiting the brushes. These are smaller issues.

Assuming all other back torque problems concerning brushes were solved, this machine would be making more energy than was required to operate it. All that is required at this point is enough energy to mechanically spin the machine. The way proposed to do this was by use of a homopolar motor. Electrical output from the homopolar generator is fed into the axis of the homopolar motor and the flowing current to its periphery spins the motor whose central shaft is attached directly to the homopolar generator (5).

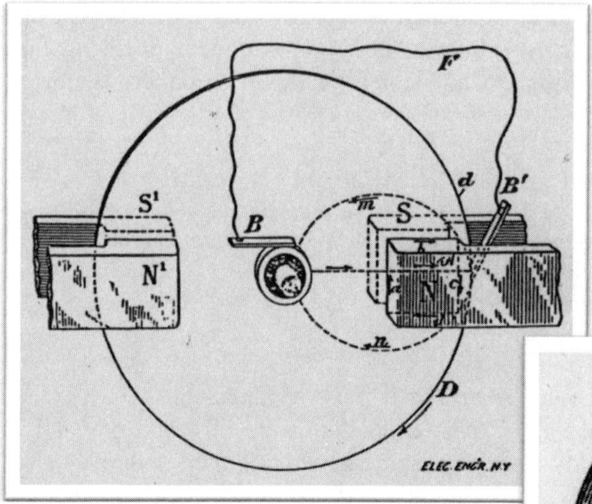

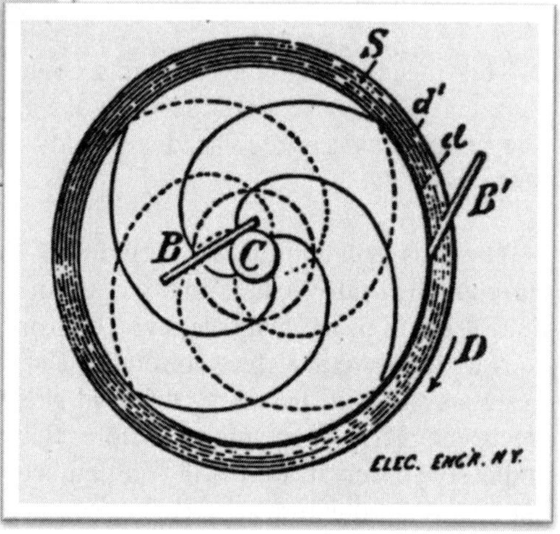

Homopolar Generator: Harnessing Eddy Currents. Note that electrical flow flow from B to B' can occur at m or n. Given the rotation of the disc D, the pathway m and resulting eddy current would diminishe the field strength of the magnets, while pathway n would actually increase the magnetic field strength and boost the electrical output. Also, along pathway m the eddy current would produce a back-torque, hampering the rotation of the disc. Pathways influencing electrical output can also be controlled by segmenting the conducting surface of the disc with non-conductive barriers, either blocking or re-routing electrical flow along them.

We are talking about something so efficient that it is approaching a free energy engine. And from its description, it could be called a "self-acting" engine. Unfortunately, Tesla had to discontinue work on this project so these ideas were never fully realized "for want of time" (4). Tesla's thoughts on this subject were in the public domain and certainly could have been further developed by anyone, including Professor Paul Boehning at the University of Breslau in 1942 as reported by Dr. Hans Nieper at his conference in Germany and in his book, cited in the last chapter. This idea could have been passed along to Dr. Bruce DePalma but apparently were lost at least at this point as far as the public understanding is concerned. A further development by Professor Boehning in 1942 along the lines discussed by Tesla would be applicable to some of the unsolved mysteries we have encountered, such as how the Searl disc managed to auto-rotate without back torque and that, as we know, is also a lost secret.

Saying a device is a free-energy device or that it is auto-rotating or that it is self-inducting is really a case of describing the same thing using different words. The Schauberger device as well as the Searl disc were said to possess these properties, but is there anything less legendary, that exists in our tangible world today, which we can point to as an example of these ideas? In other words, is there an example that would indicate that such a feat as Tesla describes is a real possibility?

Remember the three variables involved in a homopolar generator, the radius of the disc, the speed of rotation and the strength of the magnetic field? Well, there are some modifications to these ideas. As Tesla says:

> *"For a certain speed there would be a maximum energizing action; then at higher speeds, it would gradually fall off to zero and finally reverse, that is, the resultant eddy current effect would be to weaken the field. The reaction would be best demonstrated experimentally by arranging the fields N S, N' S', freely movable on an axis concentric with the shaft of the disc. If the latter were rotated as before in the direction of the arrow D, the field would be dragged in the same direction with a torque, which, up to a certain point, would go on increasing with the speed of rotation, the fall off, and, passing through zero, finally become negative; that is, the field would begin to rotate in the opposite direction to the disc." (4)*

There is an optimum speed for energy production. Production can be increased only to a point at which it starts falling away to nothing (as rotational speed continues to increase) and then reverses itself. This is because the magnetic field is being drug around in a circle by the disc. Some people say that at the poles of a magnet there exists a vortex. Well, it appears that if you spin a magnetic field a vortex certainly results. This vortex has seems to have an inertia. At high speeds the "old" magnetic field cannot keep up with the "new" position of the magnetic field. This means two magnetic fields or two overlapping positions of one magnetic field (however one wants to look at it) are interacting. When two magnetic fields interact, electrical induction takes place. In this case it is hindering electrical output much like the eddy current going the wrong way.

This sounds very much like what happens to our earth. Earth's magnetism has always been somewhat of a mystery as our molten iron-nickel core is conductive but not magnetized in the sense of a bar magnet. But its magnetic field waxes and wanes and finally reverses itself after eons just as a homopolar generator would do if its rotational speed were too fast. A disc is really just a slice of a sphere, so could earth's magnetic field be somehow connected to self-sustaining homopolar technology? Here is what Dr. Thomas Valone has to say (note: Dr. Valone uses the abbreviation OPFG meaning one piece Faraday generator, a type of homopolar generator.)

The Earth's Faraday Disk Dynamo

Self-Sustaining vs. Self-Exciting

One of the major reasons for interest in the OPFG is that the earth its self functions internally as a large OPFG. Moreover, the earth's OPFG is self-sustaining. "The critical question is how the core liquid flows to act as a dynamo. Also a self-sustaining dynamo does not require a constant supply of magnetic field, it does require a constant supply of mechanical energy to keep the conductive material moving. In the case of the earth's core this means not only that the metallic fluid must flow in the right manner but also that some energy source must sustain he flow." (here Carrigan and Gubbins, "The Source of Earth's Magnetic Field", Scientific American, Feb. 1979, page 118, is cited). Helical convection patterns called "rollers" created from conducting liquid metal are the best explanation of the mysterious secret of the earth's self-sustaining OPFG (SSOPFG)

In regards to the back torque of the earth's SSPPFG, Busse, Roberts, Lowes, and Wilkinson of the University of Newcastle upon Tyne are working on mechanical models of the earth's core to explain the changes in the fluid's speed and direction when the magnetic forces are large. A slightly different model that is being tested as well is the self-exciting OPFG (SEOPFG) that requires a spirally segmented disk and /or external current carrying coils as Tesla suggested. Since he noted that the armature current tends to demagnetize the field in a normal solid disk configuration, Tesla felt that the subdivision of the disk would be an enhancement. ....

A laboratory SEOPFG has been built by the Lowes and Wilkinson team (here Hindmarch, Lowes, Roberts and Runcorn, Magnetism and the Csomos, American Elsecier Pub. Co., 1965 is cited). Using metal rollers to simulate the earth's cylindrical eddy currents, the team found some interesting results after beginning with a few viscosity problems. "...more efficient geometry was found, so efficient that the dynamo would self-excite in a completely homogeneous state (i.e. with no insulation) at a much lower rotor speed than was believed possible." (here Carrigan and Gubbins are cited again.) Upon achieving this breakthrough, their next goal is to look into the stability of he dynamo mechanism, hoping to observe reversals of its magnetic field.

So here we are back to square one, looking for and finding a planetary model, as the Germans envisioned a field propulsion flying disc, or a model of energy generation reflecting the reality of heavenly bodies as envisioned by Dr. Paul Potter.

But we still have a couple mysteries to tie up. If a type of homopolar generator was used to produce electricity in a German U-boat, virtually nothing else would be necessary. This generator would tie into the U-boats electric drive and it could be used all by itself, without any diesel engine. All that would be needed would be a small battery for starting. But was this really the new electric submarine engine that the US Navy was secretly installing, using the sign on the door "Danger Radiation" as an ultimate cover of secrecy? This is what I heard in the early 1990's being mentioned on the Chuck Harder radio program which was syndicated all across rural America (but barred in urban areas—another story) at the time? Bill Lyne told me in private correspondence in 1999 that German submarines still held speed and "distance" records over our submarines. He also said that while he was in the military, he was told by a co-worker (circa 1957) that the US Navy was taking a second look at some kind of German highly efficient electric drive for submarines. In fact, the US Navy has taken patent applications from individual regarding new brushes for homopolar generators and/or told researchers they were to cease and desist even discussing details of such inventions, deemed essential for national security. Valone mentions three instances of such Navy restrictions in his book. (6) It is the US Navy that has this fanatic interest in homopolar generators. Why, for submarine propulsion? It will be left for the reader to reason why.

One more point regarding the US Navy but outside homopolar generators. William Lyne reminds us of the Howard Hughes Glomar Explorer and its sister ship the Glomar Challenger. These were built for the CIA and, as we all know now, used to hook onto and recover sunken Soviet submarines. Bill says they also had another purpose: to recover this German electric generator from scuttled U-boats:

> *"The Glomar Explorer, designed and built by Howard Hughes, was just another 'fishing tool'. The purpose, however, was to retrieve military and energy secrets, such as the magnetic generators powering the underwater travel of he W.W.II Nazi U-boats. Such technology was within the reach of free-lance salvers. Once these secrets hit he public domain, the oil companies and Hughes Tool Company, as we know them, may become things of the past." (7)*

One more thing: The reader will remember our mystery scientist, "Dr. Hans Ehrhardt/Engelke", a Nazi scientist working, circa 1961-1963, for the Swiss and described in an earlier chapter? He was the guy who described the exact workings of the Zippermayr fuel-air bomb and recounted an actual use of the weapon even though it was kept secret and suppressed by the United States until the late 1990's. He was the guy who described the inner workings of a laser, even before the word "laser" was coined, even describing bundling of light waves and producing a working example which melted snow miles away. Well, at that time the Swiss were also pressuring Ehrhardt/Engelke into renouncing a paper he had published titled "The New Path" where he described his idea for perpetual motion. This could have been nothing short of the Boehning homopolar motor-generator. The other mystery is what happened to Ehrhardt/Engelke when he and his family disappeared from Switzerland. It ought to be obvious by now that he got a better offer from the Third Power and so everything written by the US government with the assistance of the Swiss government using *Der Spiegel* as a vehicle, all this was just an attempt by these entities to try not look as stupid as they really were.

This chapter was the major hump, just a little more on the homopolar generator in the next chapter, but I promise it will be worth it.

In the next illustration (Figure 7), we see a suggestion for giving the disk an additional push from the generated currents by leading them through conductors that pass into coils. Here, the coils then encounter a reverse polarity magnetic field which tends to give the coils a small amount of push. This effect may not work at all but tends to lead the reader into thinking about curving the generated currents to an advantage.

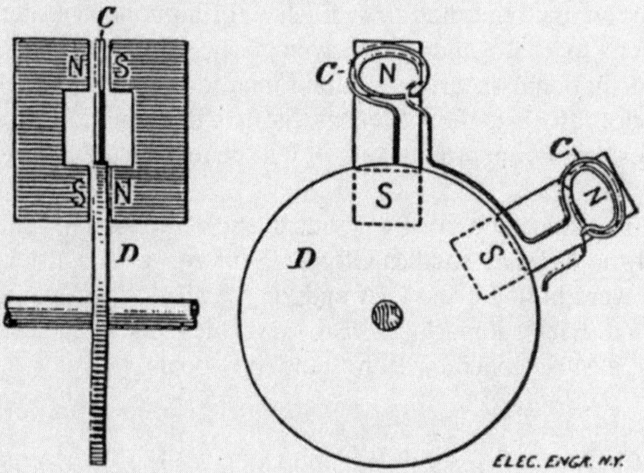

Figure 7. Possible enhancement to give discs an additional "push."

Homopolar Generator: Current Accumulator & Self-Acting Machine? This is from page 86 of the *Homopolar Handbook*, by Thomas Valone, M.A., P.E., now Ph.D. The caption explains how the disc itself increases the magnetic field strengths through the use of a small coil. The configuration may tend to push the disc between them, as a rail gun pushes a projectile.

Literature Cited

1. **X., Michael (Michael X. Barton), 1960**, *We Want You: Is Hitler Alive?,* page 36, Saucerian Books, Clarksville, WV., USA
2. **Lyne, William R., 1999**, *Space Aliens from the Pentagon* (3rd Edition), pages 283 and 284, Creatopia Productions, Lamy, NM., USA
3. **Tesla, Nikola, 2000**, *Nikola Tesla collected German And American Patents*, pages 292-294, MVV Peiting, Peiting, Germany
4. **Valone, Thomas, M.A., P.E. (now Ph.D.), 1994**, *The Homopolar Handbook A definitive Guide to Faraday Disk and N-Machine Technologies*, pages 171-172 (Dr. Valone reproduces the whole Electrical Engineer article by Tesla), Integrity Research Institute, Washington, D.C., USA
5. **Valone, Thomas, M.A., P.E. (now Ph.D.), 1994**, page 93
6. **Valone, Thomas, M.A., P.E. (now Ph.D., 1994**, pages iv, 71 and 145
7. **Lyne, William, R., 1993**, *Space Aliens from the Pentagon*, page 175, Creatopia Productions, Inc., Lamy, NM. USA

PART THREE: ZUSAMMENFASSUNG

PUTTING IT ALL TOGETHER

The reader may recall mention being made of an article in *Mench und Schichsal* magazine by Claude Schweikhart from 1952, almost sixty years ago, talking about the Emrich - Team, the first investigative body ever to look into the esoteric Reich and the "Third Power", and their mention of a "Laboratory of Death" in Greenland, probably at Beaver Dam, and another statement concerning flying U-boats? Translating, the passage reads:

> *"Interestingly enough the Emerich - Team recorded in such documents, obviously working together with the Third Power-hunting Yugoslavian radio news service, the existence of a "Laboratory of Death" somewhere in Greenland which was designated a city of technical satanism and in 1951 is to have tested a flying undersea boat." (1)*

This comes from a long time ago and from something less than a scientific journal. It is "something", whatever it is, but it is not conclusive on its own. Probably because of the way the UFO discussion was framed at the time, the whole idea of the Third Reich having a hand in UFO/USO matters was completely forgotten. It was just not fashionable to look in this direction at the time. The modern era of inquiry into the high technology of Nazi Germany only began in the middle to late 1980's and then only hesitatingly. One of those first to do so was writer O. Bergmann who published two short books propounding the idea that later German flying discs were field propulsion powered and that there is absolutely no difference between a flying saucer and a flying U-boat at this point, they are exactly one and the same, and that these devices made their first appearance at the very end of the Second World War.

Bergmann bolstered his argument with the now familiar "Vril" and "Haunebu" diagrams, in fact he was the first to publish them, and with testimony from all over the world, covering decades, of mystery submersibles and of UFO's entering and leaving the water. Again, a passage from the first of Bergmann's books bears repeating:

> *"At sometime and someplace, at secret U-boat bases outside the German motherland, U-boats of the German Navy must have been weighed out, and,*

during the great withdrawal in April/May 1945, missing U-boats must have been equipped with new revolutionary technology and also must have been converted with electromagnetic propulsion. With this, those (U-boats) may, (have been) arranged with the same possibilities and technologies as the German flying discs (called UFOs). (2)

Bergmann goes on and on making this point. As an example, another passage:

"UFOs or USOs are certainly not only observed within the seas and oceans and rivers, on the contrary also occasionally diving and surfacing on inland lakes, yes, even in ponds. We need not bother ourselves any more concerning the confusion on differing reports, if it is to be called only UFO, USO or still U-boat because (John) Keel had it completely correct, with the same electromagnetic propulsion it can be what it wants to be, the initial water craft would be able to operate in the air, as other flying craft, as well as the water. The two mediums, air and water, are interchangeable if one is fitted with this phenomenal propulsion, concerning which we have already more closely read in Hugin-Schrift: 'Geheime Wunderwaffen' Bd. III. They could maneuver mutually well in the air or water." (3)

The reference cited by Bergmann is the only older such modern reference, coming from D.H. Haarmann, 1983-1985.

So what do we have here? We have a revolutionary electromagnetic engine that was available to the Germans at the very end of the war. To more fully explain this, we must go right back into homopolar generators, this time to the work of Dr. Bruce DePalma (1935-1997).

Dr. Bruce DePalma was educated at M.I.T. and Harvard. DePalma made a breakthrough in the world of homopolar generators (HPG) by inventing a one-piece HPG that he named the "N machine". DePalm combined the field magnets and the conducting disc into one. The disc contained the magnets and both spun as the original disc of the HPG. In fact, the disc can be a magnet. So all that is visible is a flywheel-like device, spinning on its shaft, with two brushes forming the electrical circuit and the electric motor supplying power to the spinning shaft. In fact, the N machine used a homopolar motor but in the motor, the magnets were not mounted on the wheel.

With his N machine, Dr. DePalma made claims of over-unity or near over-unity, off and on again, all the while making improvements in the design. The point here is not to delve into the ins and outs of HPGs but instead to focus on the origin of DePalma's idea, for DePalma claims that the inspiration for the one-piece HPG came to him from an extraterrestrial source, which is called the "Sunburst Material" in the literature. This material seems to have influenced DePalma greatly and thereafter built his one-piece HPG. The Sunburst Material and its proponents lace their discussion with New Age and religious connotations, if not outright language. In this passage, an earthman is taken aboard and alien ship and given a tour, including the powerplant. It is as follows (4):

"During the course of this conversation we had been descending in an elevator, finally arriving at the level which contained the ship's propulsion drive units. This level was gigantic and spanned the entire diameter of the ship's hull. Standing on a walk-way, we looked down on the drive systems which filled the whole immense area."

At this point an alien apparently, (allegedly) speaks:

"My Son, the propulsion system which drives our mother Mu is patterned after the perfect design of The Great Central SuN-SoN. The application of vortexes by Devine Spirit on its infinite body of life force, as you know, generated the first ignition of Light. The visible expanding sphere of cession and all forces and images existing in it were projected outward from the center of The Great Central SuN-Son. A spinning, centripetal vortex projected into Spirit's infinite body of life-energy, producing a whirlpool. This thought-produced whirlpool began drawing Spirit's life-energy particles towards its center. Spirit's life-energy particles moving towards this center created directional lines of force for the pulling effects of magnetic attraction to operate on. This created a perpetual flow of life-energy particles into the vortex from the Eternal Sea of Life Energy. This accumulation of masses of life energy particles at this center of vortex, under tremendous pressure and friction, produced light and images. The masses of life energy particles were now shaped by Devine Consciousness into the images and forces Spirit wanted to see."

Minus New Age and religious imagery, substituting ether for "life-energy", we find the underlying Black Sun concept from the days of the 3rd Reich. This imagery is discarded for the next paragraphs, which reminds me of Dr. Paul Potter:

"The propulsion unit on this ship operates upon the same devine principles. To create a vortex that would operate in this physical dimension in a similar manner, we must spin a physical object, which is, or which can be, magnetized. Spinning a magnetized object, we would create a vortex that would induce the energy in space to move towards its center. As the energy particles in space are drawn into the vortex by magnetic attraction, they would take orbital positioning around the center of the magnetic core. The accumulation of energy particles around the spinning magnetic center would generate a high-density magnetic field. With this condition we can create two poles, one at the center of the magnetic core, and one on the perimeter of the magnetic field. Here we can perpetually draw off energy in the form of positive and negative electrical currents. This the principle on which our propulsion units operate.

The outside perimeter of each disc carries twelve magnets. The simultaneous clockwise and counterclockwise rotation of these two discs creates two spinning magnetic fields. Here we can draw off electrical current from the central hubs on which the spin and the rapidly rotating outside perimeter. The generation of a perpetual flow of electrical energy from each disc will continue as long as the discs rotate. The space between the two discs is the area in which both spinning vortexes contact each other.. It is here that the two spinning magnetic fields create a gyroscopic effect on each other. The magnetic fields generated by the two discs are so intense that any other gravitational or magnetic lines of force are bent around this force field. Therefore, the object that contains the generators of this magnetic and gyroscopic effect creates its own gravity. The object, or in this case, the spaceship, generates its own force field which becomes so intense that the ship's hull exists in an anti-gravity space all its own."

Yes, it is similar to Dr. Paul Potter's work but Dr. Potter would have gone on to explain the underlying physics, the positive electrical forces that are positrons while the negative electrical forces are electrons. They are both generated by magnetic lines of force connecting and being torn apart by the rotating discs, only to reconnect and disconnect, endlessly. Positrons are anti-matter. These positrons are of such attractive-repulsive magnitude that the Biefield-Brown Effect (5) looks like a shadow in comparison and they can be made to collect on one side of these rotating discs while their opposite charge, the electrons, collect on the other side. The "spaceship" falls into the positive side, or rather, is driven which a huge force. And, do I have to say it, the Wewelsburg Black Sun symbol as an abstraction of the "twelve magnets", spirally segmented in the manner suggested by Tesla?

We pick up our "alien" narrator, mid-paragraph:

"Sometime in the future you could construct one half of the ship's drive systems and have an unlimited supply of electrical energy. This system would require no out-side sources of energy to run it, such as fossil fuels or atomic power. That generator would be self-perpetuating as it would produce more energy than it would take to run it! You would, therefore, have an unlimited supply of totally free energy."

So one disc is the energy generator, two disc equal the field propulsion unit. And the way this is worded, it does not sound like the two-disc version is free energy, which was reserved for the one-disc version. I say this because there would be an energy cost to magnetic reconnection concept. Dr. Thomas Valone did run some tests in which two homopolar generators were run facing one another. (6) He found there was an increase of electric current production when they were run "together" but a 40% drop when they were run opposing each other. It is not stated in this study if these were like or opposing poles which were being run together nor was this test to measure positrons nor was it done to test field propulsion. This test was only designed to measure electrical output. We might deduce, however, that the running of opposed rotating magnets in the manner of the Sunburst machine would expend energy, not produce it.

The other deduction which can be made is that, now, we know precisely why the U.S. Navy and the Department Of Defense so heavily monitors and appropriates advances in homopolar generator research. They use it themselves and perhaps on a submarine and simply do not want the remainder of humanity to have such an advance. This also explains the Bergmann hypothesis that any field propulsion saucer can also be a submarine. Unfortunately, this seems to apply only to the saucer-shape, necessary for power production and not the typical submarine shape. Maybe we can figure out other shapes later.

One more thing needs to be said about the Sunburst Material that some readers have already picked up on. That is its resemblance to the theory for field propulsion put forth by the Vril Society. For the best explanation of the device allegedly used by the Vril Society, we go directly to the most authoritative source, Norbert Juergen-Ratthofer and Ralf Ettl in their book on the subject, Das Vril Projekt. In that work the "Jenseitsmachine" or "Jenseitsflugmachine" is described. This word "Jenseits" means, " beyond"; "across", or "on the other side". I don't think I am too far off in translating it "Interdimension" in this particular instance. With that caveat, the translation is as follows:

> *"In the year 1922 the Project "Jenseitsmachine" (Interdimenstional machine) was begun and now designated as the "Jenseitsmachine". In the summer of this year a barn was built in a small region in the vicinity of Munich. A portion of these grounds were dug up, cracks in the plank-walls caulked. An additional shed was built. In this shed there soon collected itself all possible strange, technical, single parts...the "Jenseitsflugmacine" was set into production.*
>
> *It consisted of a disc of eight meters in diameter, over which a parallel lying disc of 6.5 meters in diameter was situated, and there under a further disc of seven meters in diameter. These three discs were set in the middle of a 1.8-meter diameter hole, in which, the 2.4-meter high propulsion assembly was mounted. Below the middle-body ran into a cone-shaped point, form that ran a huge pendulum reaching into the cellar that provided for the stabilization of the device.*
>
> *In active conditions presumably the top and bottom discs rotated in a counter-rotation direction in order first of all to build an electromagnetic rotation field and thereby at the same time to generate that "intercosmic vibration", which reigns in the dimensional sphere of "Green Lands". According to the principle of affinity of vibrations (resonance? —translator) shall, through this, the fundamental conditions for the "interdimensional flight" is built. The power assembly, the propulsion for the dimensional flight machine is as described: a peculiarly composed battery. Allegedly it concerned a special high-energy condenser for short interval energy-pulse values and served as a starter for the three discs, which, to be sure, formed at the same time, a special electric motor as well as an electric generator. The statements concerning the Jenseitsflugmachine are in any even insufficient, it is even possible that known misleading information was disseminated in order to guarantee secrecy." (7)*

Summarizing more of the text, the device was tested for two years. It was financed through German industry under the code name "JFM". The authors go on to say:

"With certainty the "Vril Power Unit" came from the "Jenseitsflugmachine" brought forth formally as the 'Schumann SM-Levitator'. (8)

Again summarizing, in 1924 the device was brought to Augsburg and stored. This was perhaps at the Messerschmitt Works. Fifteen years later the first Haunebu (according to these writers) was first tested. Again translating:

" 'The Jenseitsmachine' would be thereafter also the foundation of the 'Thule-Triebwerk' ". (9)

The Jenseitsmachine differs from the Sunburst machine in that on the later only two counter-rotating magnetic fields were used. It is obvious from the discussing concerning the starter that the Jenseitsmachine is said to function as something like a homopolar motor-generator. Also, in this original telling of the tale, the word "Tachyon" or its derivatives are not used. In fact, it looks like this word "Thule-Tachyonator" seems to have first appeared in O. Bergmann's first book of 1988 and then only preceded with the publisher, Hugin Gesellschaft's disclaimer. This word "Tachyon" is not a German word. The Germans of the Nazi period would certainly have coined a word originating in their own language for such a new development. As it is, the word "Tachyon" was coined in the mid-1960's by Dr. Gerald Feinberg and I have not found it in print until 1977. (10) (11) Since the original source did not include this word, the original can not be discredited out of hand as can the alleged technical drawings. (12) But it is interesting to note that only the Haunebu drawings are associated with this word "Tachyon", while the Vril references (the type of craft under discussion here) describe the propulsion unit as "Schumann-Levitator" (13).

What has been done in this book so far is to discuss specific issues such as secret bases, secret technology, and U-boats while discussing theory and means for one type of field propulsion German flying disc in a less pointed way. What should be done now is to review all those ideas and assemble them in a straight-line manner so that what is being presented is perfectly clear.

It was noted that at least two German writers, D. H. Haarmann and O. Bergmann, the two earliest writers on the subject of both German saucers and mystery U-boats in our modern era, both say that the final German flying discs at the very end of the war functioned just as planets and heavenly bodies do. The rotate and it is in this rotation by which electromagnetic forces are generated by which gravity is overcome. They point to the rotating ring seen in these very late, and probably still experimental, flying saucers as part of the levitation mechanism.

From here we are guided by Renato Vesco, writing even earlier, toward a German firm which would have to have been involved in such work, Kreiselgeraete GmbH. This very word "Kreiselgeraete" means "gyro-devices" in English, and so Vesco's reference is clear. A flying saucer whose very body is in a high state of rotation, would need the technical know-how of a firm accustomed to dealing with exactly this type of force.

A Combined Intelligence Objectives file on Kreiselgeraete, GmbH. was obtained from the US government using the FOIA. It was a report actually done during the war, rather than a post-war white wash that sometimes occurs. It relied on a prisoner of war's testimony. Besides the plant in Berlin, Kreiselgeraete had a secret facility in Nieder Einiedel. That second, secret facility did experimental work in Lodz, Poland in association with another firm, Askania. The work done at this largely underground facility of Askania-Mitte was on "aircraft engines". Neither firm, Kreiselgeraete nor Askania made pistons, or crankshafts or propellers or even jet engines, yet they were working on aero-engines. How is that possible? These precision instrument makers could only have been working on aero-engines if those engines involved technology of which they were the masters as opposed to one of the usual German aircraft makers. This leads us to the conclusion that the engines involved were not only secret but also unusual.

Next we consider the work of Dr. Paul Potter in his book "Gravitational Manipulation of Domed Craft. Dr. Potter's basic idea is that what we call flying saucers operate on principles found operating in heavenly bodies. According to Dr. Potter, astrophysicists deal with these principles on a regular basis but they are largely unknown to those outside the field. Chief among these heavenly bodies are black holes and it is to black holes and their methods of energy production and manipulation that we should first turn in order to explain UFOs.

The very first of these heavenly principles of physics by which UFOs fly Dr. Potter calls magnetic reconnection. When two magnetic fields come into proximity the magnetic lines of force of both magnetic fields reach out to each other and form common bonds. As each of the magnetic fields of these two heavenly bodies are rotating, as they rotate the magnetic bonds of these magnetic lines of force are broken and immediately reform with the next line of force moving to meet it. Upon breaking and because of it, new particles are formed from the zero point. These are electrons and positrons (positive electrons).

At this point, given we are talking about a flying saucer, the electrons move outward and downward while the positrons move inward and upward. As we have seen with the Biefield-Brown Effect, the craft is pulled to the positive side. In this case, with positrons as opposed to simply positive charges as in Biefeld-Brown, the resulting forces are like Biefield-Brown on steroids, and the flying saucer immediately moves into the positron cone. In fairness to Dr. Potter, this magnetic reconnection principle is only the first and simplest of the ideas for UFO propulsion which he sets forth, but it is enough, alone, to explain the physics of German flying discs.

Dr. Potter then uses the Searl disc to explain his ideas. The idea of "reverse moment" (back torque) was raised by this writer. But this problem was allegedly solved by Dr. P. Boehning in 1942 who was said by Dr. Hans Nieper to have invented a motor (electric motor) which bypassed this problem and so had no reverse moment.

Since this concept of reverse moment or back torque involved eddy currents generated during the interaction of two magnetic fields (or a magnetic field through which a conductor is moving - or vice versa), the special situation of the Schauberger disc was discussed. It resembled the Searl disc in that little or no reverse moment or back torque was observed and both discs achieved auto-rotation once a certain speed had been achieved. Both discs also achieved levitation that was unexplained at the time it occurred.

After the war had ended, it was noted that the Nazi International set up scientific workshops in South America for the purpose of research and development of high technology. This included experimentation upon and production of flying discs. This coincided with the golden age of flying saucers in the late 1940s through the 1960s. Flying saucer accounts in and around South America abounded.

But it was also noted that a strange FBI report claimed a German inventor had discovered a new principle of "aerodynamics" and was trying to market this idea. His concept was not one based upon free energy in that he stated his method involved using motorcycle or auto engines. These engines produce movement of a spinning shaft, whose speed and torque can be harnessed for many uses but at its core is rotary motion.

The testimony of a retired colonel, known to UFO researcher Wendell Stevens was also discussed. He claimed that a German flying disc had been tested at Murdoc AFB (now Edwards AFB) in the 1950s. The basis of its propulsion, he claimed, was two counterrotating magnetic fields.

Work in homopolar generators/motors was also discussed. These electric generators were invaluable to the Germans for the production of specific electric current for rail gun experimentation as well as the electrolysis of water. Tesla's thoughts on further development of homopolar generators was available to the Germans. According to Tesla, it was possible to harness the eddy currents generated in a homopolar generator. These homopolar generators bore a resemblance to both the Searl and Schauberger machines as well as to the fundamental, planetary, descriptions of early field propulsion German flying discs by writers Haarmann and Bergmann. Harnessing eddy currents rather than fighting them would allow a back-torque free electric generator to be built. This would certainly solve all problems concerning electric generation in the world of submarines and may have been instrumental in reports of German free-energy U-boats.

These ideas about harnessing eddy currents to power homopolar generators came from exactly the same place Dr. Paul Potter got his ideas, by the motions of heavenly bodies. In the case of the homopolar generator, it was the earth itself because the earth itself is a homopolar generator and uses eddy currents to intensify its own magnetic field. In fact, Tesla suggests gradually withdrawing any energizing magnets so that the homopolar generator energizes itself.

The Sunburst Material that suggested combining the magnets and the rotor into one unit, greatly influenced Dr. Bruce DePalma's work on the N-machine. The Sunburst Material also suggested combining two opposing and counter-rotating to produce levitation. The Vril Society proposed the same idea many years before.

The positioning of two or more rotating magnetic fields in such a way that Dr. Paul Potter's magnetic reconnection occurs, (the production of electrons and positrons), Dr. Potter's explanation of it, as well as the historic and cultural setting provided in the discussion, are enough to explain the origin and development of the smaller type of German flying disc in my mind. It is also enough to explain the USO sightings in which underwater object travel at amazing speeds (since the same principles would work underwater) and also exit the water and fly in the atmosphere as would a "normal" flying disc.

The fact that the idea of magnetic reconnection came from observations of heavenly bodies, especially black holes, is the least of our surprises. It may be that this concept, if first observed in the mid-1920s by the Vril Society, was one of the fundamental linchpins in the overall Black Sun concept.

It this explains the "Vril" type or "Magnetscheibe" flying disc in the reader's mind then all that needs to be done is to explain the other type, the "Haunebu" type, which seems to have first appeared after World War Two. And perhaps this explanation will apply to some other devices also.

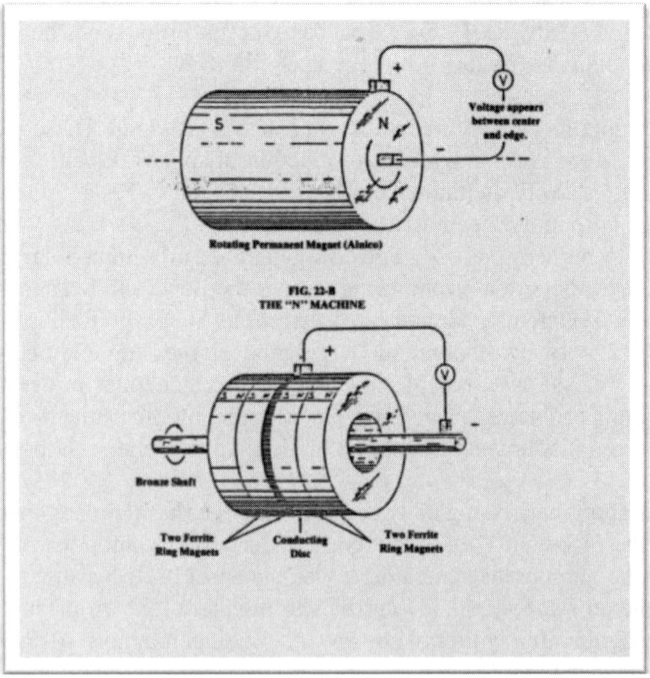

Dr. Bruce DePalma's "N"-Machine The N-machine is a type of homopolar generator in which the rotating disc or cylinder is itself a magnet. The fact that an external magnet is lacking and the magnetic disc itself is rotating has no influence on the output of the machine.

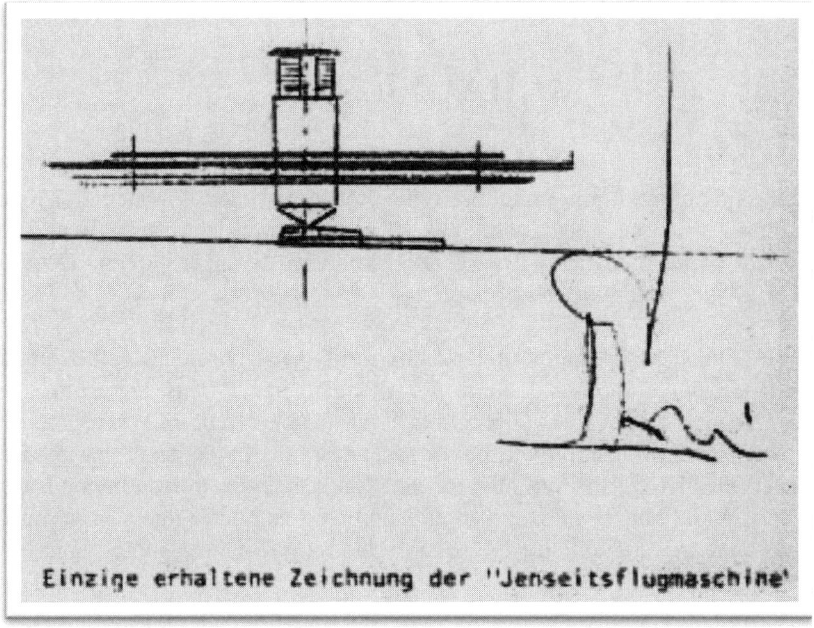

The Vril Society's *Jenseitsflugmachine*. This is the only depiction of that machine available, and originates with the material of Norbert Juergen-Rathoffer and Ralf Ettl. The three rotating discs can be seen in the drawing.

Literature Cited

1. **Schweikhart, Claude writing in Mench und Schicksal (magazine), August, 1952**, in an article titled: Um Krone und Gipfel der Welt, 6. Jahrg./NR. 10
2. **Bergmann, O., 1988**, *I Deutsche Flugscheiben und U-Boote Ueberwachen Die Weltmeere*, page 18, Hugin Gesellschaft Fuer Politisch-Philosophische Studien E. V., Wetter/Ruhr, Germany
3. **Bergmann, O., 1988**, page 20
4. **Valone, Thomas, M.A., P.E., (now Ph.D.), 1994**, *The Homopolar Handbook*, pages 138-140, Integrity Research Institute, Washington, D.C., USA
5. **Stevens, Henry, 2003**, *Hitler's Flying Saucers*, pages 134-135, Adventures Unlimited Press, Kempton, Illinois, USA (as well as many other sources discussing the Biefield-Brown Effect)
6. **Valone, Thomas, M.A., P.E. (now Ph.D.), 1994**, pages 15-17
7. **Juergen-Rathoffer, Norbert, and Ralf Ettl, 1992**, *Das Vril Projekt - Der Endkampf Der Erde!,* page 27-28, privately published.
8. *ibid.*
9. *ibid.*
10. **Stevens, Henry, 2003**, pages 221-222
11. **Feinberg, Gerald, Ph.D., 1977**, *What Is The World Made Of?,* Anchor Press/Doubleday, Garden City, NY., USA
12. **Bergmann, O., 1988**, pages 63-64 (and numerous other references including hundreds of internet sites)
13. *ibid*

HAUNEBU

As I have said before, in my mind the flying craft type called "Haunebu" is a post-war creation, at least in its operational version. A Haunebu craft is a larger flying saucer, at least 30 feet or so in diameter, with a classic dome on its upper side, and without any indication of rotating discs, wheels or parts.

There are alleged photographs of Haunebu craft that are said to date from the war years, but these photographs all come from one source. This one source was an anonymous package dropped off in England for researcher Ralf Ettl, who was working there on an unrelated project at the time. It seems that the fundamental basis—if not the entirety—of the Ettl/Juergen-Ratthofer explanation resides in this anonymous package. The date was in the late 1980's, far enough into the computer age that some kind of investigation into the authenticity or possible alteration of any photographs within it would seem in order (1).

Besides the photographs and explanation offered by Ralf Ettl and Norbert Juergen-Ratthofer, there are the numerous and worldwide eyewitness sightings, photographs and videotapings of these craft in the early 1950's. George Adamski, a Polish immigrant living in California, took excellent photographs of these objects and even offered an explanation of their presence (he believed they came from the planet Venus). Hence their alternate name, "Adamski Craft". Of course we know now much more than we did in the 1950's. We know that Venus is about 900 degrees Farenheit on its surface, and that its atmosphere contains about 97% carbon dioxide with clouds of billowing sulfuric acid. Soviet space probes were hard put to even last long enough in that atmosphere to land and make a short transmission.

So if the documented sightings of the early 1950's were not of craft from Venus, then what were they? Where did these craft come from and how did they fly? Where they came from ought to be obvious by now, but we will discuss this in more detail later. How they managed to levitate has already been answered. They levitated exactly as did the Vril craft—or Magnetscheibe—by the production of positrons through magnetic reconnection as described by Dr. Paul Potter. The Haunebu just used different technology to achieve the same ends.

The first clues come from the two scientists who did a ground floor evaluation of Karl Schappeller, his home, his home area, witnesses and the Schappeller technology itself. Their conclusion was that the technology involved was first introduced by Tesla, and that Schappeller experimented exclusively with Tesla ideas. So does this mean we ought to be looking for clues to Haunebu secrets by looking at old Tesla stuff? Why not? It already seems that Tesla has been involved in the smaller type of field propulsion German flying disc.

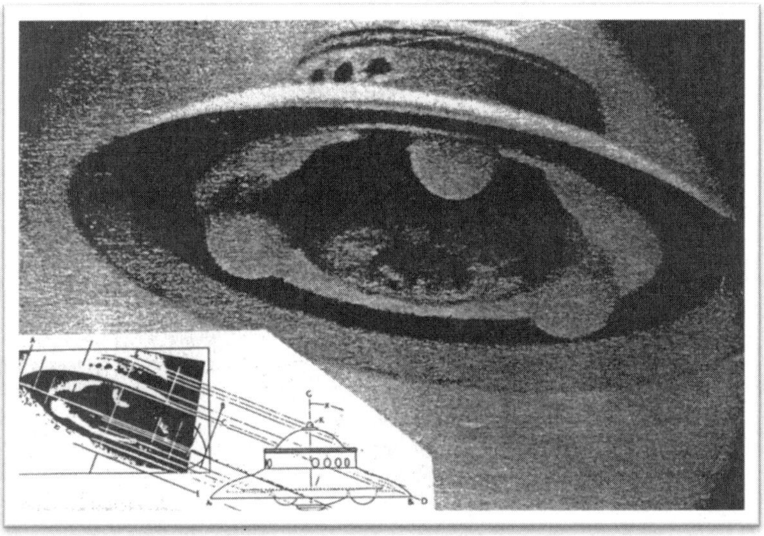

aunebu. Haunebu craft were first noticed in the early 1950's, worldwide. One of the first to photograph them extensibly as George Adamski, giving them their alternate name of "Adamski Craft" at that time. Here is Adamski's December 13, 952 photograph alongside alleged drawings of the Haunebu for comparison. Please note the three globes on the underside and e globular nature of the craft minus the surrounding disc.

But in looking through the book of Tesla patents, nothing even remotely similar seems to present itself. Nevertheless, there are a couple of clues in Tesla's writing. We have already taken a peek at both of these but they ought to be considered, now, in this present context.

> *"I was confident, however, that with properly designed machinery signals could be transmitted to any point of the globe, no matter what the distance, without the necessity of using such intermediate stations. I gained this conviction through the discovery of a singular electrical phenomenon, which I described early in 1892, in lectures delivered before some scientific societies abroad, and which I have called a 'rotating brush'. This is a bundle of light which is formed, under certain conditions, in a vacuum-bulb, and which is of a sensitiveness to magnetic and electric influences bordering, so to speak, on the supernatural. This light bundle is rapidly rotated by the earth's magnetism as many as twenty thousand times per second, the rotation in these parts being opposite to what it would be in the southern hemisphere, while in the region of the magnetic equator it should not rotate at all. In its most sensitive state, which is difficult to attain, it is responsible to electric or magnetic influences to an incredible degree. The mere stiffening of the muscles of the arm and consequent slight electrical charge in the body of an observer standing at some distance from it, will perceptibly affect it. When in this highly sensitive state it is capable of indicating the slightest*

magnetic and electrical changes taking place in the earth. The observation of this wonderful phenomenon impressed me strongly that communications at any distance could be easily effected by its means, provided that apparatus could be perfected capable of producing and electric or magnetic change of state, however small, in the terrestrial globe or envisioning medium." (2)

So here we have a bundle of light, rapidly rotating in a vacuum-bulb that is super-sensitive to other magnetic fields. Tesla mentions lecturing on the subject, a clue. Tesla goes on to explain how important this invention was to him.

"This conclusion I reached, I think, in the latter part of 1883, when I was in Paris, and it was at a time when my mind was being more and more dominated by an invention which I had evolved during the preceding year, and, which has since become known under the name of the 'rotating magnetic field'. During the few years that followed I made little headway. The commercial introduction in this country of the invention before referred to required most of my energies until 1889, when I again took up the idea of the self-acting machine." (3)

This "rotating brush" renamed "rotating magnetic field" dominated Tesla's mind for six years! Fortunately, one of the lectures Tesla gave describing this device has been found along with Tesla's diagrams explaining the device. Joining Tesla's lecture mid-stream:

"I think it best at this juncture to bring before you a phenomenon, observed by me some time ago, which to the purely scientific investigator may perhaps appear more interesting than any of the results which I have the privilege to present to you this evening.

It may be quite properly ranked among the brush phenomena — in fact, it is a brush, formed at, or near, a single terminal in high vacuum.

In bulbs provided with a conducting terminal, though it be of aluminum, the brush has but an ephemeral existence, and cannot, unfortunately, be indefinitely preserved in its most sensitive state, even in a bulb devoid of any conducting electrode. In studying the phenomenon, by all means a bulb having no leading-in wire should be used. I have found it best to use bulbs constructed as indicated in Figs. 141 and 142.

In Fig. 141 the bulb comprises an incandescent lamp glove L, in the neck of which is sealed a barometer tube b, the end of which is blown out to form a small sphere s. This sphere should be sealed as closely as possible in the centre of the large globe. Before sealing, a thin tube t, of aluminum sheet, may be slipped in the barometer tube, but it is not important to employ it.

The small hollow sphere s is filled with some conducting powder, and a wire w is cemented in the neck for the purpose of connecting the conducting powder with the generator.

The construction shown in Fig. 142 was chosen in order to remove from the brush any conducting body that might possibly affect it. The bulb consists in this case of a lamp globe L, which has a neck n, provided with a tube b and small sphere s, sealed to it , so that two entirely independent compartments are formed, as indicated in the drawing. When the bulb is in used the neck n is provided with a tinfoil coating, which is connected to the generator and acts inductively upon the moderately rarefied and highly conducted gas enclosed in the neck. From there the current passes through the tube b into the small sphere s, to act by induction upon the gas contained in the globe L.

It is of advantage to make the tube t very thick, the hole through it very small, and to blow the sphere s very thin. It is of the greatest importance that the sphere s be placed in the centre of the globe L.

Figs. 143, 144 and 145 indicate different forms, or stages, of the brush. Fig. 143 shows the brush as it first appears in a bulb provided with a conducting terminal; but, as in such a bulb it very soon disappears —- often after a few minutes —-I will confine myself to the description of the phenomenon as seen in a bulb without conducting electrode. It is observed under the following conditions;

When the globe+ L (Figs. 141 and 142) is exhausted to a very high degree, generally the bulb is not excited upon connecting the wire w (Fig.141) or the tinfoil coating of the bulb (Fig. 142) to the terminal of the induction coil. To excite it, it is usually sufficient to grasp the glove L with the hand. Intense phosphorescence then spreads at first over the glove, but soon gives place to a white, misty light. Shortly afterward one may notice that the luminosity is unevenly distributed in the globe, and after passing the current for some time the bulb appears as in Fig. 144. From this stage the phenomenon will gradually pass to that indicated in Fig. 145, after some minutes, hours, days or weeks, according as the bulb is worked. Warming the bulb or increasing the potential hastens the transit.

When the brush assumes the form indicated in Fig. 145, it might be brought to a state of extreme sensitiveness to electrostatic and magnetic influence. The bulb hanging straight down from a wire, and all objects being remote from it, the approach of the observer at a few paces from the bulb will cause the brush to fly to the opposite side, and if he walks around the bulb it will always keep on the opposite side. It may begin to spin around the terminal long before it reaches that sensitive stage. When it begins to turn around, principally, but also before, it is affected by a magnet, and at a certain stage it is susceptible to magnetic influence to an astonishing degree. A small permanent magnet, with its poles at a distance of no more than two centimeters, will affect it visibly at a distance of two meters, slowing down or accelerating the rotation according to how it is held relatively to the brush. I think I have observed that at the stage when it is most sensitive to magnetic, it is not most sensitive to electrostatic, influence. My explanation is, that the electrostatic attractions between the brush and the glass of the bulb, which retards the rotation, grows much uicker than the magnetic influence wen the intensity of the stream is increased.

When the bulb hangs with the globe L down, the rotation is always clockwise. In the southern hemisphere it would occur in the oppose direction and on the equator the brush should not turn at all. The rotation may be reversed by a magnet kept at some distance. The brush rotates best, seemingly, when it is at right angles to the lines of force of the earth. It very likely rotates, when at its maximum speed, in synchronism with the alterations, say 10,000 times a second. The rotation can be slowed down or accelerated by the approach or receding of the observer, or any conducting body, but it cannot be reversed by putting the bulb in any position. When it is in the state of the highest sensitiveness and the potential or frequency varied, the sensitiveness is rapidly diminished. Changing either of these but little will generally stop the rotation. The sensitiveness is likewise affected by the variations of temperature. To attain great sensitiveness it is necessary to have the small sphere s in the centre of the globe L, as otherwise the electrostatic action of the glass on the glove will tend to stop the rotation. The sphere s should be small and of uniform thickness; any dissymmetry of course has the effect to diminish the sensitiveness.

The fact that the brush rotates in a definite direction in a permanent magnetic field seems to show that in alternating currents of very high frequency the positive and negative impulses are not equal, but that one always preponderates over the other.

Of course, this rotation in one direction may be due to the action of the two elements of the same current upon each other, or to the action of the field produced by one of the elements upon the other, as in a series motor, without necessarily one impulse being stronger than the other. The fact that the brush turns, as far as I could observe, in any position, would speak for this view. In such case it would turn at any point of the earth's surface. But, on the other hand, it is then hard to explain why a permanent magnet should reverse the rotation, and one must assume the preponderance of impulses of one kind.

As to the cause of the formation of the brush or stream, I think it is due to the electrostatic action of the globe and the dissymmetry of the parts. If the small bulb s and the globe L were perfect concentric spheres, and the glass throughout of the same thickness and quality, I think the brush would not form, as the tendency to pass would be equal on all sides. That the formation of the stream is due to an irregularity is apparent from the fact that it has the tendency to remain in one position, and rotation occurs most generally only when it is brought out of this position by electrostatic or magnetic influence. When in an extremely sensitive state it rests in one position, most curious experiments may be performed with it. For instance, the experimenter may, by selecting a proper position, approach the hand at a certain considerable distance to the bulb, and he may cause the brush to pass off by merely stiffening the muscles of he arm. When it begins to rotate slowly, and the hands are held at a proper distance, it is impossible to make even the slightest motion without producing a visible effect upon the brush. A metal plate connected to the other terminal of the coil affects it at a great distance, slowing down the rotation often to one turn a second.

I am firmly convinced that such a brush, when we learn how to produce it properly, will prove a valuable aid in the investigation of he nature of the forces acting in an electrostatic or magnetic field. If there is any motion that is measurable going on in the space, such a brush ought to reveal it. It is so to speak, a beam of light, frictions, devoid of inertia.

I think that it may find practical applications in telegraphy. With such a brush I would be possible to send dispatches across the Atlantic, for instance, with any speed, since its sensitiveness may be so great that the slightest changes will affect it. If it were possible to make the stream more intense and very narrow, its deflections could be easily photographed.

I have been interested to find whether there is a rotation of the stream itself, or whether there is simply a stress traveling around the bulb. For this purpose I mounted a light mica fan so that its vanes were in the path of the brush. If the stream itself were rotating the fan would be spun around. I could produce no distinct rotation of the fan, although I tried the experiment repeatedly; but as the fan exerted a noticeable influence on the stream, and the apparent rotation of the latter was, in this case, never quite satisfactory, the experiment did not appear to be conclusive.

I have been unable to produce the phenomenon with the disruptive discharge coil, although every other of these phenomena can be well produced by it —- many, in fact, much better than with coils operated from an alternator. It may be possible to produce the brush by impulses of one direction, or even by a steady potential, in which case it would be still more sensitive to magnetic influence." (4)

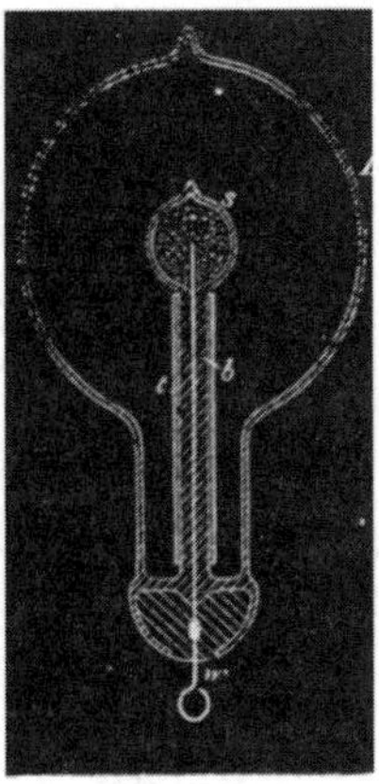

FIG. 141.

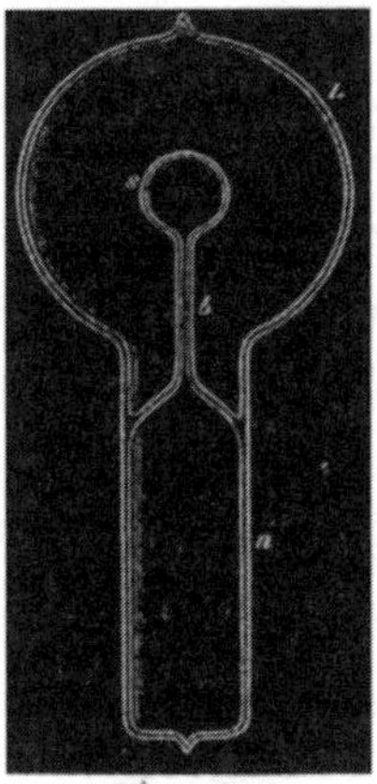

FIG. 142.

FIG. 144.

FIG. 145.

Tesla's Drawings of his "Brush". This is clearly the prototype upon which Karl Schappeller based his work. Fig. 141 shows the incandescent lamp glove *L*, in the neck a sealed barometer tube *b*, the end of which is blown out, forming a small sphere *s*, which was sealed after being filled with a conducting metallic powder. An electrical connection was made, turning the metallic powder into a rapidly-spinning plasma vortex.

We have a conductive powder inside a small glass bulb, connected to a source of electricity. Outside of this, surrounding it, we have a more or less a glass, standard vacuum tube. When connected to an electricity source, this powder instantly becomes a bright, rapidly rotating ball which is supersensitive to magnetism, electrostatics or even the human bodies own internal electric discharges.

This was apparently the phenomena which fascinated our next inventor, Karl Schappeller. Schappeller created a device consisting to outer half shells fitted together as a globe. Inside the metal is a ceramic insulating material. Also inside and pointing toward each other at the poles are two permanent iron magnets. Surrounding the hollow center is a conductive coil that evidently induces electricity. The hollow center itself is filled with what Schappeller calls "glowing magnetism" which Schappeller's student, the English engineer Cyril Davson, reports is 1000 times stronger than magnetism "of present magnetism". (5)

Schappeller's description, "glowing magnetism" is interesting since he would have never seen this phenomenon though the metal and ceramic walls. Schappeller must have started with Tesla's glass bulb method and observed this form himself first. He must have also charged two such devices at the same time in order to achieve magnetic reconnection. The two moving magnetic fields would interact, connect and disconnect their lines of force as they spun in proximity, reconnecting as they do so and as they do so producing electrons and positrons from the zero point as explained by Dr. Paul Potter. Any tendency to slow their rotation in this interaction (back torque) could be offset by an increase in potential or frequency to the two spinning brush vortices, just as Tesla says. With two such devices or one device in the company of a revolving magnetic field around it, magnetic reconnection would occur and both bulbs would begin to levitate. This is what must have perked Schappeller's interest.

Instead of using whatever name this has gone by in the past, "rotating brush", "rotating magnetic field" or "glowing magnetism" it is evident that we are speaking about what we now call plasma and in fact plasma vortices or plasmoids. This plasma, in this case has had its entropy lowered that is it is organized, as evidenced by the vortex and the symmetrical magnetic field. This plasma has been given a specific shape by the small glass bulb or by the permanent iron magnets of the Schappeller device that must hold the plasma in place at the center of the device. Something else is evident: It is rotating and has a magnetic field of its own which run from top to bottom or pole to pole of the ball of plasma. One has to wonder how different this is from what is observed in the natural world as ball lightning and if all the remarks made about German experimentation with ball lightning, both during and after the war, had some basis in fact.

Another point, there is no doubt that Schappeller envisioned a flying device resulting from his work. Davson mentions "ether ships" powered by the Schappeller device by name twice. (6) But Schappeller also built a coil into his machine which seems to have nothing to do with levitation, rather with electrical generation.

As mentioned earlier, several Europeans are researching Schappeller at the moment so I want to wait this analysis rather than commenting further myself on Schappeller. But from Schappeller this technology clearly found its way to the researchers at the Reichsarbeitsgemeinschaft (RAG), a governmental organization charged with energy independence for Germany at a time between the two World Wars. So the RAG was primarily not interested in levitation but nevertheless freely commented on this as being contained among the properties of the device they were building.

> *"The new dynamic technology will enable, in the future, electric locomotives and automobiles to be made without expensive armatures and though circuit-connection to the atmospheric voltage-net to be pushed forward. Prerequisite is that, all things considered, the installation of many sufficient amplification facilities (centers) with transmit the specific "magnetic impulse" given from the Ur-machine to the dynamic globe-elements. Novel aircraft with magneto-static propulsion and steering, which are crash proof and safe from colliding with each other could be built for a fraction of the cost of today's aircraft — and without lengthy training of every person attending (the machines)."(7)*

In conjunction with their discussion on energy production and levitation of aircraft the RAG describes how this all looks to the observer. They propose using seven globes, five surrounding one in the center with one positioned above this center globe. The five feed the center globe and when it reaches some point of saturation, specific magnetic impulses are sent the seventh. This is what they describe as an Ur-machine. The reader may recall from depictions of the Haunebu machines that there are sometimes three globes visible and presumably one or two larger ones within the body of the craft. The three smaller globes may have an additional function in steering the craft but they also may interact with the globes in the body of the craft to produce magnetic reconnection and the lift producing positrons that result.

In the chapter on repositories Switzerland was mentioned. Also found in Switzerland are the Billy Meier craft, the alleged "Pleiadian Beamships". These craft are usually depicted with multiple globes visible on the outside of the saucer as if stuck there with glue. According to the interpretation given here, these globes are just additional levitation devices. Dr. Axel Stoll minces no words in debunking the extraterrestrial hypothesis of an alleged Pleiadian woman, "Semjase", who has blonde hair, is pretty, and speaks German perfectly. Thinking that this similarity was even beyond the most extreme case of parallel evolution, Dr. Stoll moves on to the saucers themselves saying they obviously have to do with further developed Haunebu craft. (8) This is so obvious it is wondered how it could ever be disputed.

Along with the Haunebu type of saucer, this technology would also be suitable for the cigar-shaped flying craft as well as the similarly shaped underwater, unidentified submerged objects. Just as would the two counterrotating magnetic wheels of the previous homopolar generator inspired devices. For a submarine, the engine should probably be mounted in the front of the ship or perhaps one at the front and one at the rear for forwards and backwards motion. In other words William R. Lyne, all those old

German sources, D. H. Haarmann and O. Bergmann are all probably correct, U-boats can fly, sometimes.

Literature Cited

1. **Stevens, Henry, 2003**, *Hitler's Flying Saucers*, page 159, Adventures Unlimited Publishing, Kempton, Illinois, USA
2. **Tesla, Nikola, edited by David Hatcher Childress, 2000**, *The Tesla Papers Nikola Tesla on Free Energy & Wireless Transmission of Power*, page 66, Adventures Unlimited Publishing, Kempton, Illinois, USA
3. **Tesla, Nikola, edited by David Hatcher Childress, 2000**, page 56
4. **Martin, Thomas Commerford, 1995**, *The Inventions, Researches and Writings of Nikola Tesla*, Second Edition, pages 226-231, Barnes & Nobel, N.Y., NY., USA
5. **Davson, Cyril W., 1956**, *The Physics Of The Primary State Of Matter*, page 231, Neill & Co. Ltd., Edinburgh, Scotland
6. **Davson, Cyril, W., 1956**, pages 199, 240
7. **Taeufer, Johannes, 1930**, *"Vril" Die Cosmische Urkraft Wiedergebaut von Atlantis* (issued on order from the Reichsarbeitsgemeinschaft) Astrologischer Verlag Wilhelm Becker, Berlin-Steglitz, Germany
8. **Stoll, Axel, Ph.D., 2001**, *Hochtechnologie im Dritten Reich*, page 83, Amun Verlag, Schleusesiedlung, Germany

MAMAS, DON'T LET YOUR SONS GROW UP TO BE BELL-BOYS

In this chapter we will take a look at the Bell (die Glocke). We are going to look at the structure of the device itself as well as its properties. We are also going to look at the potential or possibilities of the Bell. And we are going to consider the Bell in relationship to the other devices discussed.

Dr. Joseph Farrell says:

> *"The Bell was a gateway technology, a hyper-dimensional torsion-based technology that the Nazis had developed to investigate its potential applications in three areas:*
>
> 1. *As a means to tap into the zero-point energy, or, to phrase it differently, the energy of the physical medium of space-time itself;*
> 2. *As a means to manipulate gravity itself, i.e. as an advanced prototypical field propulsion technology; and*
> 3. *As a means to the ultimate, potentially planet-busting, weapon.*
>
> *The conceptual key to the achievement of all these effects was the manipulation of rotating magnetic fields by means of the counter-rotation of a plasma within the device itself." (1)*

Please consider this last sentence again in light of the Tesla to Schappeller to Reichsarbeitsgemeinschaft connection. The Bell falls right in.

Personally, I have had many thoughts about the Bell and many changes of mind concerning it. The Bell seems to have been everything to everyone. It had to be a weapon or Hitler would not have continued funding it in the last year of the war, right? If Otto Cerney is to be believed, the Bell (Cerney does not name the device) was the subject of "experiments in time". (2) And yet the real experts on the subject, Igor Witkowski, Dr. Joseph Farrell, and aerospace expert Nick Cook all believe this device was an engine for levitation. The Bell discharged some sort of radiation that simply killed everything near it. And since there is a possibility that a radioactive substance was one of its main ingredients, a substance perhaps resembling red mercury, was it not possible that this device worked like a non-exploding neutron bomb? And finally, besides the Otto Cerney report, Dr. Axel Stoll said recently on an episode of UFO Hunters, an American TV series dealing with UFOs, that the Bell did influence time.

How could all these properties be incorporated into one device? How could any of this be explained? Everyone has had a go at this, at least as regards a flying device, so here is my take on this and if it is totally wrong, then I am sure Igor Witkowski, Dr. Joseph Farrell, Nick Cook and Dr. Axel Stoll will set the record straight.

First, let us look at the structure of the Bell. For this we are going to rely on the analysis of Dr. Joseph Farrell who often cites Igor Witkowski, the man originally giving us his information. Starting from the inside out, the Bell's inner-most component was a hollow core, forming the Bell's axis.

> *"The axis was formed by quite an unusual core, with a diameter of a dozen or so, to twenty centimeters, with its lower end fixed to 'the Bell's massive pedestal. It was made of a heavy, hard metal. Before each trial some kind of ceramic, oblong container was placed in the core (It was defined as a 'vacuum flask'...), surrounded by a layer of lead approx. 1-1.5 m long and filled with a strange, metallic substance, with a violet-gold hue..." (2)*

Around this lay two cylinders or drums that rotated in opposite directions. It is unknown if one drum rotated inside the other or one was on top of the other.

> *"The main part of 'the Bell' was made up of two massive cylinders-drums around one meter in diameter, which during the experiment spun in opposite directions a tremendous speeds. The drums were made of a silvery metal and rotated around a common axis." (4)*

> *"Mercury, this time already in pure form, was present inside the spinning cylinders. Before the start of the experiment, and perhaps also for its duration, the mercury was intensively cooled." (5)*

So the mercury inside the drums was different from the mercury inside the central cylinder. All known and or conventional compounds of mercury are solids, the mercury in the cylinder must have been charged up in a nuclear reactor and came out as a thick liquid as red mercury does. This would be yet another variant on the red mercury formula. Meanwhile, the mercury inside the cylinder/drums was conventional mercury and must have had a different purpose.

> *"The entire device, i.e. the cylinders and core was covered with the aforementioned ceramic housing, of a bell-like shape..."(6)*

At least one output from the Bell was one of some sort of high radiation. It made a noise that has been compared to that of a beehive. A strong magnetic field was detected. Electric effects were apparent as electronics in he vicinity were overloaded, presumably by induction. Finally, bluish light, bluish phosphorescence was noticed on the Bell. (7)

So what do we have here? First, let us just consider levitation. We have a device whose central core was hollow and filled with a type of special conducting material. It was connected to an electric source and ionized, forming plasma. Meanwhile, the two cylinders, filled with mercury, were set into their counterrotating motion. The mercury, an excellent conductor used for electric switches, was deeply cooled. This is obviously for a superconductor effect. Once a superconductor is charged, it remains charged with no further electrical input being necessary. This charge, circulating around and around the cylinder in the mercury would have produced a huge magnetic field. Perhaps through rotation of the highly charged cylinders, the central core ionized material was wrapped into a vortex or plasmoid. As we know from looking at the work of Tesla and Schappeller, this plasmoid generated a huge magnetic field. This huge magnetic field had two counterrotating, superconducting cylinder/drums moving through its field, each with its own huge magnetic field. The electromagnets reacting to each other and the central plasmoid are causing Dr. Paul Potter's magnetic reconnection to occur as magnetic lines of force are joined and pulled apart only to be rejoined, continually. This magnetic reconnection is generating positrons and electrons. Dr. Potter contends the positrons gather at the top of the device and the electrons at the bottom. The device or any matter falls into the positron rich area and is pushed by the electron rich area in a super Biefield-Brown Effect. Hence, we have levitation. And this form of levitation is in-line with the earlier inventions from the Searl disc to the Vril Society and their three rotating magnetic fields to Schauberger to the Reichsarbeitsgemeinschaft, to the Magnetscheibe, to the Haunebu, and perhaps even to Bergmann's electromagnetic-flying U-boats, even to Bruce DePalma's alien source. In fact, they are all exactly the same thing but achieved through different mediums.

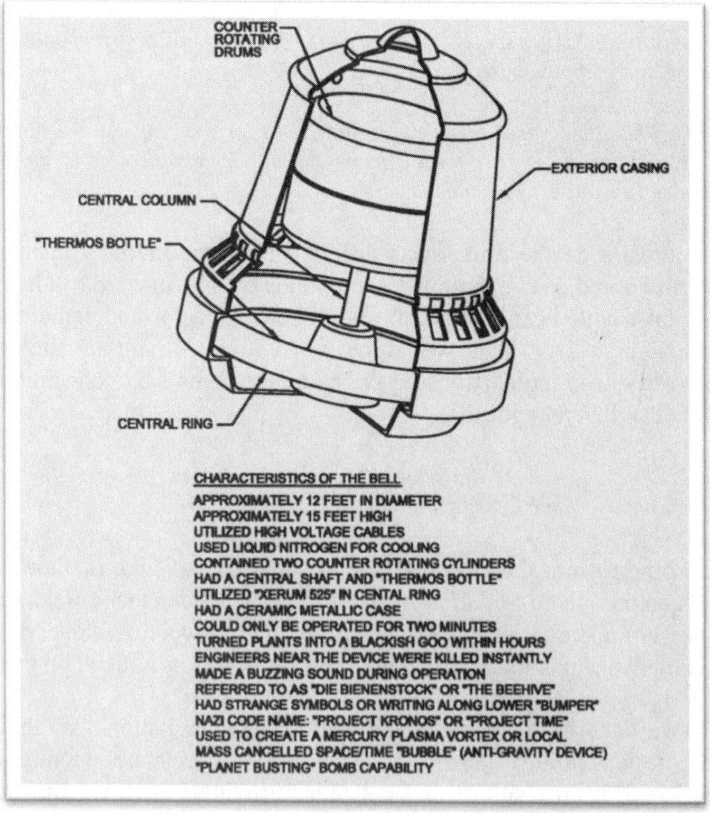

Diagram of the Bell. This is the work of researcher/writer/technical artist Michael Schratt, who is seemingly the only person combining these abilities and willing to take on such a project. The central column containing the spinning plasma vertex and the counter-rotating drums filled with mercury are clearly shown. Cooling was accomplished using liquid nitrogen.

How about a radiation weapon? Could the Germans have controlled this? In fact, the Germans certainly were leaders in ceramic material used to insulate the Bell from the two F.I.A.T. reports I have on ceramic insulators and ceramic dielectric materials.(8) Also, the Germans were leaders in the control of dangerous (radioactive) radiation, then and in the immediate post-war years. In fact zirconium shielding for the purpose of protection of human life was exclusively a German development right up until the early 1950's when it was German industry which produced the zirconium shielding for the first US nuclear submarine, the Nautilus. (9) This is physical evidence that the Germans at least thought they could control the voltage and the radiation the Bell produced.

Dr. Farrell includes a summary of Igor Witkowski's consulting physicist, Dr. Marek Demia_ski who says that the mercury vortex may have done something even more spectacular:

> *"Indeed, if the Germans 'had succeeded in aligning the axes of nuclei rotation in one direction, with the aid of a strong magnetic field then perhaps they had achieved some sort of gravitational breakthrough." (10)*

Remember, the Germans used superconducting mercury rather than ferromagnetic matterial. Soft iron contains "domains" within its structure which are aligned by magnetic means. Mercury does not. But this mercury achieved the magnetic task given it anyway and was then available for another task. It is a liquid and so may have undergone a special nuclear allignment of its own. The aligning of neutrons in the Bell and its influence on gravity is something best left to the experts in this field such as Igor Witkowski and Dr. Joseph Farrell. But, if gravity could really be influenced on its own fundamental level and not just by overpowering it as in the case of magnetic reconnection-related positron-electron pairs, well, then another mystery is solved with a new connection. Also, it seems to me that Einstein says something relating gravity to time and if gravity could be changed then to an observer standing outside the device's range, time would also be altered, would he not?

But further questions arise. What would the relationship of two Bell devices in proxmimity, operating at the same time? What would be the condition in a space surrounded by operating Bell devices? It should also be pointed out that descriptions of the Bell as well as the Schappeller device often mention transmutation of elements.

> *"The last point brings up yet another oddity in the long list of oddities associated with the Bell, and that is transmutation of elements." (11) And:*

> *"As for the reference to transmutation, this is a partly solved problem, for there exists in the Frankfurter Zeitung und Handelsblatt, for the evening edition of Friday, June 18, 1924, an article on precisely the transmutation of mercury into gold — long before the discovery of nuclear fission — by none other than Prof. Dr. Walter Gerlach! (here Dr. Farrell cites the source as The Truth About the Wunderwaffe, page 247). Gerlach speaks of such transmutation being possible*

through the bombardment of a target with 'rays' of an unspecified nature, and then goes on to speak of the scientific feasibility of alchemy! (12)

In fact, I was once contacted by a gold miner in Alaska who claimed to have built a Schappeller device to assist his gold mining operation with positive results. Did the Schappeller device somehow attract gold or was gold actually somehow produced? It is possible that there is something here. And since the underlying theory of the Black Sun is densification, organization, and transmutation such things such as gold creation from more base elements should come as no surprise.

At the top of this chapter Dr. Farrell is quoted as believing the Bell could be used as a means of tapping the zero-point or time-space itself for energy. One of Dr. Farrell's breakthroughs was seeing the relationship between the Bell and the technology of Dr. Ronald Richter. Dr. Richter in his plasma experiments at one of those Nazi labs in South America developed a method to shoot plasma through a magnetic field. Dr. Richter makes the point that this was a means to transform nuclear energy (plasma in this case) directly into electrical energy by induction but it also involved deriving energy directly from the zero-point. (13) The Bell as a "trap for a plasma vortex" or a "plasma focus" (14) just had to be doing the same thing.

Let us try another direction. As anyone can see there are plenty of possibilities here and plenty of possible sequences of events in the evolution of the Bell. Suppose we look first upon the Bell as developing from a weapon's system. But let us look at this through the eyes of the klystron-betatron. By this I mean a device of radiation and a device that controls, aims, the radiation using a magnetic field. So we have the Bell with its central hollow tube full of mercury with additions to the mercury, probably compounds of mercury that perhaps resembles red mercury. This red mercury is irradiated in an atomic reactor and the result, although different from other formulations of red mercury, is in that class of chemicals. This viscous, radioactive liquid, full of neutrons, is now poured into the Bell and energized with electricity. Plasma is formed between the anode and cathode (which where perhaps also permanent magnets as in the Schauberger device), and is warped into a long, cylindrical vortex, probably by the spinning cylinder/drum outside of the central cylinder which has been given motion and an electrical charge. The plasmoid, spinning, magnetic plasma, now generates its own monstrous magnetic field, generating eddy currents in the cylinder/drums containing mercury which are spinning around it and in counter-rotation to each other. From a weapons standpoint, a small hole could be opened at one end of the cylinder and a stream of radiation, perhaps gamma rays and X-rays, then pour out, directed by the opposing and surrounding magnetic field generated by the cylinder/drums. Like the betatron, we now have directed the radiation. As such, the Bell could be mounted on an aircraft and directed downward onto any battlefield or enemy city desired. Or, it could be mounded on a swivel as was the famous German 88 mm gun, and directed to sweep the sky of enemy bombers, just as other gamma-X-ray weapons were designed to do on a much smaller, weaker scale. The problem is the neutrons, because they were "matter" and heavy, may not have been willing to fly as directed. Instead, they seem to have radiated out in all directions as in a neutron bomb. This neutron bomb idea must have been concept number two for the

Germans, perhaps “Projekt Laternetraeger” (Project Lantern Carrier) and hardly needs any further discussion.

Or perhaps the central magnetic field could be constricted to a degree by the other two counter-rotating fields that explosives could be placed around it, as they were with the atomic bombs, detonated, compressing the central magnetic field further, resulting in a huge electromagnetic pulse weapon?

There is the theory by some that the Bell produced gravity effects, as voiced by Dr. Marek Demia_ski above. In this idea, all this rotation and magnetic interaction aligned the mercury atoms in the cylinder/drums, and some sort of gravity differential was noted. If true, this must have gotten the attention of the scientists involved and they simply must have done some on-the-spot investigation, with or without official sanction. Returning to Einstein’s ideas about the relationship between gravity and time, perhaps once this was recognized, this was the start of “Projekt Kronos”. And perhaps this is where Otto Cerney comes in. The Bell’s influence of time was the fourth concept noted in the Bell.

Let me speculate a bit. The neutrons would have “felt” the gravity effects and perhaps this is why they did not move under the influence of the magnetic field but in all directs. Could some of these neutrons have gotten stuck inside those mercury atoms? This might even be expected. Mercury does have a history regarding this. After all, charging up mercury compounds with neutrons in a nuclear reactor was the basis of red mercury. What is being discussed is transmutation. When the Bell was disassembled after each test and the mercury drained from the cylinder/drums, could some of this liquid metal have been changed into other elements by those bombarding neutrons? Could it have been radioactive material? And could there have been a byproduct? Gold was mentioned above and we will return to it one more time as this may impact the political arena. Was transmutation the fifth concept noted in the Bell?

We have no way of knowing the pathway of the energy required to spin and energize the Bell nor do we know if energy was generated, although this is what is being thought. In this it is hard not to see something approaching a homopolar generator with the central core and the spinning components in the machinery of the Bell. Perhaps a homopolar motor was in place, underground, for use as a starter motor. Perhaps auto-rotation occurred in the Bell as with the Searl and Schauberger devices, and if it happened, then the sixth concept peculiar to the Bell was as a generator of energy. Additionally, if the mercury filled cylinder drums were arranged in just the right way, as with the earth’s molten core, then feed back eddy currents might have come into play and might have even self-generated electrical energy without further input as Tesla and Farraday say was possible.

We really do not know all of what the Germans thought of the Bell. It is probably not the case that all the ideas mentioned were achieved but at least some of these concepts had to be under consideration by the Germans and they had to actively be working on at least a few of them. Also, the Bell as described, may have been a generalized demonstration device, one that was capable of many functions. Both Hans Coler and

Karl Schappeller made generalized demonstration devices. A more specific machine was to have been built according to the task at hand. Perhaps the Bell was such a demonstration machine, demonstrating many things leading to specialized "Bells" being built for specific purposes?

Let's go back to the beginning and look at this in another way. In the Dr. Paul Potter astronomical analogy, we started out with the Bell as a pulsar, a star imploding to form a black hole with two streams of gamma-X-ray radiation streaming into space from its poles as it was squeezed by magnetic and gravitational forces. The result is densification as elements are transmuted into every heavier ones and finally collapse into one big neutron under the weight of gravity into a black hole. The energy generated, every kind of energy, by a black hole is reflected in the magnetic field, the positron-electron generation and possibly even the gravity generated by the Bell. So if the gravitational effects of the Bell are as postulated, does this mean the Bell, if simply left running, would collapse into a mini-black hole or Black Sun as it would have been called at the time?

Also, it is hard not to see the relationship between the Bell and the Vril and Haunebu machines. In fact, the Bell looks like a combination of the early Vril spinning discs and the Haunebu's plasma generated magnetic field. Of course as regards levitation, this would all be the same and work the same way.

Before leaving the Bell, mention must be made of what must be its crowning story. By this I mean a story involving Otto Skorzeny! According to Dr. Farrell, citing Witkowski:

> *"...But Witkowski soon uncovered odd corroboration form another source, this time from the aide to the well-known SS commando, Otto Skorzeny, Karl Radl. Radl disclosed, in documents Witkowski uncovered at the American archives' Berlin Document Center, that Skorzeny had engaged to numerous acts of sabotage behind Russian lines in 1944 because he had 'come into contact with the 'wonder weapon' and as a result (had) 'been possessed' by the idea of 'Sonderkampf' ('Special Warfare'), regarding the use of this weapon, to such an extent, that he considered it the only sure way to win the war.*
>
> *After the war, according to the reports in the Spanish press that were soon followed by similar articles in the American press, Skorzeny had attempted to sell the secrets of this unknown Wunderwaffe to the Americans." (15)*

There is no doubt that Radl's account of events can be trusted. Radl, in many ways Skorzeny's right-hand man, was flipped by the Americans into testifying against Skorzeny after the war. In fact, Radl was the very first witness against Skorzeny. This was a thrunderbolt out of the blue and shocked Skorzeny that Radl, his friend, a man he had been to hell and back again many times, would stoop so low as to attempt to betray him. Evidently, the Americans had offered Radl a deal in exchange for testimony. They had offered SS General Gottlob Gerger immunity if he would testify against Skorzeny. Likewise, a deal was offered Werner Hunke but Hunke declined. In the end Radl's testimony only involved the theft of American uniforms and Skorzeny was acquitted of all charges anyway. (16) But Radl's turning on this friend out of fear of American reprisal serves to show how fully Radl was willing to cooperate and well as adding credibility to the story of further, secret and hidden wonder weapons and Skorzeny's attempt to sell the to the Americans.

What a scene this must have been. Imagine Otto Skorzeny, even though he was an engineer, trying to convince the Americans of a device resembling the Bell in 1946 or 1947? The Americans did not even believe Dr. Ronald Richter who was making less extreme claims and telling the Americans exactly how it was done. The Americans did not even believe Dr. Konrad Zuse's digital computer was of any value. The Americans must have thought Skorzeny had lost his mind. Well, it was a good thing for the 3rd Power that would develop a few years later that Skorzeny was completely discounted at that time. But this story does serve to establish, once again, contact between the Americans and the Nazis with the purpose of selling high technology.

The Skorzeny story reminds us that the Bell is also a human story and it brings us back to the people and organization involved, the 3rd Power. At this point we can step back for a momentary overview. Now that the issues of where the 3rd Power exists and existed, its structure, and how at least some of its technology works, we can move to a more direct discussion of how the 3rd Power works in terms of people and politics and secret technology.

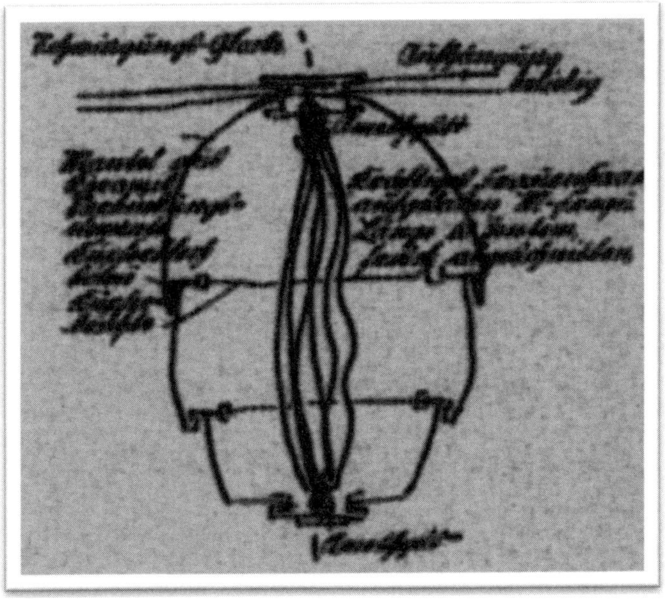

A Smoking Gun? This is a fragmentary diagram posted on the Causa Nostra website, closely identified with the beliefs of Ralf Ettl and Norbert Juergen-Rathoffer. This fragment was found sometime in the mid-1980s in Hamburg. It is important because it is not part of the hoardd given to Ralf Ettl in England and because it may document a stage in the evolution of what would become the Bell. My interpretation is a transfer of technology from Tesla to Schappeller to the Reichsarbeitsgemeinschaft to the Vril Societ to the SS. This fragment, depicting a spinning plasma vortex contained in a Bell-like sphere, is written in an old German script and is blurred. According to the proponents of their website, it was probably of Vril Society origin and a predecessor to the Bell.

Literature Cited

1. **Farrell, Joseph P., Ph.D., 2010**, *Roswell and The Reich: The Nazi Connection*, pages 361-362, Adventures Unlimited Publishing, Kempton, Illinois, USA
2. **Stevens, Henry, 2007**, *Hitler's Suppressed and Still-Secret Weapons, Science and Technology*, pages 248-257, Adventures Unlimited Publishing, Kempton, Illinois, USA
3. **Farrell, Joseph, P. Ph.D.**, 2006, *The Brotherhood Of The Bell*, page 172-173, Adventures Unlimited Publishing, Kempton, Illinois, USA. Here Farrell cites Igor Witkowski, The Truth About The Wunderwaffe, pages 232-233
4. ***ibid.***
5. ***ibid.***
6. ***ibid.***
7. **Farrell, Joseph, P., Ph.D., 2006**, pages 172-1838.
8. **FIAT Final Report No. 617** (Field Information Agency, Technical), *The Electrical And Technical Ceramic Industry of Germany*, (Supplementary Report High Dielectric Constant Insulators), by Bennett S. Ellefson, Technical Industrial Intelligence Division, U.S. Department Of Commerce and
9. **Georg, Friedrich, 2008**, "Unternehmen Patentenroub" 1945 *Die Geheimgeschichte des groessten Technologieraubs aller Zeiten*, pages 237-238, Grabert-Verlag, Tuebingen, Germany
10. **Farrell, Joseph, P., Ph.D., 2006**, page 181. Here Dr. Farrell is citing Igor Witkowski, "The Truth About the Wunderwaffe", page 247
11. **Farrell, Joseph P., Ph.D., 2006**, pages, 181, related work on page 249
12. ***ibid.***
13. **Stevens, Henry, 2006**, pages 291-292
14. **Farrell, Joseph, P., Ph.D., 2006**, page 183
15. **Farrell, Joseph, P. Ph.D., 2006**, page 172
16. **Infield, Glenn B., 1981**, pages 135-136, St. Martin's Press, N.Y., NY. USA

THE 3RD POWER IN PRACTICE

Of all the stories and accounts of the demise or disposition of Hans Kammler, the Rittermann story by far fits the post war facts the best. It fits known facts and makes sense of why the Allies never really searched for Kammler. So, assuming the correctness of the Hans Rittermann story, how would have the 3rd Power worked in reality on a day-to-day basis? What follows are my ideas on the subject. These are far from established facts, set in stone, and are presented only to inspire thoughts of those who read these words. The reader can judge where and if I go astray.

Included are also my ideas on the course of the Cold War as influenced by the 3rd Power. Likewise, this is conjecture on my part but even without evidence, I believe this version to be close to the truth. Again, this is out of need to make sense out of the utter strangeness of the fact and event pattern. As with the discussion of the 3rd Power itself, it is hoped that discussion on the topic will be inspired.

The 3rd Power is composed of three subdivisions. These are the Skorzeny organization, the Nazi International, as it is sometimes called, Dr. Hans Kammler, surviving in Prague, and the Gehlen Organization that later became the German intelligence organization, the Bundesnachrichtendienst. These three elements eventually worked in communication and together forming the 3rd Power.

We have considered the first, Skorzeny and his organization, in some detail. Besides this consideration, the work of Joseph Farrell in his books "Nazi International" and "Roswell And The Reich" should be considered to be incorporated here with the only caveat that I consider Otto Skorzeny to have been running the organization, not Martin Bormann of whom we have no real knowledge after the end of the war.

Mention should be made of the financial genius that brought Germany out of the Great Depression years before other countries emerged from this disaster. This was Dr. Haljmar Schacht. Schacht also set up the financial arrangements with the leading German firms for a post-war recovery. He also created the confusing maze of corporations and other business entities through which money was funneled and business transacted. Dr. Schacht also assisted Skorzeny in finding the money that was squirreled away and reacquiring it for the SS.

It was Skorzeny who managed the Nazi International in its permanent home of South America. Skorzeny, an engineer by profession, also would have had overall authority of "Mimes Schmiede", the laboratories and technical workshops producing the high technology invented during the Reich years. From South America, the Nazi International used its flying discs and U-boats to transport itself anywhere in the world at times when such transport was necessary.

Skorzeny himself ran this network from his "engineering office", his firm in Madrid, Spain. In fact this office was the SS post-war headquarters, the home office. Of course every intelligence agency in the world would want to tap Skorzeny's telephones. The answer was that Skorzeny traveled frequently and so could make top executive decisions the orders being passed on by courier.

At some point in the post-war world, Skorzeny would have made contact with Dr. Hans Kammler who was by then positioned in Prague. Both would have been very valuable to each other and at the very least formed some sort of working understanding. Kammler was even an older hand at surviving in the post-war world than Skorzeny, having thought of it and planning for it while Skorzeny was still opposing Soviet armies.

In accounts given by Wilhelm Landig and others, Kammler was active in Operation Avalon, the planning of a 4th Reich. (1) In this plot Kammler was not alone and in the company of other Nazi big-wigs as the 3rd Reich crumbled. This Avalon idea was based on Nazi riches that had been hidden as well as the high technology developed at this time. Plans were made to incorporate underground facilities found or created in South America as well as transporting technical specialists to these facilities. Right away it is obvious that these plans resembled the more "official" but still hidden plans enacted at the Rotes Haus meeting in Strassburg.

Additionally, another plan was created, the Z-Plan (Zukunfts-Plan or Future-Plan). (2) Kammler would have also known about this plan. And like the others it incorporated the idea of using South American underground bunkers and German secret, high technology for a "Gegenschlag", a counter-strike, presumably at the Allies after the war had ended.

This understanding comes to us through Wilhelm Landig but it is not contained in his "novels". Instead, one of the authors cited above, Heiner Gehring, was able to read Landig's private notes before he died in 1997. This was a huge coup for Gehring, a long-time researcher of German flying discs and other esoterica. Unfortunately, Gehring himself died only a few years later but not before publishing "Flugscheiben Ueber Neuschwabenland" along with long-time researcher Karl-Heinz Zunneck. These writers commented on the similarity of the two projects.

These plans and Kammler's obvious central position in them as keeper of high technology go to show how interested Dr. Hans Kammler was in life, not death. Under whatever plan, Kammler did a deal with both the Soviets and the Americans, offering his services to both. In this deal there must have been the understanding that no matter what technology was transferred to each party, an overall balance of power would have been maintained. It must have been fascinating to have worked on that equation!

Another interesting aspect of this deal must have been the basic fact that neither of the sponsoring parties, the Americans or the Soviets, knew exactly what technology was under discussion. And after awhile, after a few deals with Kammler, both sides must have known that they did not know the extent of what they did not know. The must have realized at some point that Kammler could just pull a rabbit out of a technological hat like a magic trick. Each side must have had a problem explaining the technology after they acquired it, which led to the Philip Corso trick of blaming its origin on extraterrestrials or, and probably more often, giving it to existing scientists in those countries and letting them take credit for the breakthrough. This went on to the point of allowing scientists to receive Nobel Prizes for inventions pioneered in the Third Reich. Dr. William Shockly was one who received a Nobel Prize for transistors and we will review another winner's "work" before we are through with this book.

Kammler's living arrangements must have been another issue. Kammler could not have been a true prisoner. Kammler picked Prague. Kammler spoke Czech and must have felt at home here. He must have been allowed access to Prague in general under his assumed identity. Yet he must have been shadowed everywhere he went by the CIA, KGB, Bundesnachrichtendienst and Stasi, the East German Secret Police. And all four must have known about the deal and about each other's involvement shadowing Kammler through Prague. And then there was the issue of his staff. Kammler must have wanted a personal staff because he, like Skorzney, would not have transacted real business by telephone. Hans Rittermann does say Kammler had a right hand man after 1967, a former German General named Klein. One wonders if it could have been Georg Klein whom Kammler knew and worked with on the German flying disc program after Kammler took it over. In any event, someone had to go out into the real world and retrieve technology on microfilm from time to time with the assurance that he was not being followed by the intelligence services. One can imagine a large apartment being taken over by Kammler, perhaps even something like a three story apartment complex. Some sort of cover story had to be concocted for the general population, perhaps some sort of small business allegedly being run out of this building. And because there was an obligatory tail on Kammler's ever move, including one by the Gehlen Organization that became the German intelligence service, the Bundesnachrichtendienst, there was virtually no problem in communicating with them or by extension with Skorzeny.

So a home-business setting can be imagined in which representatives of both the East and West attending or perhaps on-site with a small office or desk. Kammler would have granted an audience with them as would any businessman and in just that way deals would have been made, although for each side perhaps in private. After a deal was struck, a courier would have been dispatched and the technology retrieved from an underground storage facility or other repository known only to Kammler. Essential in this dealing would have been the understanding on the part of both East and West that there was always more that could be had. In fact, they must have understood that there was more than they knew or could even imagine. They each knew that were either the East or West to move on Kammler in any hostile manner, and remaining technology would be given to the other side. By extension, this succor extended to some extent to the Nazi International. In their complicated post-war history, various former Allied Powers had run-ins with the post-war SS as well as times of cooperation. Kammler's "home-business" must have served to smooth out these dust-ups.

What we have not discussed in detail is the Gehlen Organization that was very important to this whole system. I say system because that is exactly what it all became — not only this Kammler-Skorzeny-Gehlen relationship but also the whole East-West Cold War. It became the status quo, the way the world worked. It was the system: The "order" of its time. Reinhard Gehlen and his organization glued this world together so we need to take a closer look at this part of the system. For this we will rely upon Dr. Joseph Farrell who has recognized this from the beginning, done a great deal of research on this topic and correctly stressed the importance of Gehlen in this world and his relationship to it in his writings.

At the end of the war in Europe, Britain, France and the USA were staring into the faces of thousands upon thousands of Soviet very hard soldiers, supply lines, tanks, rocket launchers, excellent ground support aircraft, and leadership which had just managed to beat the Wehrmacht. The Soviet Union had been our ally but it was a black hole to western eyes. Now, it seems, they could become and would become a potential enemy. The Americans had no intelligence to speak of within this vast, powerful, secretive, country.

But the Nazis had a huge intelligence network within the Soviet Union which was still in place and available to be contacted but which had just become unemployed with the demise of the Third Reich. One of the brightest minds for the Americans, Allen Dulles instantly grasped the situation his country had found itself and acted. As bureau chief of the OSS, later CIA, in Zurich, Switzerland, Dulles contacted the former head of "Fremde Heere Ost" (Foreign Armies East), General Reinhard Gehlen. He offered the unemployed man and his organization a deal they could not refuse, namely employment doing exactly what they were used to doing only for a different employer, the government of the United States. Talk about unforeseen consequences! Gehlen must have had to lay down with a deep belly laugh.

But it got even better for Gehlen and his organization. Gone were the Nazis and possible fatal consequences for failure in their work. Instead, he was dealing with the Americans, babies who had come into his world of spying on the Soviets. Gehlen realized his superior position in the relationship and so was able to dictate the terms. This is reproduced by Farrell from a series of sources in which Gehlen talks in the first person:

> *"I remember the terms of the agreement well...*
>
> *1. A clandestine German intelligence organization was to be set up, using the existing potential to continue information gathering in the East just as we had been doing before. The basis for this was our common interest in a defense against communism.*
>
> *2 The German organization was to work not "for" or "under" the Americans, but "jointly" with the Americans.*

3. The organization would operate exclusively under German leadership, which would receive its directives and assignments from the Americans until a new government was established in Germany.

4. The organization was to be financed by the Americans with funds that were not to be part of the occupation costs, and in return the organization would supply all its intelligence reports to the Americans.

5. As soon as a sovereign German government was established, the government should decide whether the organization should continue to function or not, but that until such time the care and control (later referred to as "the trusteeship') of the organization would remain in American hands.

6. Should the organization at any time find itself in a position where the American and German interests diverged, it was accepted that the organization would consider the interests of Germany first." (3)

Dr. Farrell goes on to summarize this agreement just to drive its points home:

"One almost has to read this list twice in order for the full magnitude of the implications of the 'bargain' to sink in, but nonetheless the basic implication is clear: Nazi military intelligence basically remained organizationally intact after the war, was paid for by America, and it was understood in conflicts of interest, it would put German interests ahead of American interests!" (4)

Believe me, I can almost hear some Germans complaining at this juncture that a point has been missed in that Nazis are determining "German interests". They would say that after events of the war, the two were mutually exclusive. But Gehlen seems to have had no doubt. Dr. Farrell maintains, and I think correctly, that Gehlen saw it in his best interest, the surviving Nazi's best interest, and even Germany's best interest to play one side against the other, maintaining a large, as opposed to a small, Cold War division between the two which would allow more latitude for the post-war Nazi world to play as well as for himself and his organization.

"What he had cleverly done for his American handlers was to deliberately transform the political threat posed by the Soviet Union into an imminent military threat, and the "Cold Warriors" in the Pentagon responded accordingly, initiating the cold War nuclear arms race." (5)

Dr. Farrell continues:

"The purpose of all these machinations is thus immediately evident, for by locking the two postwar 'superpowers' into a stalemating arms race, more maneuvering room is created for organizations such as Gehlen's to act as the 'balance of power' and as a hidden 'third force'. (6)

The reader might remember that Skorzeny had some sort of Soviet contact. Well, Gehlen fine-tuned this concept with his double and triple agents:

> *"And if, as many researchers have proven, Gehlen's organization — the parent of the West German Bundesnachrichtendienst — was so riddled with Soviet KGB moles, then imagine the nightmarish scenario that those 'double' agents were in fact 'triple' agents, taking orders neither from the West, nor the East, but ultimately playing both sides for fools in a careful and delicate and patient dance, and taking their orders from the hidden directorate of the 'Third Position'. (7)*

And further:

> *"If it was possible for Gehlen's 'Org' to slip disinformation to the USA even if it came from 'turned' Soviet double agents within his own network, by the same token, it would have been possible to slip the Soviets disinformation about American strength and intentions through the same 'double' agents in the espionage version of the Nazi geopolitical 'Third Position'. (8)*

Gehlen is playing both sides as part of a balancing act of his own creation through the use of double and even triple agents. Surely he had agents in the East German intelligence service, "Stasi", as well. Add to this that each of these intelligence services probably penetrated the other to some extent. So, what we really have here is a balance of power on another level, the intelligence level, in which each intelligence service is part of a larger whole but each part is necessary for the whole to work — as it has worked up until that present time. Gehlen and the other intelligence services each knew this. Gehlen just always maintained the upper hand. And the Cold War just kept rolling on and on.

In the meantime the Gehlen Org was able to feed the other two elements of the 3rd Power not only political and military intelligence but also scientific/military research intelligence from SS controlled laboratories within the former Greater Reich, even those laboratories that the former Allied Powers thought they were running.

Could the 3rd Power have just sit back in an apartment house or office building in Prague and just done deals with the Soviets and Americans? Was it that easy? Would the USA and USSR have actually done deals with the Nazis? The answer is they already had done so. Remember Otto Skorzeny's deal with Winston Churchill for his letters to Mussolini in exchange for freeing SS prisoners? Those were baby steps but the principle of the deal was established. The difference now is that Dr. Hans Kammler was exchanging world-beating technology, not old love letters, and would want concessions of some considerable value in return.

Besides this interaction, the 3rd Power carried out operations throughout the third world throughout this period of time between the early 1950's and the middle 1970's.

They supplied technical aid to countries which were reluctant to go to their the Western or Eastern block. They increased the range of Scud missiles, built bunkers, dams, electrical plants, and provided high-tech assistance when asked. Sometimes they worked in conjunction with the West and/or the East and sometimes in spite of them. In fact, there were a whole series of ups and downs just with the Americans along. The year 1946-47 with Byrd's Antarctic adventure and must have been particularly bad as was the year 1952, with the Americans apparently evicting the Nazis from Beaver Dam. The 3rd Power responded with the UFO overflight of Washington, DC, probably with their newer Haunebu craft. Again, things went sour in 1957-58-59 with the atomic air burst over Neuschwabenland but this was apparently patched up with an Antarctic Treaty in 1959-60. After that, no raids or expeditions were ever launched against the extensive 3rd Power holdings and bases in South America. By then, early 1960's some lasting understanding had been reached.

Kammler's office must have been an interesting place. In fact, it must have been a microcosm of the Cold War itself, even more than the divided city of Berlin! At official meetings, probably with both the military and intelligence services of a particular country, Kammler must have been accompanied with his own special staff. There was General Klein, his right hand man. There would have been German translators even if business was conducted in German, even if both Kammler and Klein understood whatever language the opposition was using, just to get another set of ears on that opposition, looking for nuances, both before and after all the translations had been made. Then there would have been security, something for which Kammler was already known. This would have included electronic sweeps, making sure devices were not planted on the premises. Of course, Kammler's agents would have all been former SS men. And on the other side a set of similar personnel, military and intelligence, would have been present. The room must have featured political maps on the walls. Not one but a series of meetings would have been necessary for each item exchanged and each item would involve some sort of on-site visit to some secret microfilm repository after a price was agreed upon.

As far as life outside the 3rd Power for Kammler, he may have dyed his hair and/or had plastic surgery to alter his appearance. He may have roamed the streets of Prague in obscurity. As for his home-life, I know this could not be accurate, but I can not get the American TV show *Saturday Night Live's* comedy image of Christopher Walken's portrayal of "The Continental" out of my mind.

One of the first examples of technological transfer from the 3rd Power involves the Soviets. Remember, in 1957 the Soviets launched the first earth satellite named Sputnik. It was quickly followed by others of ever increasing size. Soon the Soviets were putting things in orbit weighing tons. The Americans could only put up grapefruit sized satellites or small tubes which could be lifted by one man. It was explained sometime later that a "gap" had occurred. The Americans spun it saying the Soviets had not been able to develop miniaturized nuclear warheads and so needed much larger rockets able to carry a much heavier payload. Of course it was these war-rockets that were the foundation for both the American and Soviet space programs.

The Soviets realized they needed miniaturizing nuclear technology, perhaps not for rocket payloads since this problem had been solved by monsterous rockets but for other weapons systems. The problem was solved in 1968. It was in this year that the Soviets claim to have invented red mercury, an agent that could directly detonate thermonuclear weapons (hydrogen bombs) without the need of a fission bomb (atomic bomb) that was used by the Americans for detonation purposes. With red mercury truly miniature nuclear weapons could be built. But the Soviets lied. We already know the Germans had such technology way back in the 1940's. Obviously, a technology transfer took place between the 3rd Power and the Soviets around that date, 1968.

We need to wrap-up one loose end and example of concerning this type of technological-transfer before moving on to Landig's assessment of the 1990's. Some words were left hanging in our review of the Death Ray-Melted Snow (Todesstrahlen—Schnee geschmolzen) article from *Der Spiegel* about "Dr. Hans Erhardt" which was first encountered in the discussion of possible SS repositories in Switzerland. The reader might remember that a mystery scientist calling himself "Dr. Hans Erhardt" briefly worked for the Swiss military and built a working "death ray" able to melt snow twelve kilometers, over seven miles, away. This was said to have occurred in 1961 after which the scientist disappeared in 1963 from Switzerland, mysteriously. The date for the article is July 24, 1963 (the text can be accessed online at *http://www.spiegel.de/ spiegel/print/d-46171297.html*)

Of course, problematic for the American military-industrial establishment are the dates. Dr. Charles H. Townes was credited for discovering "laser principles" ("laser" was not even in usage in Germany at the time of the "Melted Snow" article) and this was in the form of a Nobel Prize in 1964. To further confuse the issue, his brother-in-law, Dr. Arthur Schawlow, held the patent for the laser, and was also a Nobel laureate being involved with the maser. Meanwhile, the Americans kept the records for the German work on the subject, done during the war, out of sight. Fortunately, Friedrich Georg found them on microfilm and they have been since published by me and every other writer on the subject, blowing the lid off this deception.

Michel Bar-Zohar, and Israeli Professor, historian and member of the Knesset, not only mentions Dr. Erhardt's experimentation in Switzerland but also recounts a possible fielding of a laser weapon by the Germans in World War Two:

> *"There was also a vague report on the mysterious Zimmermann — the man believed to have invented the "death ray" and even to have used it effectively against the Russians in the Carpathians on 30 August 1944. The report said that he had been captured and taken to Russia just before the end of the war." (9)*

But it gets worse. That is how it is when a lie is told—thereafter, all future lies have to conform to the first one, or the liar is exposed. If one lie is exposed, well then all subsequent tales look pretty bad. Returning to the German language article from 1963, one sentence in German unravels this deception and underscores the importance of the

3rd Power to the Americans, who may have lost the laser expert, "Zimmermann" to the Soviets and needed some help catching up:

> *"Aus einer Gasplasma-Quelle gedachted der Erfinder mit grossen Hohlspiegln einen gebundelten ultravioletten Lichtstrahl herzustellen."*

Here it is in English:

> *"From a gas-plasma source the inventor thought to make a bundled ultraviolet light-ray with large concave mirrors."*

Plasma-lasers were not invented until 1964, according to the Americans. Plasma lasers are sometimes called "ion-lasers" since plasma contains the ions, matter stripped of some electrons, which is plasma. Plasma lasers were said to have been the invention of William B. Bridges, working for Hughes Research Laboratories. He was said to have discovered and patented the noble gas (argon, krypton, xenon) ion laser in that year (10). Plasma lasers work because the molecules of their original gas are "pumped" with so much energy the gas disassociates into plasma and while attempting to fall back together into a gas, this plasma issues a constant, intense stream of photons.

But the Der Spiegel article from 1963 clearly shows this alleged history to be false. And if the Americans falsified this sequence of events wrong, then they certainly have a problem with the origin of the laser also. As certain as you are reading these words, the basic and advanced technology for the laser was the product of German wartime research and development. It was developed into something which was possibly field-ready. The Americans lost the opportunity of obtaining the expert on the subject, "Zimmermann", to the Soviets and needed help. The Americans went to the 3rd Power and obtained it.

Now fast forward to the early 1980's. President Ronald Reagan wanted to build an anti-missile defense as soon as he came into office. Author Francis Fitzgerald in her book "Way Out There in the Blue" has shown that this was top-down from Reagan, not driven by the military or scientific advisors. Lasers were to be a part, a very important part, of his overall "Star Wars" (SDI) program. The problem was which kind of laser to use. Dr. Edward Teller, the "Father of the Hydrogen Bomb", and Reagan's top scientific advisor, favored and heavily lobbied for an X-ray laser. This was to be created using an atomic explosion and a utilization of this energy to produce an X-ray beam in space. President Reagan, to his credit, was dead-set against atomic weapons of any sort in space. He rejected Teller's concept.

The alternative was the "chemical laser". A chemical laser obtains its energy, not from connection to an electric current or atomic explosion, but from combining two chemicals in a reaction, producing heat. If this sounds like C-Stoff and T-Stoff, you are correct, and the Germans were the masters of this technology. Wikipedia says of chemical lasers:

"A pulsed chemical laser was demonstrated by Jerome V.V. Kasper and George C. Pimentel by 1965. First, hydrogen chloride was pumped optically so vigorously that the molecule disassociated and then recombined, leaving it in an excited state suitable for a laser." (http:en.wikipedia.org/wiki/Chemical_laser)

The relationship to the pure plasma laser is obvious. It is the chemical laser which now fuels anti-missile dreams. It is the chemical oxygen-iodine (COIL) laser mounted on Boeing jumbo-jets as the YAL-1 system, used to shoot down missiles as they ascend rather than descend.

Did the 3rd Power develop and sell this type of laser or its precursor to the Americans sometime in the 1980's? Was it with this knowledge that Ronald Reagan was able to set forth on his Star Wars program, a program that the Soviet Union was so unable to match that a kind of panic ensued, pushing a shaky economy over the edge and resulting in the demise if the Soviet Union? Of course this is not a fixed sequence of events that can be documented even if true. The question becomes one of knowing if a technological exchange was made around this time between the 3rd Power and the Reagan Administration.

To answer this question we must dip into formal logic, "modus ponens" and "modus tollens". A modus ponens statement is an "if then" statement, something like: "if there is fire then there will be smoke". A modus tollens statement reverses this logic, something like: "if there is smoke then there is fire". The latter is an old folk saying that we all recognize. This folk saying is based on the implicit understanding that fire generates smoke, not vice versa. In the case of the Reagan Administration, there are certain actions that are simply beyond comprehension unless the payment of a debt is postulated. In other words, unlike the other situations in which a specific technology can be named, (such as in Philip Corso's "alien" list), which was given up by the 3rd Power, this time there is more evidence for the payment than for the price.

The Cold War heightened during the Reagan years as fear of a huge Soviet military build up crept into American popular culture. In Europe, the Warsaw Pact countries held a vast numerical edge over the NATO countries in terms of soldiers and material. The strategy adopted by NATO in case of war was to slow the expected tidal wave of tanks, armored personnel carriers and troops with a burst of short range atomic missiles, the Pershing I and Pershing II missiles. This "tidal wave" would manifest itself on the North European Plain that ran from the Baltic to the Black Sea and, of course, right through much of Northern Germany. Germany would be turned into an atomic battleground in the event of a Warsaw Pact invasion. It would matter little to the Germans if the invasion were stopped or not, they would all certainly be dead in the exchange of tactical nuclear weaponry.

This realization did not sit well with most Germans. It led to the nuclear freeze movement. This produced demonstrations within West Germany directed at the removing all nuclear weapons from that country. Familiar names that also arose at this time include Petra Kelly and the Green Party. The new Pershing II missiles were a particular sore spot as hundreds of them as of 1983 were deployed in Germany to offset the numerical superiority of the Warsaw Pact as well as the new Soviet SS-20 multi-warhead missiles. But as of 1987 the INF Treaty between the USA and the Soviet Union was signed, removing these missiles from Germany and destroying both types of missiles. This left things where they were with the conventional might of Soviet Union and its Warsaw Pact allies able to roll into Western Europe but this time without suffering nuclear retaliation or anything new if terms of conventional opposition. This was wonderful for insuring the survival of Germany and the German people but a setback for hawkish, hard-line, anti-Soviet Americans. Ronald Reagan could have cared less about the political wishes of the Germans. So, why did Reagan do this?

At about the same time, June 12, 1987, President Ronald Reagan gave his famous "Mr. Gorbachev, tear down this wall" speech. Nobody paid any attention to this speech whatsoever at the time. The Soviets called it a "openly provocative, war-mongering speech" *(http://en.wikepedia.org/wiki/Tear_down_this_wall).*

Not even Ronald Reagan could have believed the Soviets were going to do this or let this be done at that time. So why would he even make this statement which sounded rather absurd at that time?

Maybe this is not so hard to understand at all coming off the heels of the Bitburg ceremony on May 5, 1985. Somehow, this all began as an attempt to observe the 40th anniversary of V-E Day but while in Bonn, Reagan took a side-trip to an obscure town in far Western Germany, Bitburg, and there placed flowers at the graves of German soldiers who had died there defending their country from the invading Western Allies near the end of the war, Allies including the Americans. There were no Americans buried at Bitburg. In fact, there were Waffen SS soldiers buried there. Why would President Ronald Reagan do this?

If you go to a source on this Bitburg controversy such as Wikipedia, for instance (*http://en.wikipedia.org/wiki/Bitburg*), you will find excuse after excuse with all the appropriate figures hand-wringing as they make up more excuses. No, Ronald Reagan did not owe Helmut Kohl anything. Helmut Kohl was the Prime Minister of an occupied country who had no input in what the Americans did in his country. This is amply evidenced by the Pershing missile affair. Yes, special interest groups in America had plenty of warning: The Bitburg visit was announced in February, three months in advance, yet they were unable to convince Reagan to cancel this ceremony. There simply is no conventional explanation for Reagan's behavior.

There is no explanation for the withdrawal of the Pershing missiles, for Reagan's strident pro-German "Mr. Gorbachev, tear down this wall" speech, or Reagan's special trip to lay flowers at a memorial ceremony for German soldiers, including SS soldiers, who died fighting Americans unless these acts were part of the payment for something Ronald Reagan had received. The demand for the withdrawal of Pershing missiles from German soil was something most Germans desperately wanted. The speech and ceremony were very public gestures that a new page had been turned in relations between the USA and the 3rd Power. The new relationship must have been was one in which the old animosity and low level confrontations were laid aside and a concerted effort was made by both parties to mitigate the damage done to all of Germany by the occupation of that country by all the former Allied Powers, especially the Soviets. Under the conditions of those times, this is the absolute best the 3rd Power could have done for Germany and they must have given up a considerable secret to get such a change. Nobody could have foreseen the collapse of the Soviet Union or the Reunification at that point in time, but it is most probable that the 3rd Power caused a butterfly, somewhere, to flap its wings, eventually setting this sequence of events into motion.

But new laser technology in exchange for the acts performed by President Ronald Reagan is only one possibility. If the long view is taken regarding klystron, maser and laser technology, they are all similar in that a medium is pumped with an abnormal amount of energy and then a small exit is opened out of which pours the over-excited energy, the particular radiation in question. In this klystrons are perhaps a precursor to lasers that were developed later so it is not surprising they both came from the same source. In the discussion on klystrons and related technology, the reader may have noted it was mentioned that klystron technology could be used to produce positrons. Supposing it was tweaked for this purpose alone? Then let us suppose a flying craft powered by positrons generated via klystron technology. How would this look? Well, how about mounting the klystron-positron projectors as swivel heads, mounted on the wing tips of a flying triangle? At the point where the three beams converge, that is the point into which the flying triangle moves, pushed and pulled by this super Biefield-Brown Effect. At low power, for instance, with the three beams converging over the center of the craft's gravity, it would just hang there, motionless. With variations in power and focus, any type of thre- dimensional movement is possible.

If this were the technology the Reagan Administration had received, it would account, temporally, for the appearance of flying triangles in Belgium only a couple years after "payment" had taken place. Likewise, beyond Belgium this new shape seemed to be the predominant UFO shape from that time to the present.

Or maybe it is much less complicated than this. Remember in the "Death Ray-Melted Snow" article how a discussion of Karl Schappeller was somehow grafted in and in that discussion the point seemed to have been something denigration of an alleged report of the Schappeller device's ability to synthesize gold? Remember the Alaskan gold miner's claim, made to me, that the presence of a Schappeller device at his gold mine somehow increased gold production? Remember Dr. Joseph Farrell's input that the June 18, 1924 edition of the Frankfurter Zeitung and Handelsblatt carried an article on the transmutation of mercury to gold, long before the discovery of nuclear fission? And the reader will recall that this article was written by Dr. Walther Gerlach, a top German physicist, involving some sort of special radiation? Well, maybe it was as simple as giving this secret to the Americans, allowing them to replenish the depleted gold stock in Fort Knox. This would be a tremendous strategic economic coup for the Americans, to be able to produce the very thing that defines "money" in all economies throughout the world. Never having to worry about their supply of this metal would have allowed the

Americans to spend like drunken sailors and in a real pinch, sell their inexhaustible gold reserves.

And this time-line ties into what was happening internally within the 3rd Power itself. The 3rd Power remained intact until sometime around the 1990's, in the technological sense. Wilhelm Landig had kept in contact with expatriate Reich insiders who informed him of the situation. The reader will remember the "Ruestungsesoteriker", the armament esoterics, the ultimate geeks who kept the post-war Nazi high technology, including the field propulsion flying discs in good operation. They worked out of these secret bases and through a network supplying parts and know-how toward the perpetuation of these technological wonders which resided in huge underground caverns connected to the outside world by tunnel-entrances. Well, it seems even they had limits. All machines eventually wear out. Landig informs us through our informant, Heiner Gehring, who managed a peek into his private files that:

> *"Actually, after the war, there were efforts made to build a military-technical power outside of Germany. The Base 211 in Neuschwabenland, which really was established, was certainly given up after some time. Besides the immunity situation it may have also been the dropping of the atom bomb of the USA during the Geophysical Year 1954 as a reason for the handing over of the base. Garrison and material of the Base 211 were spent to South America. Likewise, more German U-boat bases were available.*
>
> *German flying discs, so the Landig particulars let it be known, are still warehoused in South America but perhaps may not be flight worthy any more. Their propulsion was unconventional. The development of the "Haunebus" through the "Vril" Society did, in collaboration with the SS, actually take place. Certainly some of those topics that are found in the video-films in circulation are partially completely humbug. False are the reports concerning moon and Mars flights of German flying discs, the equipment was not developed for such effort. In the USA and USSR, attempts after the Second World War were made to replicate flying discs. This replica has, on propulsion, failed, which can not be reconstructed." (10)*

Dr. Hans Kammler was said to have died in 1972 according to Hans Rittermann. Otto Skorzeny died in 1975. Reinhard Gehlen died in 1979. Afterward, certainly, a younger generation of Nazis took over management of the 3rd Power. By the early-mid 1980's the Cold War was moving into its fourth decade with no end in sight or in contemplation in the minds of anyone on planet earth. Even the younger men running the 3rd Power must have been thinking about their own retirement as they were doubtless already in their 60's. It is no wonder they were more willing to divulge their secrets at this time. They were not sought criminals or marked men in any sort of way. They were free to fly first-class on commercial jets, they had no need of flying discs at this point.

The point is this post-war Nazi sub-culture existed in parallel along side of both the Eastern and Western blocks of the Cold War, interacting and influencing both of them in ways which we are now only beginning to understand. Just as Farraday and Tesla postulated a self-inducting homopolar generator, these Nazis self-inducted the Cold War to a greater or lesser extent. And in some ways, especially in terms of technology, this post-war Nazi subculture was the focuss of the conflict. And yet on the other hand, in terms of their middle position regarding communications, they were the glue which kept the Cold War from overheating. Was the 3rd Power was a balance-point, a fulcrum? Maybe this is overstating things but in the more narrow scope, especially in Europe and with high technology, it must have been important.

The 3rd Power was as much as child of the Cold War as were the Eastern and Western blocks and when one power got off this teeter-totter, shifting the world order, the existence of the 3rd Power as an active world-player became redundant. Now, twenty years later, their flying saucers rest in cold mountain storage, their U-boats rust in still-secret places, and their microfilm slowly deteriorates in hidden cashes.

Today the 3rd Power is not trying to take over the world or even become a 4th Reich. The 3rd Power was a concept for its members, and lives within friendly government officials and organizations of several countries as well as corporations and financial entities that owed a measure of their success to this 3rd Power. It also lives in the organizations who owe their roots or at least a greater part of their nourishment to Nazi ideas. This includes the Vril Society and the Karoteckia both of which, I am told by reliable sources, still exist. It also lives in the technology of those times, some of which must still be secret.

Literature Cited

1. **Gehring, Heiner and Karl-Heinz Zunneck, 2005**, *Flugscheiben Ueber Neuschwabenland Die Wahrheit ueber, Vril, "Haunebu," und die Templer-Erbengemeinschaft*, page 92, 93, Jochen Kopp Verlag, Rotenburg, Germany
2. **Gehring, Heiner and Karl-Heinz Zunneck, 2005**, page 159
3. **Farrell, Joseph P., Ph.D., 2010**, *Roswell And The Reich The Nazi Connection*, pages 346-347, Adventures Unlimited Publishing, Kempton, Illinois, USA
4. **Farrell, Joseph, P., Ph.D., 2010**, page 347
5. **Farrell, Joseph, P., Ph.D., 2010**, page 349, here Farrell cites Christopher Simpson in his book "*Blowback*:" as his source.
6. *ibid.*
7. **Farrell, Joseph P., Ph.D., 2008**, *The Nazi International*, page 243, Adventures Unlimited Publishing, Kempton, Illinois, USA
8. **Farrell, Joseph P., Ph.D., 2008**, page 244
9. **Bar-Zohar, Michael, Ph.D., 1967**, *The Hunt For German Scientist*, page 152 and 222, Avon Books, N.Y., NY., USA
10. http://en.wikipedia.org/wiki/William B. Bridges
11. **Gehring, Heiner and Karl-Heinz Zunneck, 2005**, page 183

Notes:

1. Here Heiner Gehring is giving us Landig's thoughts. The immunity comment references the lack of bacteria in the Antarctic and the waning of human immunity as a result. The International Geophysical Year was actually 1957-58. The video-films under consideration were the Norbert Juergen-Rathoffer/Ralf Ettl films: UFO's Das Dritte Reich Schlaegt Zurueck, circa 1988 and UFO's Geheimnis Des Dritten Reiches, circa 1992.

Special Thanks

To all those who have helped me, I thank you all. Some of you know full well that this book could not have been written without your input. This is certainly true for the many authors upon whom I have relied. Of those cited after the mid-1980s, most of them have helped me with personal correxpondence or conversation beyond those books.

Besides the researchers and writers, thanks also go out to those who have helped me in other ways. This includes the Czech to English translation work of Milos Vnenk who also contributed many Tesla patents and his knowledge in physics. This thanks also extends to those persons who have supplied input but who have a real life and a career ahead of them and who would find it a bit awkward to explain their names in a book about Nazis during, say, their next job interview. For these people initials or code-designations must be used but you all know who you are and are deeply thanked. These thanks also extend to Diana McCrorey for her computer assistance, to Lisa Stevens who edited the book and to the librarians who helped me prepare the illustrations.

Contact

Henry Stevens can be reached for questions or comments at:
luftscheiben@hotmail.com

Get these fascinating books from your nearest bookstore or directly from: Adventures Unlimited Press

www.adventuresunlimitedpress.com

HITLER'S SUPPRESSED AND STILL-SECRET WEAPONS, SCIENCE AND TECHNOLOGY
by Henry Stevens

In the closing months of WWII the Allies assembled mind-blowing intelligence reports of supermetals, electric guns, and ray weapons able to stop the engines of Allied aircraft—in addition to feared x-ray and laser weaponry. Chapters include: The Kammler Group; German Flying Disc Update; The Electromagnetic Vampire; Liquid Air; Synthetic Blood; German Free Energy Research; German Atomic Tests; The Fuel-Air Bomb; Supermetals; Red Mercury; Means to Stop Engines; more.

335 Pages. 6x9 Paperback. Illustrated. $19.95. Code: HSSW

THE FANTASTIC INVENTIONS OF NIKOLA TESLA
by Nikola Tesla with David Hatcher Childress

This book is a readable compendium of patents, diagrams, photos and explanations of the many incredible inventions of the originator of the modern era of electrification. In Tesla's own words are such topics as wireless transmission of power, death rays, and radio-controlled airships. In addition, rare material on a secret city built at a remote jungle site in South America by one of Tesla's students, Guglielmo Marconi. Marconi's secret group claims to have built flying saucers in the 1940s and to have gone to Mars in the early 1950s! Incredible photos of these Tesla craft are included. •His plan to transmit free electricity into the atmosphere. •How electrical devices would work using only small antennas. •Why unlimited power could be utilized anywhere on earth.

342 PAGES. 6x9 PAPERBACK. ILLUSTRATED. $16.95. CODE: FINT

PRODIGAL GENIUS
The Life of Nikola Tesla
by John J. O'Neill

This special edition of O'Neill's book has many rare photographs of Tesla and his most advanced inventions. Tesla's eccentric personality gives his life story a strange romantic quality. He made his first million before he was forty, yet gave up his royalties in a gesture of friendship, and died almost in poverty. Tesla could see an invention in 3-D, from every angle, within his mind, before it was built; how he refused to accept the Nobel Prize; his friendships with Mark Twain, George Westinghouse and competition with Thomas Edison. Tesla is revealed as a figure of genius whose influence on the world reaches into the far future.

408 pages. 6x9 Paperback. Illustrated. $18.95. Code: PRG

HAARP
The Ultimate Weapon of the Conspiracy
by Jerry Smith

The HAARP project in Alaska is one of the most controversial projects ever undertaken by the U.S. Government. At at worst, HAARP could be the most dangerous device ever created, a futuristic technology that is everything from super-beam weapon to world-wide mind control device. Topics include Over-the-Horizon Radar and HAARP, Mind Control, ELF and HAARP, The Telsa Connection, The Russian Woodpecker, GWEN & HAARP, Earth Penetrating Tomography, Weather Modification, Secret Science of the Conspiracy, more. Includes the complete 1987 Eastlund patent for his pulsed super-weapon that he claims was stolen by the HAARP Project.

256 pages. 6x9 Paperback. Illustrated. Bib. $14.95. Code: HARP

ROSWELL AND THE REICH
The Nazi Connection
By Joseph P. Farrell

Farrell has meticulously reviewed the best-known Roswell research from UFO-ET advocates and skeptics alike, as well as some little-known source material, and comes to a radically different scenario of what happened in Roswell, New Mexico in July 1947, and why the US military has continued to cover it up to this day. Farrell presents a fascinating case sure to disturb both ET believers and disbelievers, namely, that what crashed may have been representative of an independent postwar Nazi power—an extraterritorial Reich monitoring its old enemy, America, and the continuing development of the very technologies confiscated from Germany at the end of the War.

540 pages. 6x9 Paperback. Illustrated. $19.95. Code: RWR

SECRETS OF THE UNIFIED FIELD
The Philadelphia Experiment, the Nazi Bell, and the Discarded Theory
by Joseph P. Farrell

Farrell examines the now discarded Unified Field Theory. American and German wartime scientists and engineers determined that, while the theory was incomplete, it could nevertheless be engineered. Chapters include: The Meanings of "Torsion"; Wringing an Aluminum Can; The Mistake in Unified Field Theories and Their Discarding by Contemporary Physics; Three Routes to the Doomsday Weapon: Quantum Potential, Torsion, and Vortices; Tesla's Meeting with FDR; Arnold Sommerfeld and Electromagnetic Radar Stealth; Electromagnetic Phase Conjugations, Phase Conjugate Mirrors, and Templates; The Unified Field Theory, the Torsion Tensor, and Igor Witkowski's Idea of the Plasma Focus; tons more.

340 pages. 6x9 Paperback. Illustrated. $18.95. Code: SOUF

NAZI INTERNATIONAL
The Nazi's Postwar Plan to Control Finance, Conflict, Physics and Space
by Joseph P. Farrell

Beginning with prewar corporate partnerships in the USA, including some with the Bush family, he moves on to the surrender of Nazi Germany, and evacuation plans of the Germans. He then covers the vast, and still-little-known recreation of Nazi Germany in South America with help of Juan Peron, I.G. Farben and Martin Bormann. Farrell then covers Nazi Germany's penetration of the Muslim world including Wilhelm Voss and Otto Skorzeny in Gamel Abdul Nasser's Egypt before moving on to the development and control of new energy technologies including the Bariloche Fusion Project, Dr. Philo Farnsworth's Plasmator, and the work of Dr. Nikolai Kozyrev. Finally, Farrell discusses the Nazi desire to control space, and examines their connection with NASA, the esoteric meaning of NASA Mission Patches.

412 pages. 6x9 Paperback. Illustrated. $19.95. Code: NZIN

ARKTOS
The Polar Myth in Science, Symbolism & Nazi Survival
by Joscelyn Godwin

Explored are the many tales of an ancient race said to have lived in the Arctic regions, such as Thule and Hyperborea. Progressing onward, he looks at modern polar legends: including the survival of Hitler, German bases in Antarctica, UFOs, the hollow earth, and the hidden kingdoms of Agartha and Shambala. Chapters include: Prologue in Hyperborea; The Golden Age; The Northern Lights; The Arctic Homeland; The Aryan Myth; The Thule Society; The Black Order; The Hidden Lands; Agartha and the Polaires; Shambhala; The Hole at the Pole; Antarctica; more.

220 Pages. 6x9 Paperback. Illustrated. Bib. Index. $16.95. Code: ARK

REICH OF THE BLACK SUN

Nazi Secret Weapons & the Cold War Allied Legend

by Joseph P. Farrell

Why were the Allies worried about an atom bomb attack by the Germans in 1944? Why did the Soviets threaten to use poison gas against the Germans? Why did Hitler in 1945 insist that holding Prague could win the war for the Third Reich? Why did US General George Patton's Third Army race for the Skoda works at Pilsen in Czechoslovakia instead of Berlin? Why did the US Army not test the uranium atom bomb it dropped on Hiroshima? Why did the Luftwaffe fly a non-stop round trip mission to within twenty miles of New York City in 1944? *Reich of the Black Sun* takes the reader on a scientific-historical journey in order to answer these questions. Arguing that Nazi Germany actually won the race for the atom bomb in late 1944,

352 PAGES. 6x9 PAPERBACK. ILLUSTRATED. BIBLIOGRAPHY. $16.95. CODE: ROBS

THE GIZA DEATH STAR

The Paleophysics of the Great Pyramid & the Military Complex at Giza

by Joseph P. Farrell

Was the Giza complex part of a military installation over 10,000 years ago? Chapters include: An Archaeology of Mass Destruction, Thoth and Theories; The Machine Hypothesis; Pythagoras, Plato, Planck, and the Pyramid; The Weapon Hypothesis; Encoded Harmonics of the Planck Units in the Great Pyramid; High Fregquency Direct Current "Impulse" Technology; The Grand Gallery and its Crystals: Gravito-acoustic Resonators; The Other Two Large Pyramids; the "Causeways," and the "Temples"; A Phase Conjugate Howitzer; Evidence of the Use of Weapons of Mass Destruction in Ancient Times; more.

290 PAGES. 6x9 PAPERBACK. ILLUSTRATED. $16.95. CODE: GDS

THE GIZA DEATH STAR DEPLOYED

The Physics & Engineering of the Great Pyramid

by Joseph P. Farrell

Farrell expands on his thesis that the Great Pyramid was a maser, designed as a weapon and eventually deployed—with disastrous results to the solar system. Includes: Exploding Planets: A Brief History of the Exoteric and Esoteric Investigations of the Great Pyramid; No Machines, Please!; The Stargate Conspiracy; The Scalar Weapons; Message or Machine?; A Tesla Analysis of the Putative Physics and Engineering of the Giza Death Star; Cohering the Zero Point, Vacuum Energy, Flux: Feedback Loops and Tetrahedral Physics; and more.

290 PAGES. 6x9 PAPERBACK. ILLUSTRATED. $16.95. CODE: GDSD

THE GIZA DEATH STAR DESTROYED

The Ancient War For Future Science

by Joseph P. Farrell

Farrell moves on to events of the final days of the Giza Death Star and its awesome power. These final events, eventually leading up to the destruction of this giant machine, are dissected one by one, leading us to the eventual abandonment of the Giza Military Complex—an event that hurled civilization back into the Stone Age. Chapters include: The Mars-Earth Connection; The Lost "Root Races" and the Moral Reasons for the Flood; The Destruction of Krypton: The Electrodynamic Solar System, Exploding Planets and Ancient Wars; Turning the Stream of the Flood: the Origin of Secret Societies and Esoteric Traditions; The Quest to Recover Ancient Mega-Technology; Non-Equilibrium Paleophysics; Monatomic Paleophysics; Frequencies, Vortices and Mass Particles; "Acoustic" Intensity of Fields; The Pyramid of Crystals; tons more.

292 pages. 6x9 paperback. Illustrated. $16.95. Code: GDES

ATLANTIS & THE POWER SYSTEM OF THE GODS

by David Hatcher Childress and Bill Clendenon

Childress' fascinating analysis of Nikola Tesla's broadcast system in light of Edgar Cayce's "Terrible Crystal" and the obelisks of ancient Egypt and Ethiopia. Includes: Atlantis and its crystal power towers that broadcast energy; how these incredible power stations may still exist today; inventor Nikola Tesla's nearly identical system of power transmission; Mercury Proton Gyros and mercury vortex propulsion; more. Richly illustrated, and packed with evidence that Atlantis not only existed—it had a world-wide energy system more sophisticated than ours today.

246 PAGES. 6x9 PAPERBACK. ILLUSTRATED. $15.95. CODE: APSG

THE ANTI-GRAVITY HANDBOOK

edited by David Hatcher Childress

The new expanded compilation of material on Anti-Gravity, Free Energy, Flying Saucer Propulsion, UFOs, Suppressed Technology, NASA Cover-ups and more. Highly illustrated with patents, technical illustrations and photos. This revised and expanded edition has more material, including photos of Area 51, Nevada, the government's secret testing facility. This classic on weird science is back in a new format!

230 PAGES. 7x10 PAPERBACK. ILLUSTRATED. $16.95. CODE: AGH

ANTI–GRAVITY & THE WORLD GRID

Is the earth surrounded by an intricate electromagnetic grid network offering free energy? This compilation of material on ley lines and world power points contains chapters on the geography, mathematics, and light harmonics of the earth grid. Learn the purpose of ley lines and ancient megalithic structures located on the grid. Discover how the grid made the Philadelphia Experiment possible. Explore the Coral Castle and many other mysteries, including acoustic levitation, Tesla Shields and scalar wave weaponry. Browse through the section on anti-gravity patents, and research resources.

274 PAGES. 7x10 PAPERBACK. ILLUSTRATED. $14.95. CODE: AGW

ANTI–GRAVITY & THE UNIFIED FIELD

edited by David Hatcher Childress

Is Einstein's Unified Field Theory the answer to all of our energy problems? Explored in this compilation of material is how gravity, electricity and magnetism manifest from a unified field around us. Why artificial gravity is possible; secrets of UFO propulsion; free energy; Nikola Tesla and anti-gravity airships of the 20s and 30s; flying saucers as superconducting whirls of plasma; anti-mass generators; vortex propulsion; suppressed technology; government cover-ups; gravitational pulse drive; spacecraft & more.

240 PAGES. 7x10 PAPERBACK. ILLUSTRATED. $14.95. CODE: AGU

THE TIME TRAVEL HANDBOOK

A Manual of Practical Teleportation & Time Travel

edited by David Hatcher Childress

The Time Travel Handbook takes the reader beyond the government experiments and deep into the uncharted territory of early time travellers such as Nikola Tesla and Guglielmo Marconi and their alleged time travel experiments, as well as the Wilson Brothers of EMI and their connection to the Philadelphia Experiment—the U.S. Navy's forays into invisibility, time travel, and teleportation. Childress looks into the claims of time travelling individuals, and investigates the unusual claim that the pyramids on Mars were built in the future and sent back in time. A highly visual, large format book, with patents, photos and schematics. Be the first on your block to build your own time travel device!

316 PAGES. 7x10 PAPERBACK. ILLUSTRATED. $16.95. CODE: TTH

THE SS BROTHERHOOD OF THE BELL
The Nazis' Incredible Secret Technology
by Joseph P. Farrell

In 1945, a mysterious Nazi secret weapons project code-named "The Bell" left its underground bunker in lower Silesia, along with all its project documentation, and a four-star SS general named Hans Kammler. Taken aboard a massive six engine Junkers 390 ultra-long range aircraft, "The Bell," Kammler, and all project records disappeared completely, along with the gigantic aircraft. It is thought to have flown to America or Argentina. What was "The Bell"? What new physics might the Nazis have discovered with it? How far did the Nazis go after the war to protect the advanced energy technology that it represented?

456 pages. 6x9 Paperback. Illustrated.References. $16.95. Code: SSBB

SECRETS OF THE HOLY LANCE
The Spear of Destiny in History & Legend
by Jerry E. Smith

Secrets of the Holy Lance traces the Spear from its possession by Constantine, Rome's first Christian Caesar, to Charlemagne's claim that with it he ruled the Holy Roman Empire by Divine Right, and on through two thousand years of kings and emperors, until it came within Hitler's grasp—and beyond! Did it rest for a while in Antarctic ice? Is it now hidden in Europe, awaiting the next person to claim its awesome power? Neither debunking nor worshiping, *Secrets of the Holy Lance* seeks to pierce the veil of myth and mystery around the Spear. Mere belief that it was infused with magic by virtue of its shedding the Savior's blood has made men kings. But what if it's more? What are "the powers it serves"?

312 pages. 6x9 paperback. Illustrated. Bibliography. $16.95. Code: SOHL

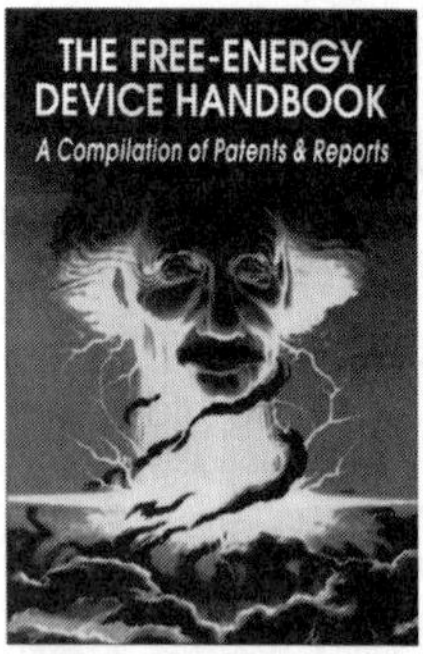

THE FREE-ENERGY DEVICE HANDBOOK
A Compilation of Patents and Reports
by David Hatcher Childress

A large-format compilation of various patents, papers, descriptions and diagrams concerning free-energy devices and systems. *The Free-Energy Device Handbook* is a visual tool for experimenters and researchers into magnetic motors and other "over-unity" devices. With chapters on the Adams Motor, the Hans Coler Generator, cold fusion, superconductors, "N" machines, space-energy generators, Nikola Tesla, T. Townsend Brown, and the latest in free-energy devices. Packed with photos, technical diagrams, patents and fascinating information, this book belongs on every science shelf.

292 pages. 8x10 Paperback. Illustrated. $16.95. Code: FEH

AXIS OF THE WORLD
The Search for the Oldest American Civilization
by Igor Witkowski

Witkowski's research reveals remnants of a high civilization that was able to exert its influence on almost the entire planet, and did so with full consciousness. Sites around South America show that this was not just one of the places influenced by this culture, but a place where they built their crowning achievements. Easter Island, in the southeastern Pacific, constitutes one of them. The Rongo-Rongo language that developed there points westward to the Indus Valley. Taken together, the facts presented by Witkowski provide a fresh, new proof that an antediluvian, great civilization flourished several millennia ago.

220 pages. 6x9 Paperback. Illustrated. References. $18.95. Code: AXOW

GRAVITATIONAL MANIPULATION OF DOMED CRAFT
UFO Propulsion Dynamics
by Paul E. Potter

Potter's precise and lavish illustrations allow the reader to enter directly into the realm of the advanced technological engineer and to understand, quite straightforwardly, the aliens' methods of energy manipulation: their methods of electrical power generation; how they purposely designed their craft to employ the kinds of energy dynamics that are exclusive to space (discoverable in our astrophysics) in order that their craft may generate both attractive and repulsive gravitational forces; their control over the mass-density matrix surrounding their craft enabling them to alter their physical dimensions and even manufacture their own frame of reference in respect to time. Includes a 16-page color insert.

624 pages. 7x10 Paperback. Illustrated. References. $24.00. Code: GMDC

TAPPING THE ZERO POINT ENERGY
Free Energy & Anti-Gravity in Today's Physics
by Moray B. King

King explains how free energy and anti-gravity are possible. The theories of the zero point energy maintain there are tremendous fluctuations of electrical field energy imbedded within the fabric of space. This book tells how, in the 1930s, inventor T. Henry Moray could produce a fifty kilowatt "free energy" machine; how an electrified plasma vortex creates anti-gravity; how the Pons/Fleischmann "cold fusion" experiment could produce tremendous heat without fusion; and how certain experiments might produce a gravitational anomaly.

180 PAGES. 5x8 PAPERBACK. ILLUSTRATED. $12.95. CODE: TAP

QUEST FOR ZERO-POINT ENERGY
Engineering Principles for "Free Energy"
by Moray B. King

King expands, with diagrams, on how free energy and anti-gravity are possible. The theories of zero point energy maintain there are tremendous fluctuations of electrical field energy embedded within the fabric of space. King explains the following topics: TFundamentals of a Zero-Point Energy Technology; Vacuum Energy Vortices; The Super Tube; Charge Clusters: The Basis of Zero-Point Energy Inventions; Vortex Filaments, Torsion Fields and the Zero-Point Energy; Transforming the Planet with a Zero-Point Energy Experiment; Dual Vortex Forms: The Key to a Large Zero-Point Energy Coherence. Packed with diagrams, patents and photos.

224 PAGES. 6x9 PAPERBACK. ILLUSTRATED. $14.95. CODE: QZPE

THE TESLA PAPERS
Nikola Tesla on Free Energy & Wireless Transmission of Power
by Nikola Tesla, edited by David Hatcher Childress

David Hatcher Childress takes us into the incredible world of Nikola Tesla and his amazing inventions. Tesla's fantastic vision of the future, including wireless power, anti-gravity, free energy and highly advanced solar power. Also included are some of the papers, patents and material collected on Tesla at the Colorado Springs Tesla Symposiums, including papers on: •The Secret History of Wireless Transmission •Tesla and the Magnifying Transmitter •Design and Construction of a Half-Wave Tesla Coil •Electrostatics: A Key to Free Energy •Progress in Zero-Point Energy Research •Electromagnetic Energy from Antennas to Atoms •Tesla's Particle Beam Technology •Fundamental Excitatory Modes of the Earth-Ionosphere Cavity

325 PAGES. 8x10 PAPERBACK. ILLUSTRATED. $16.95. CODE: TTP

ORDER FORM

10% Discount When You Order 3 or More Items!

One Adventure Place
P.O. Box 74
Kempton, Illinois 60946
United States of America
Tel.: 815-253-6390 • Fax: 815-253-6300
Email: auphq@frontiernet.net
http://www.adventuresunlimitedpress.com

ORDERING INSTRUCTIONS

- ✓ Remit by USD$ Check, Money Order or Credit Card
- ✓ Visa, Master Card, Discover & AmEx Accepted
- ✓ Paypal Payments Can Be Made To: info@wexclub.com
- ✓ Prices May Change Without Notice
- ✓ 10% Discount for 3 or more Items

SHIPPING CHARGES

United States

- ✓ Postal Book Rate { $4.00 First Item; 50¢ Each Additional Item
- ✓ POSTAL BOOK RATE Cannot Be Tracked!
- ✓ Priority Mail { $5.00 First Item; $2.00 Each Additional Item
- ✓ UPS { $6.00 First Item; $1.50 Each Additional Item

NOTE: UPS Delivery Available to Mainland USA Only

Canada

- ✓ Postal Air Mail { $10.00 First Item; $2.50 Each Additional Item
- ✓ Personal Checks or Bank Drafts MUST BE US$ and Drawn on a US Bank
- ✓ Canadian Postal Money Orders OK
- ✓ Payment MUST BE US$

All Other Countries

- ✓ Sorry, No Surface Delivery!
- ✓ Postal Air Mail { $16.00 First Item; $6.00 Each Additional Item
- ✓ Checks and Money Orders MUST BE US$ and Drawn on a US Bank or branch.
- ✓ Paypal Payments Can Be Made in US$ To: info@wexclub.com

SPECIAL NOTES

- ✓ RETAILERS: Standard Discounts Available
- ✓ BACKORDERS: We Backorder all Out-of-Stock Items Unless Otherwise Requested
- ✓ PRO FORMA INVOICES: Available on Request

ORDER ONLINE AT: www.adventuresunlimitedpress.com

Please check: ☑

☐ This is my first order ☐ I have ordered before

Name

Address

City

State/Province | Postal Code

Country

Phone day | Evening

Fax | Email

Item Code	Item Description	Qty	Total

Please check: ☑

Subtotal ▸

Less Discount-10% for 3 or more items ▸

☐ Postal-Surface — Balance ▸

☐ Postal-Air Mail (Priority in USA) — Illinois Residents 6.25% Sales Tax ▸

Previous Credit ▸

☐ UPS (Mainland USA only) — Shipping ▸

Total (check/MO in USD$ only) ▸

☐ Visa/MasterCard/Discover/American Express

Card Number

Expiration Date

10% Discount When You Order 3 or More Items!